Walt Disney's

UNCLE $CROOGE

by Carl Barks

Executive Editor: GARY GROTH
Senior Editor: J. MICHAEL CATRON
Color Editor: JASON T. MILES
Colorist: RICH TOMMASO
Series Design: JACOB COVEY
Volume Design: KEELI MCCARTHY
Production: PAUL BARESH
Editorial Consultant: DAVID GERSTEIN
Associate Publisher: ERIC REYNOLDS
Publisher: GARY GROTH

Fantagraphics Books, Inc.
7563 Lake City Way NE
Seattle, WA 98115

To receive a free catalog of more books like this, as well as an amazing variety of cutting-edge
graphic novels, classic comic book and newspaper strip collections, eclectic prose novels, uniquely insightful
cultural criticism, and other fine works of artistry, call (800) 657-1100 or visit Fantagraphics.com.
Follow us on Twitter at @fantagraphics and on Facebook at facebook.com/fantagraphics.

Special thanks to Thomas Jensen and Kim Weston

First printing, December 2014
ISBN 978-1-60699-795-6
Printed in Malaysia

Now available in this series:
Walt Disney's Donald Duck: "Christmas on Bear Mountain" (Vol. 5)
Walt Disney's Donald Duck: "The Old Castle's Secret" (Vol. 6)
Walt Disney's Donald Duck: "Lost in the Andes" (Vol. 7)
Walt Disney's Donald Duck: "Trail of the Unicorn" (Vol. 8)
Walt Disney's Donald Duck: "A Christmas for Shacktown" (Vol. 11)
Walt Disney's Uncle Scrooge: "Only a Poor Old Man" (Vol. 12)
Walt Disney's Uncle Scrooge: "The Seven Cities of Gold" (Vol. 14)
Boxed sets of some titles are available at select locations.

Walt Disney's UNCLE $CROOGE

"The Seven Cities of Gold"

by Carl Barks

FANTAGRAPHICS BOOKS

Contents

All comics stories written and drawn by Carl Barks

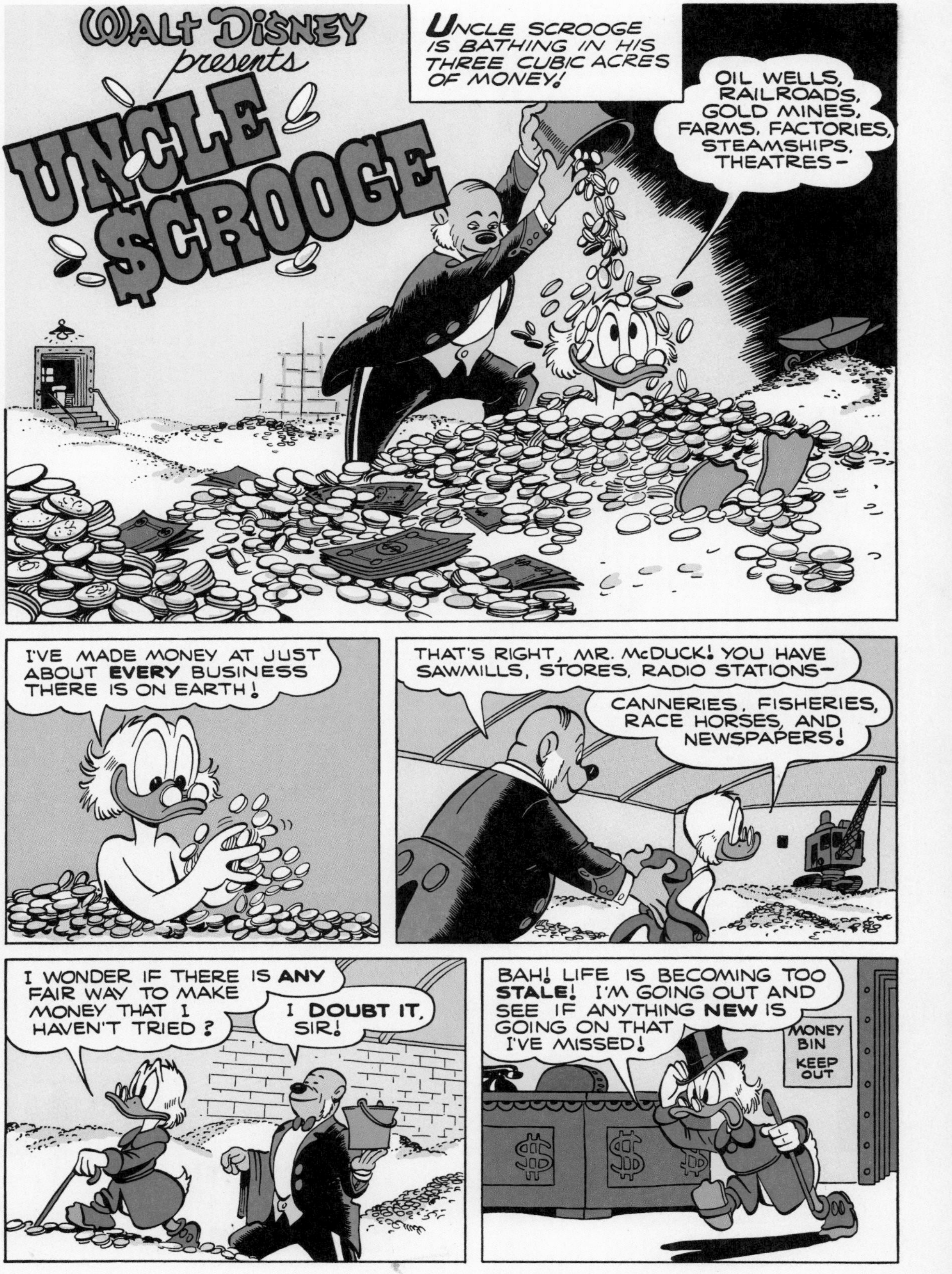
WALT DISNEY presents
UNCLE $CROOGE
UNCLE SCROOGE IS BATHING IN HIS THREE CUBIC ACRES OF MONEY!
OIL WELLS, RAILROADS, GOLD MINES, FARMS, FACTORIES, STEAMSHIPS, THEATRES–
I'VE MADE MONEY AT JUST ABOUT EVERY BUSINESS THERE IS ON EARTH!
THAT'S RIGHT, MR. McDUCK! YOU HAVE SAWMILLS, STORES, RADIO STATIONS–
CANNERIES, FISHERIES, RACE HORSES, AND NEWSPAPERS!
I WONDER IF THERE IS ANY FAIR WAY TO MAKE MONEY THAT I HAVEN'T TRIED?
I DOUBT IT, SIR!
BAH! LIFE IS BECOMING TOO STALE! I'M GOING OUT AND SEE IF ANYTHING NEW IS GOING ON THAT I'VE MISSED!
MONEY BIN
KEEP OUT

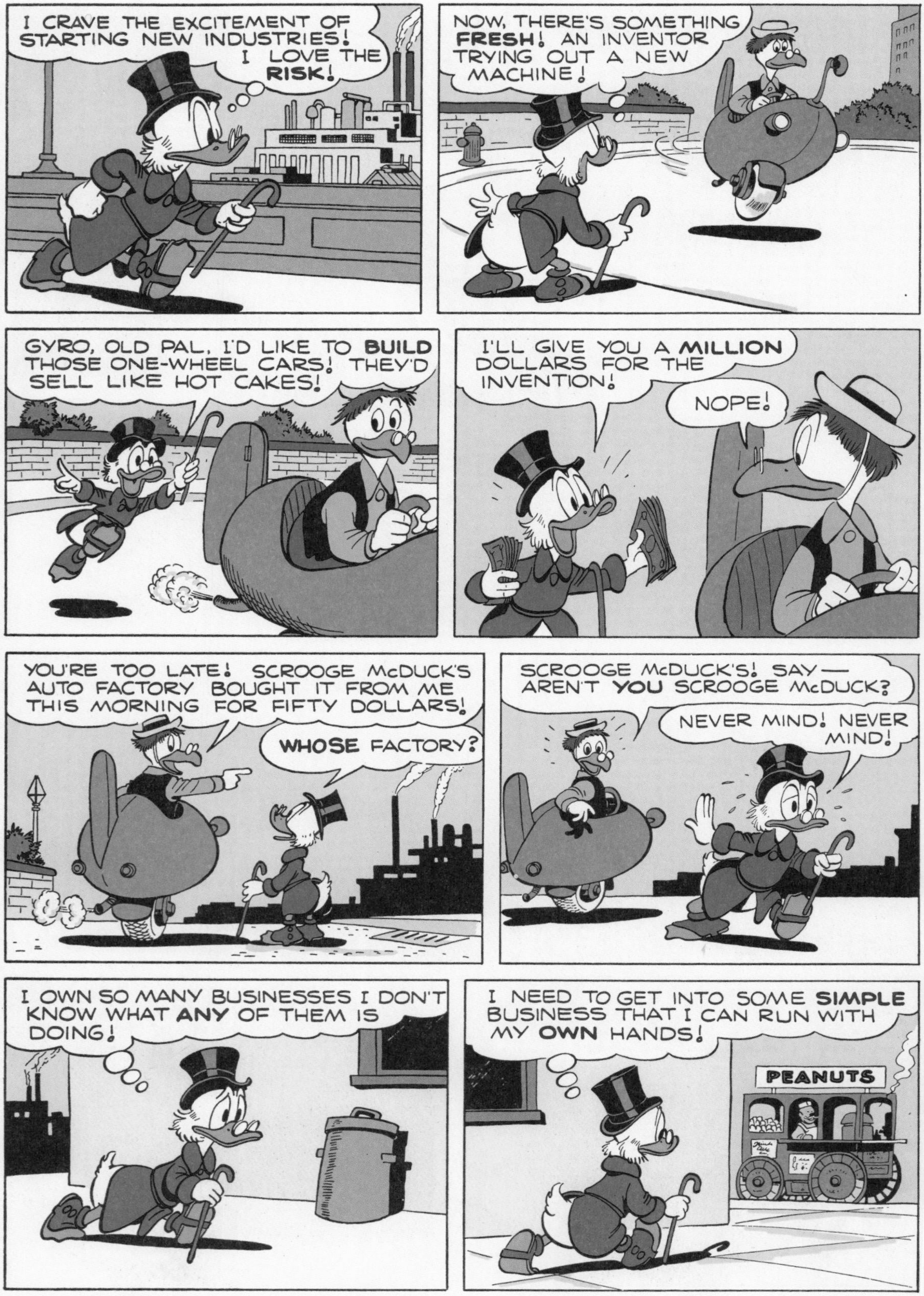
I CRAVE THE EXCITEMENT OF STARTING NEW INDUSTRIES! I LOVE THE RISK!
NOW, THERE'S SOMETHING FRESH! AN INVENTOR TRYING OUT A NEW MACHINE!
GYRO, OLD PAL, I'D LIKE TO BUILD THOSE ONE-WHEEL CARS! THEY'D SELL LIKE HOT CAKES!
I'LL GIVE YOU A MILLION DOLLARS FOR THE INVENTION!
NOPE!
YOU'RE TOO LATE! SCROOGE McDUCK'S AUTO FACTORY BOUGHT IT FROM ME THIS MORNING FOR FIFTY DOLLARS!
WHOSE FACTORY?
SCROOGE McDUCK'S! SAY— AREN'T YOU SCROOGE McDUCK?
NEVER MIND! NEVER MIND!
I OWN SO MANY BUSINESSES I DON'T KNOW WHAT ANY OF THEM IS DOING!
I NEED TO GET INTO SOME SIMPLE BUSINESS THAT I CAN RUN WITH MY OWN HANDS!
PEANUTS

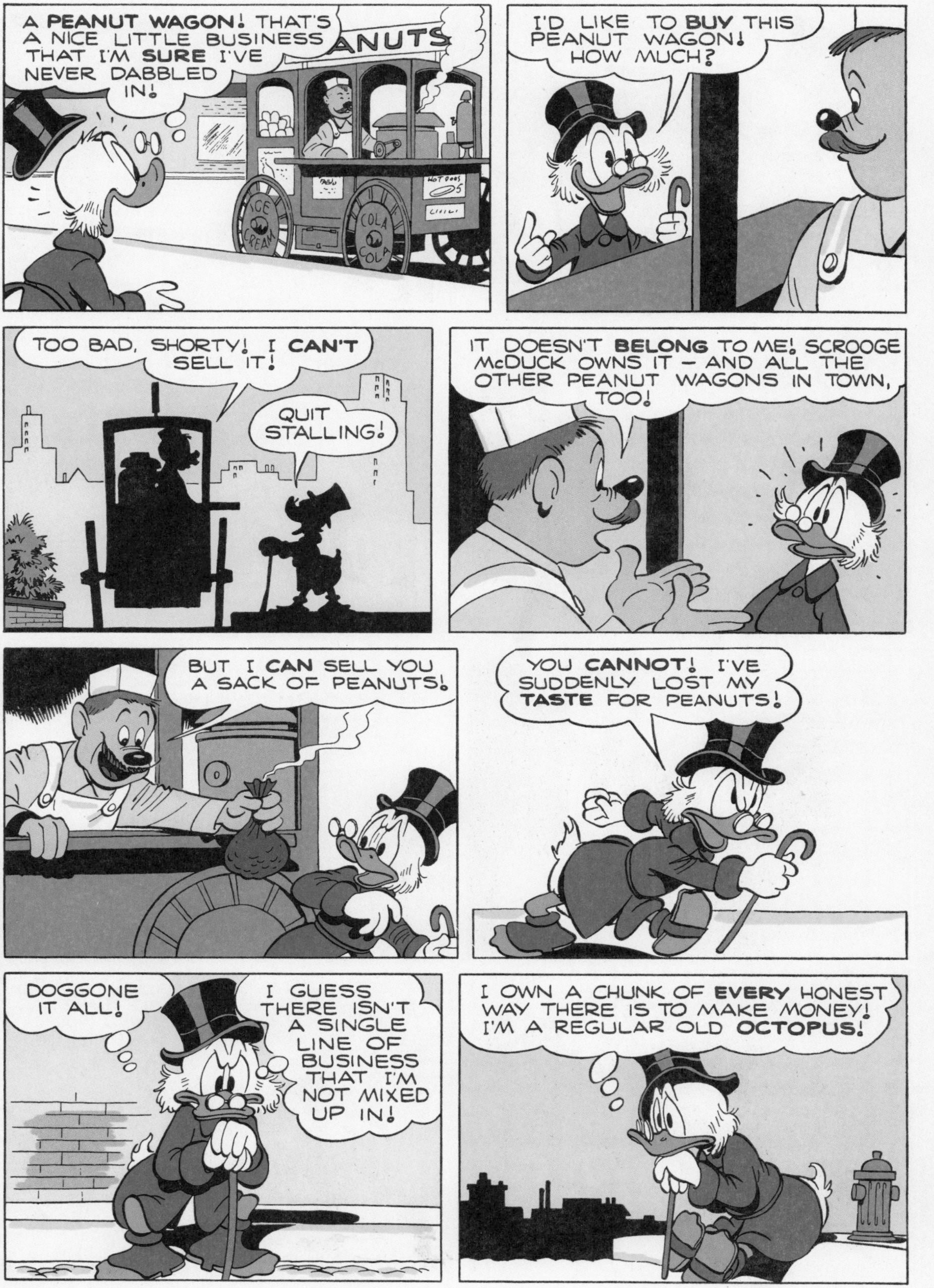
A PEANUT WAGON! THAT'S A NICE LITTLE BUSINESS THAT I'M SURE I'VE NEVER DABBLED IN!
PEANUTS
ICE CREAM
COLA COLA
HOT DOGS 5
I'D LIKE TO BUY THIS PEANUT WAGON! HOW MUCH?
TOO BAD, SHORTY! I CAN'T SELL IT!
QUIT STALLING!
IT DOESN'T BELONG TO ME! SCROOGE McDUCK OWNS IT – AND ALL THE OTHER PEANUT WAGONS IN TOWN, TOO!
BUT I CAN SELL YOU A SACK OF PEANUTS!
YOU CANNOT! I'VE SUDDENLY LOST MY TASTE FOR PEANUTS!
DOGGONE IT ALL!
I GUESS THERE ISN'T A SINGLE LINE OF BUSINESS THAT I'M NOT MIXED UP IN!
I OWN A CHUNK OF EVERY HONEST WAY THERE IS TO MAKE MONEY! I'M A REGULAR OLD OCTOPUS!

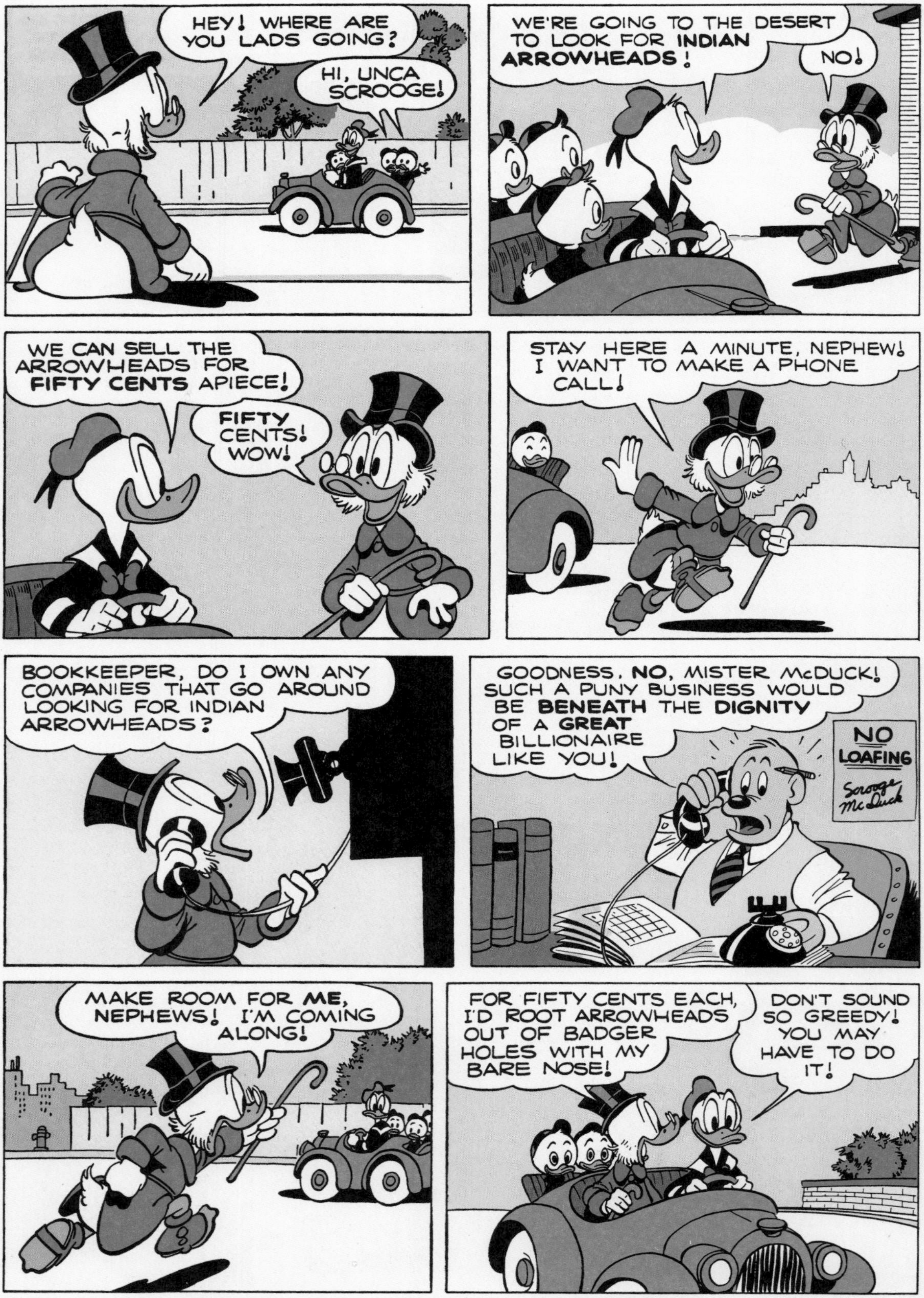
HEY! WHERE ARE YOU LADS GOING?
HI, UNCA SCROOGE!
WE'RE GOING TO THE DESERT TO LOOK FOR INDIAN ARROWHEADS!
NO!
WE CAN SELL THE ARROWHEADS FOR FIFTY CENTS APIECE!
FIFTY CENTS! WOW!
STAY HERE A MINUTE, NEPHEW! I WANT TO MAKE A PHONE CALL!
BOOKKEEPER, DO I OWN ANY COMPANIES THAT GO AROUND LOOKING FOR INDIAN ARROWHEADS?
GOODNESS, NO, MISTER McDUCK! SUCH A PUNY BUSINESS WOULD BE BENEATH THE DIGNITY OF A GREAT BILLIONAIRE LIKE YOU!
NO LOAFING
Scrooge McDuck
MAKE ROOM FOR ME, NEPHEWS! I'M COMING ALONG!
FOR FIFTY CENTS EACH, I'D ROOT ARROWHEADS OUT OF BADGER HOLES WITH MY BARE NOSE!
DON'T SOUND SO GREEDY! YOU MAY HAVE TO DO IT!

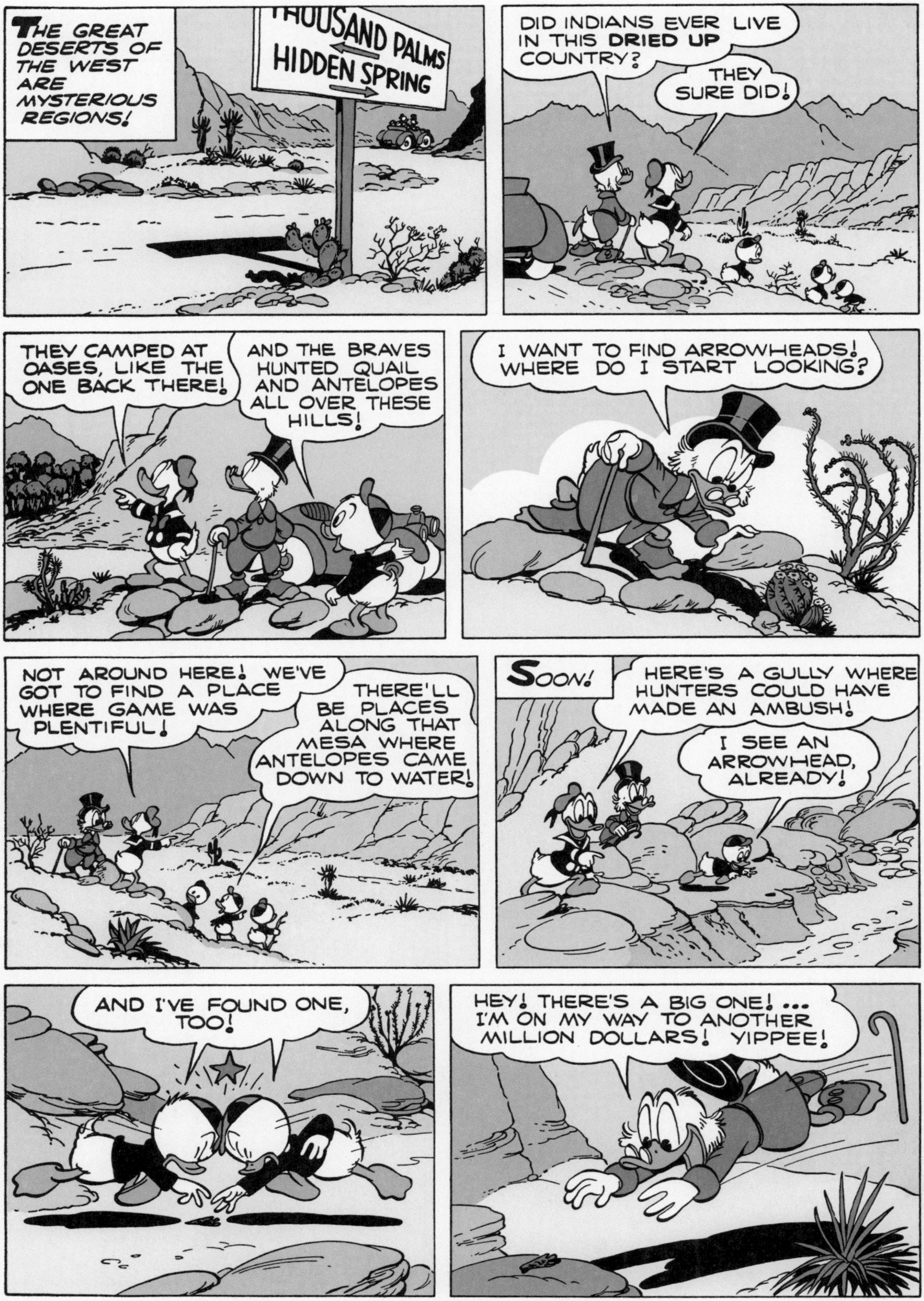
THE GREAT DESERTS OF THE WEST ARE MYSTERIOUS REGIONS!
THOUSAND PALMS
HIDDEN SPRING
DID INDIANS EVER LIVE IN THIS **DRIED UP** COUNTRY?
THEY SURE DID!
THEY CAMPED AT OASES, LIKE THE ONE BACK THERE!
AND THE BRAVES HUNTED QUAIL AND ANTELOPES ALL OVER THESE HILLS!
I WANT TO FIND ARROWHEADS! WHERE DO I START LOOKING?
NOT AROUND HERE! WE'VE GOT TO FIND A PLACE WHERE GAME WAS PLENTIFUL!
THERE'LL BE PLACES ALONG THAT MESA WHERE ANTELOPES CAME DOWN TO WATER!
SOON!
HERE'S A GULLY WHERE HUNTERS COULD HAVE MADE AN AMBUSH!
I SEE AN ARROWHEAD, ALREADY!
AND I'VE FOUND ONE, TOO!
HEY! THERE'S A BIG ONE! ... I'M ON MY WAY TO ANOTHER MILLION DOLLARS! YIPPEE!

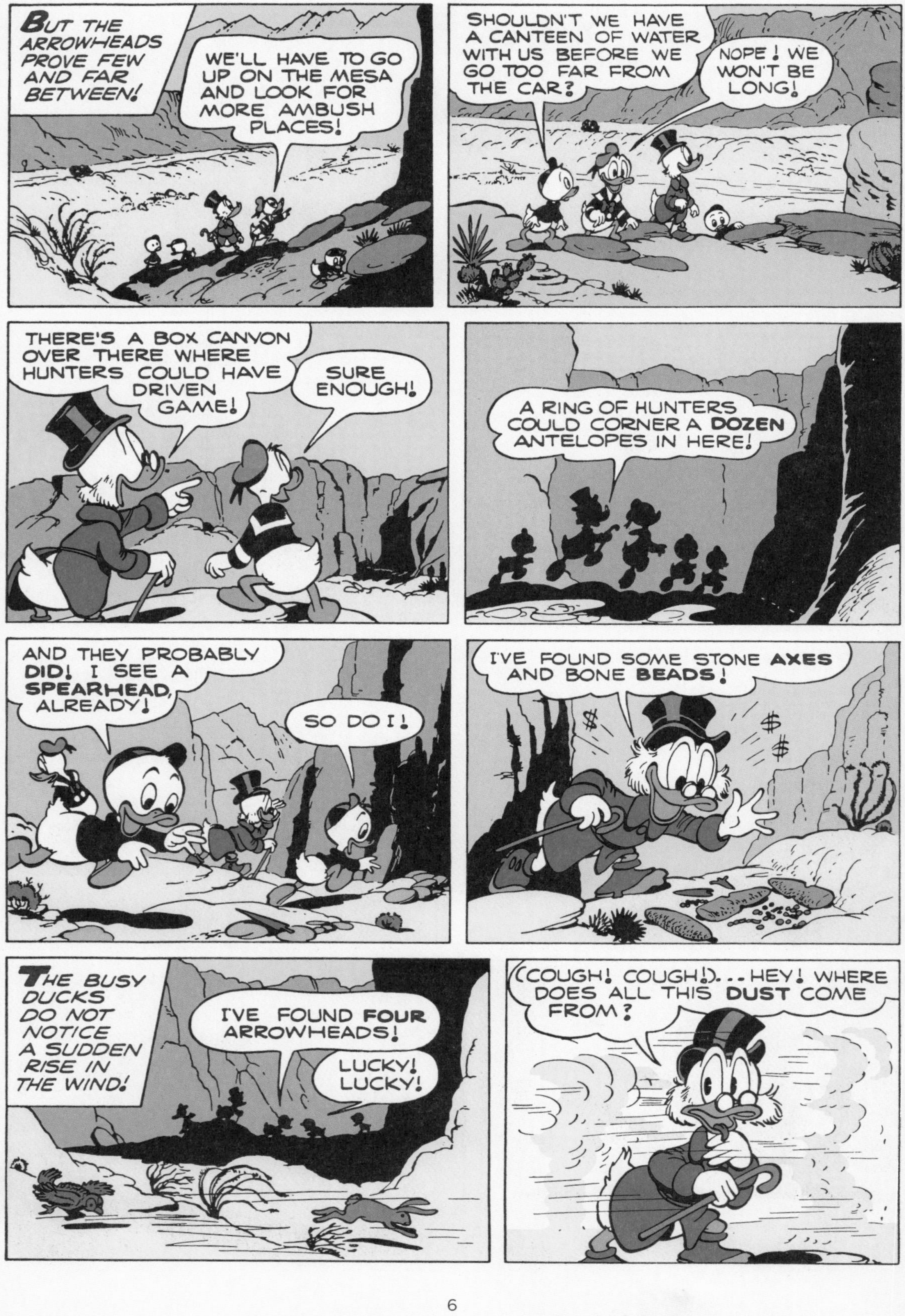
BUT THE ARROWHEADS PROVE FEW AND FAR BETWEEN!
WE'LL HAVE TO GO UP ON THE MESA AND LOOK FOR MORE AMBUSH PLACES!
SHOULDN'T WE HAVE A CANTEEN OF WATER WITH US BEFORE WE GO TOO FAR FROM THE CAR?
NOPE! WE WON'T BE LONG!
THERE'S A BOX CANYON OVER THERE WHERE HUNTERS COULD HAVE DRIVEN GAME!
SURE ENOUGH!
A RING OF HUNTERS COULD CORNER A DOZEN ANTELOPES IN HERE!
AND THEY PROBABLY DID! I SEE A SPEARHEAD, ALREADY!
SO DO I!
I'VE FOUND SOME STONE AXES AND BONE BEADS!
THE BUSY DUCKS DO NOT NOTICE A SUDDEN RISE IN THE WIND!
I'VE FOUND FOUR ARROWHEADS!
LUCKY! LUCKY!
(COUGH! COUGH!)...HEY! WHERE DOES ALL THIS DUST COME FROM?

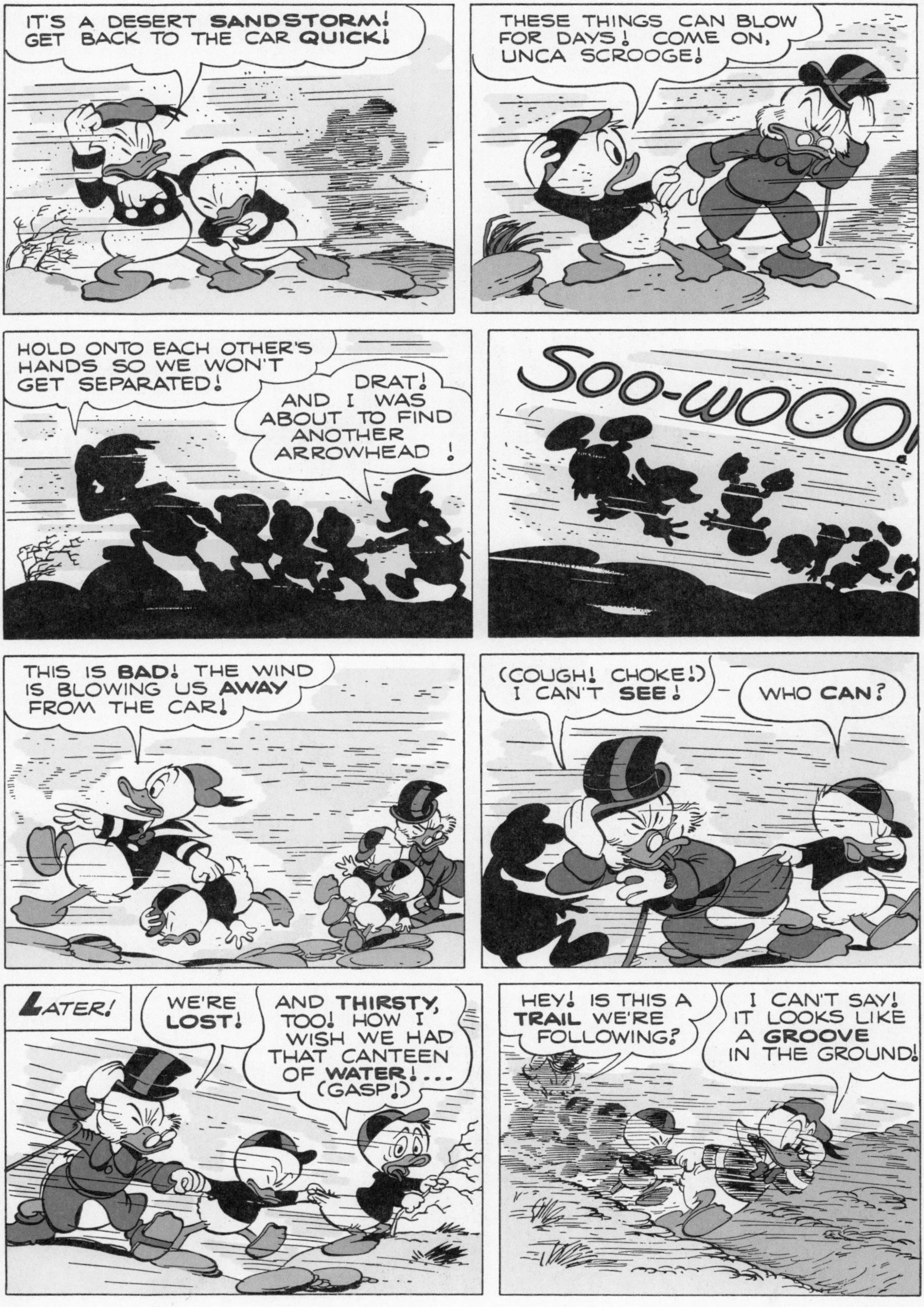
IT'S A DESERT SANDSTORM! GET BACK TO THE CAR QUICK!
THESE THINGS CAN BLOW FOR DAYS! COME ON, UNCA SCROOGE!
HOLD ONTO EACH OTHER'S HANDS SO WE WON'T GET SEPARATED!
DRAT! AND I WAS ABOUT TO FIND ANOTHER ARROWHEAD !
SOO-WOOO!
THIS IS BAD! THE WIND IS BLOWING US AWAY FROM THE CAR!
(COUGH! CHOKE!) I CAN'T SEE!
WHO CAN?
LATER!
WE'RE LOST!
AND THIRSTY, TOO! HOW I WISH WE HAD THAT CANTEEN OF WATER! ... (GASP!)
HEY! IS THIS A TRAIL WE'RE FOLLOWING?
I CAN'T SAY! IT LOOKS LIKE A GROOVE IN THE GROUND!

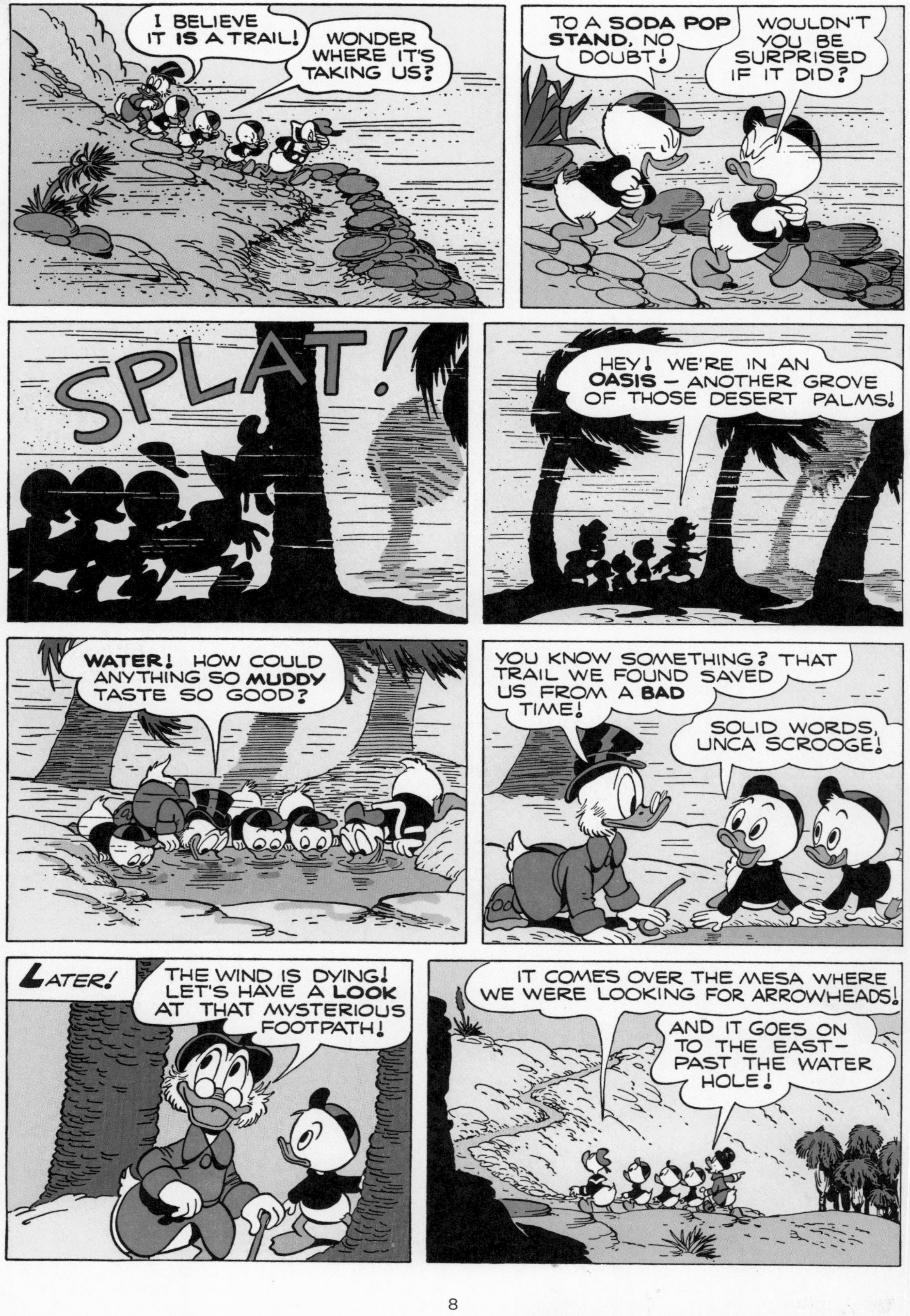

I BELIEVE IT IS A TRAIL!
WONDER WHERE IT'S TAKING US?
TO A SODA POP STAND, NO DOUBT!
WOULDN'T YOU BE SURPRISED IF IT DID?
SPLAT!
HEY! WE'RE IN AN OASIS – ANOTHER GROVE OF THOSE DESERT PALMS!
WATER! HOW COULD ANYTHING SO MUDDY TASTE SO GOOD?
YOU KNOW SOMETHING? THAT TRAIL WE FOUND SAVED US FROM A BAD TIME!
SOLID WORDS, UNCA SCROOGE!
LATER!
THE WIND IS DYING! LET'S HAVE A LOOK AT THAT MYSTERIOUS FOOTPATH!
IT COMES OVER THE MESA WHERE WE WERE LOOKING FOR ARROWHEADS!
AND IT GOES ON TO THE EAST– PAST THE WATER HOLE!

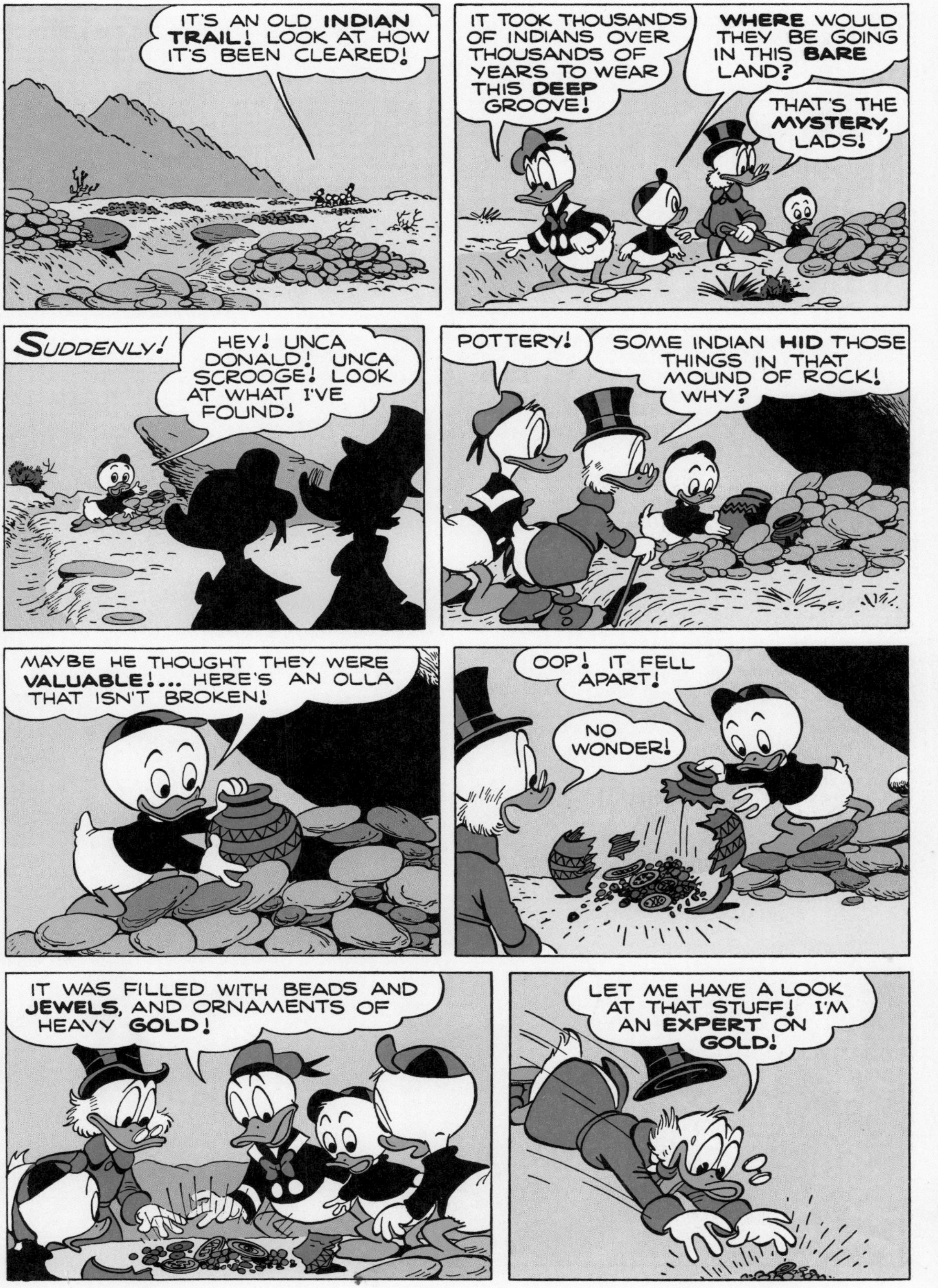
IT'S AN OLD INDIAN TRAIL! LOOK AT HOW IT'S BEEN CLEARED!
IT TOOK THOUSANDS OF INDIANS OVER THOUSANDS OF YEARS TO WEAR THIS DEEP GROOVE!
WHERE WOULD THEY BE GOING IN THIS BARE LAND?
THAT'S THE MYSTERY, LADS!
SUDDENLY!
HEY! UNCA DONALD! UNCA SCROOGE! LOOK AT WHAT I'VE FOUND!
POTTERY!
SOME INDIAN HID THOSE THINGS IN THAT MOUND OF ROCK! WHY?
MAYBE HE THOUGHT THEY WERE VALUABLE!... HERE'S AN OLLA THAT ISN'T BROKEN!
OOP! IT FELL APART!
NO WONDER!
IT WAS FILLED WITH BEADS AND JEWELS, AND ORNAMENTS OF HEAVY GOLD!
LET ME HAVE A LOOK AT THAT STUFF! I'M AN EXPERT ON GOLD!

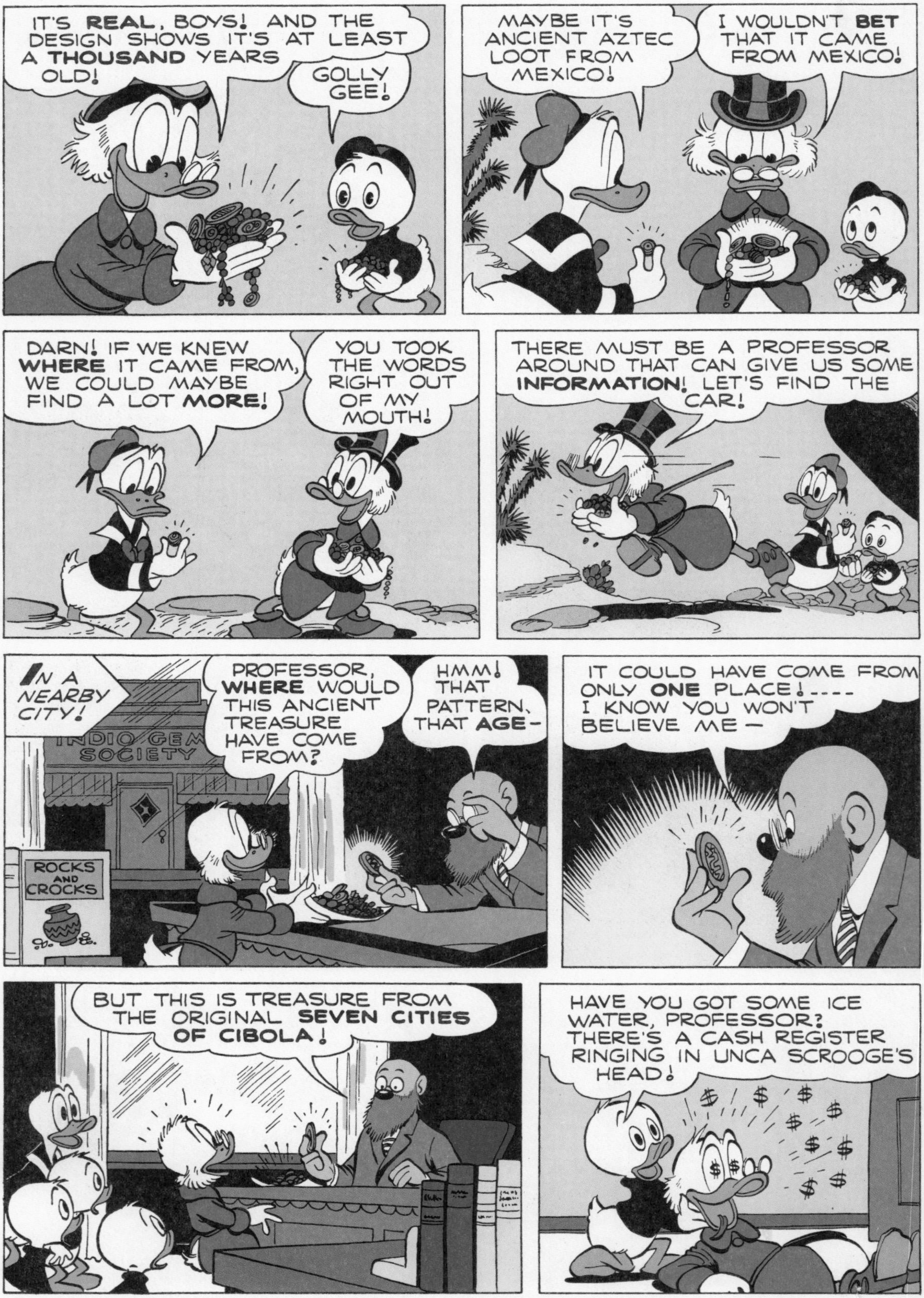
IT'S REAL, BOYS! AND THE DESIGN SHOWS IT'S AT LEAST A THOUSAND YEARS OLD!
GOLLY GEE!
MAYBE IT'S ANCIENT AZTEC LOOT FROM MEXICO!
I WOULDN'T BET THAT IT CAME FROM MEXICO!
DARN! IF WE KNEW WHERE IT CAME FROM, WE COULD MAYBE FIND A LOT MORE!
YOU TOOK THE WORDS RIGHT OUT OF MY MOUTH!
THERE MUST BE A PROFESSOR AROUND THAT CAN GIVE US SOME INFORMATION! LET'S FIND THE CAR!
IN A NEARBY CITY!
INDIO GEM SOCIETY
ROCKS AND CROCKS
PROFESSOR, WHERE WOULD THIS ANCIENT TREASURE HAVE COME FROM?
HMM! THAT PATTERN, THAT AGE-
IT COULD HAVE COME FROM ONLY ONE PLACE!---- I KNOW YOU WON'T BELIEVE ME—
BUT THIS IS TREASURE FROM THE ORIGINAL SEVEN CITIES OF CIBOLA!
HAVE YOU GOT SOME ICE WATER, PROFESSOR? THERE'S A CASH REGISTER RINGING IN UNCA SCROOGE'S HEAD!

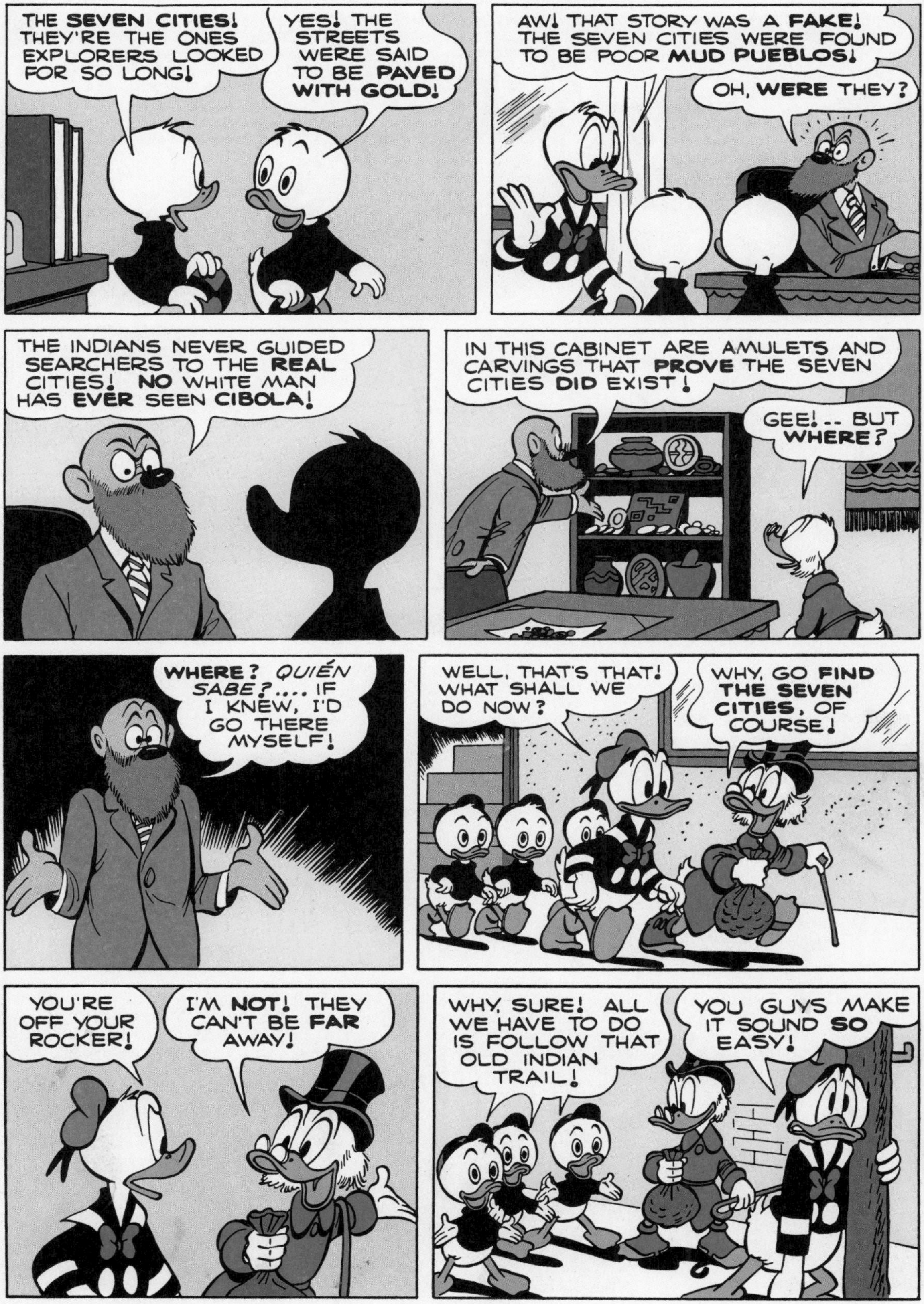
THE SEVEN CITIES! THEY'RE THE ONES EXPLORERS LOOKED FOR SO LONG!
YES! THE STREETS WERE SAID TO BE PAVED WITH GOLD!
AW! THAT STORY WAS A FAKE! THE SEVEN CITIES WERE FOUND TO BE POOR MUD PUEBLOS!
OH, WERE THEY?
THE INDIANS NEVER GUIDED SEARCHERS TO THE REAL CITIES! NO WHITE MAN HAS EVER SEEN CIBOLA!
IN THIS CABINET ARE AMULETS AND CARVINGS THAT PROVE THE SEVEN CITIES DID EXIST!
GEE! -- BUT WHERE?
WHERE? QUIÉN SABE?.... IF I KNEW, I'D GO THERE MYSELF!
WELL, THAT'S THAT! WHAT SHALL WE DO NOW?
WHY, GO FIND THE SEVEN CITIES, OF COURSE!
YOU'RE OFF YOUR ROCKER!
I'M NOT! THEY CAN'T BE FAR AWAY!
WHY, SURE! ALL WE HAVE TO DO IS FOLLOW THAT OLD INDIAN TRAIL!
YOU GUYS MAKE IT SOUND SO EASY!

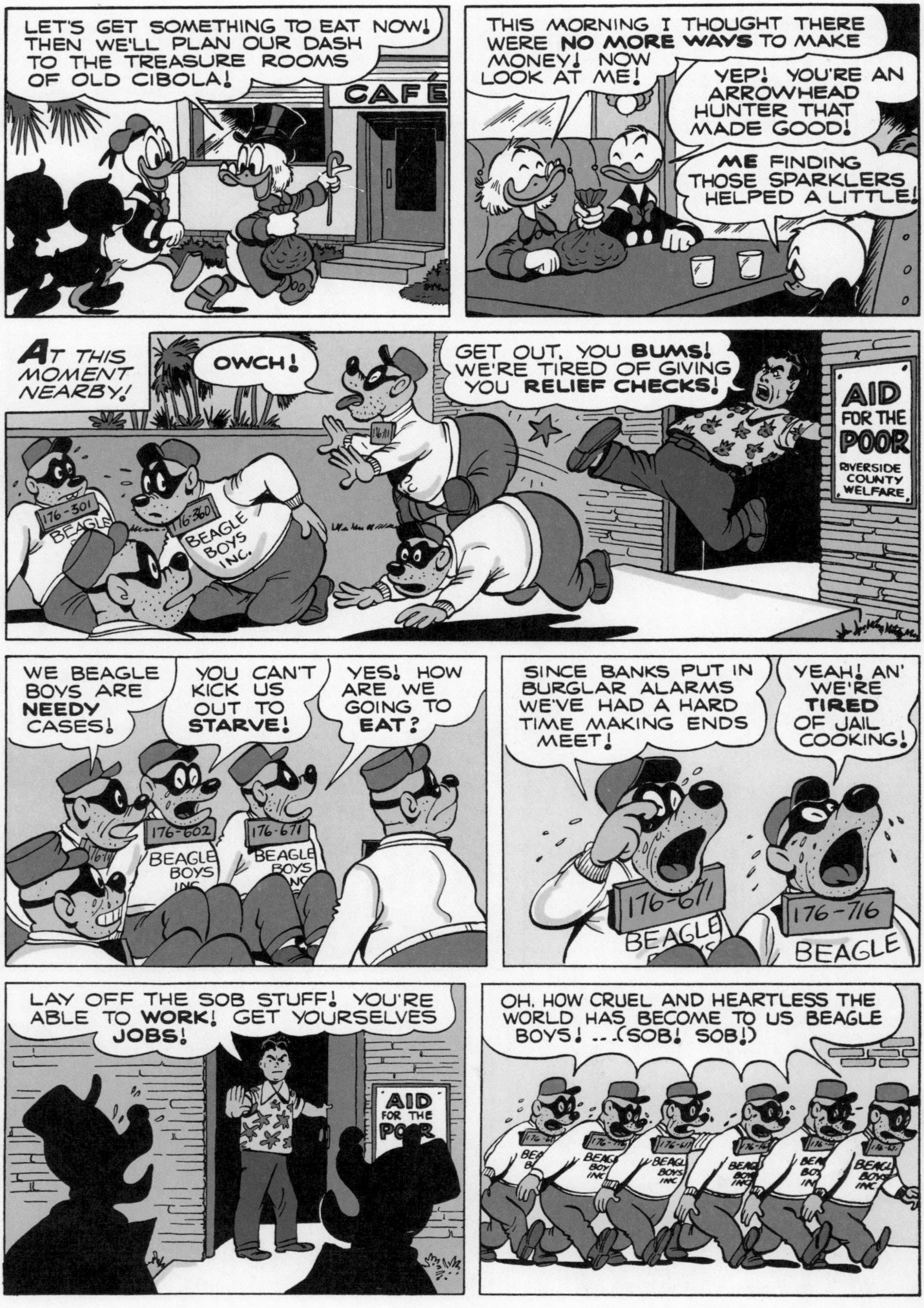

LET'S GET SOMETHING TO EAT NOW! THEN WE'LL PLAN OUR DASH TO THE TREASURE ROOMS OF OLD CIBOLA!
CAFÉ
THIS MORNING I THOUGHT THERE WERE **NO MORE WAYS** TO MAKE MONEY! NOW LOOK AT ME!
YEP! YOU'RE AN ARROWHEAD HUNTER THAT MADE GOOD!
ME FINDING THOSE SPARKLERS HELPED A LITTLE!
AT THIS MOMENT NEARBY!
OWCH!
GET OUT, YOU **BUMS**! WE'RE TIRED OF GIVING YOU **RELIEF CHECKS**!
AID FOR THE POOR
RIVERSIDE COUNTY WELFARE
176-301
176-360
BEAGLE BOYS INC.
WE BEAGLE BOYS ARE **NEEDY** CASES!
YOU CAN'T KICK US OUT TO **STARVE**!
YES! HOW ARE WE GOING TO **EAT**?
176-602
176-671
SINCE BANKS PUT IN BURGLAR ALARMS WE'VE HAD A HARD TIME MAKING ENDS MEET!
YEAH! AN' WE'RE **TIRED** OF JAIL COOKING!
176-671
176-716
BEAGLE
LAY OFF THE SOB STUFF! YOU'RE ABLE TO **WORK**! GET YOURSELVES **JOBS**!
AID FOR THE POOR
OH, HOW CRUEL AND HEARTLESS THE WORLD HAS BECOME TO US BEAGLE BOYS! ...(SOB! SOB!)

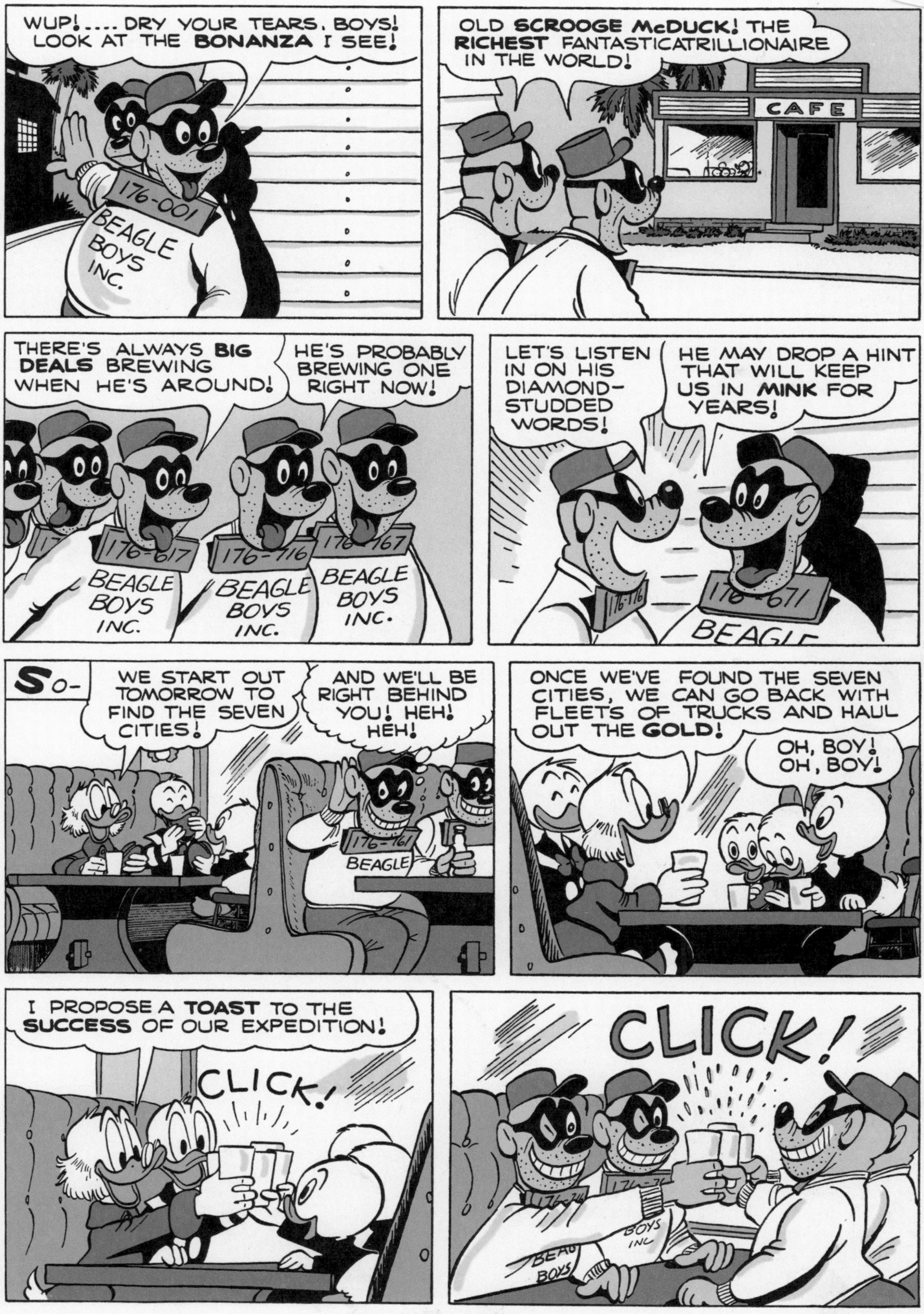
WUP! .... DRY YOUR TEARS, BOYS! LOOK AT THE BONANZA I SEE!
176-001
BEAGLE BOYS INC.
OLD SCROOGE McDUCK! THE RICHEST FANTASTICATRILLIONAIRE IN THE WORLD!
CAFE
THERE'S ALWAYS BIG DEALS BREWING WHEN HE'S AROUND!
HE'S PROBABLY BREWING ONE RIGHT NOW!
176-617
176-716
176-767
BEAGLE BOYS INC.
LET'S LISTEN IN ON HIS DIAMOND-STUDDED WORDS!
HE MAY DROP A HINT THAT WILL KEEP US IN MINK FOR YEARS!
176-671
SO-
WE START OUT TOMORROW TO FIND THE SEVEN CITIES!
AND WE'LL BE RIGHT BEHIND YOU! HEH! HEH!
176-761
BEAGLE
ONCE WE'VE FOUND THE SEVEN CITIES, WE CAN GO BACK WITH FLEETS OF TRUCKS AND HAUL OUT THE GOLD!
OH, BOY! OH, BOY!
I PROPOSE A TOAST TO THE SUCCESS OF OUR EXPEDITION!
CLICK!
CLICK!

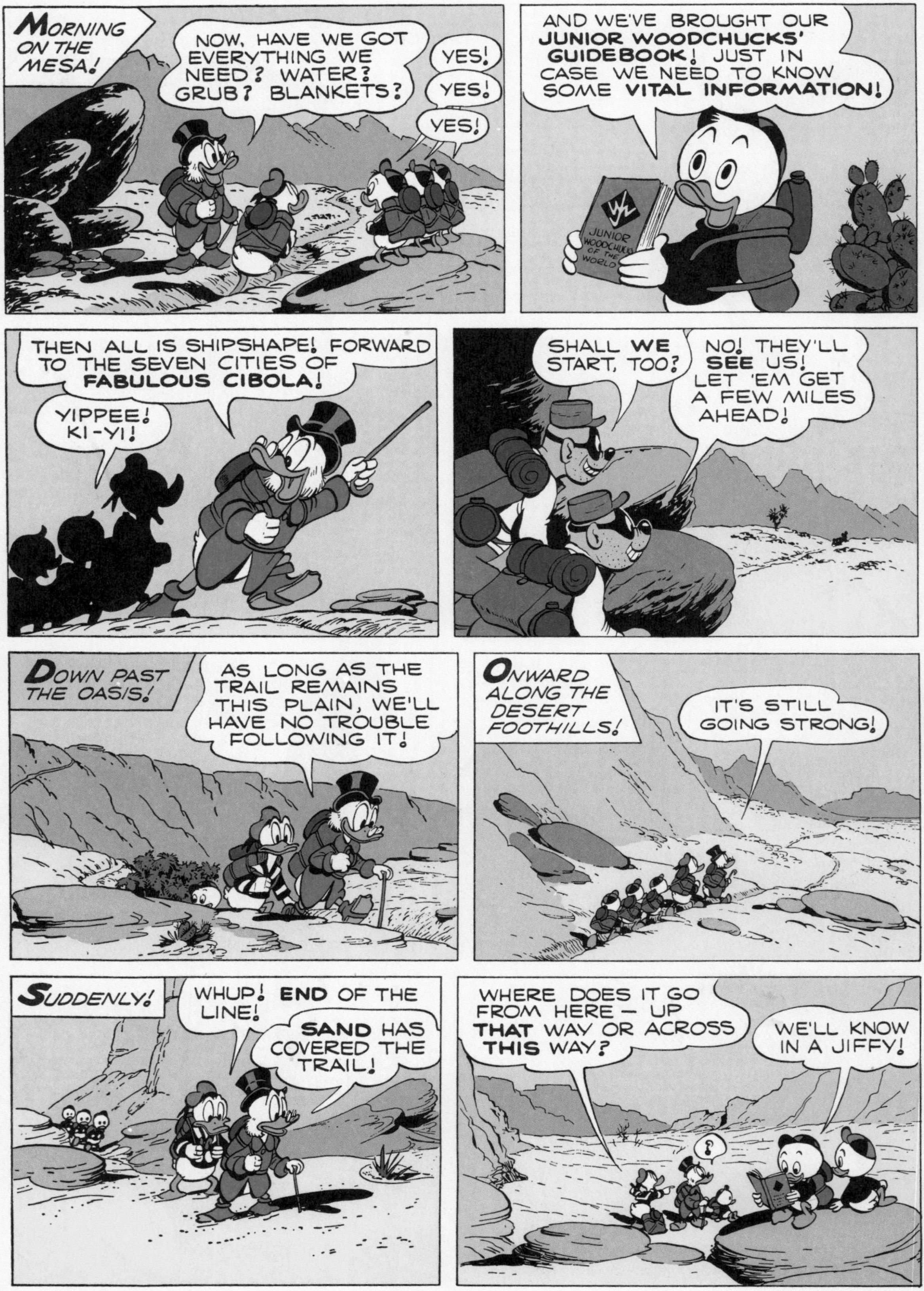
MORNING ON THE MESA!
NOW, HAVE WE GOT EVERYTHING WE NEED? WATER? GRUB? BLANKETS?
YES!
YES!
YES!
AND WE'VE BROUGHT OUR JUNIOR WOODCHUCKS' GUIDEBOOK! JUST IN CASE WE NEED TO KNOW SOME VITAL INFORMATION!
JUNIOR WOODCHUCKS OF THE WORLD
THEN ALL IS SHIPSHAPE! FORWARD TO THE SEVEN CITIES OF FABULOUS CIBOLA!
YIPPEE! KI-YI!
SHALL WE START, TOO?
NO! THEY'LL SEE US! LET 'EM GET A FEW MILES AHEAD!
DOWN PAST THE OASIS!
AS LONG AS THE TRAIL REMAINS THIS PLAIN, WE'LL HAVE NO TROUBLE FOLLOWING IT!
ONWARD ALONG THE DESERT FOOTHILLS!
IT'S STILL GOING STRONG!
SUDDENLY!
WHUP! END OF THE LINE!
SAND HAS COVERED THE TRAIL!
WHERE DOES IT GO FROM HERE — UP THAT WAY OR ACROSS THIS WAY?
WE'LL KNOW IN A JIFFY!

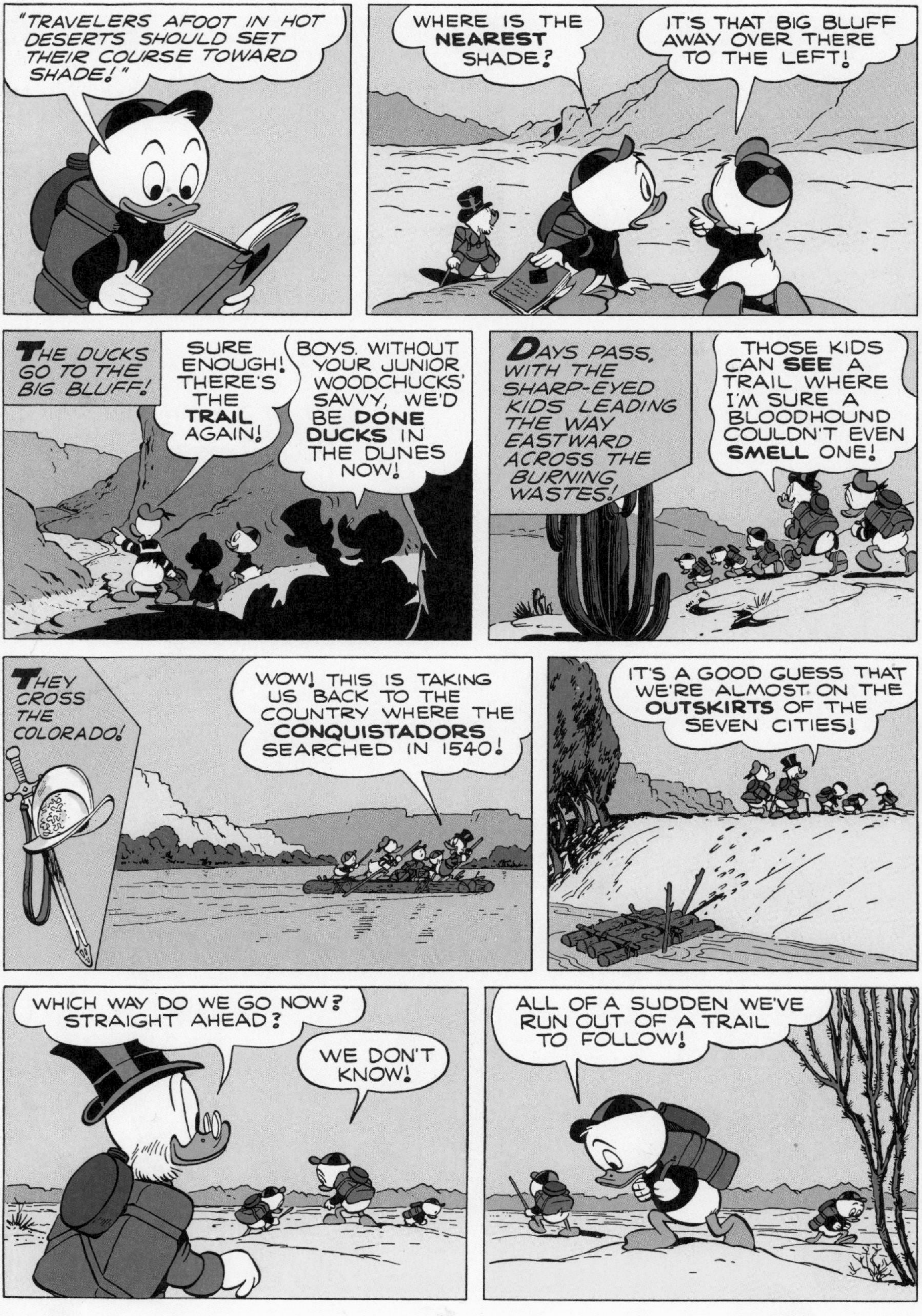
"TRAVELERS AFOOT IN HOT DESERTS SHOULD SET THEIR COURSE TOWARD SHADE!"
WHERE IS THE NEAREST SHADE?
IT'S THAT BIG BLUFF AWAY OVER THERE TO THE LEFT!
THE DUCKS GO TO THE BIG BLUFF!
SURE ENOUGH! THERE'S THE TRAIL AGAIN!
BOYS, WITHOUT YOUR JUNIOR WOODCHUCKS' SAVVY, WE'D BE DONE DUCKS IN THE DUNES NOW!
DAYS PASS, WITH THE SHARP-EYED KIDS LEADING THE WAY EASTWARD ACROSS THE BURNING WASTES!
THOSE KIDS CAN SEE A TRAIL WHERE I'M SURE A BLOODHOUND COULDN'T EVEN SMELL ONE!
THEY CROSS THE COLORADO!
WOW! THIS IS TAKING US BACK TO THE COUNTRY WHERE THE CONQUISTADORS SEARCHED IN 1540!
IT'S A GOOD GUESS THAT WE'RE ALMOST ON THE OUTSKIRTS OF THE SEVEN CITIES!
WHICH WAY DO WE GO NOW? STRAIGHT AHEAD?
WE DON'T KNOW!
ALL OF A SUDDEN WE'VE RUN OUT OF A TRAIL TO FOLLOW!

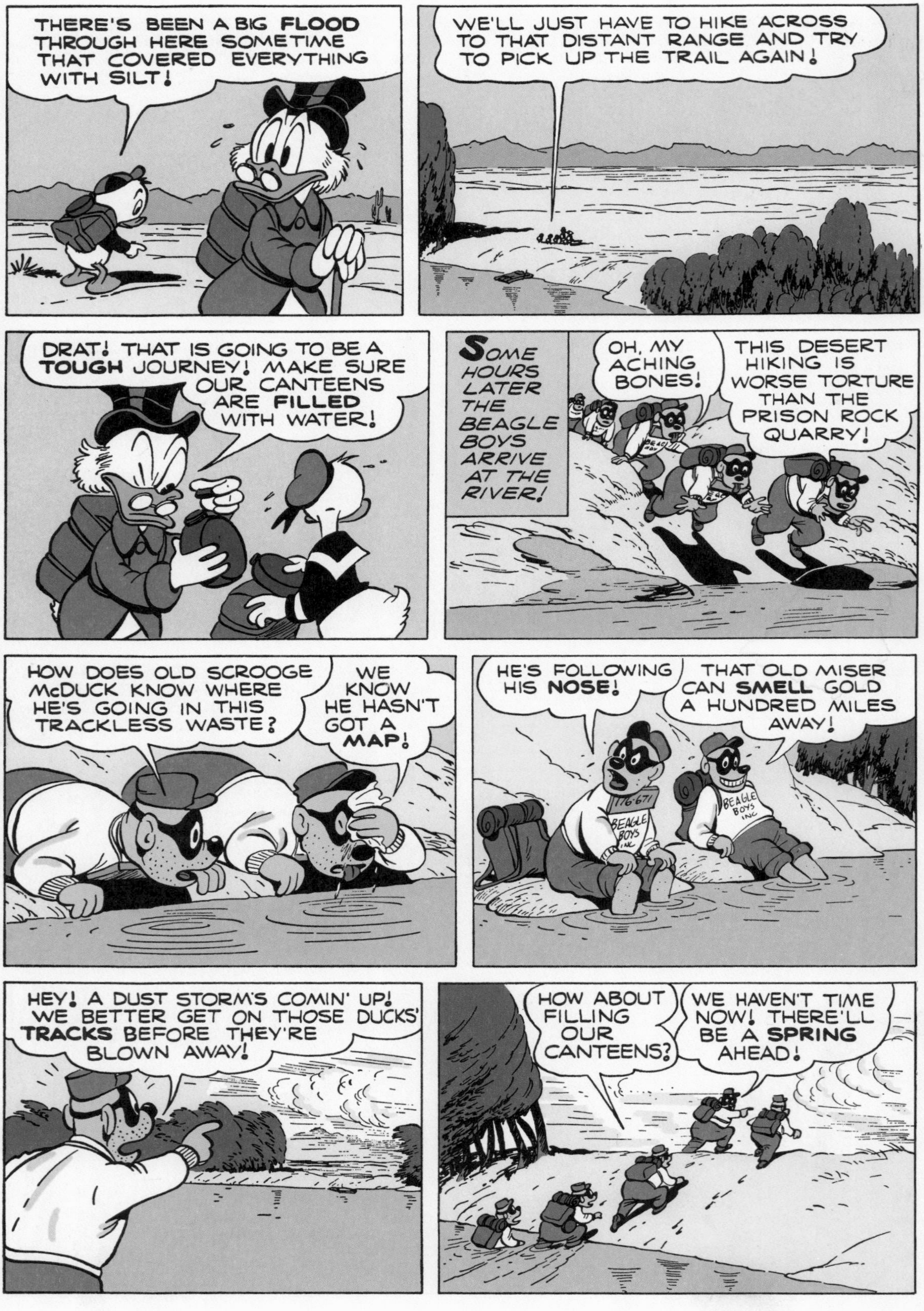
THERE'S BEEN A BIG FLOOD THROUGH HERE SOMETIME THAT COVERED EVERYTHING WITH SILT!
WE'LL JUST HAVE TO HIKE ACROSS TO THAT DISTANT RANGE AND TRY TO PICK UP THE TRAIL AGAIN!
DRAT! THAT IS GOING TO BE A TOUGH JOURNEY! MAKE SURE OUR CANTEENS ARE FILLED WITH WATER!
SOME HOURS LATER THE BEAGLE BOYS ARRIVE AT THE RIVER!
OH, MY ACHING BONES!
THIS DESERT HIKING IS WORSE TORTURE THAN THE PRISON ROCK QUARRY!
HOW DOES OLD SCROOGE McDUCK KNOW WHERE HE'S GOING IN THIS TRACKLESS WASTE?
WE KNOW HE HASN'T GOT A MAP!
HE'S FOLLOWING HIS NOSE!
THAT OLD MISER CAN SMELL GOLD A HUNDRED MILES AWAY!
176-671
BEAGLE BOYS INC
HEY! A DUST STORM'S COMIN' UP! WE BETTER GET ON THOSE DUCKS' TRACKS BEFORE THEY'RE BLOWN AWAY!
HOW ABOUT FILLING OUR CANTEENS?
WE HAVEN'T TIME NOW! THERE'LL BE A SPRING AHEAD!

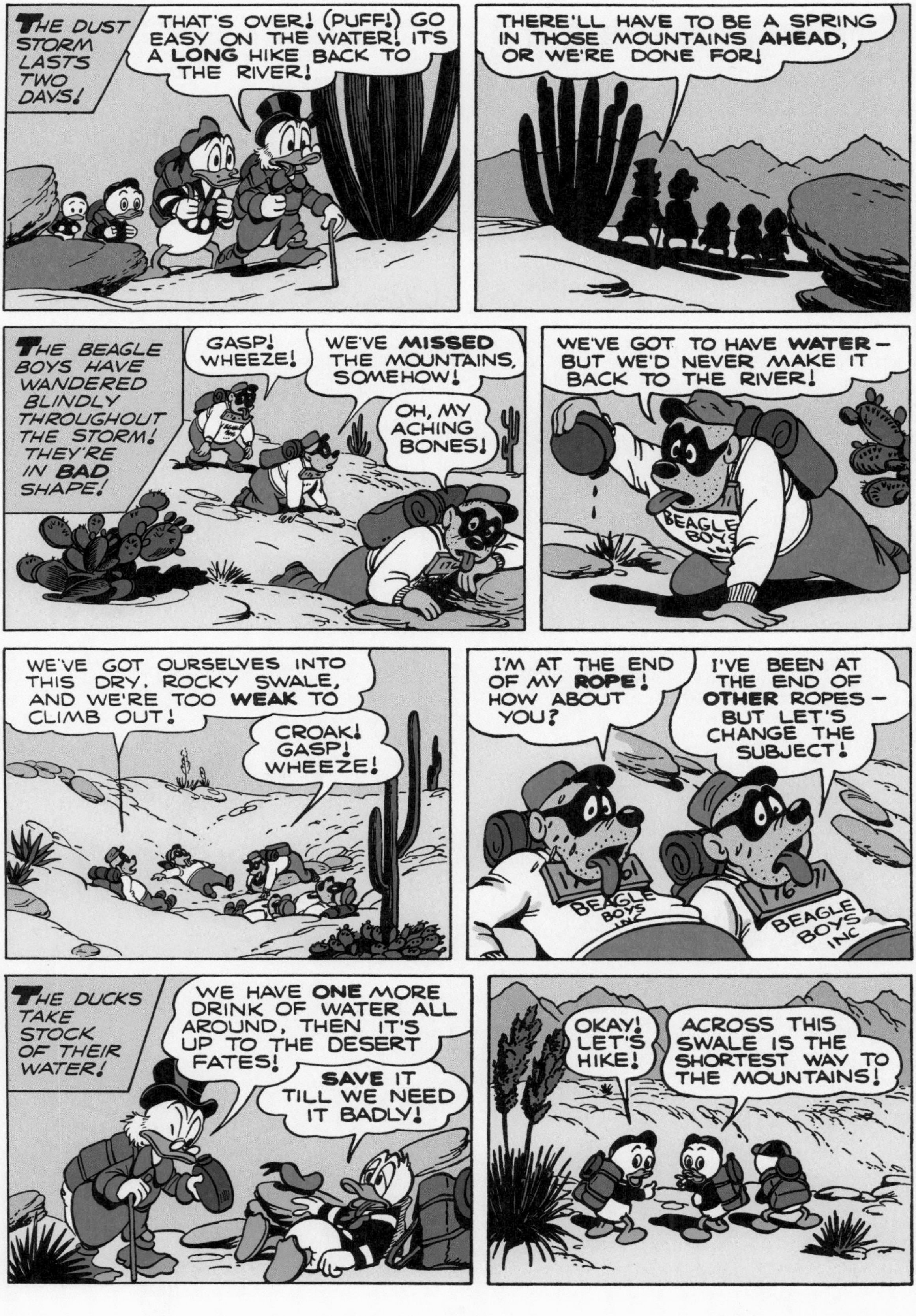
THE DUST STORM LASTS TWO DAYS!
THAT'S OVER! (PUFF!) GO EASY ON THE WATER! IT'S A LONG HIKE BACK TO THE RIVER!
THERE'LL HAVE TO BE A SPRING IN THOSE MOUNTAINS AHEAD, OR WE'RE DONE FOR!
THE BEAGLE BOYS HAVE WANDERED BLINDLY THROUGHOUT THE STORM! THEY'RE IN BAD SHAPE!
GASP! WHEEZE!
WE'VE MISSED THE MOUNTAINS, SOMEHOW!
OH, MY ACHING BONES!
WE'VE GOT TO HAVE WATER— BUT WE'D NEVER MAKE IT BACK TO THE RIVER!
BEAGLE BOYS INC
WE'VE GOT OURSELVES INTO THIS DRY, ROCKY SWALE, AND WE'RE TOO WEAK TO CLIMB OUT!
CROAK! GASP! WHEEZE!
I'M AT THE END OF MY ROPE! HOW ABOUT YOU?
I'VE BEEN AT THE END OF OTHER ROPES— BUT LET'S CHANGE THE SUBJECT!
BEAGLE BOYS INC
BEAGLE BOYS INC
THE DUCKS TAKE STOCK OF THEIR WATER!
WE HAVE ONE MORE DRINK OF WATER ALL AROUND, THEN IT'S UP TO THE DESERT FATES!
SAVE IT TILL WE NEED IT BADLY!
OKAY! LET'S HIKE!
ACROSS THIS SWALE IS THE SHORTEST WAY TO THE MOUNTAINS!

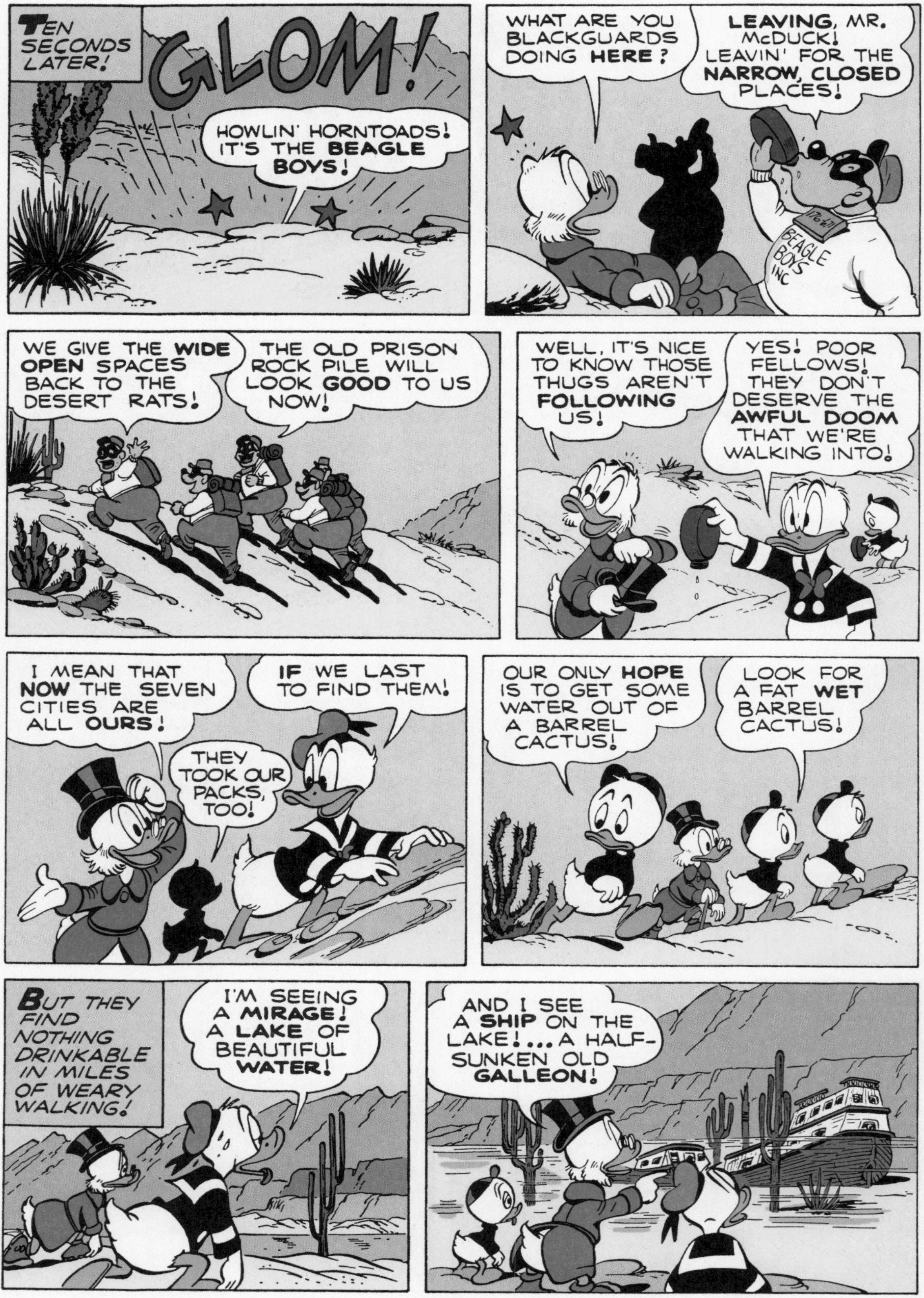
TEN SECONDS LATER!
GLOM!
HOWLIN' HORNTOADS! IT'S THE BEAGLE BOYS!
WHAT ARE YOU BLACKGUARDS DOING HERE?
LEAVING, MR. McDUCK! LEAVIN' FOR THE NARROW, CLOSED PLACES!
BEAGLE BOYS INC
WE GIVE THE WIDE OPEN SPACES BACK TO THE DESERT RATS!
THE OLD PRISON ROCK PILE WILL LOOK GOOD TO US NOW!
WELL, IT'S NICE TO KNOW THOSE THUGS AREN'T FOLLOWING US!
YES! POOR FELLOWS! THEY DON'T DESERVE THE AWFUL DOOM THAT WE'RE WALKING INTO!
I MEAN THAT NOW THE SEVEN CITIES ARE ALL OURS!
IF WE LAST TO FIND THEM!
THEY TOOK OUR PACKS, TOO!
OUR ONLY HOPE IS TO GET SOME WATER OUT OF A BARREL CACTUS!
LOOK FOR A FAT WET BARREL CACTUS!
BUT THEY FIND NOTHING DRINKABLE IN MILES OF WEARY WALKING!
I'M SEEING A MIRAGE! A LAKE OF BEAUTIFUL WATER!
AND I SEE A SHIP ON THE LAKE!...A HALF-SUNKEN OLD GALLEON!

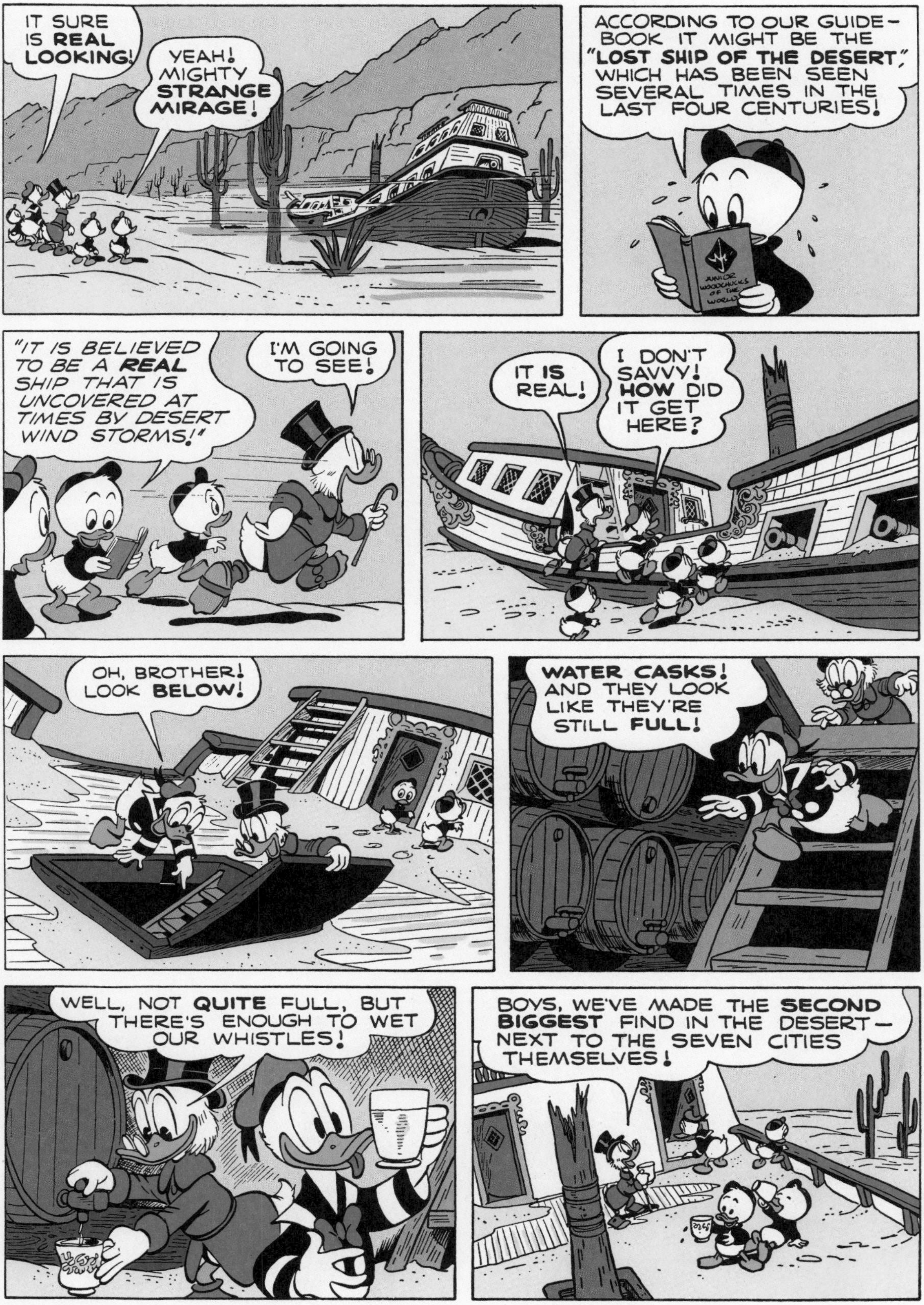
IT SURE IS REAL LOOKING!
YEAH! MIGHTY STRANGE MIRAGE!
ACCORDING TO OUR GUIDE-BOOK IT MIGHT BE THE "LOST SHIP OF THE DESERT," WHICH HAS BEEN SEEN SEVERAL TIMES IN THE LAST FOUR CENTURIES!
JUNIOR WOODCHUCKS OF THE WORLD
"IT IS BELIEVED TO BE A REAL SHIP THAT IS UNCOVERED AT TIMES BY DESERT WIND STORMS!"
I'M GOING TO SEE!
IT IS REAL!
I DON'T SAVVY! HOW DID IT GET HERE?
OH, BROTHER! LOOK BELOW!
WATER CASKS! AND THEY LOOK LIKE THEY'RE STILL FULL!
WELL, NOT QUITE FULL, BUT THERE'S ENOUGH TO WET OUR WHISTLES!
BOYS, WE'VE MADE THE SECOND BIGGEST FIND IN THE DESERT— NEXT TO THE SEVEN CITIES THEMSELVES!

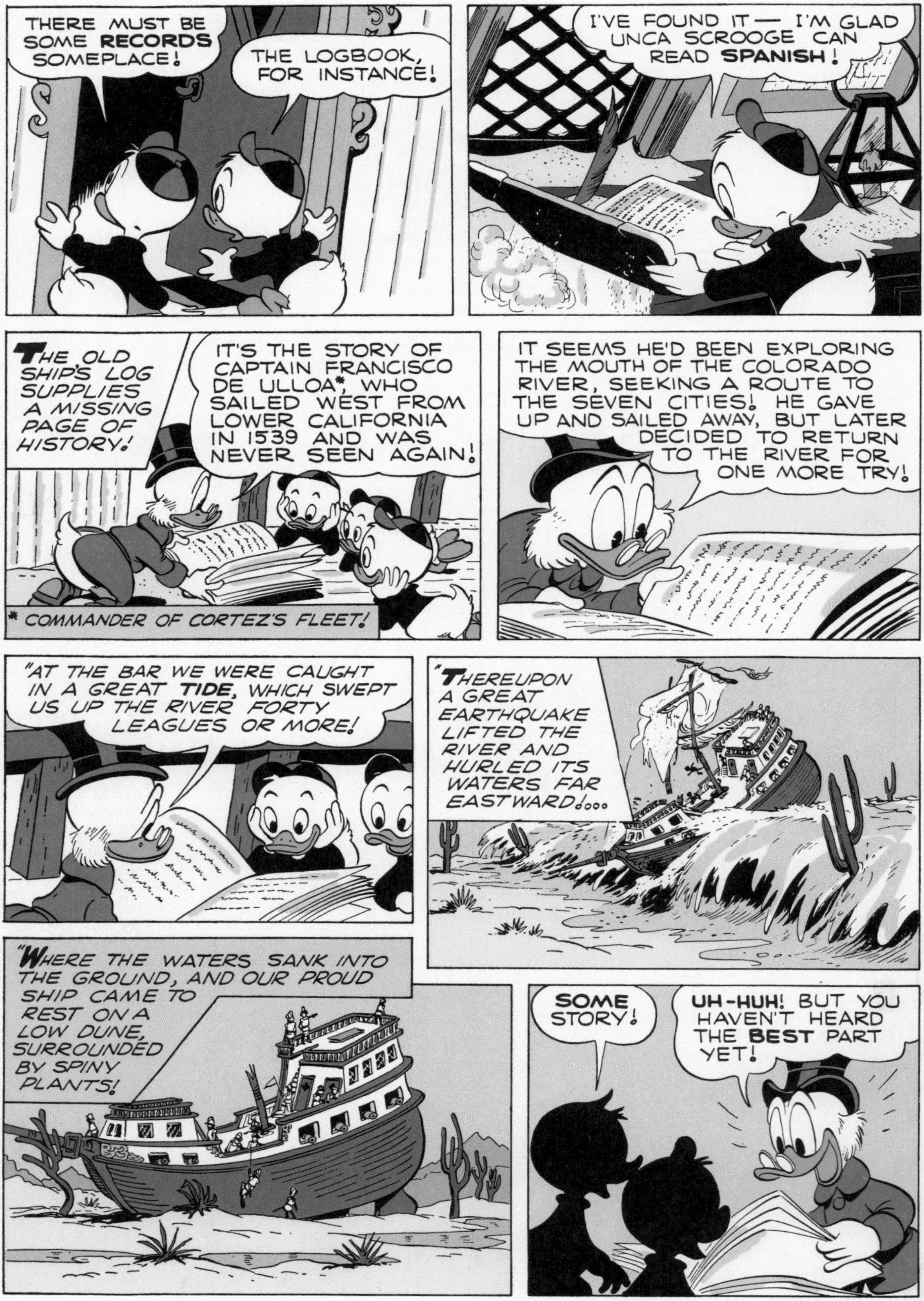
THERE MUST BE SOME **RECORDS** SOMEPLACE!
THE LOGBOOK, FOR INSTANCE!
I'VE FOUND IT — I'M GLAD UNCA SCROOGE CAN READ **SPANISH**!
THE OLD SHIP'S LOG SUPPLIES A MISSING PAGE OF HISTORY!
IT'S THE STORY OF CAPTAIN FRANCISCO DE ULLOA*, WHO SAILED WEST FROM LOWER CALIFORNIA IN 1539 AND WAS NEVER SEEN AGAIN!
* COMMANDER OF CORTEZ'S FLEET!
IT SEEMS HE'D BEEN EXPLORING THE MOUTH OF THE COLORADO RIVER, SEEKING A ROUTE TO THE SEVEN CITIES! HE GAVE UP AND SAILED AWAY, BUT LATER DECIDED TO RETURN TO THE RIVER FOR ONE MORE TRY!
"AT THE BAR WE WERE CAUGHT IN A GREAT **TIDE**, WHICH SWEPT US UP THE RIVER FORTY LEAGUES OR MORE!
"THEREUPON A GREAT EARTHQUAKE LIFTED THE RIVER AND HURLED ITS WATERS FAR EASTWARD!...
"WHERE THE WATERS SANK INTO THE GROUND, AND OUR PROUD SHIP CAME TO REST ON A LOW DUNE, SURROUNDED BY SPINY PLANTS!
SOME STORY!
UH-HUH! BUT YOU HAVEN'T HEARD THE **BEST** PART YET!

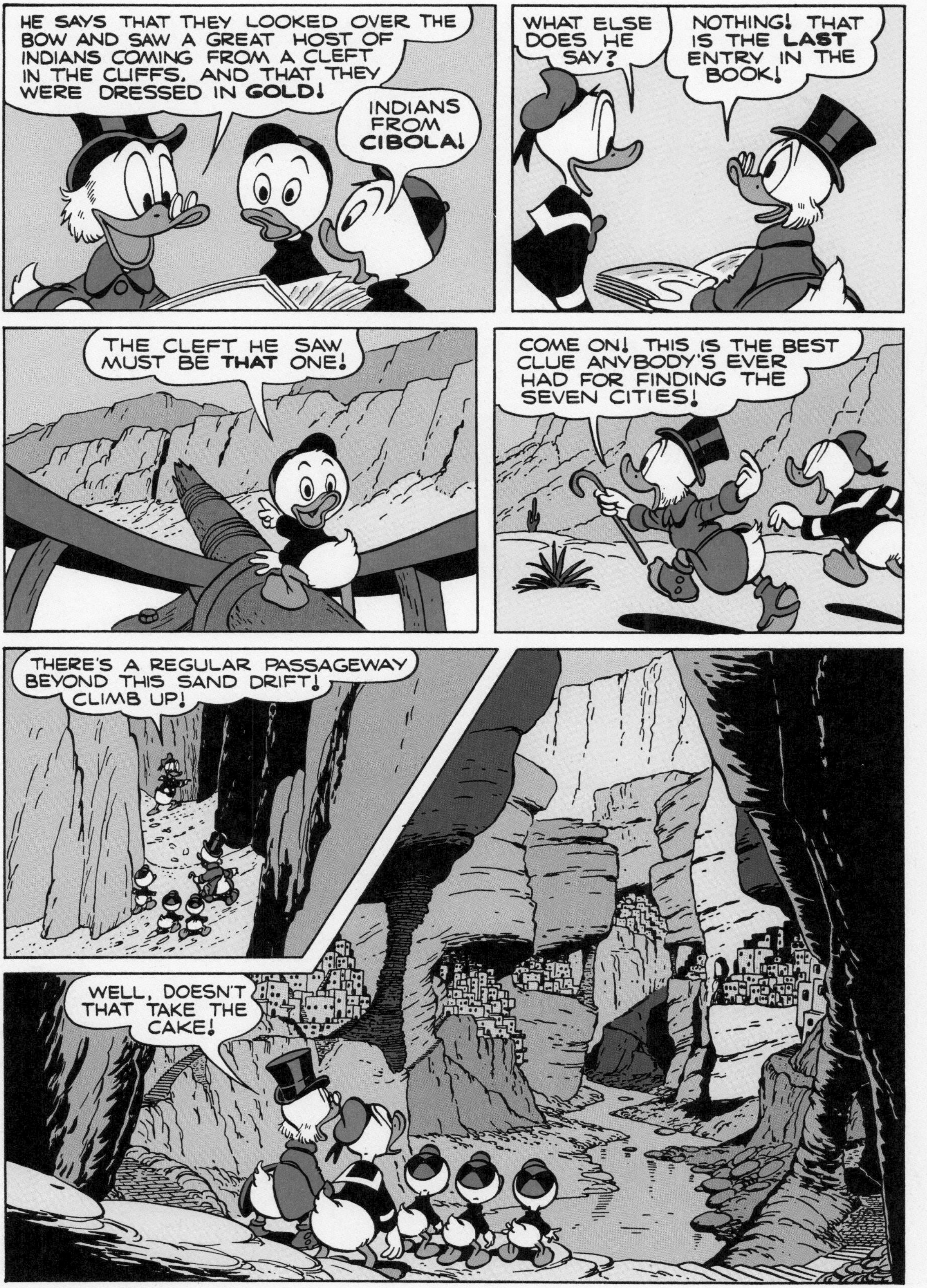
HE SAYS THAT THEY LOOKED OVER THE BOW AND SAW A GREAT HOST OF INDIANS COMING FROM A CLEFT IN THE CLIFFS, AND THAT THEY WERE DRESSED IN **GOLD**!
INDIANS FROM **CIBOLA**!
WHAT ELSE DOES HE SAY?
NOTHING! THAT IS THE **LAST** ENTRY IN THE BOOK!
THE CLEFT HE SAW MUST BE **THAT** ONE!
COME ON! THIS IS THE BEST CLUE ANYBODY'S EVER HAD FOR FINDING THE SEVEN CITIES!
THERE'S A REGULAR PASSAGEWAY BEYOND THIS SAND DRIFT! CLIMB UP!
WELL, DOESN'T THAT TAKE THE CAKE!

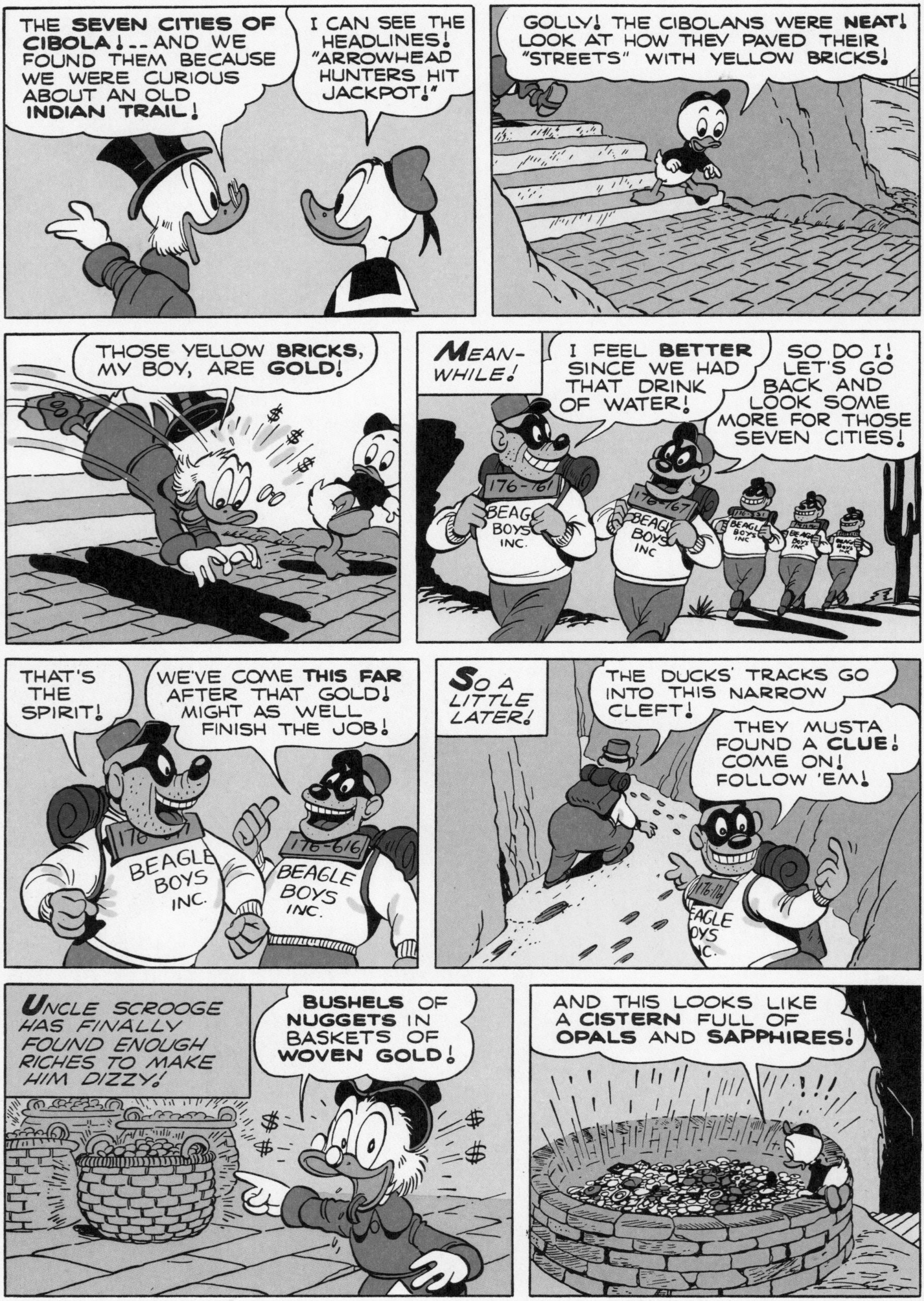
THE SEVEN CITIES OF CIBOLA! -- AND WE FOUND THEM BECAUSE WE WERE CURIOUS ABOUT AN OLD INDIAN TRAIL!
I CAN SEE THE HEADLINES! "ARROWHEAD HUNTERS HIT JACKPOT!"
GOLLY! THE CIBOLANS WERE NEAT! LOOK AT HOW THEY PAVED THEIR "STREETS" WITH YELLOW BRICKS!
THOSE YELLOW BRICKS, MY BOY, ARE GOLD!
MEANWHILE!
I FEEL BETTER SINCE WE HAD THAT DRINK OF WATER!
SO DO I! LET'S GO BACK AND LOOK SOME MORE FOR THOSE SEVEN CITIES!
176-761
BEAGLE BOYS INC.
176-767
BEAGLE BOYS INC
THAT'S THE SPIRIT!
WE'VE COME THIS FAR AFTER THAT GOLD! MIGHT AS WELL FINISH THE JOB!
BEAGLE BOYS INC.
176-616
BEAGLE BOYS INC.
SO A LITTLE LATER!
THE DUCKS' TRACKS GO INTO THIS NARROW CLEFT!
THEY MUSTA FOUND A CLUE! COME ON! FOLLOW 'EM!
UNCLE SCROOGE HAS FINALLY FOUND ENOUGH RICHES TO MAKE HIM DIZZY!
BUSHELS OF NUGGETS IN BASKETS OF WOVEN GOLD!
AND THIS LOOKS LIKE A CISTERN FULL OF OPALS AND SAPPHIRES!
!!!

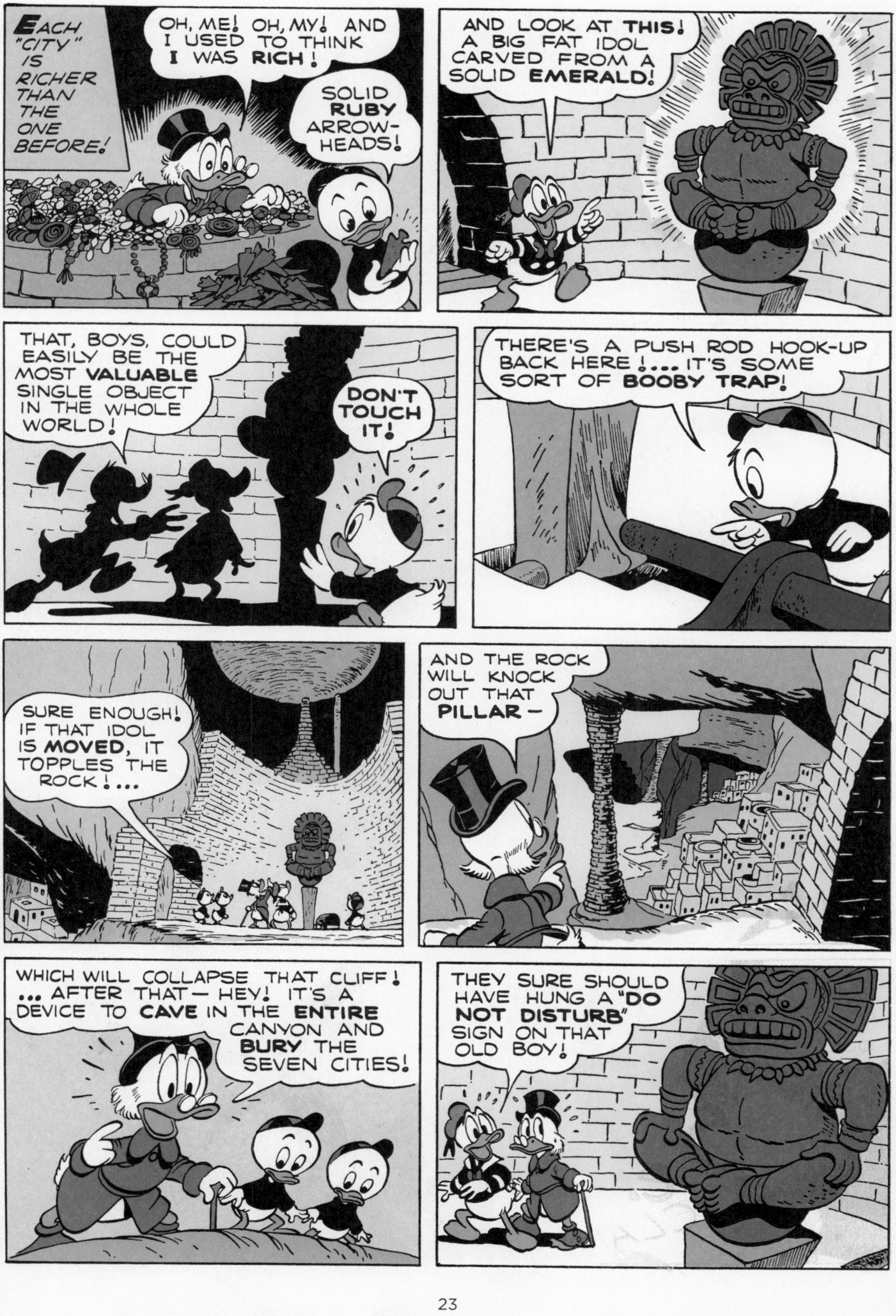
EACH "CITY" IS RICHER THAN THE ONE BEFORE!
OH, ME! OH, MY! AND I USED TO THINK I WAS RICH!
SOLID RUBY ARROW-HEADS!
AND LOOK AT THIS! A BIG FAT IDOL CARVED FROM A SOLID EMERALD!
THAT, BOYS, COULD EASILY BE THE MOST VALUABLE SINGLE OBJECT IN THE WHOLE WORLD!
DON'T TOUCH IT!
THERE'S A PUSH ROD HOOK-UP BACK HERE!... IT'S SOME SORT OF BOOBY TRAP!
SURE ENOUGH! IF THAT IDOL IS MOVED, IT TOPPLES THE ROCK!...
AND THE ROCK WILL KNOCK OUT THAT PILLAR—
WHICH WILL COLLAPSE THAT CLIFF! ... AFTER THAT— HEY! IT'S A DEVICE TO CAVE IN THE ENTIRE CANYON AND BURY THE SEVEN CITIES!
THEY SURE SHOULD HAVE HUNG A "DO NOT DISTURB" SIGN ON THAT OLD BOY!

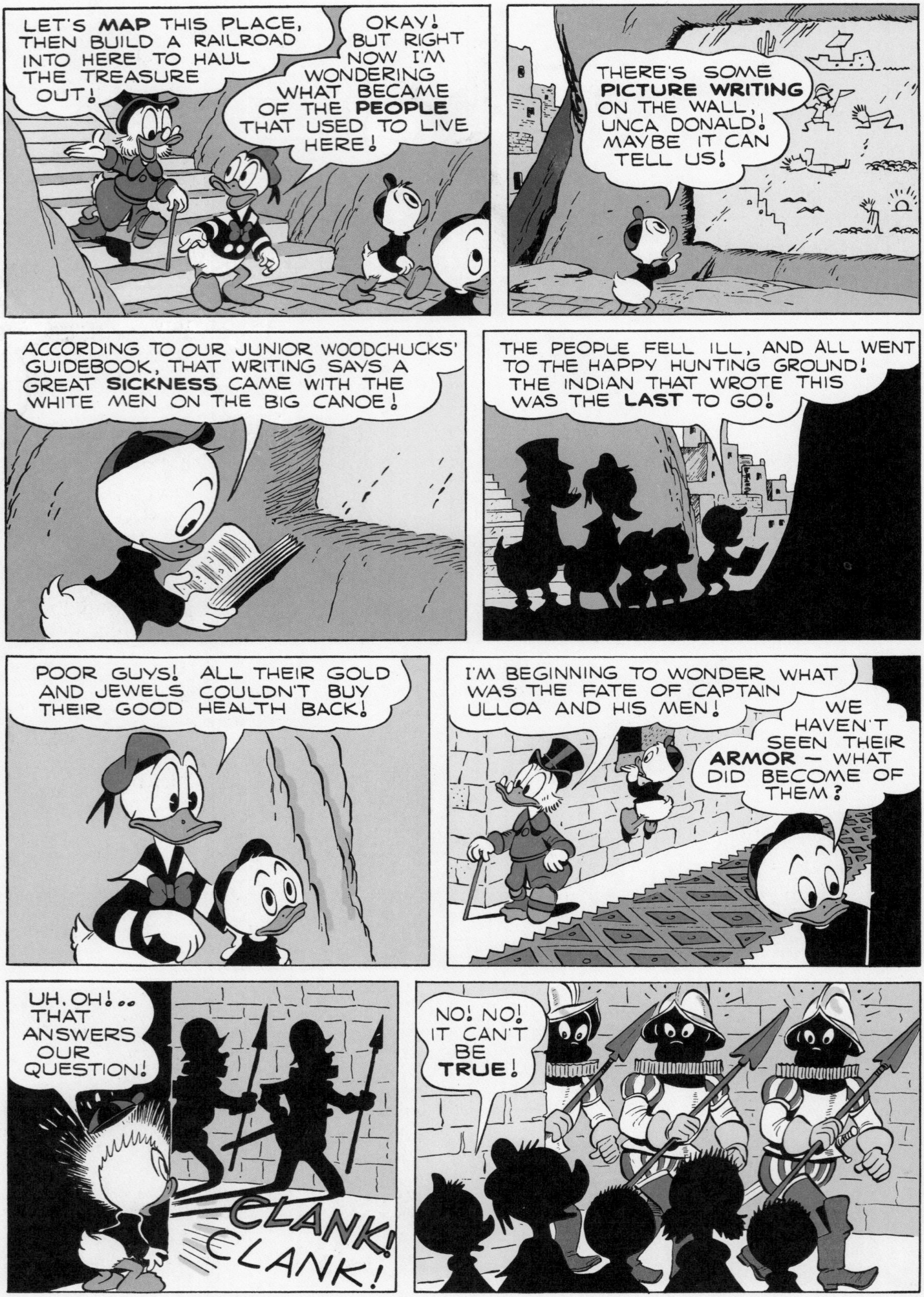
LET'S MAP THIS PLACE, THEN BUILD A RAILROAD INTO HERE TO HAUL THE TREASURE OUT!
OKAY! BUT RIGHT NOW I'M WONDERING WHAT BECAME OF THE PEOPLE THAT USED TO LIVE HERE!
THERE'S SOME PICTURE WRITING ON THE WALL, UNCA DONALD! MAYBE IT CAN TELL US!
ACCORDING TO OUR JUNIOR WOODCHUCKS' GUIDEBOOK, THAT WRITING SAYS A GREAT SICKNESS CAME WITH THE WHITE MEN ON THE BIG CANOE!
THE PEOPLE FELL ILL, AND ALL WENT TO THE HAPPY HUNTING GROUND! THE INDIAN THAT WROTE THIS WAS THE LAST TO GO!
POOR GUYS! ALL THEIR GOLD AND JEWELS COULDN'T BUY THEIR GOOD HEALTH BACK!
I'M BEGINNING TO WONDER WHAT WAS THE FATE OF CAPTAIN ULLOA AND HIS MEN!
WE HAVEN'T SEEN THEIR ARMOR — WHAT DID BECOME OF THEM?
UH, OH!.. THAT ANSWERS OUR QUESTION!
CLANK! CLANK!
NO! NO! IT CAN'T BE TRUE!

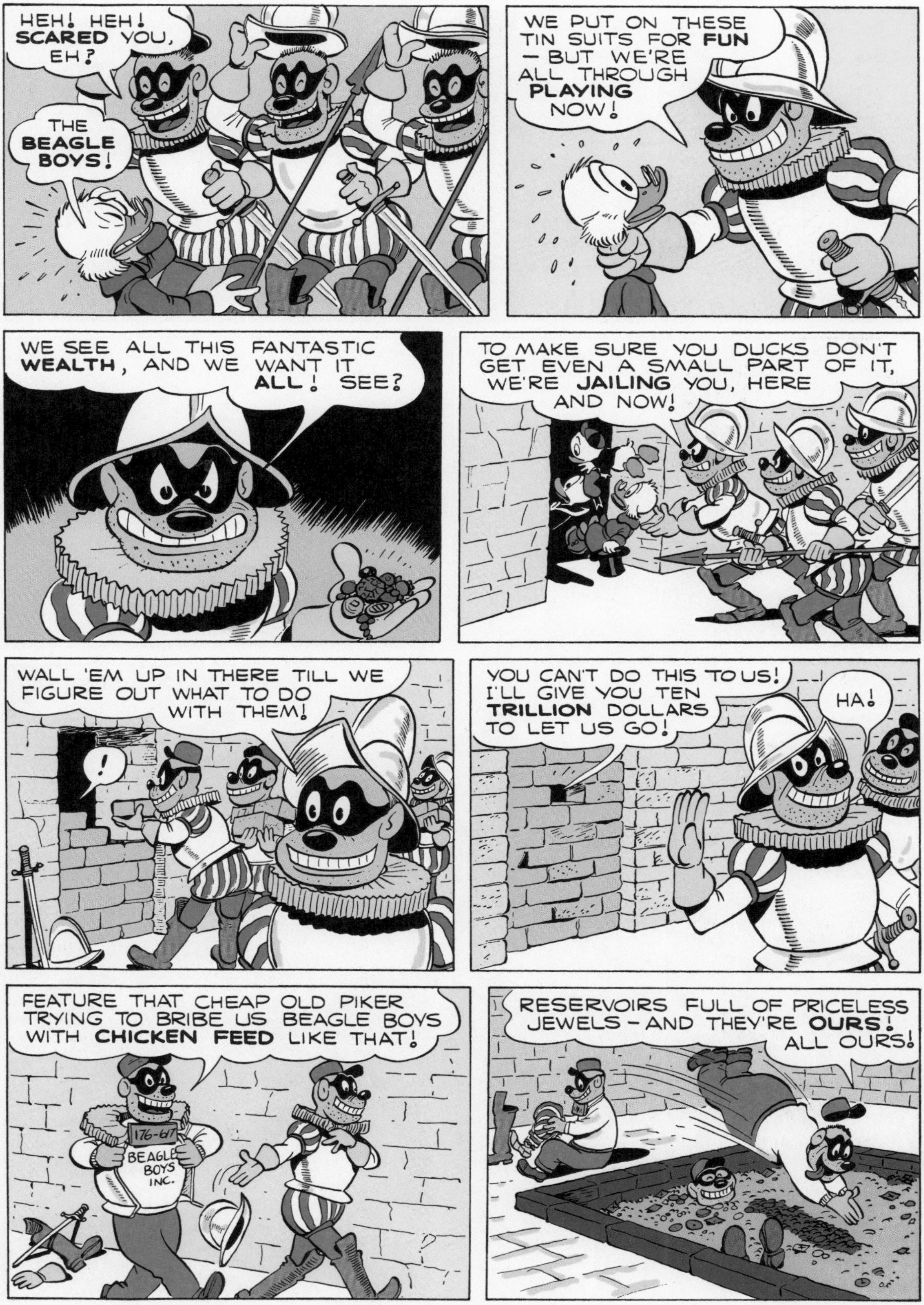
HEH! HEH! SCARED YOU, EH?
THE BEAGLE BOYS!
WE PUT ON THESE TIN SUITS FOR FUN — BUT WE'RE ALL THROUGH PLAYING NOW!
WE SEE ALL THIS FANTASTIC WEALTH, AND WE WANT IT ALL! SEE?
TO MAKE SURE YOU DUCKS DON'T GET EVEN A SMALL PART OF IT, WE'RE JAILING YOU, HERE AND NOW!
WALL 'EM UP IN THERE TILL WE FIGURE OUT WHAT TO DO WITH THEM!
!
YOU CAN'T DO THIS TO US! I'LL GIVE YOU TEN TRILLION DOLLARS TO LET US GO!
HA!
FEATURE THAT CHEAP OLD PIKER TRYING TO BRIBE US BEAGLE BOYS WITH CHICKEN FEED LIKE THAT!
176-617
BEAGLE BOYS INC.
RESERVOIRS FULL OF PRICELESS JEWELS — AND THEY'RE OURS! ALL OURS!

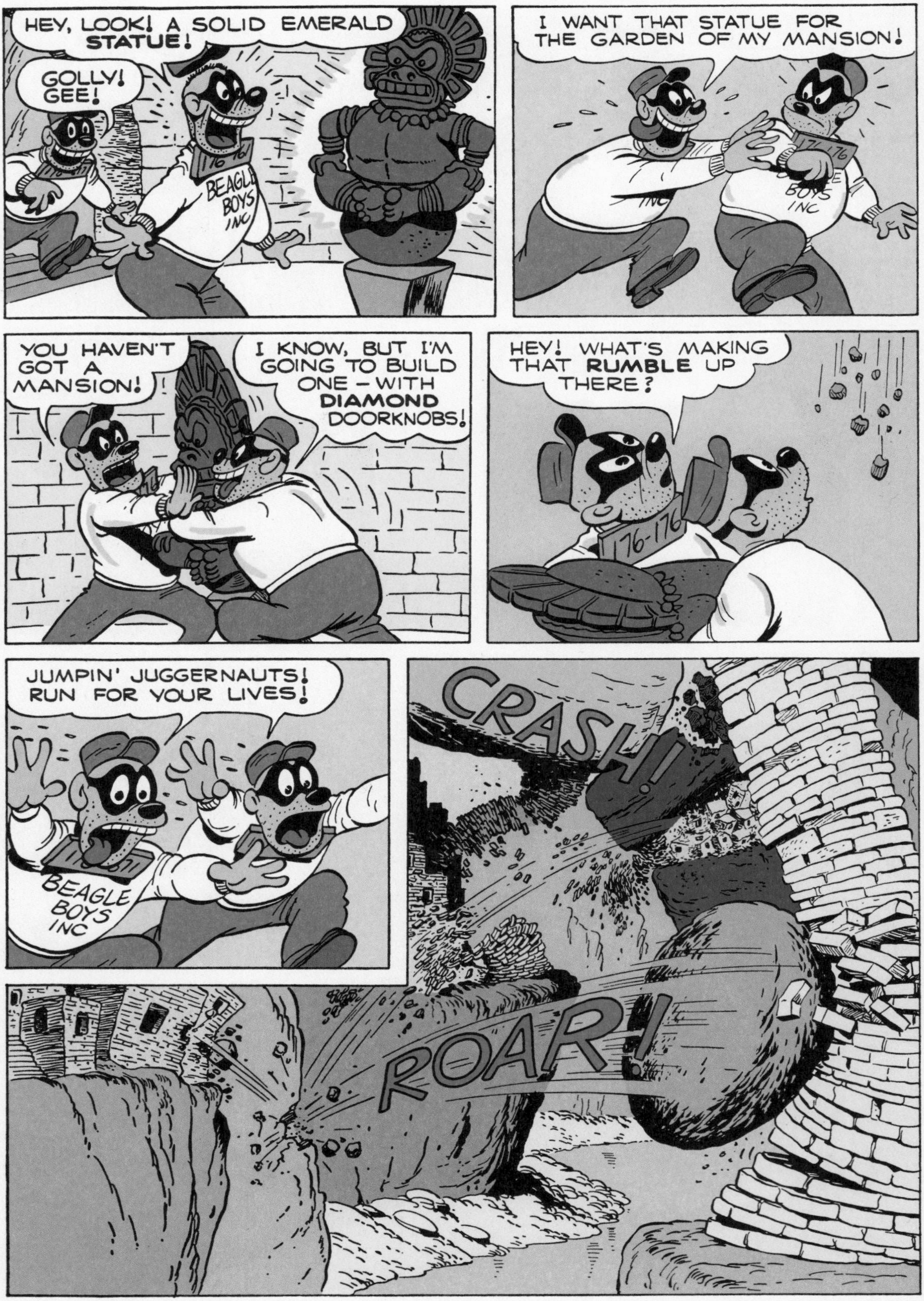
HEY, LOOK! A SOLID EMERALD STATUE!
GOLLY! GEE!
I WANT THAT STATUE FOR THE GARDEN OF MY MANSION!
YOU HAVEN'T GOT A MANSION!
I KNOW, BUT I'M GOING TO BUILD ONE – WITH DIAMOND DOORKNOBS!
HEY! WHAT'S MAKING THAT RUMBLE UP THERE?
JUMPIN' JUGGERNAUTS! RUN FOR YOUR LIVES!
CRASH!
ROAR!

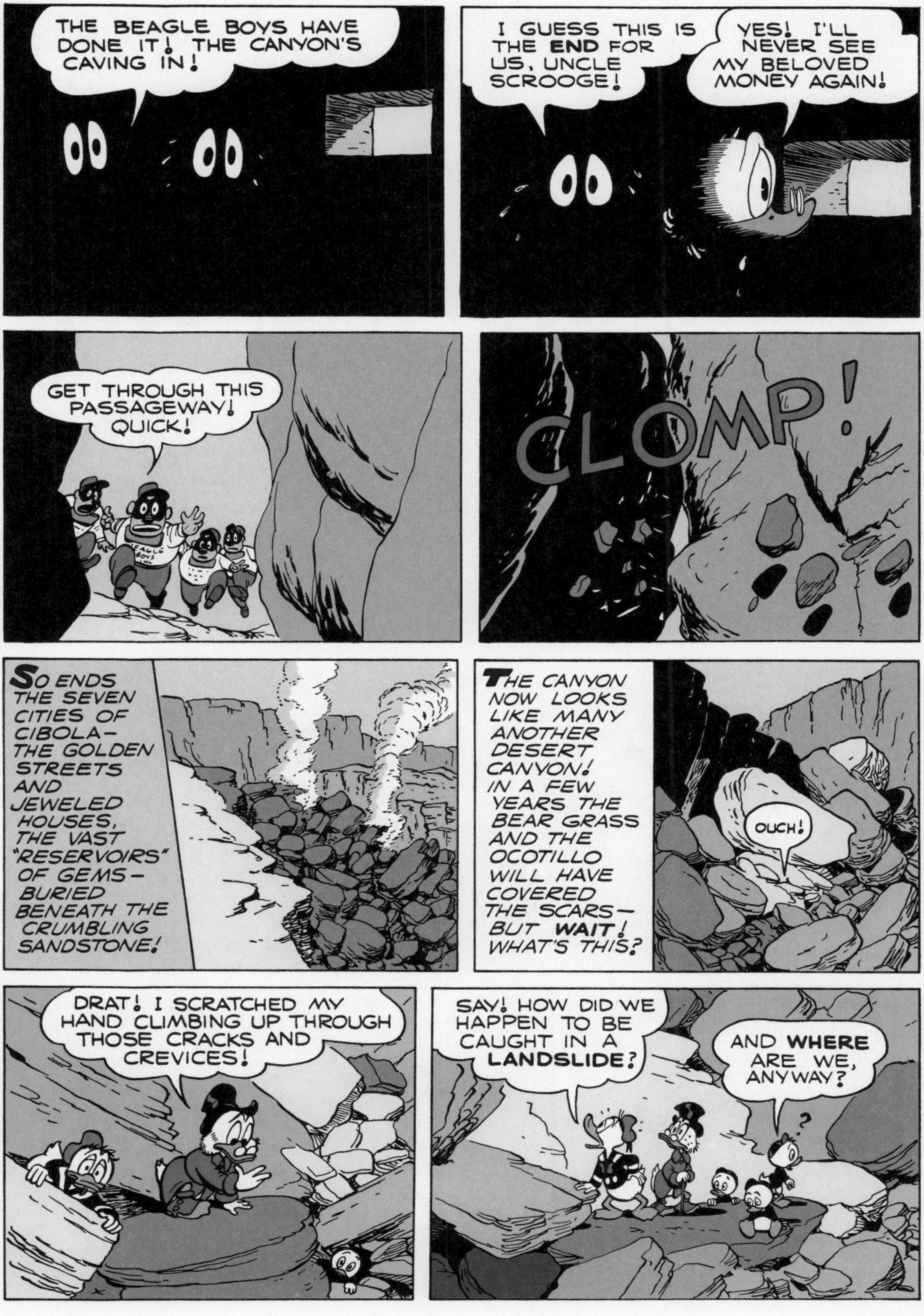
THE BEAGLE BOYS HAVE DONE IT! THE CANYON'S CAVING IN!
I GUESS THIS IS THE END FOR US, UNCLE SCROOGE!
YES! I'LL NEVER SEE MY BELOVED MONEY AGAIN!
GET THROUGH THIS PASSAGEWAY! QUICK!
BEAGLE BOYS
CLOMP!
SO ENDS THE SEVEN CITIES OF CIBOLA—THE GOLDEN STREETS AND JEWELED HOUSES, THE VAST "RESERVOIRS" OF GEMS—BURIED BENEATH THE CRUMBLING SANDSTONE!
THE CANYON NOW LOOKS LIKE MANY ANOTHER DESERT CANYON! IN A FEW YEARS THE BEAR GRASS AND THE OCOTILLO WILL HAVE COVERED THE SCARS—BUT WAIT! WHAT'S THIS?
OUCH!
DRAT! I SCRATCHED MY HAND CLIMBING UP THROUGH THOSE CRACKS AND CREVICES!
SAY! HOW DID WE HAPPEN TO BE CAUGHT IN A LANDSLIDE?
AND WHERE ARE WE, ANYWAY?
?

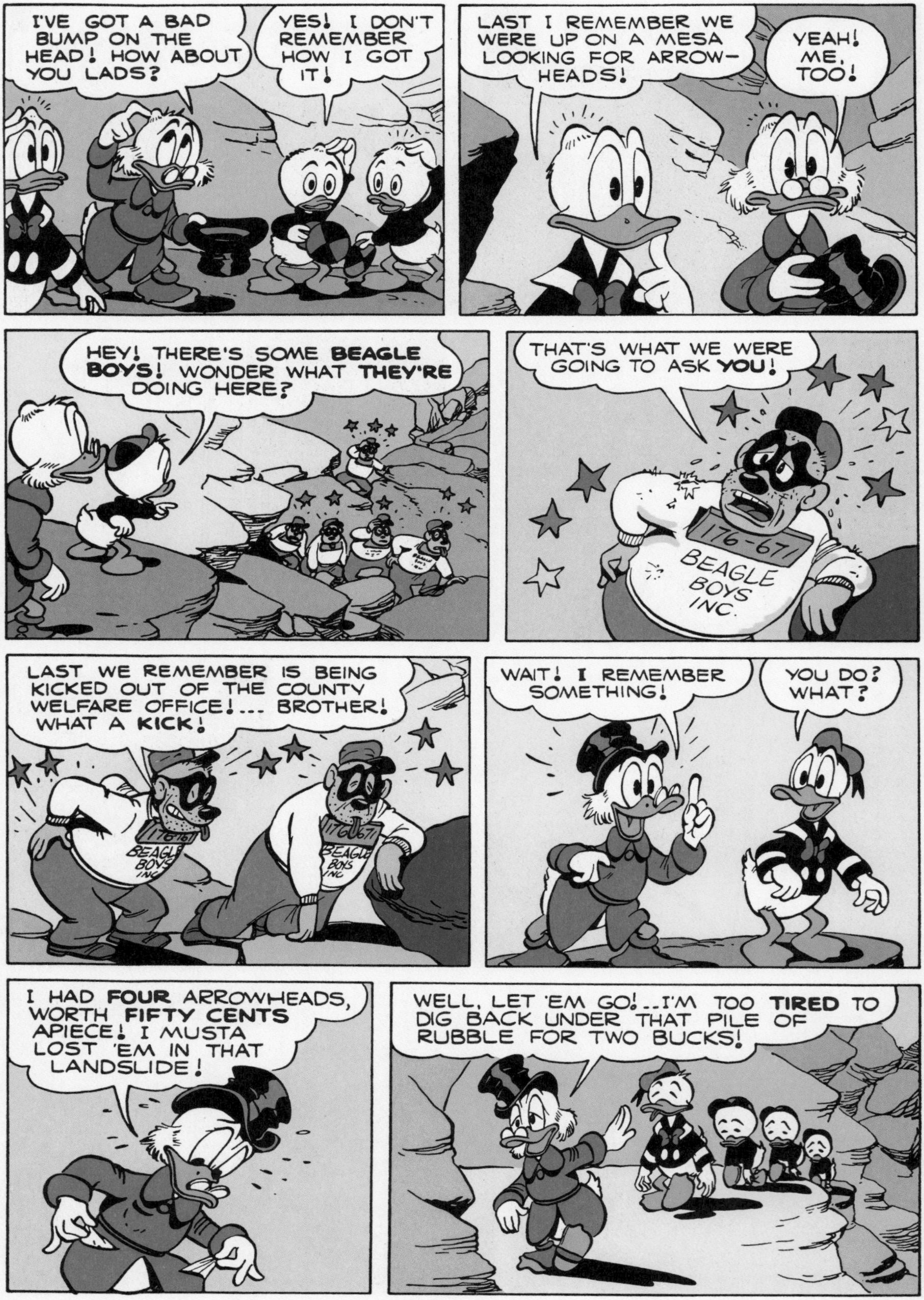

I'VE GOT A BAD BUMP ON THE HEAD! HOW ABOUT YOU LADS?
YES! I DON'T REMEMBER HOW I GOT IT!
LAST I REMEMBER WE WERE UP ON A MESA LOOKING FOR ARROW-HEADS!
YEAH! ME, TOO!
HEY! THERE'S SOME **BEAGLE BOYS**! WONDER WHAT **THEY'RE** DOING HERE?
THAT'S WHAT WE WERE GOING TO ASK **YOU**!
176-671
BEAGLE BOYS INC.
LAST WE REMEMBER IS BEING KICKED OUT OF THE COUNTY WELFARE OFFICE!... BROTHER! WHAT A **KICK**!
WAIT! **I** REMEMBER SOMETHING!
YOU DO? WHAT?
I HAD **FOUR** ARROWHEADS, WORTH **FIFTY CENTS** APIECE! I MUSTA LOST 'EM IN THAT LANDSLIDE!
WELL, LET 'EM GO!..I'M TOO **TIRED** TO DIG BACK UNDER THAT PILE OF RUBBLE FOR TWO BUCKS!

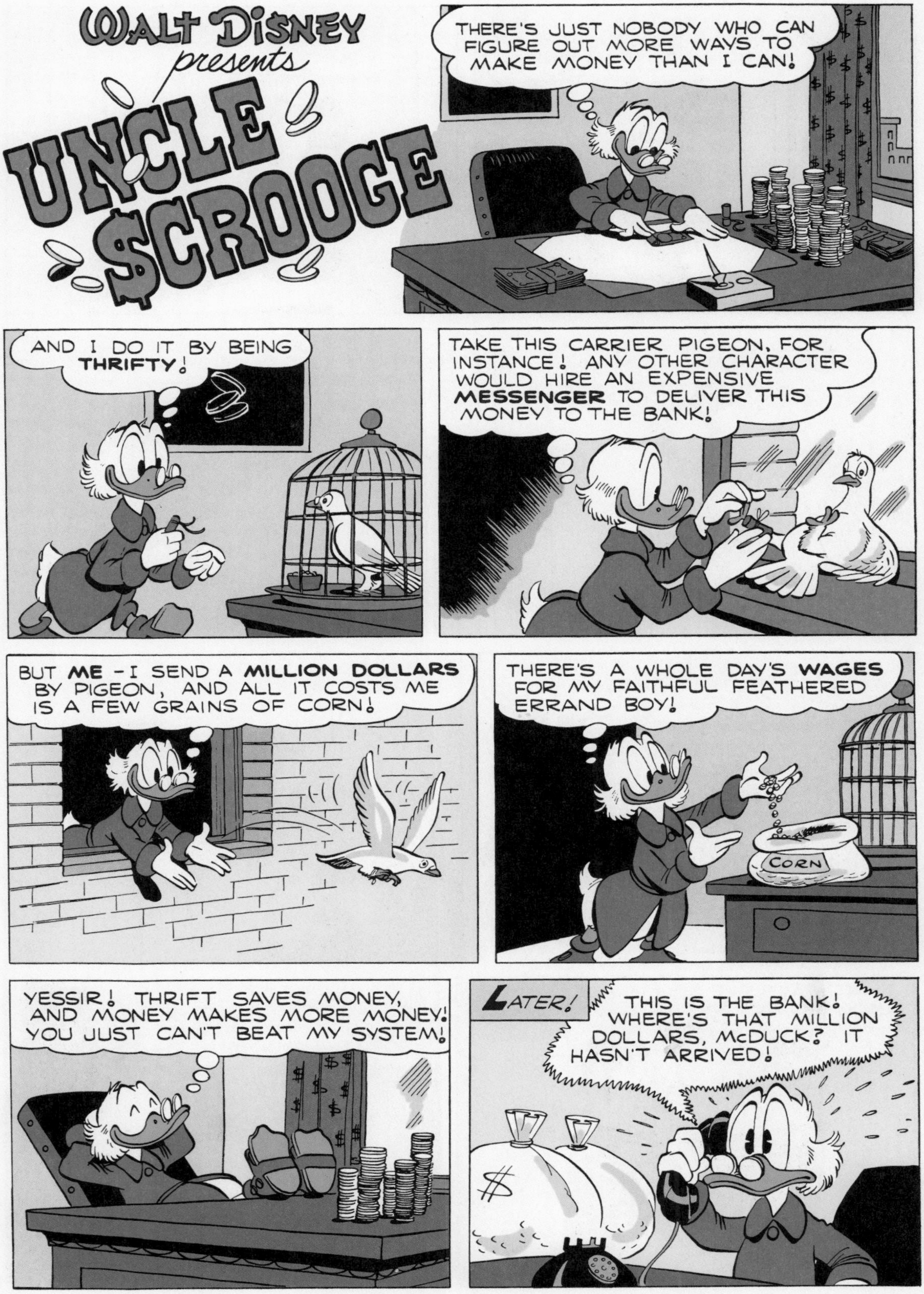
WALT DISNEY presents
UNCLE $CROOGE
THERE'S JUST NOBODY WHO CAN FIGURE OUT MORE WAYS TO MAKE MONEY THAN I CAN!
AND I DO IT BY BEING THRIFTY!
TAKE THIS CARRIER PIGEON, FOR INSTANCE! ANY OTHER CHARACTER WOULD HIRE AN EXPENSIVE MESSENGER TO DELIVER THIS MONEY TO THE BANK!
BUT ME - I SEND A MILLION DOLLARS BY PIGEON, AND ALL IT COSTS ME IS A FEW GRAINS OF CORN!
THERE'S A WHOLE DAY'S WAGES FOR MY FAITHFUL FEATHERED ERRAND BOY!
CORN
YESSIR! THRIFT SAVES MONEY, AND MONEY MAKES MORE MONEY! YOU JUST CAN'T BEAT MY SYSTEM!
LATER!
THIS IS THE BANK! WHERE'S THAT MILLION DOLLARS, McDUCK? IT HASN'T ARRIVED!

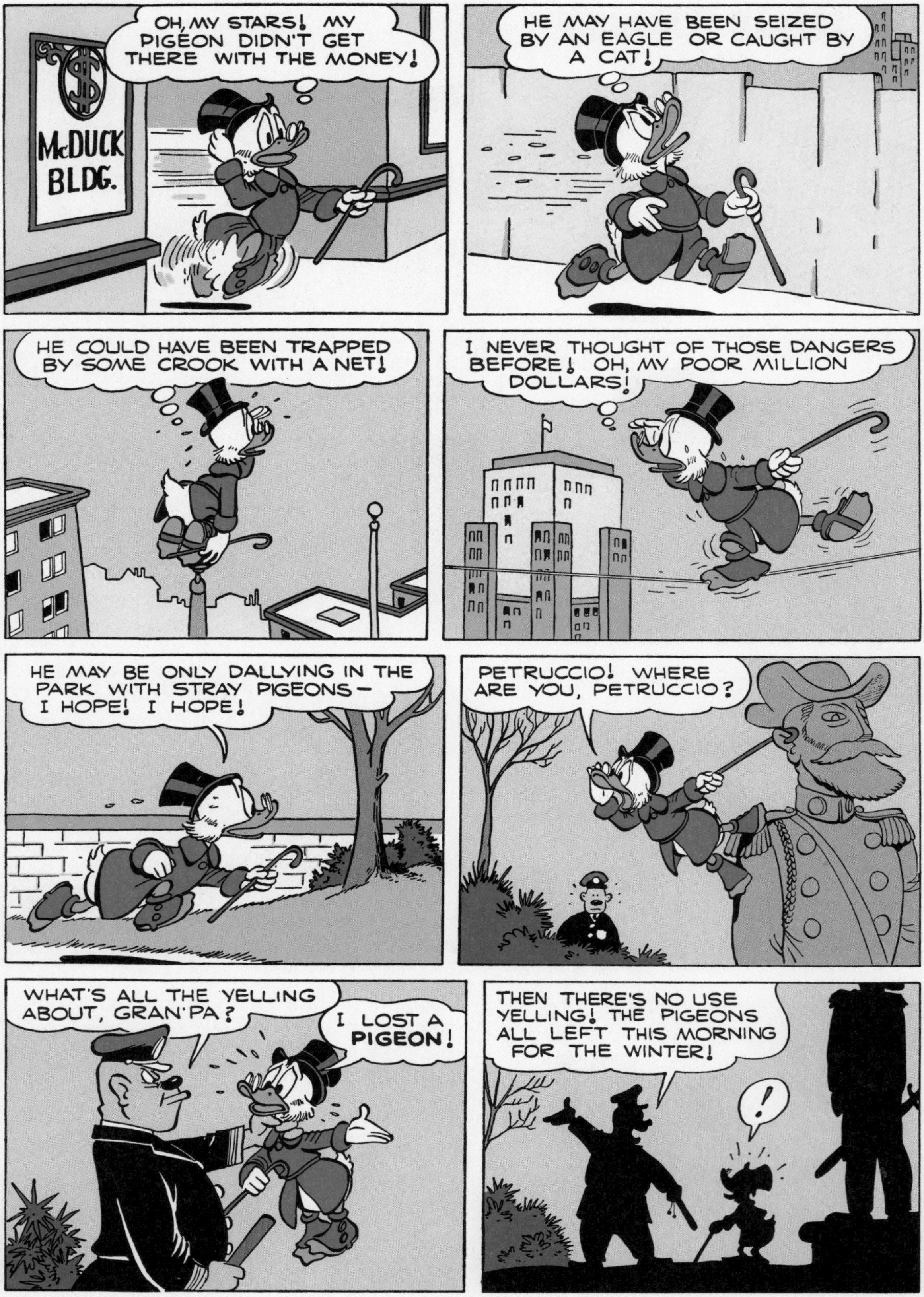
OH, MY STARS! MY PIGEON DIDN'T GET THERE WITH THE MONEY!
McDUCK BLDG.
HE MAY HAVE BEEN SEIZED BY AN EAGLE OR CAUGHT BY A CAT!
HE COULD HAVE BEEN TRAPPED BY SOME CROOK WITH A NET!
I NEVER THOUGHT OF THOSE DANGERS BEFORE! OH, MY POOR MILLION DOLLARS!
HE MAY BE ONLY DALLYING IN THE PARK WITH STRAY PIGEONS— I HOPE! I HOPE!
PETRUCCIO! WHERE ARE YOU, PETRUCCIO?
WHAT'S ALL THE YELLING ABOUT, GRAN'PA?
I LOST A **PIGEON**!
THEN THERE'S NO USE YELLING! THE PIGEONS ALL LEFT THIS MORNING FOR THE WINTER!
!

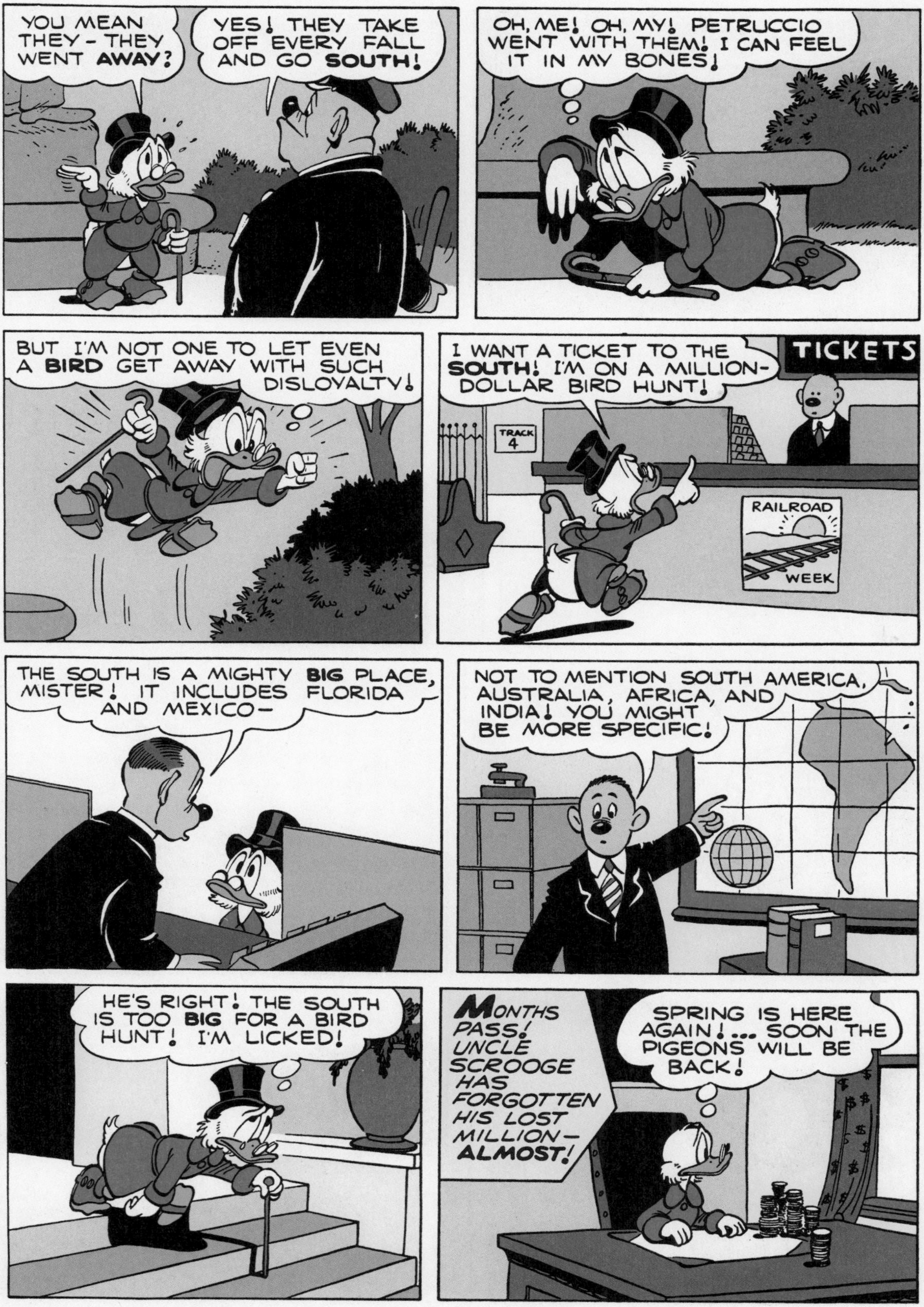

YOU MEAN THEY - THEY WENT **AWAY**?
YES! THEY TAKE OFF EVERY FALL AND GO **SOUTH**!
OH, ME! OH, MY! PETRUCCIO WENT WITH THEM! I CAN FEEL IT IN MY BONES!
BUT I'M NOT ONE TO LET EVEN A **BIRD** GET AWAY WITH SUCH DISLOYALTY!
I WANT A TICKET TO THE **SOUTH**! I'M ON A MILLION-DOLLAR BIRD HUNT!
TICKETS
TRACK 4
RAILROAD WEEK
THE SOUTH IS A MIGHTY **BIG** PLACE, MISTER! IT INCLUDES FLORIDA AND MEXICO—
NOT TO MENTION SOUTH AMERICA, AUSTRALIA, AFRICA, AND INDIA! YOU MIGHT BE MORE SPECIFIC!
HE'S RIGHT! THE SOUTH IS TOO **BIG** FOR A BIRD HUNT! I'M LICKED!
MONTHS PASS! UNCLE SCROOGE HAS FORGOTTEN HIS LOST MILLION— **ALMOST**!
SPRING IS HERE AGAIN! ... SOON THE PIGEONS WILL BE BACK!

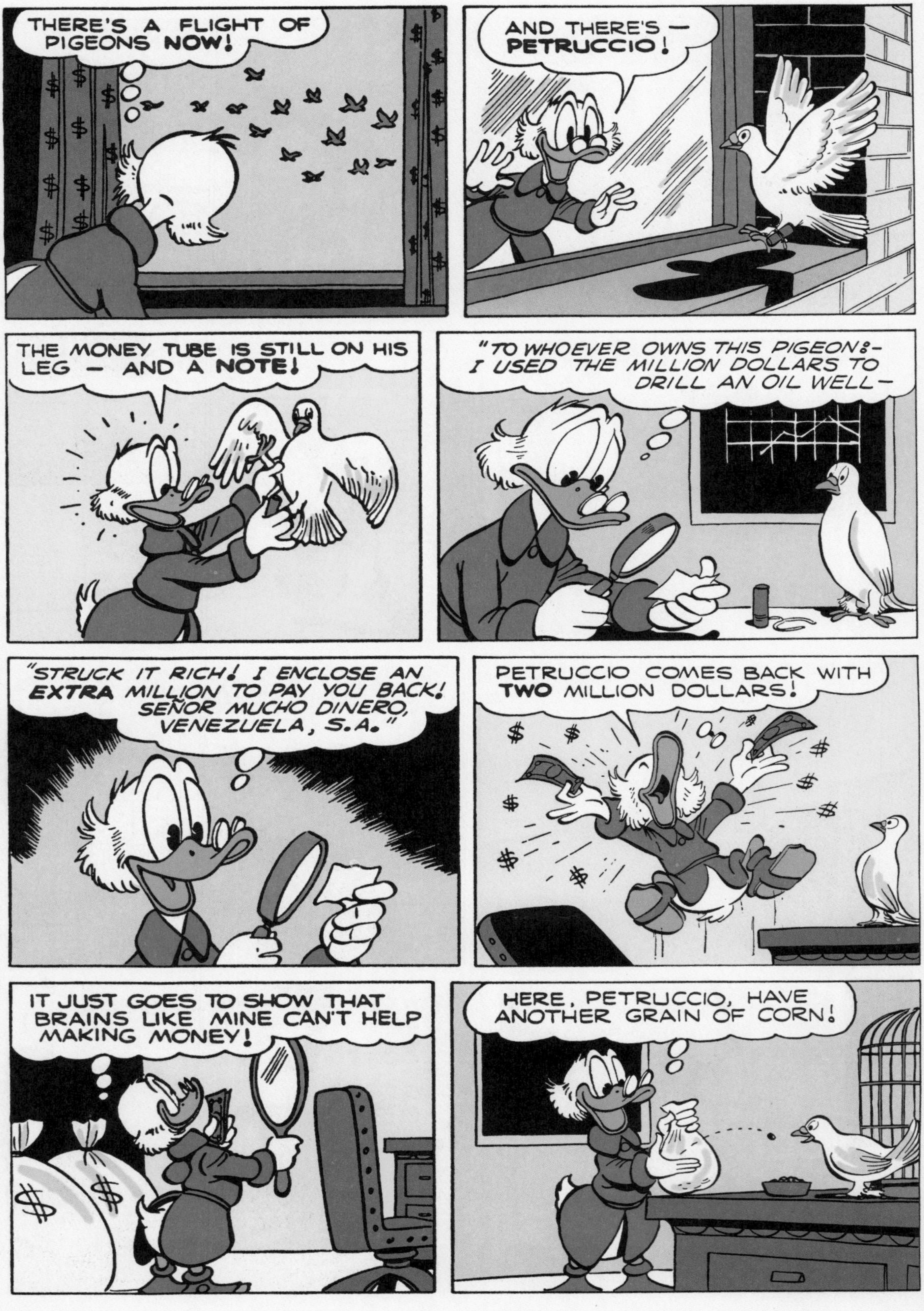
THERE'S A FLIGHT OF PIGEONS **NOW**!
AND THERE'S — **PETRUCCIO**!
THE MONEY TUBE IS STILL ON HIS LEG — AND A **NOTE**!
"TO WHOEVER OWNS THIS PIGEON:— I USED THE MILLION DOLLARS TO DRILL AN OIL WELL—
"STRUCK IT RICH! I ENCLOSE AN **EXTRA** MILLION TO PAY YOU BACK! SEÑOR MUCHO DINERO, VENEZUELA, S.A."
PETRUCCIO COMES BACK WITH **TWO** MILLION DOLLARS!
IT JUST GOES TO SHOW THAT BRAINS LIKE MINE CAN'T HELP MAKING MONEY!
HERE, PETRUCCIO, HAVE ANOTHER GRAIN OF CORN!

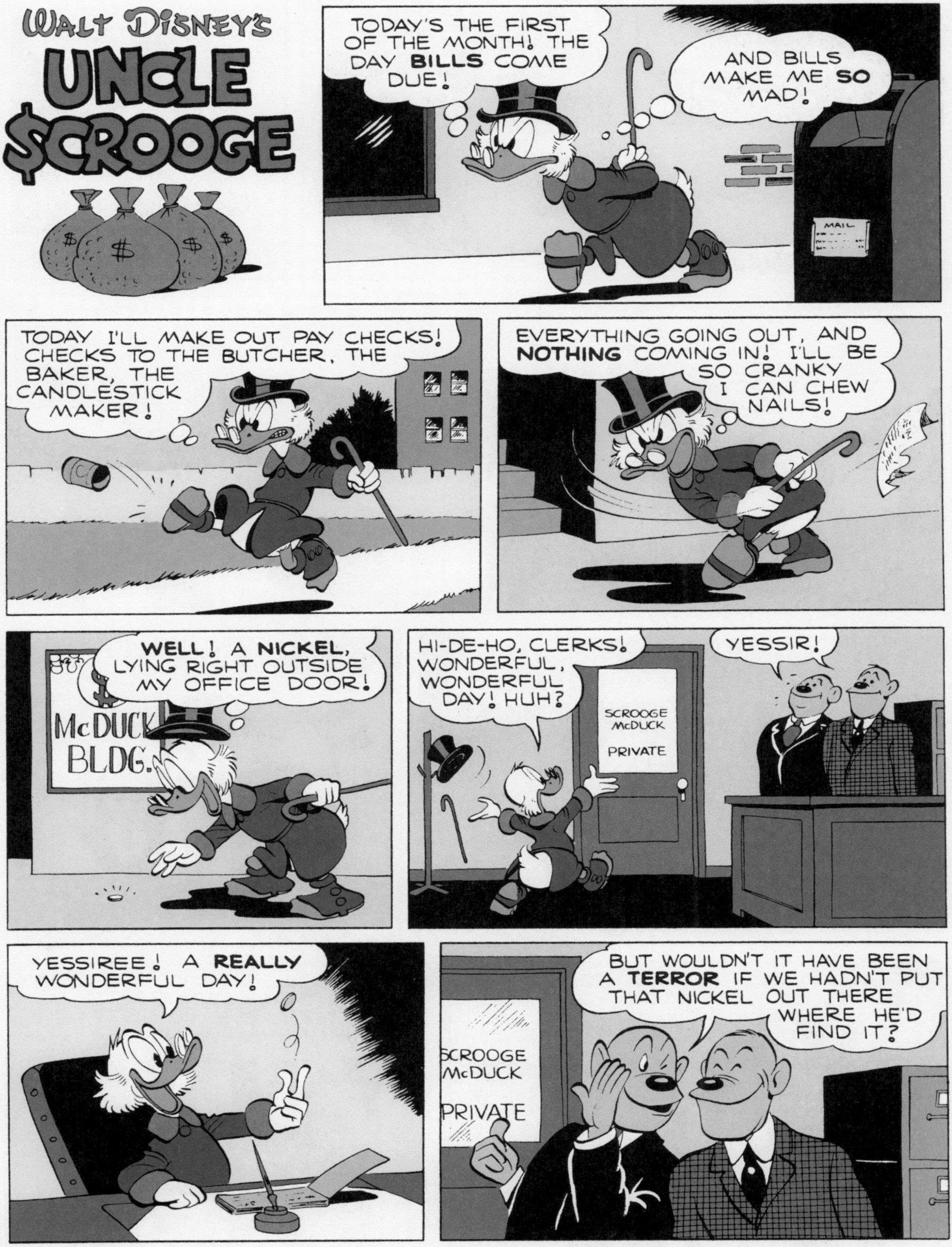
WALT DISNEY'S
UNCLE SCROOGE
TODAY'S THE FIRST OF THE MONTH! THE DAY BILLS COME DUE!
AND BILLS MAKE ME SO MAD!
MAIL
TODAY I'LL MAKE OUT PAY CHECKS! CHECKS TO THE BUTCHER, THE BAKER, THE CANDLESTICK MAKER!
EVERYTHING GOING OUT, AND NOTHING COMING IN! I'LL BE SO CRANKY I CAN CHEW NAILS!
WELL! A NICKEL, LYING RIGHT OUTSIDE MY OFFICE DOOR!
McDUCK BLDG.
HI-DE-HO, CLERKS! WONDERFUL, WONDERFUL DAY! HUH?
SCROOGE McDUCK PRIVATE
YESSIR!
YESSIREE! A REALLY WONDERFUL DAY!
BUT WOULDN'T IT HAVE BEEN A TERROR IF WE HADN'T PUT THAT NICKEL OUT THERE WHERE HE'D FIND IT?
SCROOGE McDUCK PRIVATE

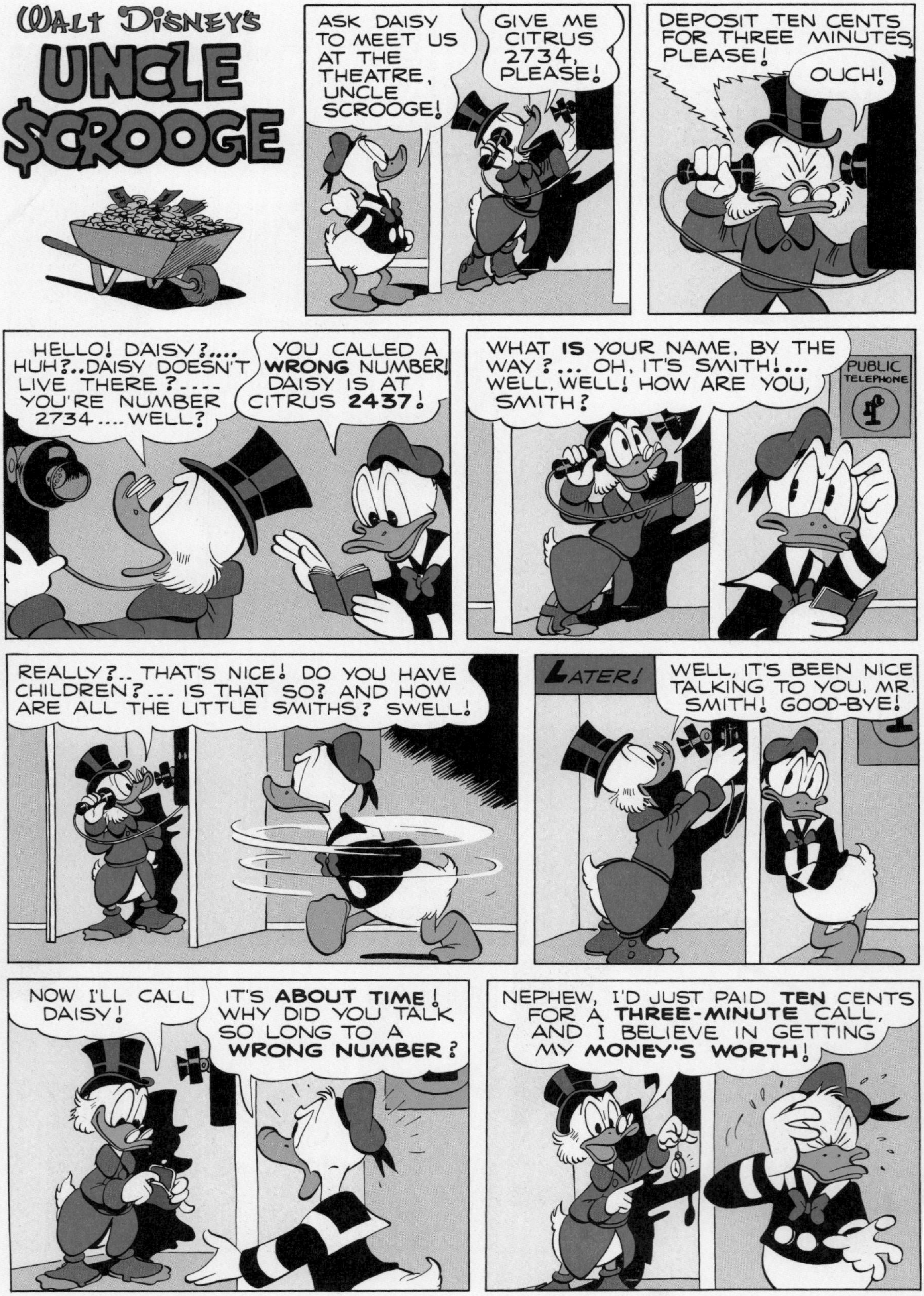
WALT DISNEY'S
UNCLE $CROOGE
ASK DAISY TO MEET US AT THE THEATRE, UNCLE SCROOGE!
GIVE ME CITRUS 2734, PLEASE!
DEPOSIT TEN CENTS FOR THREE MINUTES, PLEASE!
OUCH!
HELLO! DAISY?.... HUH?..DAISY DOESN'T LIVE THERE?.... YOU'RE NUMBER 2734....WELL?
YOU CALLED A WRONG NUMBER! DAISY IS AT CITRUS 2437!
WHAT IS YOUR NAME, BY THE WAY?... OH, IT'S SMITH!... WELL, WELL! HOW ARE YOU, SMITH?
PUBLIC TELEPHONE
REALLY?.. THAT'S NICE! DO YOU HAVE CHILDREN?... IS THAT SO? AND HOW ARE ALL THE LITTLE SMITHS? SWELL!
LATER!
WELL, IT'S BEEN NICE TALKING TO YOU, MR. SMITH! GOOD-BYE!
NOW I'LL CALL DAISY!
IT'S ABOUT TIME! WHY DID YOU TALK SO LONG TO A WRONG NUMBER?
NEPHEW, I'D JUST PAID TEN CENTS FOR A THREE-MINUTE CALL, AND I BELIEVE IN GETTING MY MONEY'S WORTH!

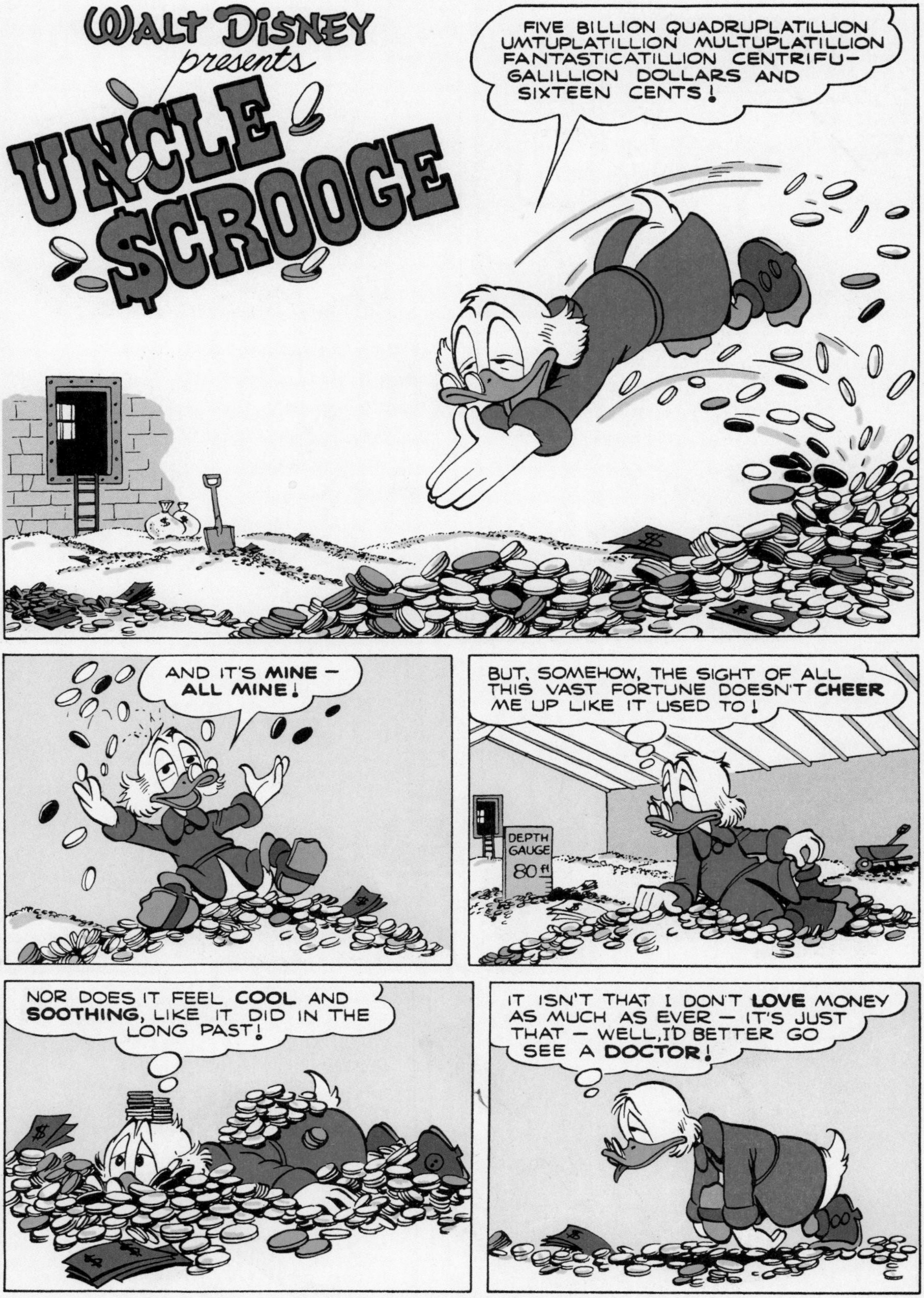
WALT DISNEY presents
UNCLE $CROOGE
FIVE BILLION QUADRUPLATILLION UMTUPLATILLION MULTUPLATILLION FANTASTICATILLION CENTRIFU-GALILLION DOLLARS AND SIXTEEN CENTS!
AND IT'S MINE — ALL MINE!
BUT, SOMEHOW, THE SIGHT OF ALL THIS VAST FORTUNE DOESN'T CHEER ME UP LIKE IT USED TO!
DEPTH GAUGE 80 ft
NOR DOES IT FEEL COOL AND SOOTHING, LIKE IT DID IN THE LONG PAST!
IT ISN'T THAT I DON'T LOVE MONEY AS MUCH AS EVER — IT'S JUST THAT — WELL, I'D BETTER GO SEE A DOCTOR!

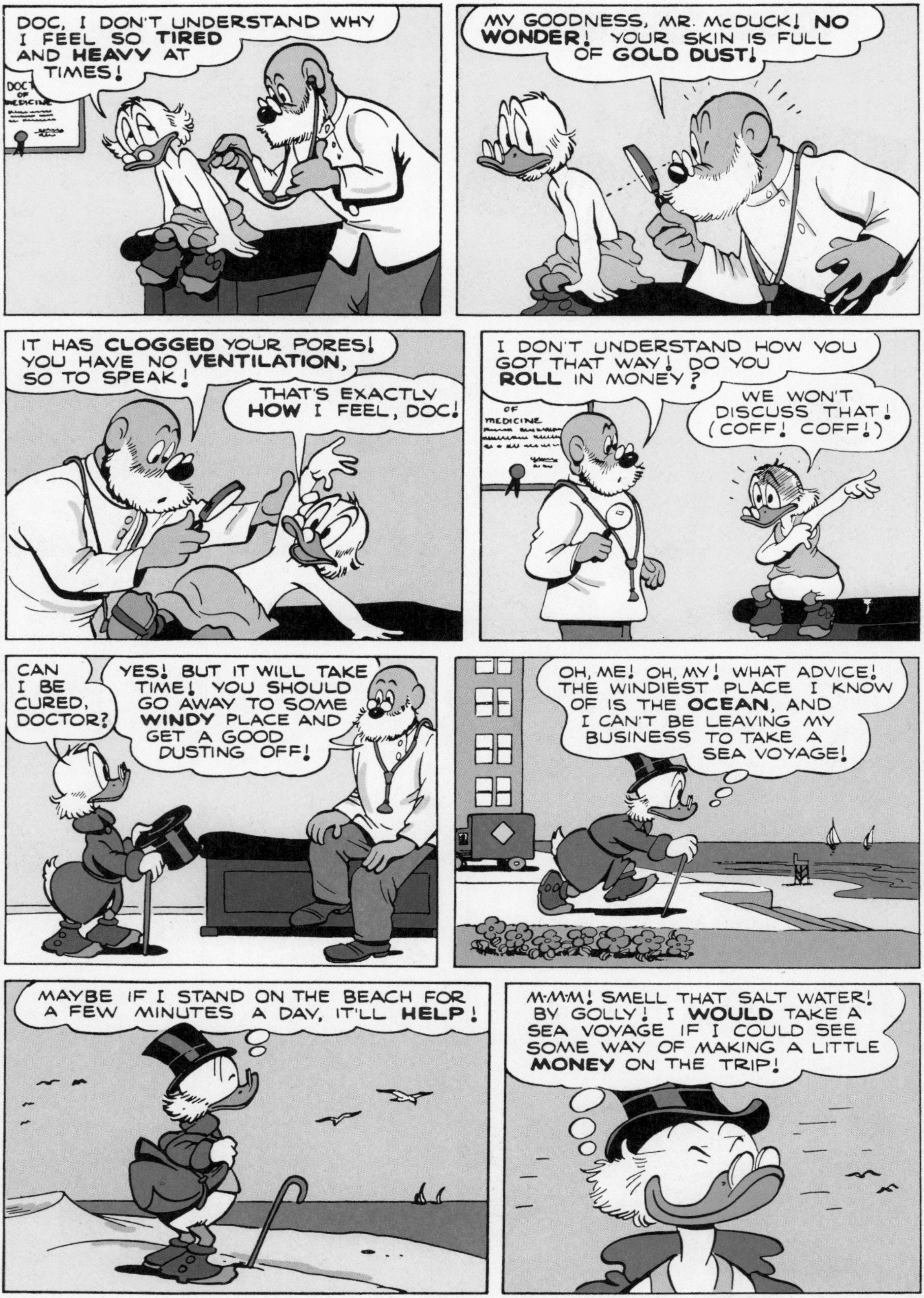
DOC, I DON'T UNDERSTAND WHY I FEEL SO TIRED AND HEAVY AT TIMES!
DOCTOR OF MEDICINE
MY GOODNESS, MR. McDUCK! NO WONDER! YOUR SKIN IS FULL OF GOLD DUST!
IT HAS CLOGGED YOUR PORES! YOU HAVE NO VENTILATION, SO TO SPEAK!
THAT'S EXACTLY HOW I FEEL, DOC!
I DON'T UNDERSTAND HOW YOU GOT THAT WAY! DO YOU ROLL IN MONEY?
OF MEDICINE
WE WON'T DISCUSS THAT! (COFF! COFF!)
CAN I BE CURED, DOCTOR?
YES! BUT IT WILL TAKE TIME! YOU SHOULD GO AWAY TO SOME WINDY PLACE AND GET A GOOD DUSTING OFF!
OH, ME! OH, MY! WHAT ADVICE! THE WINDIEST PLACE I KNOW OF IS THE OCEAN, AND I CAN'T BE LEAVING MY BUSINESS TO TAKE A SEA VOYAGE!
MAYBE IF I STAND ON THE BEACH FOR A FEW MINUTES A DAY, IT'LL HELP!
M-M-M! SMELL THAT SALT WATER! BY GOLLY! I WOULD TAKE A SEA VOYAGE IF I COULD SEE SOME WAY OF MAKING A LITTLE MONEY ON THE TRIP!

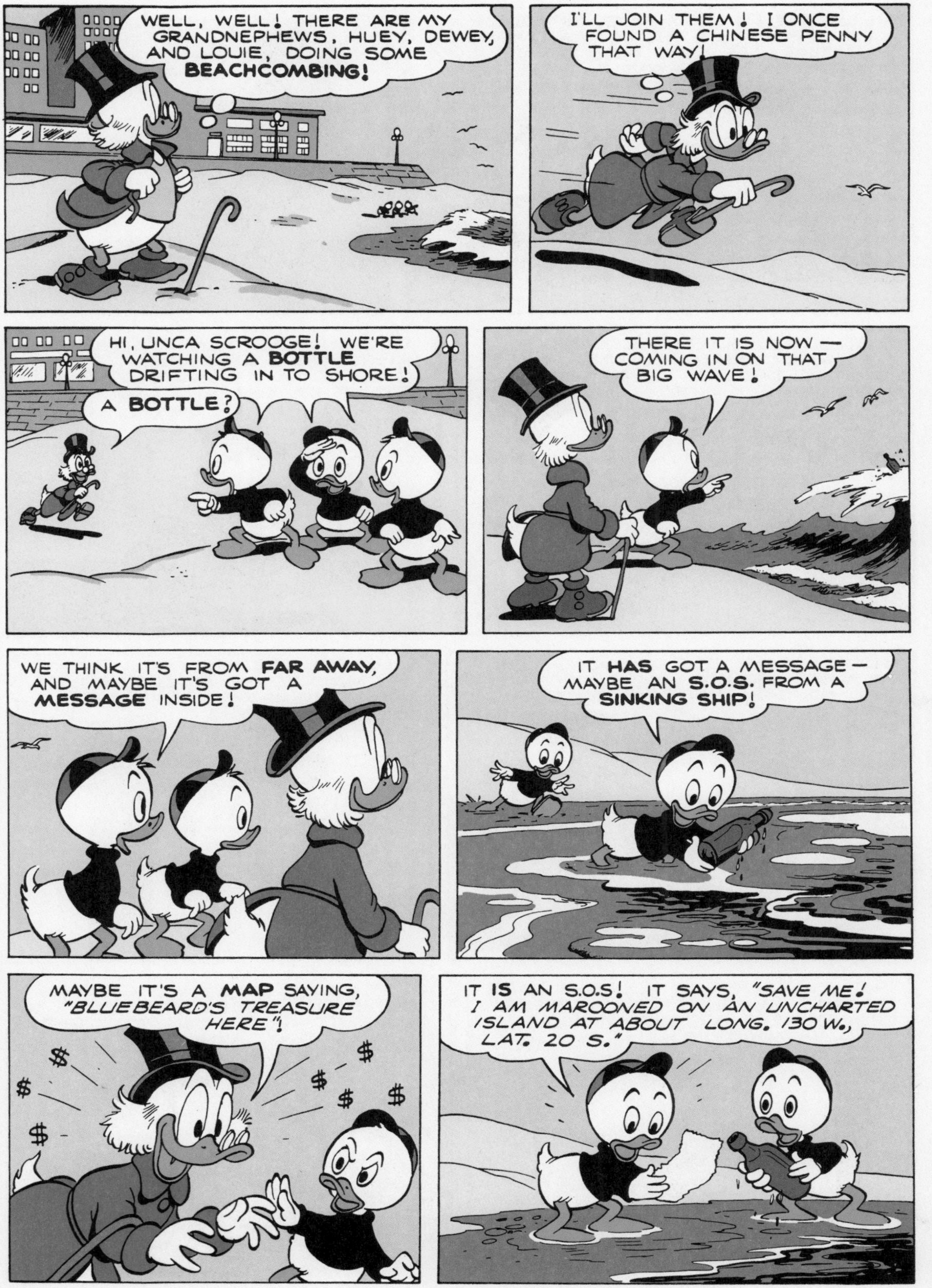
WELL, WELL! THERE ARE MY GRANDNEPHEWS, HUEY, DEWEY, AND LOUIE, DOING SOME BEACHCOMBING!
I'LL JOIN THEM! I ONCE FOUND A CHINESE PENNY THAT WAY!
HI, UNCA SCROOGE! WE'RE WATCHING A BOTTLE DRIFTING IN TO SHORE!
A BOTTLE?
THERE IT IS NOW— COMING IN ON THAT BIG WAVE!
WE THINK IT'S FROM FAR AWAY, AND MAYBE IT'S GOT A MESSAGE INSIDE!
IT HAS GOT A MESSAGE— MAYBE AN S.O.S. FROM A SINKING SHIP!
MAYBE IT'S A MAP SAYING, "BLUEBEARD'S TREASURE HERE"!
$
IT IS AN S.O.S! IT SAYS, "SAVE ME! I AM MAROONED ON AN UNCHARTED ISLAND AT ABOUT LONG. 130 W., LAT. 20 S."

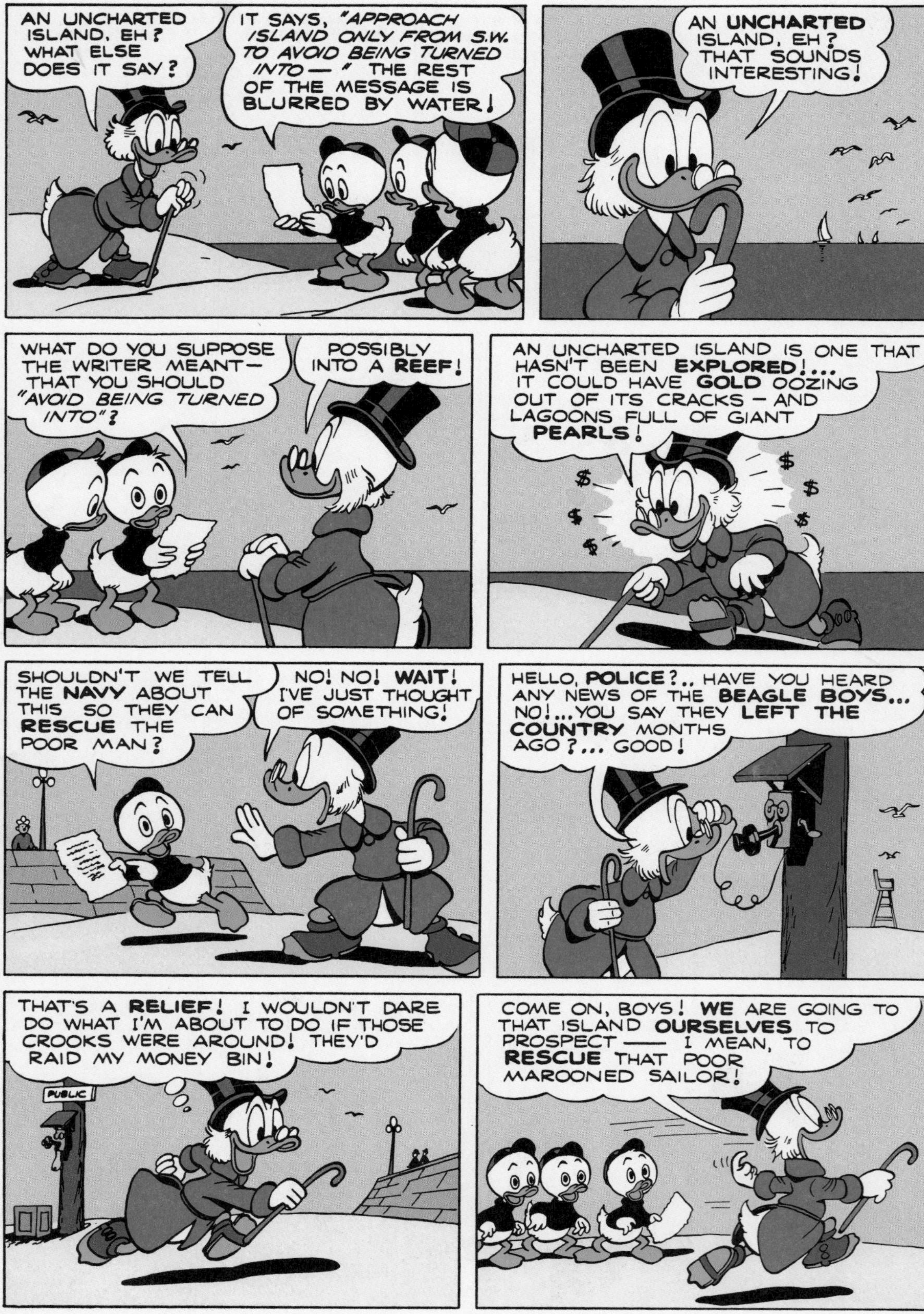
AN UNCHARTED ISLAND, EH? WHAT ELSE DOES IT SAY?
IT SAYS, "APPROACH ISLAND ONLY FROM S.W. TO AVOID BEING TURNED INTO—" THE REST OF THE MESSAGE IS BLURRED BY WATER!
AN UNCHARTED ISLAND, EH? THAT SOUNDS INTERESTING!
WHAT DO YOU SUPPOSE THE WRITER MEANT— THAT YOU SHOULD "AVOID BEING TURNED INTO"?
POSSIBLY INTO A REEF!
AN UNCHARTED ISLAND IS ONE THAT HASN'T BEEN EXPLORED!... IT COULD HAVE GOLD OOZING OUT OF ITS CRACKS — AND LAGOONS FULL OF GIANT PEARLS!
SHOULDN'T WE TELL THE NAVY ABOUT THIS SO THEY CAN RESCUE THE POOR MAN?
NO! NO! WAIT! I'VE JUST THOUGHT OF SOMETHING!
HELLO, POLICE?.. HAVE YOU HEARD ANY NEWS OF THE BEAGLE BOYS... NO!...YOU SAY THEY LEFT THE COUNTRY MONTHS AGO?... GOOD!
THAT'S A RELIEF! I WOULDN'T DARE DO WHAT I'M ABOUT TO DO IF THOSE CROOKS WERE AROUND! THEY'D RAID MY MONEY BIN!
PUBLIC
COME ON, BOYS! WE ARE GOING TO THAT ISLAND OURSELVES TO PROSPECT —— I MEAN, TO RESCUE THAT POOR MAROONED SAILOR!

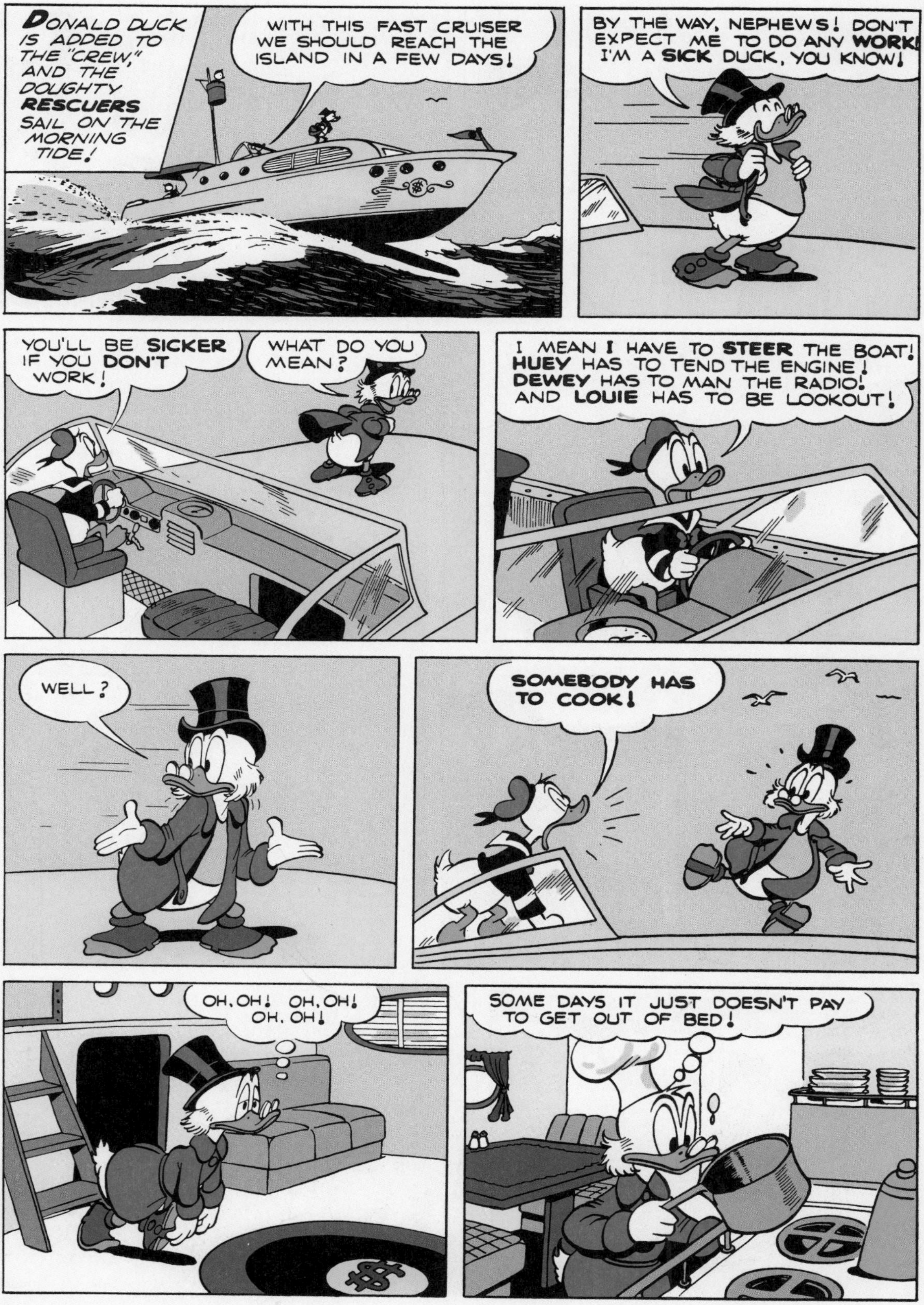
DONALD DUCK IS ADDED TO THE "CREW," AND THE DOUGHTY RESCUERS SAIL ON THE MORNING TIDE!
WITH THIS FAST CRUISER WE SHOULD REACH THE ISLAND IN A FEW DAYS!
BY THE WAY, NEPHEWS! DON'T EXPECT ME TO DO ANY WORK! I'M A SICK DUCK, YOU KNOW!
YOU'LL BE SICKER IF YOU DON'T WORK!
WHAT DO YOU MEAN?
I MEAN I HAVE TO STEER THE BOAT! HUEY HAS TO TEND THE ENGINE! DEWEY HAS TO MAN THE RADIO! AND LOUIE HAS TO BE LOOKOUT!
WELL?
SOMEBODY HAS TO COOK!
OH, OH! OH, OH! OH, OH!
SOME DAYS IT JUST DOESN'T PAY TO GET OUT OF BED!

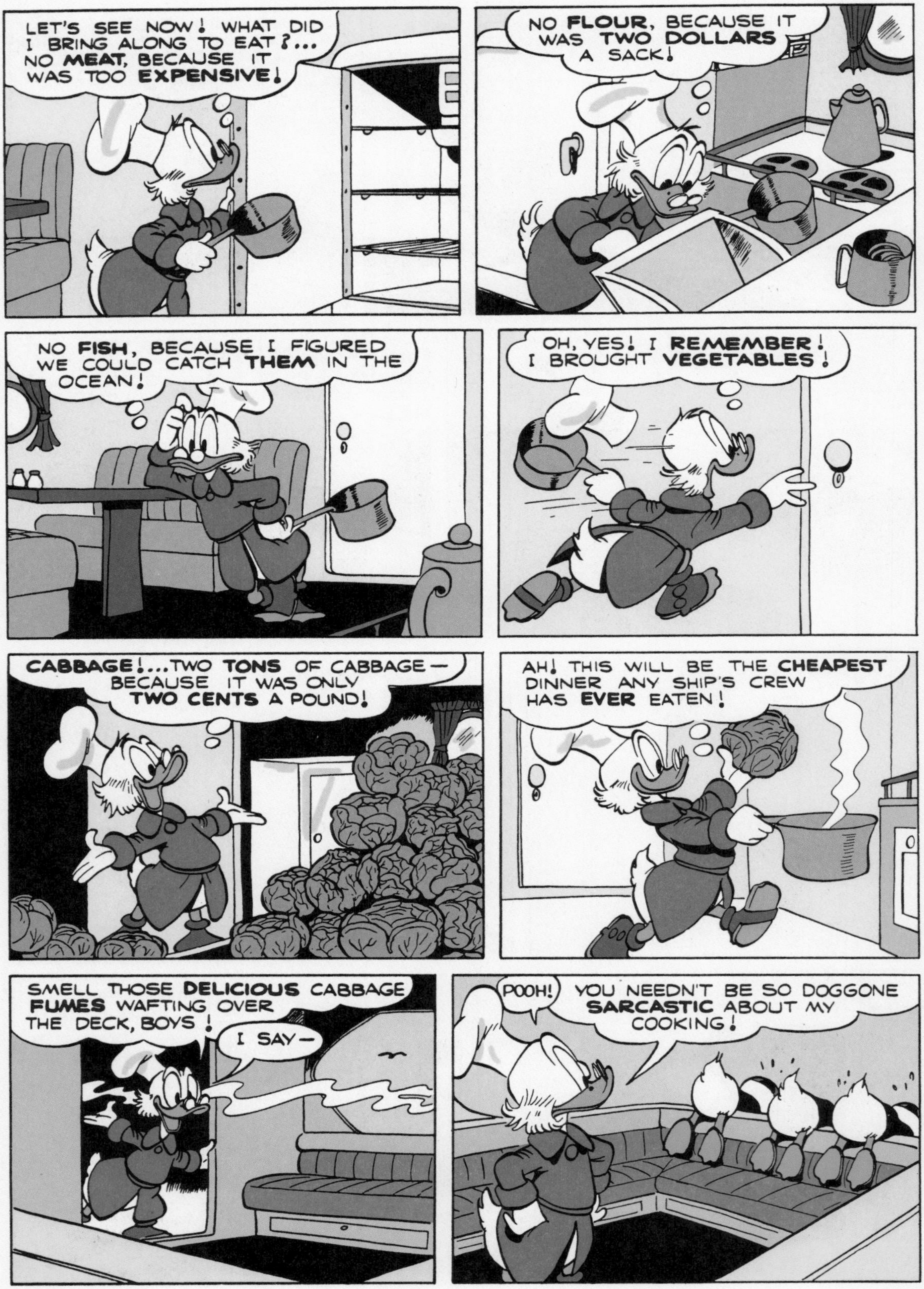

LET'S SEE NOW! WHAT DID I BRING ALONG TO EAT?... NO MEAT, BECAUSE IT WAS TOO EXPENSIVE!
NO FLOUR, BECAUSE IT WAS TWO DOLLARS A SACK!
NO FISH, BECAUSE I FIGURED WE COULD CATCH THEM IN THE OCEAN!
OH, YES! I REMEMBER! I BROUGHT VEGETABLES!
CABBAGE!...TWO TONS OF CABBAGE— BECAUSE IT WAS ONLY TWO CENTS A POUND!
AH! THIS WILL BE THE CHEAPEST DINNER ANY SHIP'S CREW HAS EVER EATEN!
SMELL THOSE DELICIOUS CABBAGE FUMES WAFTING OVER THE DECK, BOYS!
I SAY—
POOH!
YOU NEEDN'T BE SO DOGGONE SARCASTIC ABOUT MY COOKING!

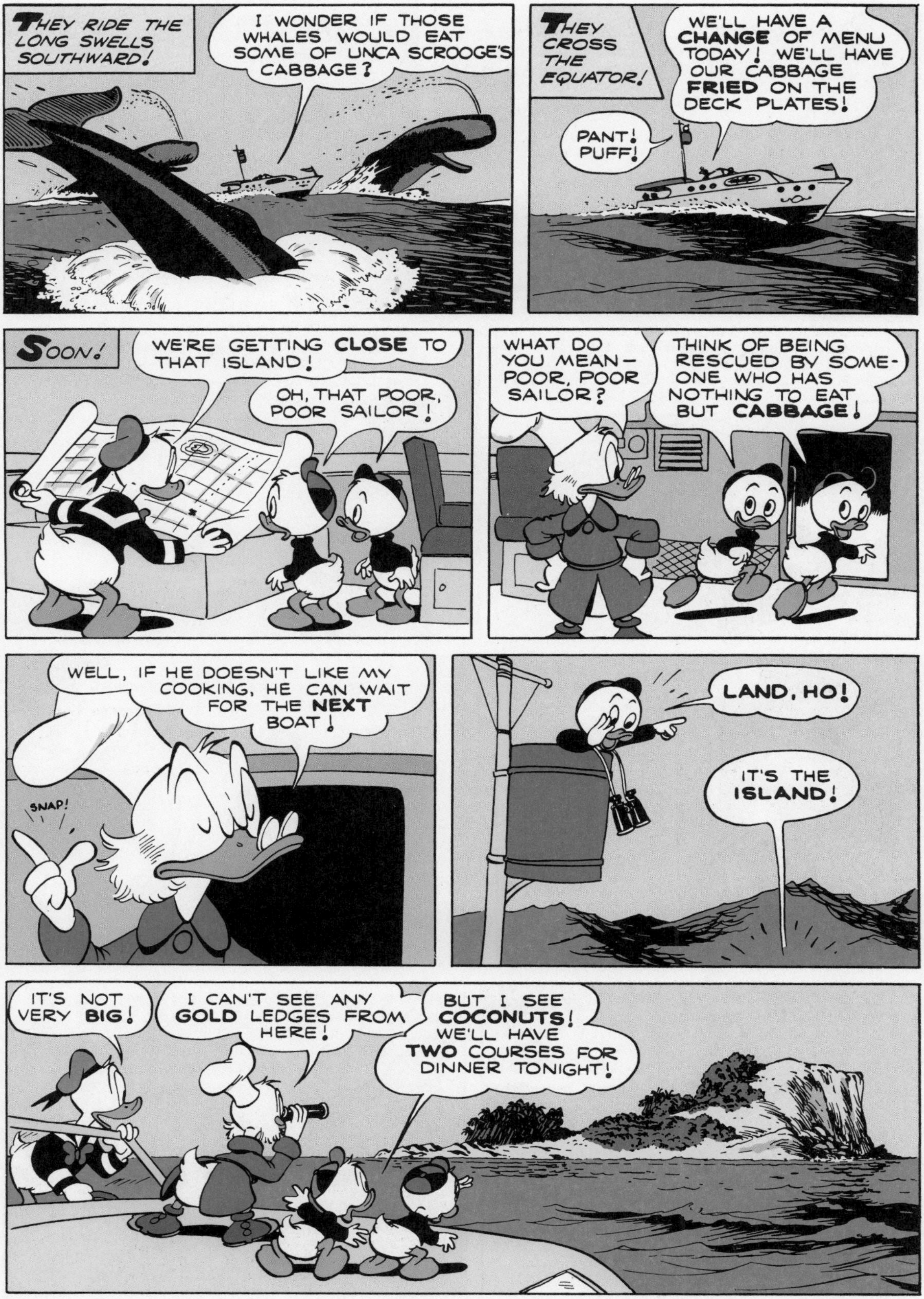
THEY RIDE THE LONG SWELLS SOUTHWARD!
I WONDER IF THOSE WHALES WOULD EAT SOME OF UNCA SCROOGE'S CABBAGE?
THEY CROSS THE EQUATOR!
WE'LL HAVE A CHANGE OF MENU TODAY! WE'LL HAVE OUR CABBAGE FRIED ON THE DECK PLATES!
PANT! PUFF!
SOON!
WE'RE GETTING CLOSE TO THAT ISLAND!
OH, THAT POOR, POOR SAILOR!
WHAT DO YOU MEAN—POOR, POOR SAILOR?
THINK OF BEING RESCUED BY SOME-ONE WHO HAS NOTHING TO EAT BUT CABBAGE!
WELL, IF HE DOESN'T LIKE MY COOKING, HE CAN WAIT FOR THE NEXT BOAT!
SNAP!
LAND, HO!
IT'S THE ISLAND!
IT'S NOT VERY BIG!
I CAN'T SEE ANY GOLD LEDGES FROM HERE!
BUT I SEE COCONUTS! WE'LL HAVE TWO COURSES FOR DINNER TONIGHT!

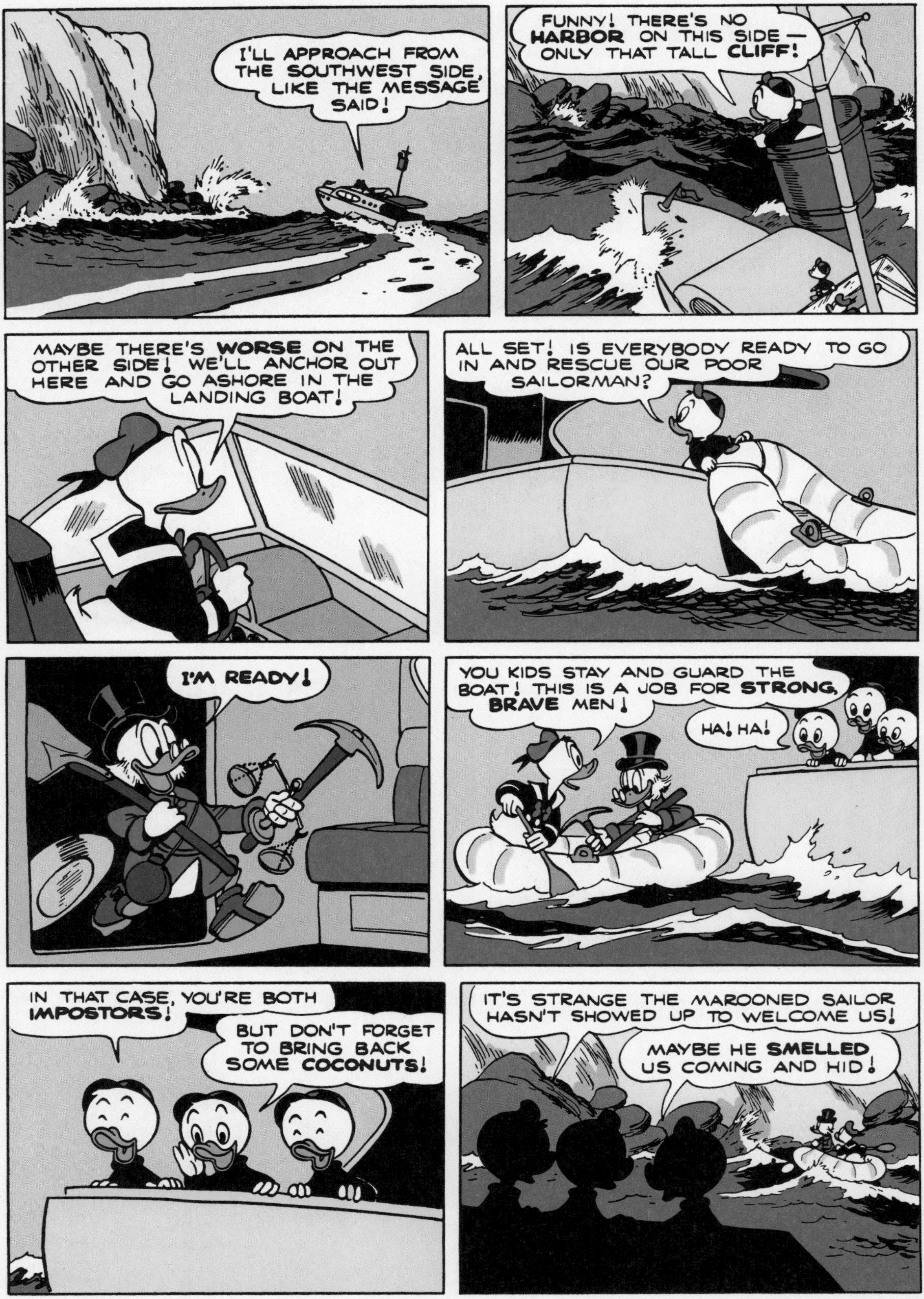
I'LL APPROACH FROM THE SOUTHWEST SIDE, LIKE THE MESSAGE SAID!
FUNNY! THERE'S NO HARBOR ON THIS SIDE— ONLY THAT TALL CLIFF!
MAYBE THERE'S WORSE ON THE OTHER SIDE! WE'LL ANCHOR OUT HERE AND GO ASHORE IN THE LANDING BOAT!
ALL SET! IS EVERYBODY READY TO GO IN AND RESCUE OUR POOR SAILORMAN?
I'M READY!
YOU KIDS STAY AND GUARD THE BOAT! THIS IS A JOB FOR STRONG, BRAVE MEN!
HA! HA!
IN THAT CASE, YOU'RE BOTH IMPOSTORS!
BUT DON'T FORGET TO BRING BACK SOME COCONUTS!
IT'S STRANGE THE MAROONED SAILOR HASN'T SHOWED UP TO WELCOME US!
MAYBE HE SMELLED US COMING AND HID!

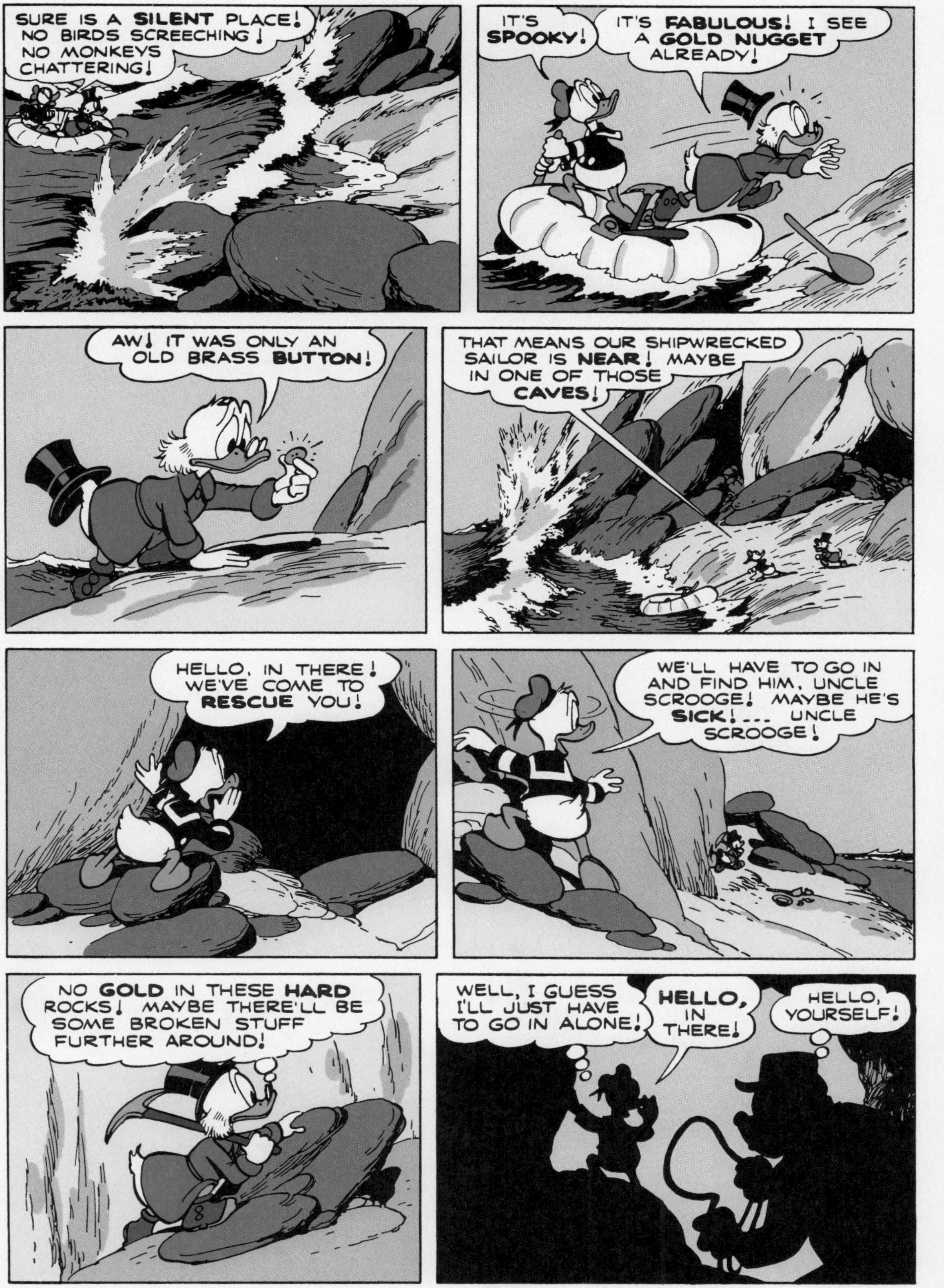
SURE IS A SILENT PLACE! NO BIRDS SCREECHING! NO MONKEYS CHATTERING!
IT'S SPOOKY!
IT'S FABULOUS! I SEE A GOLD NUGGET ALREADY!
AW! IT WAS ONLY AN OLD BRASS BUTTON!
THAT MEANS OUR SHIPWRECKED SAILOR IS NEAR! MAYBE IN ONE OF THOSE CAVES!
HELLO, IN THERE! WE'VE COME TO RESCUE YOU!
WE'LL HAVE TO GO IN AND FIND HIM, UNCLE SCROOGE! MAYBE HE'S SICK! ... UNCLE SCROOGE!
NO GOLD IN THESE HARD ROCKS! MAYBE THERE'LL BE SOME BROKEN STUFF FURTHER AROUND!
WELL, I GUESS I'LL JUST HAVE TO GO IN ALONE!
HELLO, IN THERE!
HELLO, YOURSELF!

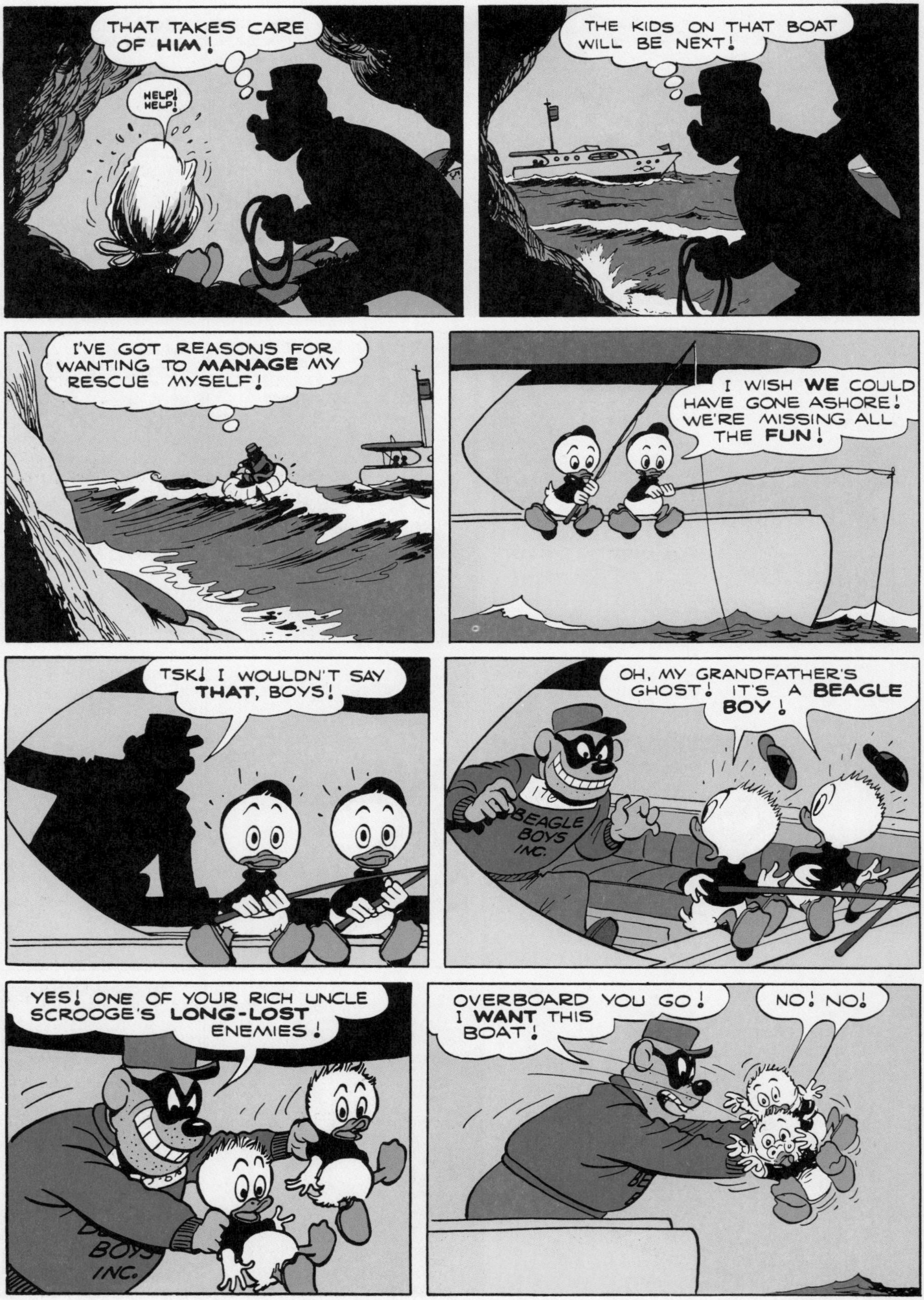
THAT TAKES CARE OF HIM!
HELP! HELP!
THE KIDS ON THAT BOAT WILL BE NEXT!
I'VE GOT REASONS FOR WANTING TO MANAGE MY RESCUE MYSELF!
I WISH WE COULD HAVE GONE ASHORE! WE'RE MISSING ALL THE FUN!
TSK! I WOULDN'T SAY THAT, BOYS!
OH, MY GRANDFATHER'S GHOST! IT'S A BEAGLE BOY!
BEAGLE BOYS INC.
YES! ONE OF YOUR RICH UNCLE SCROOGE'S LONG-LOST ENEMIES!
BOYS INC.
OVERBOARD YOU GO! I WANT THIS BOAT!
NO! NO!

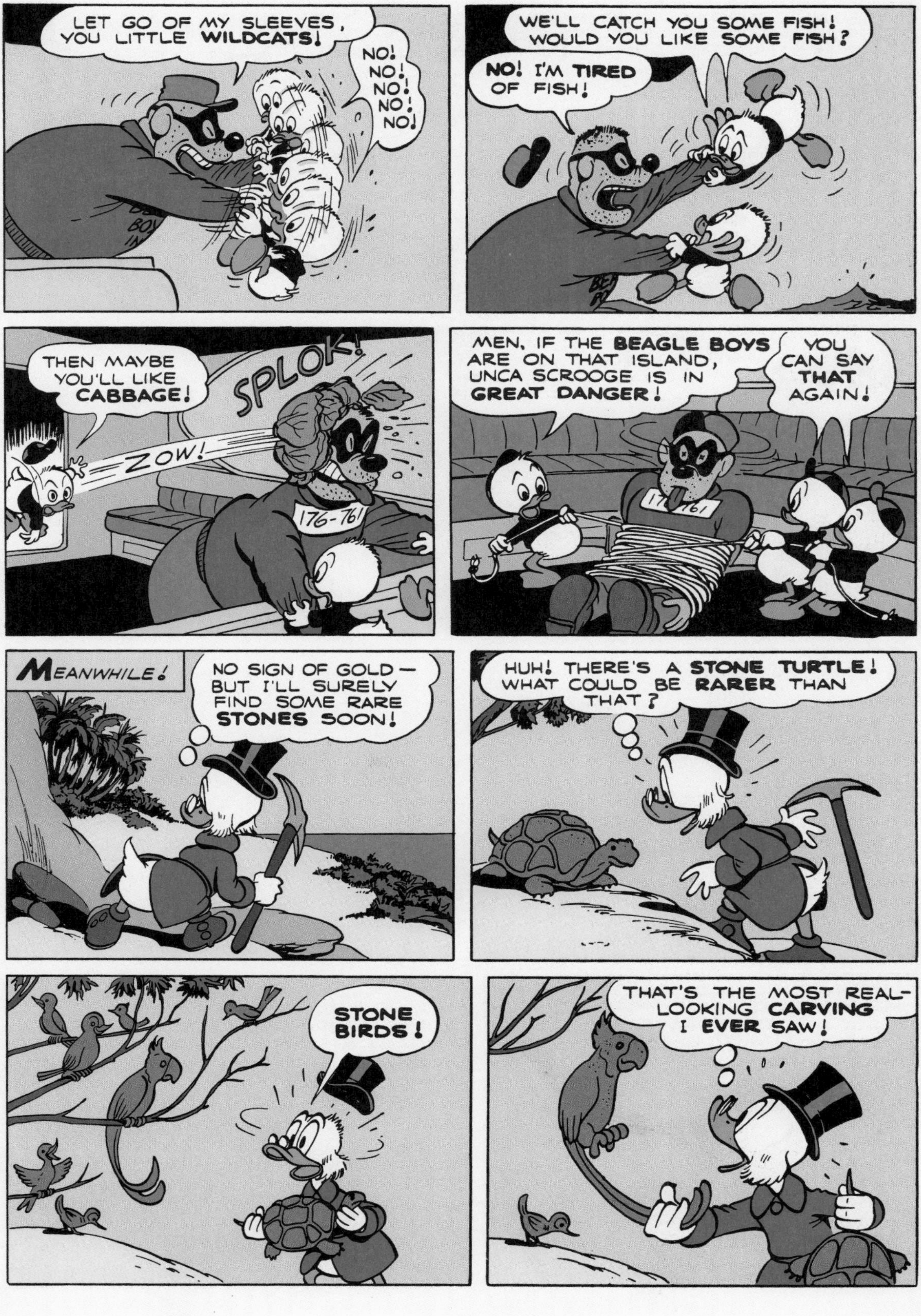
LET GO OF MY SLEEVES, YOU LITTLE WILDCATS!
NO! NO! NO! NO! NO!
WE'LL CATCH YOU SOME FISH! WOULD YOU LIKE SOME FISH?
NO! I'M TIRED OF FISH!
THEN MAYBE YOU'LL LIKE CABBAGE!
SPLOK!
ZOW!
176-761
MEN, IF THE BEAGLE BOYS ARE ON THAT ISLAND, UNCA SCROOGE IS IN GREAT DANGER!
YOU CAN SAY THAT AGAIN!
MEANWHILE!
NO SIGN OF GOLD— BUT I'LL SURELY FIND SOME RARE STONES SOON!
HUH! THERE'S A STONE TURTLE! WHAT COULD BE RARER THAN THAT?
STONE BIRDS!
THAT'S THE MOST REAL-LOOKING CARVING I EVER SAW!

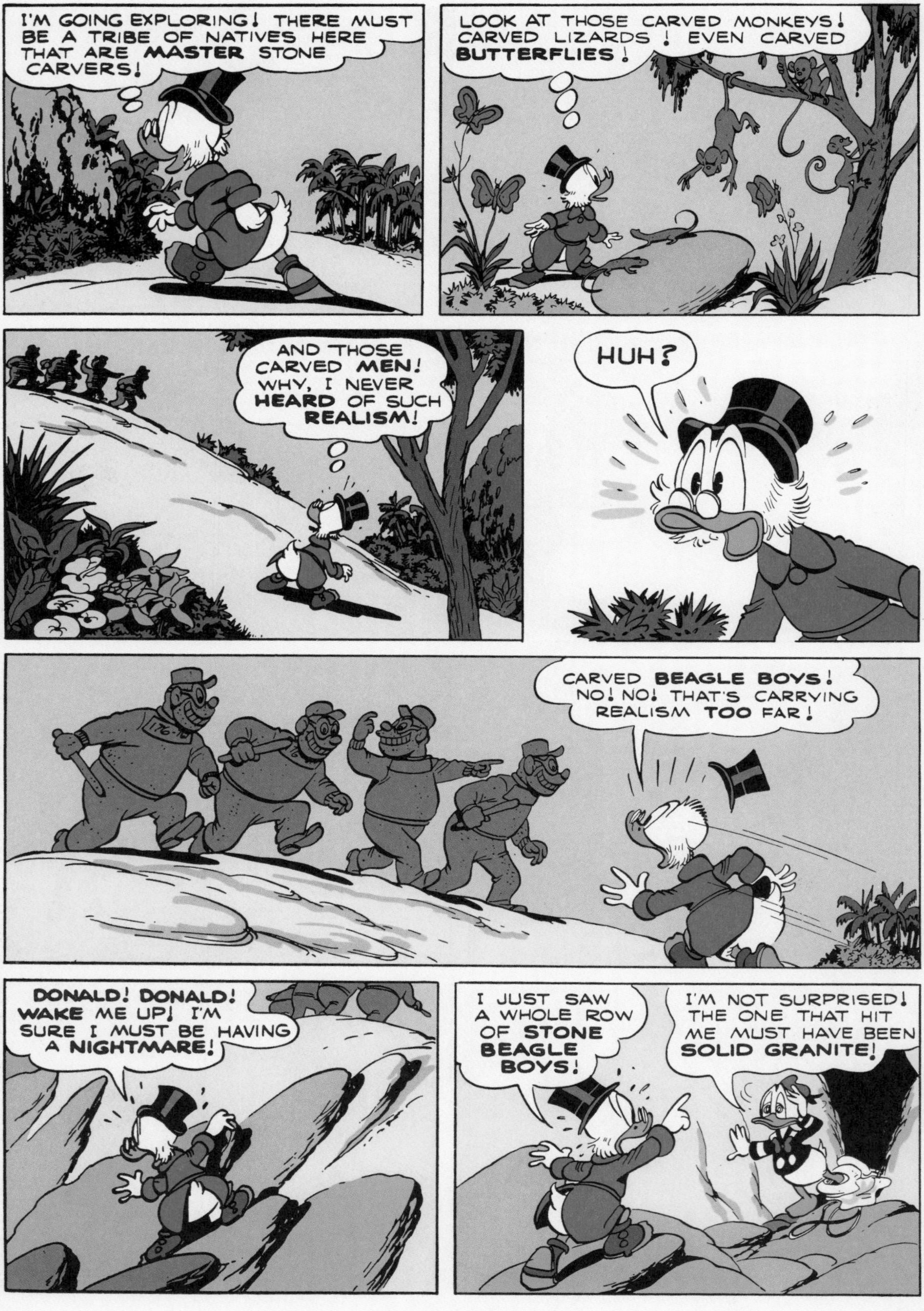
I'M GOING EXPLORING! THERE MUST BE A TRIBE OF NATIVES HERE THAT ARE **MASTER** STONE CARVERS!
LOOK AT THOSE CARVED MONKEYS! CARVED LIZARDS! EVEN CARVED **BUTTERFLIES**!
AND THOSE CARVED **MEN**! WHY, I NEVER **HEARD** OF SUCH **REALISM**!
HUH?
176-167
CARVED **BEAGLE BOYS**! NO! NO! THAT'S CARRYING REALISM **TOO** FAR!
DONALD! DONALD! WAKE ME UP! I'M SURE I MUST BE HAVING A **NIGHTMARE**!
I JUST SAW A WHOLE ROW OF **STONE BEAGLE BOYS**!
I'M NOT SURPRISED! THE ONE THAT HIT ME MUST HAVE BEEN **SOLID GRANITE**!

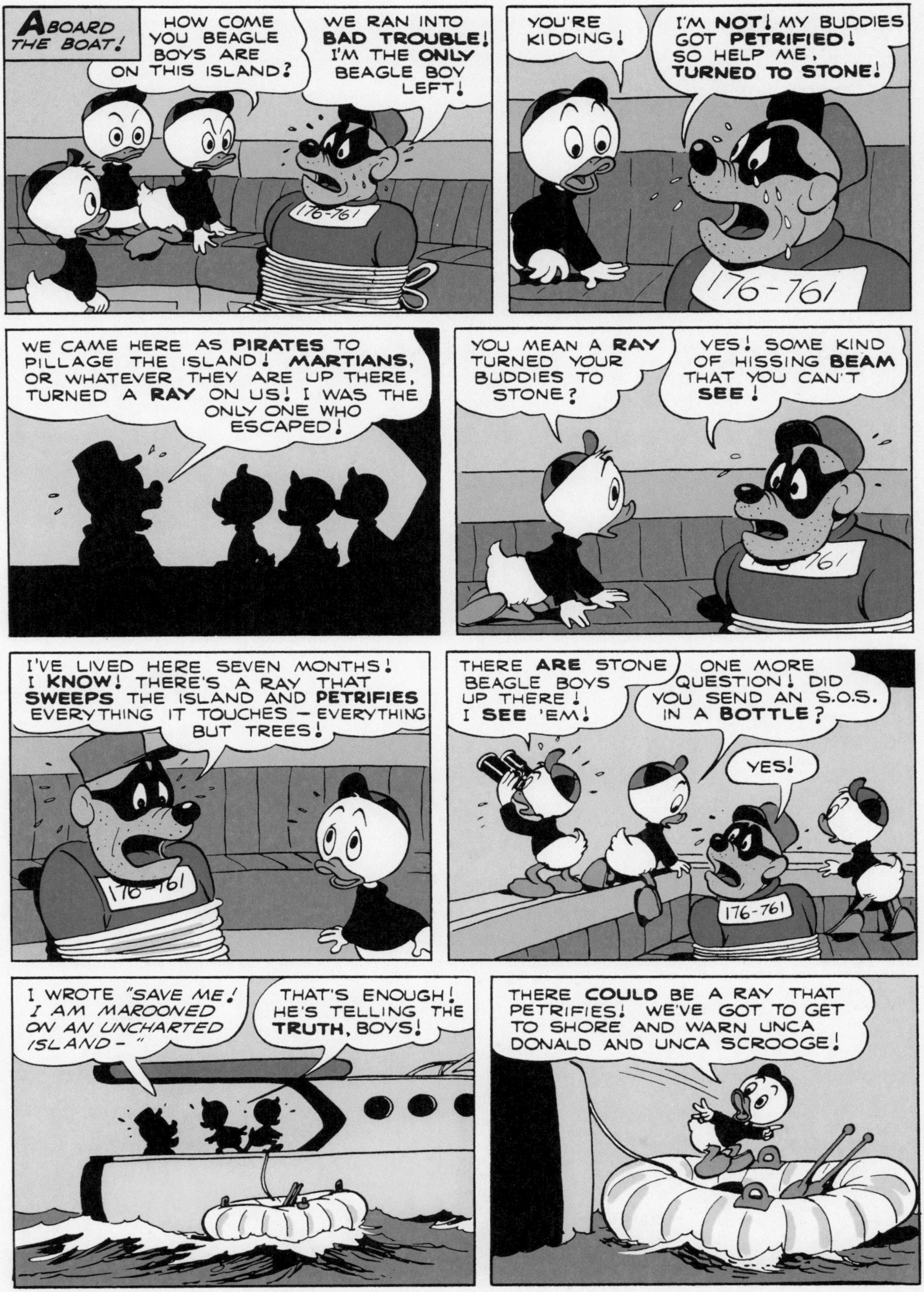
ABOARD THE BOAT!
HOW COME YOU BEAGLE BOYS ARE ON THIS ISLAND?
WE RAN INTO BAD TROUBLE! I'M THE ONLY BEAGLE BOY LEFT!
176-761
YOU'RE KIDDING!
I'M NOT! MY BUDDIES GOT PETRIFIED! SO HELP ME, TURNED TO STONE!
176-761
WE CAME HERE AS PIRATES TO PILLAGE THE ISLAND! MARTIANS, OR WHATEVER THEY ARE UP THERE, TURNED A RAY ON US! I WAS THE ONLY ONE WHO ESCAPED!
YOU MEAN A RAY TURNED YOUR BUDDIES TO STONE?
YES! SOME KIND OF HISSING BEAM THAT YOU CAN'T SEE!
I'VE LIVED HERE SEVEN MONTHS! I KNOW! THERE'S A RAY THAT SWEEPS THE ISLAND AND PETRIFIES EVERYTHING IT TOUCHES — EVERYTHING BUT TREES!
176-761
THERE ARE STONE BEAGLE BOYS UP THERE! I SEE 'EM!
ONE MORE QUESTION! DID YOU SEND AN S.O.S. IN A BOTTLE?
YES!
176-761
I WROTE "SAVE ME! I AM MAROONED ON AN UNCHARTED ISLAND—"
THAT'S ENOUGH! HE'S TELLING THE TRUTH, BOYS!
THERE COULD BE A RAY THAT PETRIFIES! WE'VE GOT TO GET TO SHORE AND WARN UNCA DONALD AND UNCA SCROOGE!

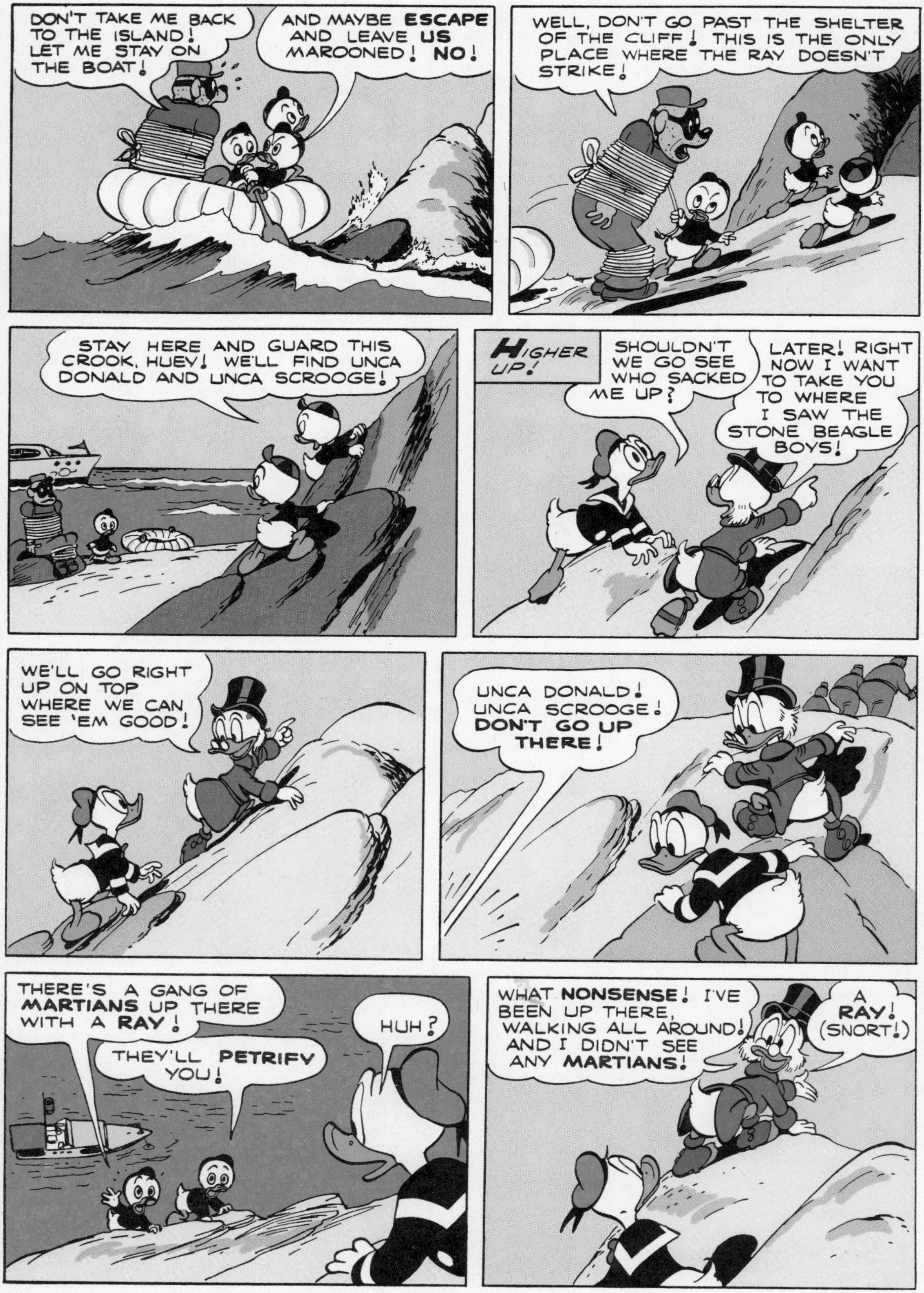
DON'T TAKE ME BACK TO THE ISLAND! LET ME STAY ON THE BOAT!
AND MAYBE **ESCAPE** AND LEAVE **US** MAROONED! **NO**!
WELL, DON'T GO PAST THE SHELTER OF THE CLIFF! THIS IS THE ONLY PLACE WHERE THE RAY DOESN'T STRIKE!
STAY HERE AND GUARD THIS CROOK, HUEY! WE'LL FIND UNCA DONALD AND UNCA SCROOGE!
HIGHER UP!
SHOULDN'T WE GO SEE WHO SACKED ME UP?
LATER! RIGHT NOW I WANT TO TAKE YOU TO WHERE I SAW THE STONE BEAGLE BOYS!
WE'LL GO RIGHT UP ON TOP WHERE WE CAN SEE 'EM GOOD!
UNCA DONALD! UNCA SCROOGE! **DON'T GO UP THERE**!
THERE'S A GANG OF **MARTIANS** UP THERE WITH A **RAY**!
THEY'LL **PETRIFY** YOU!
HUH?
WHAT **NONSENSE**! I'VE BEEN UP THERE, WALKING ALL AROUND! AND I DIDN'T SEE ANY **MARTIANS**!
A **RAY**! (SNORT!)

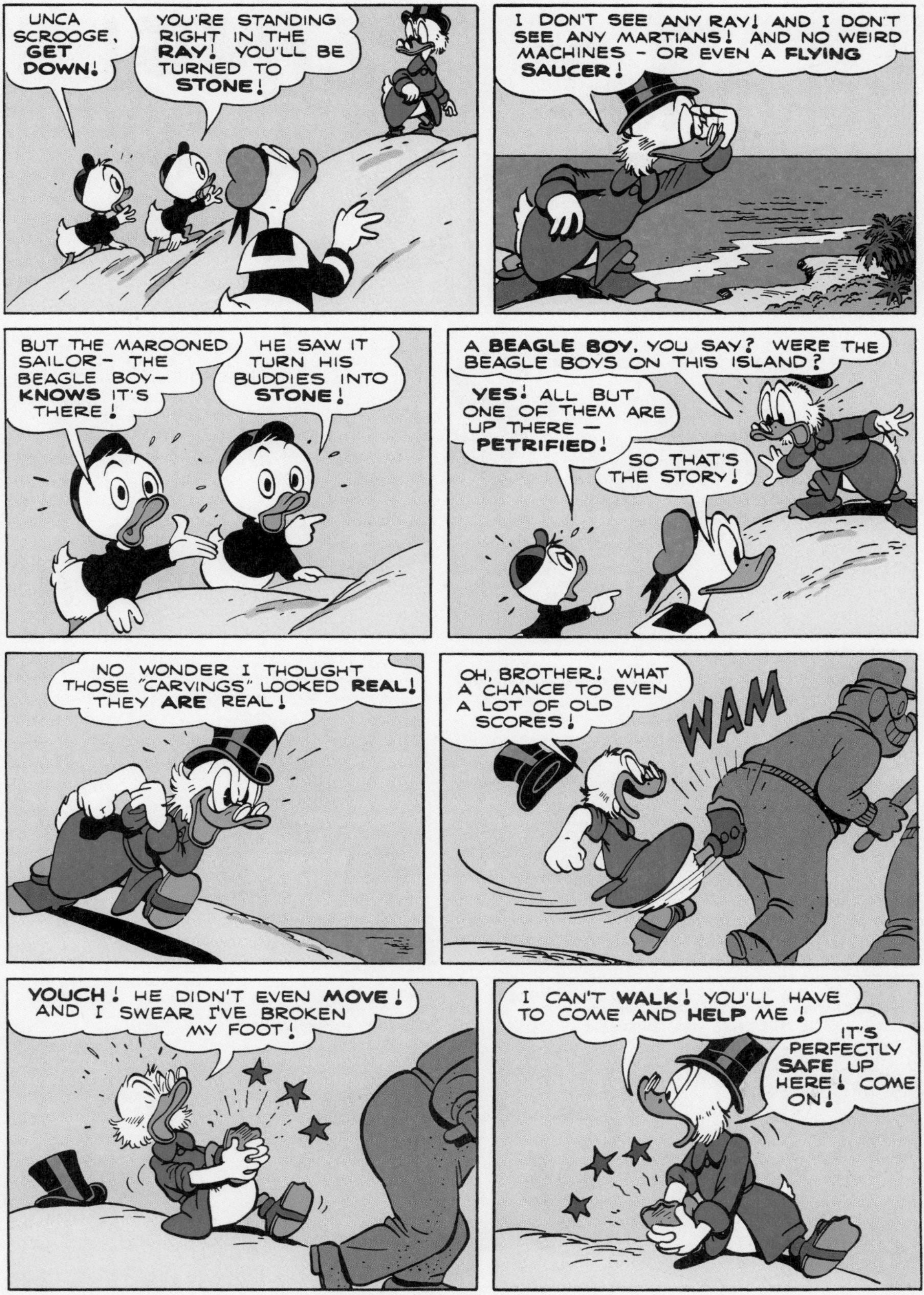
UNCA SCROOGE, GET DOWN!
YOU'RE STANDING RIGHT IN THE RAY! YOU'LL BE TURNED TO STONE!
I DON'T SEE ANY RAY! AND I DON'T SEE ANY MARTIANS! AND NO WEIRD MACHINES - OR EVEN A FLYING SAUCER!
BUT THE MAROONED SAILOR- THE BEAGLE BOY- KNOWS IT'S THERE!
HE SAW IT TURN HIS BUDDIES INTO STONE!
A BEAGLE BOY, YOU SAY? WERE THE BEAGLE BOYS ON THIS ISLAND?
YES! ALL BUT ONE OF THEM ARE UP THERE — PETRIFIED!
SO THAT'S THE STORY!
NO WONDER I THOUGHT THOSE "CARVINGS" LOOKED REAL! THEY ARE REAL!
OH, BROTHER! WHAT A CHANCE TO EVEN A LOT OF OLD SCORES!
WAM
YOUCH! HE DIDN'T EVEN MOVE! AND I SWEAR I'VE BROKEN MY FOOT!
I CAN'T WALK! YOU'LL HAVE TO COME AND HELP ME!
IT'S PERFECTLY SAFE UP HERE! COME ON!

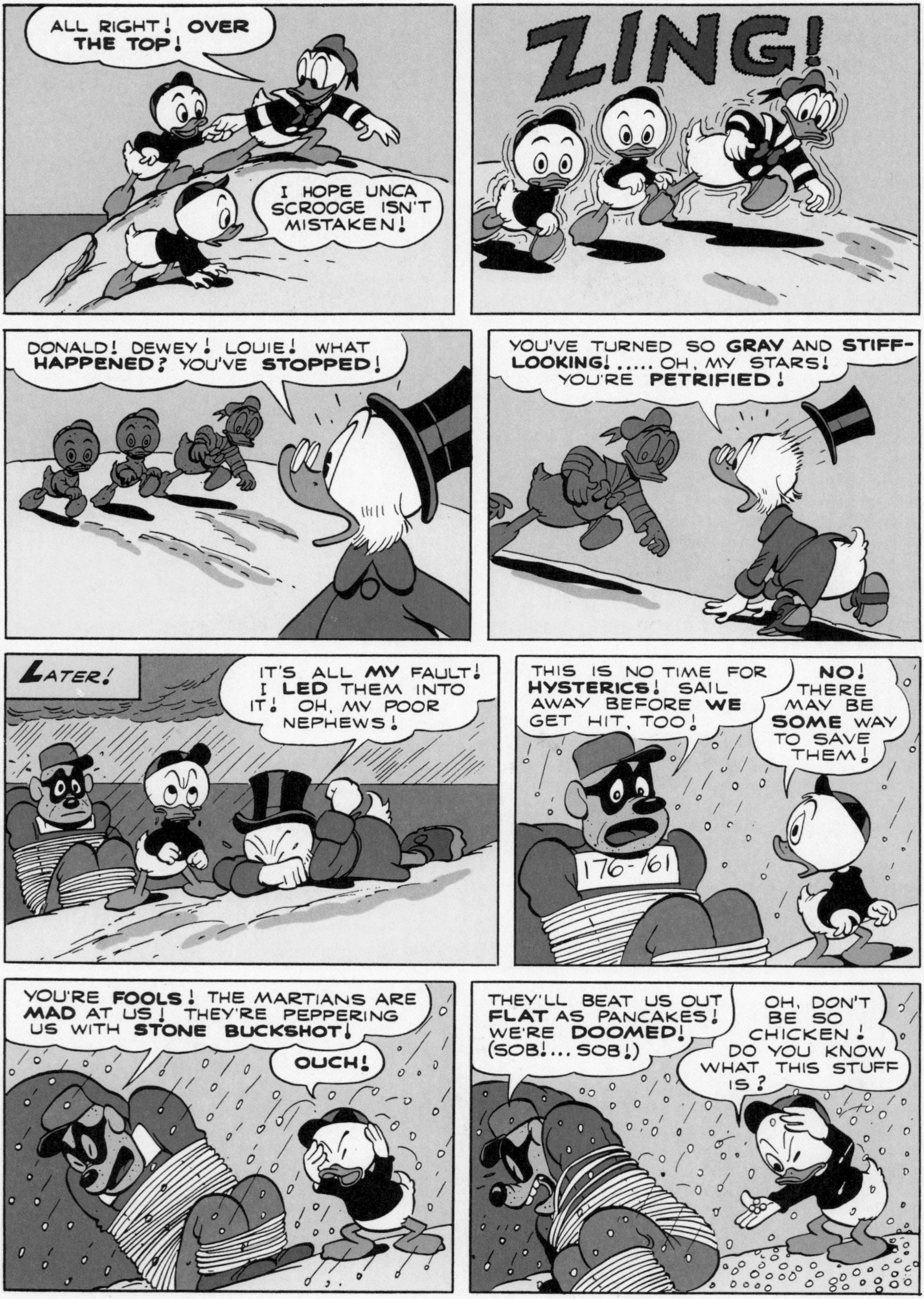
ALL RIGHT! OVER THE TOP!
I HOPE UNCA SCROOGE ISN'T MISTAKEN!
ZING!
DONALD! DEWEY! LOUIE! WHAT HAPPENED? YOU'VE STOPPED!
YOU'VE TURNED SO GRAY AND STIFF-LOOKING! ..... OH, MY STARS! YOU'RE PETRIFIED!
LATER!
IT'S ALL MY FAULT! I LED THEM INTO IT! OH, MY POOR NEPHEWS!
THIS IS NO TIME FOR HYSTERICS! SAIL AWAY BEFORE WE GET HIT, TOO!
NO! THERE MAY BE SOME WAY TO SAVE THEM!
176-161
YOU'RE FOOLS! THE MARTIANS ARE MAD AT US! THEY'RE PEPPERING US WITH STONE BUCKSHOT!
OUCH!
THEY'LL BEAT US OUT FLAT AS PANCAKES! WE'RE DOOMED! (SOB!... SOB!)
OH, DON'T BE SO CHICKEN! DO YOU KNOW WHAT THIS STUFF IS?

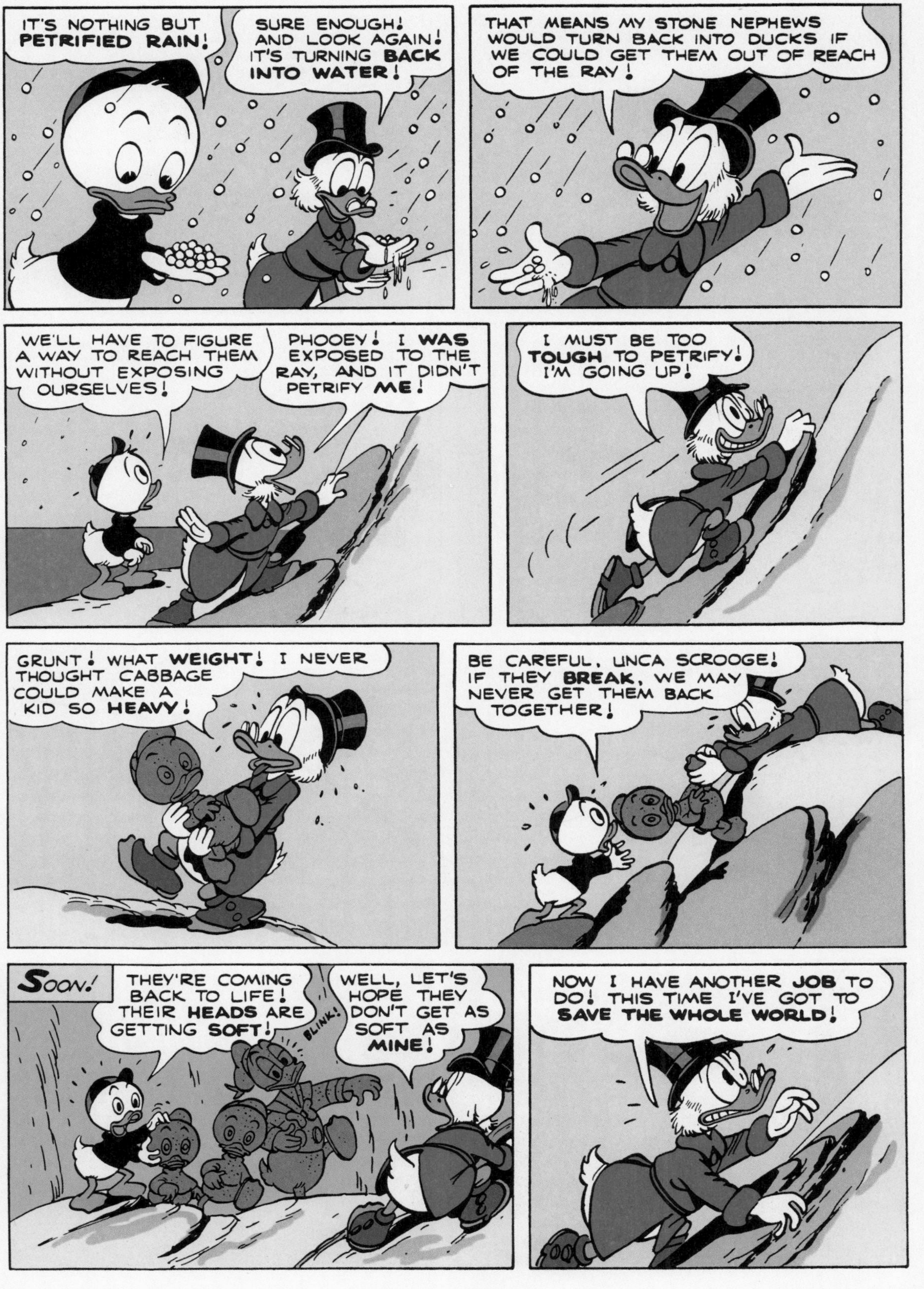
IT'S NOTHING BUT PETRIFIED RAIN!
SURE ENOUGH! AND LOOK AGAIN! IT'S TURNING BACK INTO WATER!
THAT MEANS MY STONE NEPHEWS WOULD TURN BACK INTO DUCKS IF WE COULD GET THEM OUT OF REACH OF THE RAY!
WE'LL HAVE TO FIGURE A WAY TO REACH THEM WITHOUT EXPOSING OURSELVES!
PHOOEY! I WAS EXPOSED TO THE RAY, AND IT DIDN'T PETRIFY ME!
I MUST BE TOO TOUGH TO PETRIFY! I'M GOING UP!
GRUNT! WHAT WEIGHT! I NEVER THOUGHT CABBAGE COULD MAKE A KID SO HEAVY!
BE CAREFUL, UNCA SCROOGE! IF THEY BREAK, WE MAY NEVER GET THEM BACK TOGETHER!
SOON!
THEY'RE COMING BACK TO LIFE! THEIR HEADS ARE GETTING SOFT!
BLINK!
WELL, LET'S HOPE THEY DON'T GET AS SOFT AS MINE!
NOW I HAVE ANOTHER JOB TO DO! THIS TIME I'VE GOT TO SAVE THE WHOLE WORLD!

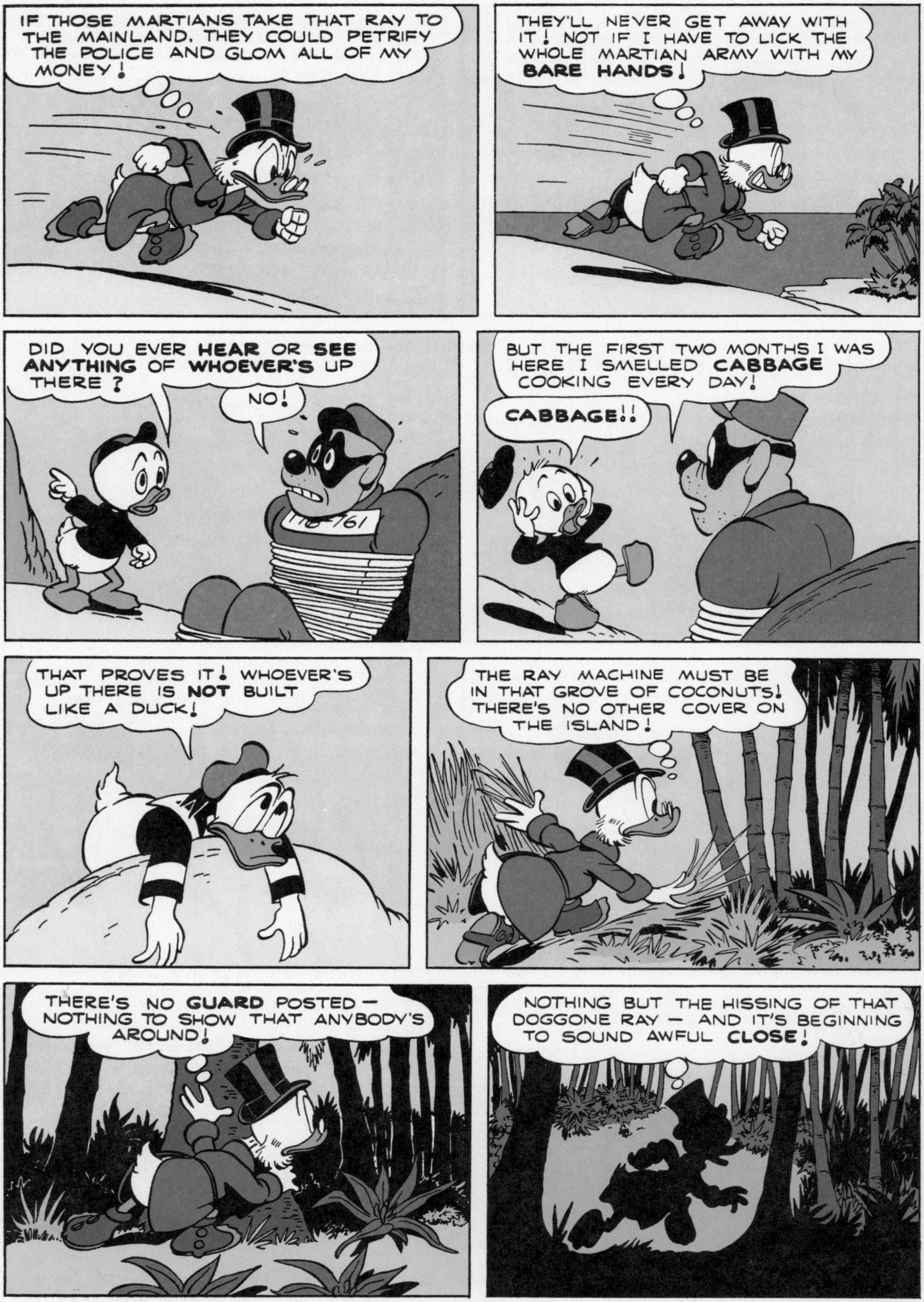
IF THOSE MARTIANS TAKE THAT RAY TO THE MAINLAND, THEY COULD PETRIFY THE POLICE AND GLOM ALL OF MY MONEY!
THEY'LL NEVER GET AWAY WITH IT! NOT IF I HAVE TO LICK THE WHOLE MARTIAN ARMY WITH MY BARE HANDS!
DID YOU EVER HEAR OR SEE ANYTHING OF WHOEVER'S UP THERE?
NO!
176-761
BUT THE FIRST TWO MONTHS I WAS HERE I SMELLED CABBAGE COOKING EVERY DAY!
CABBAGE!!
THAT PROVES IT! WHOEVER'S UP THERE IS NOT BUILT LIKE A DUCK!
THE RAY MACHINE MUST BE IN THAT GROVE OF COCONUTS! THERE'S NO OTHER COVER ON THE ISLAND!
THERE'S NO GUARD POSTED — NOTHING TO SHOW THAT ANYBODY'S AROUND!
NOTHING BUT THE HISSING OF THAT DOGGONE RAY — AND IT'S BEGINNING TO SOUND AWFUL CLOSE!

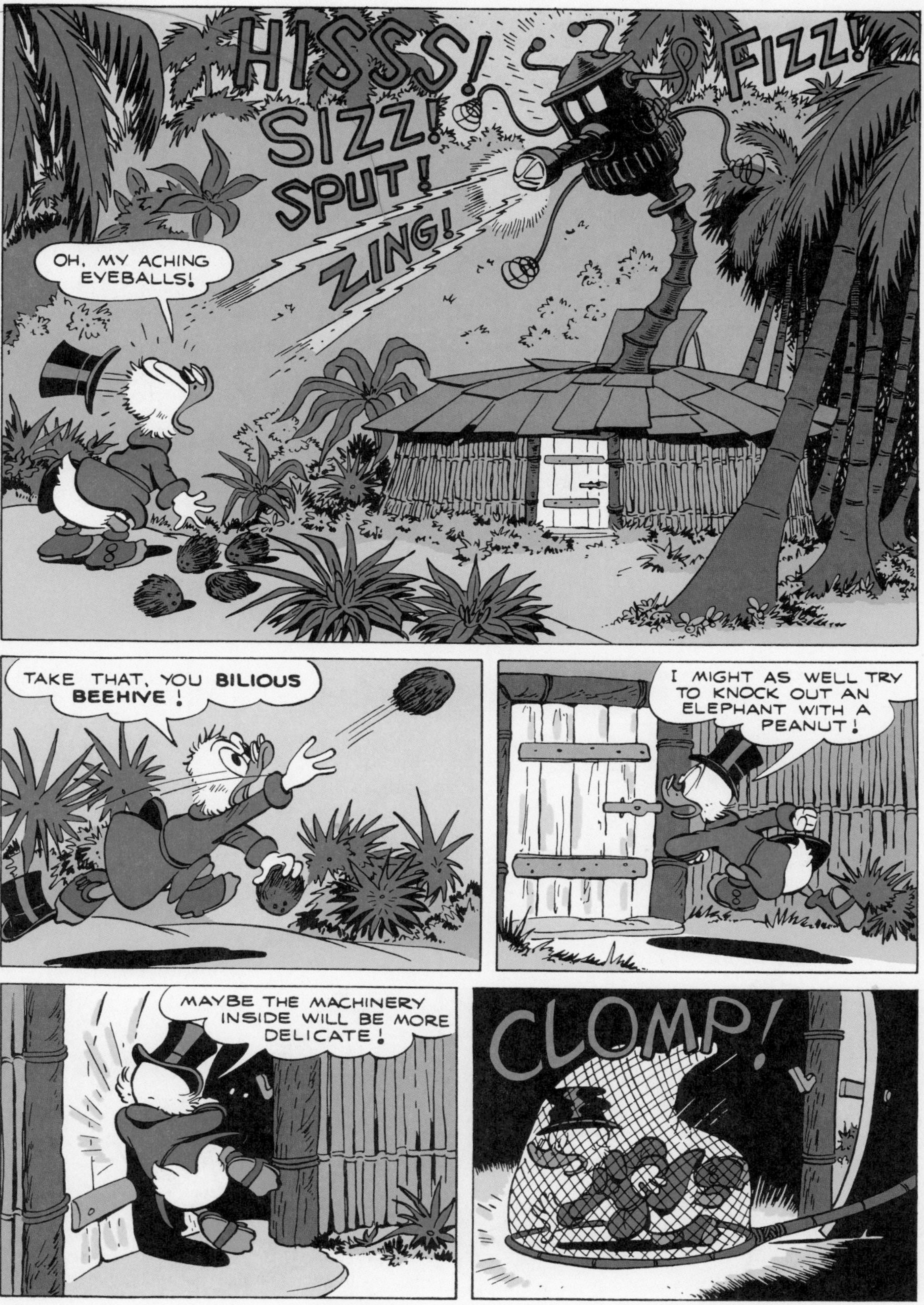
HISSS!
FIZZ!
SIZZ!
SPUT!
ZING!
OH, MY ACHING EYEBALLS!
TAKE THAT, YOU **BILIOUS BEEHIVE**!
I MIGHT AS WELL TRY TO KNOCK OUT AN ELEPHANT WITH A PEANUT!
MAYBE THE MACHINERY INSIDE WILL BE MORE DELICATE!
CLOMP!

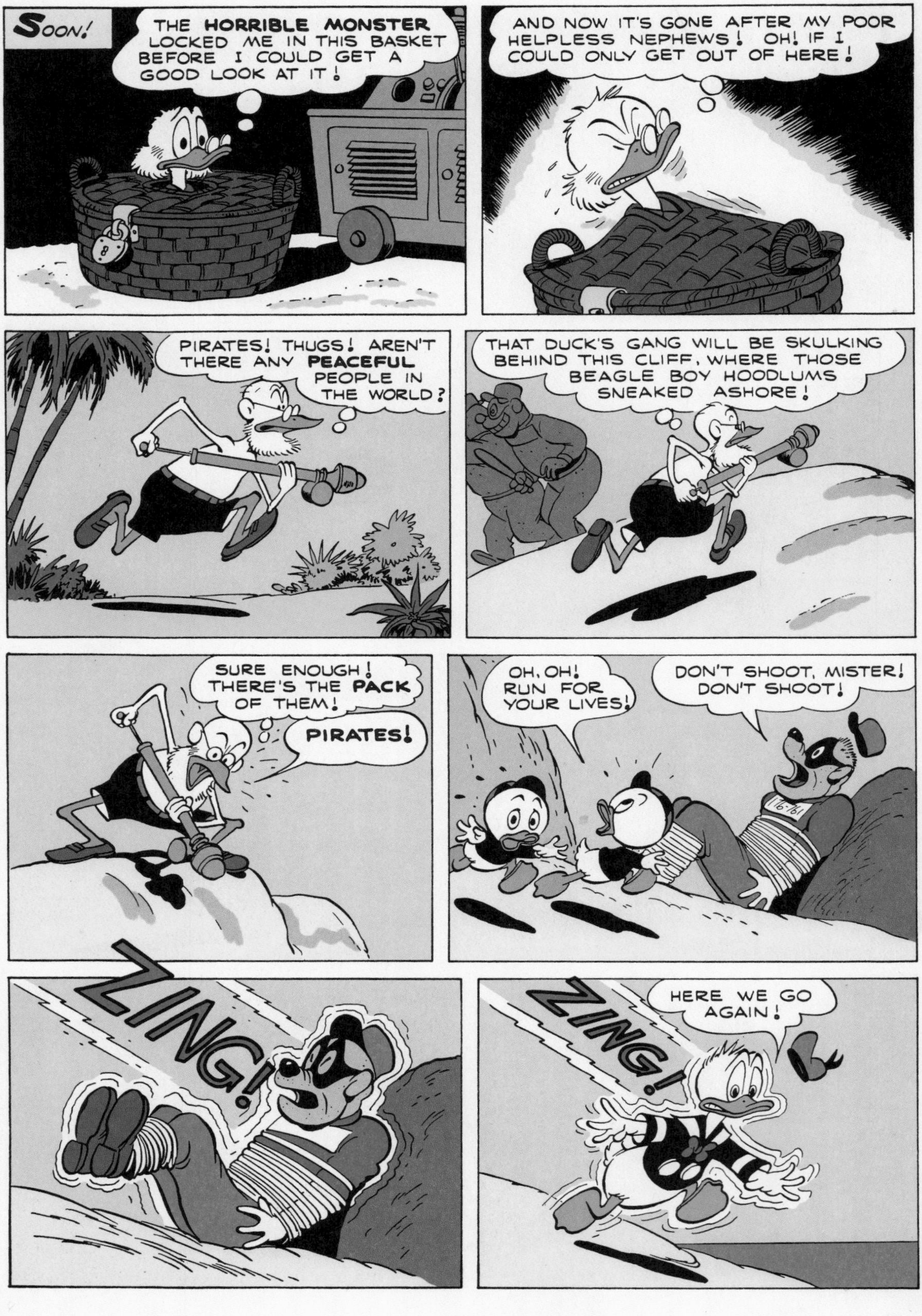
SOON!
THE HORRIBLE MONSTER LOCKED ME IN THIS BASKET BEFORE I COULD GET A GOOD LOOK AT IT!
AND NOW IT'S GONE AFTER MY POOR HELPLESS NEPHEWS! OH! IF I COULD ONLY GET OUT OF HERE!
PIRATES! THUGS! AREN'T THERE ANY PEACEFUL PEOPLE IN THE WORLD?
THAT DUCK'S GANG WILL BE SKULKING BEHIND THIS CLIFF, WHERE THOSE BEAGLE BOY HOODLUMS SNEAKED ASHORE!
SURE ENOUGH! THERE'S THE PACK OF THEM!
PIRATES!
OH, OH! RUN FOR YOUR LIVES!
DON'T SHOOT, MISTER! DON'T SHOOT!
176-761
ZING!
ZING!
HERE WE GO AGAIN!

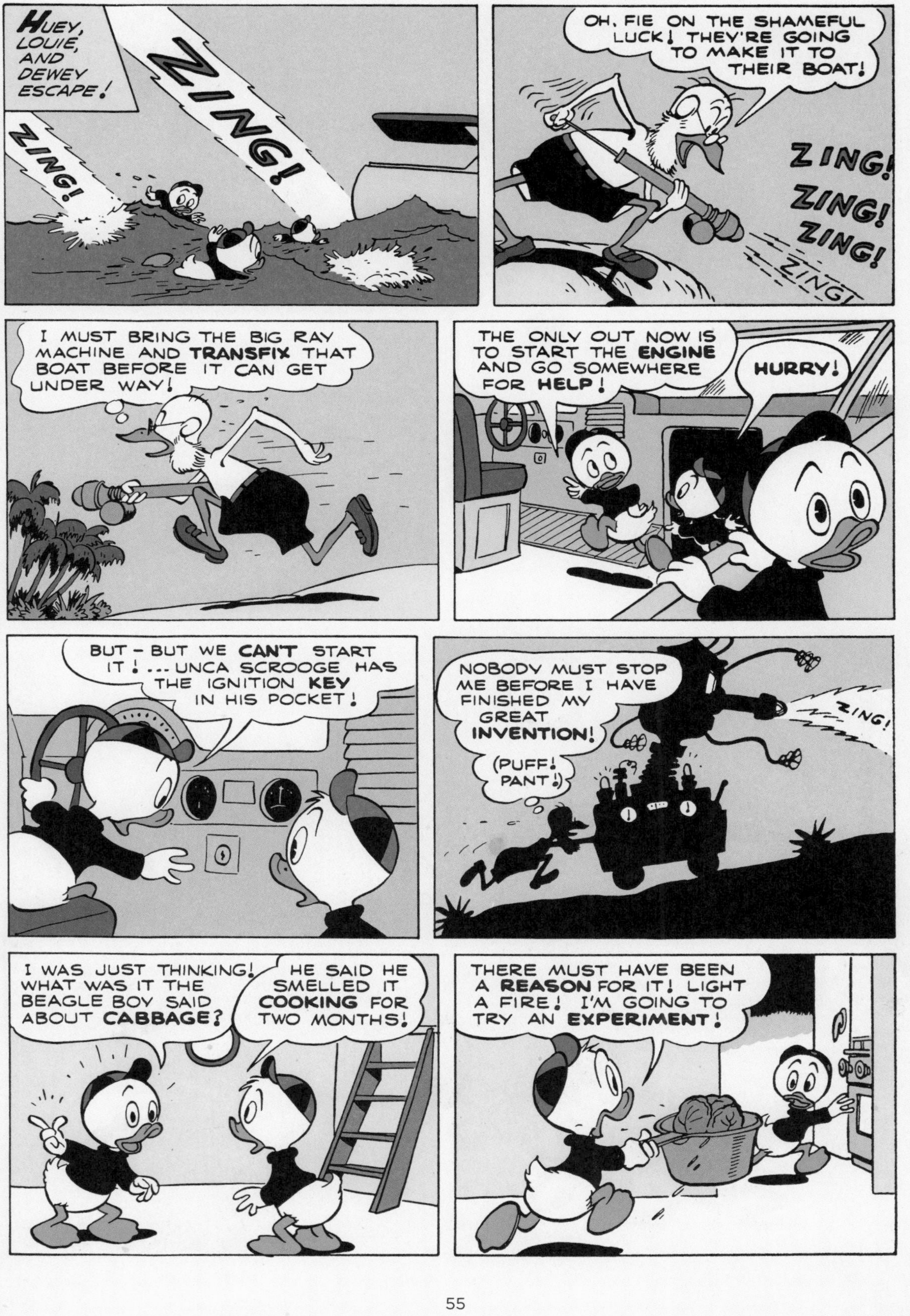
HUEY, LOUIE, AND DEWEY ESCAPE!
ZING!
ZING!
OH, FIE ON THE SHAMEFUL LUCK! THEY'RE GOING TO MAKE IT TO THEIR BOAT!
ZING!
ZING!
ZING!
ZING!
I MUST BRING THE BIG RAY MACHINE AND TRANSFIX THAT BOAT BEFORE IT CAN GET UNDER WAY!
THE ONLY OUT NOW IS TO START THE ENGINE AND GO SOMEWHERE FOR HELP!
HURRY!
BUT – BUT WE CAN'T START IT! ... UNCA SCROOGE HAS THE IGNITION KEY IN HIS POCKET!
NOBODY MUST STOP ME BEFORE I HAVE FINISHED MY GREAT INVENTION!
(PUFF! PANT!)
ZING!
I WAS JUST THINKING! WHAT WAS IT THE BEAGLE BOY SAID ABOUT CABBAGE?
HE SAID HE SMELLED IT COOKING FOR TWO MONTHS!
THERE MUST HAVE BEEN A REASON FOR IT! LIGHT A FIRE! I'M GOING TO TRY AN EXPERIMENT!

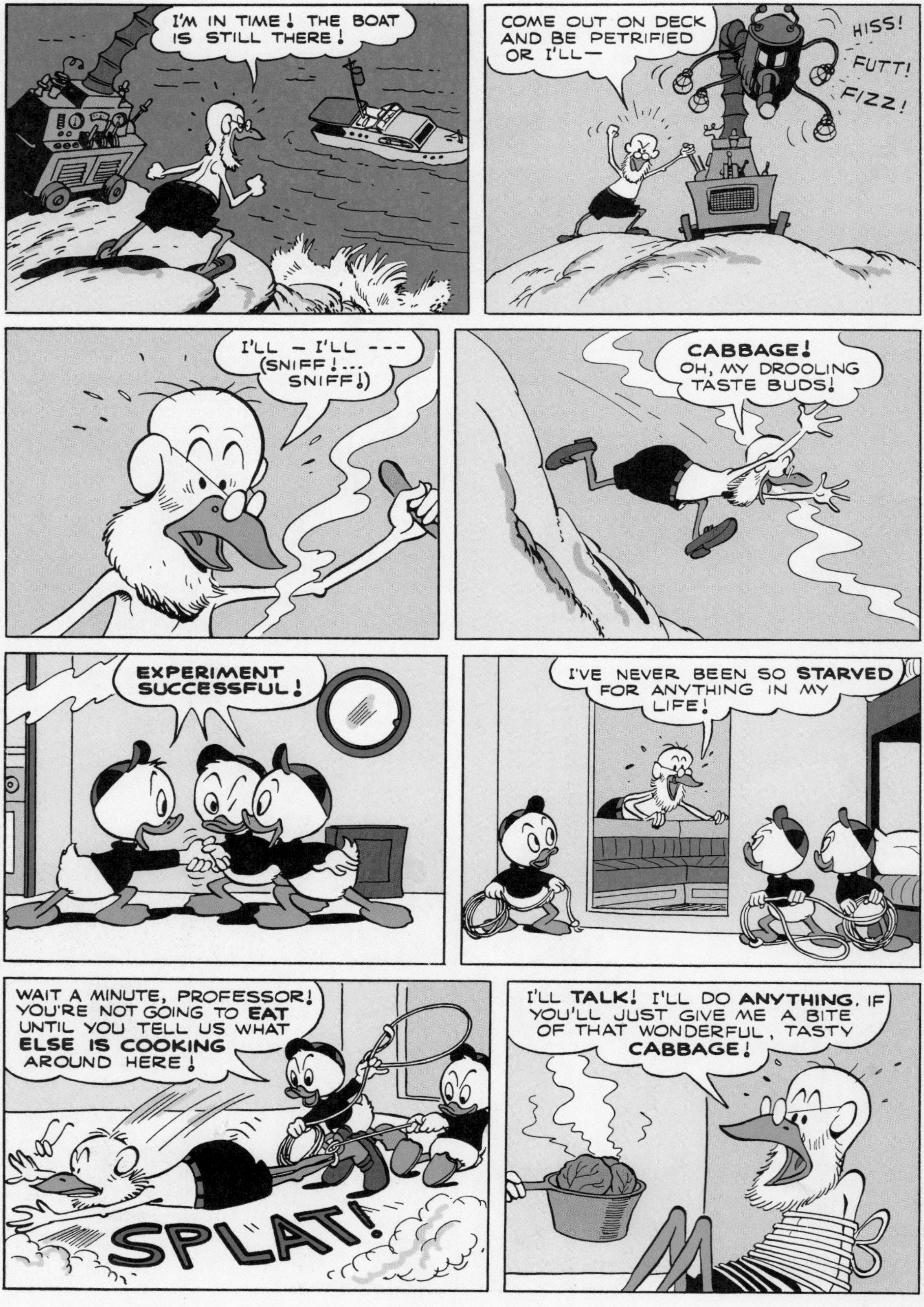
I'M IN TIME! THE BOAT IS STILL THERE!
COME OUT ON DECK AND BE PETRIFIED OR I'LL—
HISS!
FUTT!
FIZZ!
I'LL — I'LL --- (SNIFF!... SNIFF!)
CABBAGE! OH, MY DROOLING TASTE BUDS!
EXPERIMENT SUCCESSFUL!
I'VE NEVER BEEN SO STARVED FOR ANYTHING IN MY LIFE!
WAIT A MINUTE, PROFESSOR! YOU'RE NOT GOING TO EAT UNTIL YOU TELL US WHAT ELSE IS COOKING AROUND HERE!
SPLAT!
I'LL TALK! I'LL DO ANYTHING, IF YOU'LL JUST GIVE ME A BITE OF THAT WONDERFUL, TASTY CABBAGE!

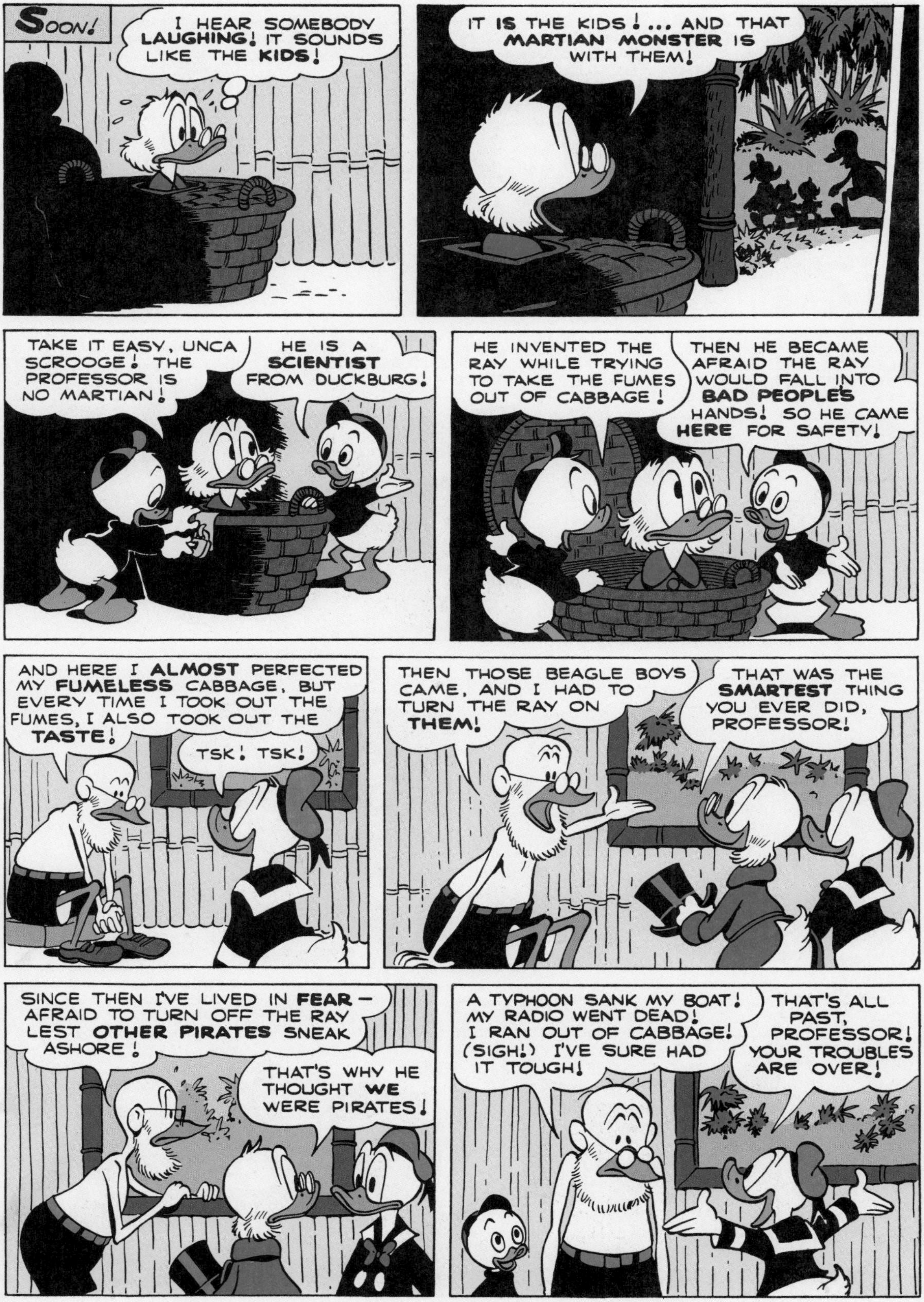
SOON!
I HEAR SOMEBODY LAUGHING! IT SOUNDS LIKE THE KIDS!
IT IS THE KIDS! ... AND THAT MARTIAN MONSTER IS WITH THEM!
TAKE IT EASY, UNCA SCROOGE! THE PROFESSOR IS NO MARTIAN!
HE IS A SCIENTIST FROM DUCKBURG!
HE INVENTED THE RAY WHILE TRYING TO TAKE THE FUMES OUT OF CABBAGE!
THEN HE BECAME AFRAID THE RAY WOULD FALL INTO BAD PEOPLE'S HANDS! SO HE CAME HERE FOR SAFETY!
AND HERE I ALMOST PERFECTED MY FUMELESS CABBAGE, BUT EVERY TIME I TOOK OUT THE FUMES, I ALSO TOOK OUT THE TASTE!
TSK! TSK!
THEN THOSE BEAGLE BOYS CAME, AND I HAD TO TURN THE RAY ON THEM!
THAT WAS THE SMARTEST THING YOU EVER DID, PROFESSOR!
SINCE THEN I'VE LIVED IN FEAR — AFRAID TO TURN OFF THE RAY LEST OTHER PIRATES SNEAK ASHORE!
THAT'S WHY HE THOUGHT WE WERE PIRATES!
A TYPHOON SANK MY BOAT! MY RADIO WENT DEAD! I RAN OUT OF CABBAGE! (SIGH!) I'VE SURE HAD IT TOUGH!
THAT'S ALL PAST, PROFESSOR! YOUR TROUBLES ARE OVER!

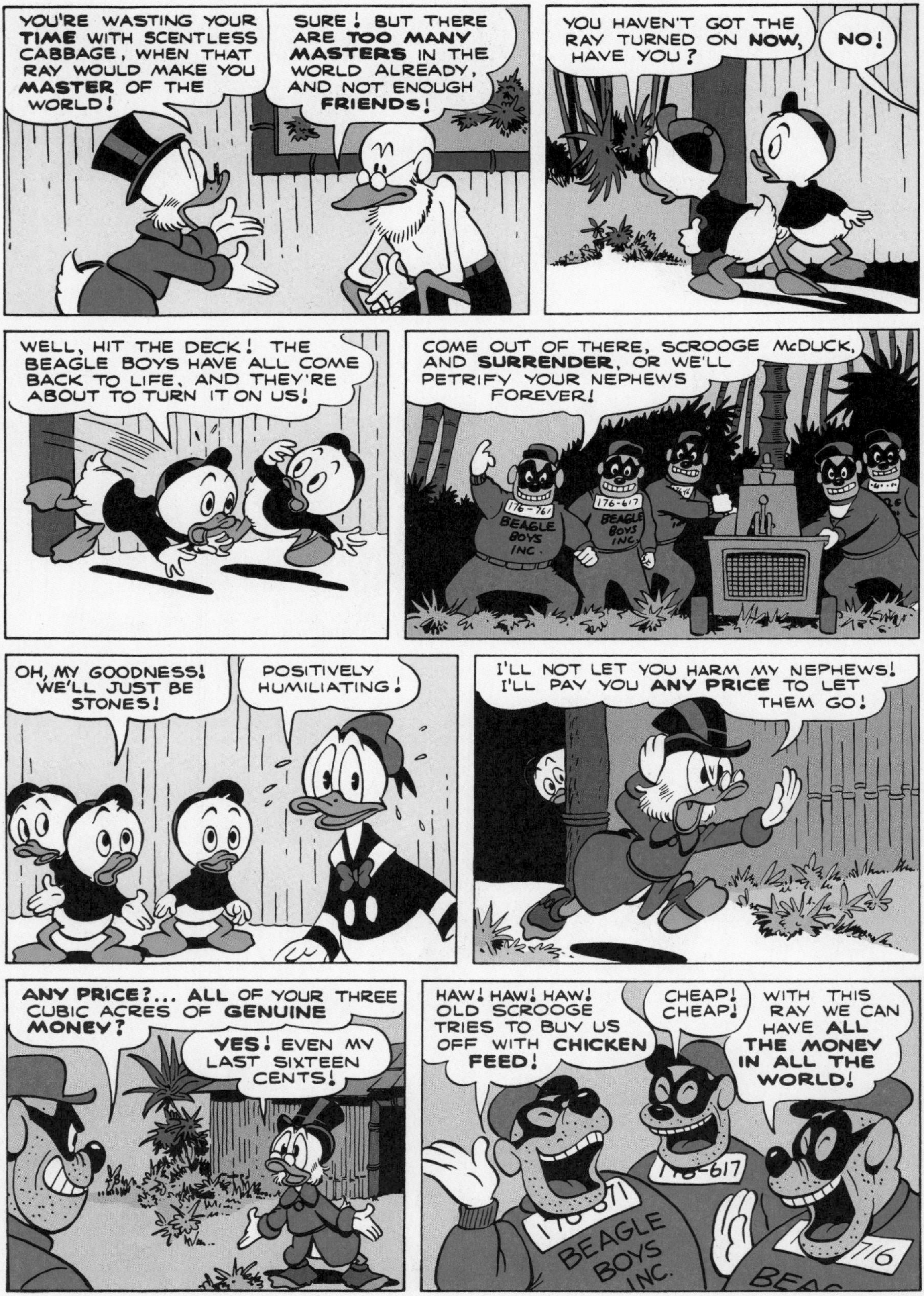
YOU'RE WASTING YOUR TIME WITH SCENTLESS CABBAGE, WHEN THAT RAY WOULD MAKE YOU MASTER OF THE WORLD!
SURE! BUT THERE ARE TOO MANY MASTERS IN THE WORLD ALREADY, AND NOT ENOUGH FRIENDS!
YOU HAVEN'T GOT THE RAY TURNED ON NOW, HAVE YOU?
NO!
WELL, HIT THE DECK! THE BEAGLE BOYS HAVE ALL COME BACK TO LIFE, AND THEY'RE ABOUT TO TURN IT ON US!
COME OUT OF THERE, SCROOGE McDUCK, AND SURRENDER, OR WE'LL PETRIFY YOUR NEPHEWS FOREVER!
176-761
BEAGLE BOYS INC.
176-617
BEAGLE BOYS INC.
OH, MY GOODNESS! WE'LL JUST BE STONES!
POSITIVELY HUMILIATING!
I'LL NOT LET YOU HARM MY NEPHEWS! I'LL PAY YOU ANY PRICE TO LET THEM GO!
ANY PRICE?... ALL OF YOUR THREE CUBIC ACRES OF GENUINE MONEY?
YES! EVEN MY LAST SIXTEEN CENTS!
HAW! HAW! HAW! OLD SCROOGE TRIES TO BUY US OFF WITH CHICKEN FEED!
CHEAP! CHEAP!
WITH THIS RAY WE CAN HAVE ALL THE MONEY IN ALL THE WORLD!
176-617
BEAGLE BOYS INC.
716

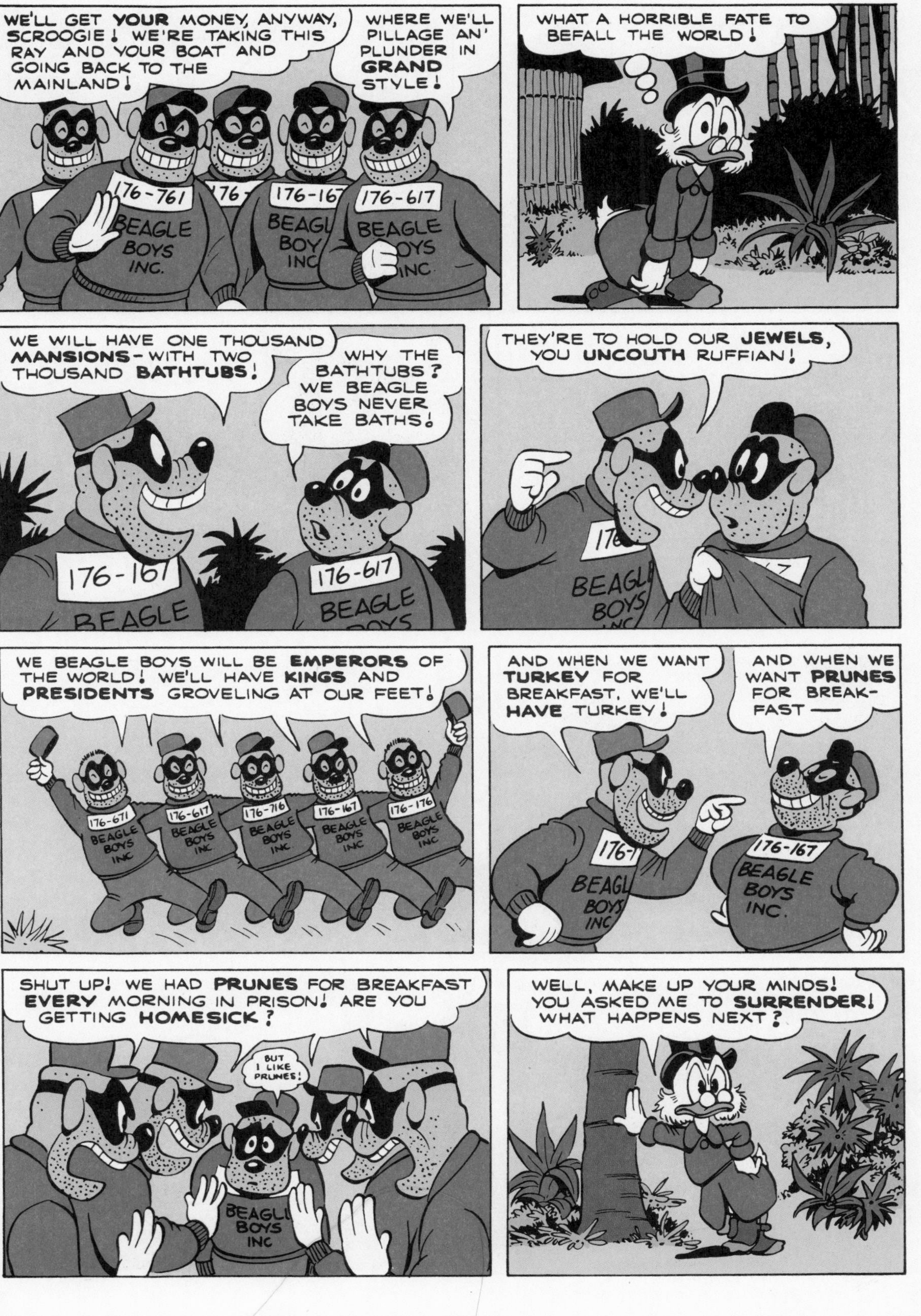

WE'LL GET **YOUR** MONEY, ANYWAY, SCROOGIE! WE'RE TAKING THIS RAY AND YOUR BOAT AND GOING BACK TO THE MAINLAND!
WHERE WE'LL PILLAGE AN' PLUNDER IN **GRAND** STYLE!
176-761
176-167
176-617
BEAGLE BOYS INC.
WHAT A HORRIBLE FATE TO BEFALL THE WORLD!
WE WILL HAVE ONE THOUSAND **MANSIONS**– WITH TWO THOUSAND **BATHTUBS**!
WHY THE BATHTUBS? WE BEAGLE BOYS NEVER TAKE BATHS!
176-167
176-617
THEY'RE TO HOLD OUR **JEWELS**, YOU **UNCOUTH** RUFFIAN!
WE BEAGLE BOYS WILL BE **EMPERORS** OF THE WORLD! WE'LL HAVE **KINGS** AND **PRESIDENTS** GROVELING AT OUR FEET!
176-671
176-617
176-716
176-167
176-176
AND WHEN WE WANT **TURKEY** FOR BREAKFAST, WE'LL **HAVE** TURKEY!
AND WHEN WE WANT **PRUNES** FOR BREAK-FAST —
176-167
BEAGLE BOYS INC.
SHUT UP! WE HAD **PRUNES** FOR BREAKFAST **EVERY** MORNING IN PRISON! ARE YOU GETTING **HOMESICK**?
BUT I LIKE PRUNES!
BEAGLE BOYS INC
WELL, MAKE UP YOUR MINDS! YOU ASKED ME TO **SURRENDER**! WHAT HAPPENS NEXT?

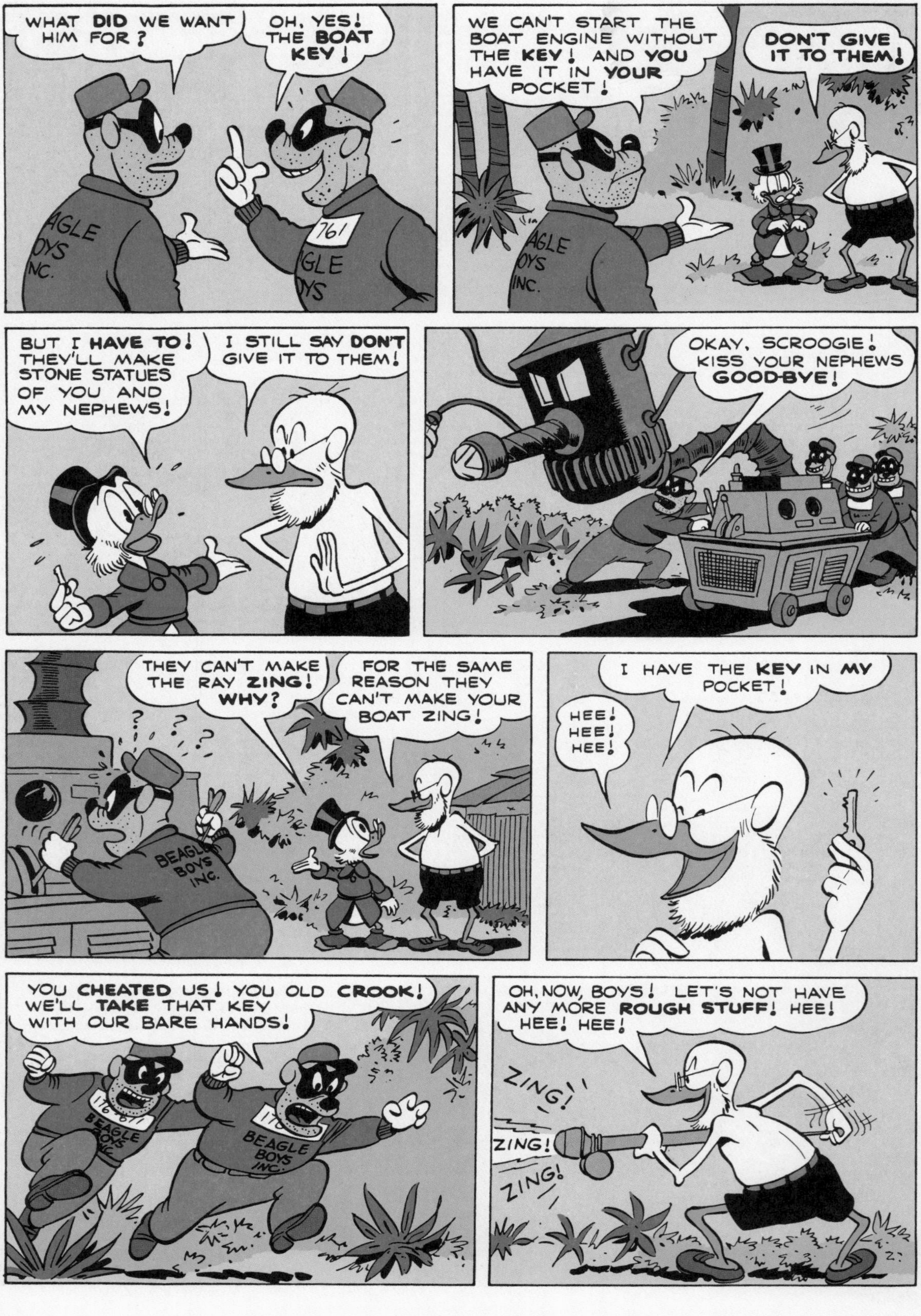
WHAT DID WE WANT HIM FOR?
OH, YES! THE BOAT KEY!
761
WE CAN'T START THE BOAT ENGINE WITHOUT THE KEY! AND YOU HAVE IT IN YOUR POCKET!
DON'T GIVE IT TO THEM!
BUT I HAVE TO! THEY'LL MAKE STONE STATUES OF YOU AND MY NEPHEWS!
I STILL SAY DON'T GIVE IT TO THEM!
OKAY, SCROOGIE! KISS YOUR NEPHEWS GOOD-BYE!
THEY CAN'T MAKE THE RAY ZING! WHY?
FOR THE SAME REASON THEY CAN'T MAKE YOUR BOAT ZING!
BEAGLE BOYS INC.
I HAVE THE KEY IN MY POCKET!
HEE! HEE! HEE!
YOU CHEATED US! YOU OLD CROOK! WE'LL TAKE THAT KEY WITH OUR BARE HANDS!
BEAGLE BOYS INC.
OH, NOW, BOYS! LET'S NOT HAVE ANY MORE ROUGH STUFF! HEE! HEE! HEE!
ZING!
ZING!
ZING!

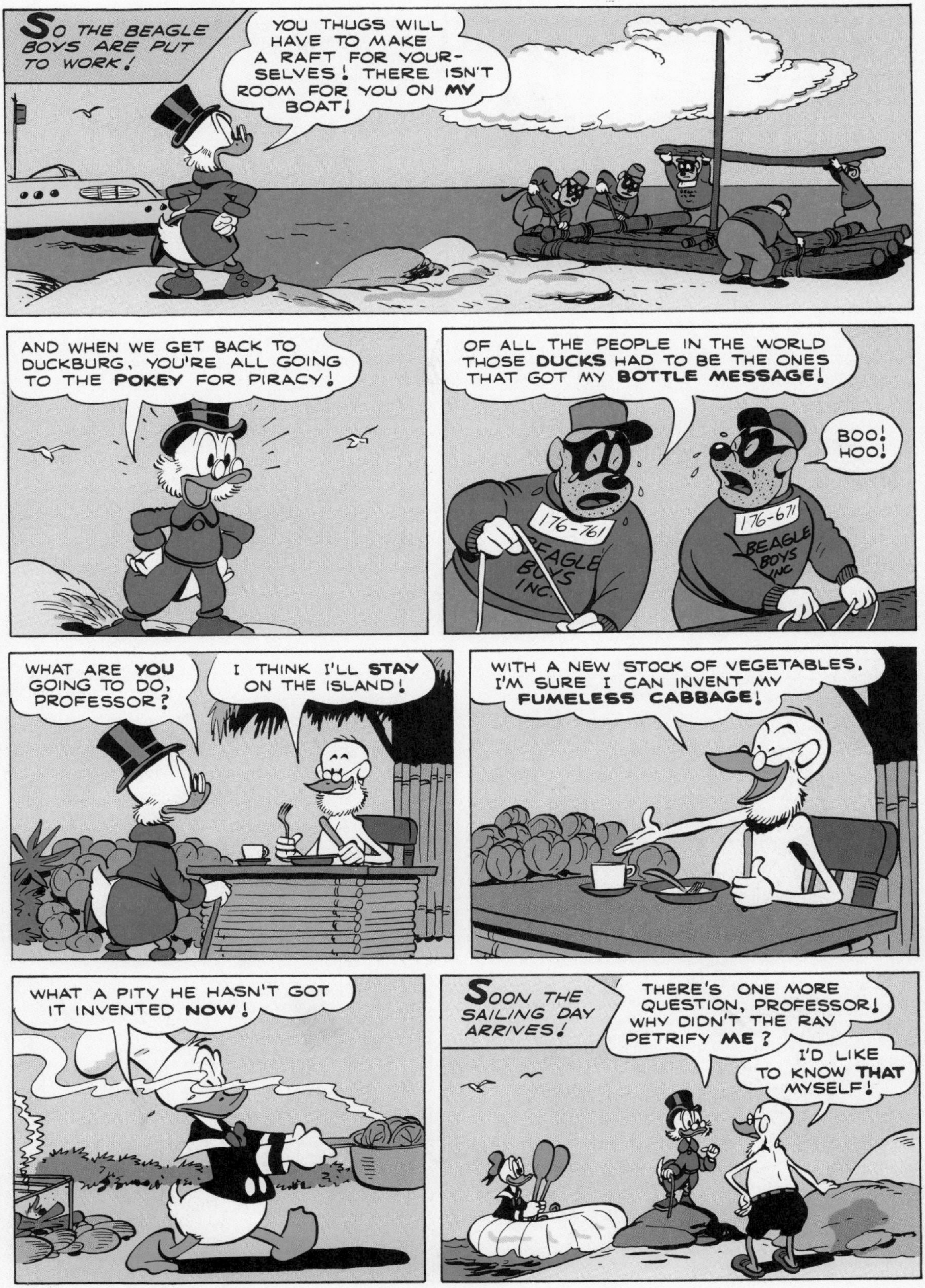
SO THE BEAGLE BOYS ARE PUT TO WORK!
YOU THUGS WILL HAVE TO MAKE A RAFT FOR YOURSELVES! THERE ISN'T ROOM FOR YOU ON MY BOAT!
AND WHEN WE GET BACK TO DUCKBURG, YOU'RE ALL GOING TO THE POKEY FOR PIRACY!
OF ALL THE PEOPLE IN THE WORLD THOSE DUCKS HAD TO BE THE ONES THAT GOT MY BOTTLE MESSAGE!
BOO! HOO!
176-761
BEAGLE BOYS INC.
176-671
BEAGLE BOYS INC
WHAT ARE YOU GOING TO DO, PROFESSOR?
I THINK I'LL STAY ON THE ISLAND!
WITH A NEW STOCK OF VEGETABLES, I'M SURE I CAN INVENT MY FUMELESS CABBAGE!
WHAT A PITY HE HASN'T GOT IT INVENTED NOW!
SOON THE SAILING DAY ARRIVES!
THERE'S ONE MORE QUESTION, PROFESSOR! WHY DIDN'T THE RAY PETRIFY ME?
I'D LIKE TO KNOW THAT MYSELF!

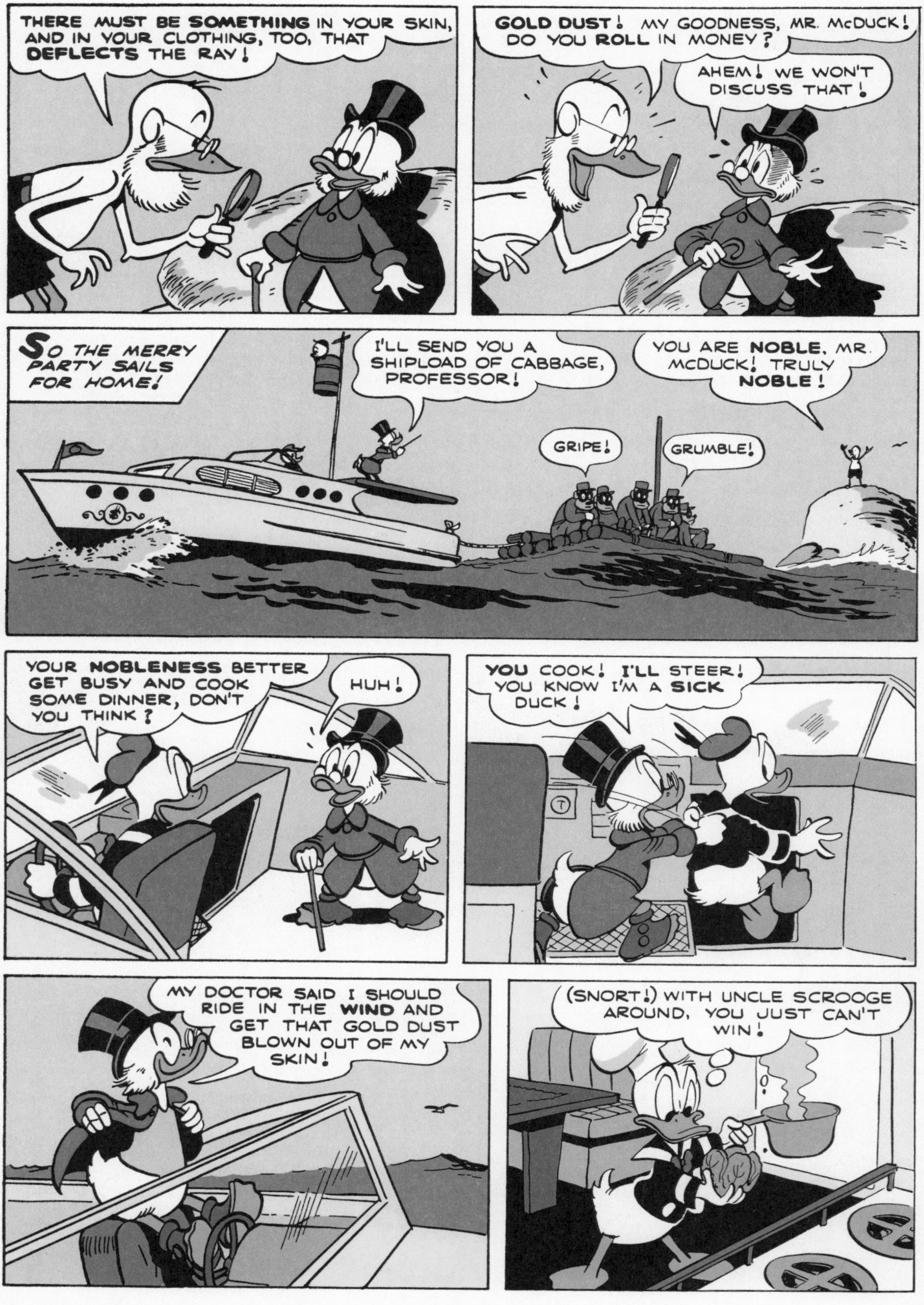
THERE MUST BE SOMETHING IN YOUR SKIN, AND IN YOUR CLOTHING, TOO, THAT DEFLECTS THE RAY!
GOLD DUST! MY GOODNESS, MR. McDUCK! DO YOU ROLL IN MONEY?
AHEM! WE WON'T DISCUSS THAT!
SO THE MERRY PARTY SAILS FOR HOME!
I'LL SEND YOU A SHIPLOAD OF CABBAGE, PROFESSOR!
YOU ARE NOBLE, MR. McDUCK! TRULY NOBLE!
GRIPE!
GRUMBLE!
YOUR NOBLENESS BETTER GET BUSY AND COOK SOME DINNER, DON'T YOU THINK?
HUH!
YOU COOK! I'LL STEER! YOU KNOW I'M A SICK DUCK!
MY DOCTOR SAID I SHOULD RIDE IN THE WIND AND GET THAT GOLD DUST BLOWN OUT OF MY SKIN!
(SNORT!) WITH UNCLE SCROOGE AROUND, YOU JUST CAN'T WIN!

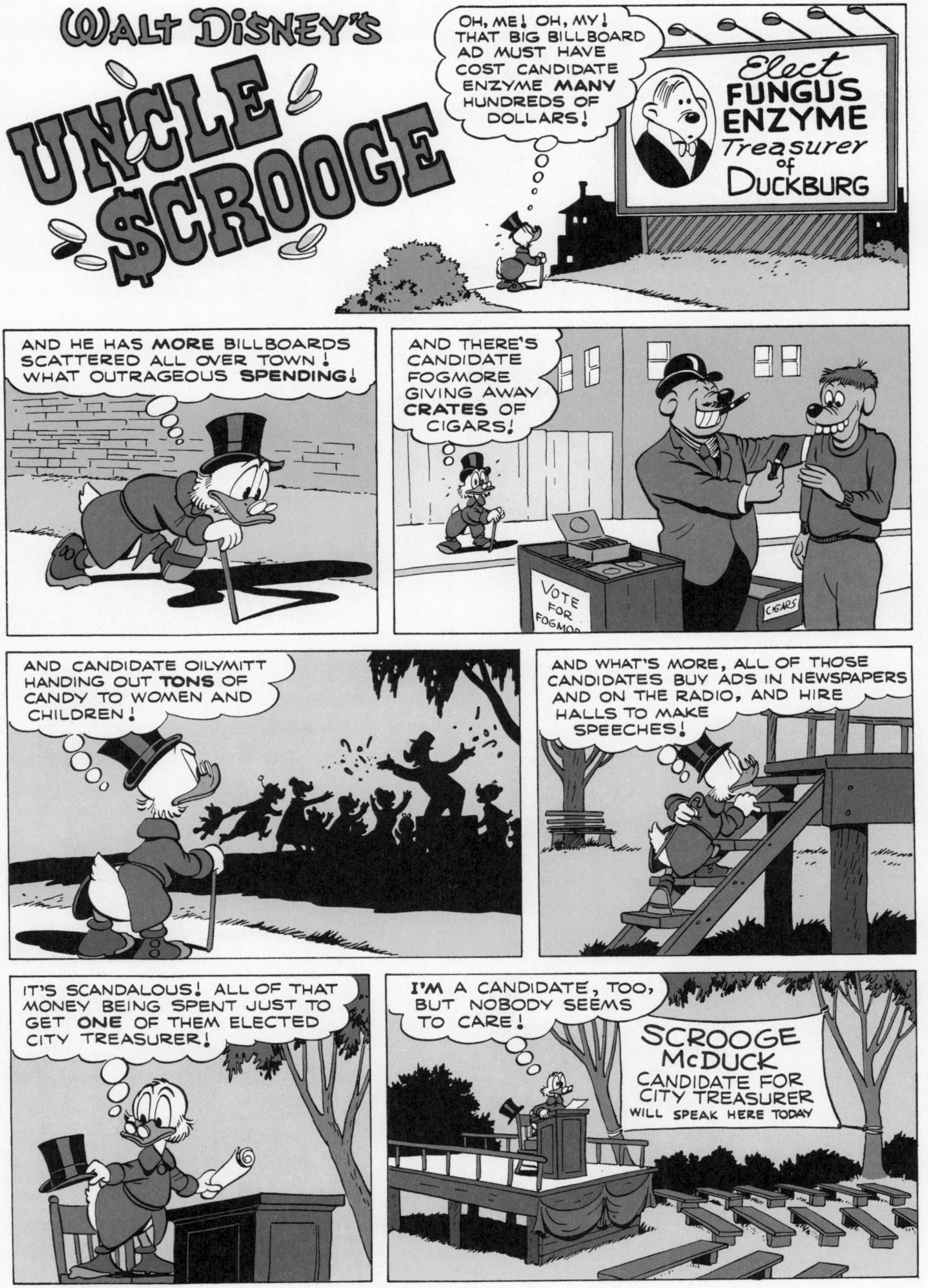
WALT DISNEY'S
UNCLE $CROOGE
OH, ME! OH, MY! THAT BIG BILLBOARD AD MUST HAVE COST CANDIDATE ENZYME MANY HUNDREDS OF DOLLARS!
Elect FUNGUS ENZYME Treasurer of DUCKBURG
AND HE HAS MORE BILLBOARDS SCATTERED ALL OVER TOWN! WHAT OUTRAGEOUS SPENDING!
AND THERE'S CANDIDATE FOGMORE GIVING AWAY CRATES OF CIGARS!
CIGARS
AND CANDIDATE OILYMITT HANDING OUT TONS OF CANDY TO WOMEN AND CHILDREN!
AND WHAT'S MORE, ALL OF THOSE CANDIDATES BUY ADS IN NEWSPAPERS AND ON THE RADIO, AND HIRE HALLS TO MAKE SPEECHES!
IT'S SCANDALOUS! ALL OF THAT MONEY BEING SPENT JUST TO GET ONE OF THEM ELECTED CITY TREASURER!
I'M A CANDIDATE, TOO, BUT NOBODY SEEMS TO CARE!
SCROOGE McDUCK CANDIDATE FOR CITY TREASURER WILL SPEAK HERE TODAY

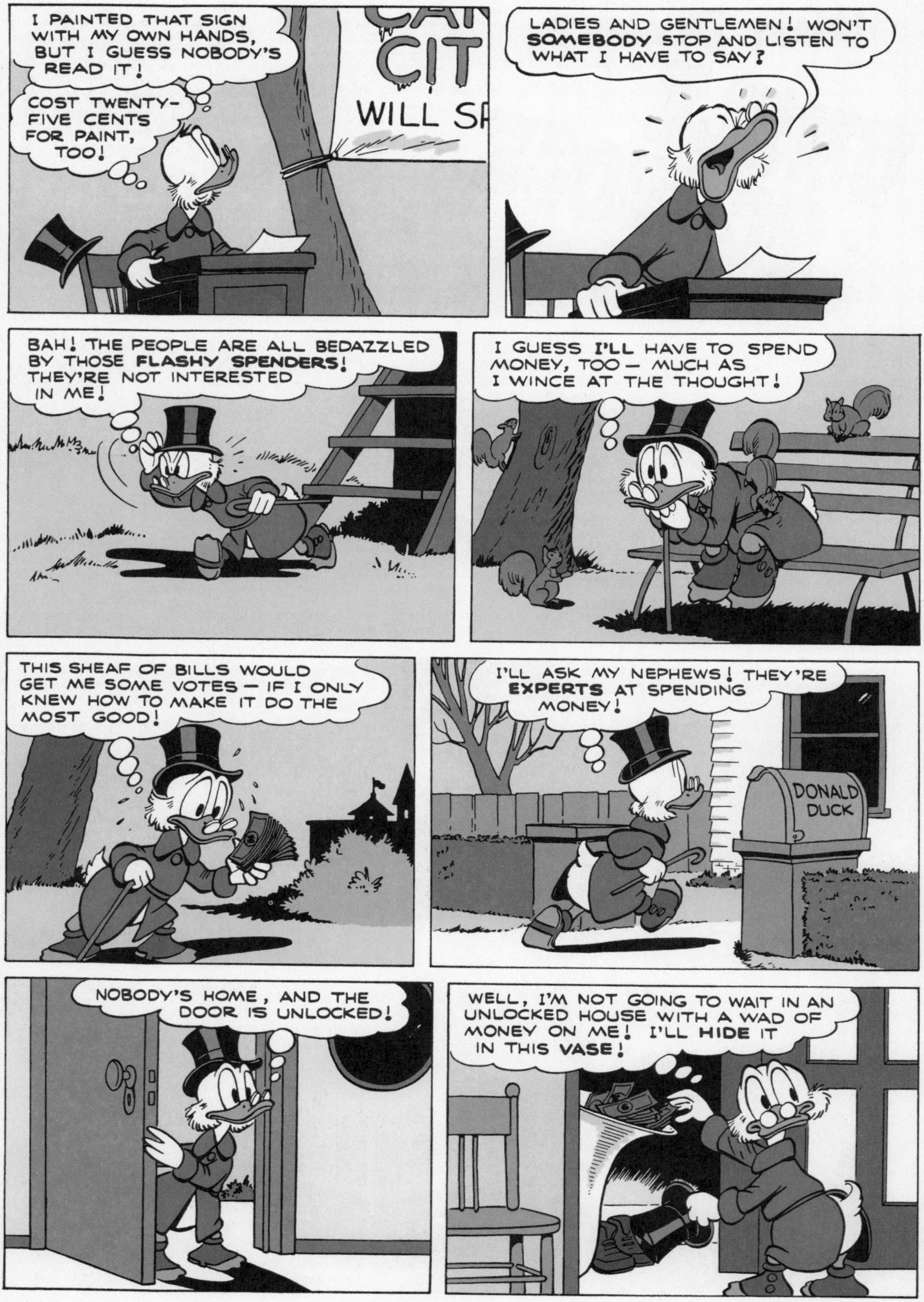
I PAINTED THAT SIGN WITH MY OWN HANDS, BUT I GUESS NOBODY'S READ IT!
COST TWENTY-FIVE CENTS FOR PAINT, TOO!
CIT
WILL S
LADIES AND GENTLEMEN! WON'T **SOMEBODY** STOP AND LISTEN TO WHAT I HAVE TO SAY?
BAH! THE PEOPLE ARE ALL BEDAZZLED BY THOSE **FLASHY SPENDERS**! THEY'RE NOT INTERESTED IN ME!
I GUESS **I'LL** HAVE TO SPEND MONEY, TOO — MUCH AS I WINCE AT THE THOUGHT!
THIS SHEAF OF BILLS WOULD GET ME SOME VOTES — IF I ONLY KNEW HOW TO MAKE IT DO THE MOST GOOD!
I'LL ASK MY NEPHEWS! THEY'RE **EXPERTS** AT SPENDING MONEY!
DONALD DUCK
NOBODY'S HOME, AND THE DOOR IS UNLOCKED!
WELL, I'M NOT GOING TO WAIT IN AN UNLOCKED HOUSE WITH A WAD OF MONEY ON ME! I'LL **HIDE** IT IN THIS **VASE**!

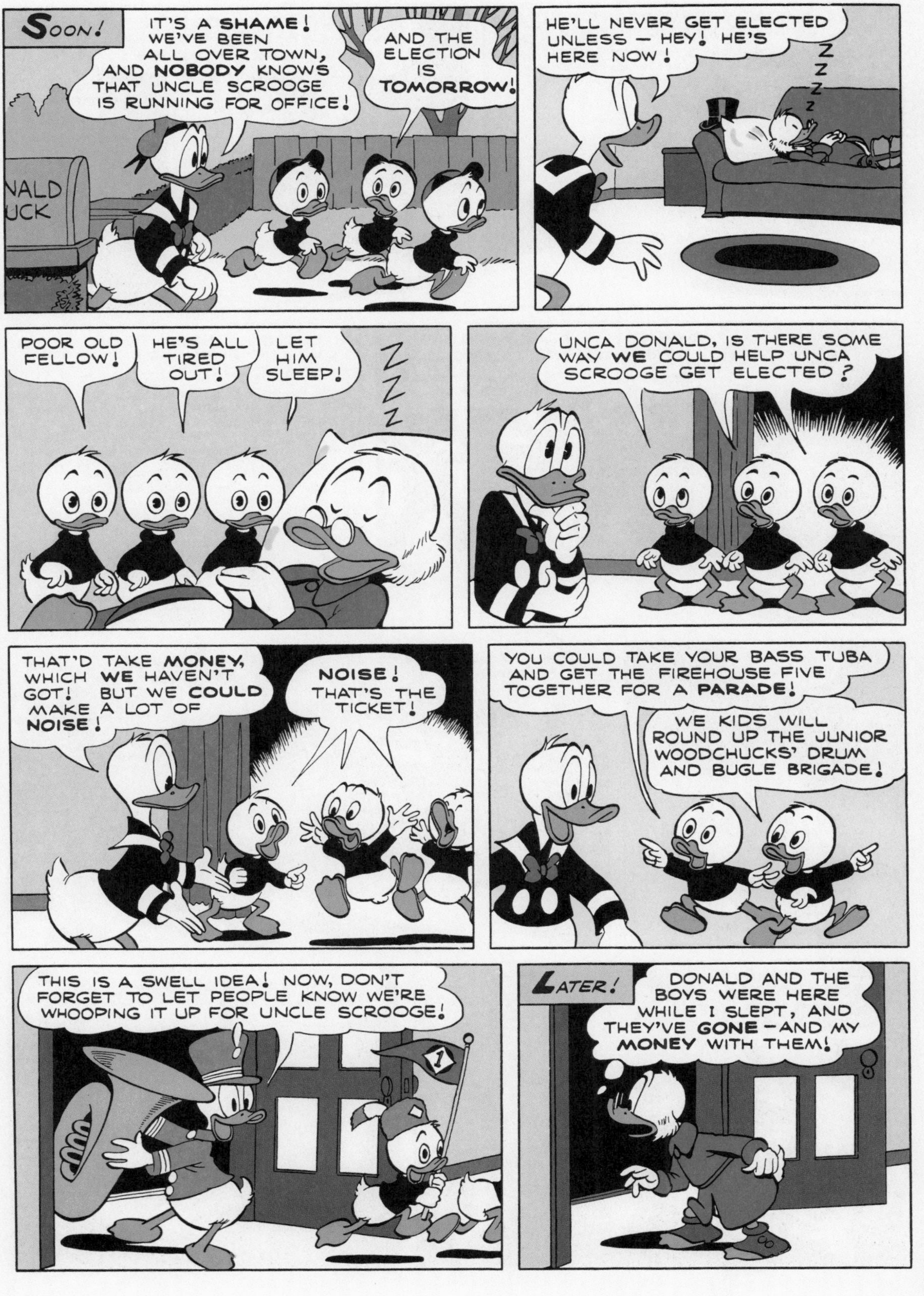
SOON!
IT'S A SHAME! WE'VE BEEN ALL OVER TOWN, AND NOBODY KNOWS THAT UNCLE SCROOGE IS RUNNING FOR OFFICE!
AND THE ELECTION IS TOMORROW!
NALD
UCK
HE'LL NEVER GET ELECTED UNLESS — HEY! HE'S HERE NOW!
Z Z Z Z
POOR OLD FELLOW!
HE'S ALL TIRED OUT!
LET HIM SLEEP!
Z Z Z
UNCA DONALD, IS THERE SOME WAY WE COULD HELP UNCA SCROOGE GET ELECTED?
THAT'D TAKE MONEY, WHICH WE HAVEN'T GOT! BUT WE COULD MAKE A LOT OF NOISE!
NOISE! THAT'S THE TICKET!
YOU COULD TAKE YOUR BASS TUBA AND GET THE FIREHOUSE FIVE TOGETHER FOR A PARADE!
WE KIDS WILL ROUND UP THE JUNIOR WOODCHUCKS' DRUM AND BUGLE BRIGADE!
THIS IS A SWELL IDEA! NOW, DON'T FORGET TO LET PEOPLE KNOW WE'RE WHOOPING IT UP FOR UNCLE SCROOGE!
1
LATER!
DONALD AND THE BOYS WERE HERE WHILE I SLEPT, AND THEY'VE GONE—AND MY MONEY WITH THEM!

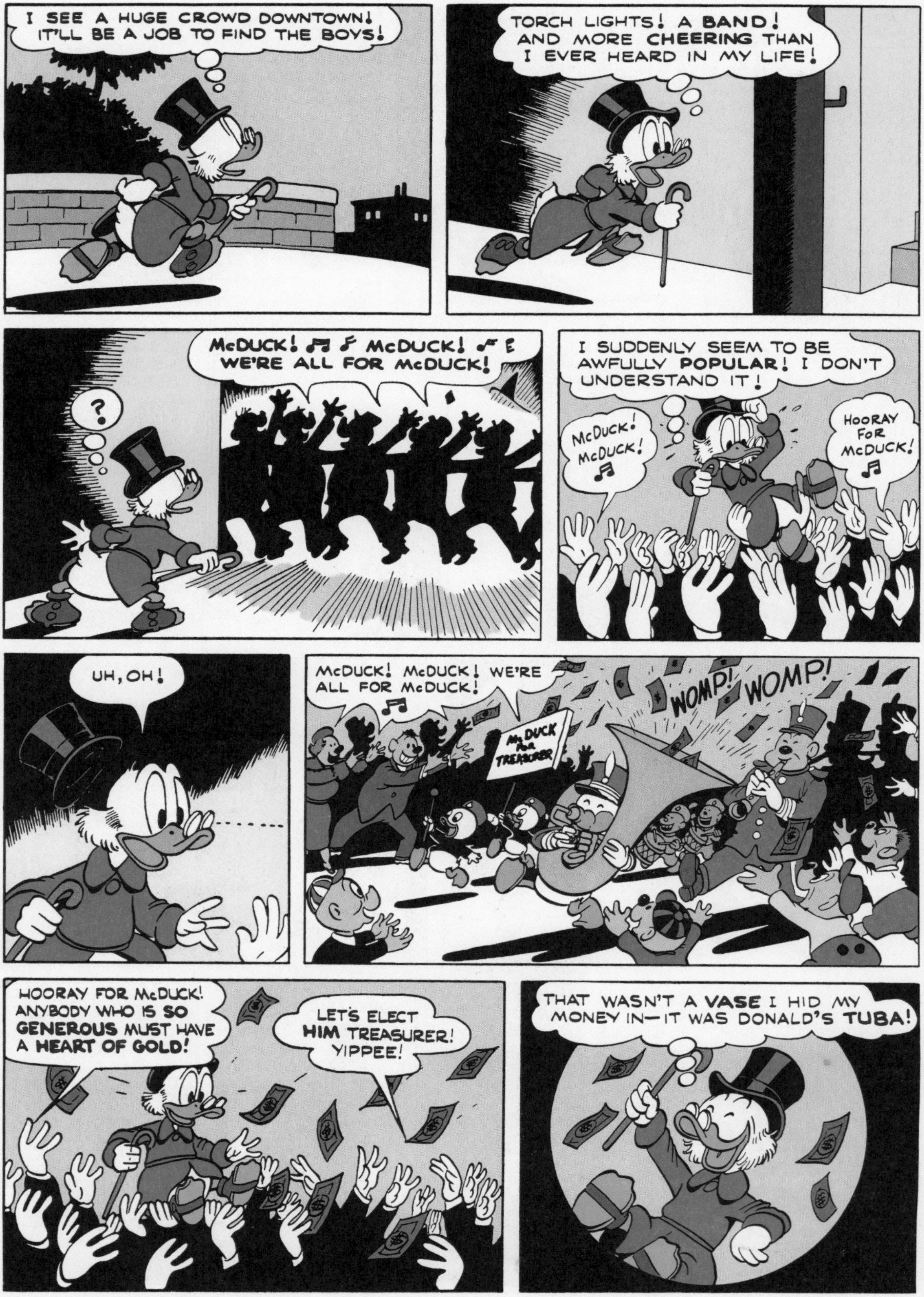
I SEE A HUGE CROWD DOWNTOWN! IT'LL BE A JOB TO FIND THE BOYS!
TORCH LIGHTS! A BAND! AND MORE CHEERING THAN I EVER HEARD IN MY LIFE!
?
McDUCK! McDUCK! WE'RE ALL FOR McDUCK!
I SUDDENLY SEEM TO BE AWFULLY POPULAR! I DON'T UNDERSTAND IT!
McDUCK! McDUCK!
HOORAY FOR McDUCK!
UH, OH!
McDUCK! McDUCK! WE'RE ALL FOR McDUCK!
WOMP! WOMP!
McDUCK FOR TREASURER
HOORAY FOR McDUCK! ANYBODY WHO IS SO GENEROUS MUST HAVE A HEART OF GOLD!
LET'S ELECT HIM TREASURER! YIPPEE!
THAT WASN'T A VASE I HID MY MONEY IN— IT WAS DONALD'S TUBA!

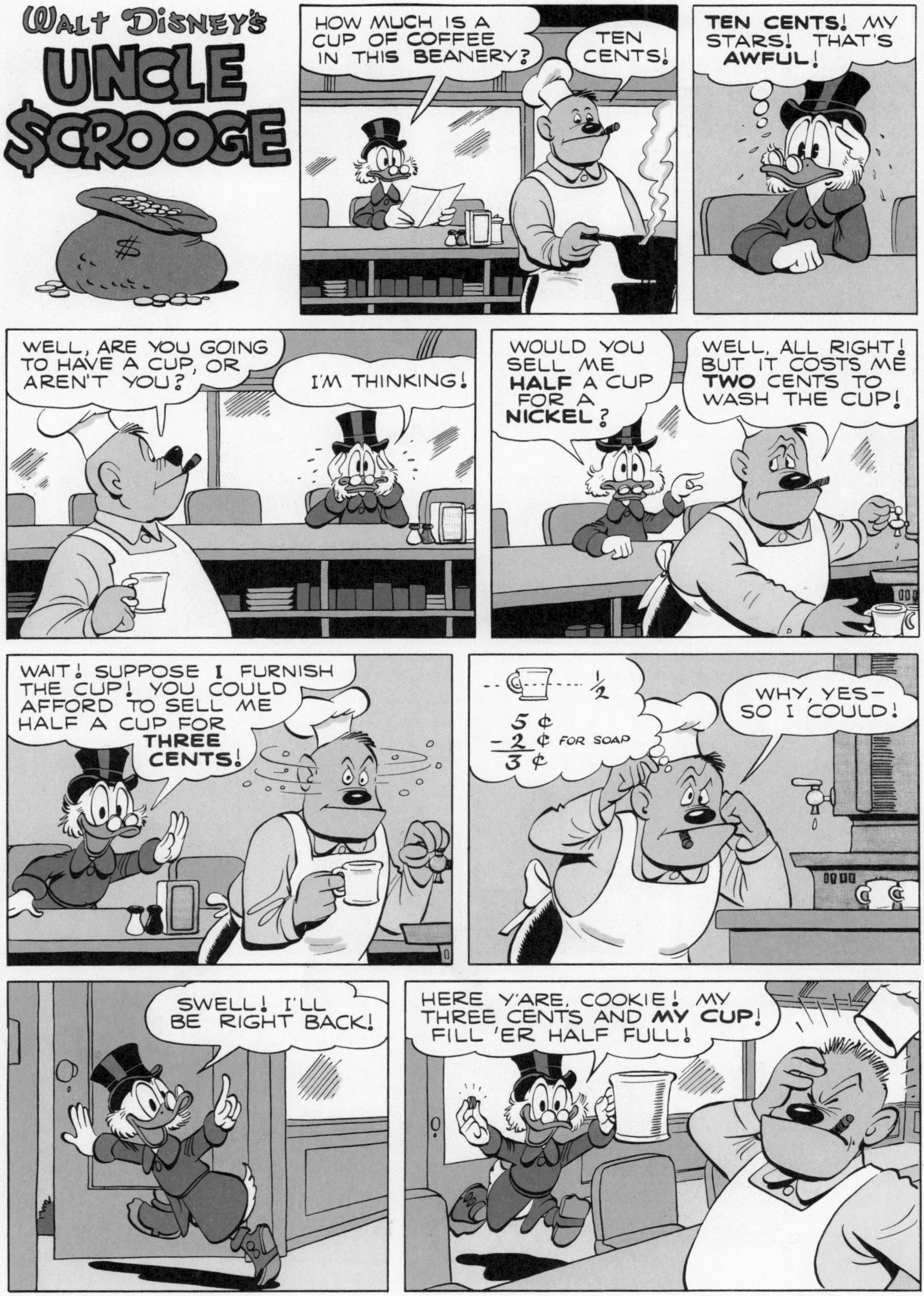
WALT DISNEY'S
UNCLE $CROOGE
HOW MUCH IS A CUP OF COFFEE IN THIS BEANERY?
TEN CENTS!
TEN CENTS! MY STARS! THAT'S AWFUL!
WELL, ARE YOU GOING TO HAVE A CUP, OR AREN'T YOU?
I'M THINKING!
WOULD YOU SELL ME HALF A CUP FOR A NICKEL?
WELL, ALL RIGHT! BUT IT COSTS ME TWO CENTS TO WASH THE CUP!
WAIT! SUPPOSE I FURNISH THE CUP! YOU COULD AFFORD TO SELL ME HALF A CUP FOR THREE CENTS!
1/2
5 ¢
- 2 ¢ FOR SOAP
3 ¢
WHY, YES— SO I COULD!
SWELL! I'LL BE RIGHT BACK!
HERE Y'ARE, COOKIE! MY THREE CENTS AND MY CUP! FILL 'ER HALF FULL!

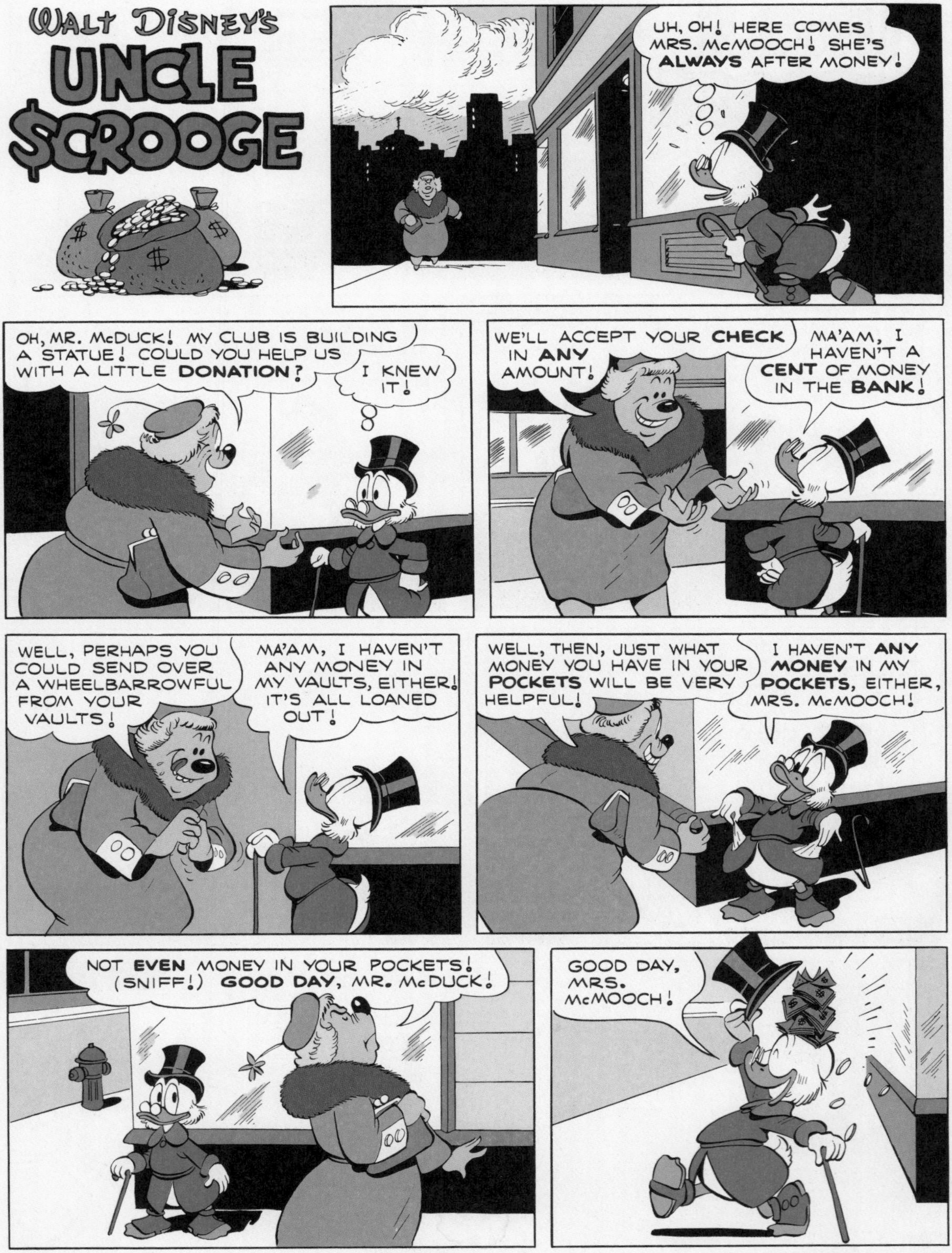

WALT DISNEY'S
UNCLE $CROOGE
UH, OH! HERE COMES MRS. McMOOCH! SHE'S ALWAYS AFTER MONEY!
OH, MR. McDUCK! MY CLUB IS BUILDING A STATUE! COULD YOU HELP US WITH A LITTLE DONATION?
I KNEW IT!
WE'LL ACCEPT YOUR CHECK IN ANY AMOUNT!
MA'AM, I HAVEN'T A CENT OF MONEY IN THE BANK!
WELL, PERHAPS YOU COULD SEND OVER A WHEELBARROWFUL FROM YOUR VAULTS!
MA'AM, I HAVEN'T ANY MONEY IN MY VAULTS, EITHER! IT'S ALL LOANED OUT!
WELL, THEN, JUST WHAT MONEY YOU HAVE IN YOUR POCKETS WILL BE VERY HELPFUL!
I HAVEN'T ANY MONEY IN MY POCKETS, EITHER, MRS. McMOOCH!
NOT EVEN MONEY IN YOUR POCKETS! (SNIFF!) GOOD DAY, MR. McDUCK!
GOOD DAY, MRS. McMOOCH!

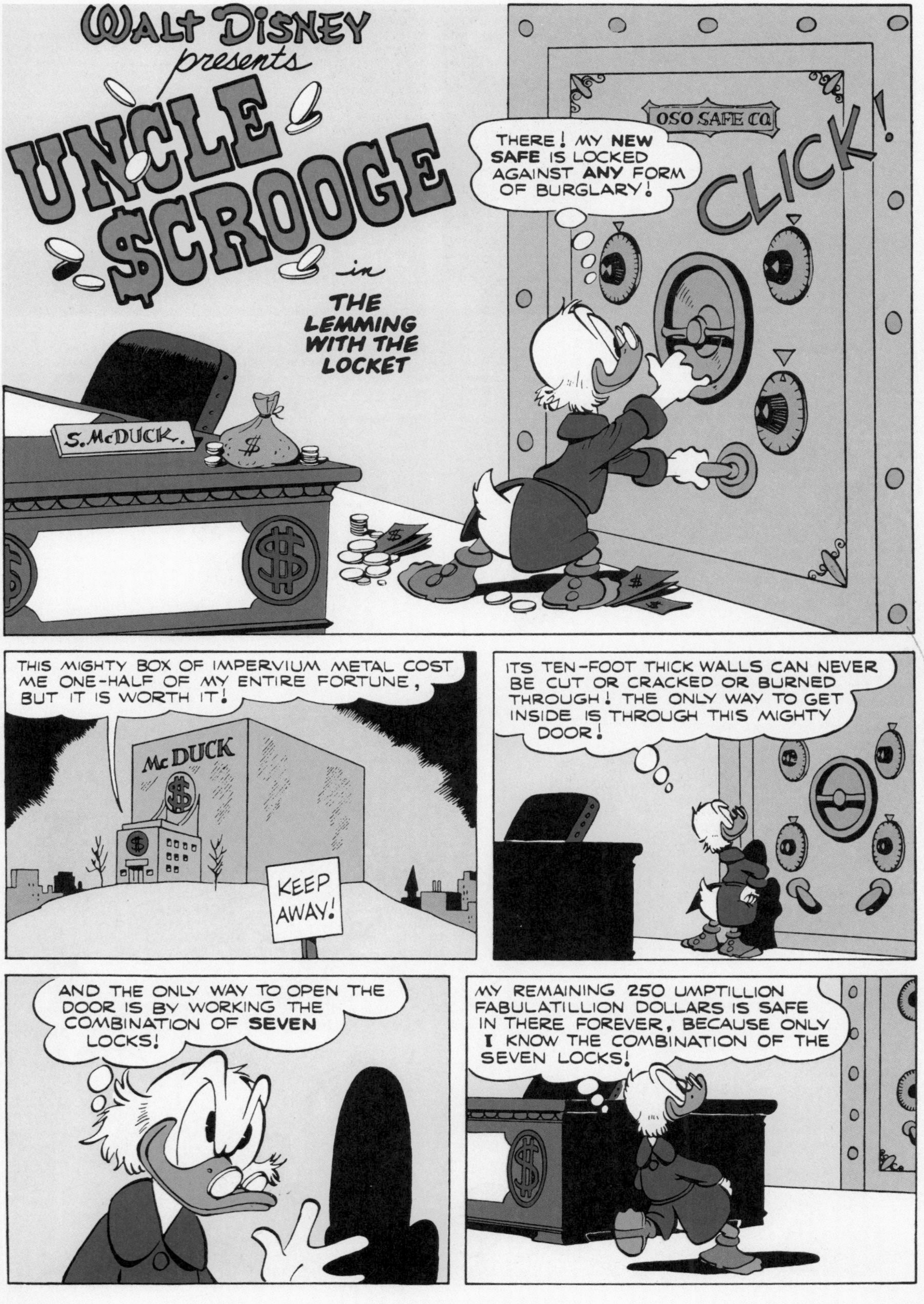
WALT DISNEY
presents
UNCLE $CROOGE
in
THE LEMMING WITH THE LOCKET
OSO SAFE CO.
THERE! MY NEW SAFE IS LOCKED AGAINST ANY FORM OF BURGLARY!
CLICK!
S. McDUCK
THIS MIGHTY BOX OF IMPERVIUM METAL COST ME ONE-HALF OF MY ENTIRE FORTUNE, BUT IT IS WORTH IT!
McDUCK
KEEP AWAY!
ITS TEN-FOOT THICK WALLS CAN NEVER BE CUT OR CRACKED OR BURNED THROUGH! THE ONLY WAY TO GET INSIDE IS THROUGH THIS MIGHTY DOOR!
AND THE ONLY WAY TO OPEN THE DOOR IS BY WORKING THE COMBINATION OF SEVEN LOCKS!
MY REMAINING 250 UMPTILLION FABULATILLION DOLLARS IS SAFE IN THERE FOREVER, BECAUSE ONLY I KNOW THE COMBINATION OF THE SEVEN LOCKS!

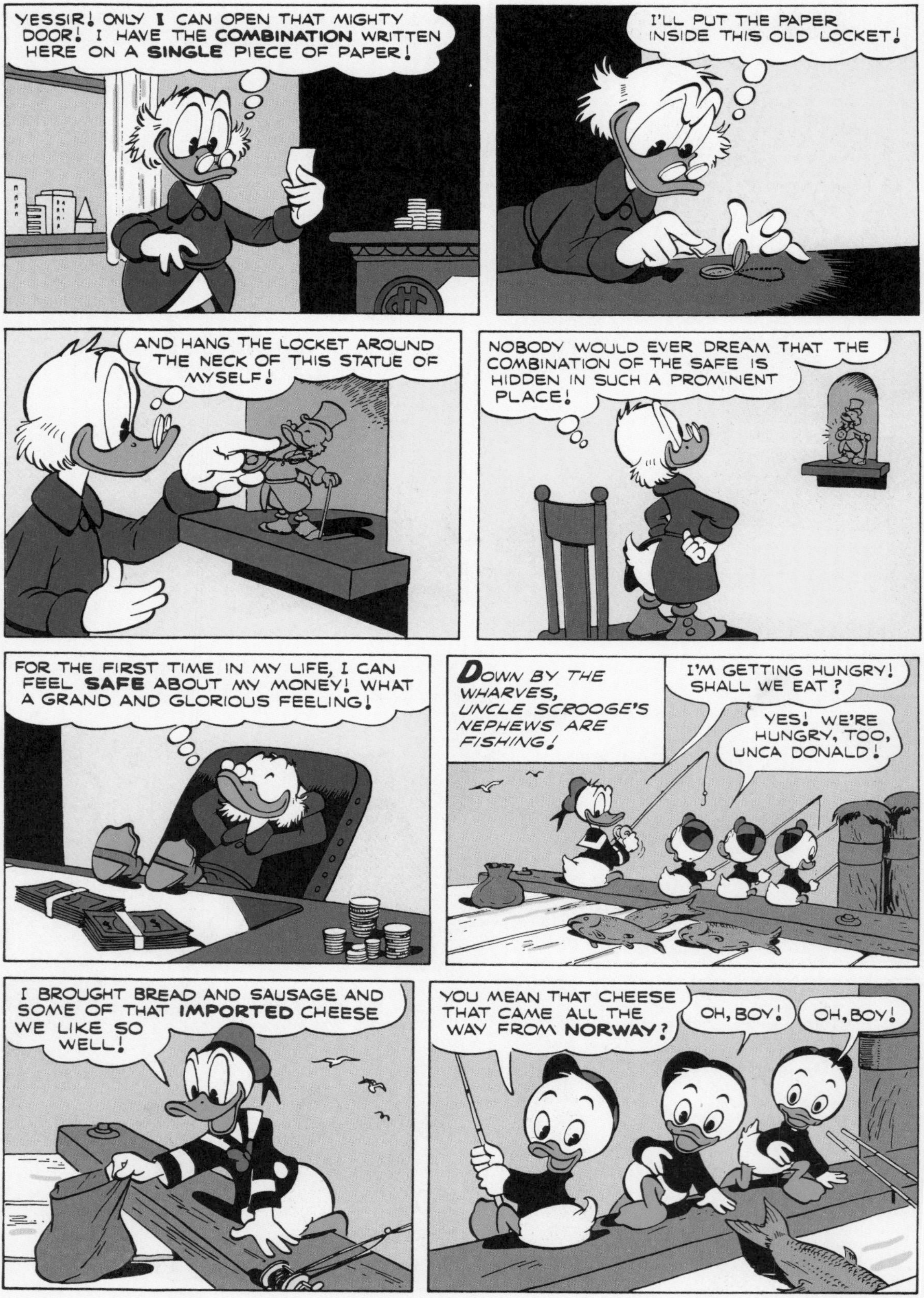

YESSIR! ONLY I CAN OPEN THAT MIGHTY DOOR! I HAVE THE COMBINATION WRITTEN HERE ON A SINGLE PIECE OF PAPER!
I'LL PUT THE PAPER INSIDE THIS OLD LOCKET!
AND HANG THE LOCKET AROUND THE NECK OF THIS STATUE OF MYSELF!
NOBODY WOULD EVER DREAM THAT THE COMBINATION OF THE SAFE IS HIDDEN IN SUCH A PROMINENT PLACE!
FOR THE FIRST TIME IN MY LIFE, I CAN FEEL SAFE ABOUT MY MONEY! WHAT A GRAND AND GLORIOUS FEELING!
DOWN BY THE WHARVES, UNCLE SCROOGE'S NEPHEWS ARE FISHING!
I'M GETTING HUNGRY! SHALL WE EAT?
YES! WE'RE HUNGRY, TOO, UNCA DONALD!
I BROUGHT BREAD AND SAUSAGE AND SOME OF THAT IMPORTED CHEESE WE LIKE SO WELL!
YOU MEAN THAT CHEESE THAT CAME ALL THE WAY FROM NORWAY?
OH, BOY!
OH, BOY!

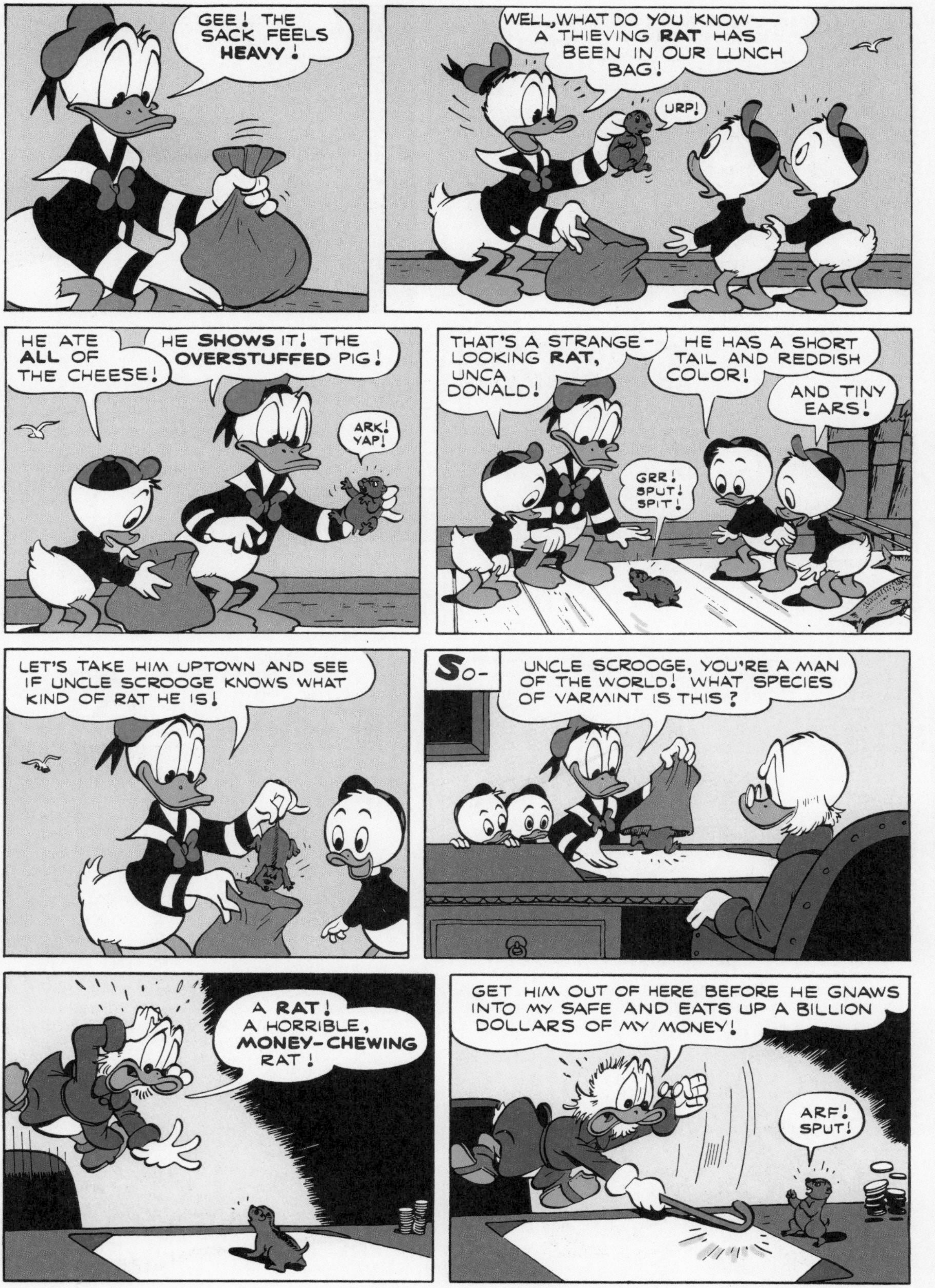
GEE! THE SACK FEELS HEAVY!
WELL, WHAT DO YOU KNOW— A THIEVING RAT HAS BEEN IN OUR LUNCH BAG!
URP!
HE ATE ALL OF THE CHEESE!
HE SHOWS IT! THE OVERSTUFFED PIG!
ARK! YAP!
THAT'S A STRANGE-LOOKING RAT, UNCA DONALD!
HE HAS A SHORT TAIL AND REDDISH COLOR!
AND TINY EARS!
GRR! SPUT! SPIT!
LET'S TAKE HIM UPTOWN AND SEE IF UNCLE SCROOGE KNOWS WHAT KIND OF RAT HE IS!
SO-
UNCLE SCROOGE, YOU'RE A MAN OF THE WORLD! WHAT SPECIES OF VARMINT IS THIS?
A RAT! A HORRIBLE, MONEY-CHEWING RAT!
GET HIM OUT OF HERE BEFORE HE GNAWS INTO MY SAFE AND EATS UP A BILLION DOLLARS OF MY MONEY!
ARF! SPUT!

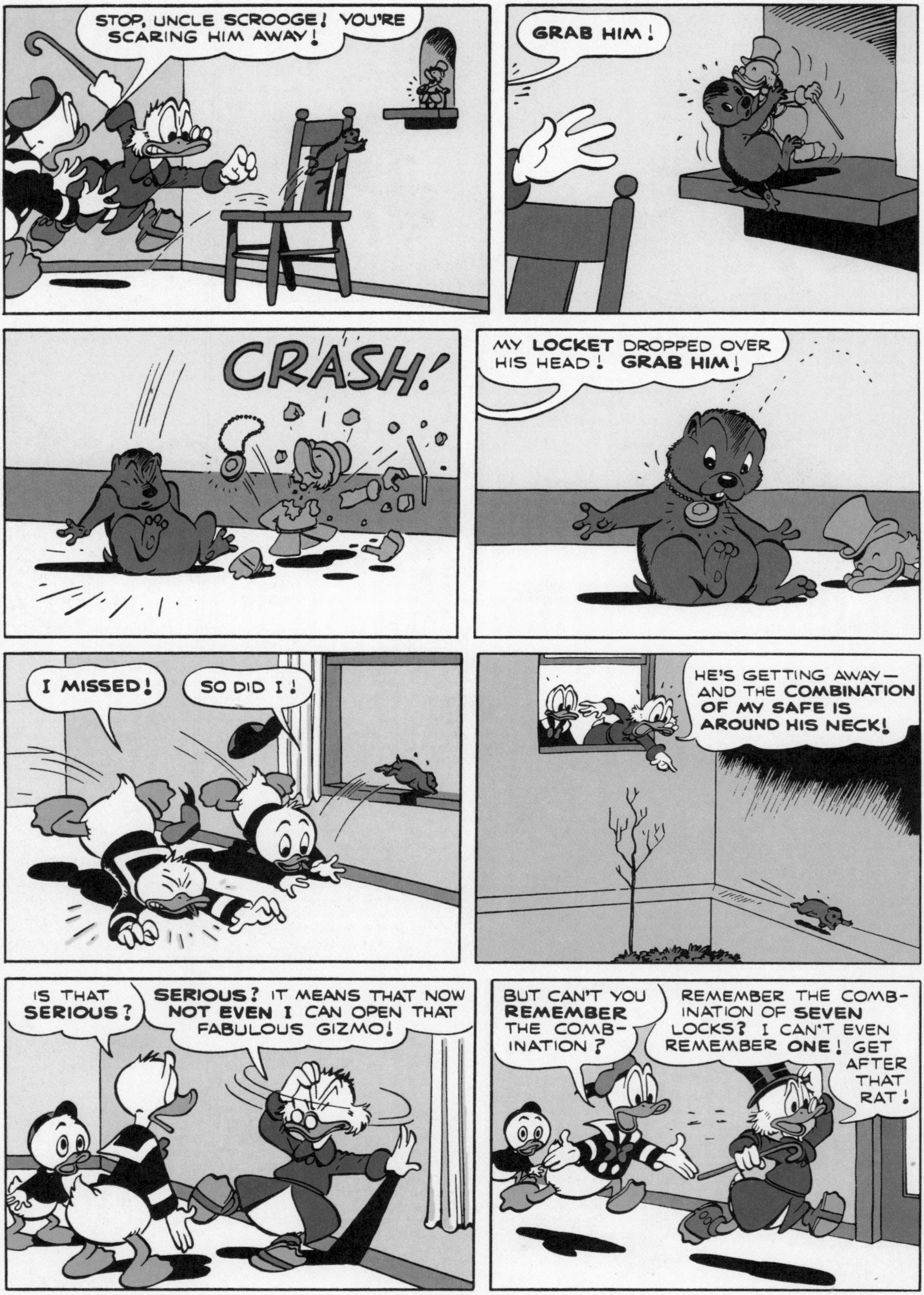
STOP, UNCLE SCROOGE! YOU'RE SCARING HIM AWAY!
GRAB HIM!
CRASH!
MY LOCKET DROPPED OVER HIS HEAD! GRAB HIM!
I MISSED!
SO DID I!
HE'S GETTING AWAY— AND THE COMBINATION OF MY SAFE IS AROUND HIS NECK!
IS THAT SERIOUS?
SERIOUS? IT MEANS THAT NOW NOT EVEN I CAN OPEN THAT FABULOUS GIZMO!
BUT CAN'T YOU REMEMBER THE COMBINATION?
REMEMBER THE COMBINATION OF SEVEN LOCKS? I CAN'T EVEN REMEMBER ONE! GET AFTER THAT RAT!

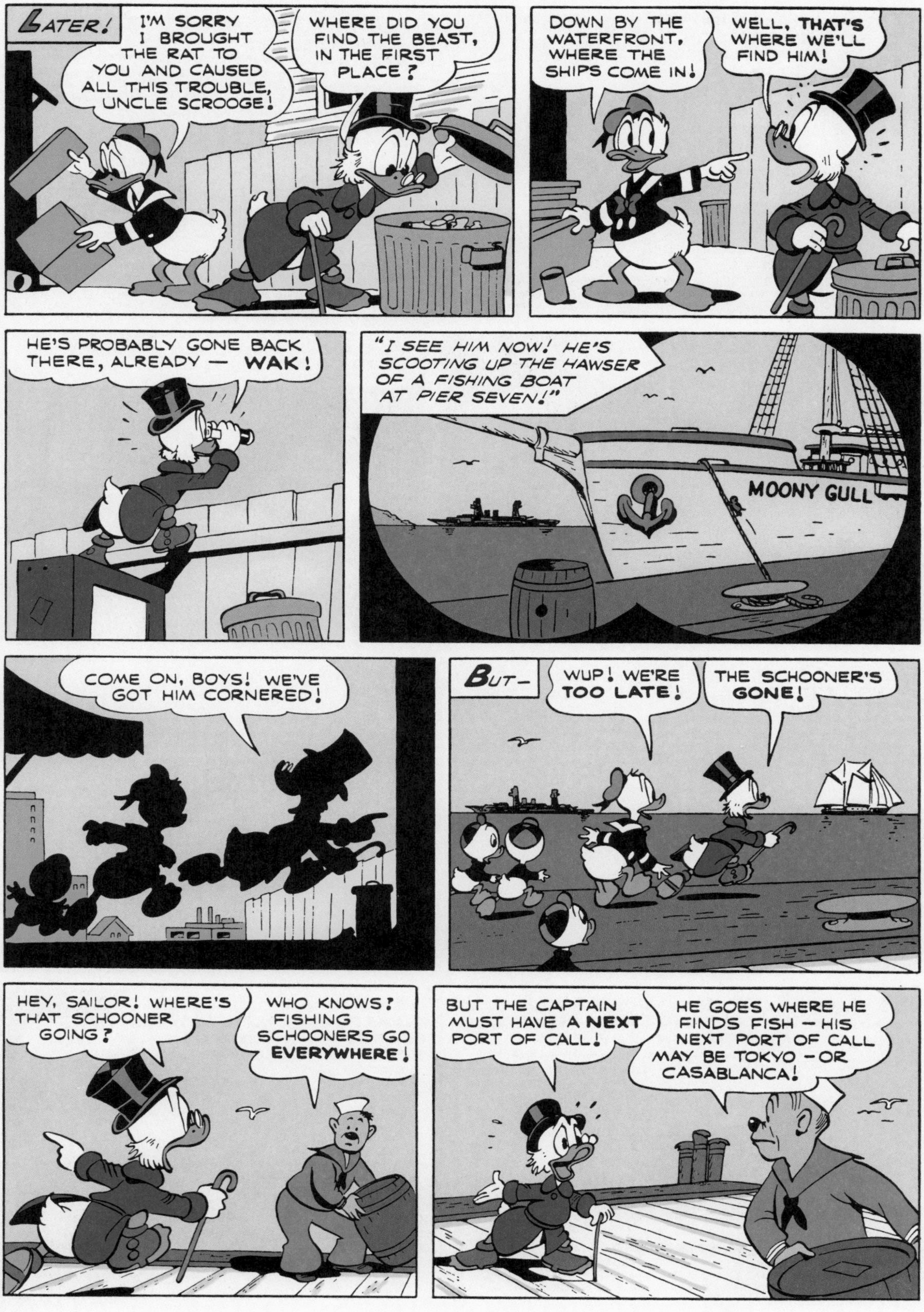
LATER!
I'M SORRY I BROUGHT THE RAT TO YOU AND CAUSED ALL THIS TROUBLE, UNCLE SCROOGE!
WHERE DID YOU FIND THE BEAST, IN THE FIRST PLACE?
DOWN BY THE WATERFRONT, WHERE THE SHIPS COME IN!
WELL, THAT'S WHERE WE'LL FIND HIM!
HE'S PROBABLY GONE BACK THERE, ALREADY — WAK!
"I SEE HIM NOW! HE'S SCOOTING UP THE HAWSER OF A FISHING BOAT AT PIER SEVEN!"
MOONY GULL
COME ON, BOYS! WE'VE GOT HIM CORNERED!
BUT—
WUP! WE'RE TOO LATE!
THE SCHOONER'S GONE!
HEY, SAILOR! WHERE'S THAT SCHOONER GOING?
WHO KNOWS? FISHING SCHOONERS GO EVERYWHERE!
BUT THE CAPTAIN MUST HAVE A NEXT PORT OF CALL!
HE GOES WHERE HE FINDS FISH — HIS NEXT PORT OF CALL MAY BE TOKYO — OR CASABLANCA!

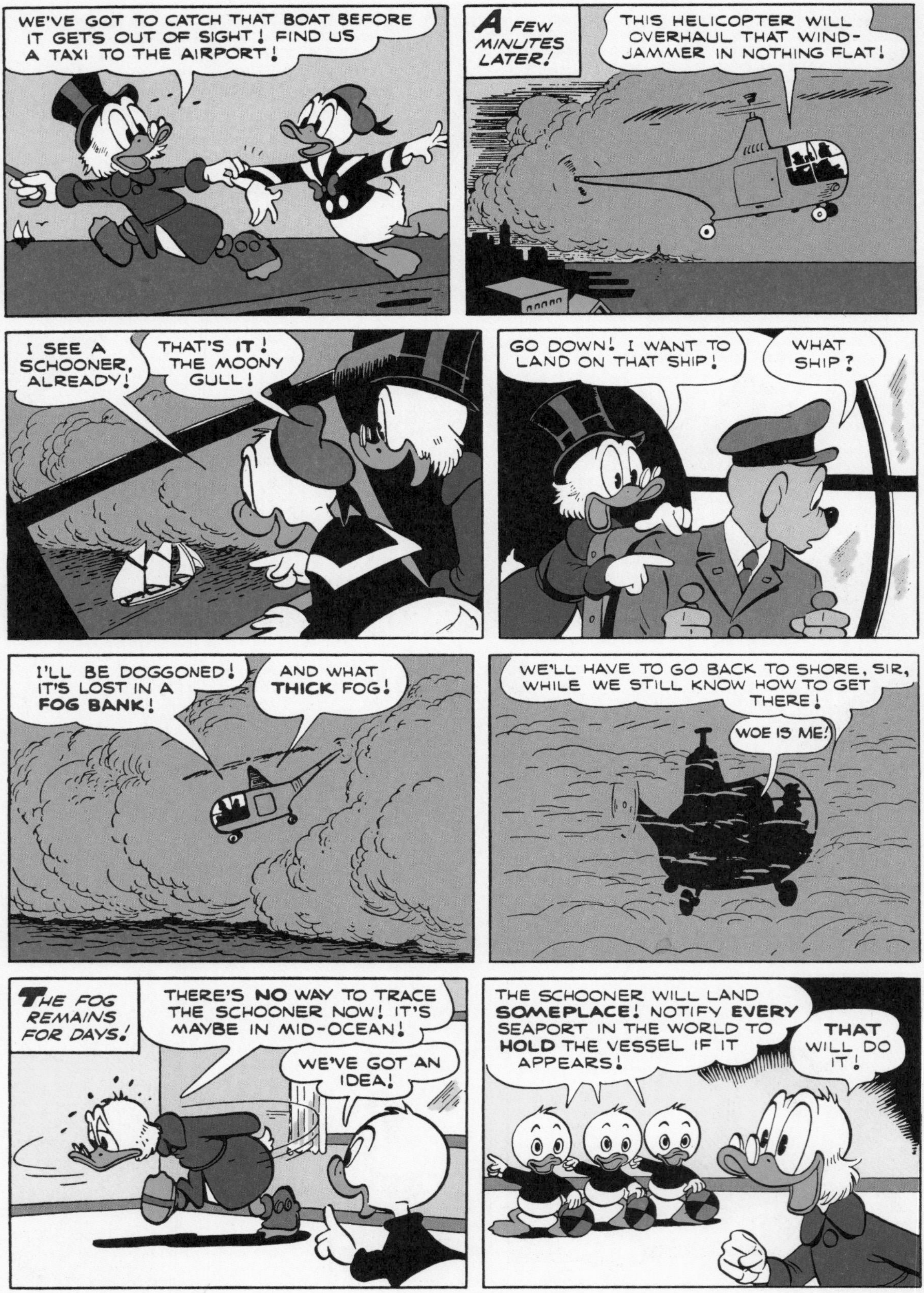
WE'VE GOT TO CATCH THAT BOAT BEFORE IT GETS OUT OF SIGHT! FIND US A TAXI TO THE AIRPORT!
A FEW MINUTES LATER!
THIS HELICOPTER WILL OVERHAUL THAT WIND-JAMMER IN NOTHING FLAT!
I SEE A SCHOONER, ALREADY!
THAT'S IT! THE MOONY GULL!
GO DOWN! I WANT TO LAND ON THAT SHIP!
WHAT SHIP?
I'LL BE DOGGONED! IT'S LOST IN A FOG BANK!
AND WHAT THICK FOG!
WE'LL HAVE TO GO BACK TO SHORE, SIR, WHILE WE STILL KNOW HOW TO GET THERE!
WOE IS ME!
THE FOG REMAINS FOR DAYS!
THERE'S NO WAY TO TRACE THE SCHOONER NOW! IT'S MAYBE IN MID-OCEAN!
WE'VE GOT AN IDEA!
THE SCHOONER WILL LAND SOMEPLACE! NOTIFY EVERY SEAPORT IN THE WORLD TO HOLD THE VESSEL IF IT APPEARS!
THAT WILL DO IT!

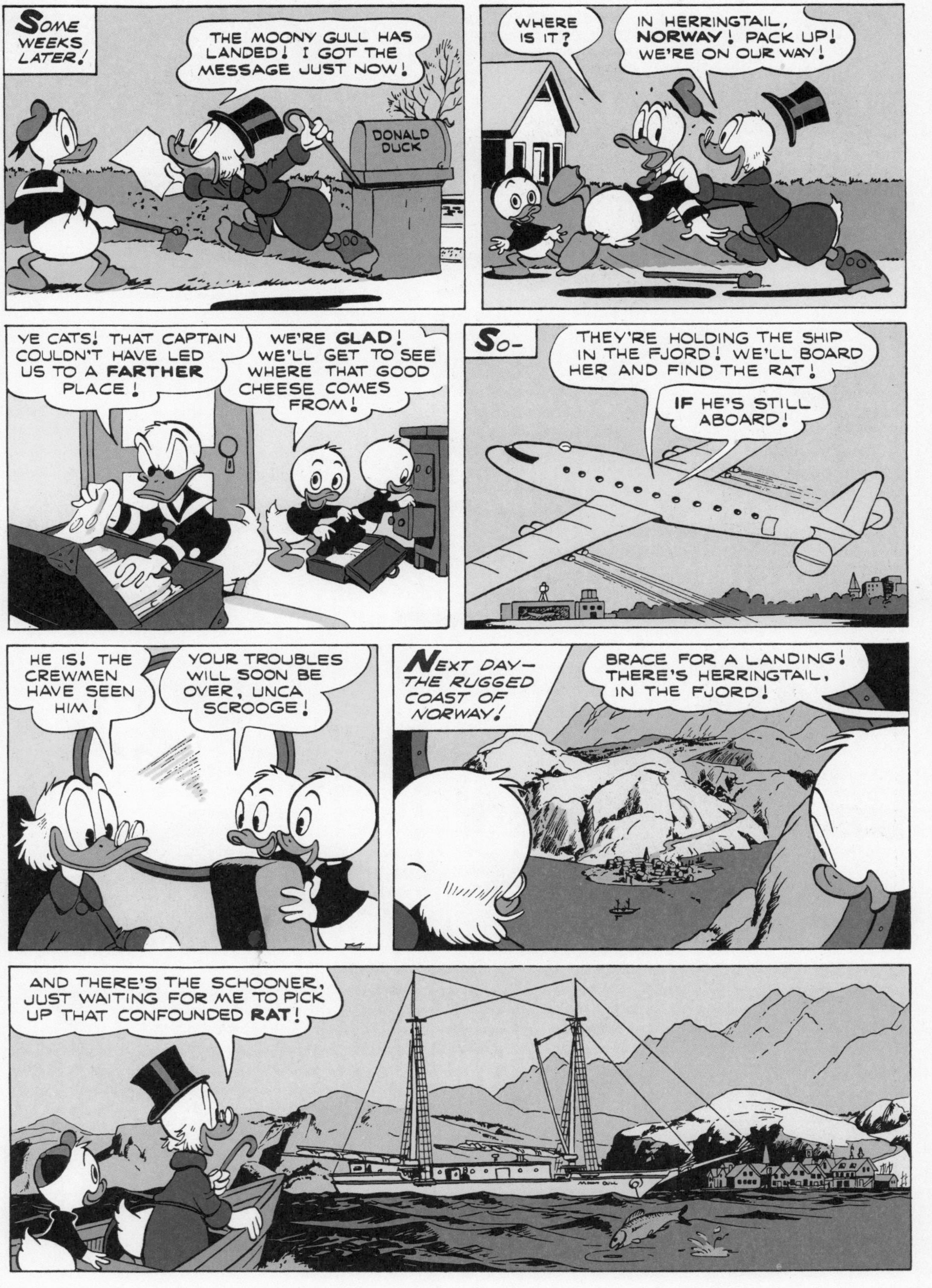
SOME WEEKS LATER!
THE MOONY GULL HAS LANDED! I GOT THE MESSAGE JUST NOW!
DONALD DUCK
WHERE IS IT?
IN HERRINGTAIL, NORWAY! PACK UP! WE'RE ON OUR WAY!
YE CATS! THAT CAPTAIN COULDN'T HAVE LED US TO A FARTHER PLACE!
WE'RE GLAD! WE'LL GET TO SEE WHERE THAT GOOD CHEESE COMES FROM!
SO-
THEY'RE HOLDING THE SHIP IN THE FJORD! WE'LL BOARD HER AND FIND THE RAT!
IF HE'S STILL ABOARD!
HE IS! THE CREWMEN HAVE SEEN HIM!
YOUR TROUBLES WILL SOON BE OVER, UNCA SCROOGE!
NEXT DAY— THE RUGGED COAST OF NORWAY!
BRACE FOR A LANDING! THERE'S HERRINGTAIL, IN THE FJORD!
AND THERE'S THE SCHOONER, JUST WAITING FOR ME TO PICK UP THAT CONFOUNDED RAT!

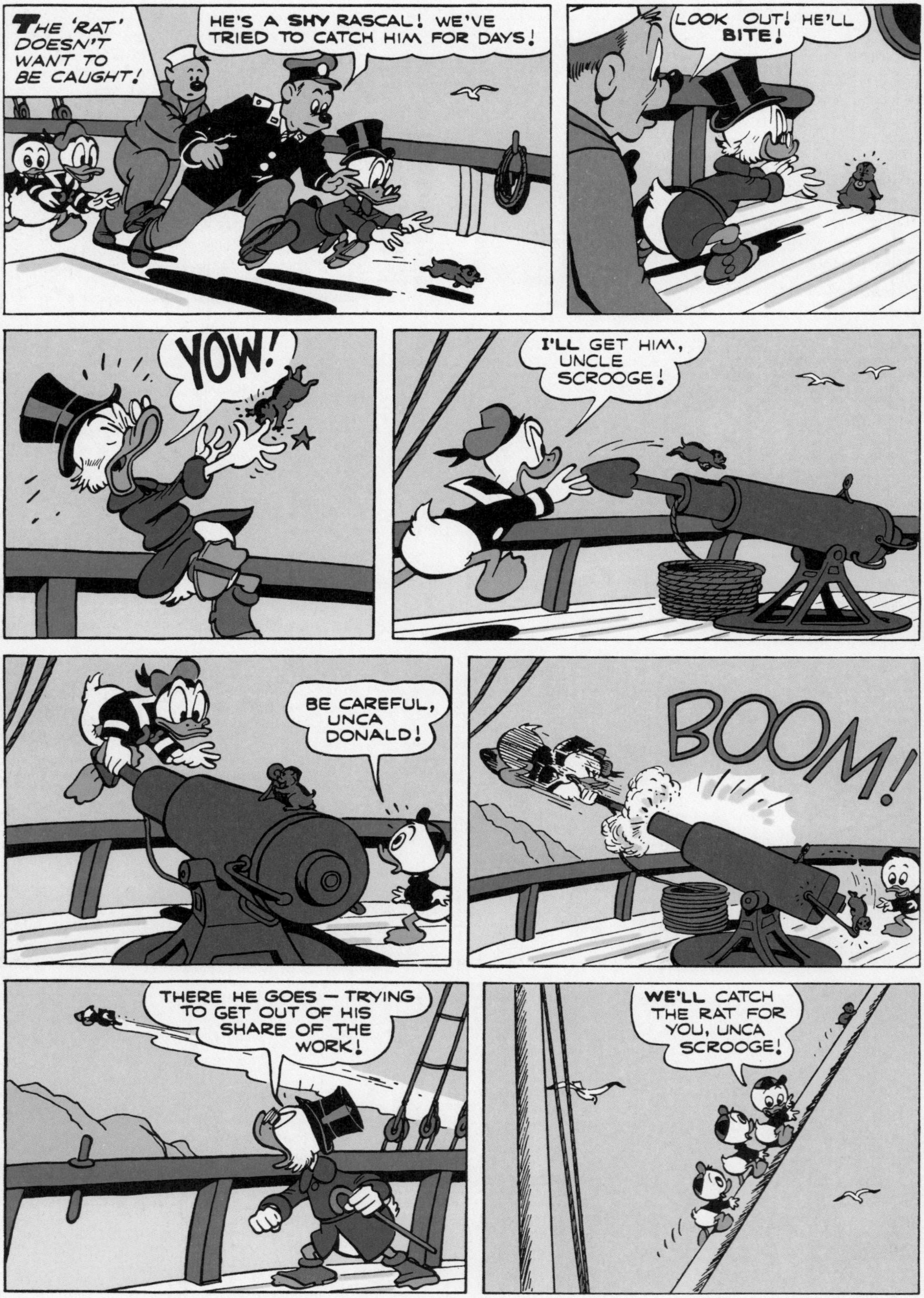

THE 'RAT' DOESN'T WANT TO BE CAUGHT!
HE'S A SHY RASCAL! WE'VE TRIED TO CATCH HIM FOR DAYS!
LOOK OUT! HE'LL BITE!
YOW!
I'LL GET HIM, UNCLE SCROOGE!
BE CAREFUL, UNCA DONALD!
BOOM!
THERE HE GOES — TRYING TO GET OUT OF HIS SHARE OF THE WORK!
WE'LL CATCH THE RAT FOR YOU, UNCA SCROOGE!

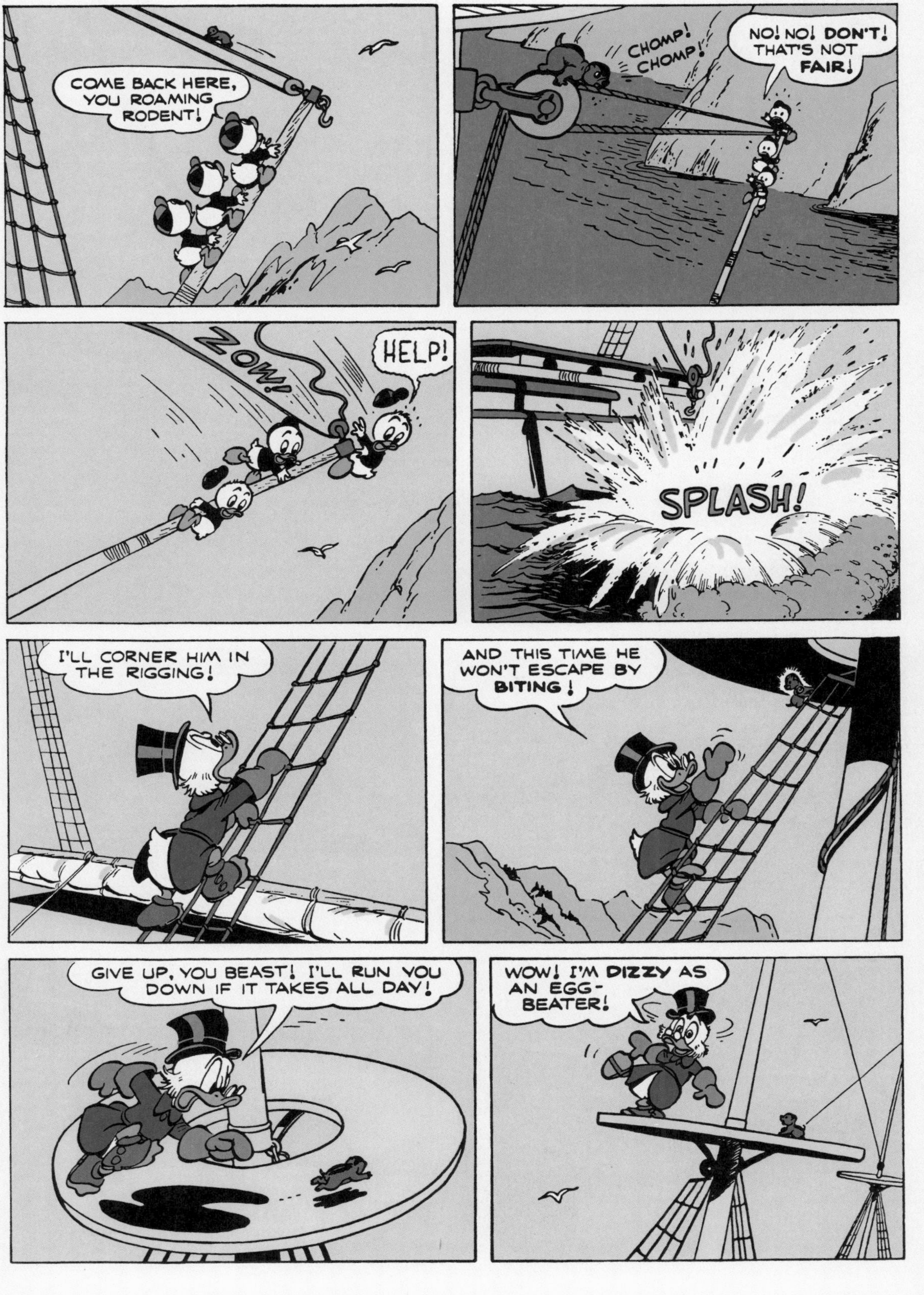
COME BACK HERE, YOU ROAMING RODENT!
CHOMP! CHOMP!
NO! NO! DON'T! THAT'S NOT FAIR!
ZOW!
HELP!
SPLASH!
I'LL CORNER HIM IN THE RIGGING!
AND THIS TIME HE WON'T ESCAPE BY BITING!
GIVE UP, YOU BEAST! I'LL RUN YOU DOWN IF IT TAKES ALL DAY!
WOW! I'M DIZZY AS AN EGG-BEATER!

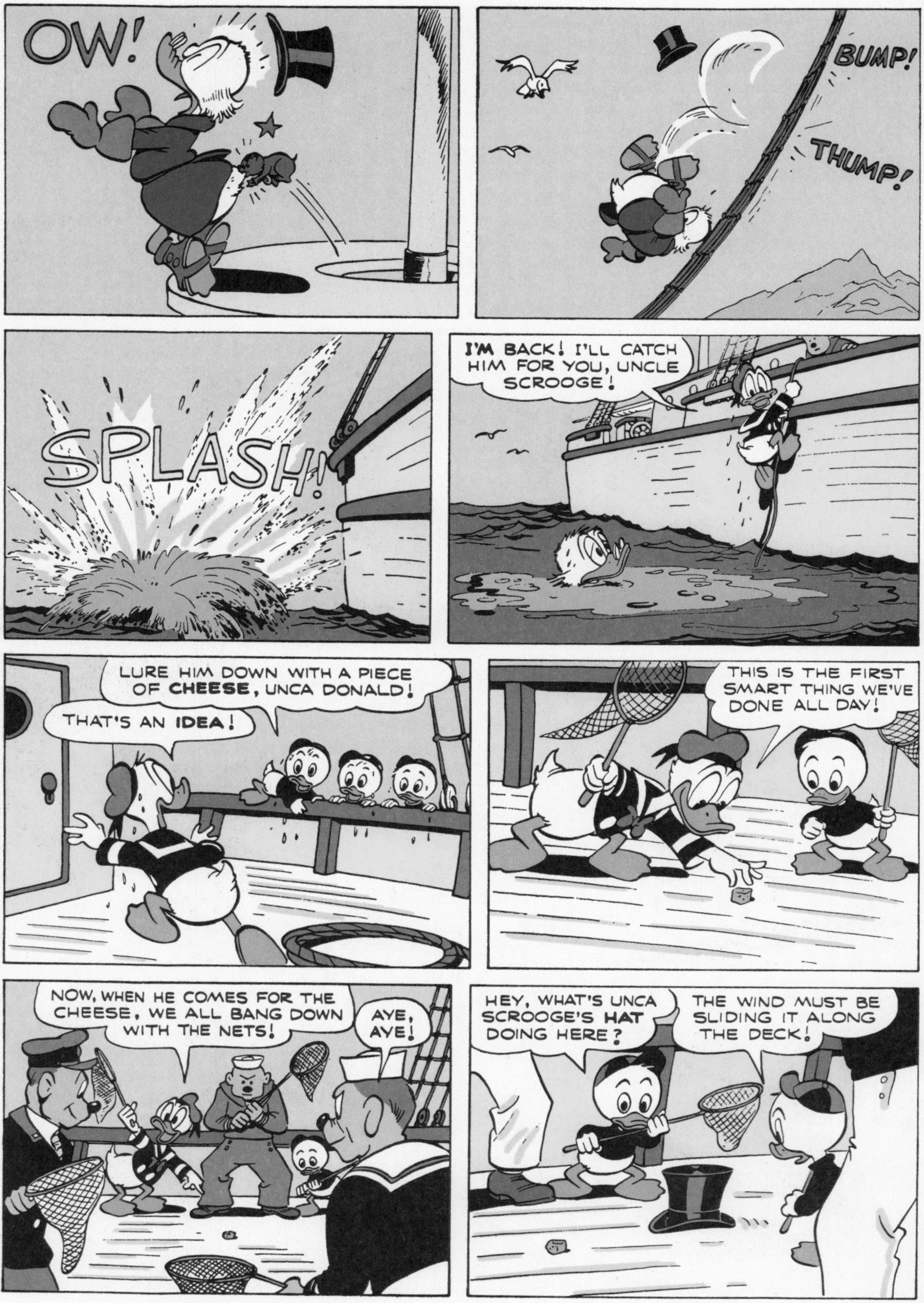
OW!
BUMP!
THUMP!
SPLASH!
I'M BACK! I'LL CATCH HIM FOR YOU, UNCLE SCROOGE!
LURE HIM DOWN WITH A PIECE OF CHEESE, UNCA DONALD!
THAT'S AN IDEA!
THIS IS THE FIRST SMART THING WE'VE DONE ALL DAY!
NOW, WHEN HE COMES FOR THE CHEESE, WE ALL BANG DOWN WITH THE NETS!
AYE, AYE!
HEY, WHAT'S UNCA SCROOGE'S HAT DOING HERE?
THE WIND MUST BE SLIDING IT ALONG THE DECK!

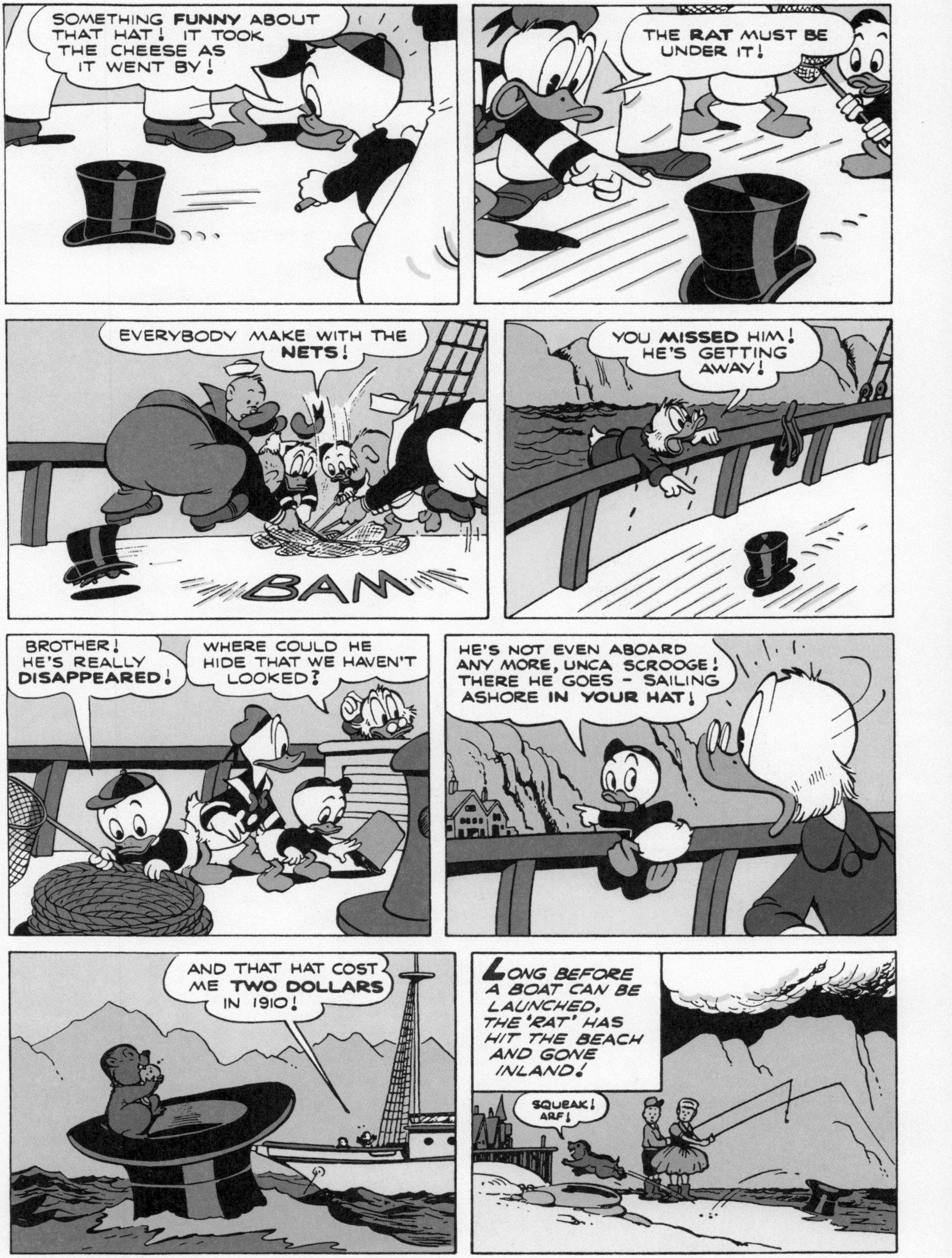
SOMETHING FUNNY ABOUT THAT HAT! IT TOOK THE CHEESE AS IT WENT BY!
THE RAT MUST BE UNDER IT!
EVERYBODY MAKE WITH THE NETS!
BAM
YOU MISSED HIM! HE'S GETTING AWAY!
BROTHER! HE'S REALLY DISAPPEARED!
WHERE COULD HE HIDE THAT WE HAVEN'T LOOKED?
HE'S NOT EVEN ABOARD ANY MORE, UNCA SCROOGE! THERE HE GOES - SAILING ASHORE IN YOUR HAT!
AND THAT HAT COST ME TWO DOLLARS IN 1910!
LONG BEFORE A BOAT CAN BE LAUNCHED, THE 'RAT' HAS HIT THE BEACH AND GONE INLAND!
SQUEAK! ARF!

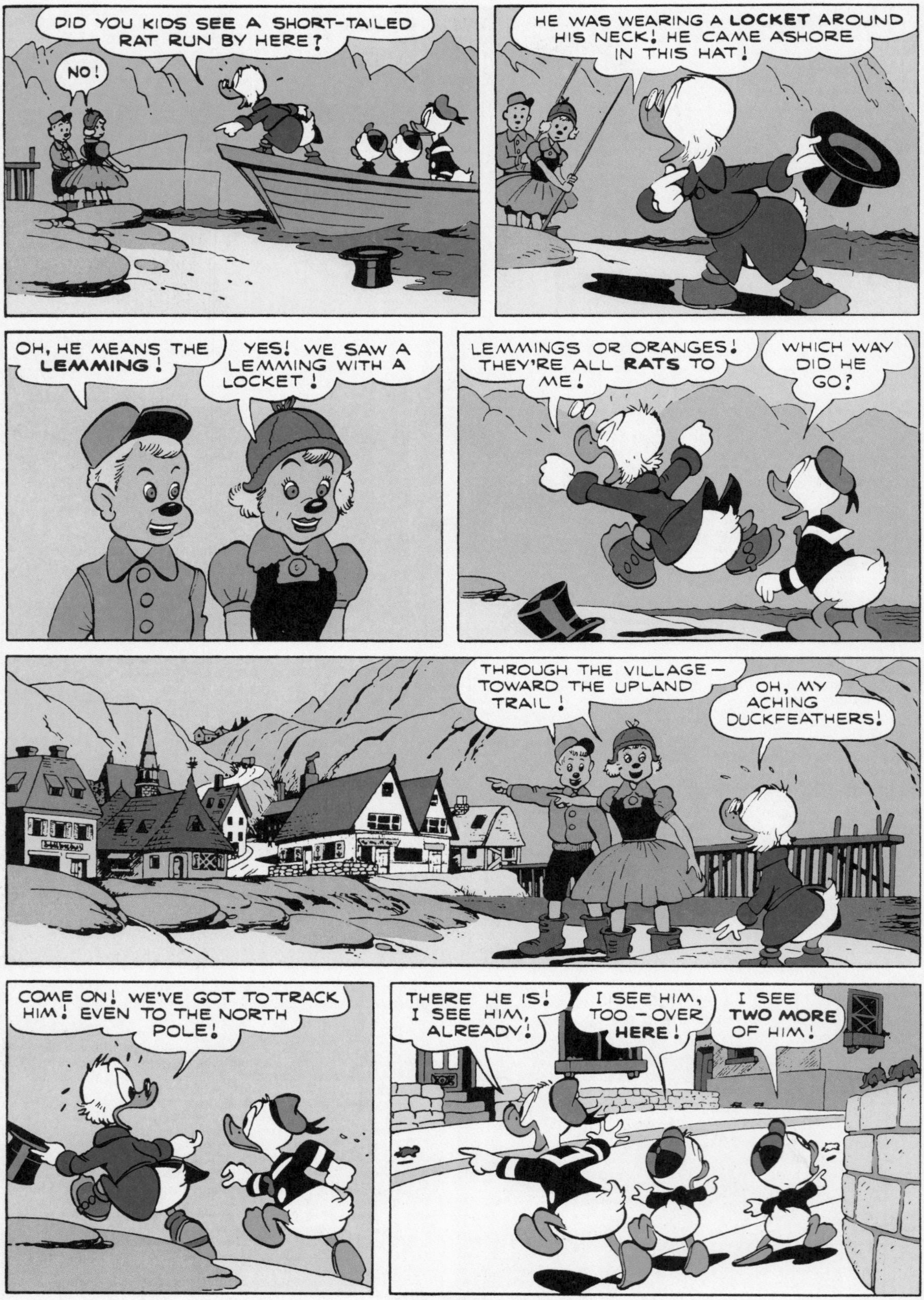

DID YOU KIDS SEE A SHORT-TAILED RAT RUN BY HERE?
NO!
HE WAS WEARING A **LOCKET** AROUND HIS NECK! HE CAME ASHORE IN THIS HAT!
OH, HE MEANS THE **LEMMING**!
YES! WE SAW A LEMMING WITH A LOCKET!
LEMMINGS OR ORANGES! THEY'RE ALL **RATS** TO ME!
WHICH WAY DID HE GO?
THROUGH THE VILLAGE— TOWARD THE UPLAND TRAIL!
OH, MY ACHING DUCKFEATHERS!
COME ON! WE'VE GOT TO TRACK HIM! EVEN TO THE NORTH POLE!
THERE HE IS! I SEE HIM, ALREADY!
I SEE HIM, TOO — OVER **HERE**!
I SEE **TWO MORE** OF HIM!

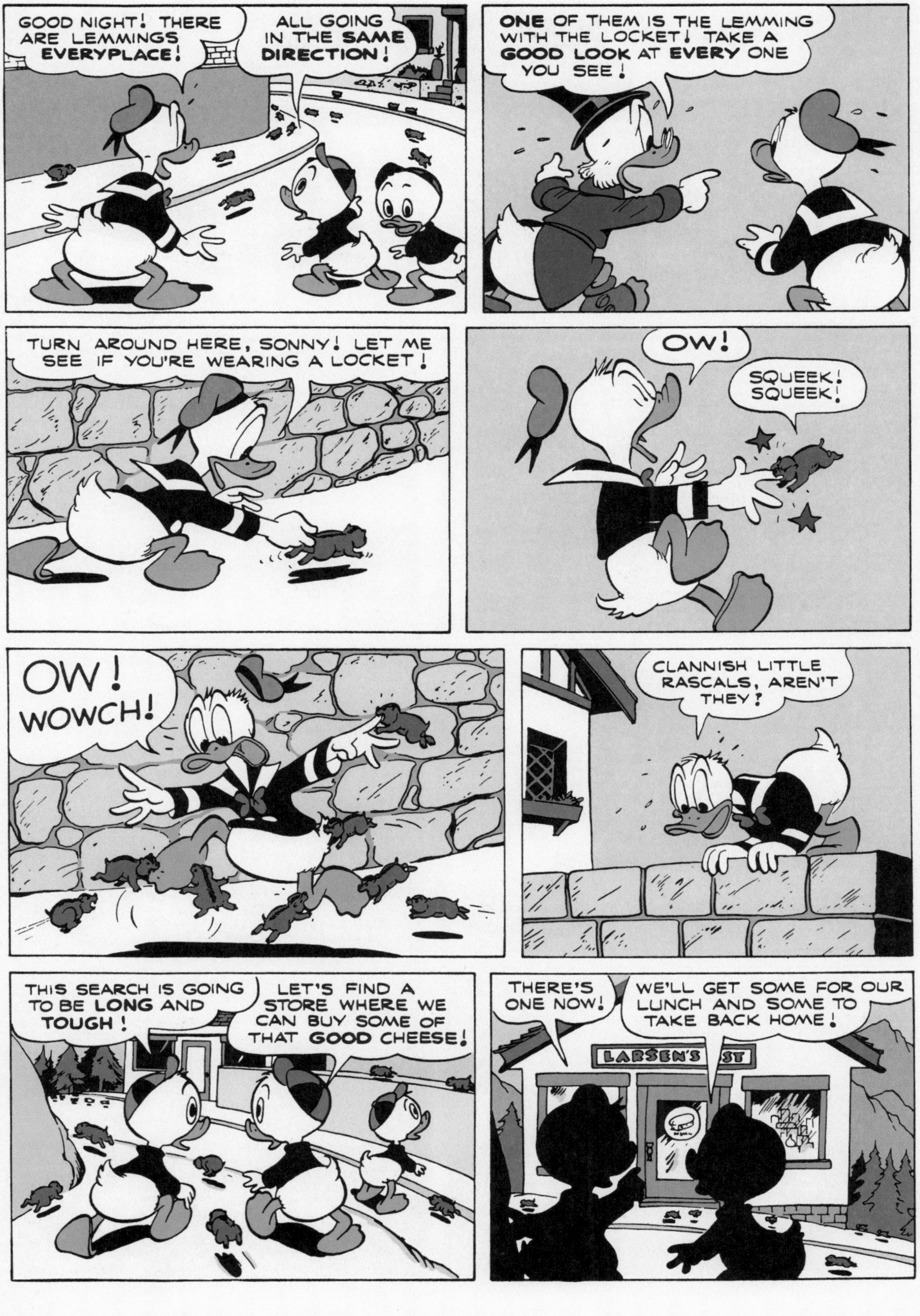
GOOD NIGHT! THERE ARE LEMMINGS EVERYPLACE!
ALL GOING IN THE SAME DIRECTION!
ONE OF THEM IS THE LEMMING WITH THE LOCKET! TAKE A GOOD LOOK AT EVERY ONE YOU SEE!
TURN AROUND HERE, SONNY! LET ME SEE IF YOU'RE WEARING A LOCKET!
OW!
SQUEEK! SQUEEK!
OW! WOWCH!
CLANNISH LITTLE RASCALS, AREN'T THEY?
THIS SEARCH IS GOING TO BE LONG AND TOUGH!
LET'S FIND A STORE WHERE WE CAN BUY SOME OF THAT GOOD CHEESE!
THERE'S ONE NOW!
WE'LL GET SOME FOR OUR LUNCH AND SOME TO TAKE BACK HOME!
LARSEN'S

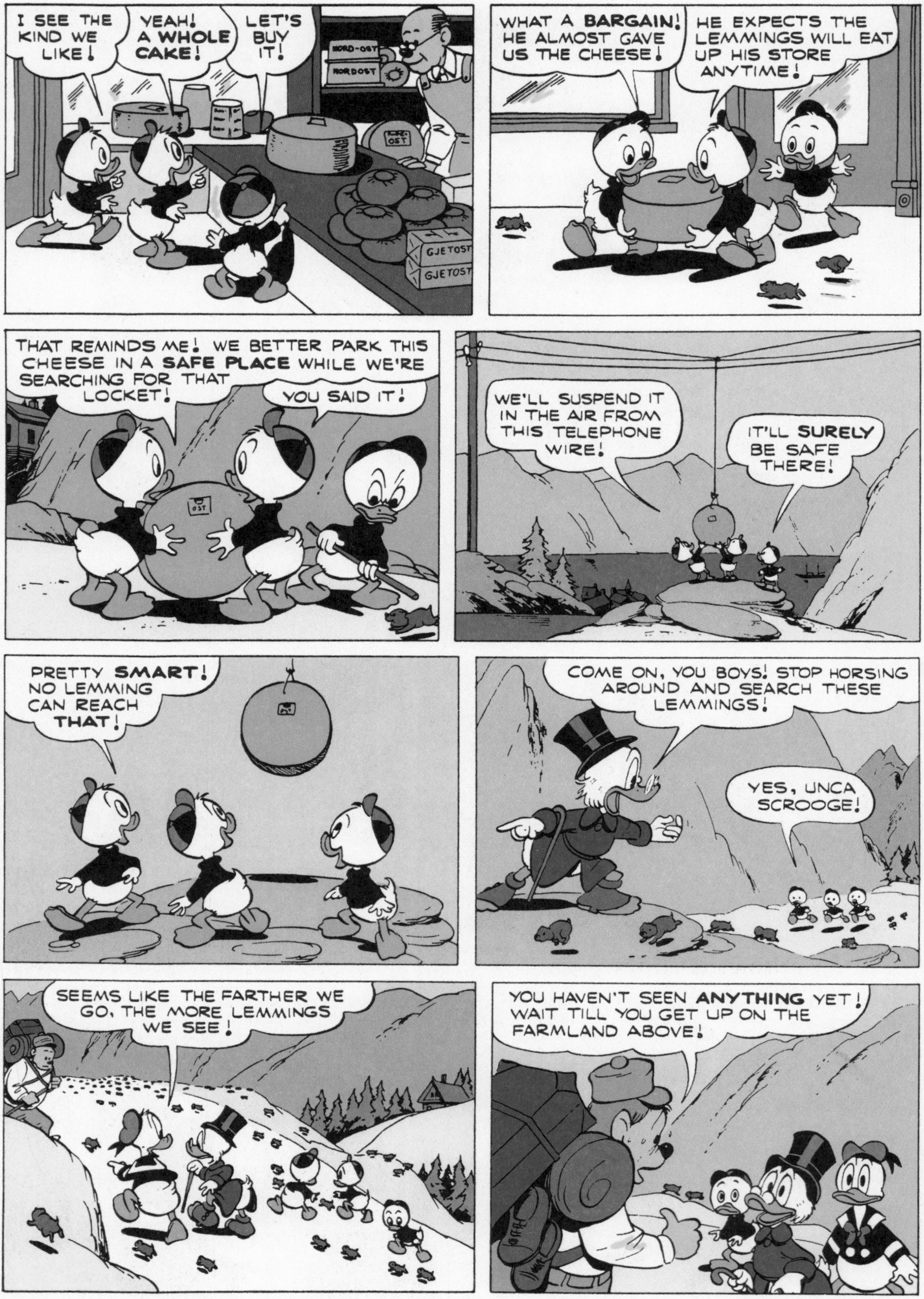
I SEE THE KIND WE LIKE!
YEAH! A **WHOLE CAKE**!
LET'S BUY IT!
NORD-OST
NORDOST
GJETOST
GJETOST
WHAT A **BARGAIN**! HE ALMOST GAVE US THE CHEESE!
HE EXPECTS THE LEMMINGS WILL EAT UP HIS STORE ANYTIME!
THAT REMINDS ME! WE BETTER PARK THIS CHEESE IN A **SAFE PLACE** WHILE WE'RE SEARCHING FOR THAT LOCKET!
YOU SAID IT!
WE'LL SUSPEND IT IN THE AIR FROM THIS TELEPHONE WIRE!
IT'LL **SURELY** BE SAFE THERE!
PRETTY **SMART**! NO LEMMING CAN REACH **THAT**!
COME ON, YOU BOYS! STOP HORSING AROUND AND SEARCH THESE LEMMINGS!
YES, UNCA SCROOGE!
SEEMS LIKE THE FARTHER WE GO, THE MORE LEMMINGS WE SEE!
YOU HAVEN'T SEEN **ANYTHING** YET! WAIT TILL YOU GET UP ON THE FARMLAND ABOVE!

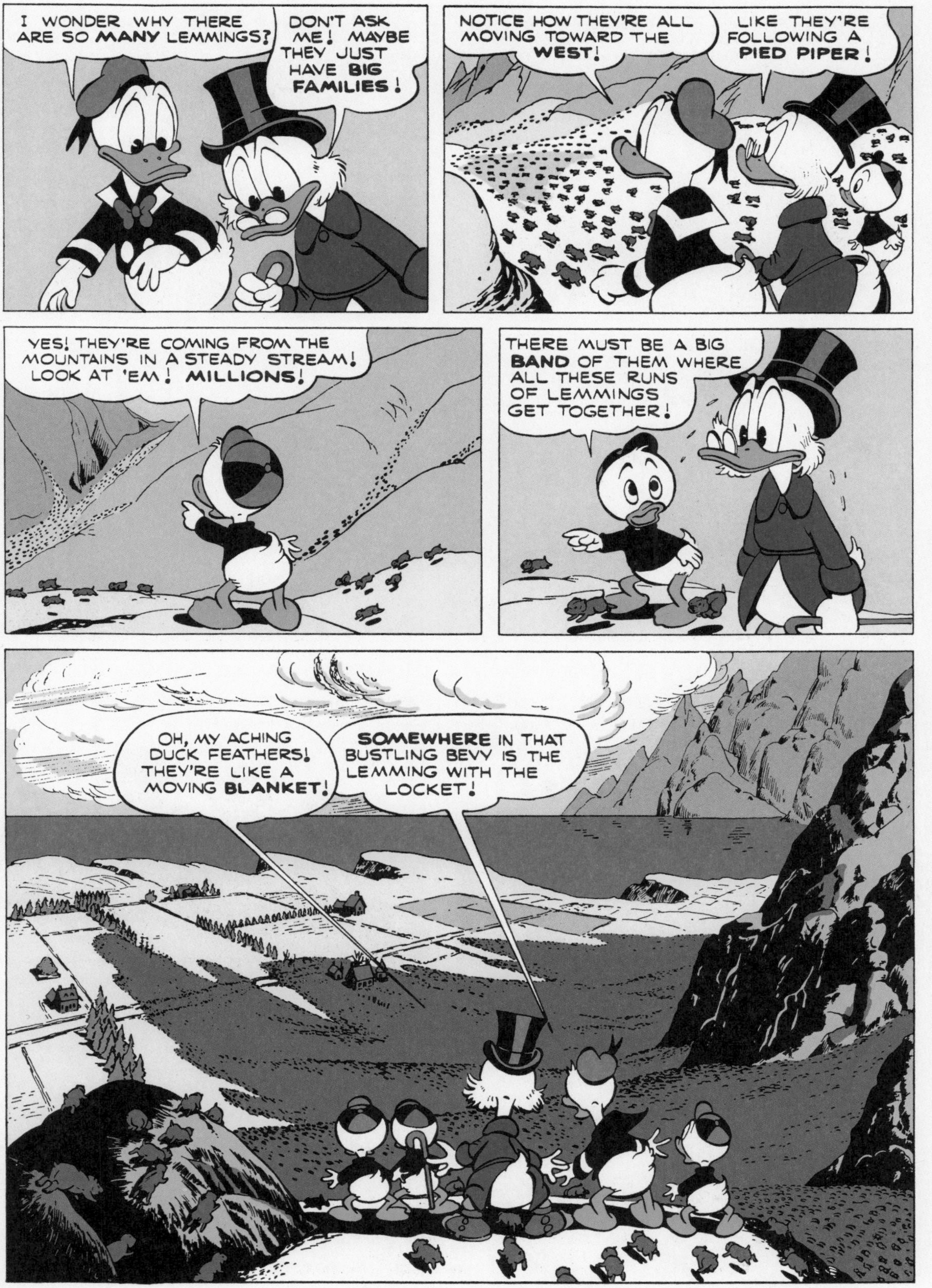
I WONDER WHY THERE ARE SO MANY LEMMINGS?
DON'T ASK ME! MAYBE THEY JUST HAVE BIG FAMILIES!
NOTICE HOW THEY'RE ALL MOVING TOWARD THE WEST!
LIKE THEY'RE FOLLOWING A PIED PIPER!
YES! THEY'RE COMING FROM THE MOUNTAINS IN A STEADY STREAM! LOOK AT 'EM! MILLIONS!
THERE MUST BE A BIG BAND OF THEM WHERE ALL THESE RUNS OF LEMMINGS GET TOGETHER!
OH, MY ACHING DUCK FEATHERS! THEY'RE LIKE A MOVING BLANKET!
SOMEWHERE IN THAT BUSTLING BEVY IS THE LEMMING WITH THE LOCKET!

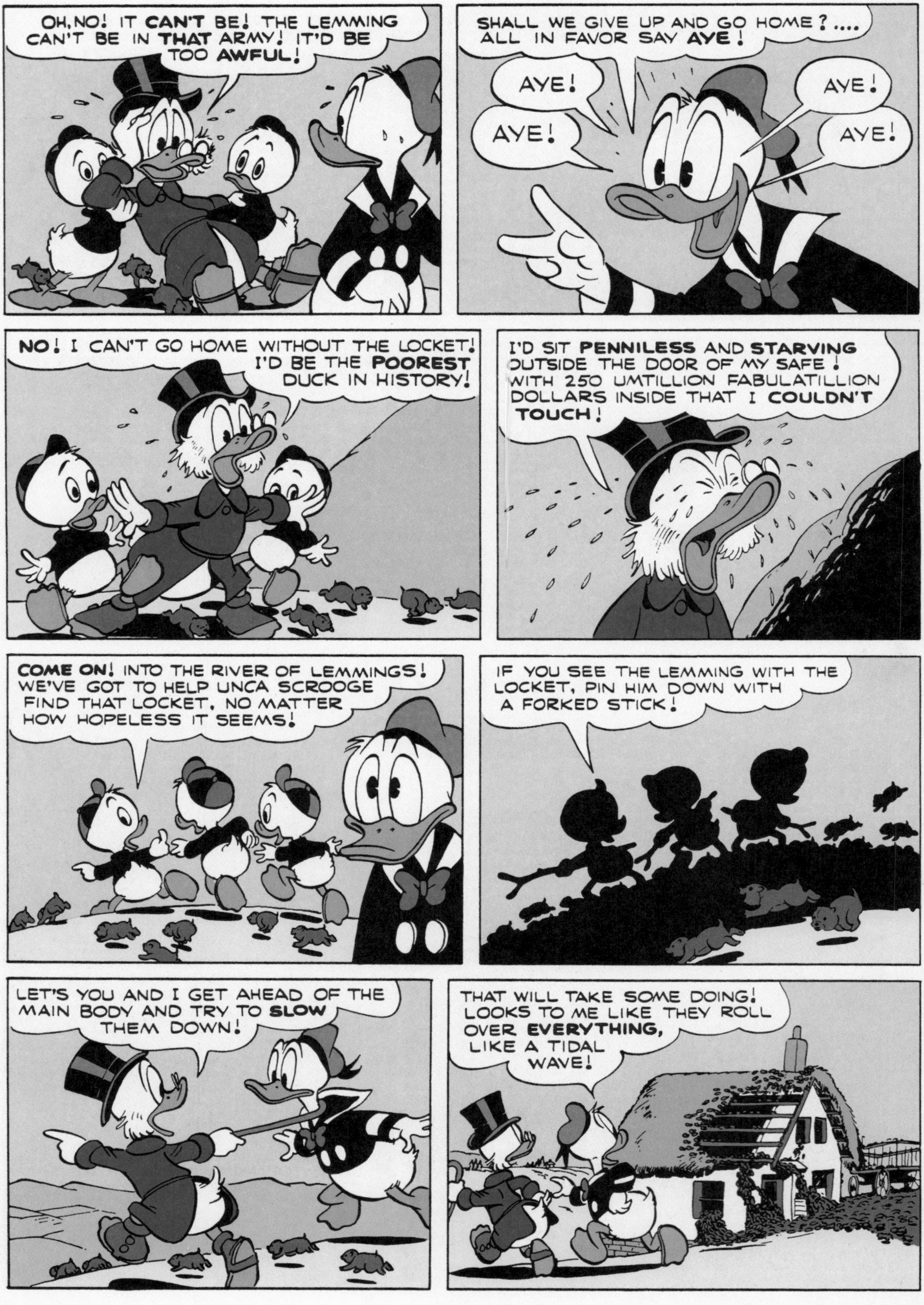

OH, NO! IT CAN'T BE! THE LEMMING CAN'T BE IN THAT ARMY! IT'D BE TOO AWFUL!
SHALL WE GIVE UP AND GO HOME?.... ALL IN FAVOR SAY AYE!
AYE!
AYE!
AYE!
AYE!
NO! I CAN'T GO HOME WITHOUT THE LOCKET! I'D BE THE POOREST DUCK IN HISTORY!
I'D SIT PENNILESS AND STARVING OUTSIDE THE DOOR OF MY SAFE! WITH 250 UMTILLION FABULATILLION DOLLARS INSIDE THAT I COULDN'T TOUCH!
COME ON! INTO THE RIVER OF LEMMINGS! WE'VE GOT TO HELP UNCA SCROOGE FIND THAT LOCKET, NO MATTER HOW HOPELESS IT SEEMS!
IF YOU SEE THE LEMMING WITH THE LOCKET, PIN HIM DOWN WITH A FORKED STICK!
LET'S YOU AND I GET AHEAD OF THE MAIN BODY AND TRY TO SLOW THEM DOWN!
THAT WILL TAKE SOME DOING! LOOKS TO ME LIKE THEY ROLL OVER EVERYTHING, LIKE A TIDAL WAVE!

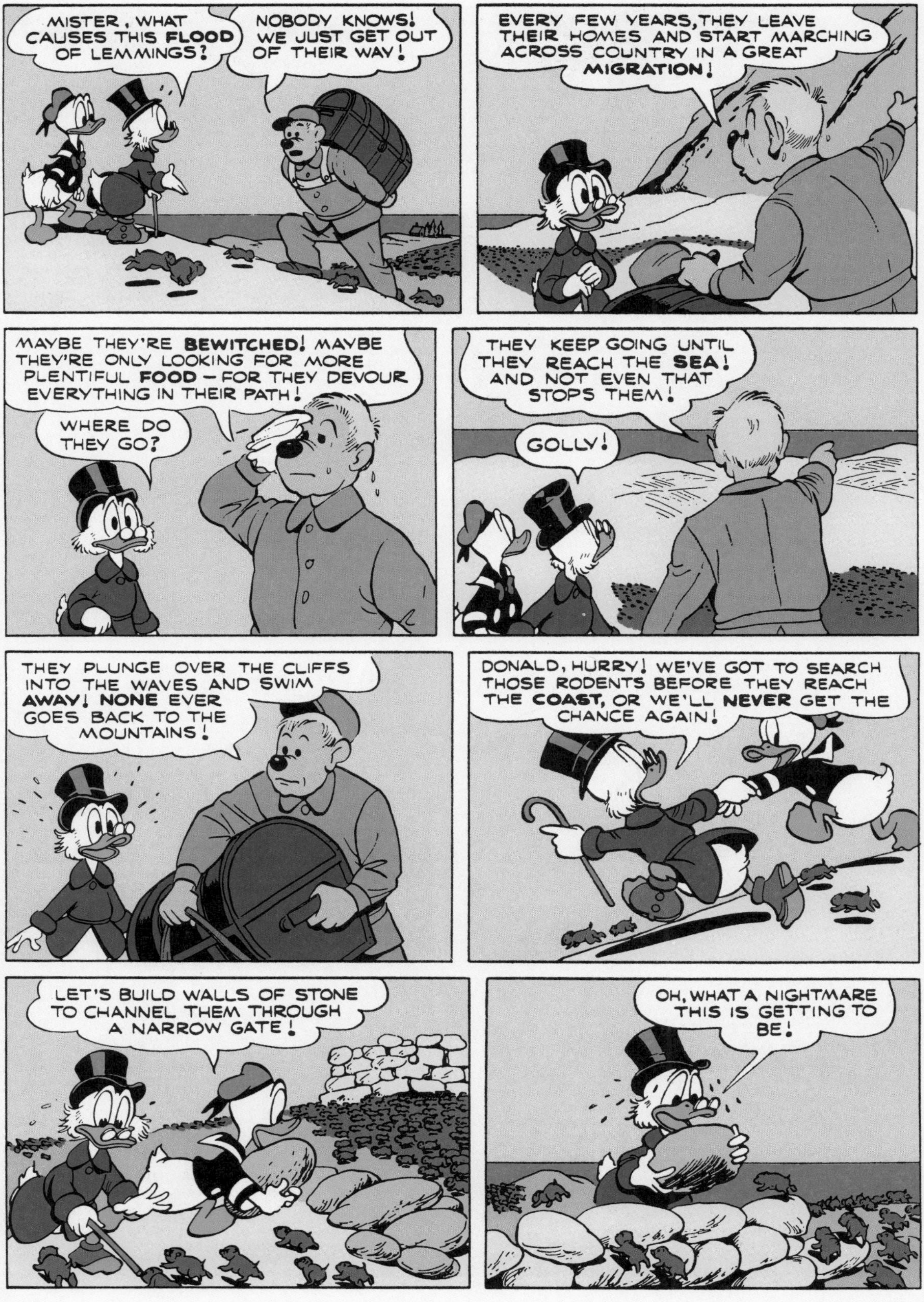

MISTER, WHAT CAUSES THIS FLOOD OF LEMMINGS?
NOBODY KNOWS! WE JUST GET OUT OF THEIR WAY!
EVERY FEW YEARS, THEY LEAVE THEIR HOMES AND START MARCHING ACROSS COUNTRY IN A GREAT MIGRATION!
MAYBE THEY'RE BEWITCHED! MAYBE THEY'RE ONLY LOOKING FOR MORE PLENTIFUL FOOD — FOR THEY DEVOUR EVERYTHING IN THEIR PATH!
WHERE DO THEY GO?
THEY KEEP GOING UNTIL THEY REACH THE SEA! AND NOT EVEN THAT STOPS THEM!
GOLLY!
THEY PLUNGE OVER THE CLIFFS INTO THE WAVES AND SWIM AWAY! NONE EVER GOES BACK TO THE MOUNTAINS!
DONALD, HURRY! WE'VE GOT TO SEARCH THOSE RODENTS BEFORE THEY REACH THE COAST, OR WE'LL NEVER GET THE CHANCE AGAIN!
LET'S BUILD WALLS OF STONE TO CHANNEL THEM THROUGH A NARROW GATE!
OH, WHAT A NIGHTMARE THIS IS GETTING TO BE!

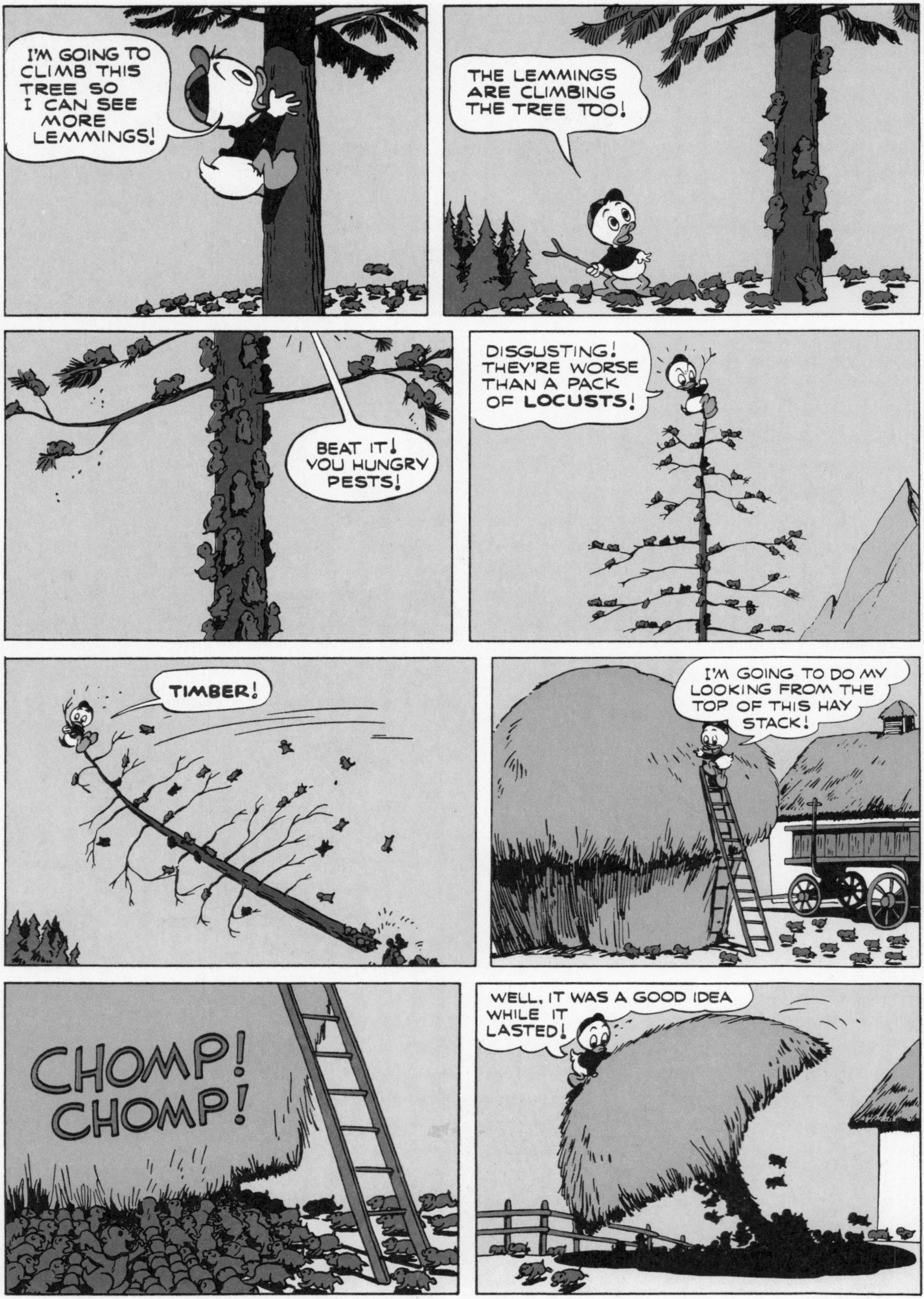
I'M GOING TO CLIMB THIS TREE SO I CAN SEE MORE LEMMINGS!
THE LEMMINGS ARE CLIMBING THE TREE TOO!
BEAT IT! YOU HUNGRY PESTS!
DISGUSTING! THEY'RE WORSE THAN A PACK OF **LOCUSTS**!
TIMBER!
I'M GOING TO DO MY LOOKING FROM THE TOP OF THIS HAY STACK!
CHOMP! CHOMP!
WELL, IT WAS A GOOD IDEA WHILE IT LASTED!

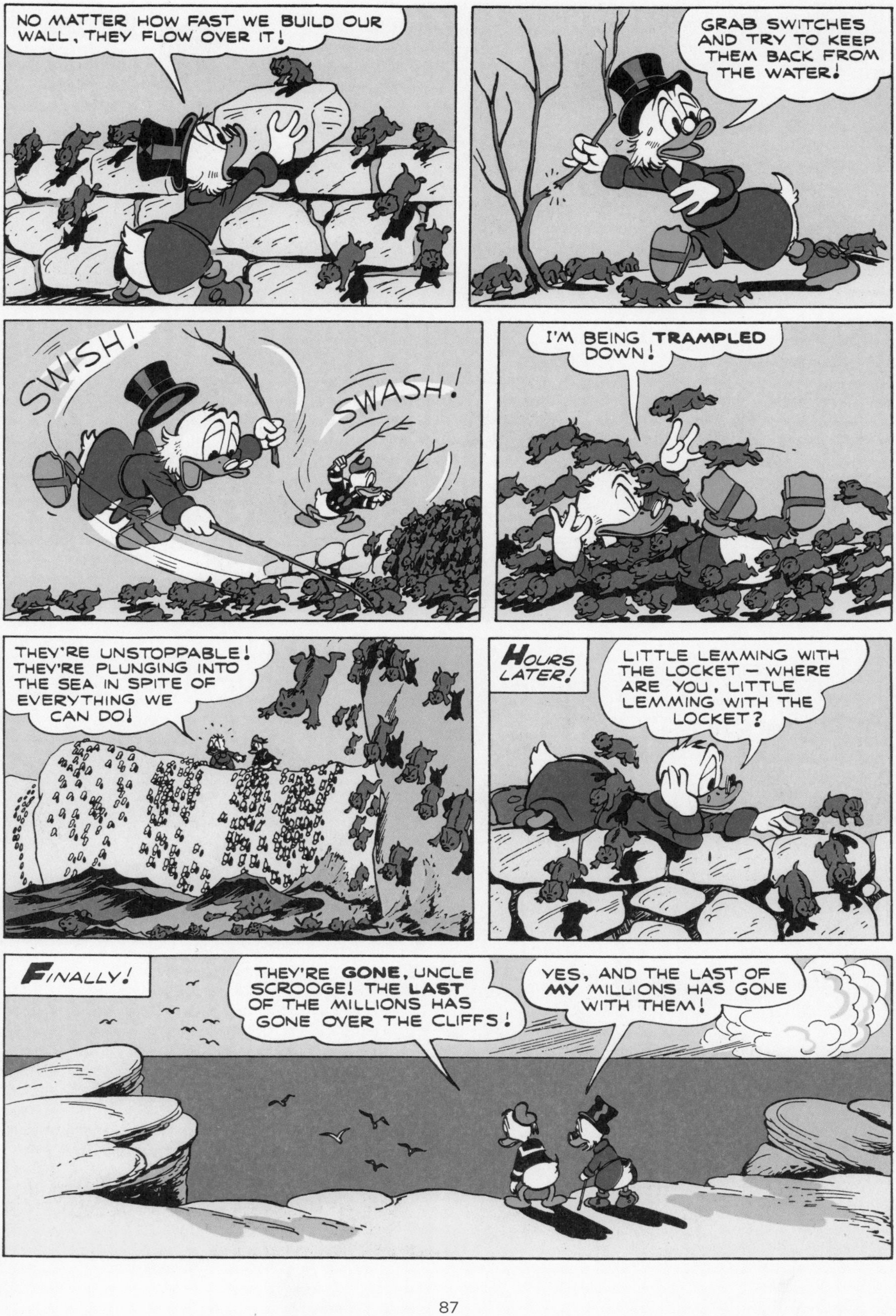

NO MATTER HOW FAST WE BUILD OUR WALL, THEY FLOW OVER IT!
GRAB SWITCHES AND TRY TO KEEP THEM BACK FROM THE WATER!
SWISH!
SWASH!
I'M BEING **TRAMPLED** DOWN!
THEY'RE UNSTOPPABLE! THEY'RE PLUNGING INTO THE SEA IN SPITE OF EVERYTHING WE CAN DO!
HOURS LATER!
LITTLE LEMMING WITH THE LOCKET — WHERE ARE YOU, LITTLE LEMMING WITH THE LOCKET?
FINALLY!
THEY'RE **GONE**, UNCLE SCROOGE! THE **LAST** OF THE MILLIONS HAS GONE OVER THE CLIFFS!
YES, AND THE LAST OF **MY** MILLIONS HAS GONE WITH THEM!

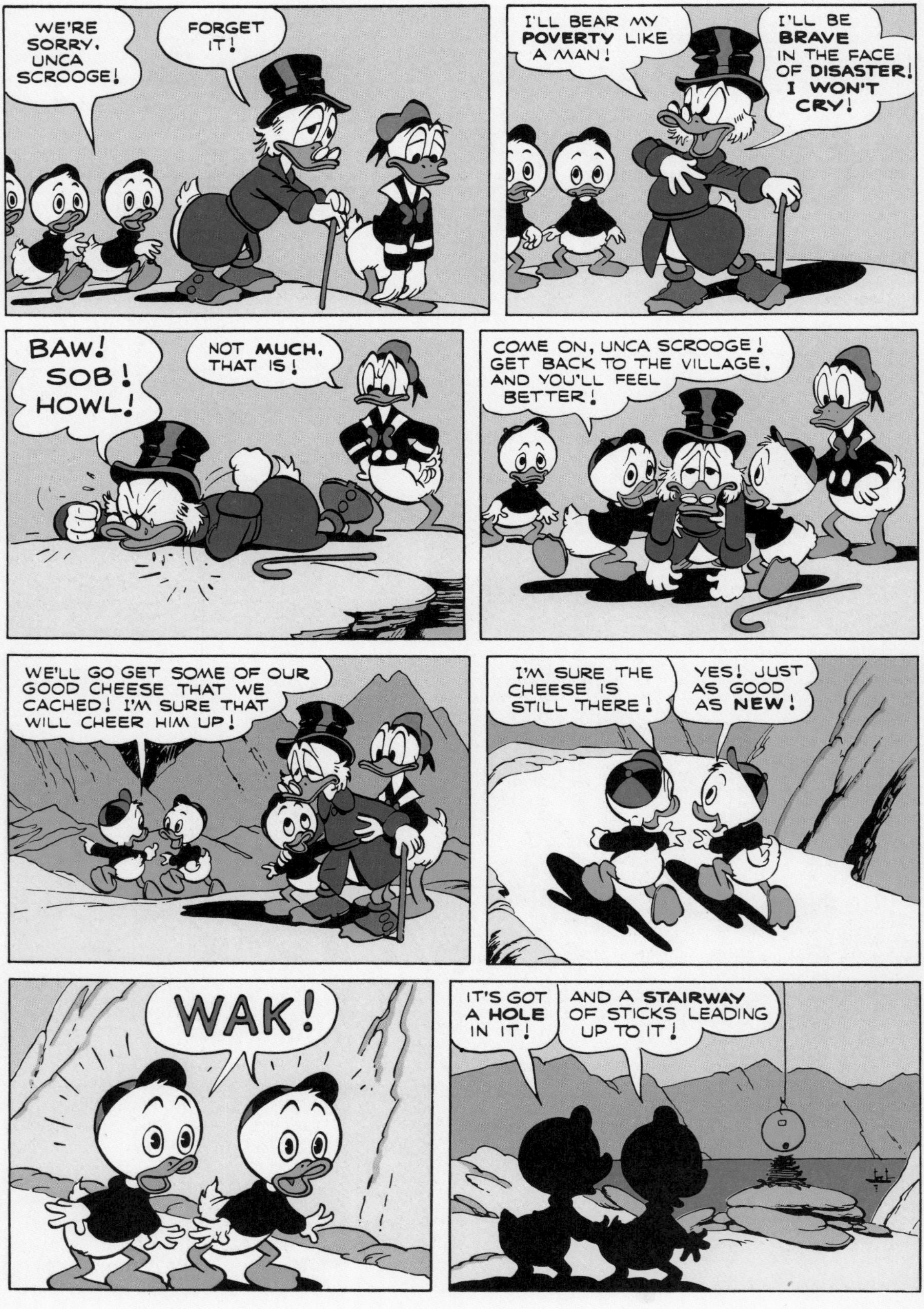

WE'RE SORRY, UNCA SCROOGE!
FORGET IT!
I'LL BEAR MY POVERTY LIKE A MAN!
I'LL BE BRAVE IN THE FACE OF DISASTER! I WON'T CRY!
BAW! SOB! HOWL!
NOT MUCH, THAT IS!
COME ON, UNCA SCROOGE! GET BACK TO THE VILLAGE, AND YOU'LL FEEL BETTER!
WE'LL GO GET SOME OF OUR GOOD CHEESE THAT WE CACHED! I'M SURE THAT WILL CHEER HIM UP!
I'M SURE THE CHEESE IS STILL THERE!
YES! JUST AS GOOD AS NEW!
WAK!
IT'S GOT A HOLE IN IT!
AND A STAIRWAY OF STICKS LEADING UP TO IT!

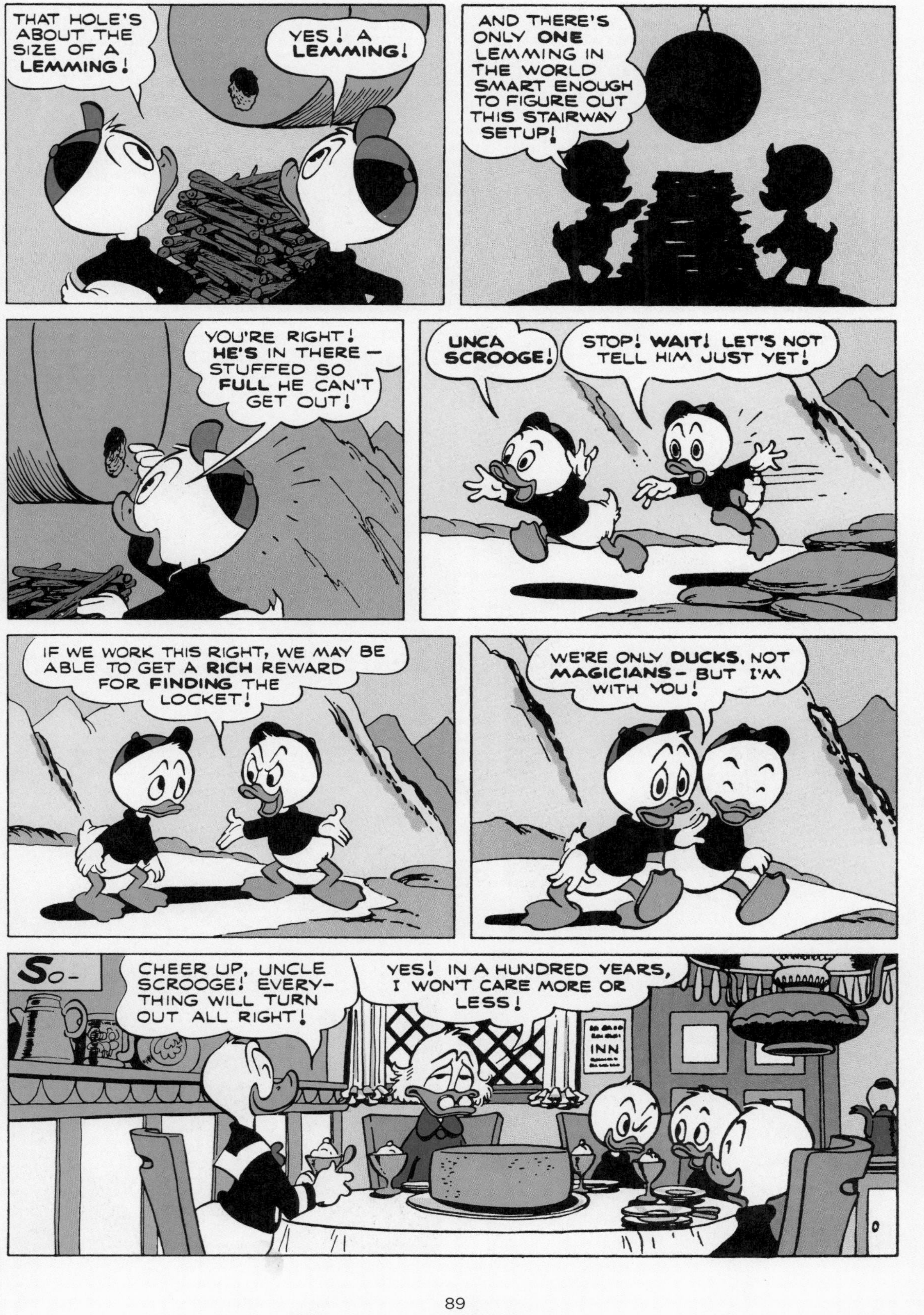
THAT HOLE'S ABOUT THE SIZE OF A LEMMING!
YES! A LEMMING!
AND THERE'S ONLY ONE LEMMING IN THE WORLD SMART ENOUGH TO FIGURE OUT THIS STAIRWAY SETUP!
YOU'RE RIGHT! HE'S IN THERE— STUFFED SO FULL HE CAN'T GET OUT!
UNCA SCROOGE!
STOP! WAIT! LET'S NOT TELL HIM JUST YET!
IF WE WORK THIS RIGHT, WE MAY BE ABLE TO GET A RICH REWARD FOR FINDING THE LOCKET!
WE'RE ONLY DUCKS, NOT MAGICIANS— BUT I'M WITH YOU!
SO-
CHEER UP, UNCLE SCROOGE! EVERYTHING WILL TURN OUT ALL RIGHT!
YES! IN A HUNDRED YEARS, I WON'T CARE MORE OR LESS!
INN

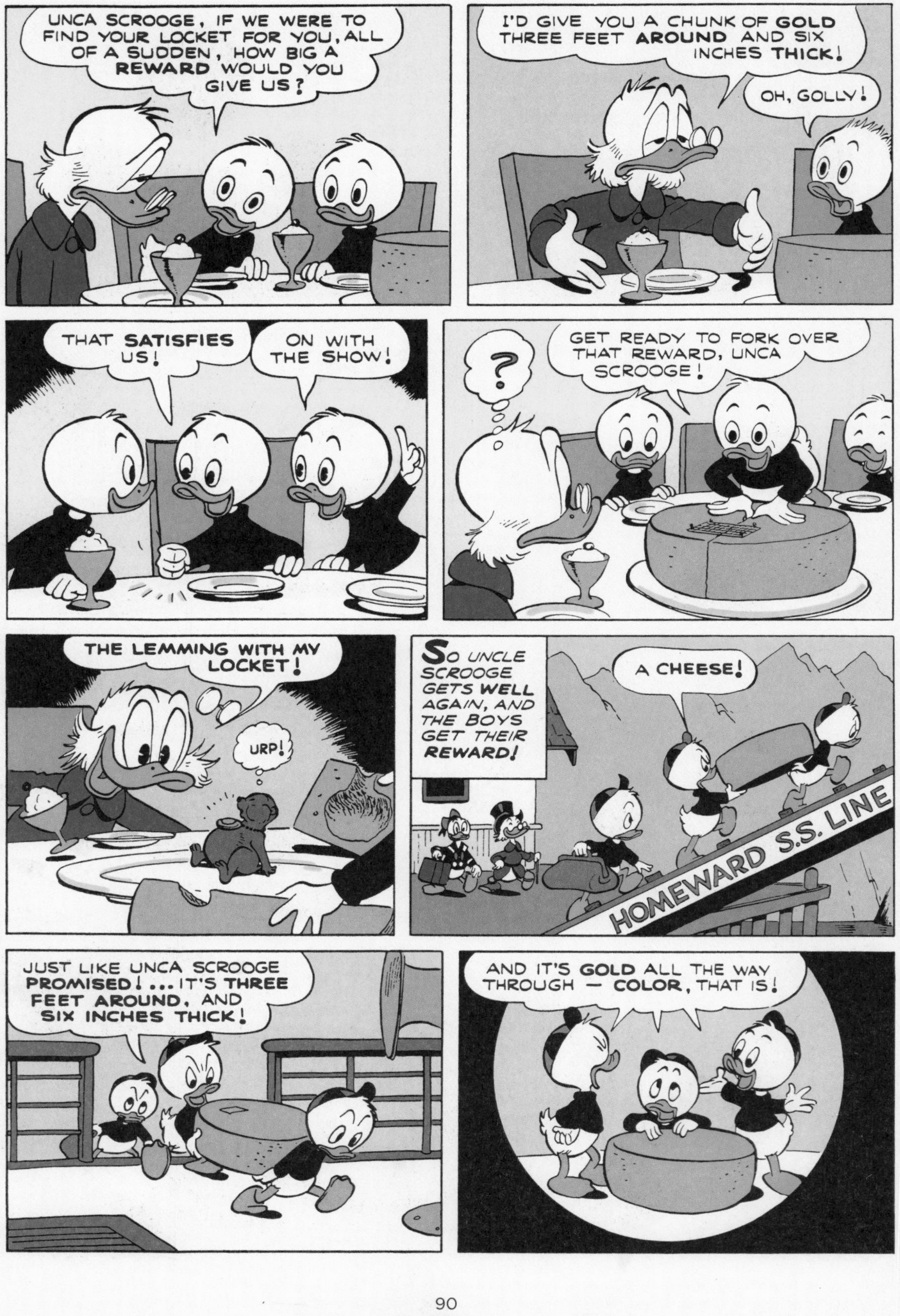
UNCA SCROOGE, IF WE WERE TO FIND YOUR LOCKET FOR YOU, ALL OF A SUDDEN, HOW BIG A REWARD WOULD YOU GIVE US?
I'D GIVE YOU A CHUNK OF GOLD THREE FEET AROUND AND SIX INCHES THICK!
OH, GOLLY!
THAT SATISFIES US!
ON WITH THE SHOW!
?
GET READY TO FORK OVER THAT REWARD, UNCA SCROOGE!
THE LEMMING WITH MY LOCKET!
URP!
SO UNCLE SCROOGE GETS WELL AGAIN, AND THE BOYS GET THEIR REWARD!
A CHEESE!
HOMEWARD S.S. LINE
JUST LIKE UNCA SCROOGE PROMISED! ... IT'S THREE FEET AROUND, AND SIX INCHES THICK!
AND IT'S GOLD ALL THE WAY THROUGH — COLOR, THAT IS!

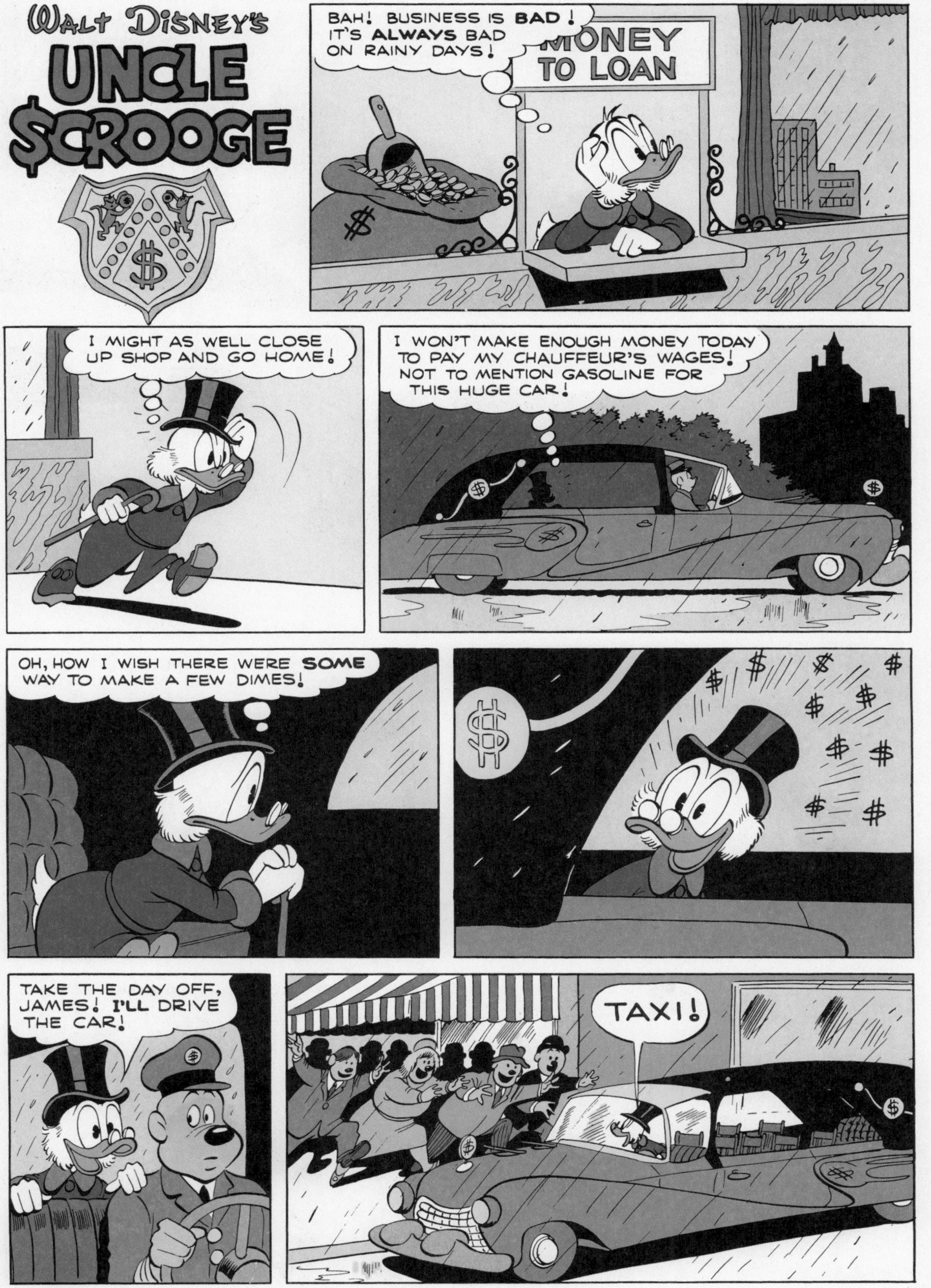
WALT DISNEY'S
UNCLE $CROOGE
BAH! BUSINESS IS **BAD**! IT'S **ALWAYS** BAD ON RAINY DAYS!
MONEY TO LOAN
I MIGHT AS WELL CLOSE UP SHOP AND GO HOME!
I WON'T MAKE ENOUGH MONEY TODAY TO PAY MY CHAUFFEUR'S WAGES! NOT TO MENTION GASOLINE FOR THIS HUGE CAR!
OH, HOW I WISH THERE WERE **SOME** WAY TO MAKE A FEW DIMES!
TAKE THE DAY OFF, JAMES! **I'LL** DRIVE THE CAR!
TAXI!

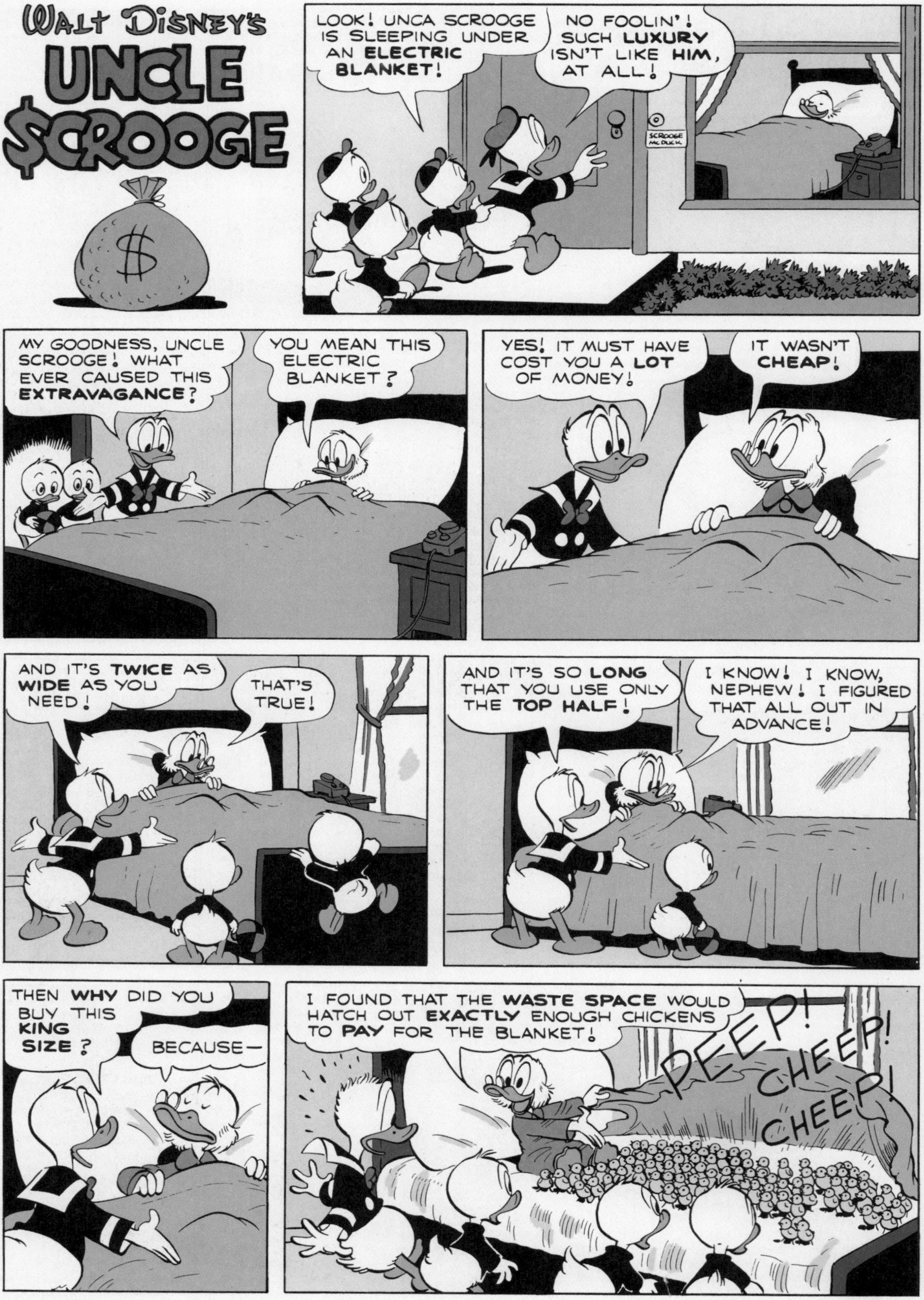
WALT DISNEY'S
UNCLE $CROOGE
LOOK! UNCA SCROOGE IS SLEEPING UNDER AN ELECTRIC BLANKET!
NO FOOLIN'! SUCH LUXURY ISN'T LIKE HIM, AT ALL!
SCROOGE McDUCK
MY GOODNESS, UNCLE SCROOGE! WHAT EVER CAUSED THIS EXTRAVAGANCE?
YOU MEAN THIS ELECTRIC BLANKET?
YES! IT MUST HAVE COST YOU A LOT OF MONEY!
IT WASN'T CHEAP!
AND IT'S TWICE AS WIDE AS YOU NEED!
THAT'S TRUE!
AND IT'S SO LONG THAT YOU USE ONLY THE TOP HALF!
I KNOW! I KNOW, NEPHEW! I FIGURED THAT ALL OUT IN ADVANCE!
THEN WHY DID YOU BUY THIS KING SIZE?
BECAUSE—
I FOUND THAT THE WASTE SPACE WOULD HATCH OUT EXACTLY ENOUGH CHICKENS TO PAY FOR THE BLANKET!
PEEP!
CHEEP!
CHEEP!

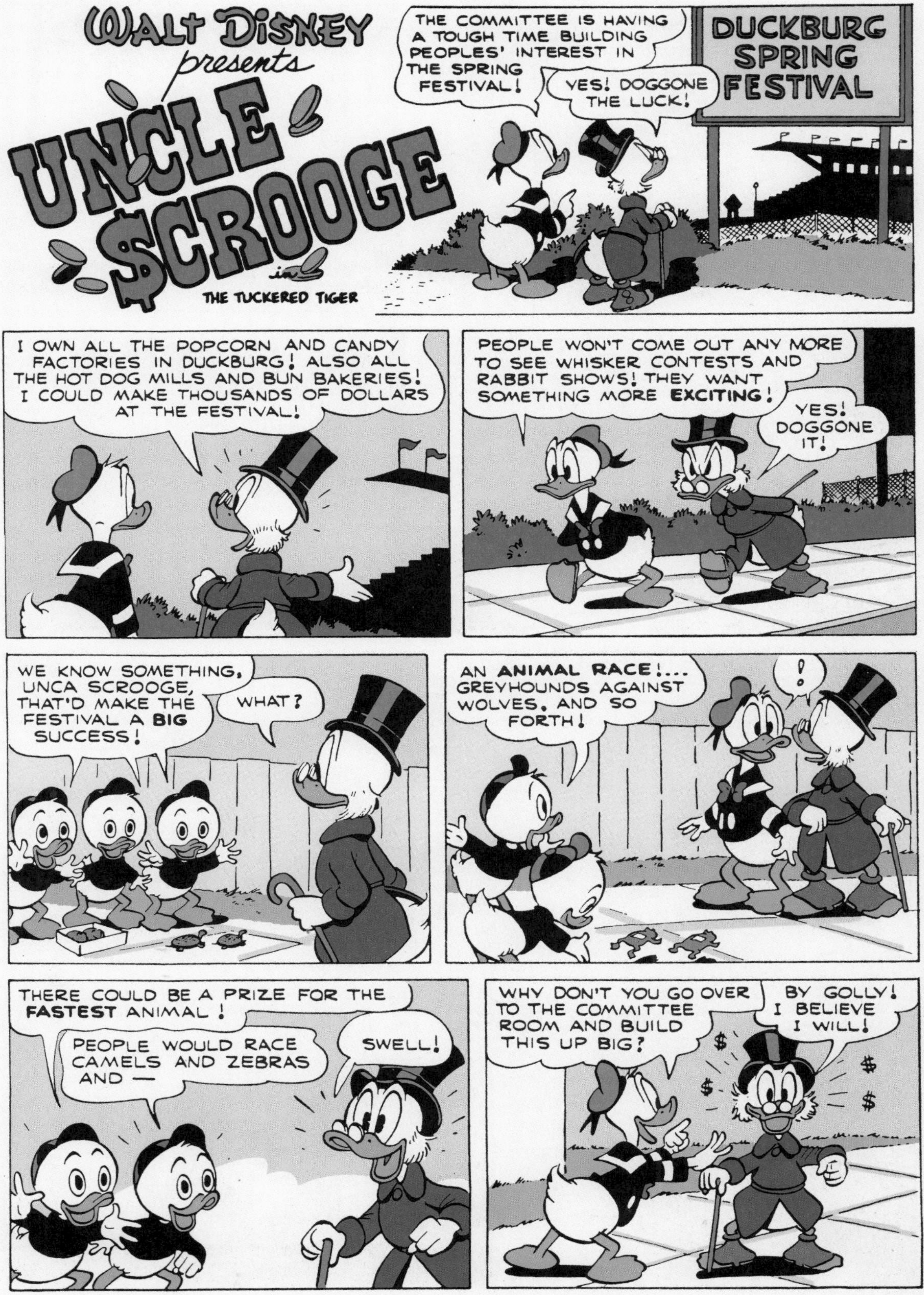
WALT DISNEY presents
UNCLE $CROOGE
in
THE TUCKERED TIGER
THE COMMITTEE IS HAVING A TOUGH TIME BUILDING PEOPLES' INTEREST IN THE SPRING FESTIVAL!
YES! DOGGONE THE LUCK!
DUCKBURG SPRING FESTIVAL
I OWN ALL THE POPCORN AND CANDY FACTORIES IN DUCKBURG! ALSO ALL THE HOT DOG MILLS AND BUN BAKERIES! I COULD MAKE THOUSANDS OF DOLLARS AT THE FESTIVAL!
PEOPLE WON'T COME OUT ANY MORE TO SEE WHISKER CONTESTS AND RABBIT SHOWS! THEY WANT SOMETHING MORE EXCITING!
YES! DOGGONE IT!
WE KNOW SOMETHING, UNCA SCROOGE, THAT'D MAKE THE FESTIVAL A BIG SUCCESS!
WHAT?
AN ANIMAL RACE!... GREYHOUNDS AGAINST WOLVES, AND SO FORTH!
!
THERE COULD BE A PRIZE FOR THE FASTEST ANIMAL!
PEOPLE WOULD RACE CAMELS AND ZEBRAS AND —
SWELL!
WHY DON'T YOU GO OVER TO THE COMMITTEE ROOM AND BUILD THIS UP BIG?
BY GOLLY! I BELIEVE I WILL!

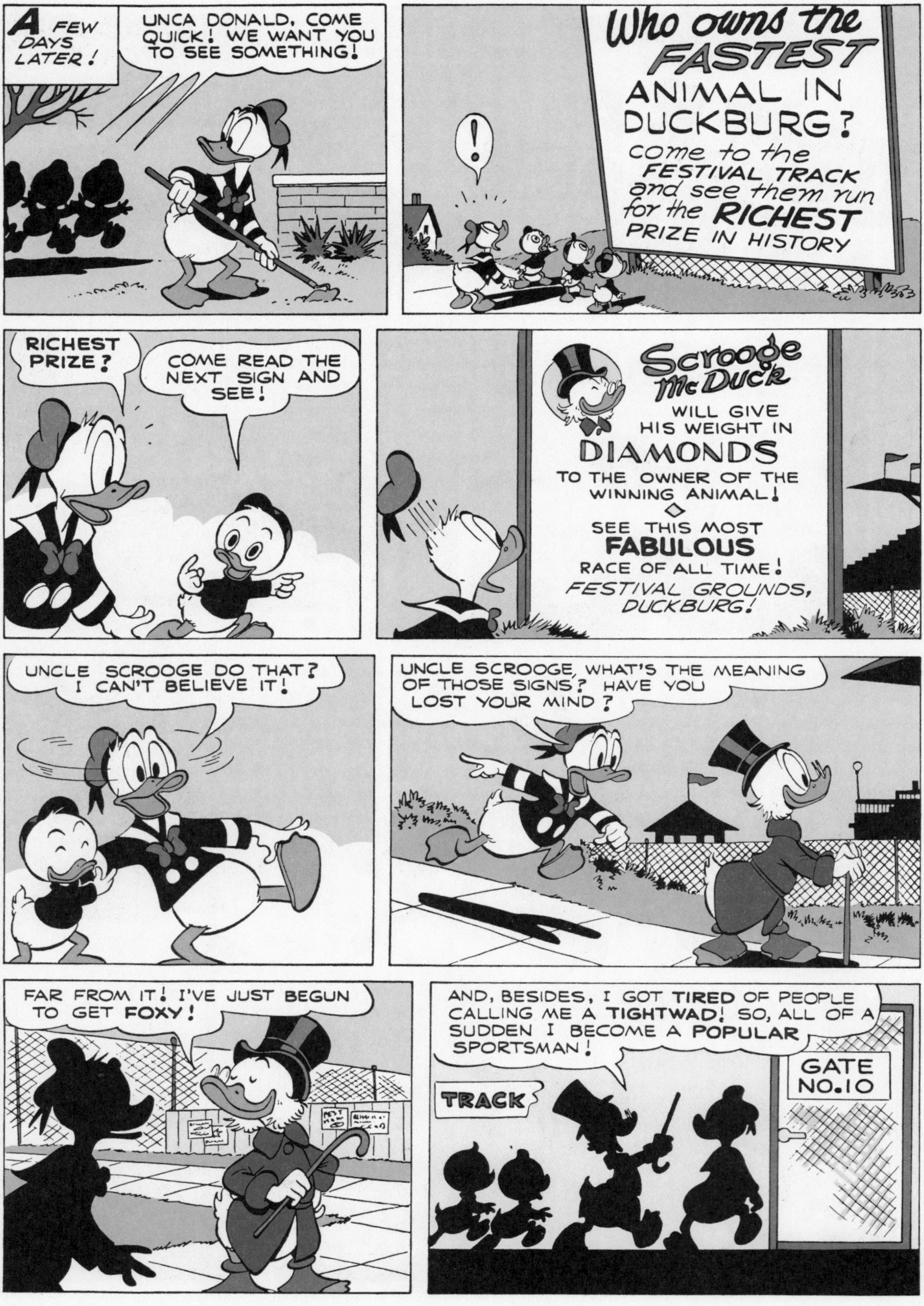

A FEW DAYS LATER!
UNCA DONALD, COME QUICK! WE WANT YOU TO SEE SOMETHING!
!
Who owns the FASTEST ANIMAL IN DUCKBURG? come to the FESTIVAL TRACK and see them run for the RICHEST PRIZE IN HISTORY
RICHEST PRIZE?
COME READ THE NEXT SIGN AND SEE!
Scrooge McDuck WILL GIVE HIS WEIGHT IN DIAMONDS TO THE OWNER OF THE WINNING ANIMAL!
SEE THIS MOST FABULOUS RACE OF ALL TIME! FESTIVAL GROUNDS, DUCKBURG!
UNCLE SCROOGE DO THAT? I CAN'T BELIEVE IT!
UNCLE SCROOGE, WHAT'S THE MEANING OF THOSE SIGNS? HAVE YOU LOST YOUR MIND?
FAR FROM IT! I'VE JUST BEGUN TO GET FOXY!
AND, BESIDES, I GOT TIRED OF PEOPLE CALLING ME A TIGHTWAD! SO, ALL OF A SUDDEN I BECOME A POPULAR SPORTSMAN!
TRACK
GATE NO.10

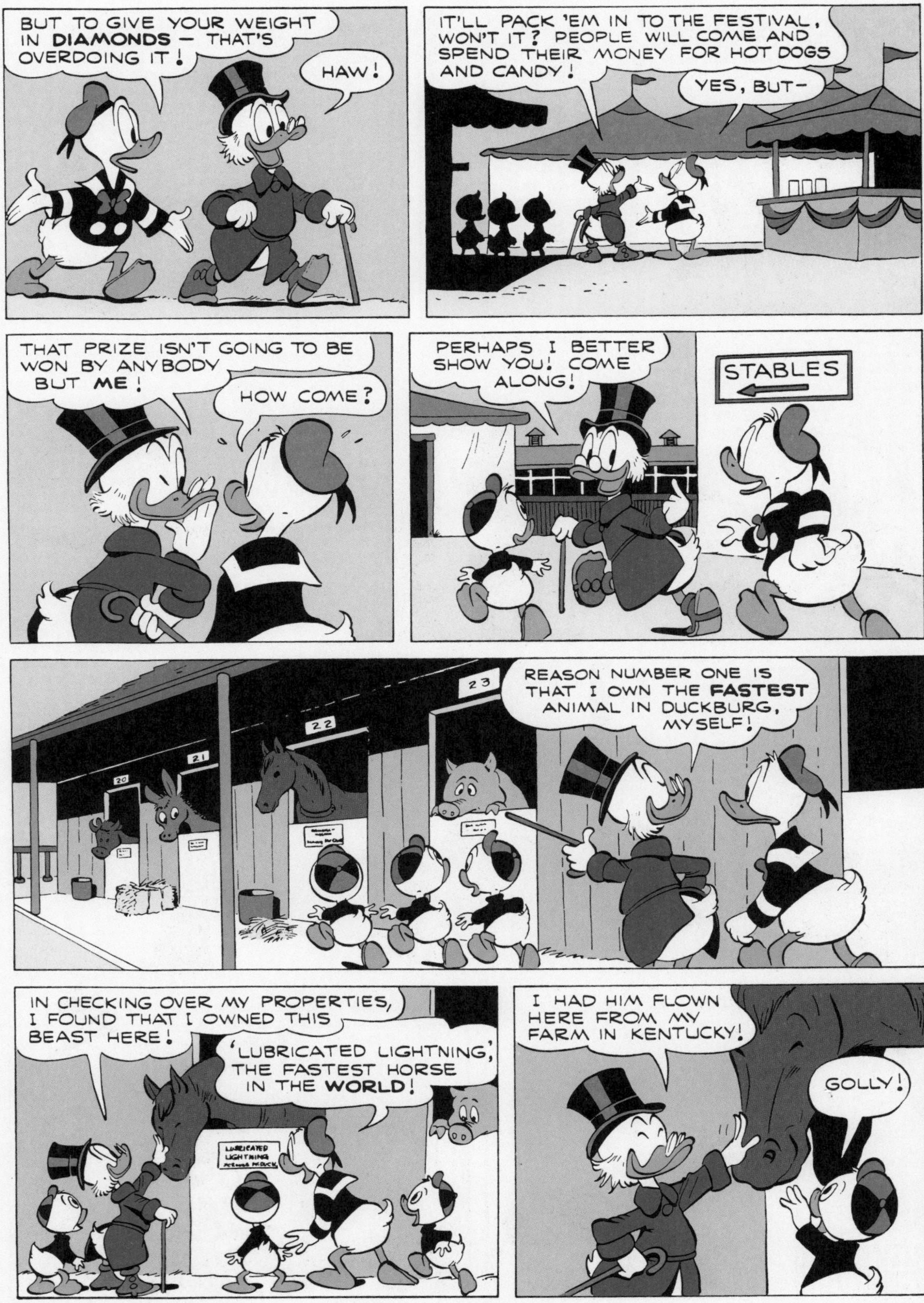
BUT TO GIVE YOUR WEIGHT IN **DIAMONDS** — THAT'S OVERDOING IT!
HAW!
IT'LL PACK 'EM IN TO THE FESTIVAL, WON'T IT? PEOPLE WILL COME AND SPEND THEIR MONEY FOR HOT DOGS AND CANDY!
YES, BUT–
THAT PRIZE ISN'T GOING TO BE WON BY ANYBODY BUT **ME**!
HOW COME?
PERHAPS I BETTER SHOW YOU! COME ALONG!
STABLES
REASON NUMBER ONE IS THAT I OWN THE **FASTEST** ANIMAL IN DUCKBURG, MYSELF!
IN CHECKING OVER MY PROPERTIES, I FOUND THAT I OWNED THIS BEAST HERE!
'LUBRICATED LIGHTNING', THE FASTEST HORSE IN THE **WORLD**!
I HAD HIM FLOWN HERE FROM MY FARM IN KENTUCKY!
GOLLY!

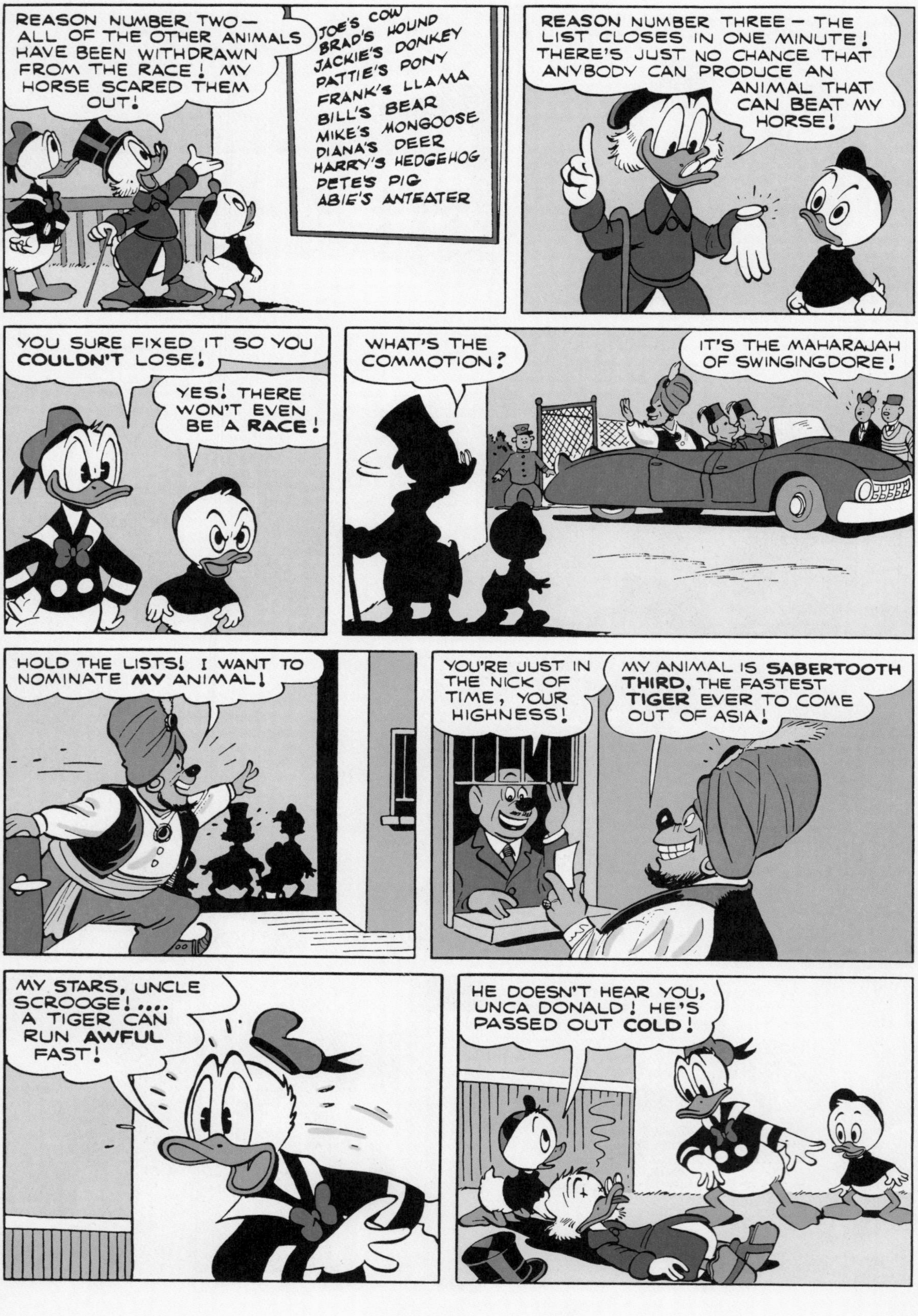
REASON NUMBER TWO— ALL OF THE OTHER ANIMALS HAVE BEEN WITHDRAWN FROM THE RACE! MY HORSE SCARED THEM OUT!
JOE'S COW
BRAD'S HOUND
JACKIE'S DONKEY
PATTIE'S PONY
FRANK'S LLAMA
BILL'S BEAR
MIKE'S MONGOOSE
DIANA'S DEER
HARRY'S HEDGEHOG
PETE'S PIG
ABIE'S ANTEATER
REASON NUMBER THREE — THE LIST CLOSES IN ONE MINUTE! THERE'S JUST NO CHANCE THAT ANYBODY CAN PRODUCE AN ANIMAL THAT CAN BEAT MY HORSE!
YOU SURE FIXED IT SO YOU COULDN'T LOSE!
YES! THERE WON'T EVEN BE A RACE!
WHAT'S THE COMMOTION?
IT'S THE MAHARAJAH OF SWINGINGDORE!
HOLD THE LISTS! I WANT TO NOMINATE MY ANIMAL!
YOU'RE JUST IN THE NICK OF TIME, YOUR HIGHNESS!
MY ANIMAL IS SABERTOOTH THIRD, THE FASTEST TIGER EVER TO COME OUT OF ASIA!
MY STARS, UNCLE SCROOGE!.... A TIGER CAN RUN AWFUL FAST!
HE DOESN'T HEAR YOU, UNCA DONALD! HE'S PASSED OUT COLD!

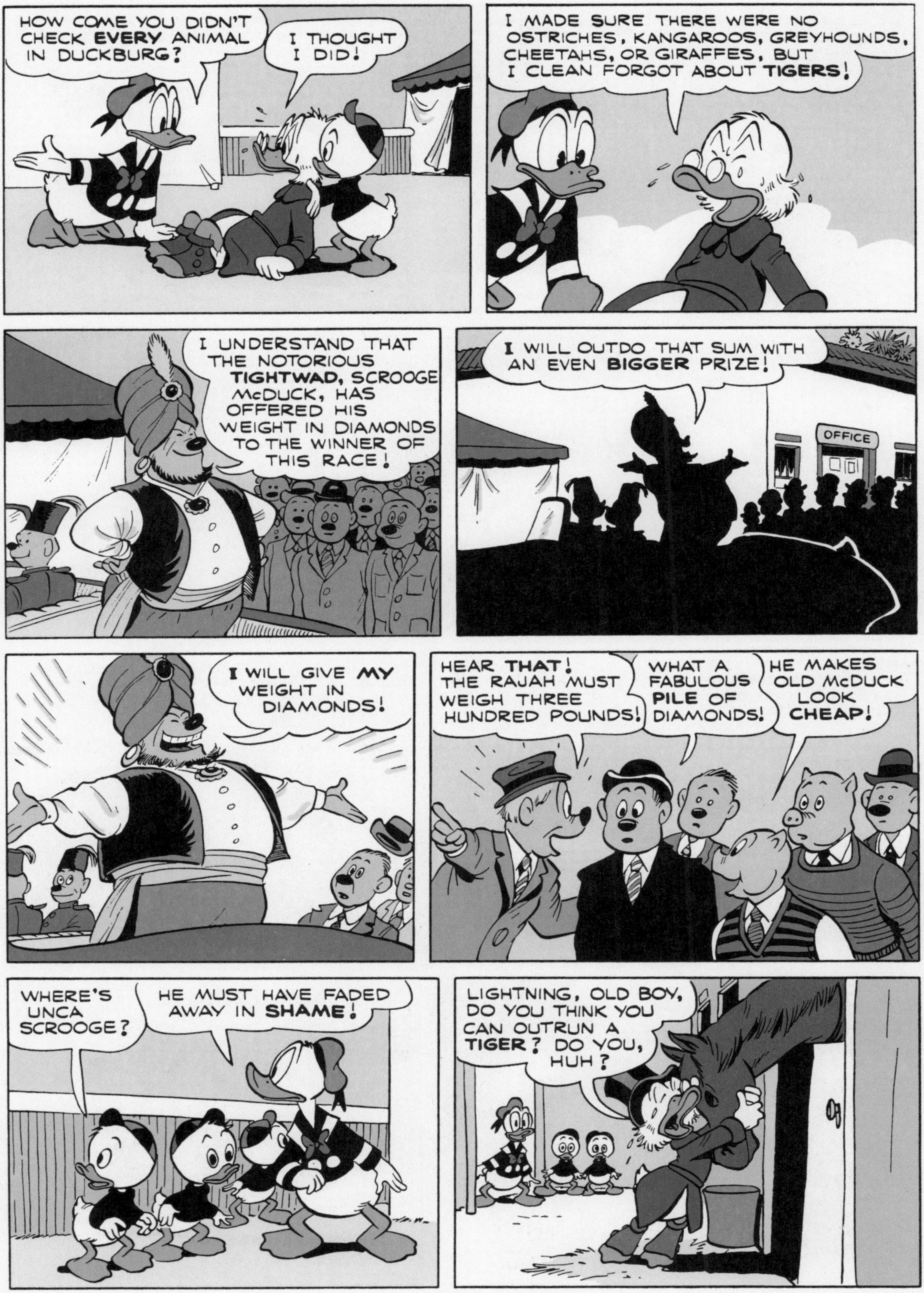
HOW COME YOU DIDN'T CHECK EVERY ANIMAL IN DUCKBURG?
I THOUGHT I DID!
I MADE SURE THERE WERE NO OSTRICHES, KANGAROOS, GREYHOUNDS, CHEETAHS, OR GIRAFFES, BUT I CLEAN FORGOT ABOUT TIGERS!
I UNDERSTAND THAT THE NOTORIOUS TIGHTWAD, SCROOGE McDUCK, HAS OFFERED HIS WEIGHT IN DIAMONDS TO THE WINNER OF THIS RACE!
I WILL OUTDO THAT SUM WITH AN EVEN BIGGER PRIZE!
OFFICE
I WILL GIVE MY WEIGHT IN DIAMONDS!
HEAR THAT! THE RAJAH MUST WEIGH THREE HUNDRED POUNDS!
WHAT A FABULOUS PILE OF DIAMONDS!
HE MAKES OLD McDUCK LOOK CHEAP!
WHERE'S UNCA SCROOGE?
HE MUST HAVE FADED AWAY IN SHAME!
LIGHTNING, OLD BOY, DO YOU THINK YOU CAN OUTRUN A TIGER? DO YOU, HUH?

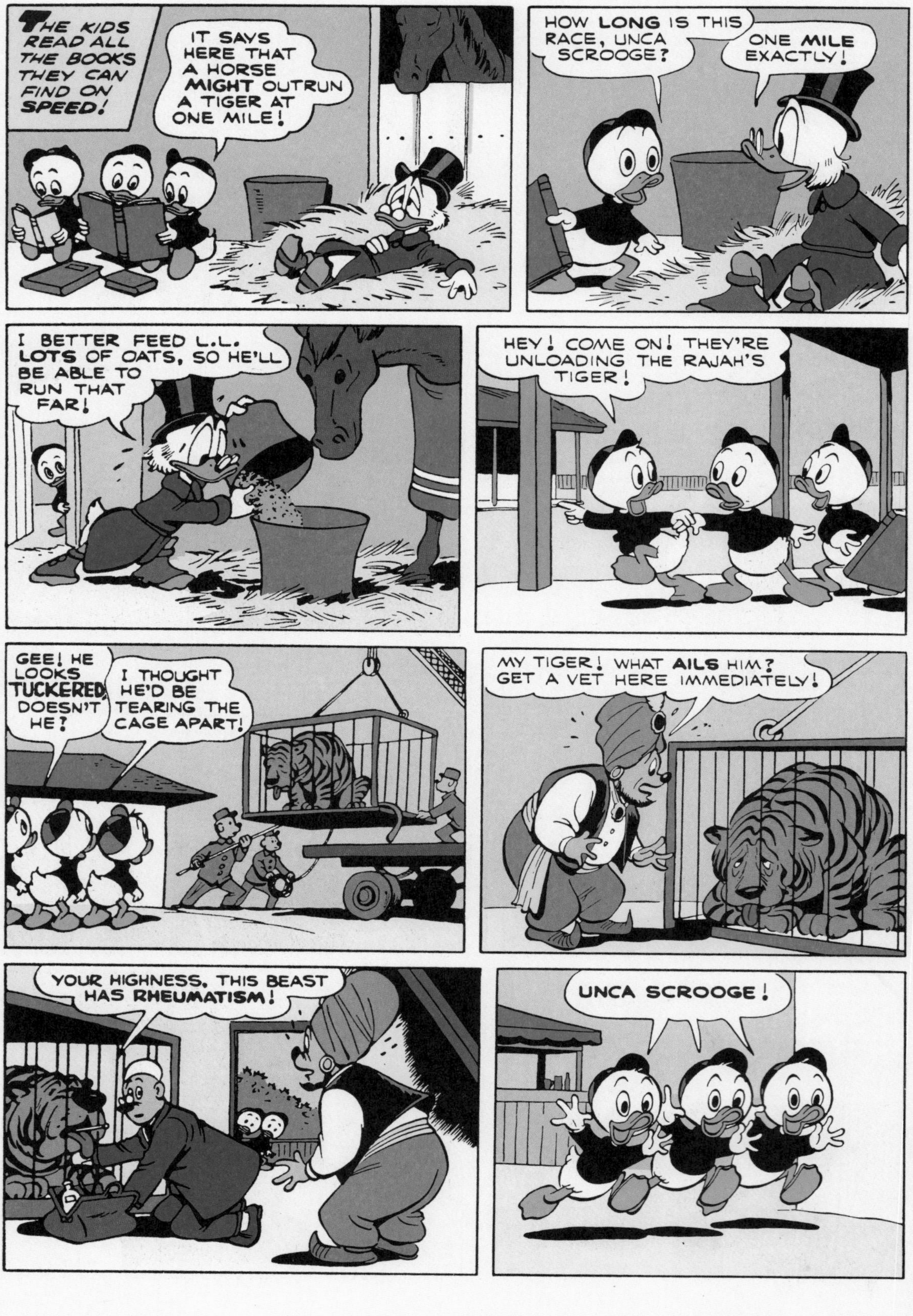
THE KIDS READ ALL THE BOOKS THEY CAN FIND ON SPEED!
IT SAYS HERE THAT A HORSE MIGHT OUTRUN A TIGER AT ONE MILE!
HOW LONG IS THIS RACE, UNCA SCROOGE?
ONE MILE EXACTLY!
I BETTER FEED L.L. LOTS OF OATS, SO HE'LL BE ABLE TO RUN THAT FAR!
HEY! COME ON! THEY'RE UNLOADING THE RAJAH'S TIGER!
GEE! HE LOOKS TUCKERED, DOESN'T HE?
I THOUGHT HE'D BE TEARING THE CAGE APART!
MY TIGER! WHAT AILS HIM? GET A VET HERE IMMEDIATELY!
YOUR HIGHNESS, THIS BEAST HAS RHEUMATISM!
UNCA SCROOGE!

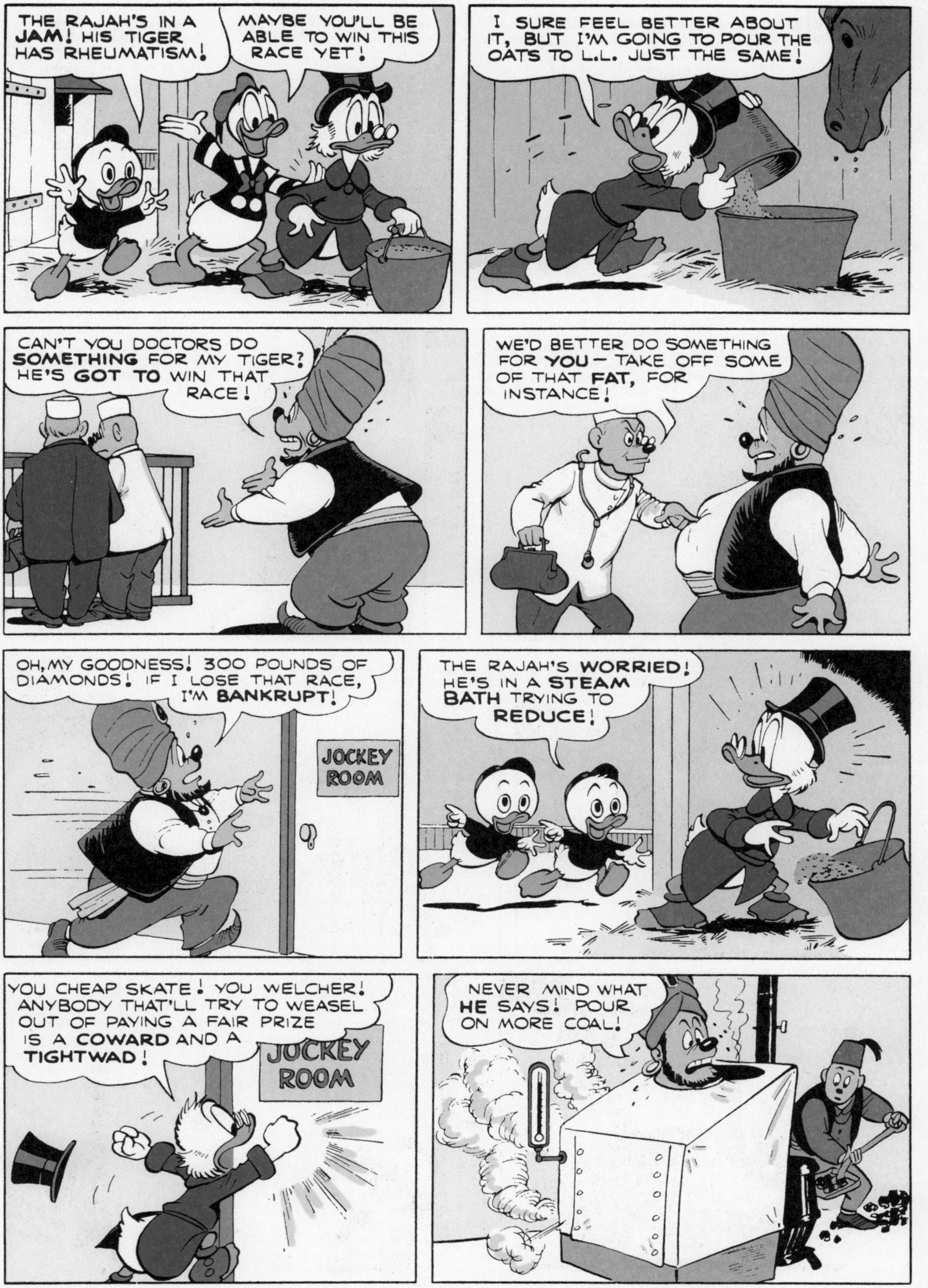

THE RAJAH'S IN A JAM! HIS TIGER HAS RHEUMATISM!
MAYBE YOU'LL BE ABLE TO WIN THIS RACE YET!
I SURE FEEL BETTER ABOUT IT, BUT I'M GOING TO POUR THE OATS TO L.L. JUST THE SAME!
CAN'T YOU DOCTORS DO SOMETHING FOR MY TIGER? HE'S GOT TO WIN THAT RACE!
WE'D BETTER DO SOMETHING FOR YOU — TAKE OFF SOME OF THAT FAT, FOR INSTANCE!
OH, MY GOODNESS! 300 POUNDS OF DIAMONDS! IF I LOSE THAT RACE, I'M BANKRUPT!
JOCKEY ROOM
THE RAJAH'S WORRIED! HE'S IN A STEAM BATH TRYING TO REDUCE!
YOU CHEAP SKATE! YOU WELCHER! ANYBODY THAT'LL TRY TO WEASEL OUT OF PAYING A FAIR PRIZE IS A COWARD AND A TIGHTWAD!
JOCKEY ROOM
NEVER MIND WHAT HE SAYS! POUR ON MORE COAL!

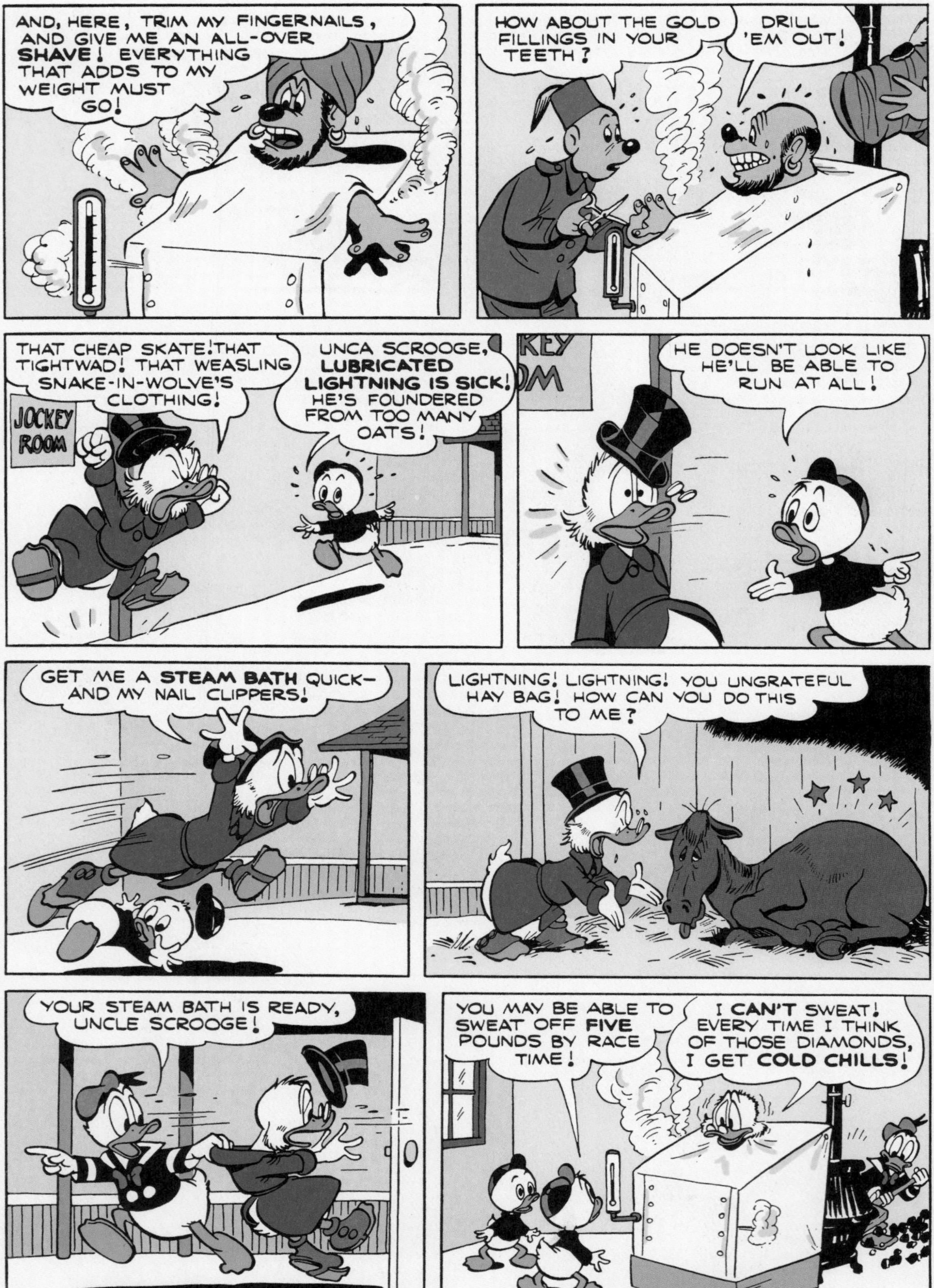
AND, HERE, TRIM MY FINGERNAILS, AND GIVE ME AN ALL-OVER SHAVE! EVERYTHING THAT ADDS TO MY WEIGHT MUST GO!
HOW ABOUT THE GOLD FILLINGS IN YOUR TEETH?
DRILL 'EM OUT!
THAT CHEAP SKATE! THAT TIGHTWAD! THAT WEASLING SNAKE-IN-WOLVE'S CLOTHING!
JOCKEY ROOM
UNCA SCROOGE, LUBRICATED LIGHTNING IS SICK! HE'S FOUNDERED FROM TOO MANY OATS!
HE DOESN'T LOOK LIKE HE'LL BE ABLE TO RUN AT ALL!
GET ME A STEAM BATH QUICK— AND MY NAIL CLIPPERS!
LIGHTNING! LIGHTNING! YOU UNGRATEFUL HAY BAG! HOW CAN YOU DO THIS TO ME?
YOUR STEAM BATH IS READY, UNCLE SCROOGE!
YOU MAY BE ABLE TO SWEAT OFF FIVE POUNDS BY RACE TIME!
I CAN'T SWEAT! EVERY TIME I THINK OF THOSE DIAMONDS, I GET COLD CHILLS!

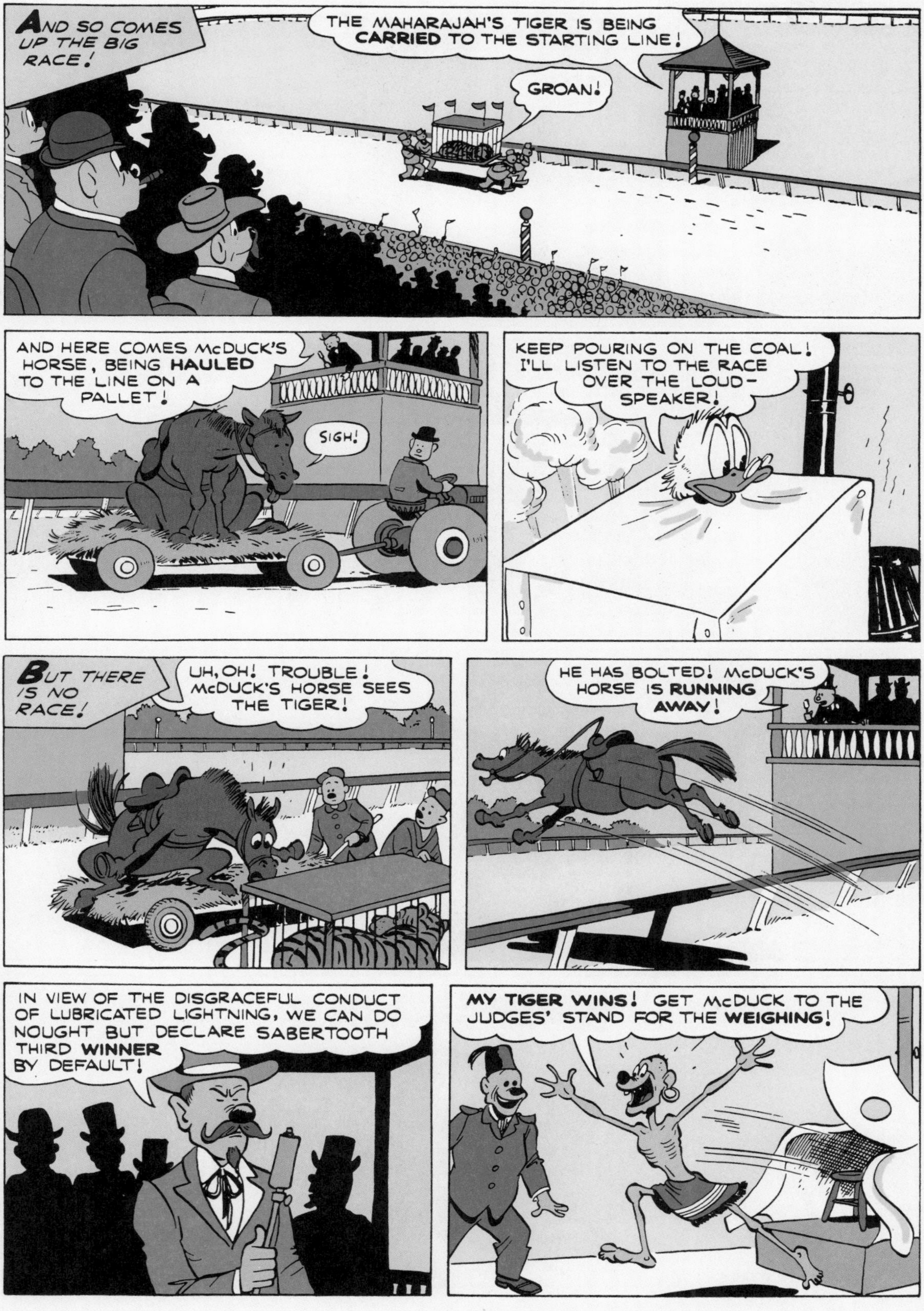
AND SO COMES UP THE BIG RACE!
THE MAHARAJAH'S TIGER IS BEING CARRIED TO THE STARTING LINE!
GROAN!
AND HERE COMES McDUCK'S HORSE, BEING HAULED TO THE LINE ON A PALLET!
SIGH!
KEEP POURING ON THE COAL! I'LL LISTEN TO THE RACE OVER THE LOUD-SPEAKER!
BUT THERE IS NO RACE!
UH, OH! TROUBLE! McDUCK'S HORSE SEES THE TIGER!
HE HAS BOLTED! McDUCK'S HORSE IS RUNNING AWAY!
IN VIEW OF THE DISGRACEFUL CONDUCT OF LUBRICATED LIGHTNING, WE CAN DO NOUGHT BUT DECLARE SABERTOOTH THIRD WINNER BY DEFAULT!
MY TIGER WINS! GET McDUCK TO THE JUDGES' STAND FOR THE WEIGHING!

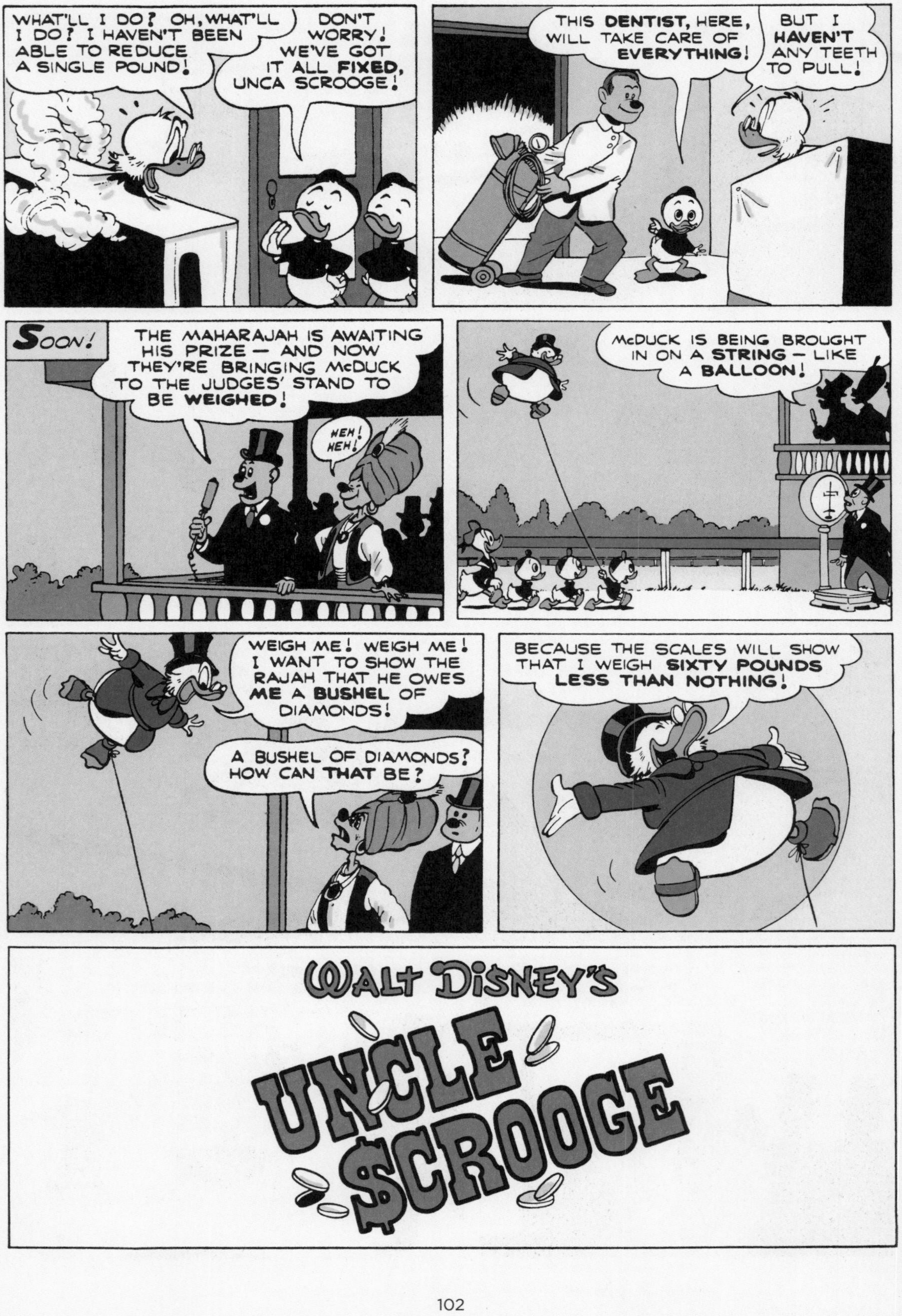
WHAT'LL I DO? OH, WHAT'LL I DO? I HAVEN'T BEEN ABLE TO REDUCE A SINGLE POUND!
DON'T WORRY! WE'VE GOT IT ALL FIXED, UNCA SCROOGE!
THIS DENTIST, HERE, WILL TAKE CARE OF EVERYTHING!
BUT I HAVEN'T ANY TEETH TO PULL!
SOON!
THE MAHARAJAH IS AWAITING HIS PRIZE — AND NOW THEY'RE BRINGING McDUCK TO THE JUDGES' STAND TO BE WEIGHED!
NEH! NEH!
McDUCK IS BEING BROUGHT IN ON A STRING — LIKE A BALLOON!
WEIGH ME! WEIGH ME! I WANT TO SHOW THE RAJAH THAT HE OWES ME A BUSHEL OF DIAMONDS!
A BUSHEL OF DIAMONDS? HOW CAN THAT BE?
BECAUSE THE SCALES WILL SHOW THAT I WEIGH SIXTY POUNDS LESS THAN NOTHING!

WALT DISNEY'S UNCLE $CROOGE

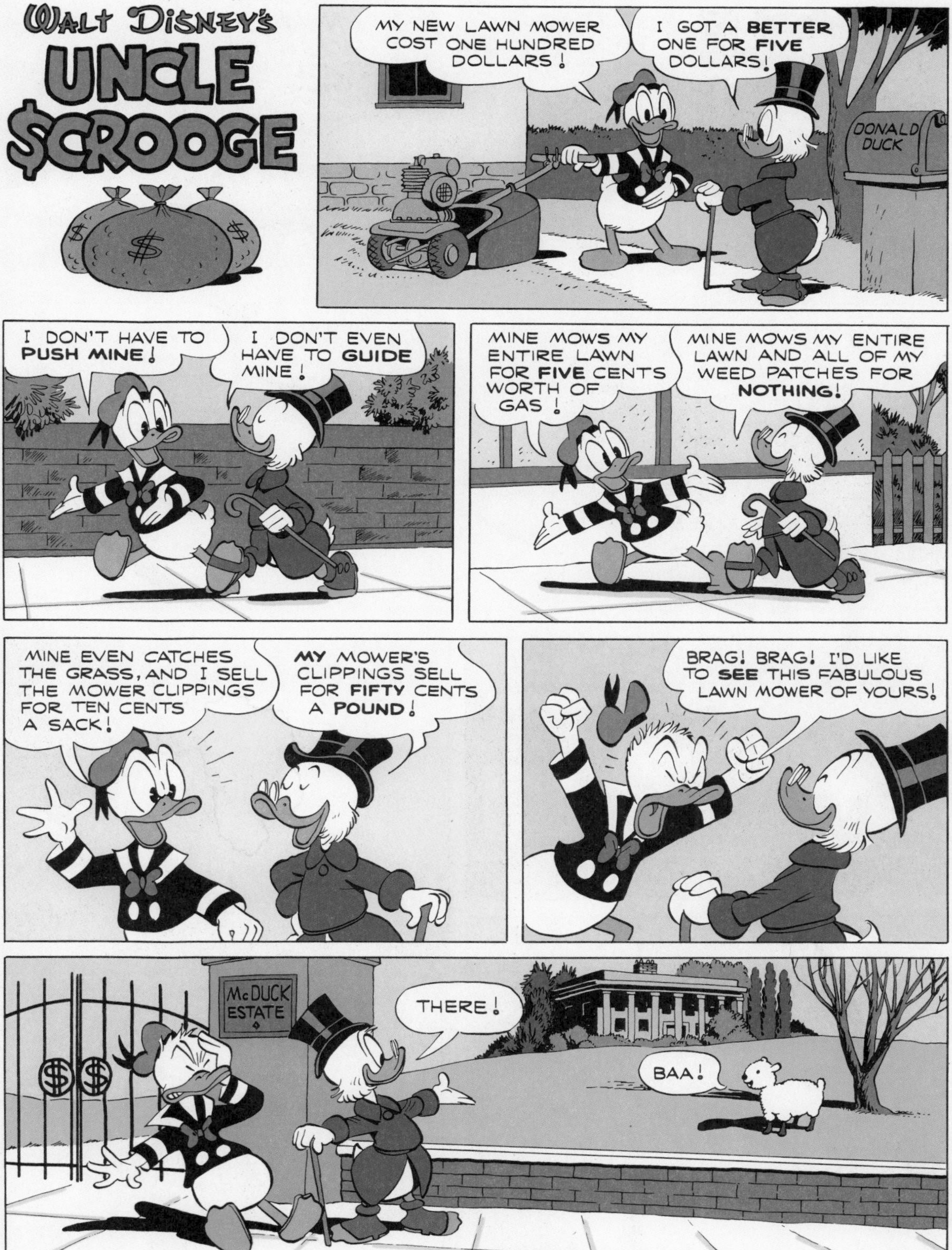
WALT DISNEY'S
UNCLE $CROOGE
MY NEW LAWN MOWER COST ONE HUNDRED DOLLARS!
I GOT A BETTER ONE FOR FIVE DOLLARS!
DONALD DUCK
I DON'T HAVE TO PUSH MINE!
I DON'T EVEN HAVE TO GUIDE MINE!
MINE MOWS MY ENTIRE LAWN FOR FIVE CENTS WORTH OF GAS!
MINE MOWS MY ENTIRE LAWN AND ALL OF MY WEED PATCHES FOR NOTHING!
MINE EVEN CATCHES THE GRASS, AND I SELL THE MOWER CLIPPINGS FOR TEN CENTS A SACK!
MY MOWER'S CLIPPINGS SELL FOR FIFTY CENTS A POUND!
BRAG! BRAG! I'D LIKE TO SEE THIS FABULOUS LAWN MOWER OF YOURS!
McDUCK ESTATE
THERE!
BAA!

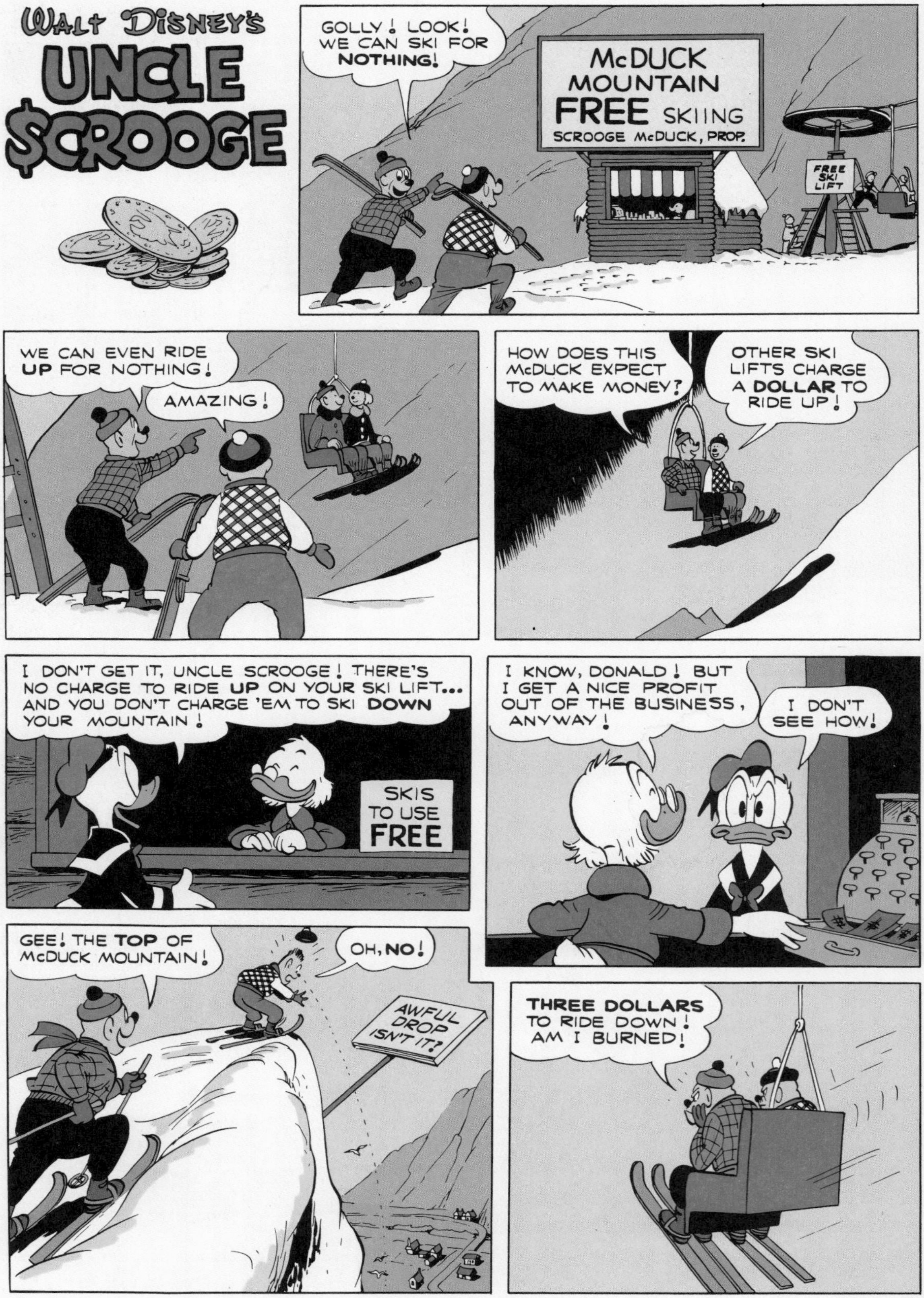

WALT DISNEY'S
UNCLE $CROOGE
GOLLY! LOOK! WE CAN SKI FOR NOTHING!
McDUCK MOUNTAIN FREE SKIING SCROOGE McDUCK, PROP.
FREE SKI LIFT
WE CAN EVEN RIDE UP FOR NOTHING!
AMAZING!
HOW DOES THIS McDUCK EXPECT TO MAKE MONEY?
OTHER SKI LIFTS CHARGE A DOLLAR TO RIDE UP!
I DON'T GET IT, UNCLE SCROOGE! THERE'S NO CHARGE TO RIDE UP ON YOUR SKI LIFT... AND YOU DON'T CHARGE 'EM TO SKI DOWN YOUR MOUNTAIN!
SKIS TO USE FREE
I KNOW, DONALD! BUT I GET A NICE PROFIT OUT OF THE BUSINESS, ANYWAY!
I DON'T SEE HOW!
GEE! THE TOP OF McDUCK MOUNTAIN!
OH, NO!
AWFUL DROP ISN'T IT?
THREE DOLLARS TO RIDE DOWN! AM I BURNED!

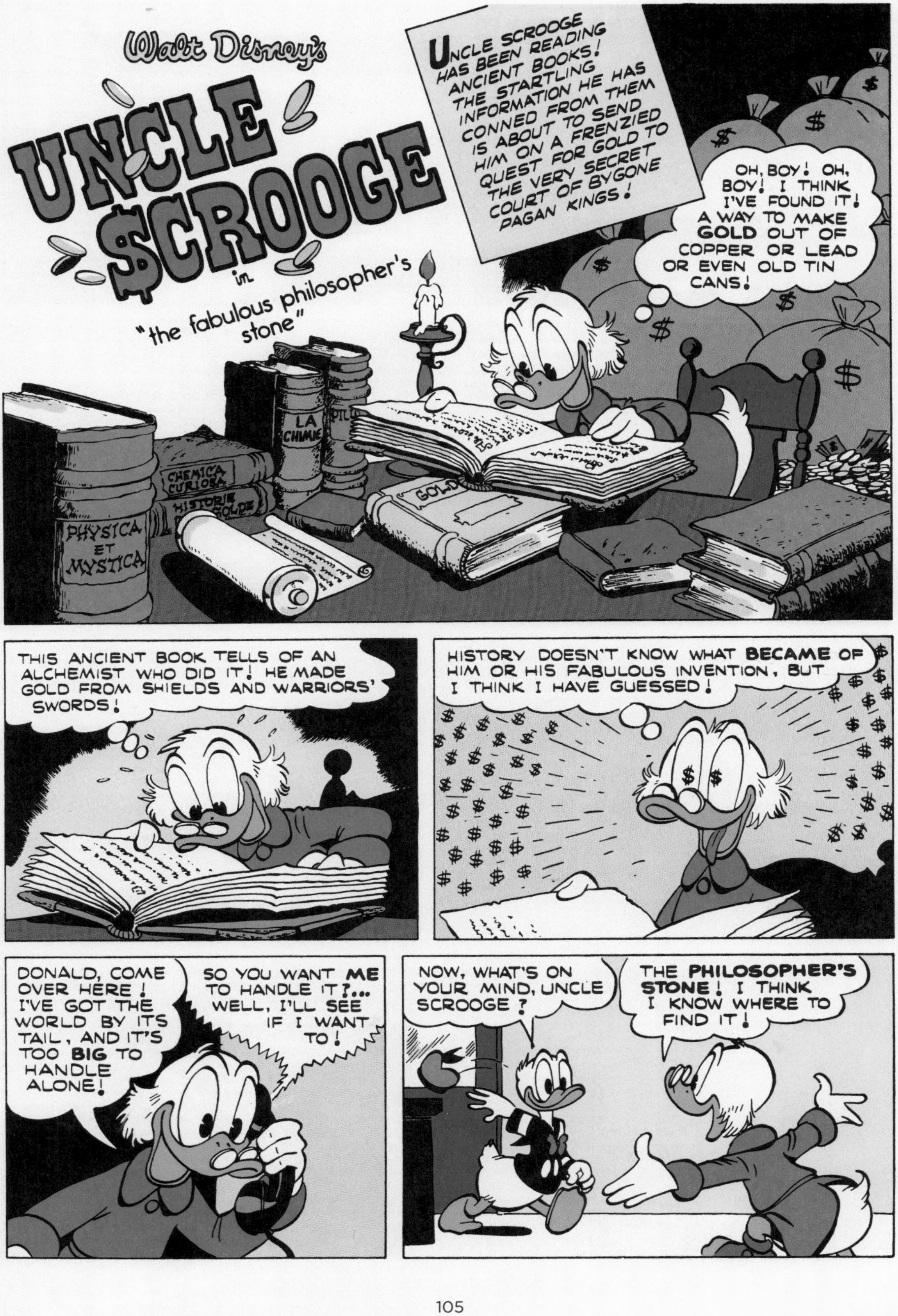

Walt Disney's
UNCLE $CROOGE
in
"the fabulous philosopher's stone"
UNCLE SCROOGE HAS BEEN READING ANCIENT BOOKS! THE STARTLING INFORMATION HE HAS CONNED FROM THEM IS ABOUT TO SEND HIM ON A FRENZIED QUEST FOR GOLD TO THE VERY SECRET COURT OF BYGONE PAGAN KINGS!
OH, BOY! OH, BOY! I THINK I'VE FOUND IT! A WAY TO MAKE GOLD OUT OF COPPER OR LEAD OR EVEN OLD TIN CANS!
LA CHIMIE
CHEMICA CURIOSA
HISTORIE
PHYSICA ET MYSTICA
GOLD
THIS ANCIENT BOOK TELLS OF AN ALCHEMIST WHO DID IT! HE MADE GOLD FROM SHIELDS AND WARRIORS' SWORDS!
HISTORY DOESN'T KNOW WHAT BECAME OF HIM OR HIS FABULOUS INVENTION, BUT I THINK I HAVE GUESSED!
DONALD, COME OVER HERE! I'VE GOT THE WORLD BY ITS TAIL, AND IT'S TOO BIG TO HANDLE ALONE!
SO YOU WANT ME TO HANDLE IT?... WELL, I'LL SEE IF I WANT TO!
NOW, WHAT'S ON YOUR MIND, UNCLE SCROOGE?
THE PHILOSOPHER'S STONE! I THINK I KNOW WHERE TO FIND IT!

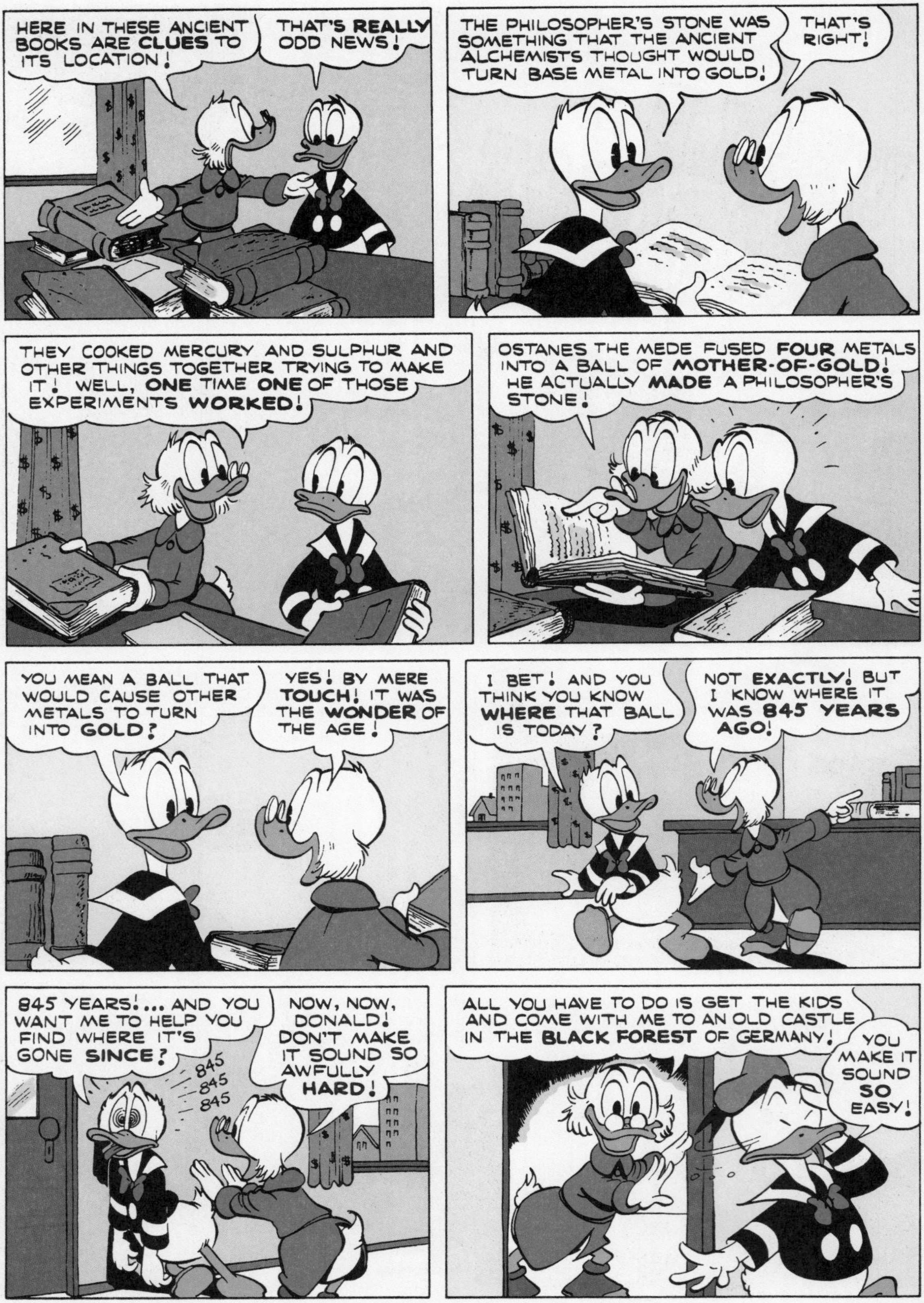
HERE IN THESE ANCIENT BOOKS ARE CLUES TO ITS LOCATION!
THAT'S REALLY ODD NEWS!
THE PHILOSOPHER'S STONE WAS SOMETHING THAT THE ANCIENT ALCHEMISTS THOUGHT WOULD TURN BASE METAL INTO GOLD!
THAT'S RIGHT!
THEY COOKED MERCURY AND SULPHUR AND OTHER THINGS TOGETHER TRYING TO MAKE IT! WELL, ONE TIME ONE OF THOSE EXPERIMENTS WORKED!
OSTANES THE MEDE FUSED FOUR METALS INTO A BALL OF MOTHER-OF-GOLD! HE ACTUALLY MADE A PHILOSOPHER'S STONE!
YOU MEAN A BALL THAT WOULD CAUSE OTHER METALS TO TURN INTO GOLD?
YES! BY MERE TOUCH! IT WAS THE WONDER OF THE AGE!
I BET! AND YOU THINK YOU KNOW WHERE THAT BALL IS TODAY?
NOT EXACTLY! BUT I KNOW WHERE IT WAS 845 YEARS AGO!
845 YEARS!... AND YOU WANT ME TO HELP YOU FIND WHERE IT'S GONE SINCE?
845
845
845
NOW, NOW, DONALD! DON'T MAKE IT SOUND SO AWFULLY HARD!
ALL YOU HAVE TO DO IS GET THE KIDS AND COME WITH ME TO AN OLD CASTLE IN THE BLACK FOREST OF GERMANY!
YOU MAKE IT SOUND SO EASY!

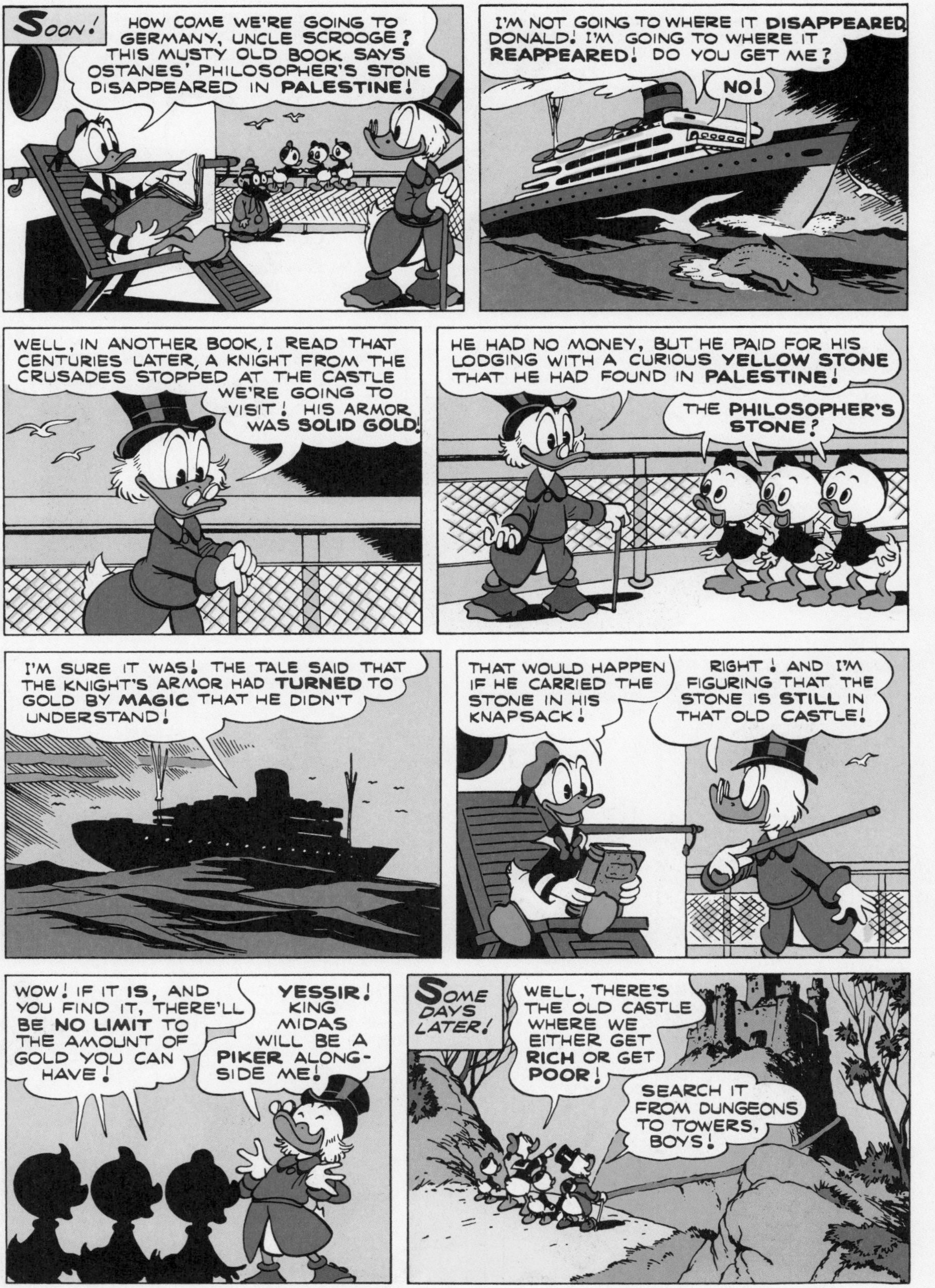
SOON!
HOW COME WE'RE GOING TO GERMANY, UNCLE SCROOGE? THIS MUSTY OLD BOOK SAYS OSTANES' PHILOSOPHER'S STONE DISAPPEARED IN PALESTINE!
I'M NOT GOING TO WHERE IT DISAPPEARED, DONALD! I'M GOING TO WHERE IT REAPPEARED! DO YOU GET ME?
NO!
WELL, IN ANOTHER BOOK, I READ THAT CENTURIES LATER, A KNIGHT FROM THE CRUSADES STOPPED AT THE CASTLE WE'RE GOING TO VISIT! HIS ARMOR WAS SOLID GOLD!
HE HAD NO MONEY, BUT HE PAID FOR HIS LODGING WITH A CURIOUS YELLOW STONE THAT HE HAD FOUND IN PALESTINE!
THE PHILOSOPHER'S STONE?
I'M SURE IT WAS! THE TALE SAID THAT THE KNIGHT'S ARMOR HAD TURNED TO GOLD BY MAGIC THAT HE DIDN'T UNDERSTAND!
THAT WOULD HAPPEN IF HE CARRIED THE STONE IN HIS KNAPSACK!
RIGHT! AND I'M FIGURING THAT THE STONE IS STILL IN THAT OLD CASTLE!
WOW! IF IT IS, AND YOU FIND IT, THERE'LL BE NO LIMIT TO THE AMOUNT OF GOLD YOU CAN HAVE!
YESSIR! KING MIDAS WILL BE A PIKER ALONGSIDE ME!
SOME DAYS LATER!
WELL, THERE'S THE OLD CASTLE WHERE WE EITHER GET RICH OR GET POOR!
SEARCH IT FROM DUNGEONS TO TOWERS, BOYS!

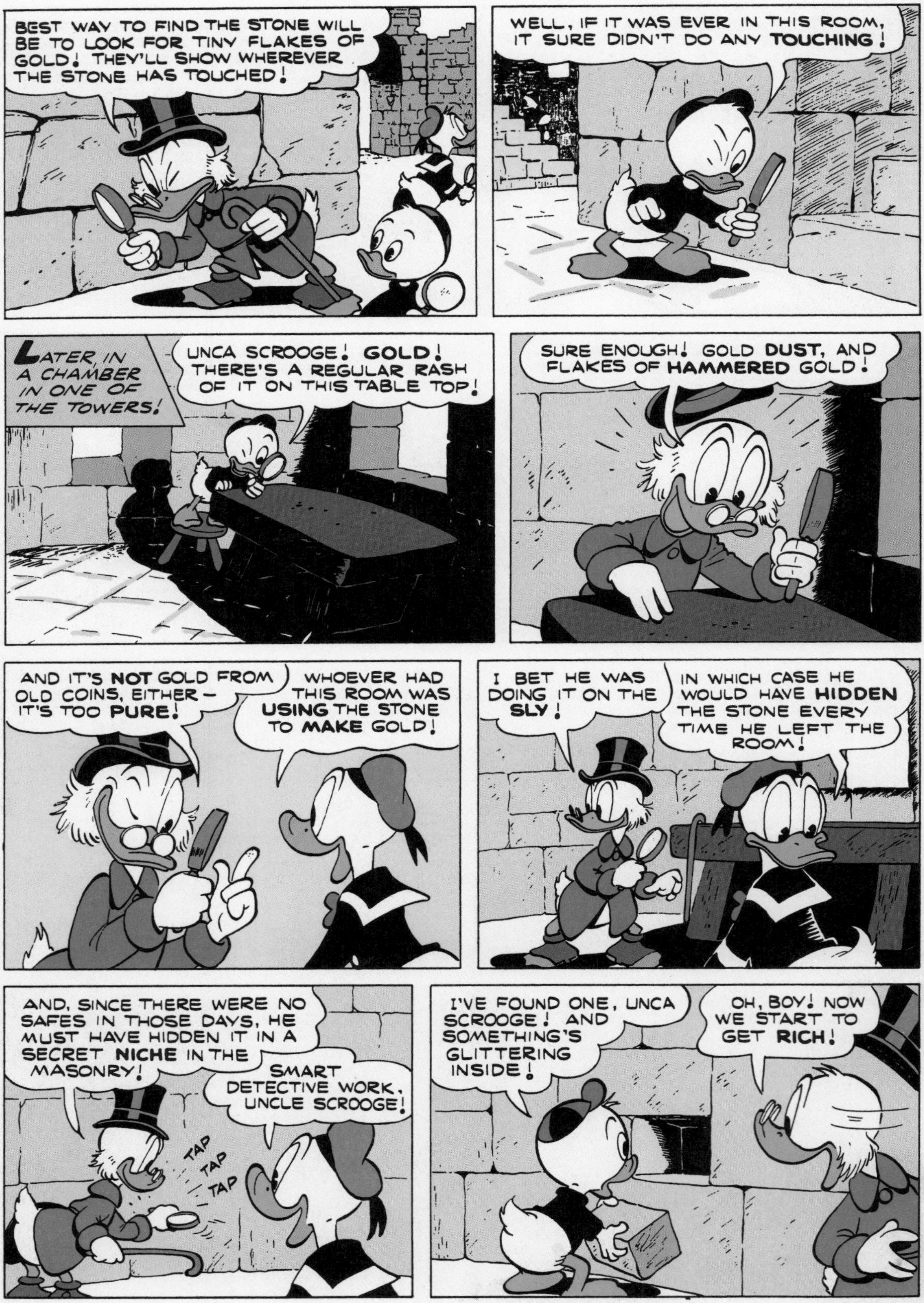
BEST WAY TO FIND THE STONE WILL BE TO LOOK FOR TINY FLAKES OF GOLD! THEY'LL SHOW WHEREVER THE STONE HAS TOUCHED!
WELL, IF IT WAS EVER IN THIS ROOM, IT SURE DIDN'T DO ANY TOUCHING!
LATER, IN A CHAMBER IN ONE OF THE TOWERS!
UNCA SCROOGE! GOLD! THERE'S A REGULAR RASH OF IT ON THIS TABLE TOP!
SURE ENOUGH! GOLD DUST, AND FLAKES OF HAMMERED GOLD!
AND IT'S NOT GOLD FROM OLD COINS, EITHER— IT'S TOO PURE!
WHOEVER HAD THIS ROOM WAS USING THE STONE TO MAKE GOLD!
I BET HE WAS DOING IT ON THE SLY!
IN WHICH CASE HE WOULD HAVE HIDDEN THE STONE EVERY TIME HE LEFT THE ROOM!
AND, SINCE THERE WERE NO SAFES IN THOSE DAYS, HE MUST HAVE HIDDEN IT IN A SECRET NICHE IN THE MASONRY!
SMART DETECTIVE WORK, UNCLE SCROOGE!
TAP
TAP
TAP
I'VE FOUND ONE, UNCA SCROOGE! AND SOMETHING'S GLITTERING INSIDE!
OH, BOY! NOW WE START TO GET RICH!

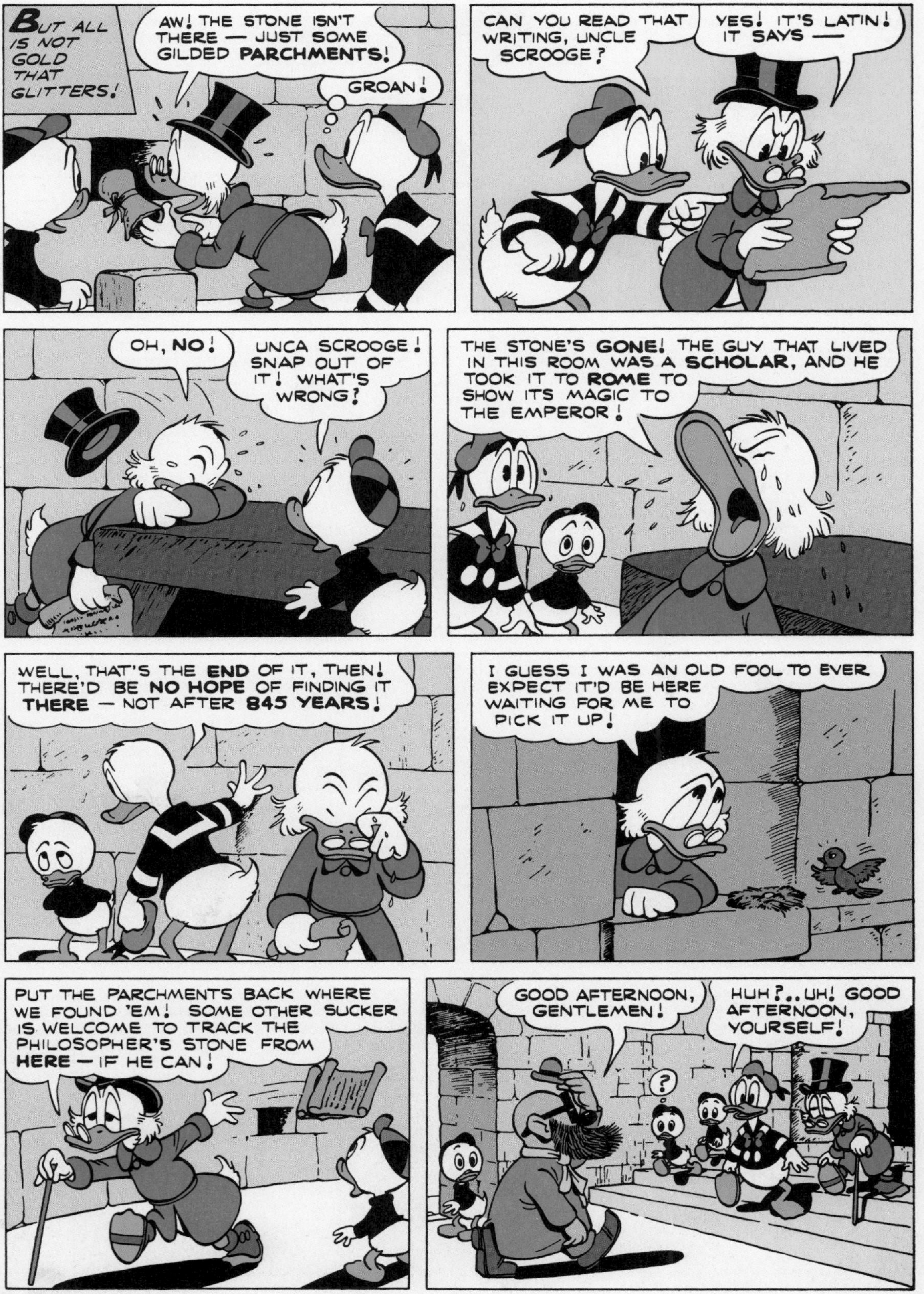
BUT ALL IS NOT GOLD THAT GLITTERS!
AW! THE STONE ISN'T THERE — JUST SOME GILDED PARCHMENTS!
GROAN!
CAN YOU READ THAT WRITING, UNCLE SCROOGE?
YES! IT'S LATIN! IT SAYS —
OH, NO!
UNCA SCROOGE! SNAP OUT OF IT! WHAT'S WRONG?
THE STONE'S GONE! THE GUY THAT LIVED IN THIS ROOM WAS A SCHOLAR, AND HE TOOK IT TO ROME TO SHOW ITS MAGIC TO THE EMPEROR!
WELL, THAT'S THE END OF IT, THEN! THERE'D BE NO HOPE OF FINDING IT THERE — NOT AFTER 845 YEARS!
I GUESS I WAS AN OLD FOOL TO EVER EXPECT IT'D BE HERE WAITING FOR ME TO PICK IT UP!
PUT THE PARCHMENTS BACK WHERE WE FOUND 'EM! SOME OTHER SUCKER IS WELCOME TO TRACK THE PHILOSOPHER'S STONE FROM HERE — IF HE CAN!
GOOD AFTERNOON, GENTLEMEN!
?
HUH?..UH! GOOD AFTERNOON, YOURSELF!

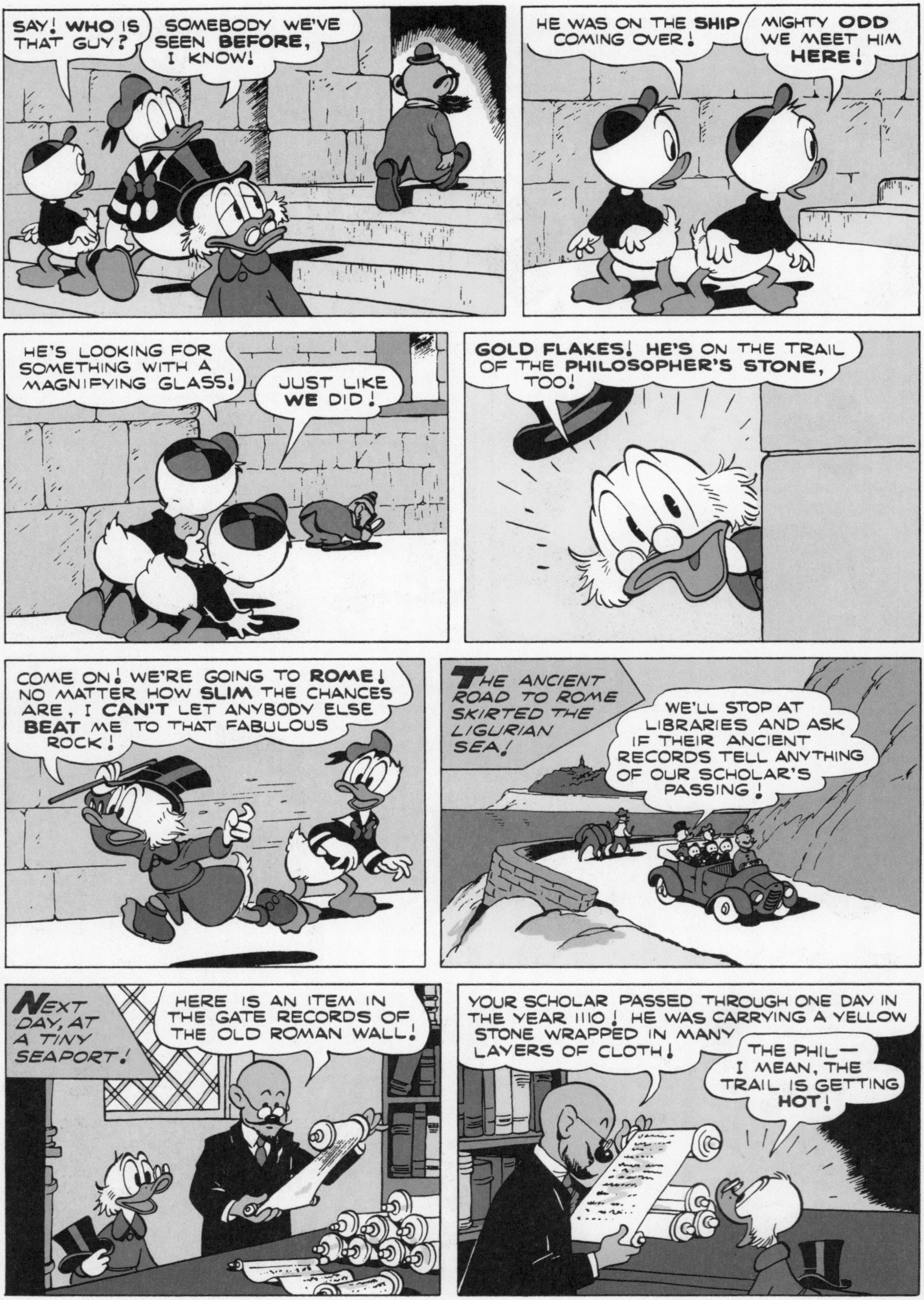
SAY! WHO IS THAT GUY?
SOMEBODY WE'VE SEEN BEFORE, I KNOW!
HE WAS ON THE SHIP COMING OVER!
MIGHTY ODD WE MEET HIM HERE!
HE'S LOOKING FOR SOMETHING WITH A MAGNIFYING GLASS!
JUST LIKE WE DID!
GOLD FLAKES! HE'S ON THE TRAIL OF THE PHILOSOPHER'S STONE, TOO!
COME ON! WE'RE GOING TO ROME! NO MATTER HOW SLIM THE CHANCES ARE, I CAN'T LET ANYBODY ELSE BEAT ME TO THAT FABULOUS ROCK!
THE ANCIENT ROAD TO ROME SKIRTED THE LIGURIAN SEA!
WE'LL STOP AT LIBRARIES AND ASK IF THEIR ANCIENT RECORDS TELL ANYTHING OF OUR SCHOLAR'S PASSING!
NEXT DAY, AT A TINY SEAPORT!
HERE IS AN ITEM IN THE GATE RECORDS OF THE OLD ROMAN WALL!
YOUR SCHOLAR PASSED THROUGH ONE DAY IN THE YEAR 1110! HE WAS CARRYING A YELLOW STONE WRAPPED IN MANY LAYERS OF CLOTH!
THE PHIL— I MEAN, THE TRAIL IS GETTING HOT!

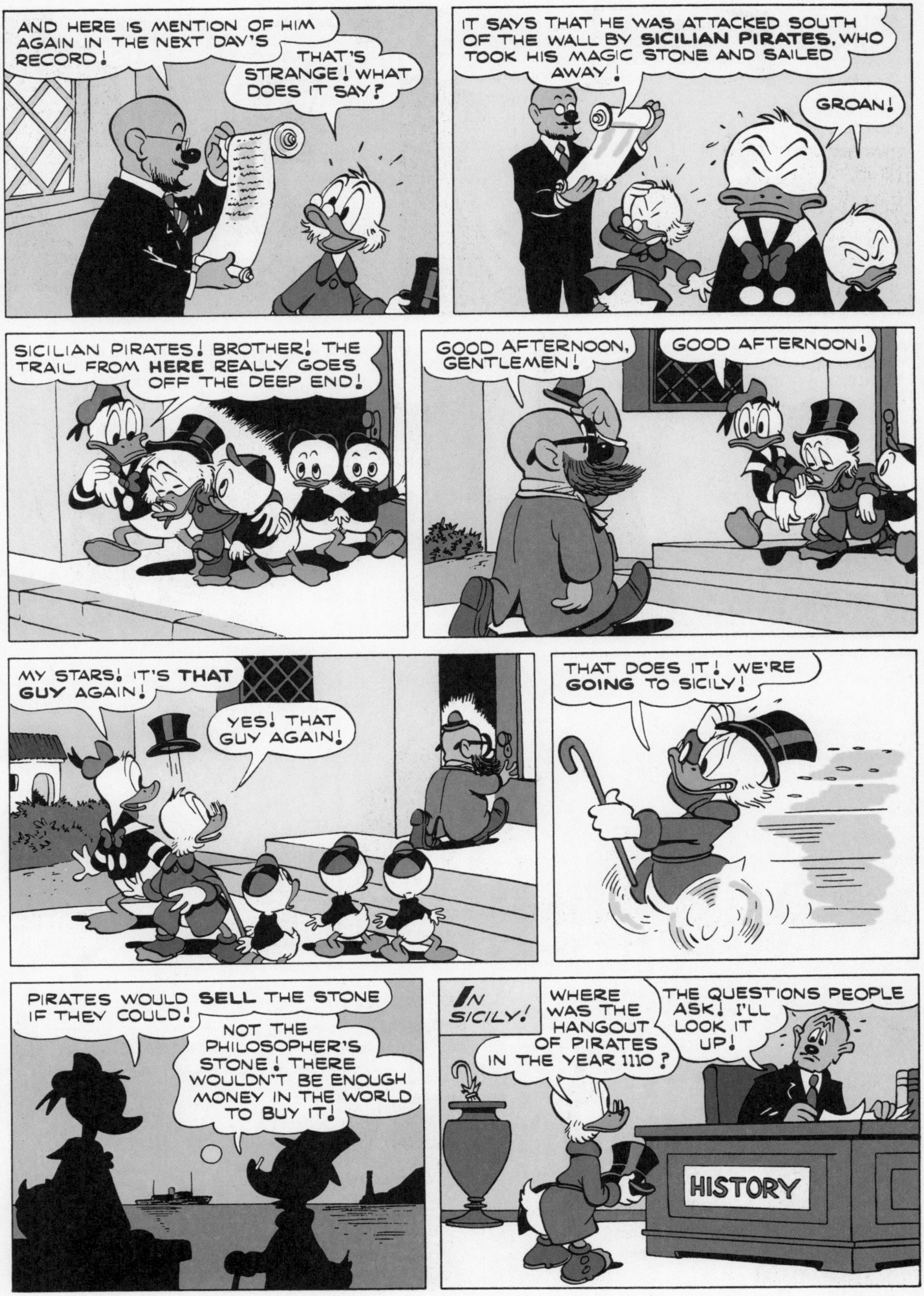
AND HERE IS MENTION OF HIM AGAIN IN THE NEXT DAY'S RECORD!
THAT'S STRANGE! WHAT DOES IT SAY?
IT SAYS THAT HE WAS ATTACKED SOUTH OF THE WALL BY SICILIAN PIRATES, WHO TOOK HIS MAGIC STONE AND SAILED AWAY!
GROAN!
SICILIAN PIRATES! BROTHER! THE TRAIL FROM HERE REALLY GOES OFF THE DEEP END!
GOOD AFTERNOON, GENTLEMEN!
GOOD AFTERNOON!
MY STARS! IT'S THAT GUY AGAIN!
YES! THAT GUY AGAIN!
THAT DOES IT! WE'RE GOING TO SICILY!
PIRATES WOULD SELL THE STONE IF THEY COULD!
NOT THE PHILOSOPHER'S STONE! THERE WOULDN'T BE ENOUGH MONEY IN THE WORLD TO BUY IT!
IN SICILY!
WHERE WAS THE HANGOUT OF PIRATES IN THE YEAR 1110?
THE QUESTIONS PEOPLE ASK! I'LL LOOK IT UP!
HISTORY

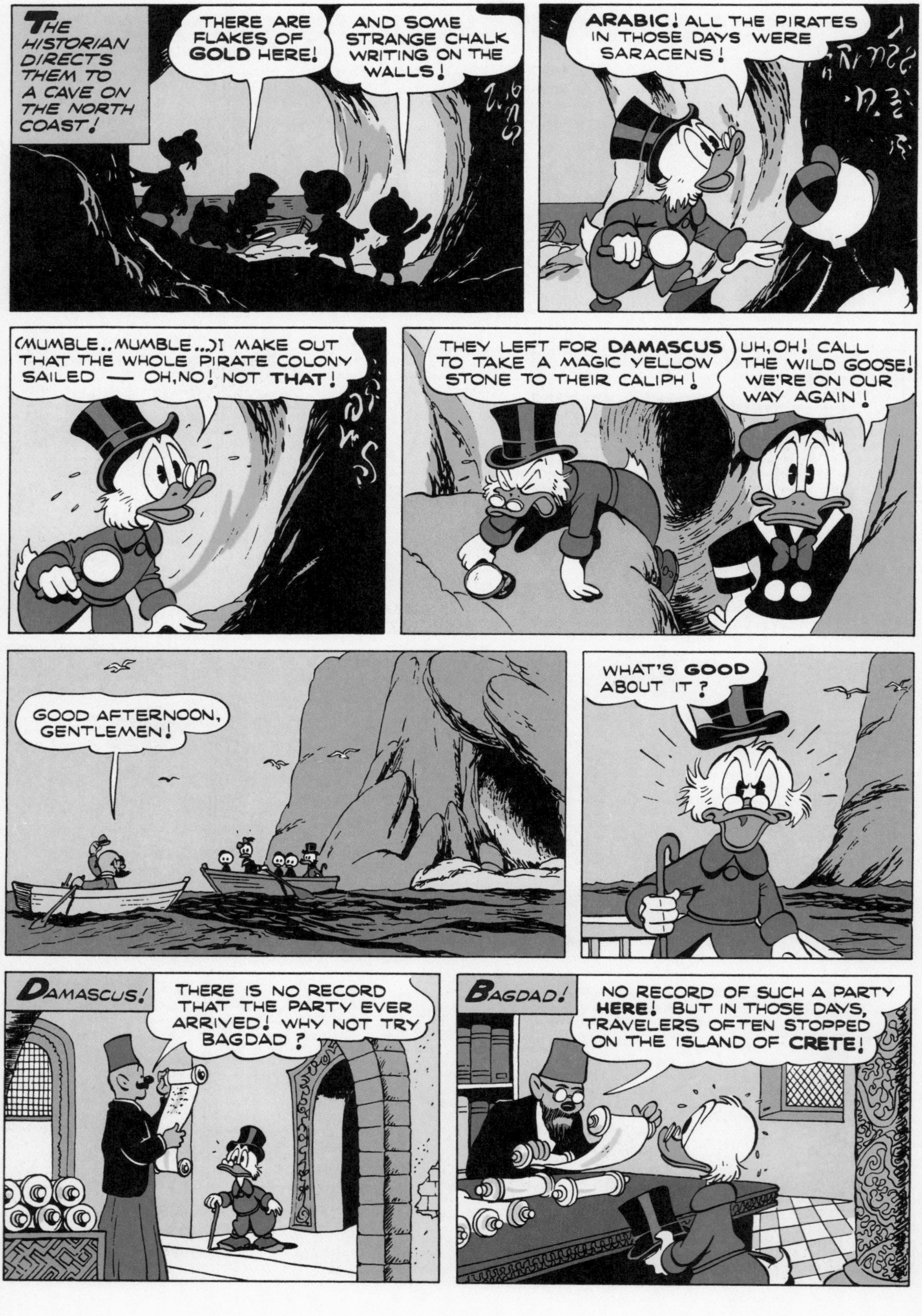
THE HISTORIAN DIRECTS THEM TO A CAVE ON THE NORTH COAST!
THERE ARE FLAKES OF GOLD HERE!
AND SOME STRANGE CHALK WRITING ON THE WALLS!
ARABIC! ALL THE PIRATES IN THOSE DAYS WERE SARACENS!
(MUMBLE.. MUMBLE...) I MAKE OUT THAT THE WHOLE PIRATE COLONY SAILED — OH, NO! NOT THAT!
THEY LEFT FOR DAMASCUS TO TAKE A MAGIC YELLOW STONE TO THEIR CALIPH!
UH, OH! CALL THE WILD GOOSE! WE'RE ON OUR WAY AGAIN!
GOOD AFTERNOON, GENTLEMEN!
WHAT'S GOOD ABOUT IT?
DAMASCUS!
THERE IS NO RECORD THAT THE PARTY EVER ARRIVED! WHY NOT TRY BAGDAD?
BAGDAD!
NO RECORD OF SUCH A PARTY HERE! BUT IN THOSE DAYS, TRAVELERS OFTEN STOPPED ON THE ISLAND OF CRETE!

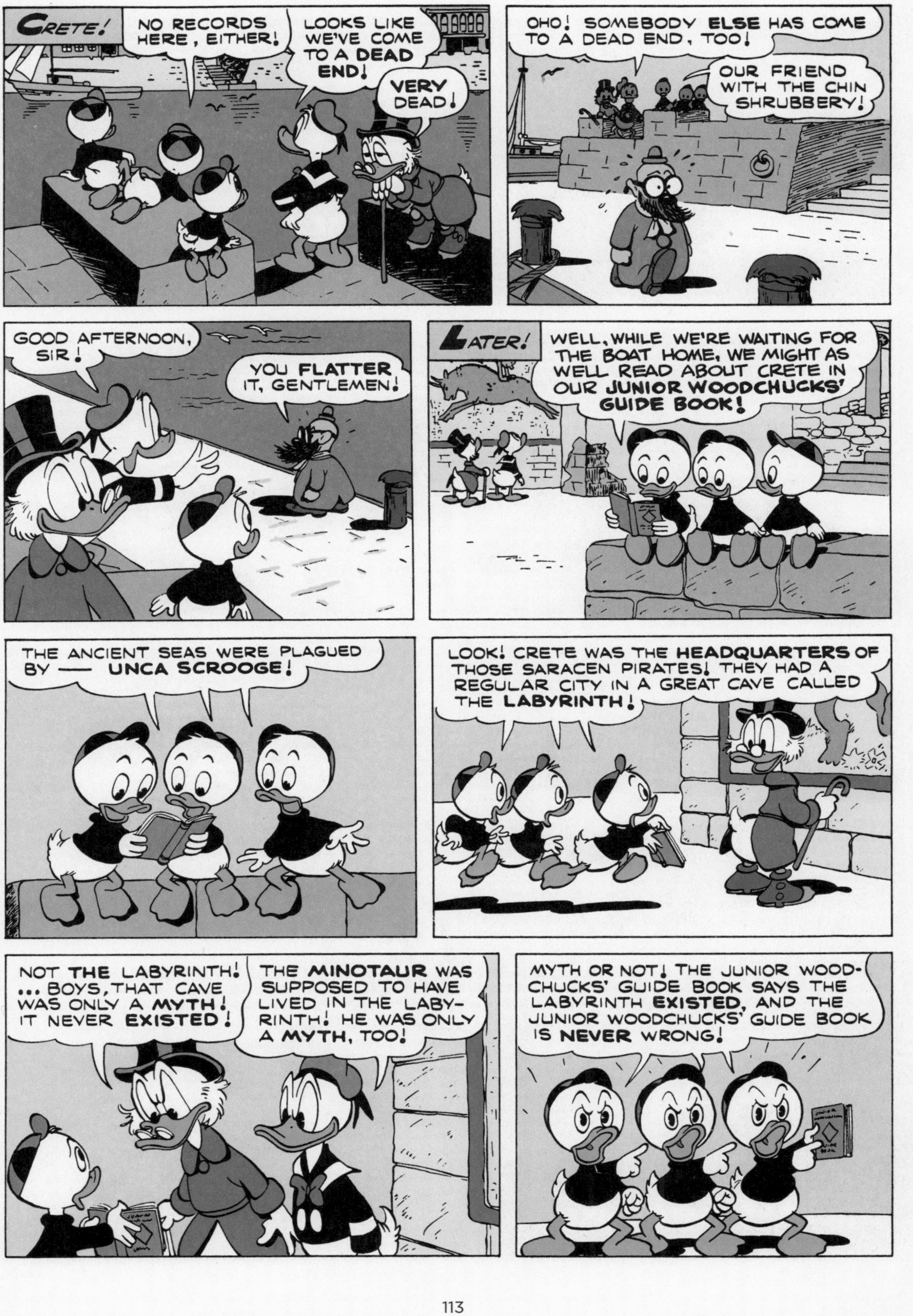
CRETE!
NO RECORDS HERE, EITHER!
LOOKS LIKE WE'VE COME TO A DEAD END!
VERY DEAD!
OHO! SOMEBODY ELSE HAS COME TO A DEAD END, TOO!
OUR FRIEND WITH THE CHIN SHRUBBERY!
GOOD AFTERNOON, SIR!
YOU FLATTER IT, GENTLEMEN!
LATER!
WELL, WHILE WE'RE WAITING FOR THE BOAT HOME, WE MIGHT AS WELL READ ABOUT CRETE IN OUR JUNIOR WOODCHUCKS' GUIDE BOOK!
THE ANCIENT SEAS WERE PLAGUED BY — UNCA SCROOGE!
LOOK! CRETE WAS THE HEADQUARTERS OF THOSE SARACEN PIRATES! THEY HAD A REGULAR CITY IN A GREAT CAVE CALLED THE LABYRINTH!
NOT THE LABYRINTH! ... BOYS, THAT CAVE WAS ONLY A MYTH! IT NEVER EXISTED!
THE MINOTAUR WAS SUPPOSED TO HAVE LIVED IN THE LABYRINTH! HE WAS ONLY A MYTH, TOO!
MYTH OR NOT! THE JUNIOR WOODCHUCKS' GUIDE BOOK SAYS THE LABYRINTH EXISTED, AND THE JUNIOR WOODCHUCKS' GUIDE BOOK IS NEVER WRONG!

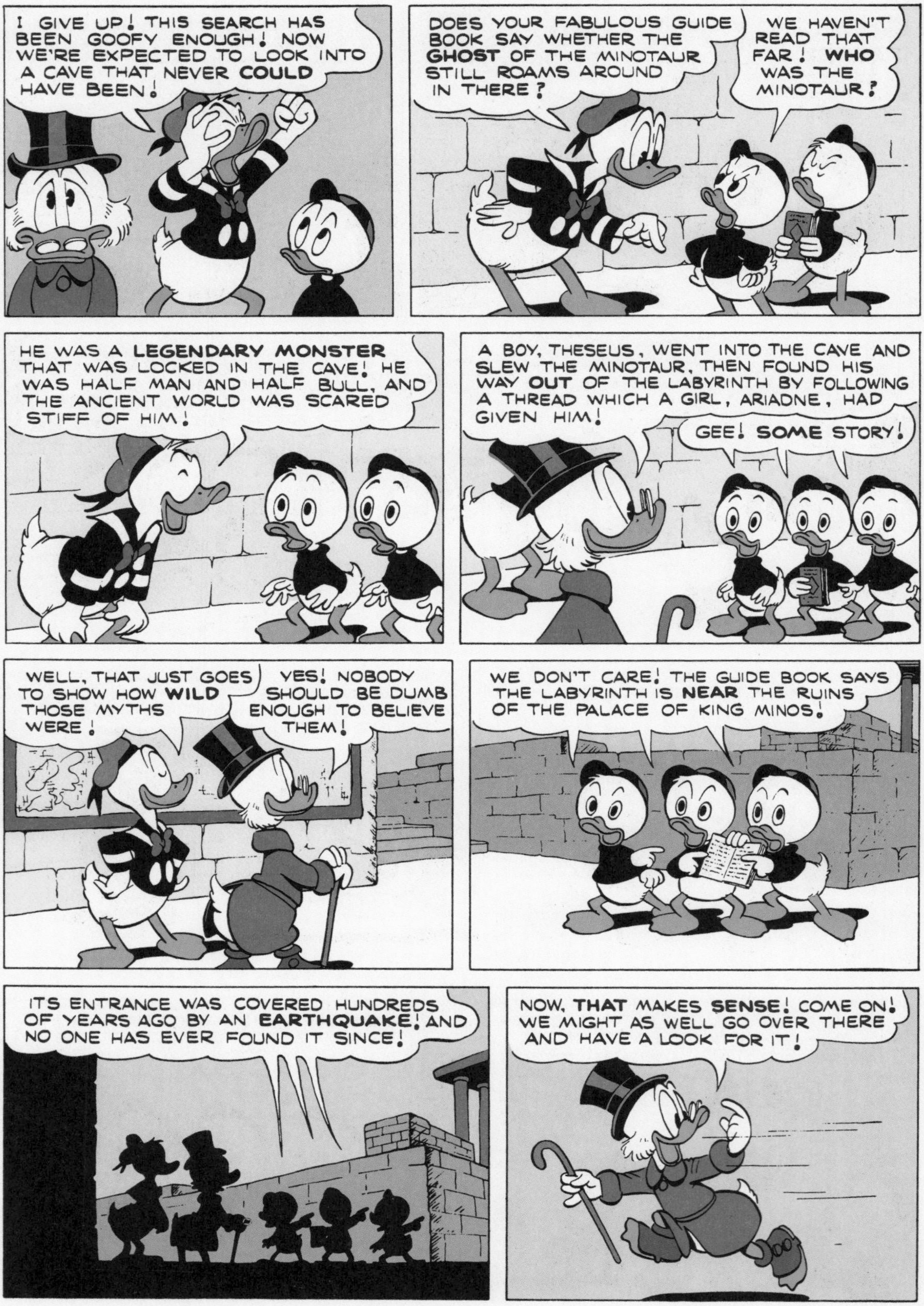
I GIVE UP! THIS SEARCH HAS BEEN GOOFY ENOUGH! NOW WE'RE EXPECTED TO LOOK INTO A CAVE THAT NEVER COULD HAVE BEEN!
DOES YOUR FABULOUS GUIDE BOOK SAY WHETHER THE GHOST OF THE MINOTAUR STILL ROAMS AROUND IN THERE?
WE HAVEN'T READ THAT FAR! WHO WAS THE MINOTAUR?
HE WAS A LEGENDARY MONSTER THAT WAS LOCKED IN THE CAVE! HE WAS HALF MAN AND HALF BULL, AND THE ANCIENT WORLD WAS SCARED STIFF OF HIM!
A BOY, THESEUS, WENT INTO THE CAVE AND SLEW THE MINOTAUR, THEN FOUND HIS WAY OUT OF THE LABYRINTH BY FOLLOWING A THREAD WHICH A GIRL, ARIADNE, HAD GIVEN HIM!
GEE! SOME STORY!
WELL, THAT JUST GOES TO SHOW HOW WILD THOSE MYTHS WERE!
YES! NOBODY SHOULD BE DUMB ENOUGH TO BELIEVE THEM!
WE DON'T CARE! THE GUIDE BOOK SAYS THE LABYRINTH IS NEAR THE RUINS OF THE PALACE OF KING MINOS!
ITS ENTRANCE WAS COVERED HUNDREDS OF YEARS AGO BY AN EARTHQUAKE! AND NO ONE HAS EVER FOUND IT SINCE!
NOW, THAT MAKES SENSE! COME ON! WE MIGHT AS WELL GO OVER THERE AND HAVE A LOOK FOR IT!

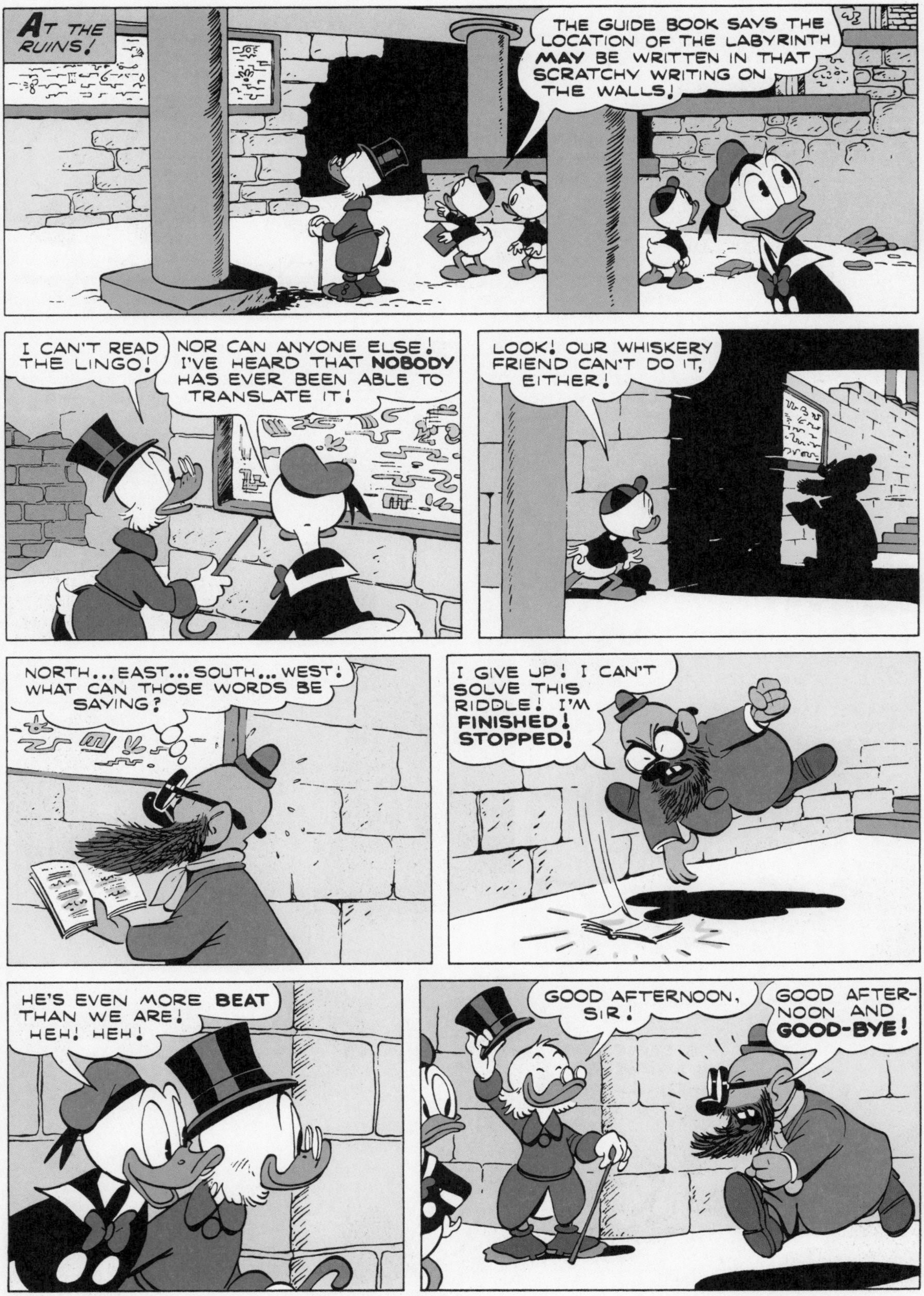

AT THE RUINS!
THE GUIDE BOOK SAYS THE LOCATION OF THE LABYRINTH **MAY** BE WRITTEN IN THAT SCRATCHY WRITING ON THE WALLS!
I CAN'T READ THE LINGO!
NOR CAN ANYONE ELSE! I'VE HEARD THAT **NOBODY** HAS EVER BEEN ABLE TO TRANSLATE IT!
LOOK! OUR WHISKERY FRIEND CAN'T DO IT, EITHER!
NORTH... EAST... SOUTH... WEST! WHAT CAN THOSE WORDS BE SAYING?
I GIVE UP! I CAN'T SOLVE THIS RIDDLE! I'M **FINISHED! STOPPED!**
HE'S EVEN MORE **BEAT** THAN WE ARE! HEH! HEH!
GOOD AFTERNOON, SIR!
GOOD AFTER-NOON AND **GOOD-BYE!**

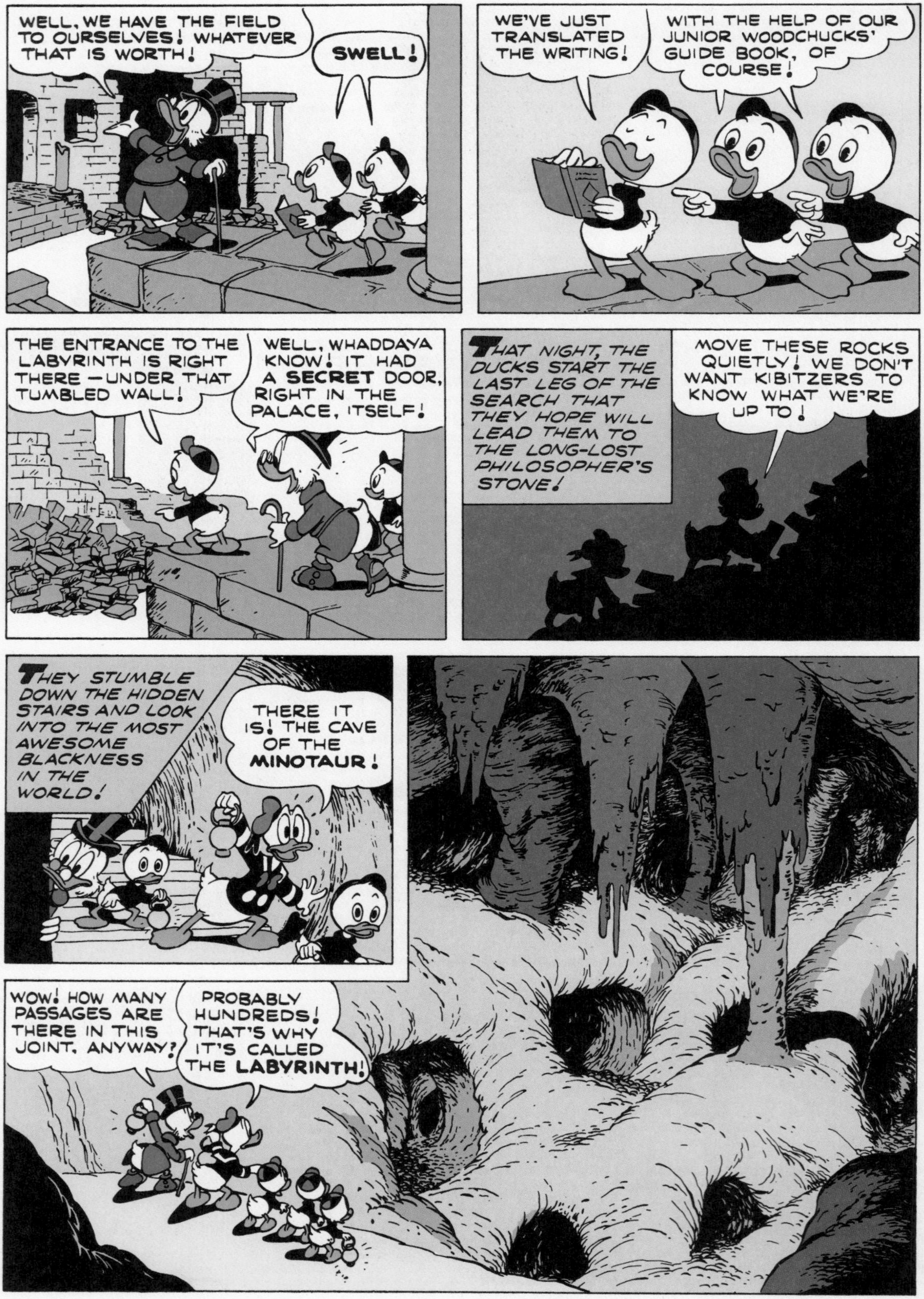

WELL, WE HAVE THE FIELD TO OURSELVES! WHATEVER THAT IS WORTH!
SWELL!
WE'VE JUST TRANSLATED THE WRITING!
WITH THE HELP OF OUR JUNIOR WOODCHUCKS' GUIDE BOOK, OF COURSE!
THE ENTRANCE TO THE LABYRINTH IS RIGHT THERE—UNDER THAT TUMBLED WALL!
WELL, WHADDAYA KNOW! IT HAD A SECRET DOOR, RIGHT IN THE PALACE, ITSELF!
THAT NIGHT, THE DUCKS START THE LAST LEG OF THE SEARCH THAT THEY HOPE WILL LEAD THEM TO THE LONG-LOST PHILOSOPHER'S STONE!
MOVE THESE ROCKS QUIETLY! WE DON'T WANT KIBITZERS TO KNOW WHAT WE'RE UP TO!
THEY STUMBLE DOWN THE HIDDEN STAIRS AND LOOK INTO THE MOST AWESOME BLACKNESS IN THE WORLD!
THERE IT IS! THE CAVE OF THE MINOTAUR!
WOW! HOW MANY PASSAGES ARE THERE IN THIS JOINT, ANYWAY?
PROBABLY HUNDREDS! THAT'S WHY IT'S CALLED THE LABYRINTH!

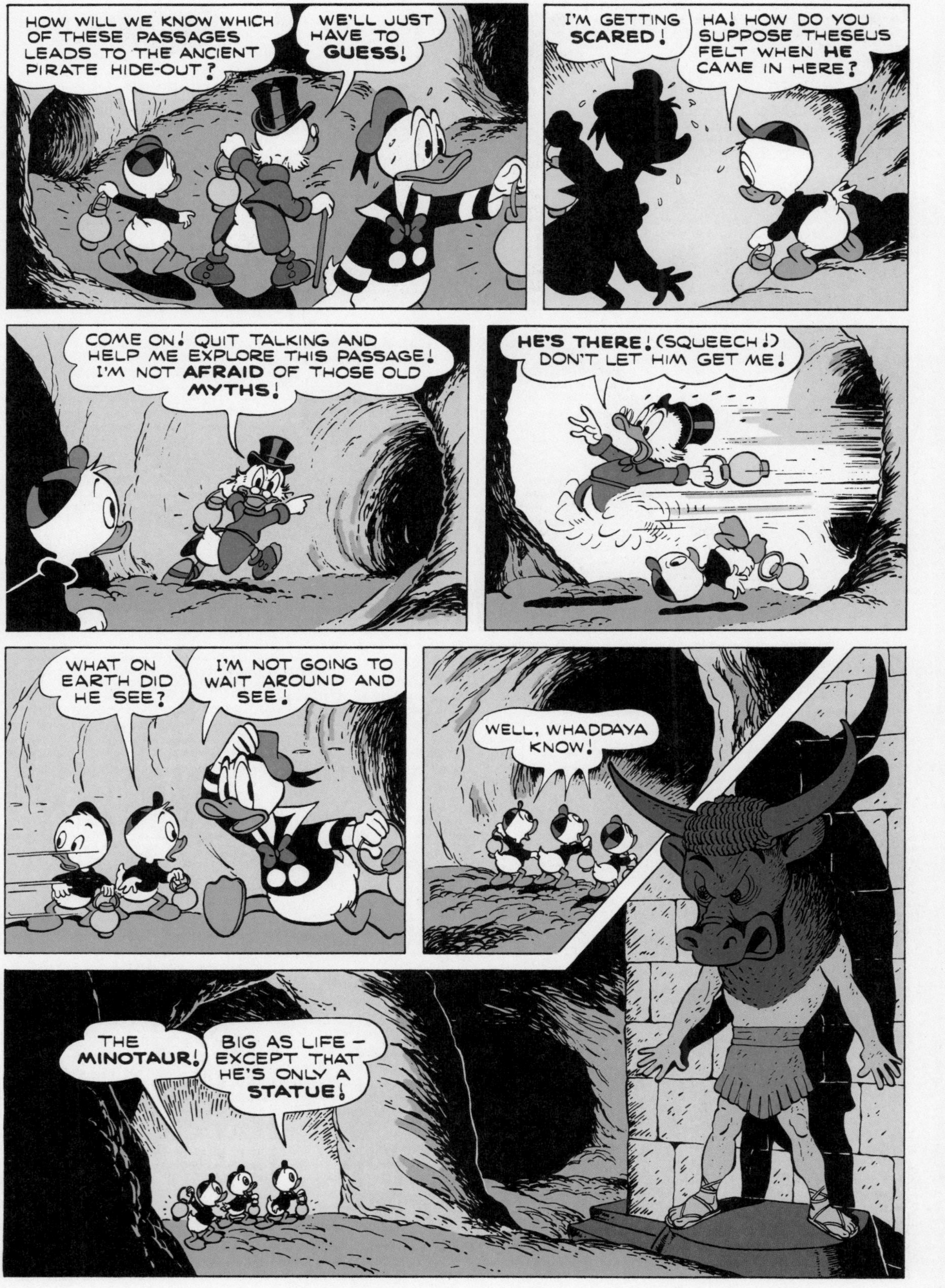
HOW WILL WE KNOW WHICH OF THESE PASSAGES LEADS TO THE ANCIENT PIRATE HIDE-OUT?
WE'LL JUST HAVE TO GUESS!
I'M GETTING SCARED!
HA! HOW DO YOU SUPPOSE THESEUS FELT WHEN HE CAME IN HERE?
COME ON! QUIT TALKING AND HELP ME EXPLORE THIS PASSAGE! I'M NOT AFRAID OF THOSE OLD MYTHS!
HE'S THERE! (SQUEECH!) DON'T LET HIM GET ME!
WHAT ON EARTH DID HE SEE?
I'M NOT GOING TO WAIT AROUND AND SEE!
WELL, WHADDAYA KNOW!
THE MINOTAUR!
BIG AS LIFE — EXCEPT THAT HE'S ONLY A STATUE!

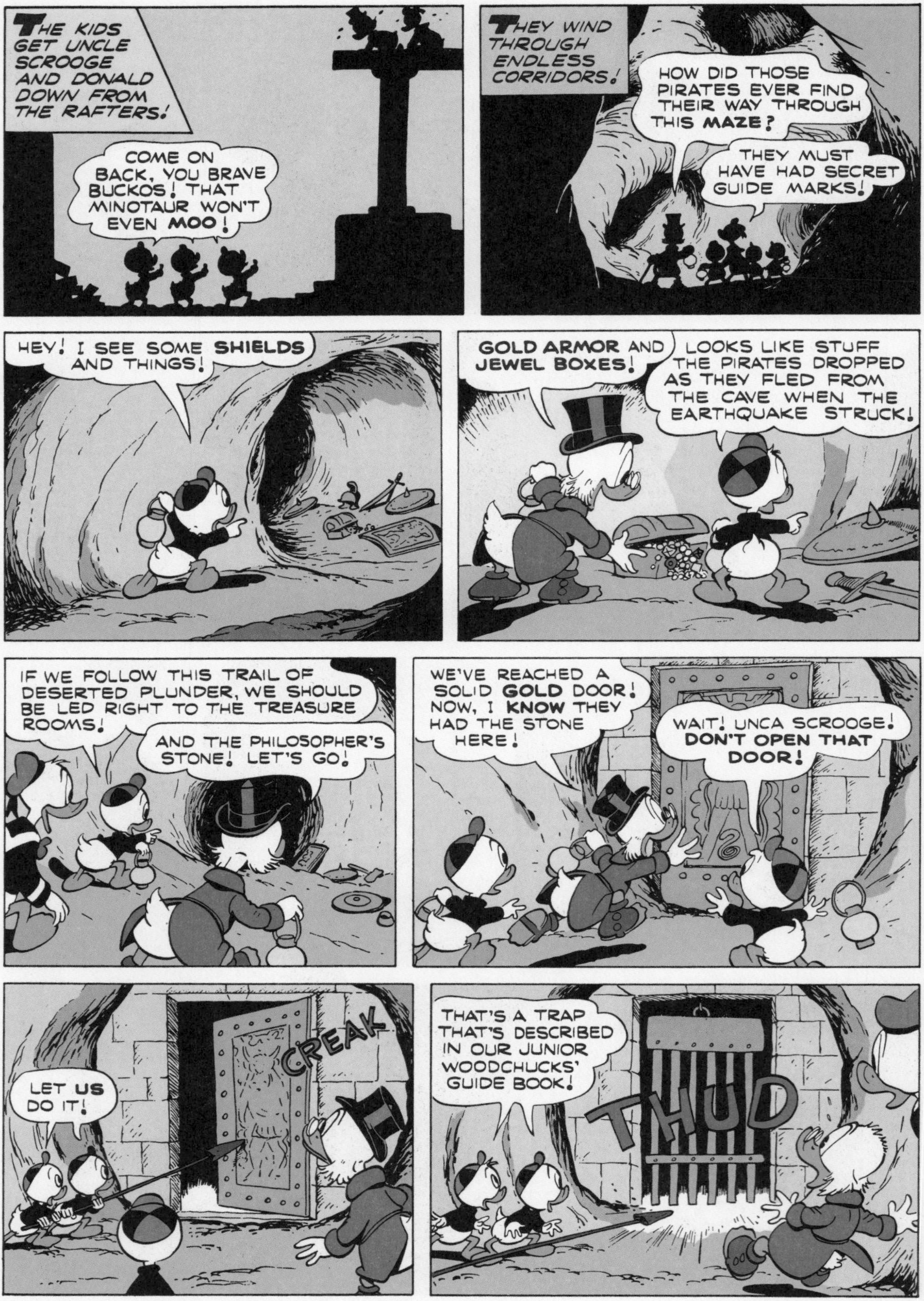
THE KIDS GET UNCLE SCROOGE AND DONALD DOWN FROM THE RAFTERS!
COME ON BACK, YOU BRAVE BUCKOS! THAT MINOTAUR WON'T EVEN MOO!
THEY WIND THROUGH ENDLESS CORRIDORS!
HOW DID THOSE PIRATES EVER FIND THEIR WAY THROUGH THIS MAZE?
THEY MUST HAVE HAD SECRET GUIDE MARKS!
HEY! I SEE SOME SHIELDS AND THINGS!
GOLD ARMOR AND JEWEL BOXES!
LOOKS LIKE STUFF THE PIRATES DROPPED AS THEY FLED FROM THE CAVE WHEN THE EARTHQUAKE STRUCK!
IF WE FOLLOW THIS TRAIL OF DESERTED PLUNDER, WE SHOULD BE LED RIGHT TO THE TREASURE ROOMS!
AND THE PHILOSOPHER'S STONE! LET'S GO!
WE'VE REACHED A SOLID GOLD DOOR! NOW, I KNOW THEY HAD THE STONE HERE!
WAIT! UNCA SCROOGE! DON'T OPEN THAT DOOR!
LET US DO IT!
CREAK
THAT'S A TRAP THAT'S DESCRIBED IN OUR JUNIOR WOODCHUCKS' GUIDE BOOK!
THUD

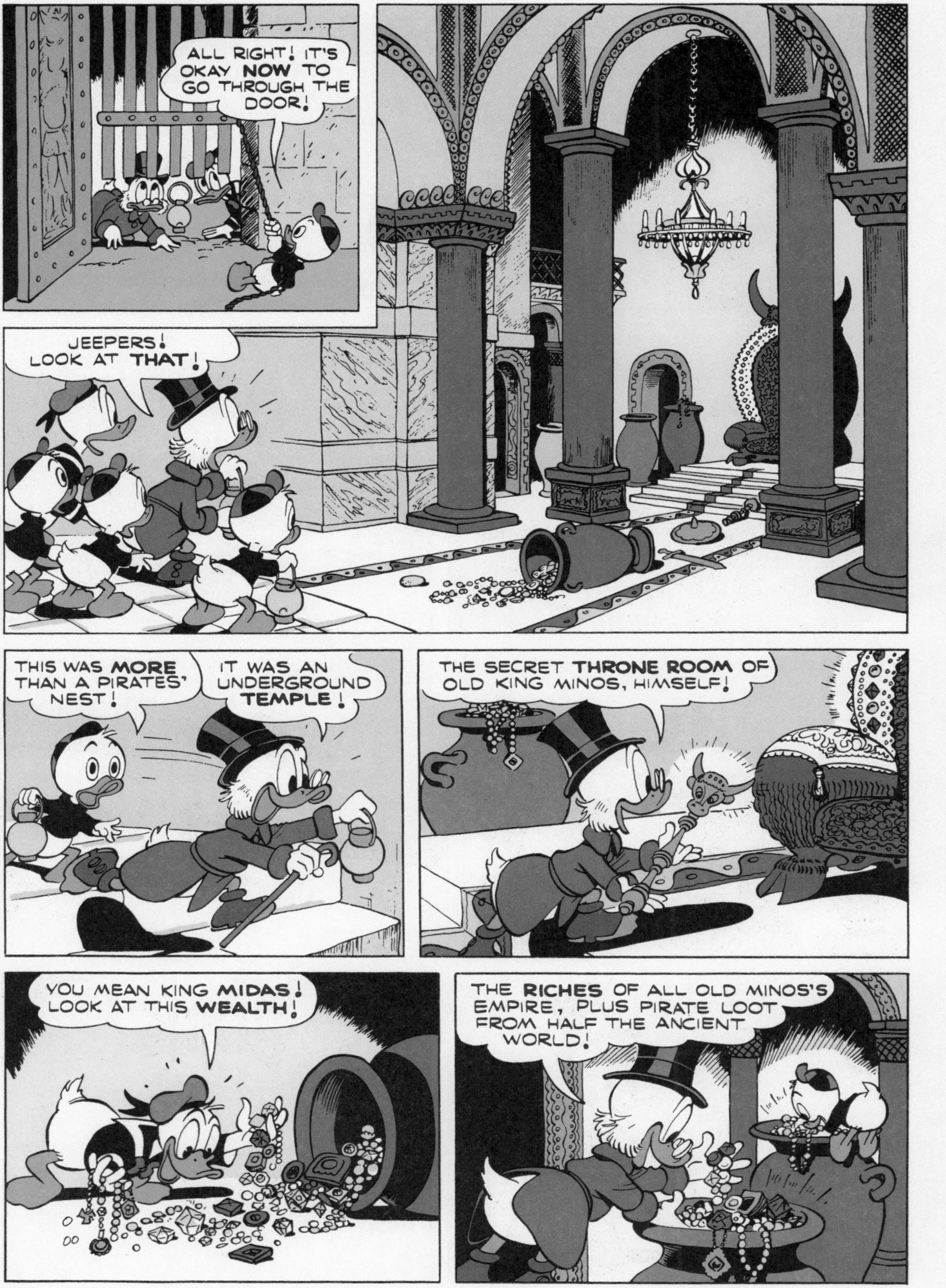
ALL RIGHT! IT'S OKAY NOW TO GO THROUGH THE DOOR!
JEEPERS! LOOK AT THAT!
THIS WAS MORE THAN A PIRATES' NEST!
IT WAS AN UNDERGROUND TEMPLE!
THE SECRET THRONE ROOM OF OLD KING MINOS, HIMSELF!
YOU MEAN KING MIDAS! LOOK AT THIS WEALTH!
THE RICHES OF ALL OLD MINOS'S EMPIRE, PLUS PIRATE LOOT FROM HALF THE ANCIENT WORLD!

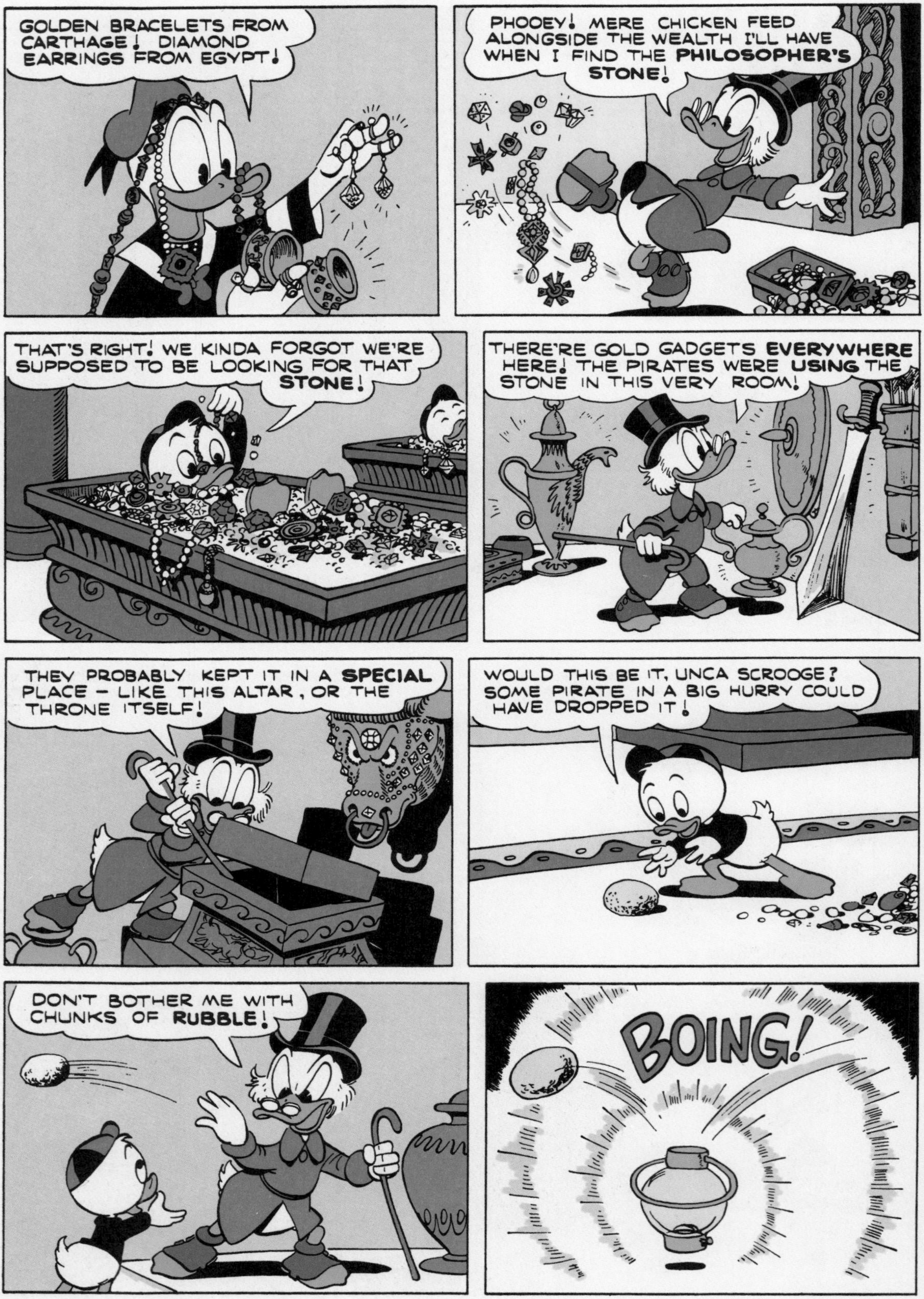
GOLDEN BRACELETS FROM CARTHAGE! DIAMOND EARRINGS FROM EGYPT!
PHOOEY! MERE CHICKEN FEED ALONGSIDE THE WEALTH I'LL HAVE WHEN I FIND THE **PHILOSOPHER'S STONE**!
THAT'S RIGHT! WE KINDA FORGOT WE'RE SUPPOSED TO BE LOOKING FOR THAT **STONE**!
THERE'RE GOLD GADGETS **EVERYWHERE** HERE! THE PIRATES WERE **USING** THE STONE IN THIS VERY ROOM!
THEY PROBABLY KEPT IT IN A **SPECIAL** PLACE – LIKE THIS ALTAR, OR THE THRONE ITSELF!
WOULD THIS BE IT, UNCA SCROOGE? SOME PIRATE IN A BIG HURRY COULD HAVE DROPPED IT!
DON'T BOTHER ME WITH CHUNKS OF **RUBBLE**!
BOING!

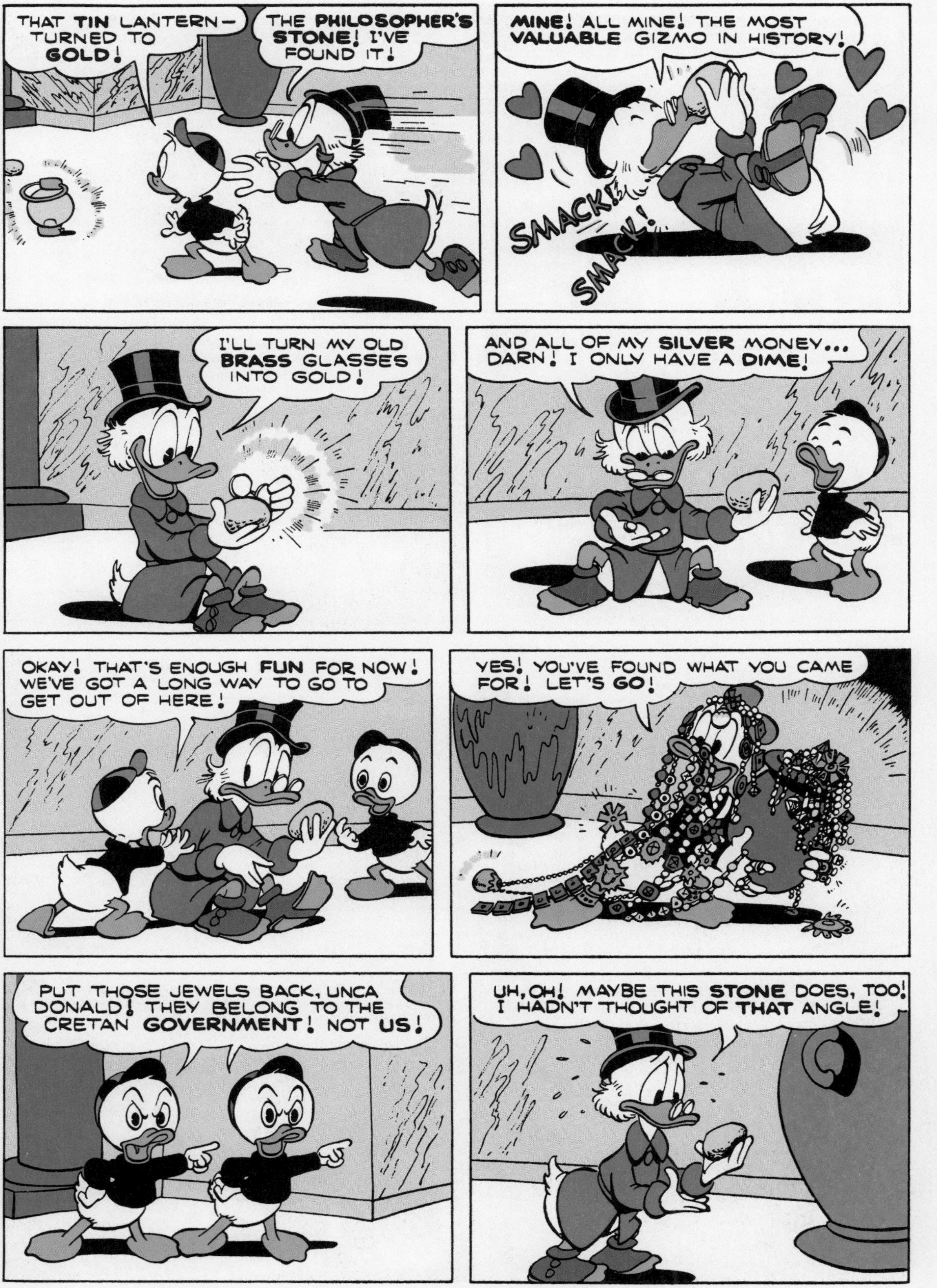
THAT TIN LANTERN— TURNED TO GOLD!
THE PHILOSOPHER'S STONE! I'VE FOUND IT!
MINE! ALL MINE! THE MOST VALUABLE GIZMO IN HISTORY!
SMACK!
SMACK!
I'LL TURN MY OLD BRASS GLASSES INTO GOLD!
AND ALL OF MY SILVER MONEY... DARN! I ONLY HAVE A DIME!
OKAY! THAT'S ENOUGH FUN FOR NOW! WE'VE GOT A LONG WAY TO GO TO GET OUT OF HERE!
YES! YOU'VE FOUND WHAT YOU CAME FOR! LET'S GO!
PUT THOSE JEWELS BACK, UNCA DONALD! THEY BELONG TO THE CRETAN GOVERNMENT! NOT US!
UH, OH! MAYBE THIS STONE DOES, TOO! I HADN'T THOUGHT OF THAT ANGLE!

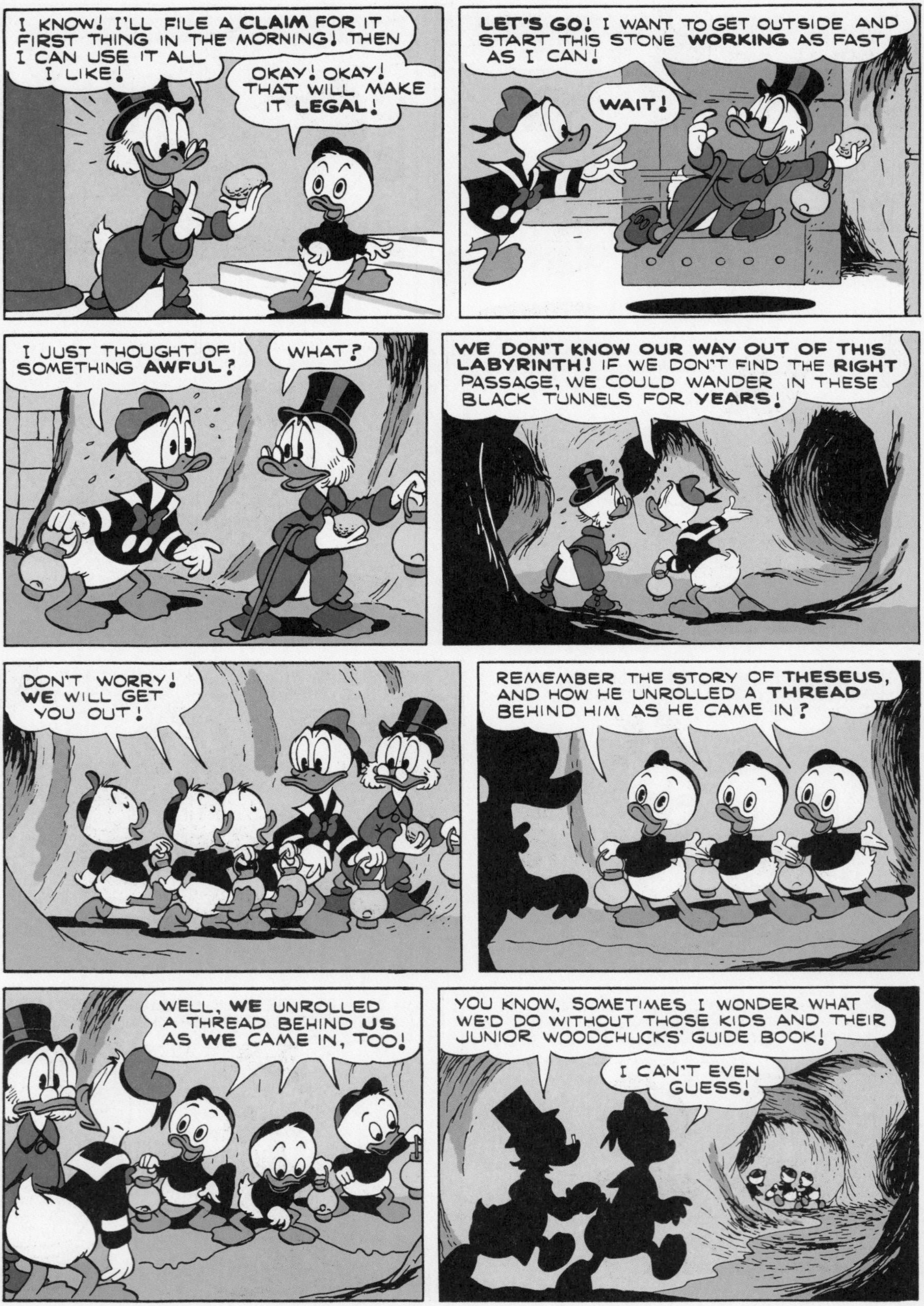
I KNOW! I'LL FILE A CLAIM FOR IT FIRST THING IN THE MORNING! THEN I CAN USE IT ALL I LIKE!
OKAY! OKAY! THAT WILL MAKE IT LEGAL!
LET'S GO! I WANT TO GET OUTSIDE AND START THIS STONE WORKING AS FAST AS I CAN!
WAIT!
I JUST THOUGHT OF SOMETHING AWFUL?
WHAT?
WE DON'T KNOW OUR WAY OUT OF THIS LABYRINTH! IF WE DON'T FIND THE RIGHT PASSAGE, WE COULD WANDER IN THESE BLACK TUNNELS FOR YEARS!
DON'T WORRY! WE WILL GET YOU OUT!
REMEMBER THE STORY OF THESEUS, AND HOW HE UNROLLED A THREAD BEHIND HIM AS HE CAME IN?
WELL, WE UNROLLED A THREAD BEHIND US AS WE CAME IN, TOO!
YOU KNOW, SOMETIMES I WONDER WHAT WE'D DO WITHOUT THOSE KIDS AND THEIR JUNIOR WOODCHUCKS' GUIDE BOOK!
I CAN'T EVEN GUESS!

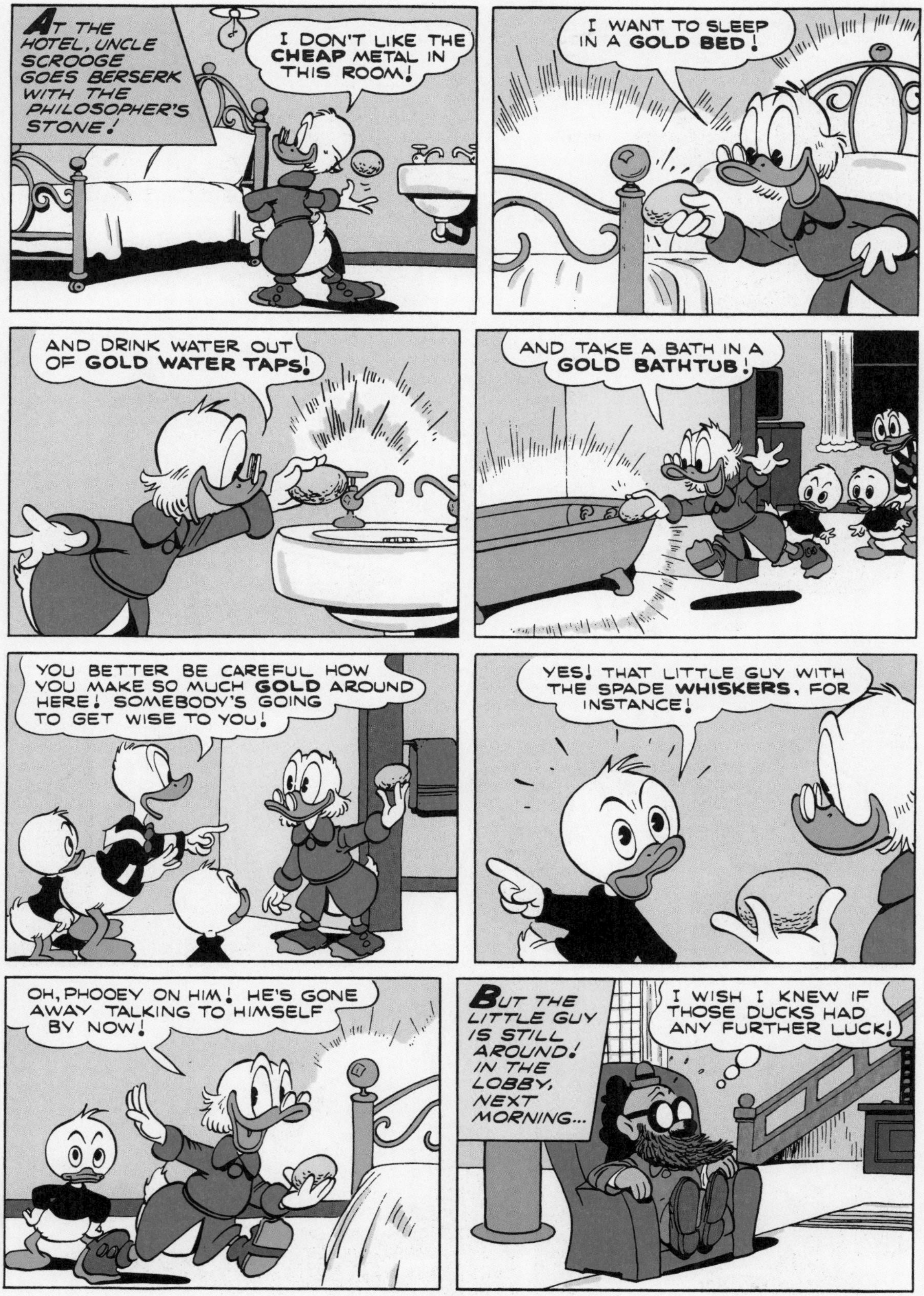
AT THE HOTEL, UNCLE SCROOGE GOES BERSERK WITH THE PHILOSOPHER'S STONE!
I DON'T LIKE THE CHEAP METAL IN THIS ROOM!
I WANT TO SLEEP IN A GOLD BED!
AND DRINK WATER OUT OF GOLD WATER TAPS!
AND TAKE A BATH IN A GOLD BATHTUB!
YOU BETTER BE CAREFUL HOW YOU MAKE SO MUCH GOLD AROUND HERE! SOMEBODY'S GOING TO GET WISE TO YOU!
YES! THAT LITTLE GUY WITH THE SPADE WHISKERS, FOR INSTANCE!
OH, PHOOEY ON HIM! HE'S GONE AWAY TALKING TO HIMSELF BY NOW!
BUT THE LITTLE GUY IS STILL AROUND! IN THE LOBBY, NEXT MORNING...
I WISH I KNEW IF THOSE DUCKS HAD ANY FURTHER LUCK!

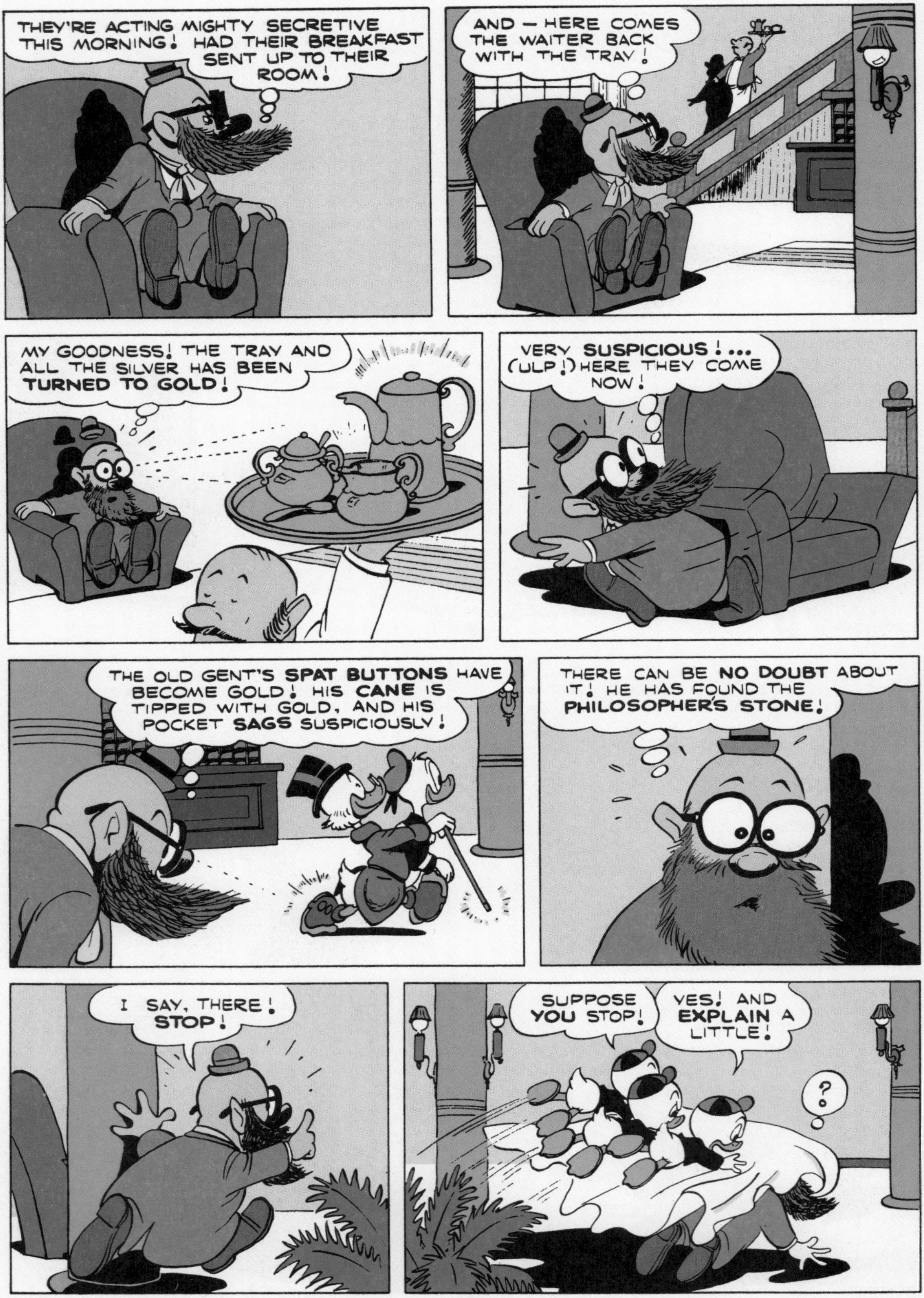
THEY'RE ACTING MIGHTY SECRETIVE THIS MORNING! HAD THEIR BREAKFAST SENT UP TO THEIR ROOM!
AND — HERE COMES THE WAITER BACK WITH THE TRAY!
MY GOODNESS! THE TRAY AND ALL THE SILVER HAS BEEN TURNED TO GOLD!
VERY SUSPICIOUS!... (ULP!) HERE THEY COME NOW!
THE OLD GENT'S SPAT BUTTONS HAVE BECOME GOLD! HIS CANE IS TIPPED WITH GOLD, AND HIS POCKET SAGS SUSPICIOUSLY!
THERE CAN BE NO DOUBT ABOUT IT! HE HAS FOUND THE PHILOSOPHER'S STONE!
I SAY, THERE! STOP!
SUPPOSE YOU STOP!
YES! AND EXPLAIN A LITTLE!
?

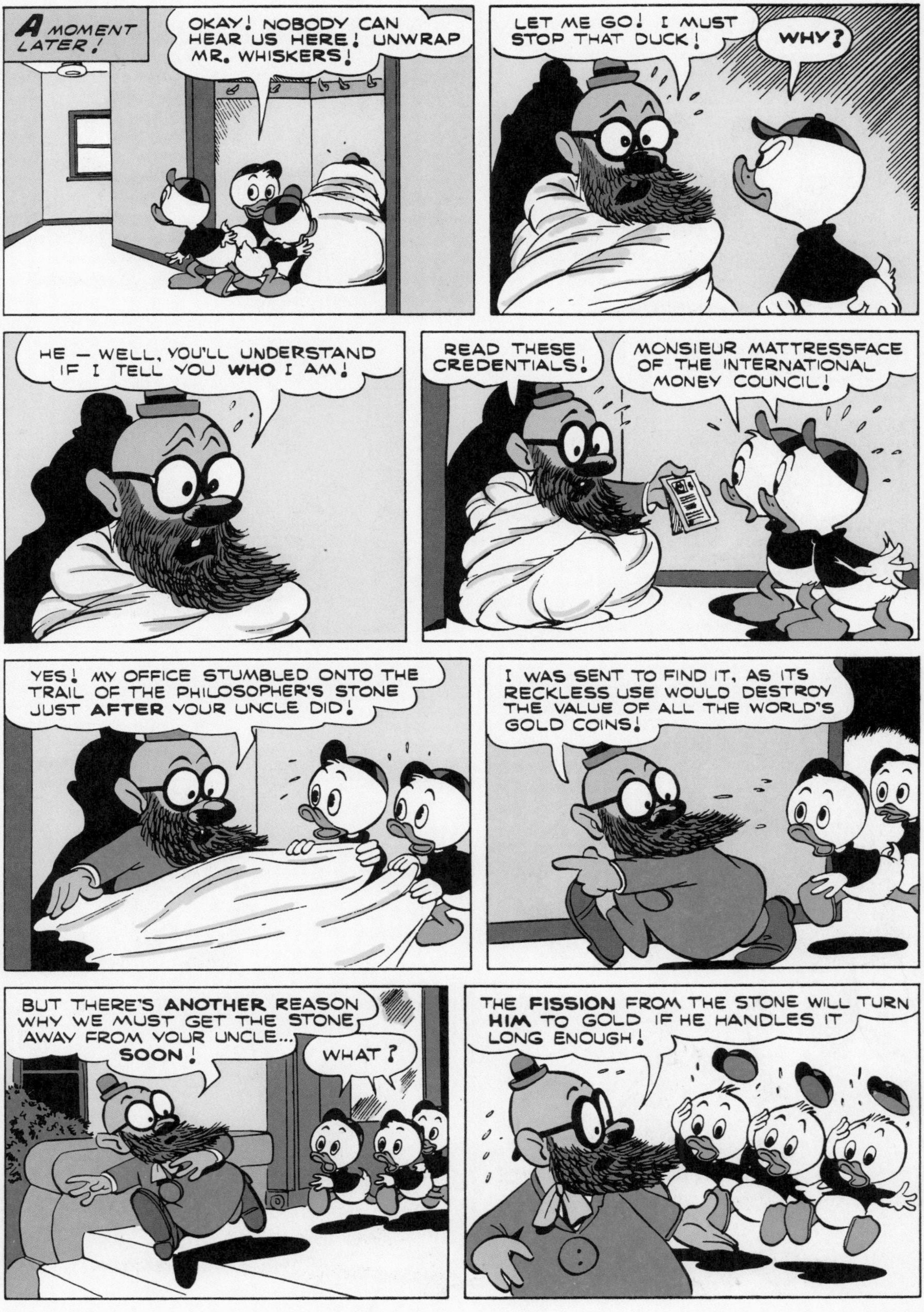
A MOMENT LATER!
OKAY! NOBODY CAN HEAR US HERE! UNWRAP MR. WHISKERS!
LET ME GO! I MUST STOP THAT DUCK!
WHY?
HE — WELL, YOU'LL UNDERSTAND IF I TELL YOU WHO I AM!
READ THESE CREDENTIALS!
MONSIEUR MATTRESSFACE OF THE INTERNATIONAL MONEY COUNCIL!
YES! MY OFFICE STUMBLED ONTO THE TRAIL OF THE PHILOSOPHER'S STONE JUST AFTER YOUR UNCLE DID!
I WAS SENT TO FIND IT, AS ITS RECKLESS USE WOULD DESTROY THE VALUE OF ALL THE WORLD'S GOLD COINS!
BUT THERE'S ANOTHER REASON WHY WE MUST GET THE STONE AWAY FROM YOUR UNCLE... SOON!
WHAT?
THE FISSION FROM THE STONE WILL TURN HIM TO GOLD IF HE HANDLES IT LONG ENOUGH!

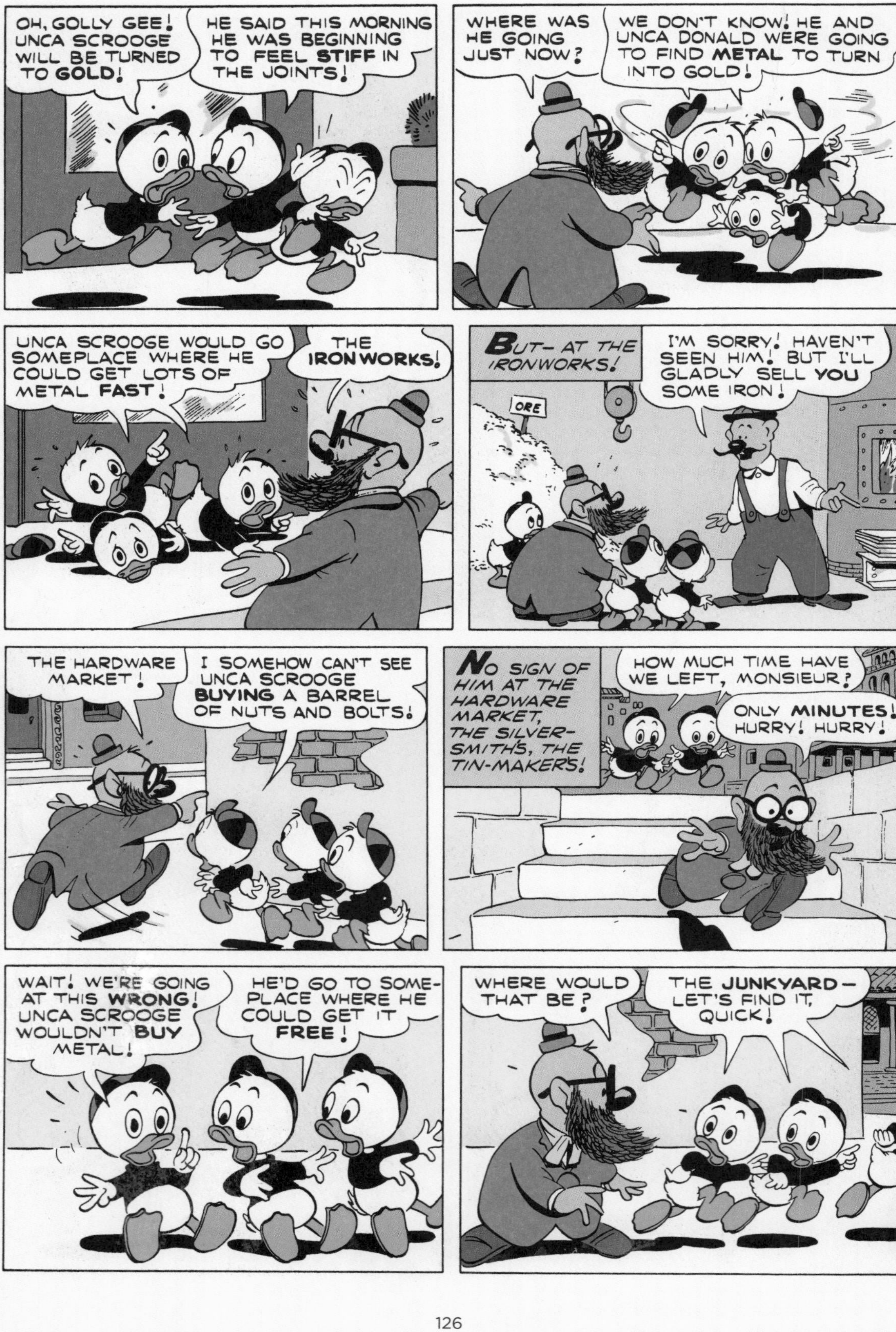
OH, GOLLY GEE! UNCA SCROOGE WILL BE TURNED TO GOLD!
HE SAID THIS MORNING HE WAS BEGINNING TO FEEL STIFF IN THE JOINTS!
WHERE WAS HE GOING JUST NOW?
WE DON'T KNOW! HE AND UNCA DONALD WERE GOING TO FIND METAL TO TURN INTO GOLD!
UNCA SCROOGE WOULD GO SOMEPLACE WHERE HE COULD GET LOTS OF METAL FAST!
THE IRONWORKS!
BUT— AT THE IRONWORKS!
I'M SORRY! HAVEN'T SEEN HIM! BUT I'LL GLADLY SELL YOU SOME IRON!
ORE
THE HARDWARE MARKET!
I SOMEHOW CAN'T SEE UNCA SCROOGE BUYING A BARREL OF NUTS AND BOLTS!
NO SIGN OF HIM AT THE HARDWARE MARKET, THE SILVER-SMITH'S, THE TIN-MAKER'S!
HOW MUCH TIME HAVE WE LEFT, MONSIEUR?
ONLY MINUTES! HURRY! HURRY!
WAIT! WE'RE GOING AT THIS WRONG! UNCA SCROOGE WOULDN'T BUY METAL!
HE'D GO TO SOME-PLACE WHERE HE COULD GET IT FREE!
WHERE WOULD THAT BE?
THE JUNKYARD— LET'S FIND IT, QUICK!

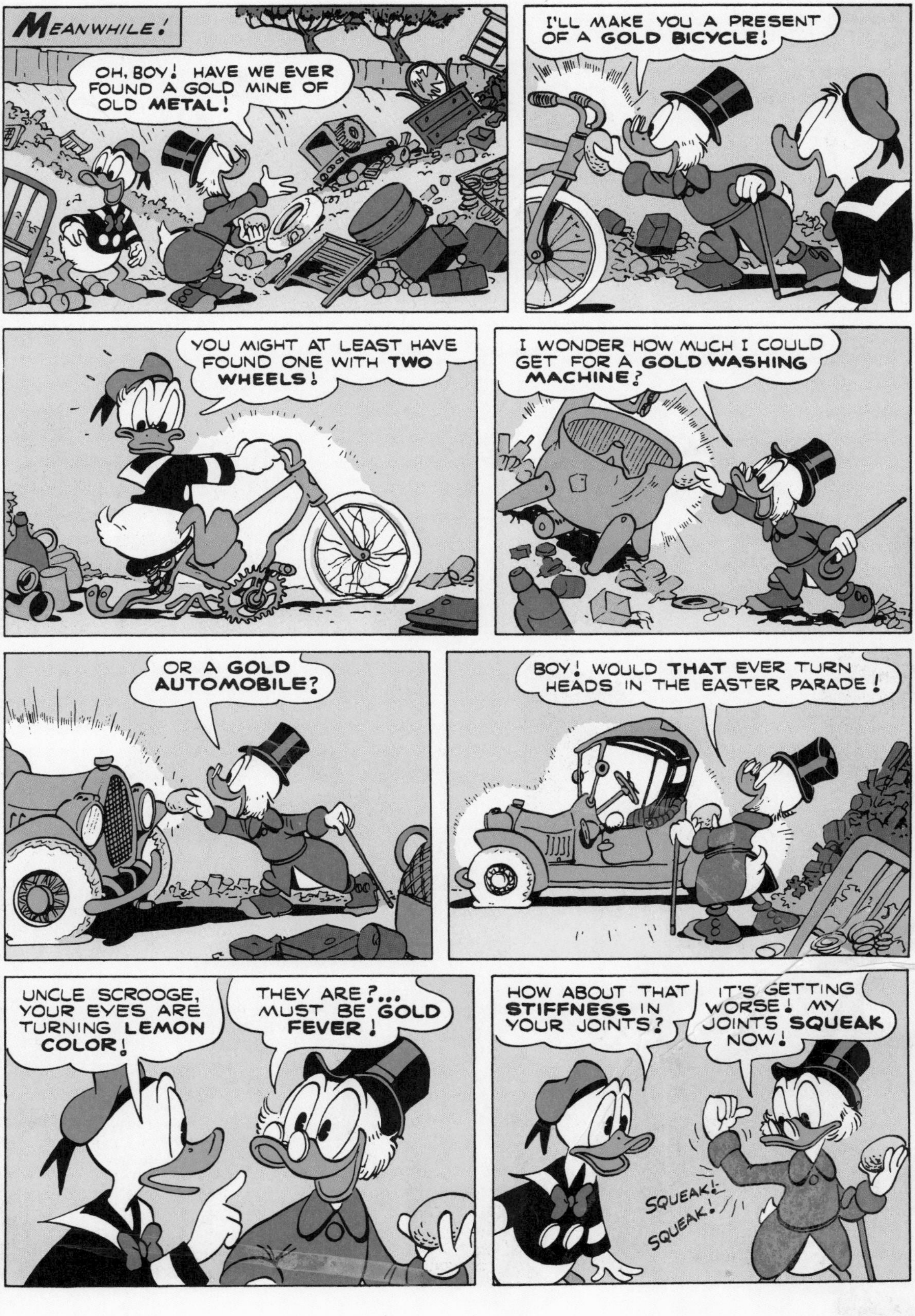
MEANWHILE!
OH, BOY! HAVE WE EVER FOUND A GOLD MINE OF OLD METAL!
I'LL MAKE YOU A PRESENT OF A GOLD BICYCLE!
YOU MIGHT AT LEAST HAVE FOUND ONE WITH TWO WHEELS!
I WONDER HOW MUCH I COULD GET FOR A GOLD WASHING MACHINE?
OR A GOLD AUTOMOBILE?
BOY! WOULD THAT EVER TURN HEADS IN THE EASTER PARADE!
UNCLE SCROOGE, YOUR EYES ARE TURNING LEMON COLOR!
THEY ARE?... MUST BE GOLD FEVER!
HOW ABOUT THAT STIFFNESS IN YOUR JOINTS?
IT'S GETTING WORSE! MY JOINTS SQUEAK NOW!
SQUEAK! SQUEAK!

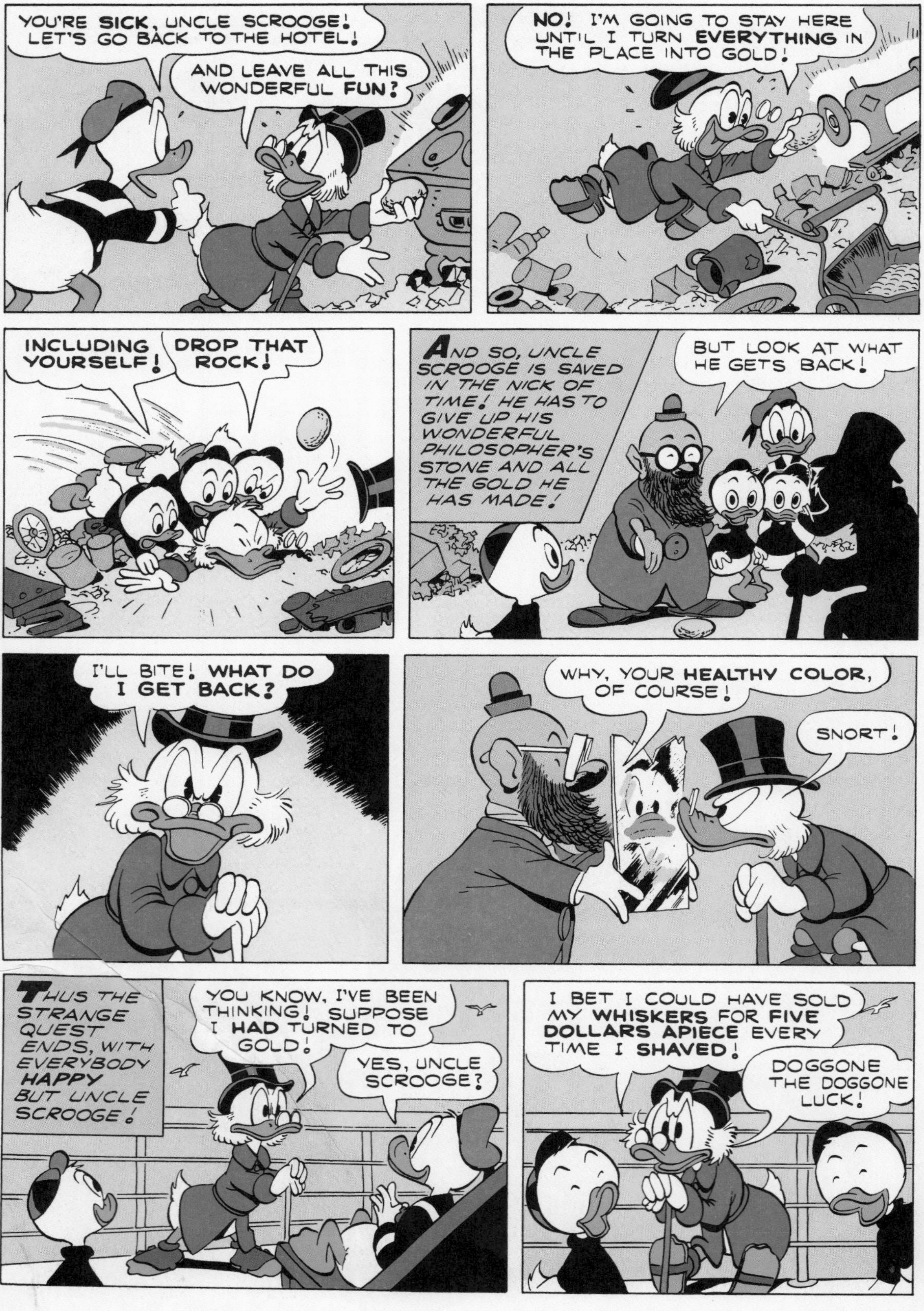
YOU'RE SICK, UNCLE SCROOGE! LET'S GO BACK TO THE HOTEL!
AND LEAVE ALL THIS WONDERFUL FUN?
NO! I'M GOING TO STAY HERE UNTIL I TURN EVERYTHING IN THE PLACE INTO GOLD!
INCLUDING YOURSELF!
DROP THAT ROCK!
AND SO, UNCLE SCROOGE IS SAVED IN THE NICK OF TIME! HE HAS TO GIVE UP HIS WONDERFUL PHILOSOPHER'S STONE AND ALL THE GOLD HE HAS MADE!
BUT LOOK AT WHAT HE GETS BACK!
I'LL BITE! WHAT DO I GET BACK?
WHY, YOUR HEALTHY COLOR, OF COURSE!
SNORT!
THUS THE STRANGE QUEST ENDS, WITH EVERYBODY HAPPY BUT UNCLE SCROOGE!
YOU KNOW, I'VE BEEN THINKING! SUPPOSE I HAD TURNED TO GOLD!
YES, UNCLE SCROOGE?
I BET I COULD HAVE SOLD MY WHISKERS FOR FIVE DOLLARS APIECE EVERY TIME I SHAVED!
DOGGONE THE DOGGONE LUCK!

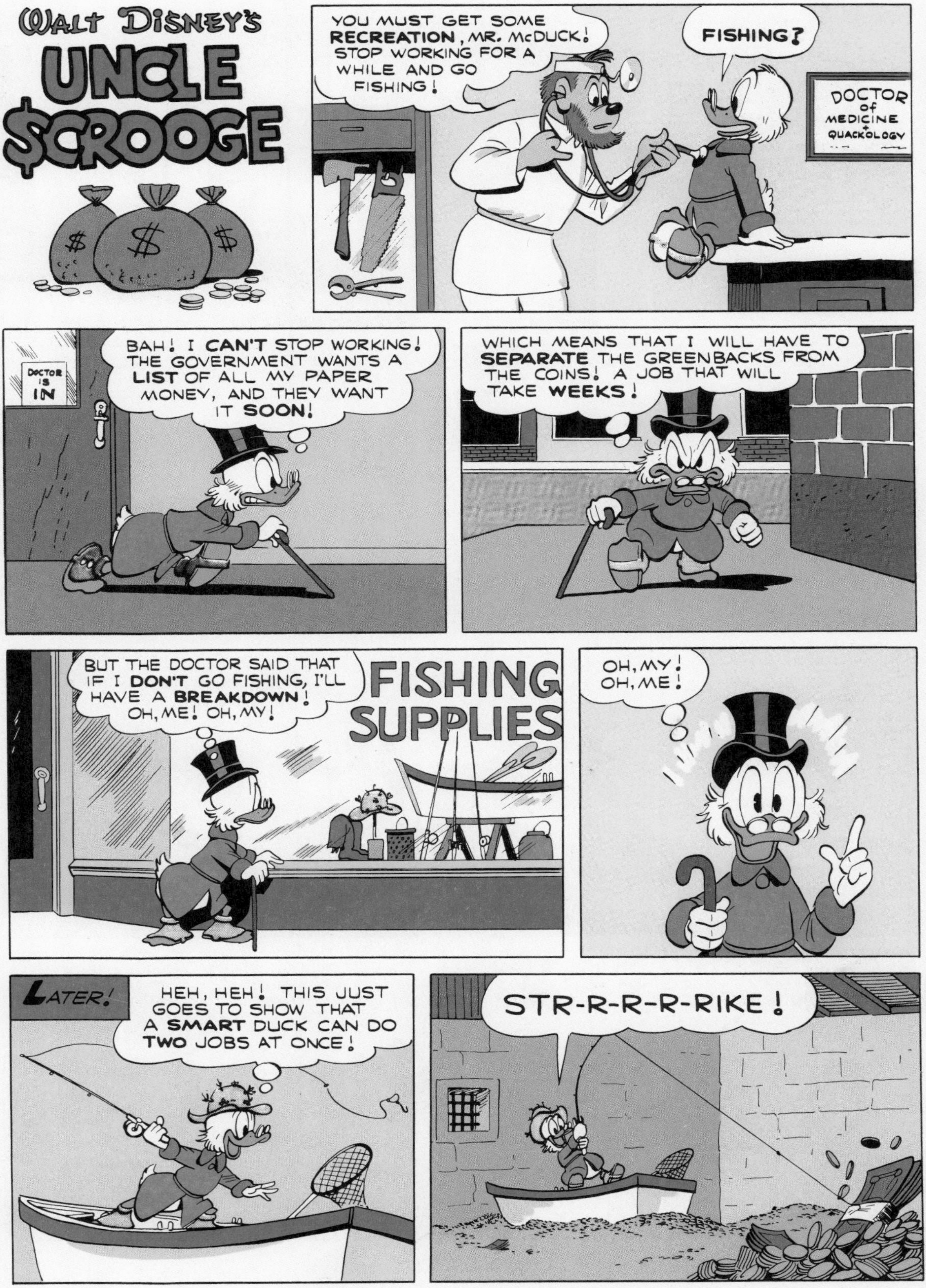
WALT DISNEY'S
UNCLE $CROOGE
YOU MUST GET SOME RECREATION, MR. McDUCK! STOP WORKING FOR A WHILE AND GO FISHING!
FISHING?
DOCTOR of MEDICINE + QUACKOLOGY
DOCTOR IS IN
BAH! I CAN'T STOP WORKING! THE GOVERNMENT WANTS A LIST OF ALL MY PAPER MONEY, AND THEY WANT IT SOON!
WHICH MEANS THAT I WILL HAVE TO SEPARATE THE GREENBACKS FROM THE COINS! A JOB THAT WILL TAKE WEEKS!
BUT THE DOCTOR SAID THAT IF I DON'T GO FISHING, I'LL HAVE A BREAKDOWN! OH, ME! OH, MY!
FISHING SUPPLIES
OH, MY! OH, ME!
LATER!
HEH, HEH! THIS JUST GOES TO SHOW THAT A SMART DUCK CAN DO TWO JOBS AT ONCE!
STR-R-R-R-RIKE!

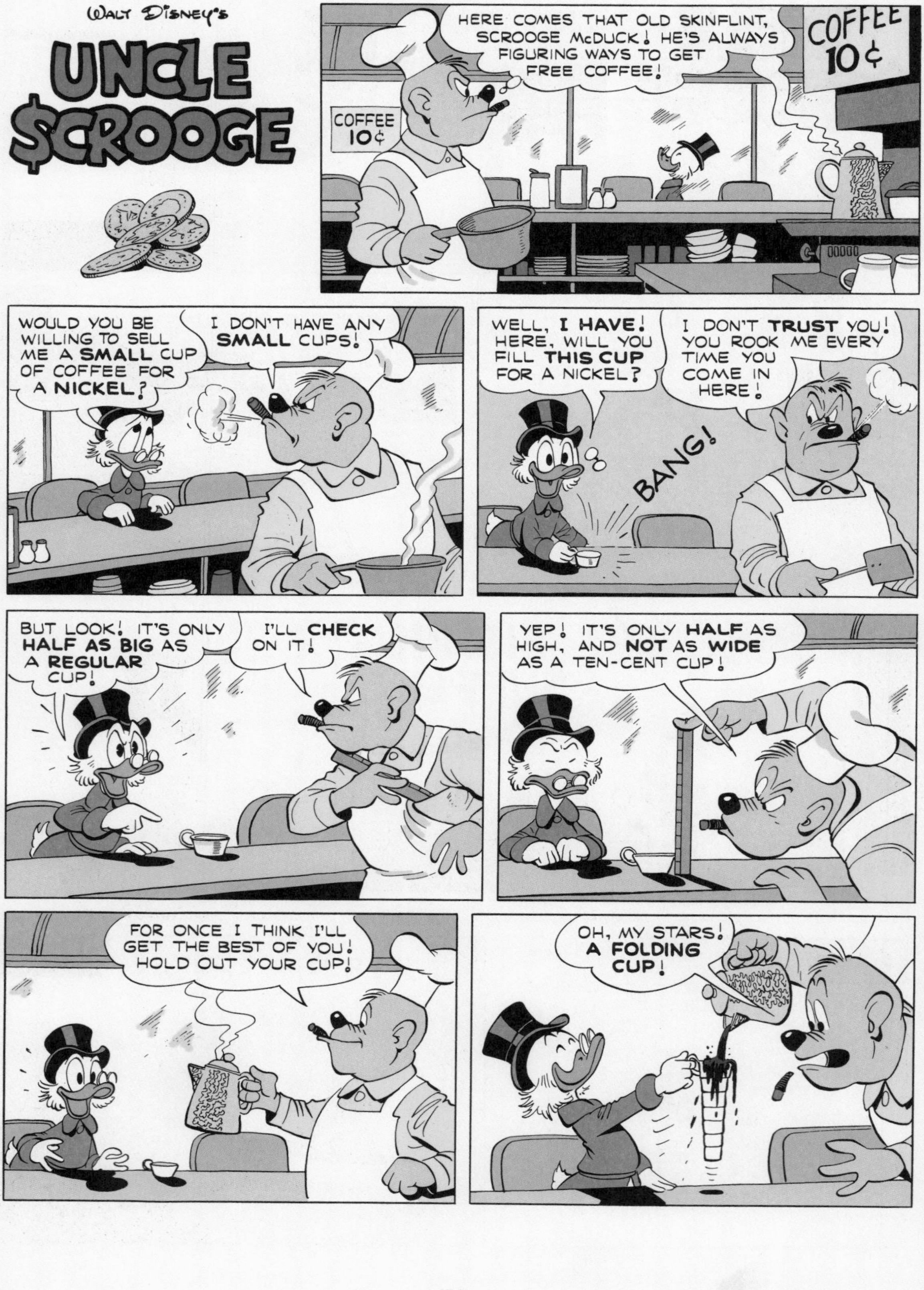
WALT DISNEY'S
UNCLE $CROOGE
HERE COMES THAT OLD SKINFLINT, SCROOGE McDUCK! HE'S ALWAYS FIGURING WAYS TO GET FREE COFFEE!
COFFEE 10¢
COFFEE 10¢
WOULD YOU BE WILLING TO SELL ME A SMALL CUP OF COFFEE FOR A NICKEL?
I DON'T HAVE ANY SMALL CUPS!
WELL, I HAVE! HERE, WILL YOU FILL THIS CUP FOR A NICKEL?
I DON'T TRUST YOU! YOU ROOK ME EVERY TIME YOU COME IN HERE!
BANG!
BUT LOOK! IT'S ONLY HALF AS BIG AS A REGULAR CUP!
I'LL CHECK ON IT!
YEP! IT'S ONLY HALF AS HIGH, AND NOT AS WIDE AS A TEN-CENT CUP!
FOR ONCE I THINK I'LL GET THE BEST OF YOU! HOLD OUT YOUR CUP!
OH, MY STARS! A FOLDING CUP!

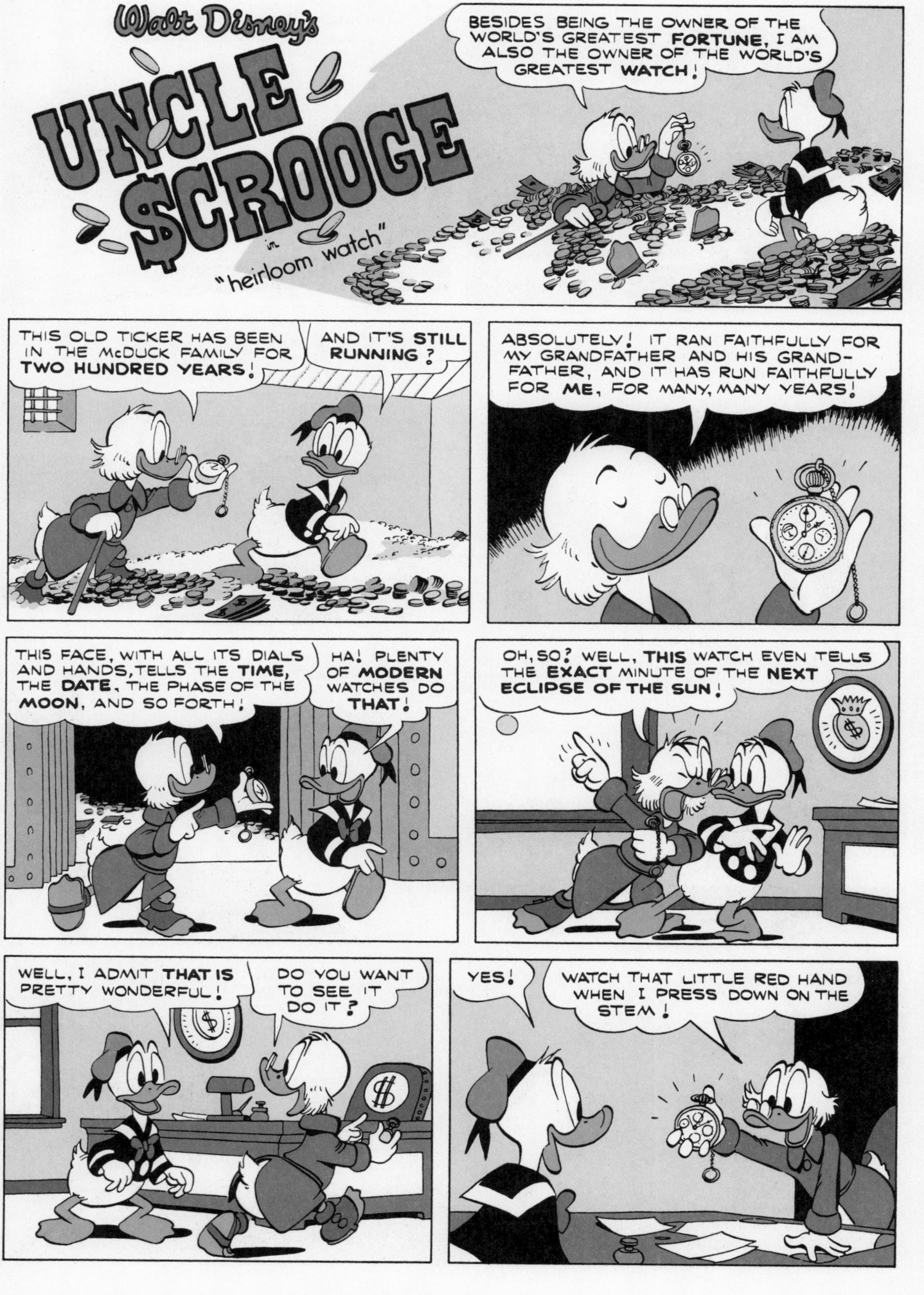
Walt Disney's
UNCLE $CROOGE
in "heirloom watch"
BESIDES BEING THE OWNER OF THE WORLD'S GREATEST FORTUNE, I AM ALSO THE OWNER OF THE WORLD'S GREATEST WATCH!
THIS OLD TICKER HAS BEEN IN THE McDUCK FAMILY FOR TWO HUNDRED YEARS!
AND IT'S STILL RUNNING?
ABSOLUTELY! IT RAN FAITHFULLY FOR MY GRANDFATHER AND HIS GRAND-FATHER, AND IT HAS RUN FAITHFULLY FOR ME, FOR MANY, MANY YEARS!
THIS FACE, WITH ALL ITS DIALS AND HANDS, TELLS THE TIME, THE DATE, THE PHASE OF THE MOON, AND SO FORTH!
HA! PLENTY OF MODERN WATCHES DO THAT!
OH, SO? WELL, THIS WATCH EVEN TELLS THE EXACT MINUTE OF THE NEXT ECLIPSE OF THE SUN!
WELL, I ADMIT THAT IS PRETTY WONDERFUL!
DO YOU WANT TO SEE IT DO IT?
YES!
WATCH THAT LITTLE RED HAND WHEN I PRESS DOWN ON THE STEM!

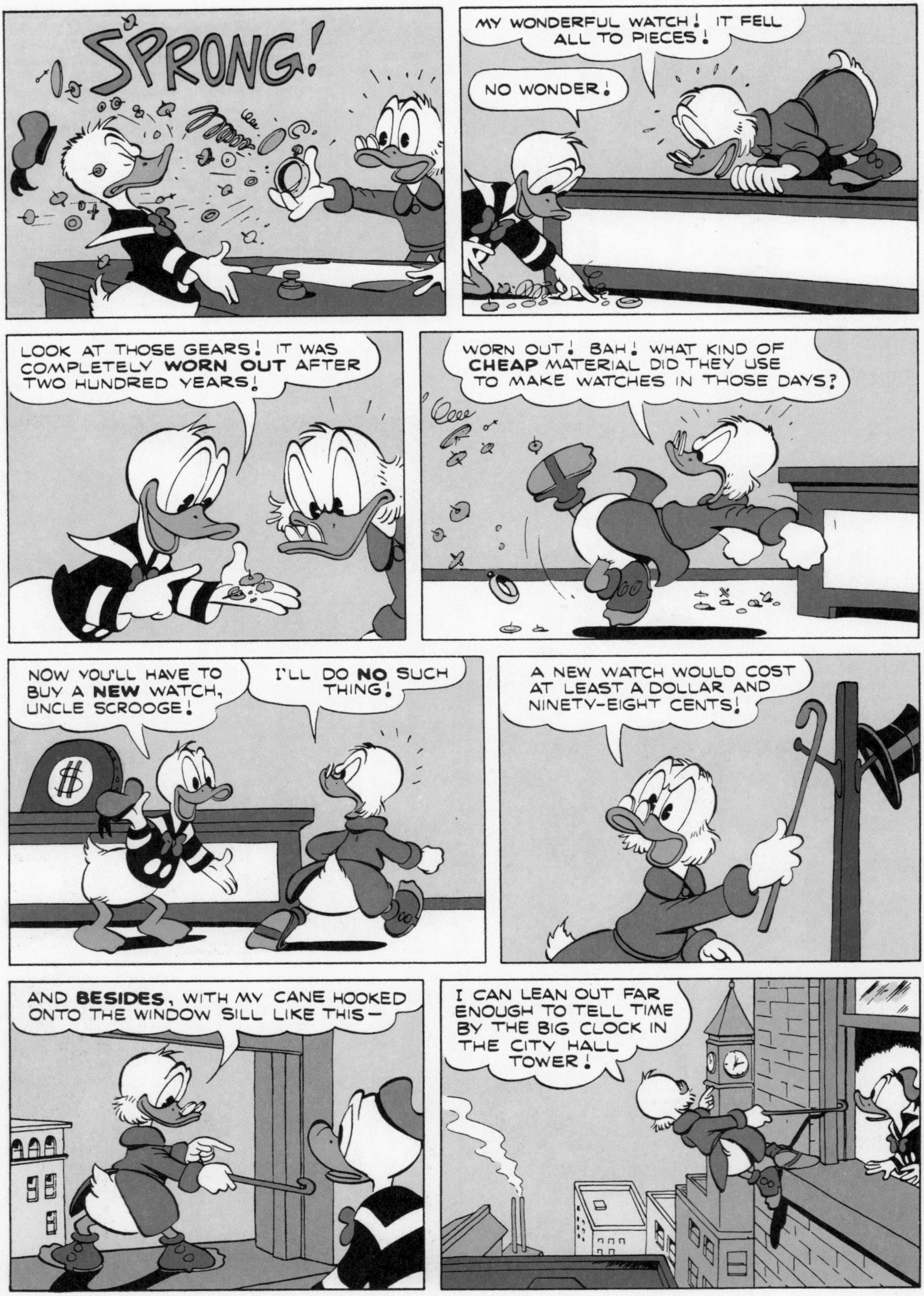

SPRONG!
MY WONDERFUL WATCH! IT FELL ALL TO PIECES!
NO WONDER!
LOOK AT THOSE GEARS! IT WAS COMPLETELY **WORN OUT** AFTER TWO HUNDRED YEARS!
WORN OUT! BAH! WHAT KIND OF **CHEAP** MATERIAL DID THEY USE TO MAKE WATCHES IN THOSE DAYS?
NOW YOU'LL HAVE TO BUY A **NEW** WATCH, UNCLE SCROOGE!
I'LL DO **NO** SUCH THING!
A NEW WATCH WOULD COST AT LEAST A DOLLAR AND NINETY-EIGHT CENTS!
AND **BESIDES**, WITH MY CANE HOOKED ONTO THE WINDOW SILL LIKE THIS—
I CAN LEAN OUT FAR ENOUGH TO TELL TIME BY THE BIG CLOCK IN THE CITY HALL TOWER!

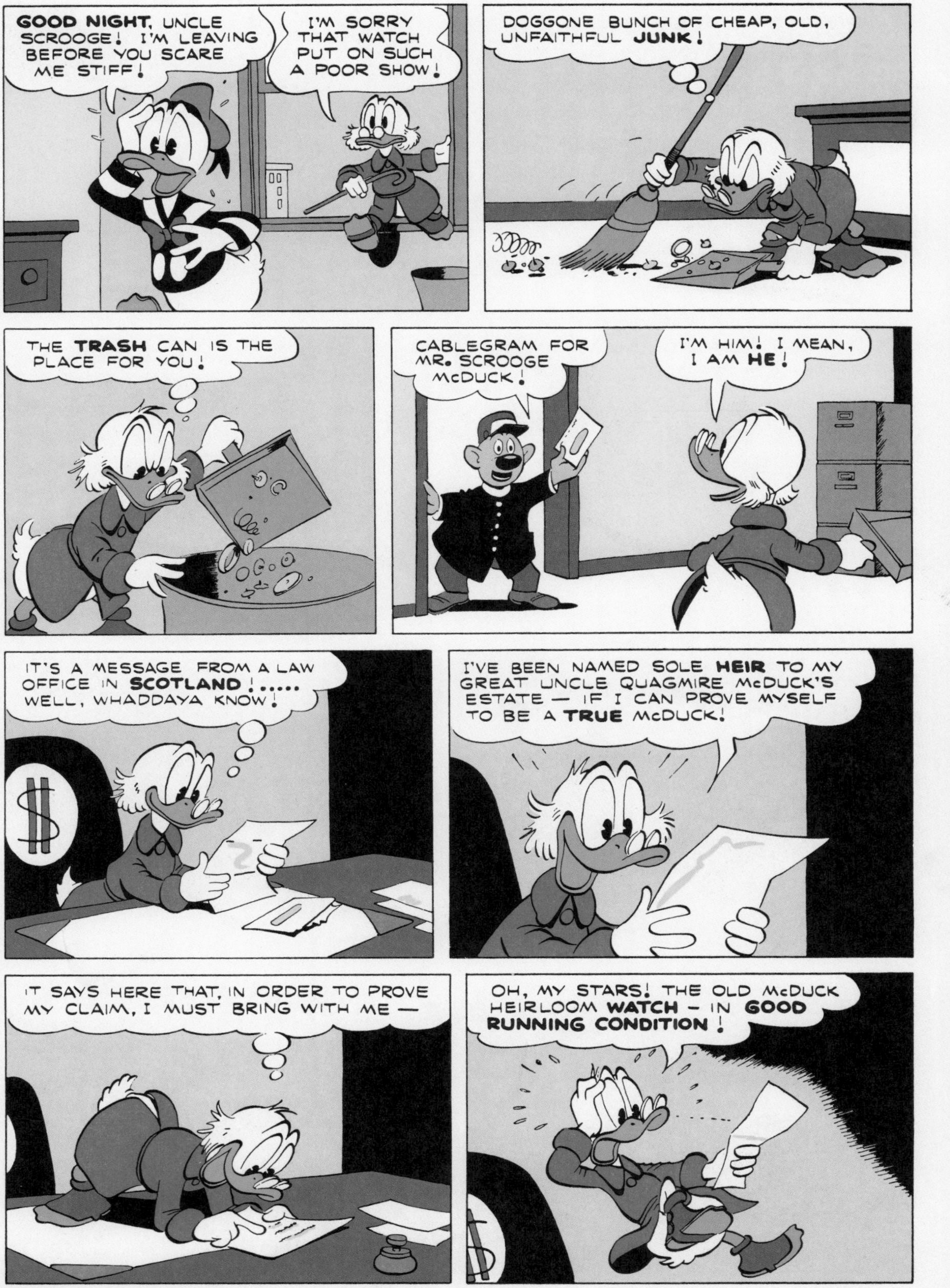
GOOD NIGHT, UNCLE SCROOGE! I'M LEAVING BEFORE YOU SCARE ME STIFF!
I'M SORRY THAT WATCH PUT ON SUCH A POOR SHOW!
DOGGONE BUNCH OF CHEAP, OLD, UNFAITHFUL JUNK!
THE TRASH CAN IS THE PLACE FOR YOU!
CABLEGRAM FOR MR. SCROOGE McDUCK!
I'M HIM! I MEAN, I AM HE!
IT'S A MESSAGE FROM A LAW OFFICE IN SCOTLAND!..... WELL, WHADDAYA KNOW!
I'VE BEEN NAMED SOLE HEIR TO MY GREAT UNCLE QUAGMIRE McDUCK'S ESTATE — IF I CAN PROVE MYSELF TO BE A TRUE McDUCK!
IT SAYS HERE THAT, IN ORDER TO PROVE MY CLAIM, I MUST BRING WITH ME —
OH, MY STARS! THE OLD McDUCK HEIRLOOM WATCH — IN GOOD RUNNING CONDITION!

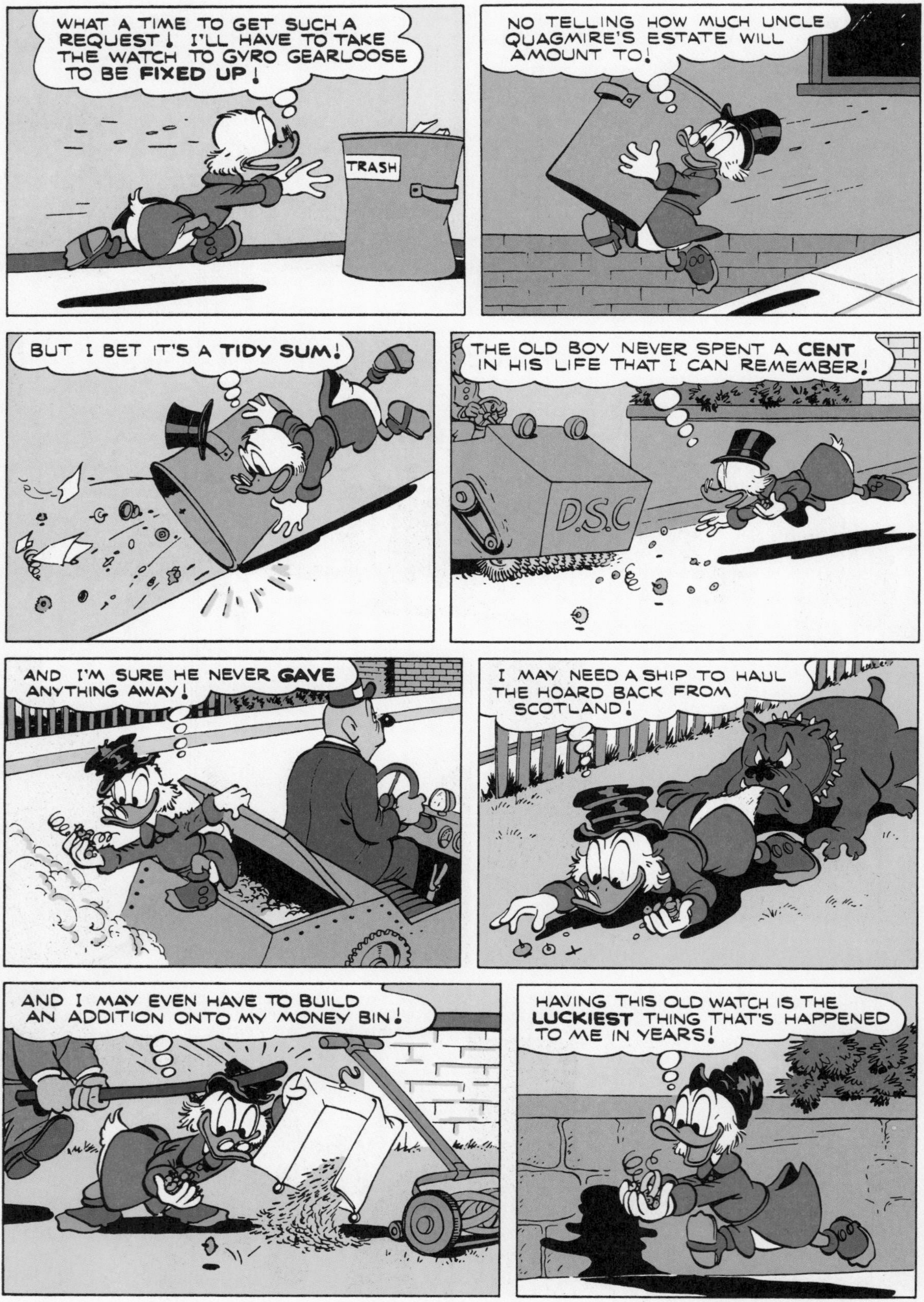
WHAT A TIME TO GET SUCH A REQUEST! I'LL HAVE TO TAKE THE WATCH TO GYRO GEARLOOSE TO BE FIXED UP!
TRASH
NO TELLING HOW MUCH UNCLE QUAGMIRE'S ESTATE WILL AMOUNT TO!
BUT I BET IT'S A TIDY SUM!
THE OLD BOY NEVER SPENT A CENT IN HIS LIFE THAT I CAN REMEMBER!
D.S.C
AND I'M SURE HE NEVER GAVE ANYTHING AWAY!
I MAY NEED A SHIP TO HAUL THE HOARD BACK FROM SCOTLAND!
AND I MAY EVEN HAVE TO BUILD AN ADDITION ONTO MY MONEY BIN!
HAVING THIS OLD WATCH IS THE LUCKIEST THING THAT'S HAPPENED TO ME IN YEARS!

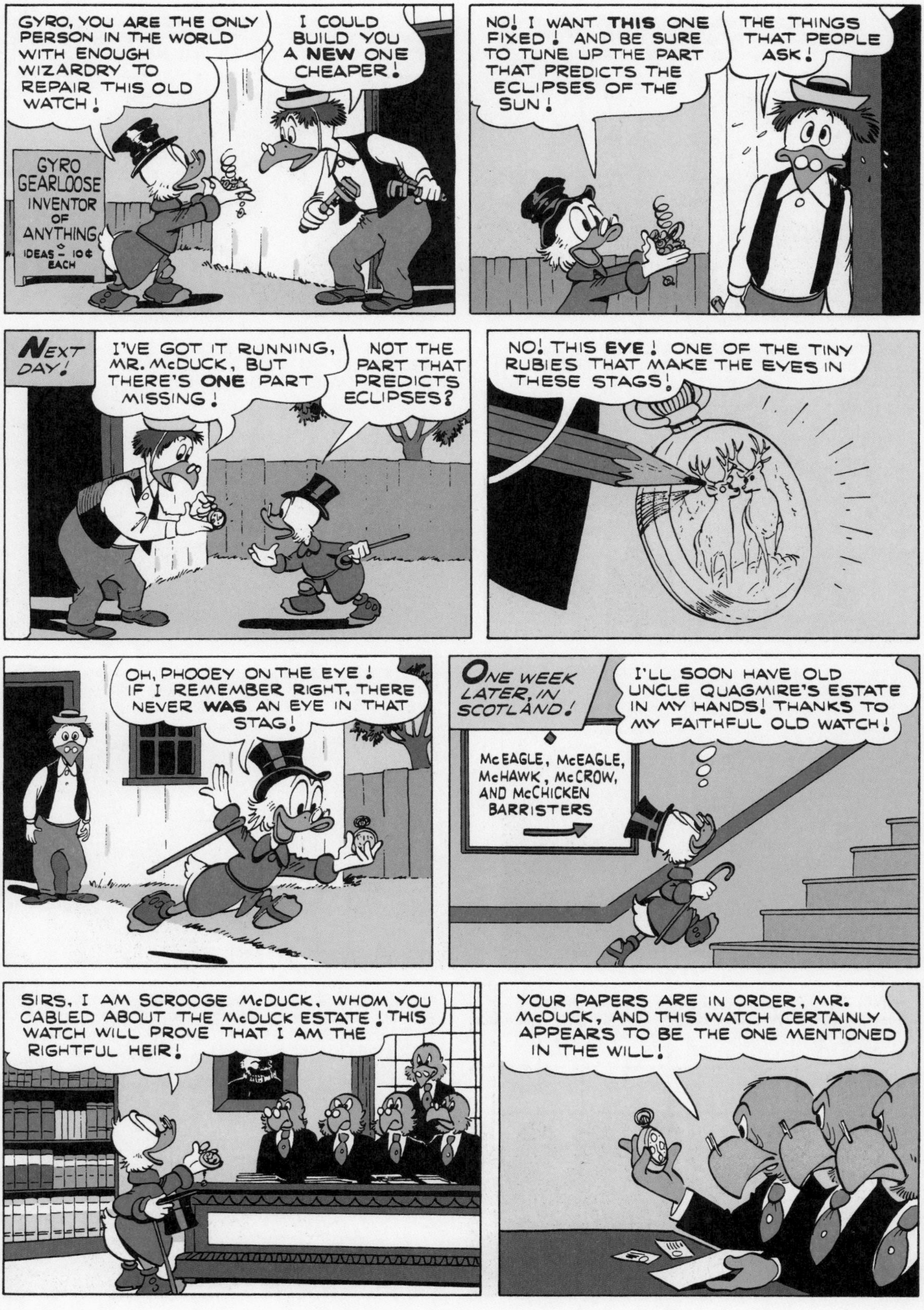
GYRO, YOU ARE THE ONLY PERSON IN THE WORLD WITH ENOUGH WIZARDRY TO REPAIR THIS OLD WATCH!
I COULD BUILD YOU A NEW ONE CHEAPER!
GYRO GEARLOOSE INVENTOR OF ANYTHING IDEAS - 10¢ EACH
NO! I WANT THIS ONE FIXED! AND BE SURE TO TUNE UP THE PART THAT PREDICTS THE ECLIPSES OF THE SUN!
THE THINGS THAT PEOPLE ASK!
NEXT DAY!
I'VE GOT IT RUNNING, MR. McDUCK, BUT THERE'S ONE PART MISSING!
NOT THE PART THAT PREDICTS ECLIPSES?
NO! THIS EYE! ONE OF THE TINY RUBIES THAT MAKE THE EYES IN THESE STAGS!
OH, PHOOEY ON THE EYE! IF I REMEMBER RIGHT, THERE NEVER WAS AN EYE IN THAT STAG!
ONE WEEK LATER, IN SCOTLAND!
I'LL SOON HAVE OLD UNCLE QUAGMIRE'S ESTATE IN MY HANDS! THANKS TO MY FAITHFUL OLD WATCH!
McEAGLE, McEAGLE, McHAWK, McCROW, AND McCHICKEN BARRISTERS
SIRS, I AM SCROOGE McDUCK, WHOM YOU CABLED ABOUT THE McDUCK ESTATE! THIS WATCH WILL PROVE THAT I AM THE RIGHTFUL HEIR!
YOUR PAPERS ARE IN ORDER, MR. McDUCK, AND THIS WATCH CERTAINLY APPEARS TO BE THE ONE MENTIONED IN THE WILL!

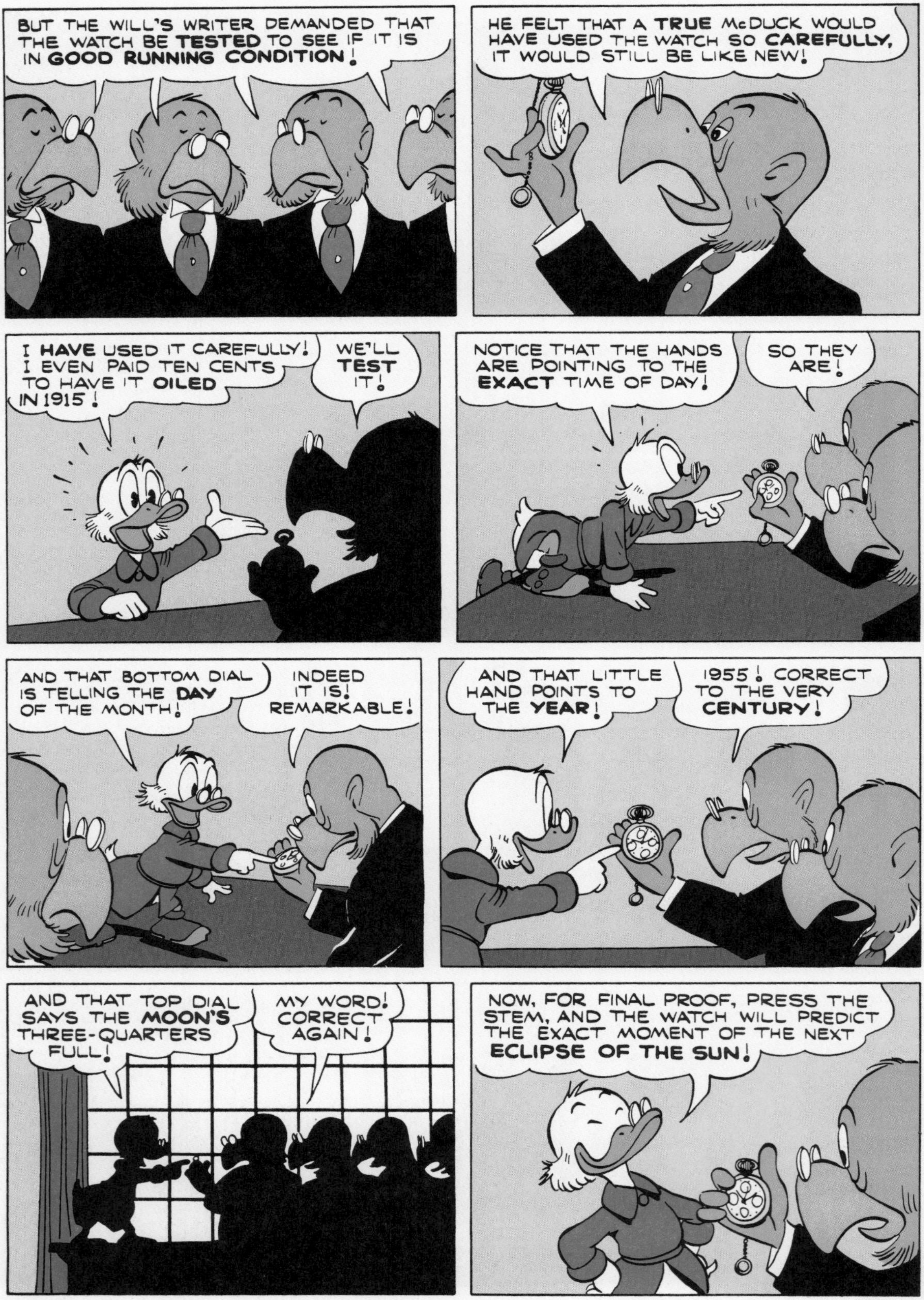
BUT THE WILL'S WRITER DEMANDED THAT THE WATCH BE **TESTED** TO SEE IF IT IS IN **GOOD RUNNING CONDITION**!
HE FELT THAT A **TRUE** McDUCK WOULD HAVE USED THE WATCH SO **CAREFULLY**, IT WOULD STILL BE LIKE NEW!
I **HAVE** USED IT CAREFULLY! I EVEN PAID TEN CENTS TO HAVE IT **OILED** IN 1915!
WE'LL **TEST** IT!
NOTICE THAT THE HANDS ARE POINTING TO THE **EXACT** TIME OF DAY!
SO THEY ARE!
AND THAT BOTTOM DIAL IS TELLING THE **DAY** OF THE MONTH!
INDEED IT IS! REMARKABLE!
AND THAT LITTLE HAND POINTS TO THE **YEAR**!
1955! CORRECT TO THE VERY **CENTURY**!
AND THAT TOP DIAL SAYS THE **MOON'S** THREE-QUARTERS FULL!
MY WORD! CORRECT AGAIN!
NOW, FOR FINAL PROOF, PRESS THE STEM, AND THE WATCH WILL PREDICT THE EXACT MOMENT OF THE NEXT **ECLIPSE OF THE SUN**!

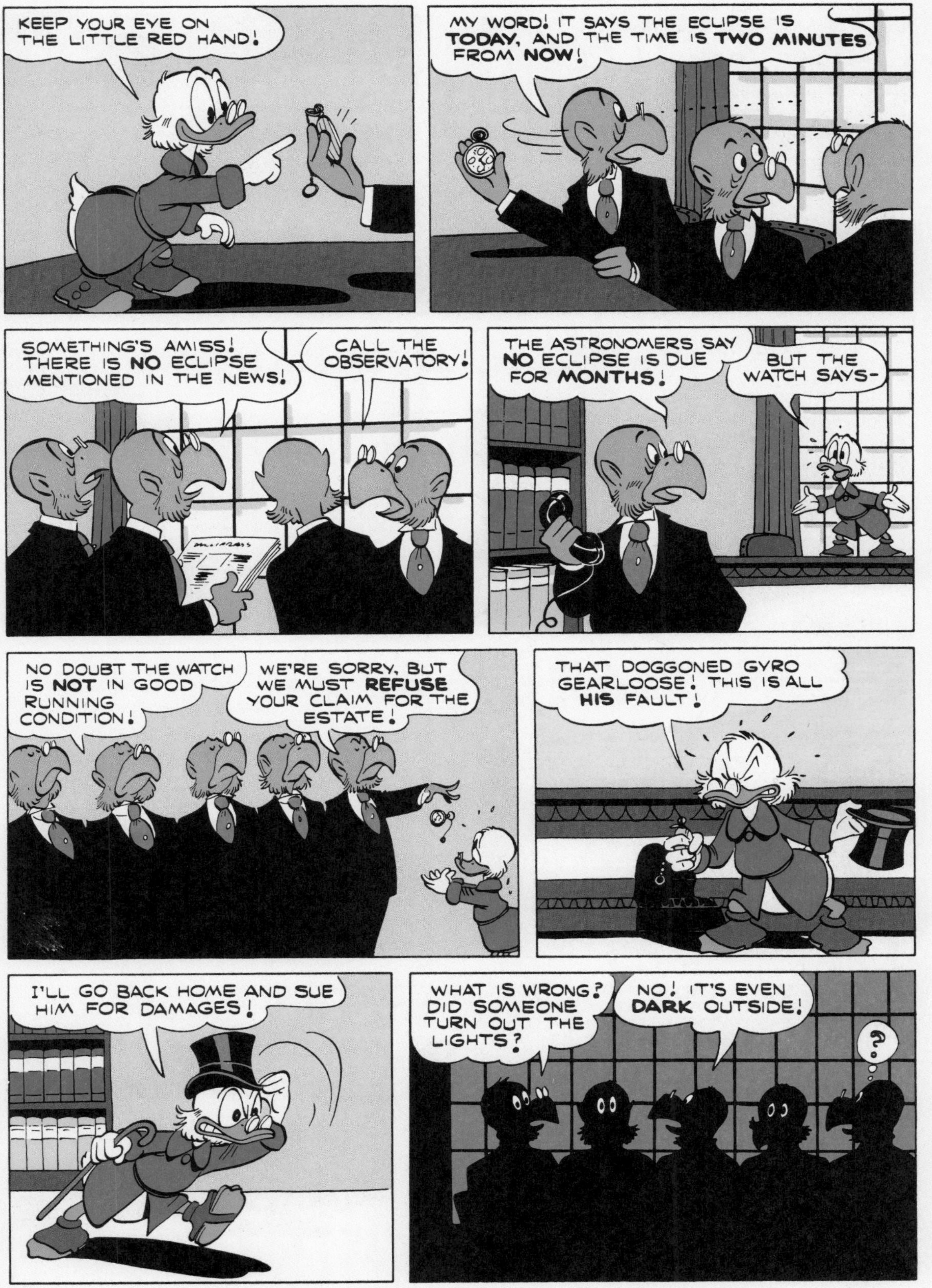
KEEP YOUR EYE ON THE LITTLE RED HAND!
MY WORD! IT SAYS THE ECLIPSE IS **TODAY**, AND THE TIME IS **TWO MINUTES** FROM **NOW**!
SOMETHING'S AMISS! THERE IS **NO** ECLIPSE MENTIONED IN THE NEWS!
CALL THE OBSERVATORY!
THE ASTRONOMERS SAY **NO** ECLIPSE IS DUE FOR **MONTHS**!
BUT THE WATCH SAYS-
NO DOUBT THE WATCH IS **NOT** IN GOOD RUNNING CONDITION!
WE'RE SORRY, BUT WE MUST **REFUSE** YOUR CLAIM FOR THE ESTATE!
THAT DOGGONED GYRO GEARLOOSE! THIS IS ALL **HIS** FAULT!
I'LL GO BACK HOME AND SUE HIM FOR DAMAGES!
WHAT IS WRONG? DID SOMEONE TURN OUT THE LIGHTS?
NO! IT'S EVEN **DARK** OUTSIDE!
?

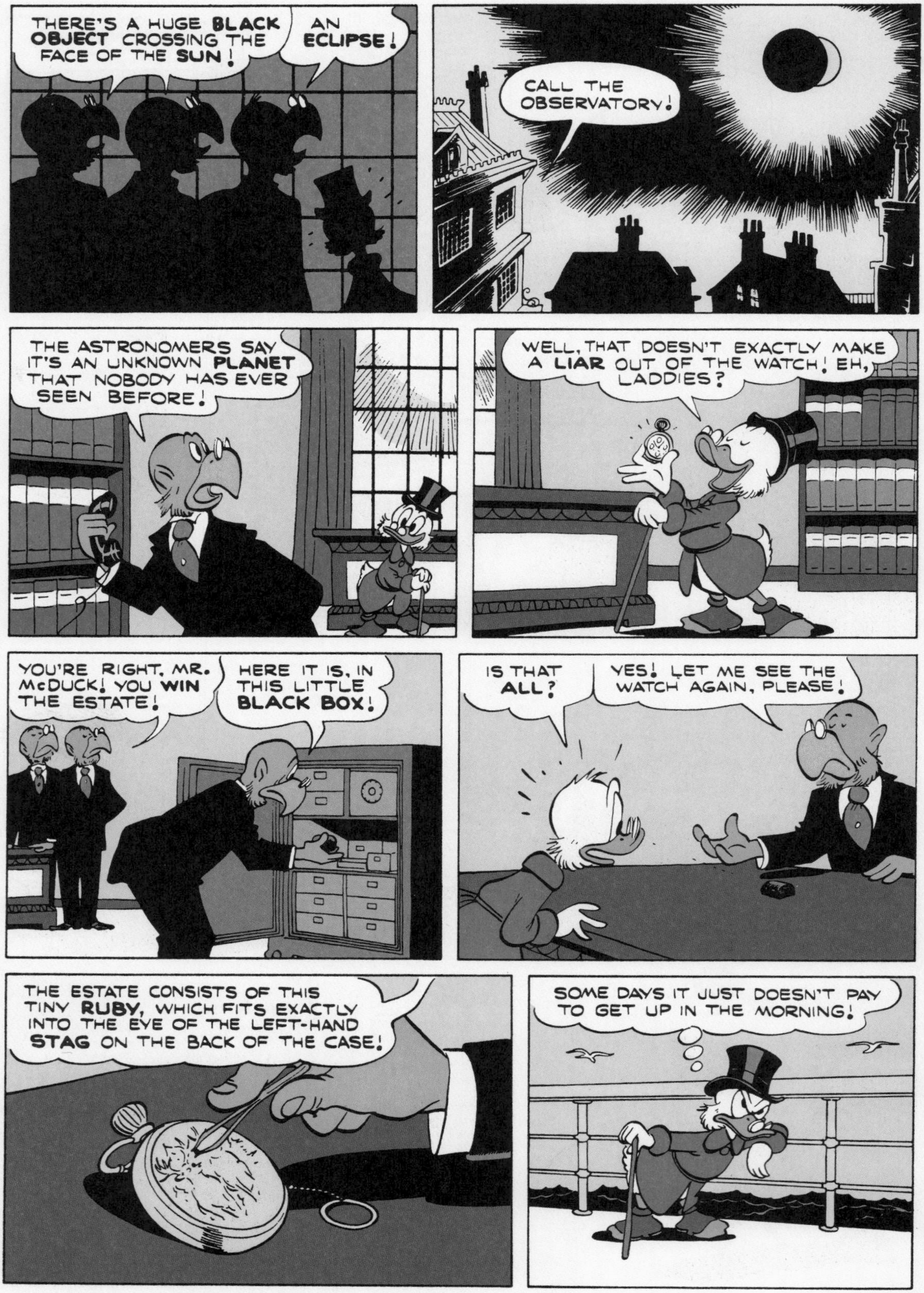
THERE'S A HUGE BLACK OBJECT CROSSING THE FACE OF THE SUN!
AN ECLIPSE!
CALL THE OBSERVATORY!
THE ASTRONOMERS SAY IT'S AN UNKNOWN PLANET THAT NOBODY HAS EVER SEEN BEFORE!
WELL, THAT DOESN'T EXACTLY MAKE A LIAR OUT OF THE WATCH! EH, LADDIES?
YOU'RE RIGHT, MR. McDUCK! YOU WIN THE ESTATE!
HERE IT IS, IN THIS LITTLE BLACK BOX!
IS THAT ALL?
YES! LET ME SEE THE WATCH AGAIN, PLEASE!
THE ESTATE CONSISTS OF THIS TINY RUBY, WHICH FITS EXACTLY INTO THE EYE OF THE LEFT-HAND STAG ON THE BACK OF THE CASE!
SOME DAYS IT JUST DOESN'T PAY TO GET UP IN THE MORNING!

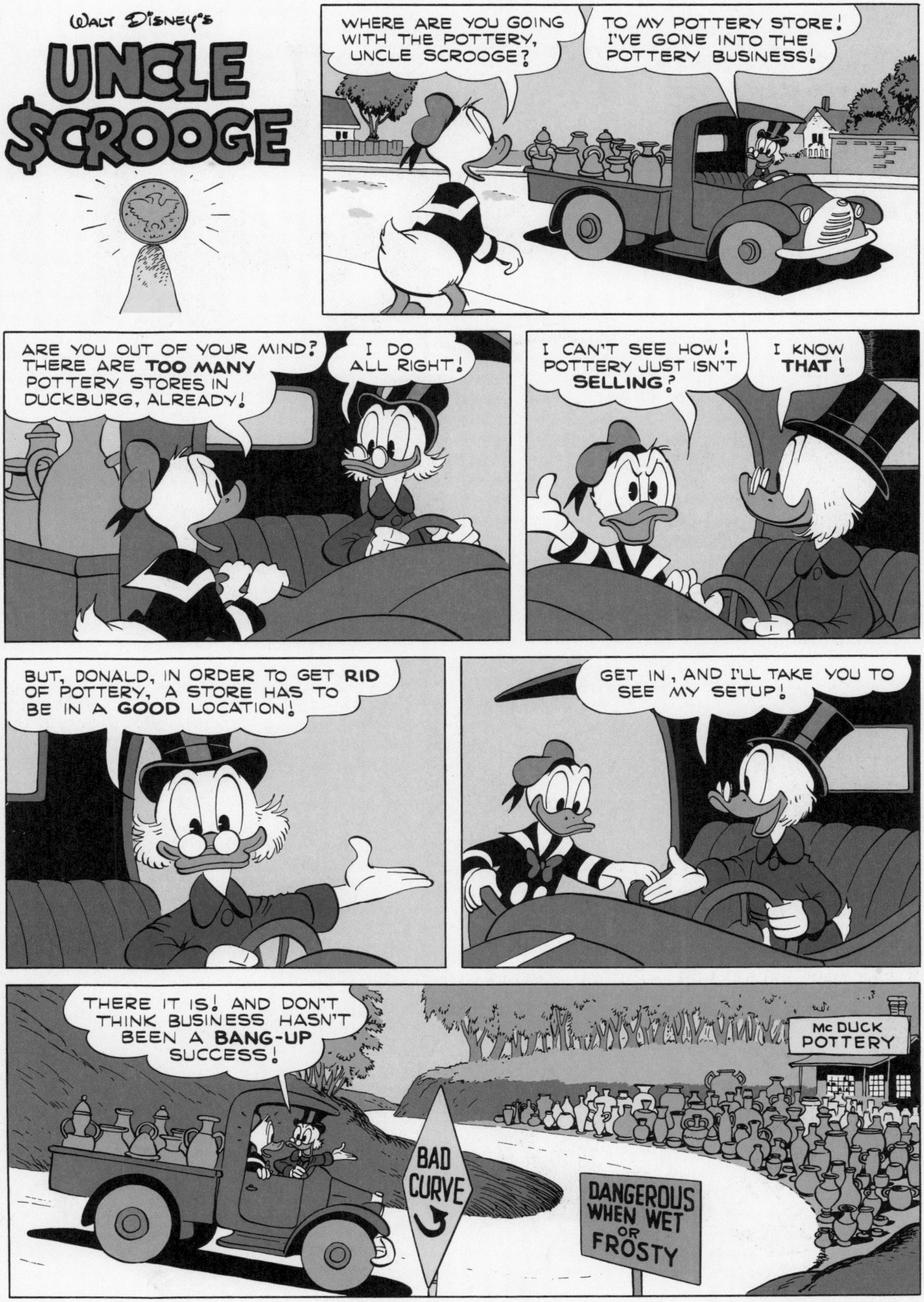
WALT DISNEY'S
UNCLE $CROOGE
WHERE ARE YOU GOING WITH THE POTTERY, UNCLE SCROOGE?
TO MY POTTERY STORE! I'VE GONE INTO THE POTTERY BUSINESS!
ARE YOU OUT OF YOUR MIND? THERE ARE TOO MANY POTTERY STORES IN DUCKBURG, ALREADY!
I DO ALL RIGHT!
I CAN'T SEE HOW! POTTERY JUST ISN'T SELLING?
I KNOW THAT!
BUT, DONALD, IN ORDER TO GET RID OF POTTERY, A STORE HAS TO BE IN A GOOD LOCATION!
GET IN, AND I'LL TAKE YOU TO SEE MY SETUP!
THERE IT IS! AND DON'T THINK BUSINESS HASN'T BEEN A BANG-UP SUCCESS!
McDUCK POTTERY
BAD CURVE
DANGEROUS WHEN WET OR FROSTY

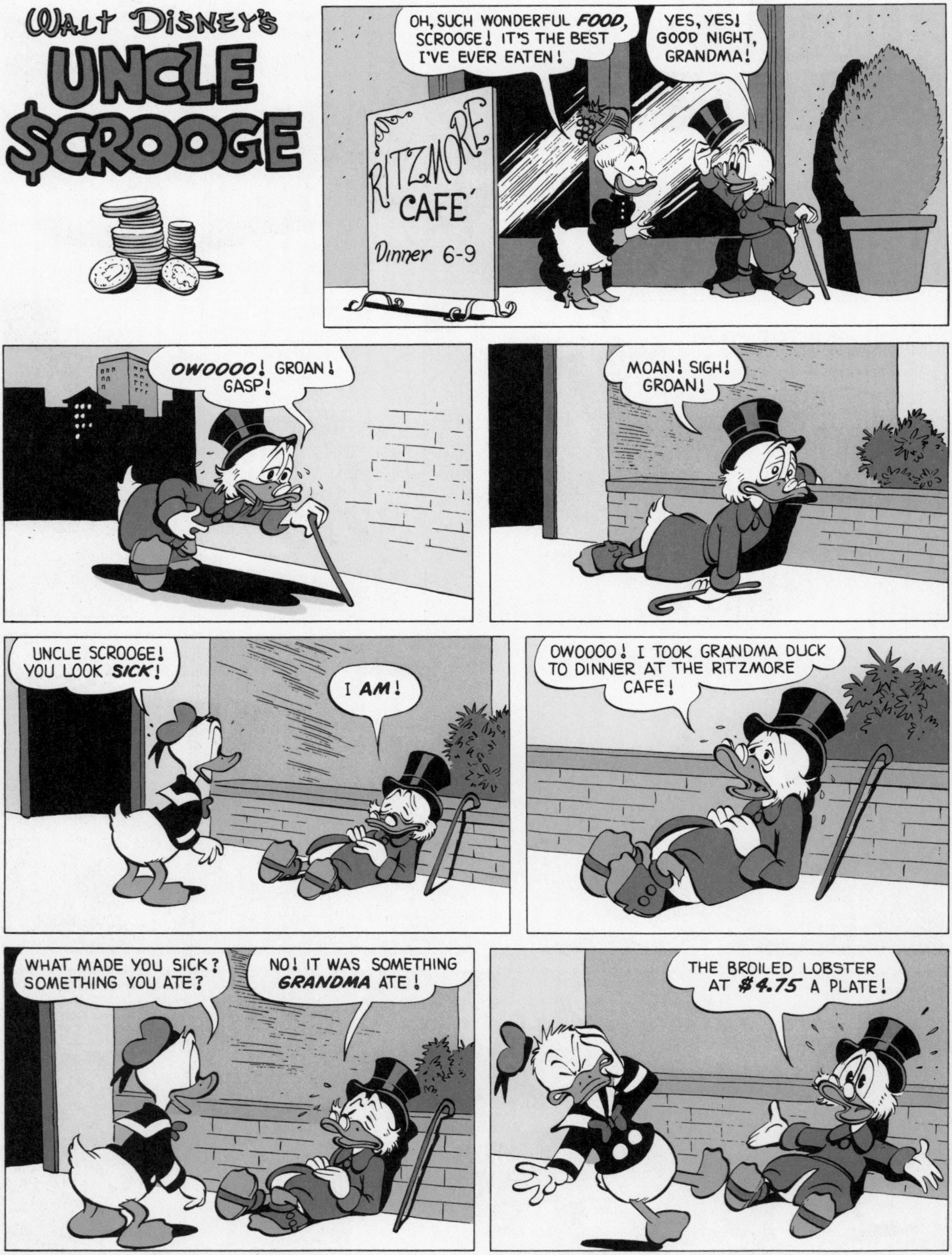
WALT DISNEY'S
UNCLE $CROOGE
OH, SUCH WONDERFUL FOOD, SCROOGE! IT'S THE BEST I'VE EVER EATEN!
YES, YES! GOOD NIGHT, GRANDMA!
RITZMORE CAFÉ
Dinner 6-9
OWOOOO! GROAN! GASP!
MOAN! SIGH! GROAN!
UNCLE SCROOGE! YOU LOOK SICK!
I AM!
OWOOOO! I TOOK GRANDMA DUCK TO DINNER AT THE RITZMORE CAFE!
WHAT MADE YOU SICK? SOMETHING YOU ATE?
NO! IT WAS SOMETHING GRANDMA ATE!
THE BROILED LOBSTER AT $4.75 A PLATE!

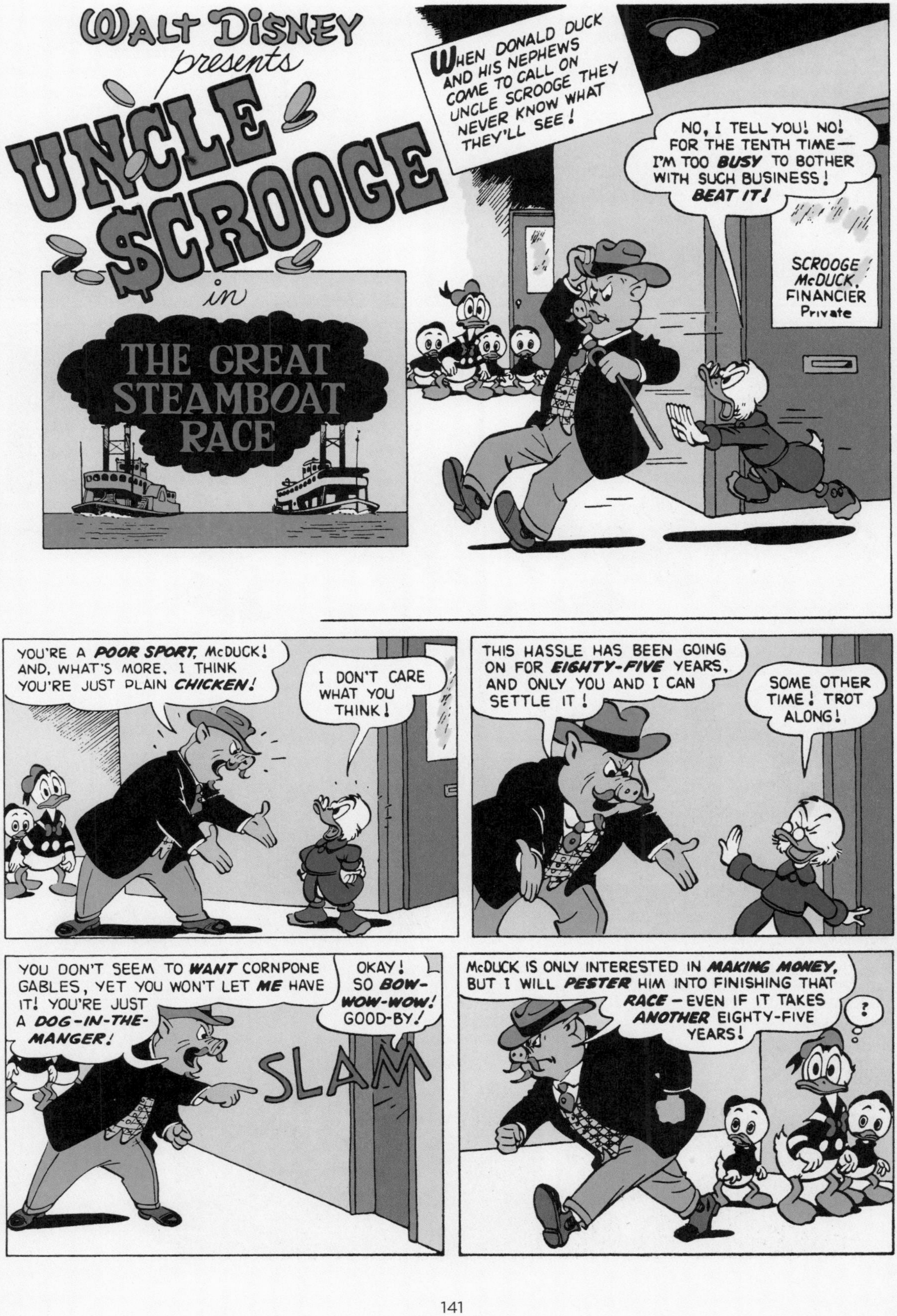
WALT DISNEY
presents
UNCLE $CROOGE
in
THE GREAT STEAMBOAT RACE
WHEN DONALD DUCK AND HIS NEPHEWS COME TO CALL ON UNCLE SCROOGE THEY NEVER KNOW WHAT THEY'LL SEE!
NO, I TELL YOU! NO! FOR THE TENTH TIME— I'M TOO BUSY TO BOTHER WITH SUCH BUSINESS! BEAT IT!
SCROOGE McDUCK, FINANCIER Private
YOU'RE A POOR SPORT, McDUCK! AND, WHAT'S MORE, I THINK YOU'RE JUST PLAIN CHICKEN!
I DON'T CARE WHAT YOU THINK!
THIS HASSLE HAS BEEN GOING ON FOR EIGHTY-FIVE YEARS, AND ONLY YOU AND I CAN SETTLE IT!
SOME OTHER TIME! TROT ALONG!
YOU DON'T SEEM TO WANT CORNPONE GABLES, YET YOU WON'T LET ME HAVE IT! YOU'RE JUST A DOG-IN-THE-MANGER!
OKAY! SO BOW-WOW-WOW! GOOD-BY!
SLAM
McDUCK IS ONLY INTERESTED IN MAKING MONEY, BUT I WILL PESTER HIM INTO FINISHING THAT RACE—EVEN IF IT TAKES ANOTHER EIGHTY-FIVE YEARS!
?

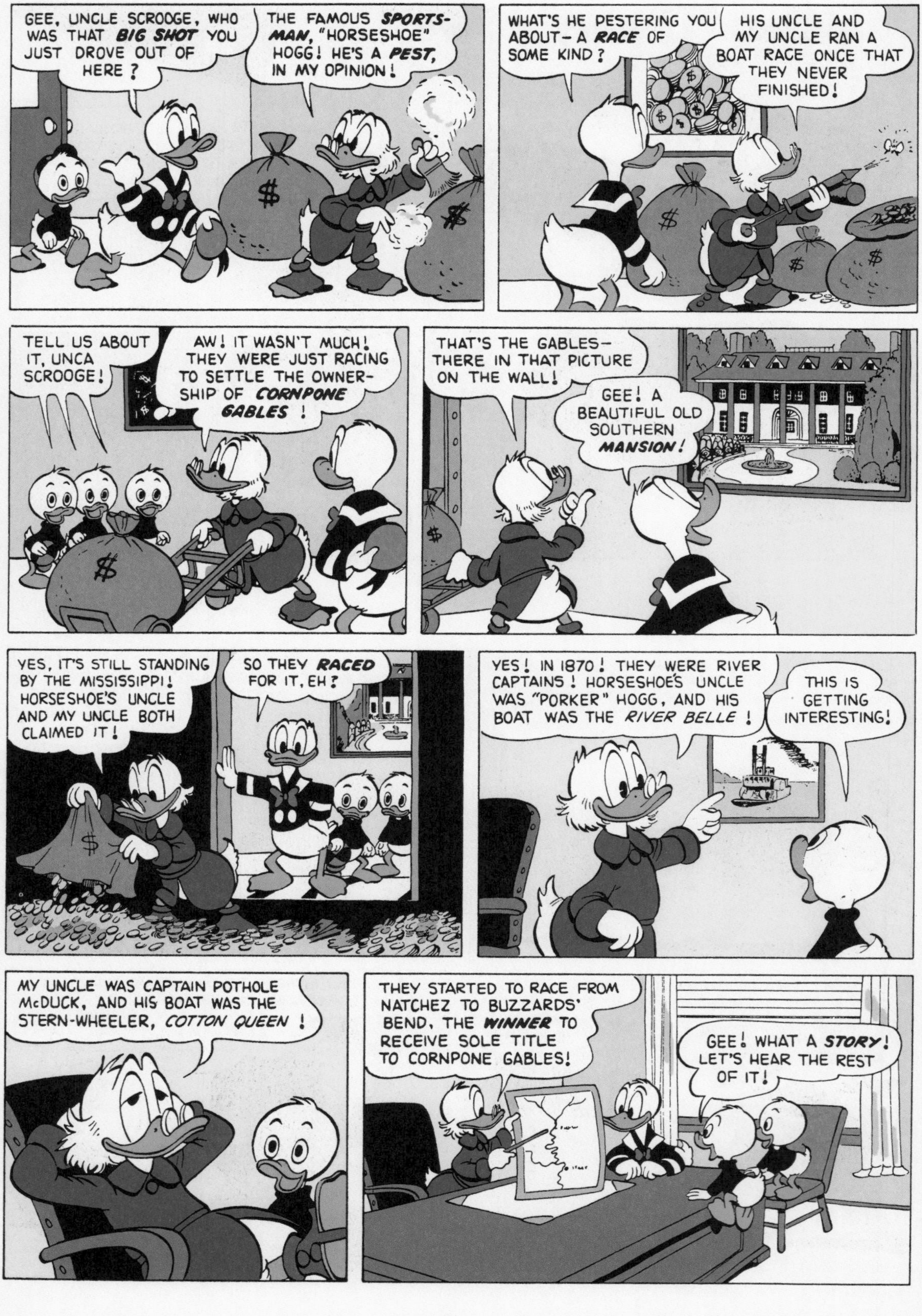
GEE, UNCLE SCROOGE, WHO WAS THAT BIG SHOT YOU JUST DROVE OUT OF HERE?
THE FAMOUS SPORTSMAN, "HORSESHOE" HOGG! HE'S A PEST, IN MY OPINION!
WHAT'S HE PESTERING YOU ABOUT—A RACE OF SOME KIND?
HIS UNCLE AND MY UNCLE RAN A BOAT RACE ONCE THAT THEY NEVER FINISHED!
TELL US ABOUT IT, UNCA SCROOGE!
AW! IT WASN'T MUCH! THEY WERE JUST RACING TO SETTLE THE OWNERSHIP OF CORNPONE GABLES!
THAT'S THE GABLES—THERE IN THAT PICTURE ON THE WALL!
GEE! A BEAUTIFUL OLD SOUTHERN MANSION!
YES, IT'S STILL STANDING BY THE MISSISSIPPI! HORSESHOE'S UNCLE AND MY UNCLE BOTH CLAIMED IT!
SO THEY RACED FOR IT, EH?
YES! IN 1870! THEY WERE RIVER CAPTAINS! HORSESHOE'S UNCLE WAS "PORKER" HOGG, AND HIS BOAT WAS THE RIVER BELLE!
THIS IS GETTING INTERESTING!
MY UNCLE WAS CAPTAIN POTHOLE McDUCK, AND HIS BOAT WAS THE STERN-WHEELER, COTTON QUEEN!
THEY STARTED TO RACE FROM NATCHEZ TO BUZZARDS' BEND, THE WINNER TO RECEIVE SOLE TITLE TO CORNPONE GABLES!
GEE! WHAT A STORY! LET'S HEAR THE REST OF IT!

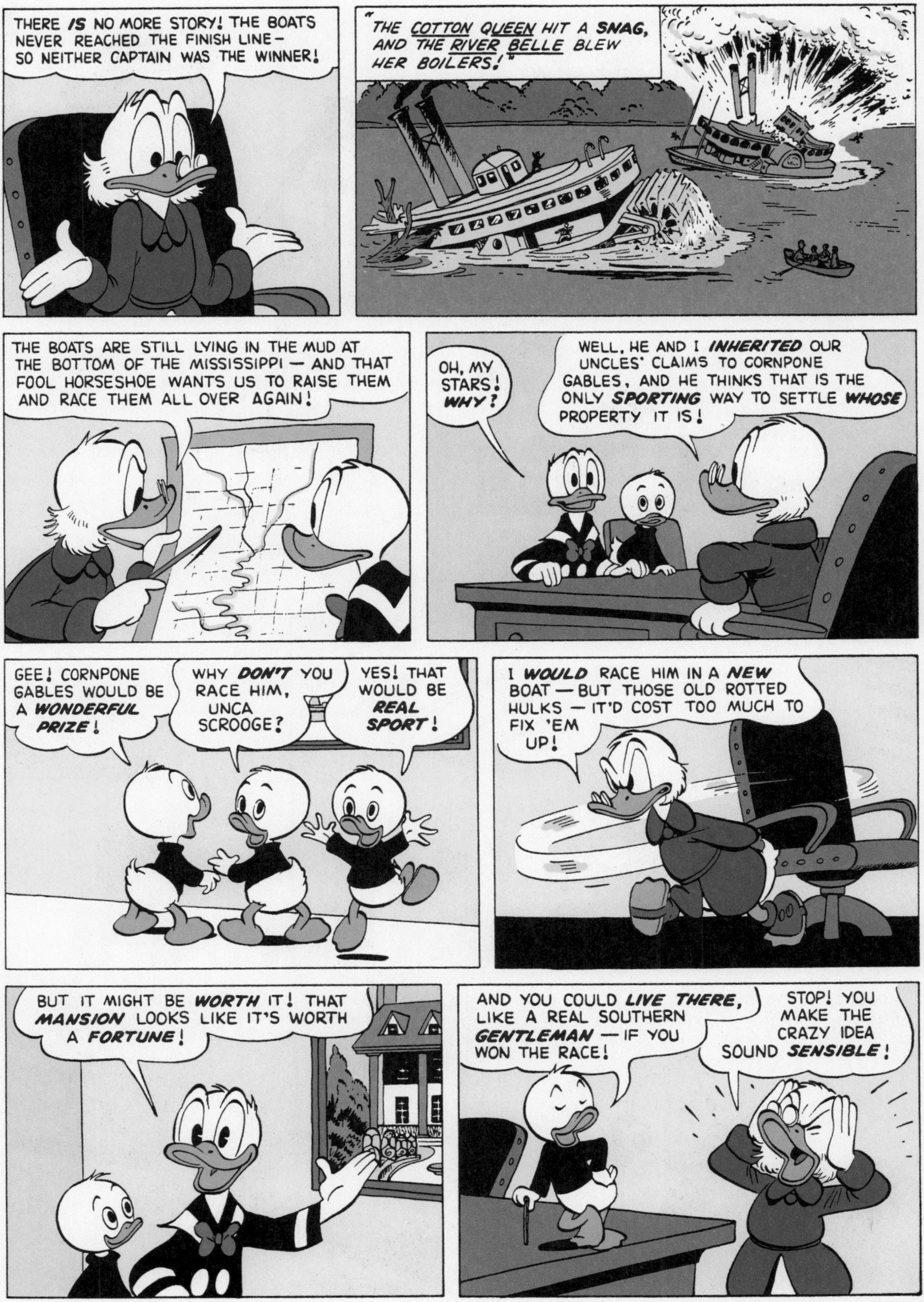
THERE IS NO MORE STORY! THE BOATS NEVER REACHED THE FINISH LINE— SO NEITHER CAPTAIN WAS THE WINNER!
"THE COTTON QUEEN HIT A SNAG, AND THE RIVER BELLE BLEW HER BOILERS!"
THE BOATS ARE STILL LYING IN THE MUD AT THE BOTTOM OF THE MISSISSIPPI — AND THAT FOOL HORSESHOE WANTS US TO RAISE THEM AND RACE THEM ALL OVER AGAIN!
OH, MY STARS! WHY?
WELL, HE AND I INHERITED OUR UNCLES' CLAIMS TO CORNPONE GABLES, AND HE THINKS THAT IS THE ONLY SPORTING WAY TO SETTLE WHOSE PROPERTY IT IS!
GEE! CORNPONE GABLES WOULD BE A WONDERFUL PRIZE!
WHY DON'T YOU RACE HIM, UNCA SCROOGE?
YES! THAT WOULD BE REAL SPORT!
I WOULD RACE HIM IN A NEW BOAT — BUT THOSE OLD ROTTED HULKS — IT'D COST TOO MUCH TO FIX 'EM UP!
BUT IT MIGHT BE WORTH IT! THAT MANSION LOOKS LIKE IT'S WORTH A FORTUNE!
AND YOU COULD LIVE THERE, LIKE A REAL SOUTHERN GENTLEMAN — IF YOU WON THE RACE!
STOP! YOU MAKE THE CRAZY IDEA SOUND SENSIBLE!

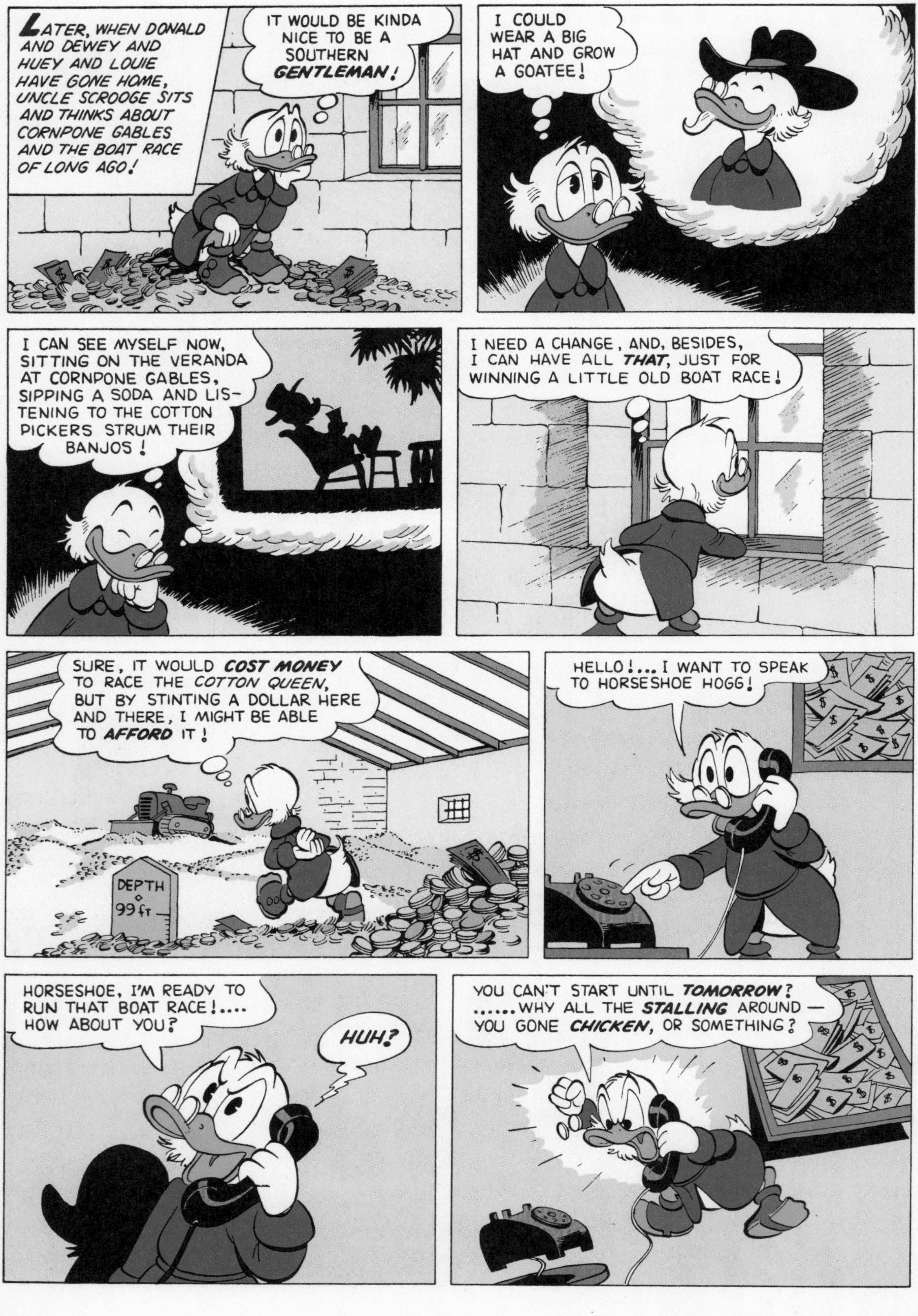
LATER, WHEN DONALD AND DEWEY AND HUEY AND LOUIE HAVE GONE HOME, UNCLE SCROOGE SITS AND THINKS ABOUT CORNPONE GABLES AND THE BOAT RACE OF LONG AGO!
IT WOULD BE KINDA NICE TO BE A SOUTHERN GENTLEMAN!
I COULD WEAR A BIG HAT AND GROW A GOATEE!
I CAN SEE MYSELF NOW, SITTING ON THE VERANDA AT CORNPONE GABLES, SIPPING A SODA AND LISTENING TO THE COTTON PICKERS STRUM THEIR BANJOS!
I NEED A CHANGE, AND, BESIDES, I CAN HAVE ALL THAT, JUST FOR WINNING A LITTLE OLD BOAT RACE!
SURE, IT WOULD COST MONEY TO RACE THE COTTON QUEEN, BUT BY STINTING A DOLLAR HERE AND THERE, I MIGHT BE ABLE TO AFFORD IT!
DEPTH 99 ft
HELLO!... I WANT TO SPEAK TO HORSESHOE HOGG!
HORSESHOE, I'M READY TO RUN THAT BOAT RACE!.... HOW ABOUT YOU?
HUH?
YOU CAN'T START UNTIL TOMORROW? ......WHY ALL THE STALLING AROUND — YOU GONE CHICKEN, OR SOMETHING?

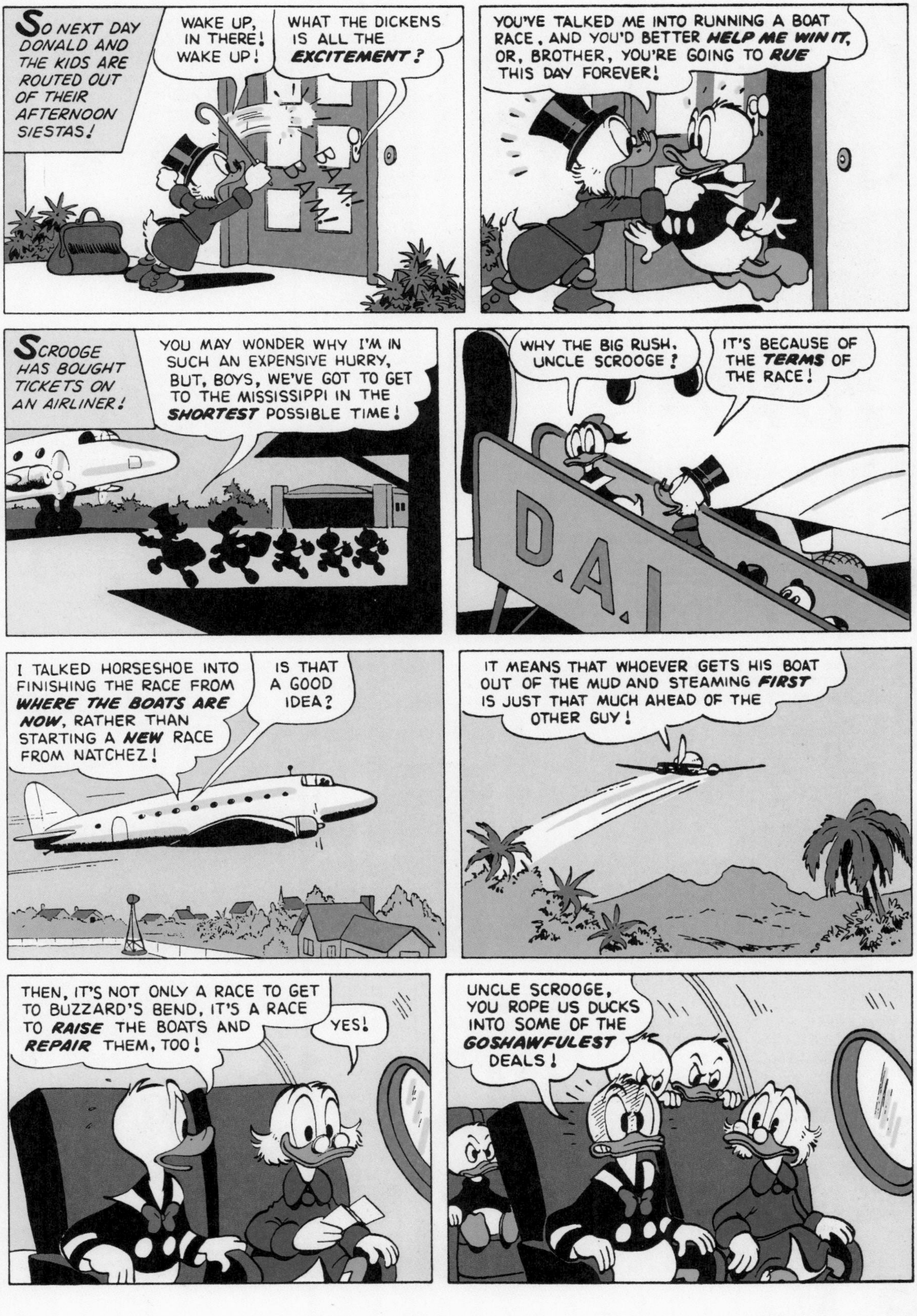
SO NEXT DAY DONALD AND THE KIDS ARE ROUTED OUT OF THEIR AFTERNOON SIESTAS!
WAKE UP, IN THERE! WAKE UP!
WHAT THE DICKENS IS ALL THE EXCITEMENT?
BAM! BAM!
YOU'VE TALKED ME INTO RUNNING A BOAT RACE, AND YOU'D BETTER HELP ME WIN IT, OR, BROTHER, YOU'RE GOING TO RUE THIS DAY FOREVER!
SCROOGE HAS BOUGHT TICKETS ON AN AIRLINER!
YOU MAY WONDER WHY I'M IN SUCH AN EXPENSIVE HURRY, BUT, BOYS, WE'VE GOT TO GET TO THE MISSISSIPPI IN THE SHORTEST POSSIBLE TIME!
WHY THE BIG RUSH, UNCLE SCROOGE?
IT'S BECAUSE OF THE TERMS OF THE RACE!
D.A.L
I TALKED HORSESHOE INTO FINISHING THE RACE FROM WHERE THE BOATS ARE NOW, RATHER THAN STARTING A NEW RACE FROM NATCHEZ!
IS THAT A GOOD IDEA?
IT MEANS THAT WHOEVER GETS HIS BOAT OUT OF THE MUD AND STEAMING FIRST IS JUST THAT MUCH AHEAD OF THE OTHER GUY!
THEN, IT'S NOT ONLY A RACE TO GET TO BUZZARD'S BEND, IT'S A RACE TO RAISE THE BOATS AND REPAIR THEM, TOO!
YES!
UNCLE SCROOGE, YOU ROPE US DUCKS INTO SOME OF THE GOSHAWFULEST DEALS!

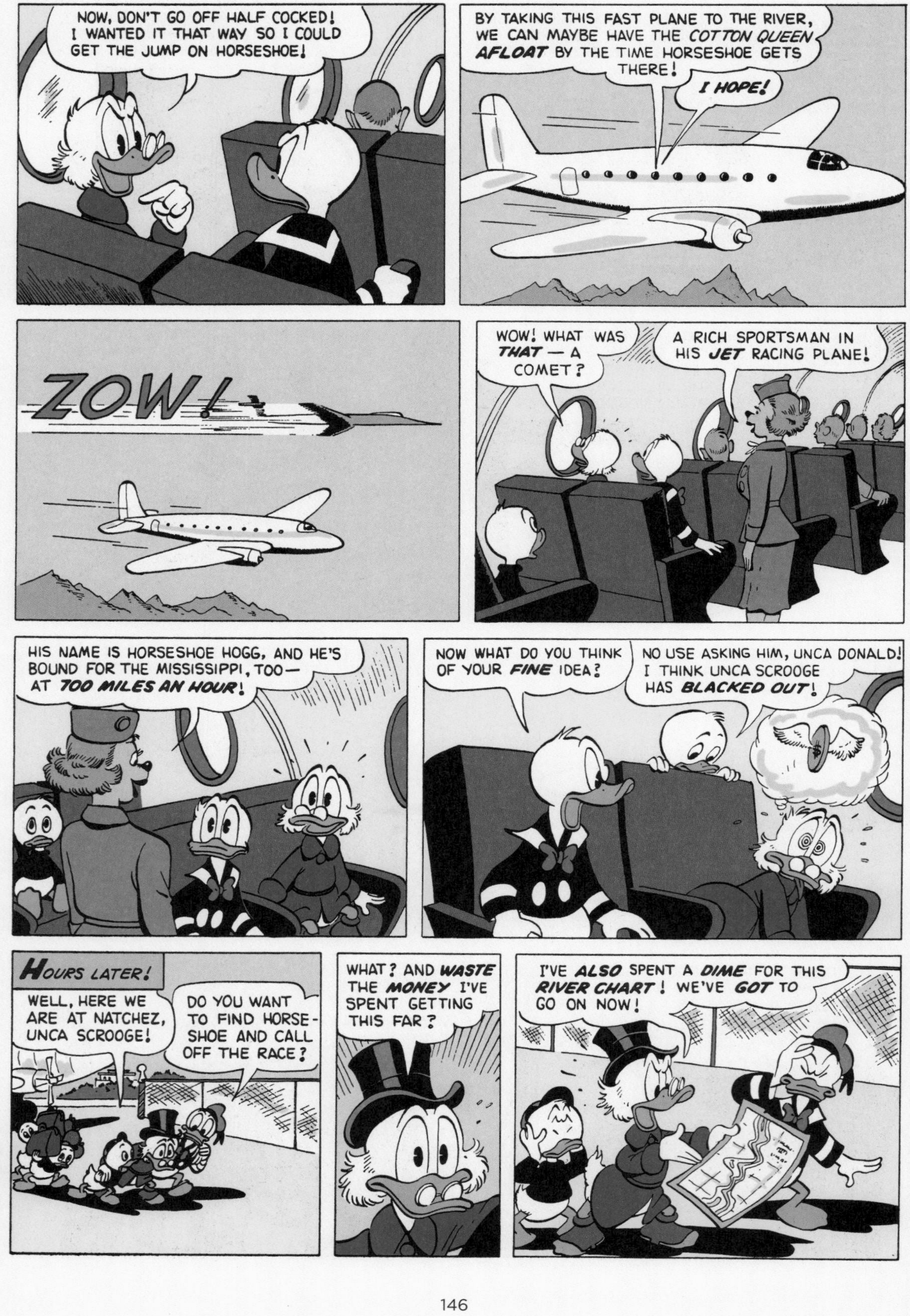
NOW, DON'T GO OFF HALF COCKED! I WANTED IT THAT WAY SO I COULD GET THE JUMP ON HORSESHOE!
BY TAKING THIS FAST PLANE TO THE RIVER, WE CAN MAYBE HAVE THE COTTON QUEEN AFLOAT BY THE TIME HORSESHOE GETS THERE!
I HOPE!
ZOW!
WOW! WHAT WAS THAT — A COMET?
A RICH SPORTSMAN IN HIS JET RACING PLANE!
HIS NAME IS HORSESHOE HOGG, AND HE'S BOUND FOR THE MISSISSIPPI, TOO— AT 700 MILES AN HOUR!
NOW WHAT DO YOU THINK OF YOUR FINE IDEA?
NO USE ASKING HIM, UNCA DONALD! I THINK UNCA SCROOGE HAS BLACKED OUT!
HOURS LATER!
WELL, HERE WE ARE AT NATCHEZ, UNCA SCROOGE!
DO YOU WANT TO FIND HORSE-SHOE AND CALL OFF THE RACE?
WHAT? AND WASTE THE MONEY I'VE SPENT GETTING THIS FAR?
I'VE ALSO SPENT A DIME FOR THIS RIVER CHART! WE'VE GOT TO GO ON NOW!

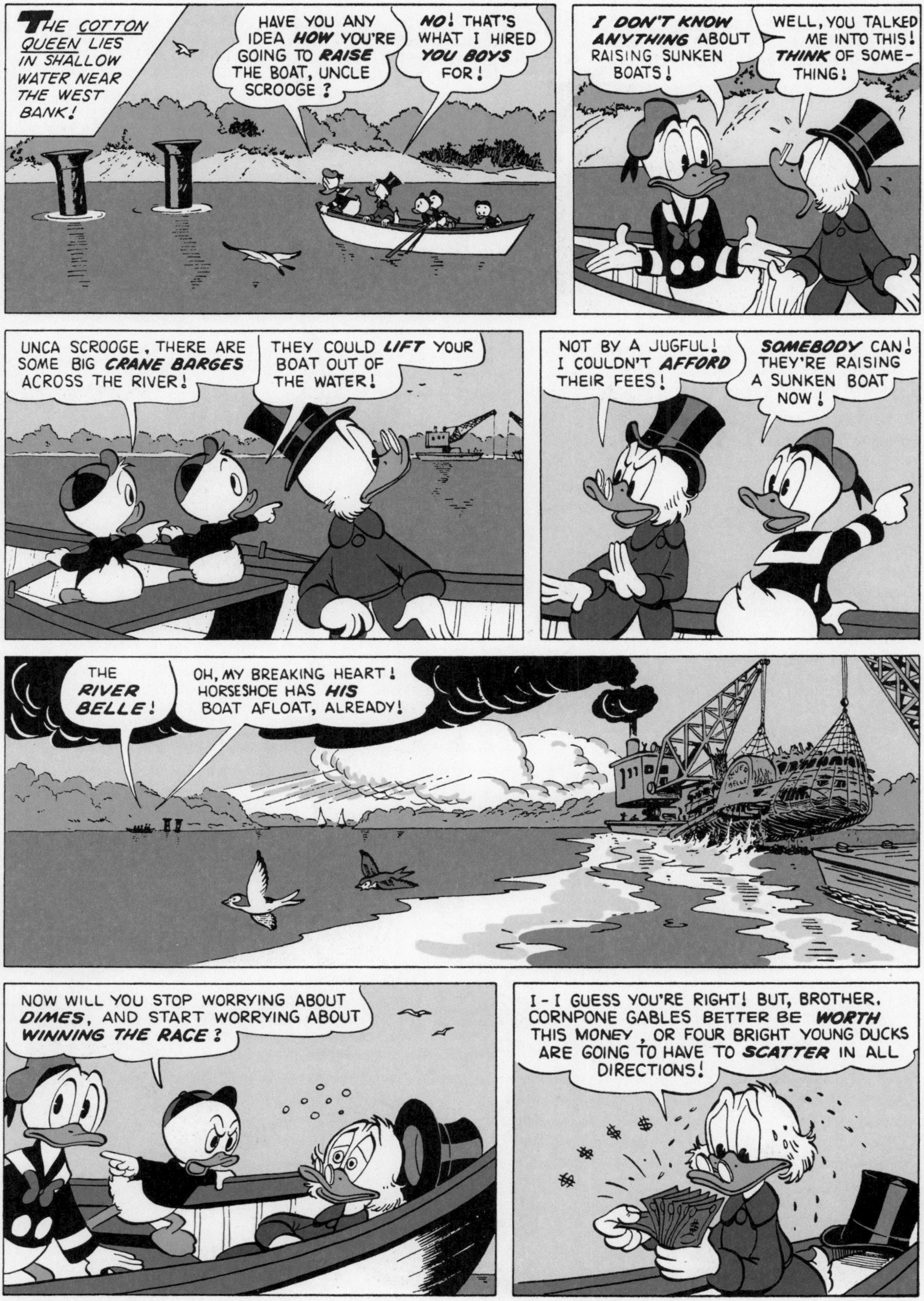
THE COTTON QUEEN LIES IN SHALLOW WATER NEAR THE WEST BANK!
HAVE YOU ANY IDEA HOW YOU'RE GOING TO RAISE THE BOAT, UNCLE SCROOGE?
NO! THAT'S WHAT I HIRED YOU BOYS FOR!
I DON'T KNOW ANYTHING ABOUT RAISING SUNKEN BOATS!
WELL, YOU TALKED ME INTO THIS! THINK OF SOMETHING!
UNCA SCROOGE, THERE ARE SOME BIG CRANE BARGES ACROSS THE RIVER!
THEY COULD LIFT YOUR BOAT OUT OF THE WATER!
NOT BY A JUGFUL! I COULDN'T AFFORD THEIR FEES!
SOMEBODY CAN! THEY'RE RAISING A SUNKEN BOAT NOW!
THE RIVER BELLE!
OH, MY BREAKING HEART! HORSESHOE HAS HIS BOAT AFLOAT, ALREADY!
NOW WILL YOU STOP WORRYING ABOUT DIMES, AND START WORRYING ABOUT WINNING THE RACE?
I-I GUESS YOU'RE RIGHT! BUT, BROTHER, CORNPONE GABLES BETTER BE WORTH THIS MONEY, OR FOUR BRIGHT YOUNG DUCKS ARE GOING TO HAVE TO SCATTER IN ALL DIRECTIONS!

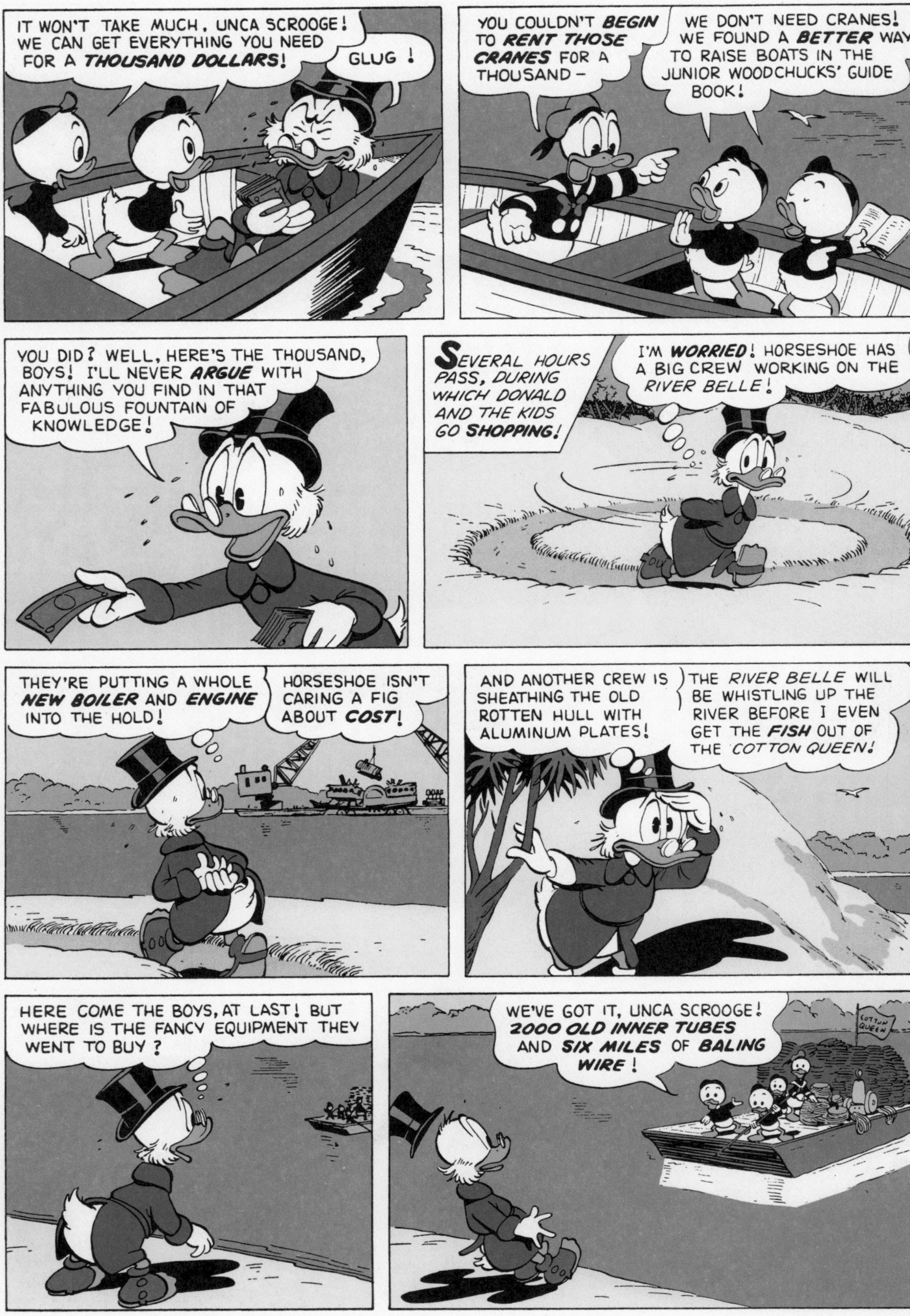

IT WON'T TAKE MUCH, UNCA SCROOGE! WE CAN GET EVERYTHING YOU NEED FOR A **THOUSAND DOLLARS**!
GLUG!
YOU COULDN'T **BEGIN** TO **RENT THOSE CRANES** FOR A THOUSAND –
WE DON'T NEED CRANES! WE FOUND A **BETTER** WAY TO RAISE BOATS IN THE JUNIOR WOODCHUCKS' GUIDE BOOK!
YOU DID? WELL, HERE'S THE THOUSAND, BOYS! I'LL NEVER **ARGUE** WITH ANYTHING YOU FIND IN THAT FABULOUS FOUNTAIN OF KNOWLEDGE!
SEVERAL HOURS PASS, DURING WHICH DONALD AND THE KIDS GO **SHOPPING**!
I'M **WORRIED**! HORSESHOE HAS A BIG CREW WORKING ON THE *RIVER BELLE*!
THEY'RE PUTTING A WHOLE **NEW BOILER** AND **ENGINE** INTO THE HOLD!
HORSESHOE ISN'T CARING A FIG ABOUT **COST**!
AND ANOTHER CREW IS SHEATHING THE OLD ROTTEN HULL WITH ALUMINUM PLATES!
THE *RIVER BELLE* WILL BE WHISTLING UP THE RIVER BEFORE I EVEN GET THE **FISH** OUT OF THE *COTTON QUEEN*!
HERE COME THE BOYS, AT LAST! BUT WHERE IS THE FANCY EQUIPMENT THEY WENT TO BUY?
WE'VE GOT IT, UNCA SCROOGE! **2000 OLD INNER TUBES** AND **SIX MILES** OF **BALING WIRE**!

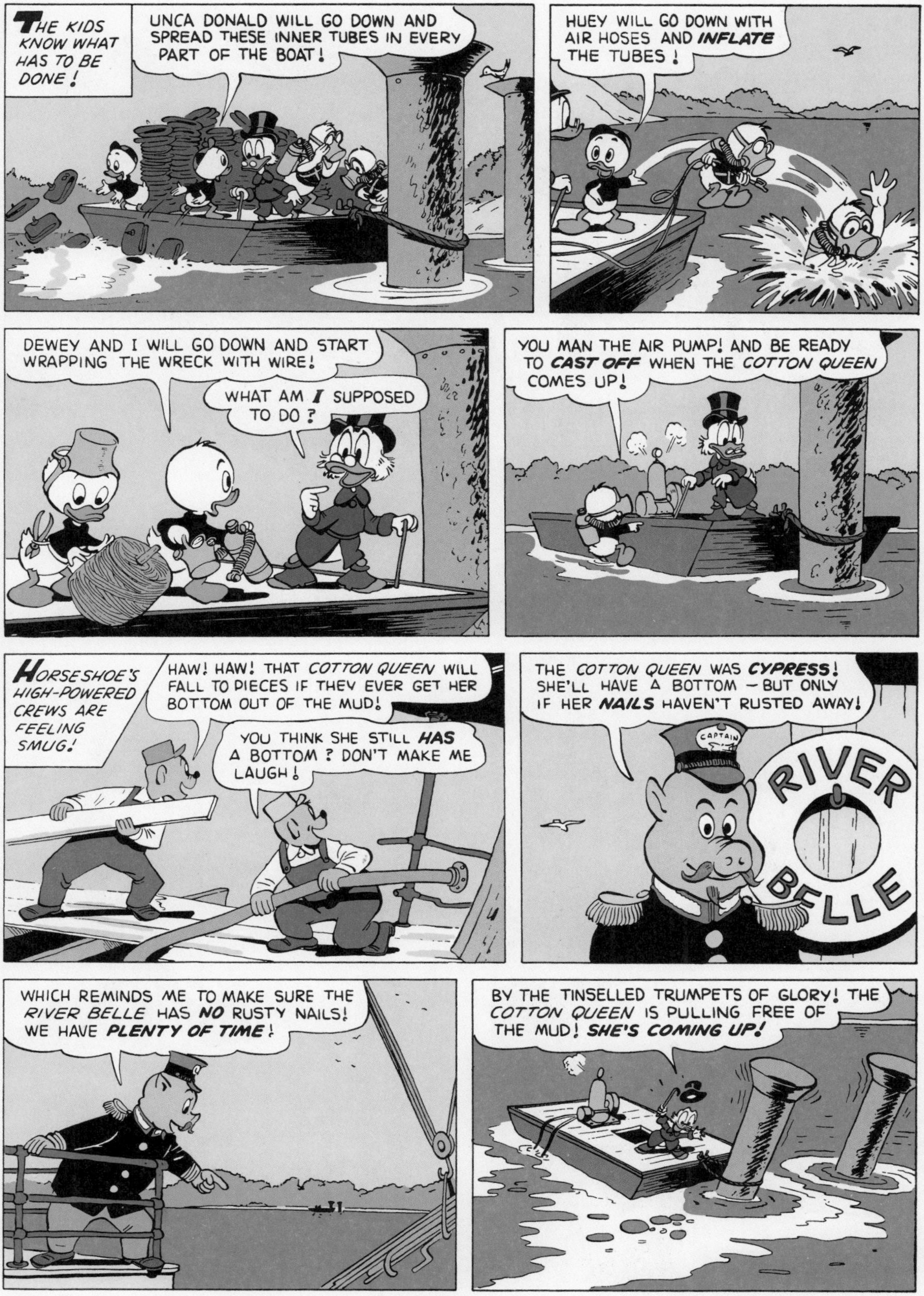
THE KIDS KNOW WHAT HAS TO BE DONE!
UNCA DONALD WILL GO DOWN AND SPREAD THESE INNER TUBES IN EVERY PART OF THE BOAT!
HUEY WILL GO DOWN WITH AIR HOSES AND INFLATE THE TUBES!
DEWEY AND I WILL GO DOWN AND START WRAPPING THE WRECK WITH WIRE!
WHAT AM I SUPPOSED TO DO?
YOU MAN THE AIR PUMP! AND BE READY TO CAST OFF WHEN THE COTTON QUEEN COMES UP!
HORSESHOE'S HIGH-POWERED CREWS ARE FEELING SMUG!
HAW! HAW! THAT COTTON QUEEN WILL FALL TO PIECES IF THEY EVER GET HER BOTTOM OUT OF THE MUD!
YOU THINK SHE STILL HAS A BOTTOM? DON'T MAKE ME LAUGH!
THE COTTON QUEEN WAS CYPRESS! SHE'LL HAVE A BOTTOM — BUT ONLY IF HER NAILS HAVEN'T RUSTED AWAY!
CAPTAIN
RIVER BELLE
WHICH REMINDS ME TO MAKE SURE THE RIVER BELLE HAS NO RUSTY NAILS! WE HAVE PLENTY OF TIME!
BY THE TINSELLED TRUMPETS OF GLORY! THE COTTON QUEEN IS PULLING FREE OF THE MUD! SHE'S COMING UP!

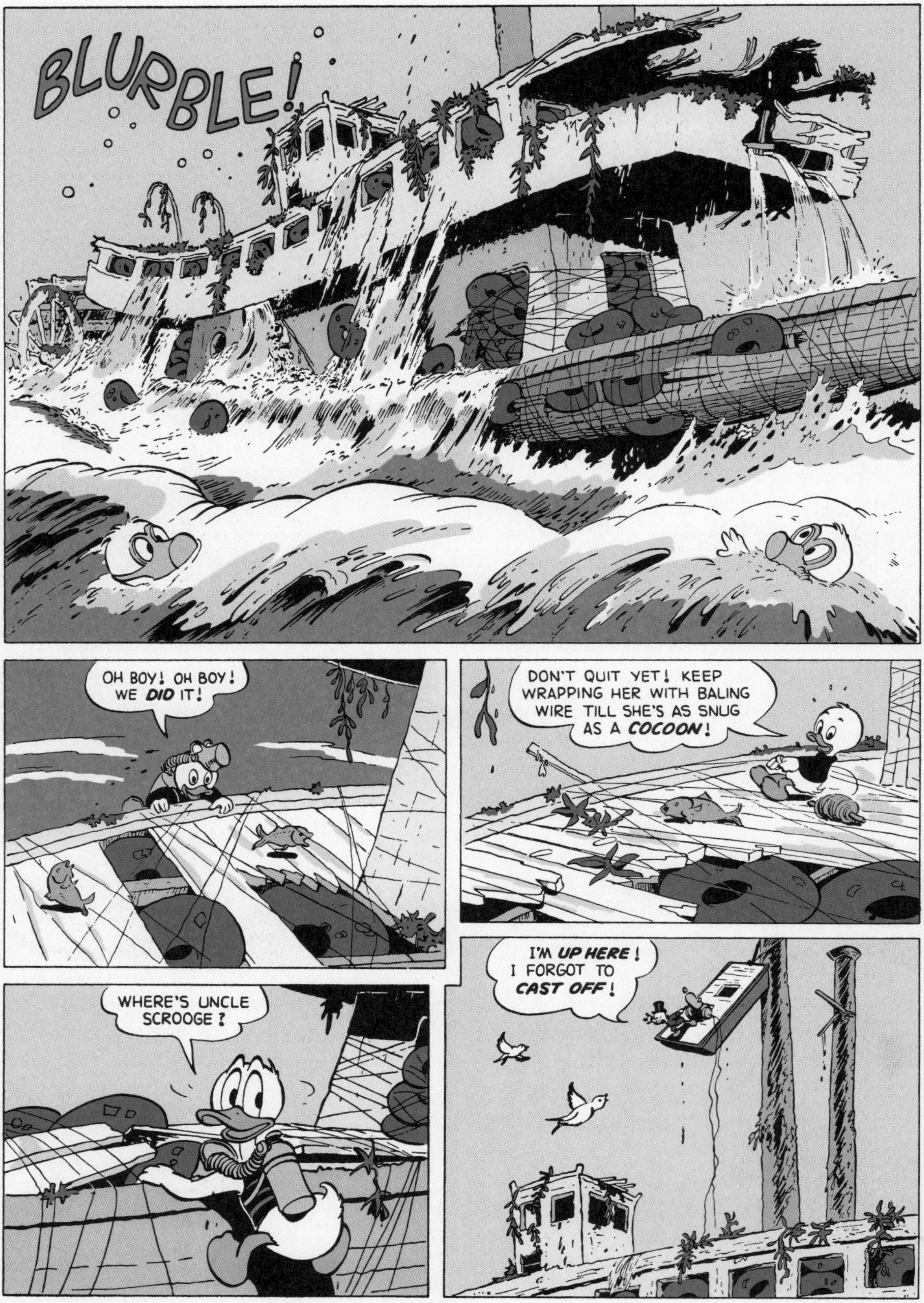
BLURBLE!
OH BOY! OH BOY! WE DID IT!
DON'T QUIT YET! KEEP WRAPPING HER WITH BALING WIRE TILL SHE'S AS SNUG AS A COCOON!
WHERE'S UNCLE SCROOGE?
I'M UP HERE! I FORGOT TO CAST OFF!

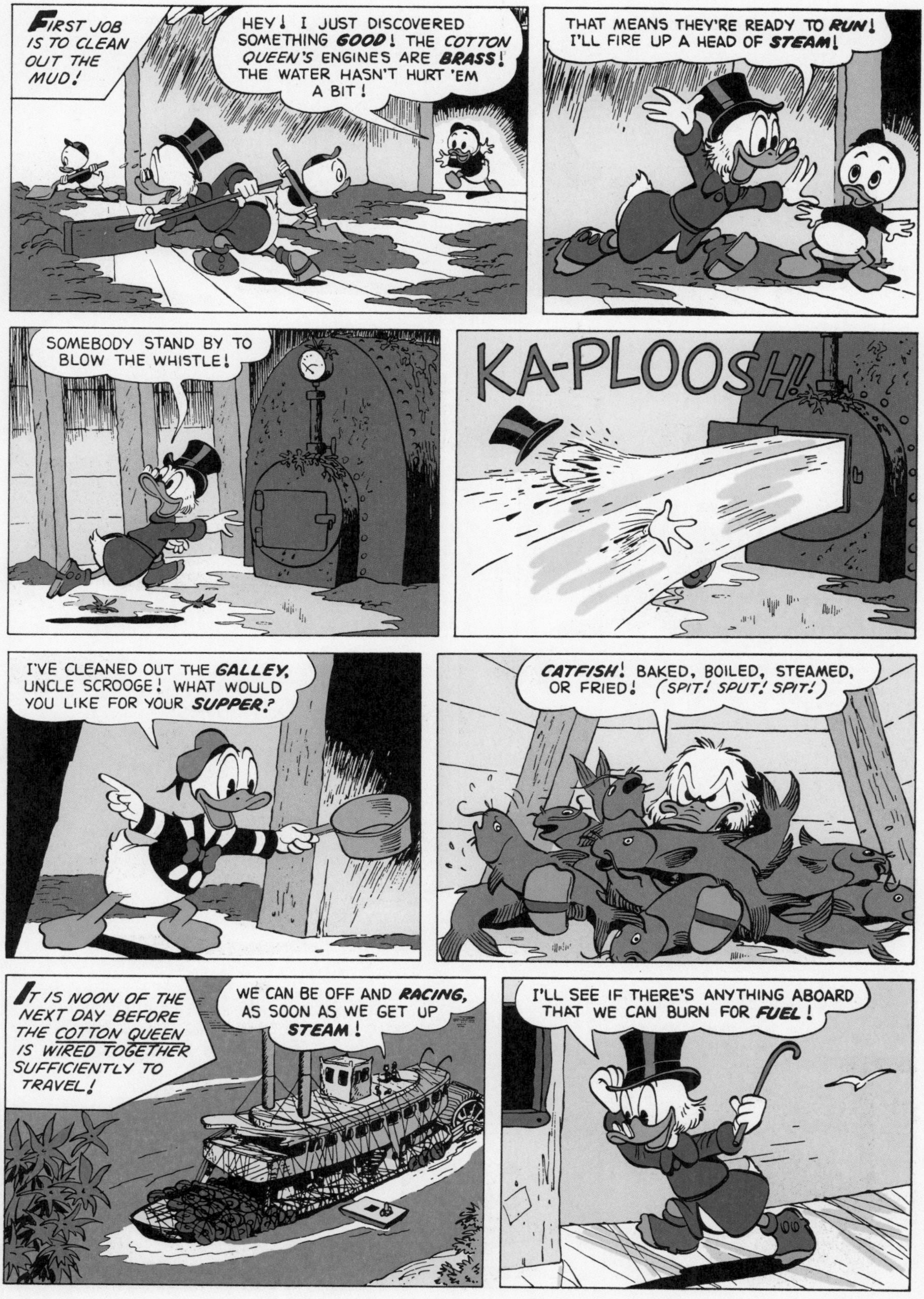
FIRST JOB IS TO CLEAN OUT THE MUD!
HEY! I JUST DISCOVERED SOMETHING GOOD! THE COTTON QUEEN'S ENGINES ARE BRASS! THE WATER HASN'T HURT 'EM A BIT!
THAT MEANS THEY'RE READY TO RUN! I'LL FIRE UP A HEAD OF STEAM!
SOMEBODY STAND BY TO BLOW THE WHISTLE!
KA-PLOOSH!
I'VE CLEANED OUT THE GALLEY, UNCLE SCROOGE! WHAT WOULD YOU LIKE FOR YOUR SUPPER?
CATFISH! BAKED, BOILED, STEAMED, OR FRIED! (SPIT! SPUT! SPIT!)
IT IS NOON OF THE NEXT DAY BEFORE THE COTTON QUEEN IS WIRED TOGETHER SUFFICIENTLY TO TRAVEL!
WE CAN BE OFF AND RACING, AS SOON AS WE GET UP STEAM!
I'LL SEE IF THERE'S ANYTHING ABOARD THAT WE CAN BURN FOR FUEL!

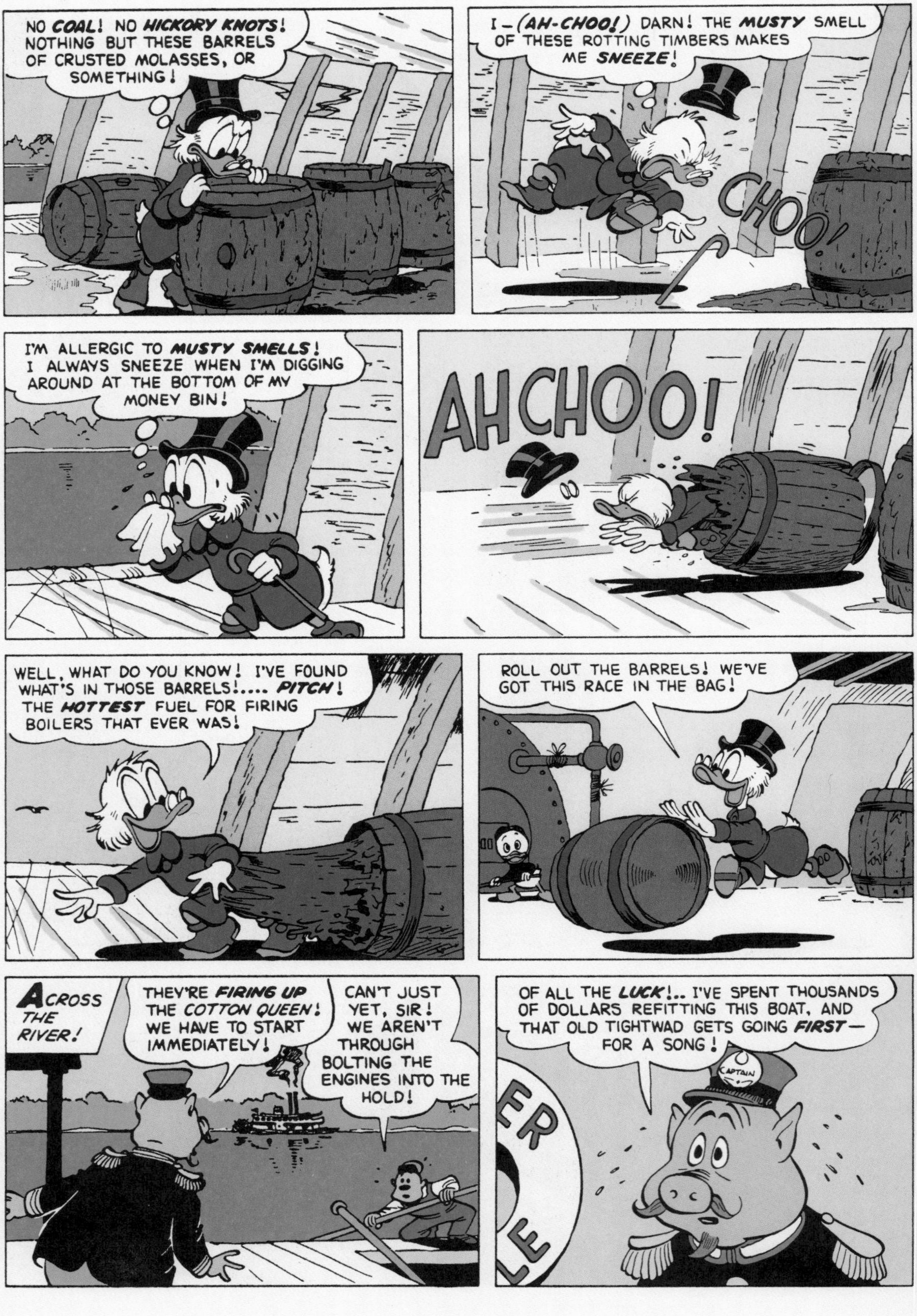
NO COAL! NO HICKORY KNOTS! NOTHING BUT THESE BARRELS OF CRUSTED MOLASSES, OR SOMETHING!
I–(AH-CHOO!) DARN! THE MUSTY SMELL OF THESE ROTTING TIMBERS MAKES ME SNEEZE!
CHOO!
I'M ALLERGIC TO MUSTY SMELLS! I ALWAYS SNEEZE WHEN I'M DIGGING AROUND AT THE BOTTOM OF MY MONEY BIN!
AHCHOO!
WELL, WHAT DO YOU KNOW! I'VE FOUND WHAT'S IN THOSE BARRELS!.... PITCH! THE HOTTEST FUEL FOR FIRING BOILERS THAT EVER WAS!
ROLL OUT THE BARRELS! WE'VE GOT THIS RACE IN THE BAG!
ACROSS THE RIVER!
THEY'RE FIRING UP THE COTTON QUEEN! WE HAVE TO START IMMEDIATELY!
CAN'T JUST YET, SIR! WE AREN'T THROUGH BOLTING THE ENGINES INTO THE HOLD!
OF ALL THE LUCK!.. I'VE SPENT THOUSANDS OF DOLLARS REFITTING THIS BOAT, AND THAT OLD TIGHTWAD GETS GOING FIRST— FOR A SONG!
CAPTAIN

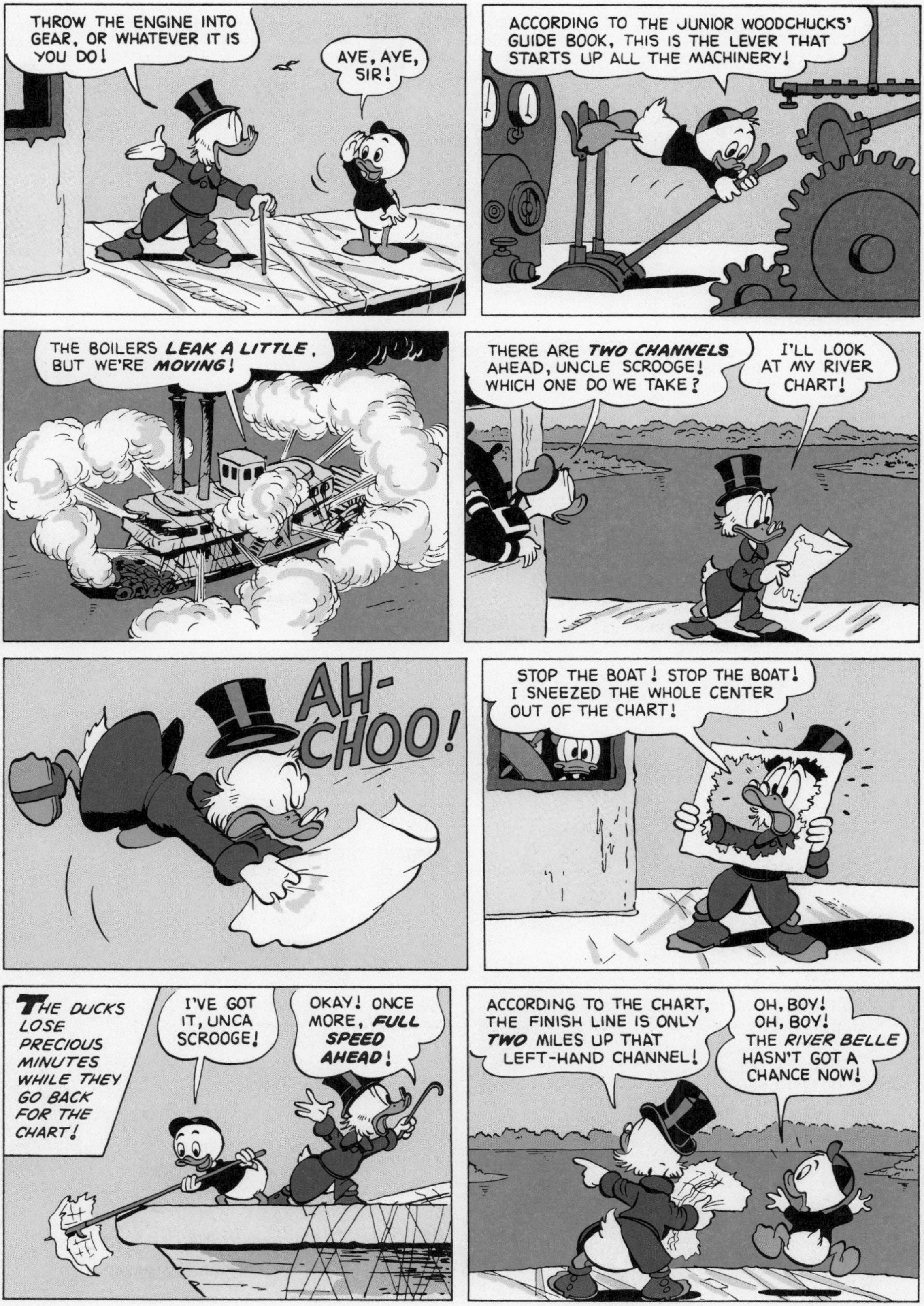
THROW THE ENGINE INTO GEAR, OR WHATEVER IT IS YOU DO!
AYE, AYE, SIR!
ACCORDING TO THE JUNIOR WOODCHUCKS' GUIDE BOOK, THIS IS THE LEVER THAT STARTS UP ALL THE MACHINERY!
THE BOILERS LEAK A LITTLE, BUT WE'RE MOVING!
THERE ARE TWO CHANNELS AHEAD, UNCLE SCROOGE! WHICH ONE DO WE TAKE?
I'LL LOOK AT MY RIVER CHART!
AH-CHOO!
STOP THE BOAT! STOP THE BOAT! I SNEEZED THE WHOLE CENTER OUT OF THE CHART!
THE DUCKS LOSE PRECIOUS MINUTES WHILE THEY GO BACK FOR THE CHART!
I'VE GOT IT, UNCA SCROOGE!
OKAY! ONCE MORE, FULL SPEED AHEAD!
ACCORDING TO THE CHART, THE FINISH LINE IS ONLY TWO MILES UP THAT LEFT-HAND CHANNEL!
OH, BOY! OH, BOY! THE RIVER BELLE HASN'T GOT A CHANCE NOW!

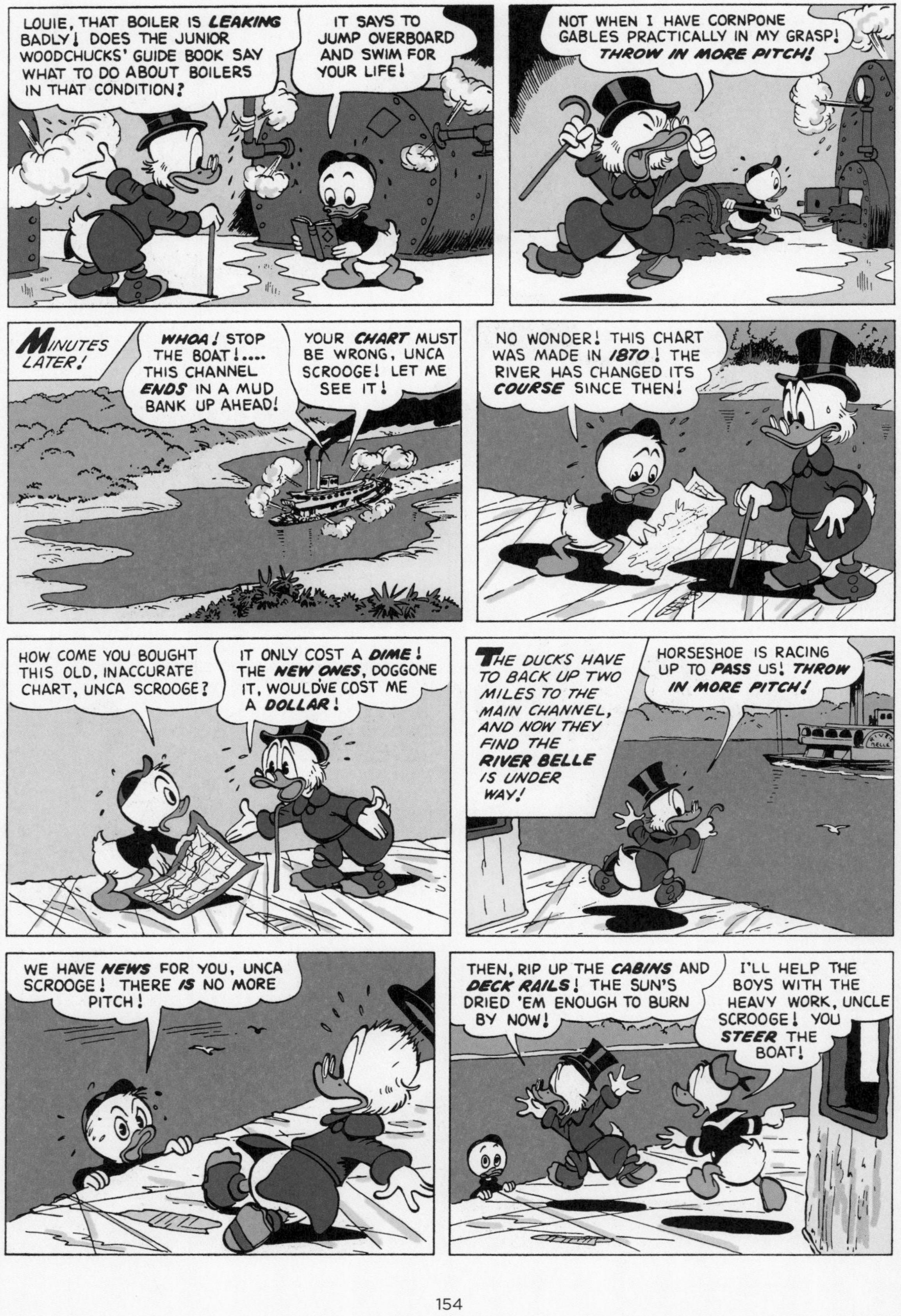
LOUIE, THAT BOILER IS LEAKING BADLY! DOES THE JUNIOR WOODCHUCKS' GUIDE BOOK SAY WHAT TO DO ABOUT BOILERS IN THAT CONDITION?
IT SAYS TO JUMP OVERBOARD AND SWIM FOR YOUR LIFE!
NOT WHEN I HAVE CORNPONE GABLES PRACTICALLY IN MY GRASP! THROW IN MORE PITCH!
MINUTES LATER!
WHOA! STOP THE BOAT!.... THIS CHANNEL ENDS IN A MUD BANK UP AHEAD!
YOUR CHART MUST BE WRONG, UNCA SCROOGE! LET ME SEE IT!
NO WONDER! THIS CHART WAS MADE IN 1870! THE RIVER HAS CHANGED ITS COURSE SINCE THEN!
HOW COME YOU BOUGHT THIS OLD, INACCURATE CHART, UNCA SCROOGE?
IT ONLY COST A DIME! THE NEW ONES, DOGGONE IT, WOULD'VE COST ME A DOLLAR!
THE DUCKS HAVE TO BACK UP TWO MILES TO THE MAIN CHANNEL, AND NOW THEY FIND THE RIVER BELLE IS UNDER WAY!
HORSESHOE IS RACING UP TO PASS US! THROW IN MORE PITCH!
WE HAVE NEWS FOR YOU, UNCA SCROOGE! THERE IS NO MORE PITCH!
THEN, RIP UP THE CABINS AND DECK RAILS! THE SUN'S DRIED 'EM ENOUGH TO BURN BY NOW!
I'LL HELP THE BOYS WITH THE HEAVY WORK, UNCLE SCROOGE! YOU STEER THE BOAT!

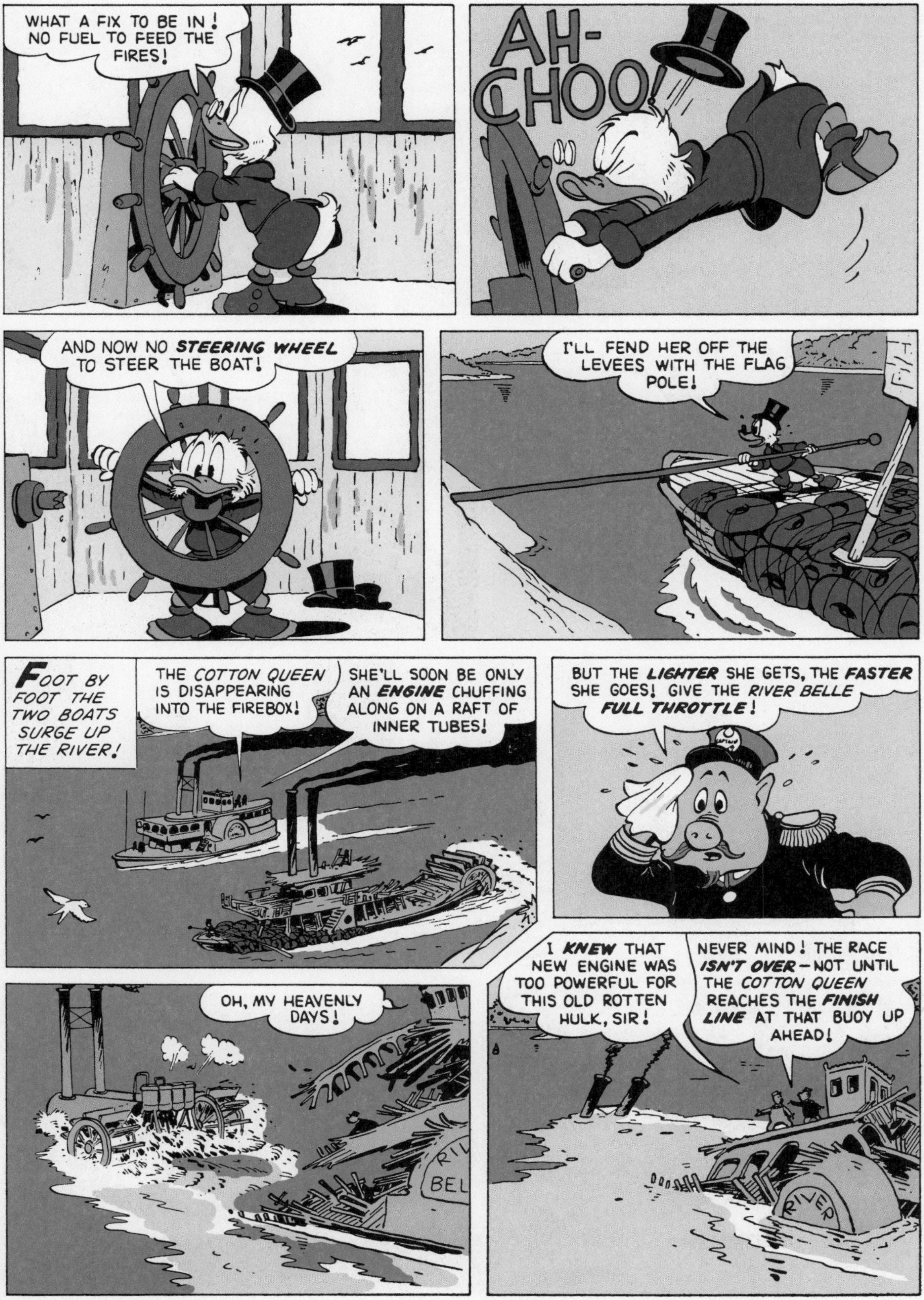
WHAT A FIX TO BE IN! NO FUEL TO FEED THE FIRES!
AH-CHOO!
AND NOW NO STEERING WHEEL TO STEER THE BOAT!
I'LL FEND HER OFF THE LEVEES WITH THE FLAG POLE!
FOOT BY FOOT THE TWO BOATS SURGE UP THE RIVER!
THE COTTON QUEEN IS DISAPPEARING INTO THE FIREBOX!
SHE'LL SOON BE ONLY AN ENGINE CHUFFING ALONG ON A RAFT OF INNER TUBES!
BUT THE LIGHTER SHE GETS, THE FASTER SHE GOES! GIVE THE RIVER BELLE FULL THROTTLE!
OH, MY HEAVENLY DAYS!
I KNEW THAT NEW ENGINE WAS TOO POWERFUL FOR THIS OLD ROTTEN HULK, SIR!
NEVER MIND! THE RACE ISN'T OVER—NOT UNTIL THE COTTON QUEEN REACHES THE FINISH LINE AT THAT BUOY UP AHEAD!
RIVER

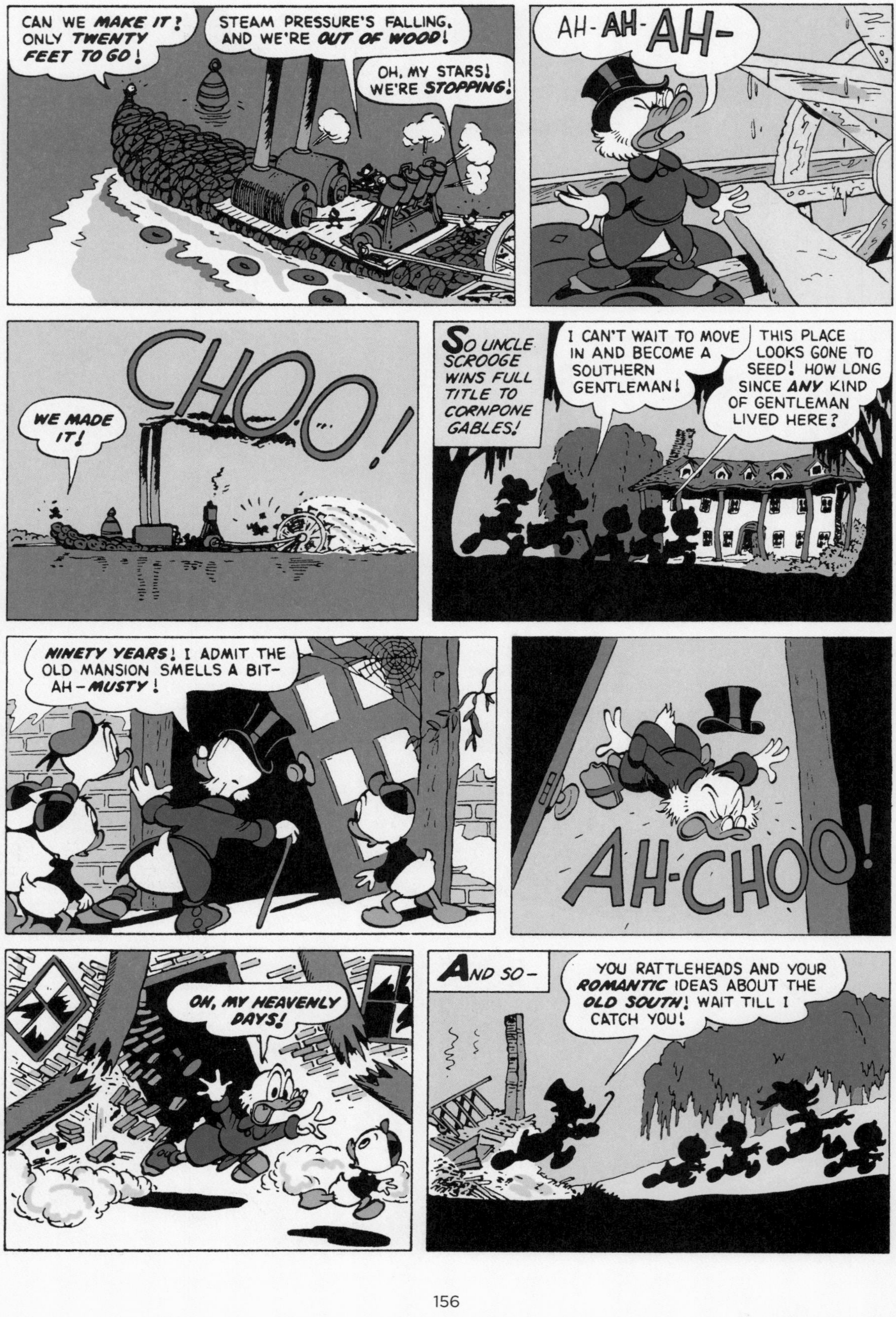
CAN WE MAKE IT? ONLY TWENTY FEET TO GO!
STEAM PRESSURE'S FALLING, AND WE'RE OUT OF WOOD!
OH, MY STARS! WE'RE STOPPING!
AH-AH-AH-
CHOO!
WE MADE IT!
SO UNCLE SCROOGE WINS FULL TITLE TO CORNPONE GABLES!
I CAN'T WAIT TO MOVE IN AND BECOME A SOUTHERN GENTLEMAN!
THIS PLACE LOOKS GONE TO SEED! HOW LONG SINCE ANY KIND OF GENTLEMAN LIVED HERE?
NINETY YEARS! I ADMIT THE OLD MANSION SMELLS A BIT-AH-MUSTY!
AH-CHOO!
OH, MY HEAVENLY DAYS!
AND SO-
YOU RATTLEHEADS AND YOUR ROMANTIC IDEAS ABOUT THE OLD SOUTH! WAIT TILL I CATCH YOU!

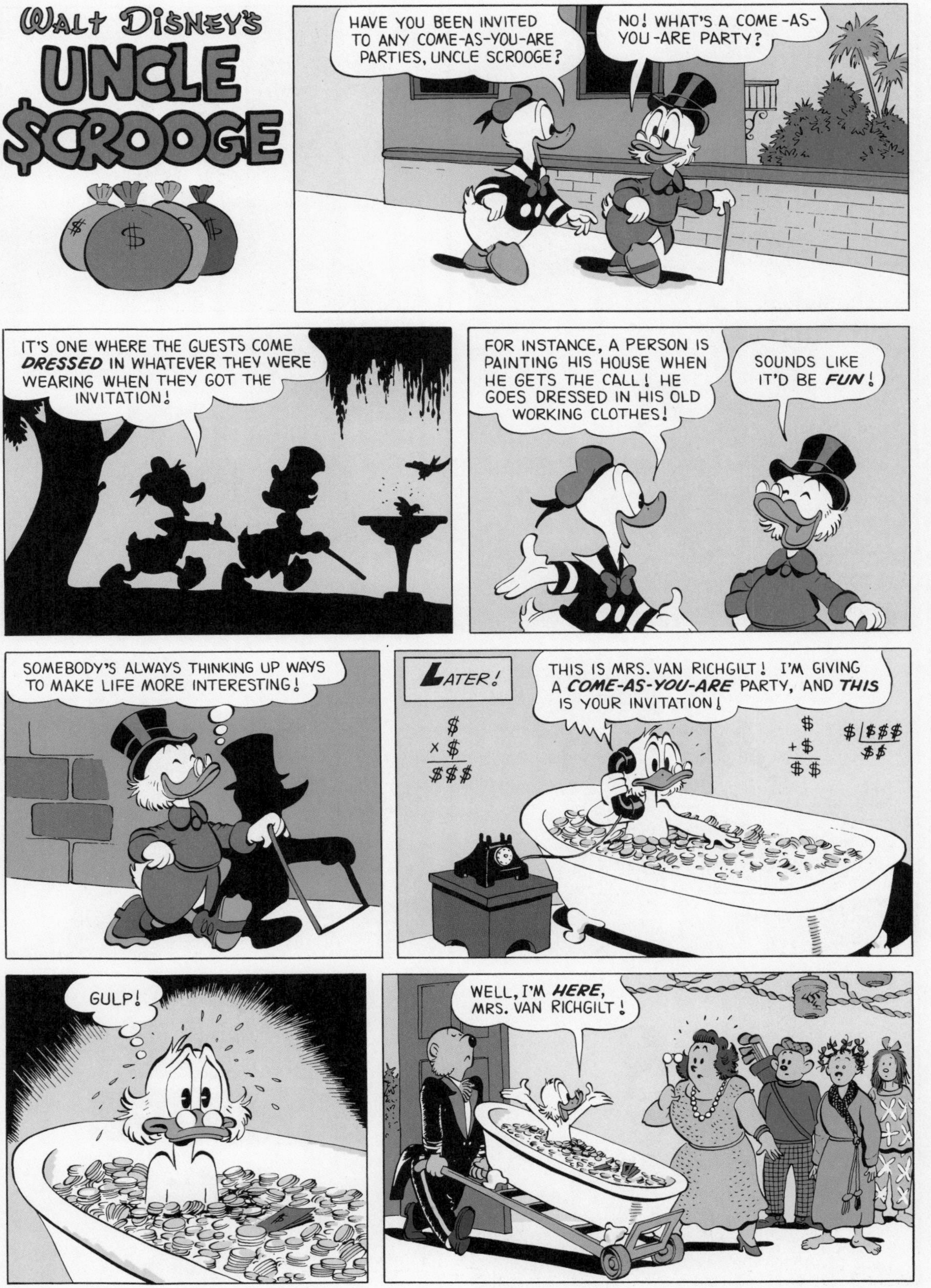
WALT DISNEY'S
UNCLE $CROOGE
HAVE YOU BEEN INVITED TO ANY COME-AS-YOU-ARE PARTIES, UNCLE SCROOGE?
NO! WHAT'S A COME-AS-YOU-ARE PARTY?
IT'S ONE WHERE THE GUESTS COME DRESSED IN WHATEVER THEY WERE WEARING WHEN THEY GOT THE INVITATION!
FOR INSTANCE, A PERSON IS PAINTING HIS HOUSE WHEN HE GETS THE CALL! HE GOES DRESSED IN HIS OLD WORKING CLOTHES!
SOUNDS LIKE IT'D BE FUN!
SOMEBODY'S ALWAYS THINKING UP WAYS TO MAKE LIFE MORE INTERESTING!
LATER!
THIS IS MRS. VAN RICHGILT! I'M GIVING A COME-AS-YOU-ARE PARTY, AND THIS IS YOUR INVITATION!
GULP!
WELL, I'M HERE, MRS. VAN RICHGILT!

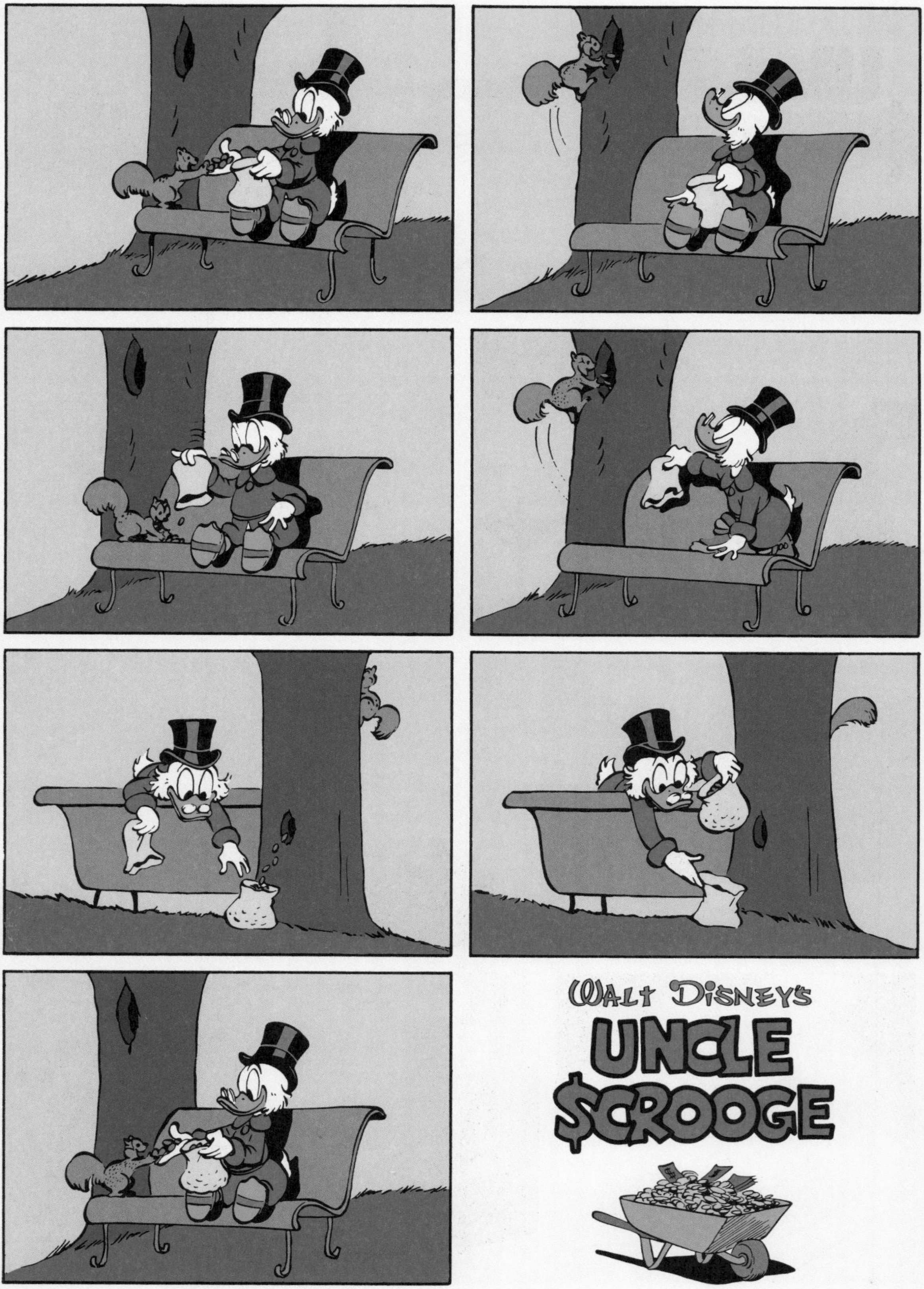
WALT DISNEY'S
UNCLE
$CROOGE

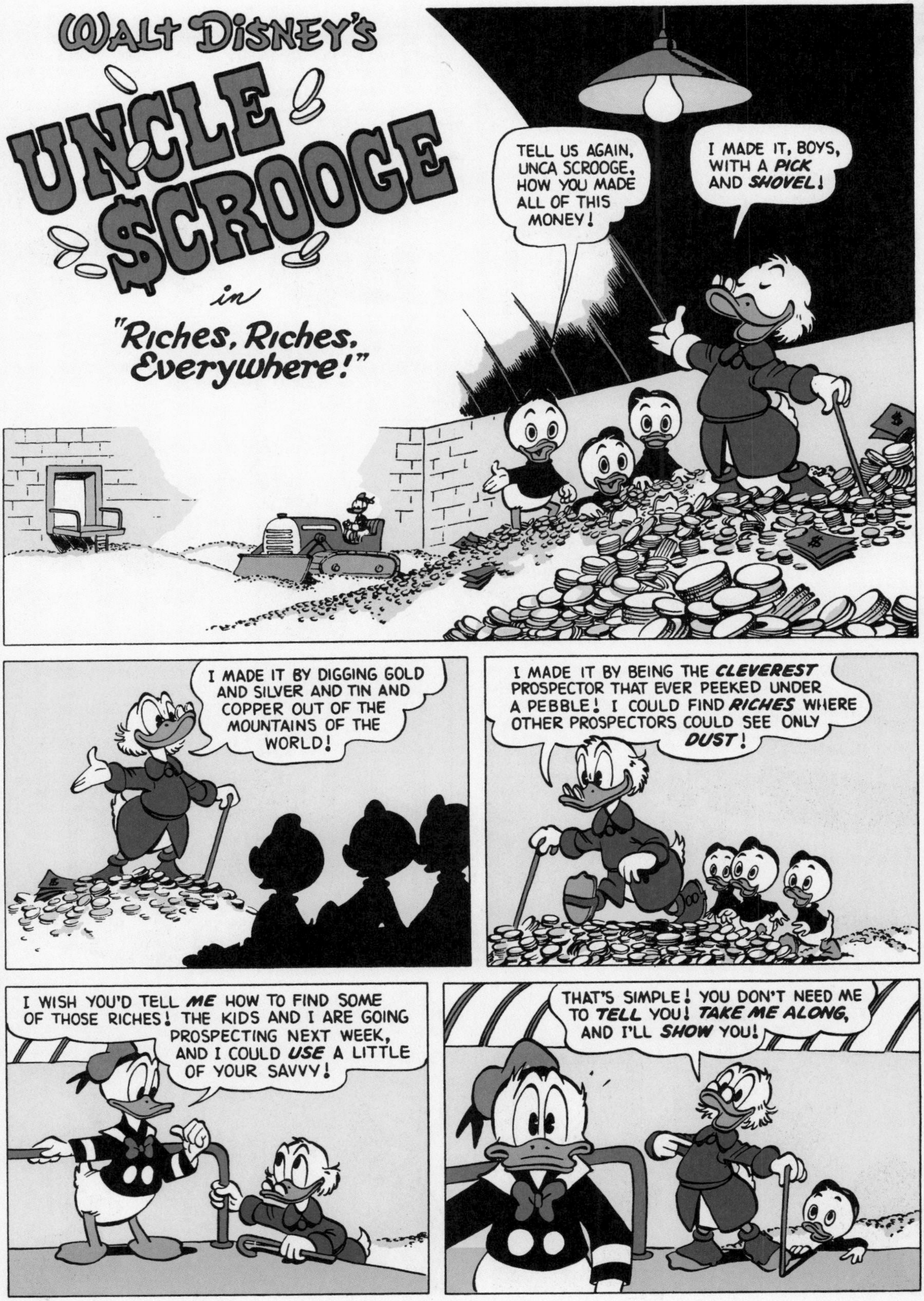
Walt Disney's
Uncle $crooge
in
"Riches, Riches, Everywhere!"
TELL US AGAIN, UNCA SCROOGE, HOW YOU MADE ALL OF THIS MONEY!
I MADE IT, BOYS, WITH A PICK AND SHOVEL!
I MADE IT BY DIGGING GOLD AND SILVER AND TIN AND COPPER OUT OF THE MOUNTAINS OF THE WORLD!
I MADE IT BY BEING THE CLEVEREST PROSPECTOR THAT EVER PEEKED UNDER A PEBBLE! I COULD FIND RICHES WHERE OTHER PROSPECTORS COULD SEE ONLY DUST!
I WISH YOU'D TELL ME HOW TO FIND SOME OF THOSE RICHES! THE KIDS AND I ARE GOING PROSPECTING NEXT WEEK, AND I COULD USE A LITTLE OF YOUR SAVVY!
THAT'S SIMPLE! YOU DON'T NEED ME TO TELL YOU! TAKE ME ALONG, AND I'LL SHOW YOU!

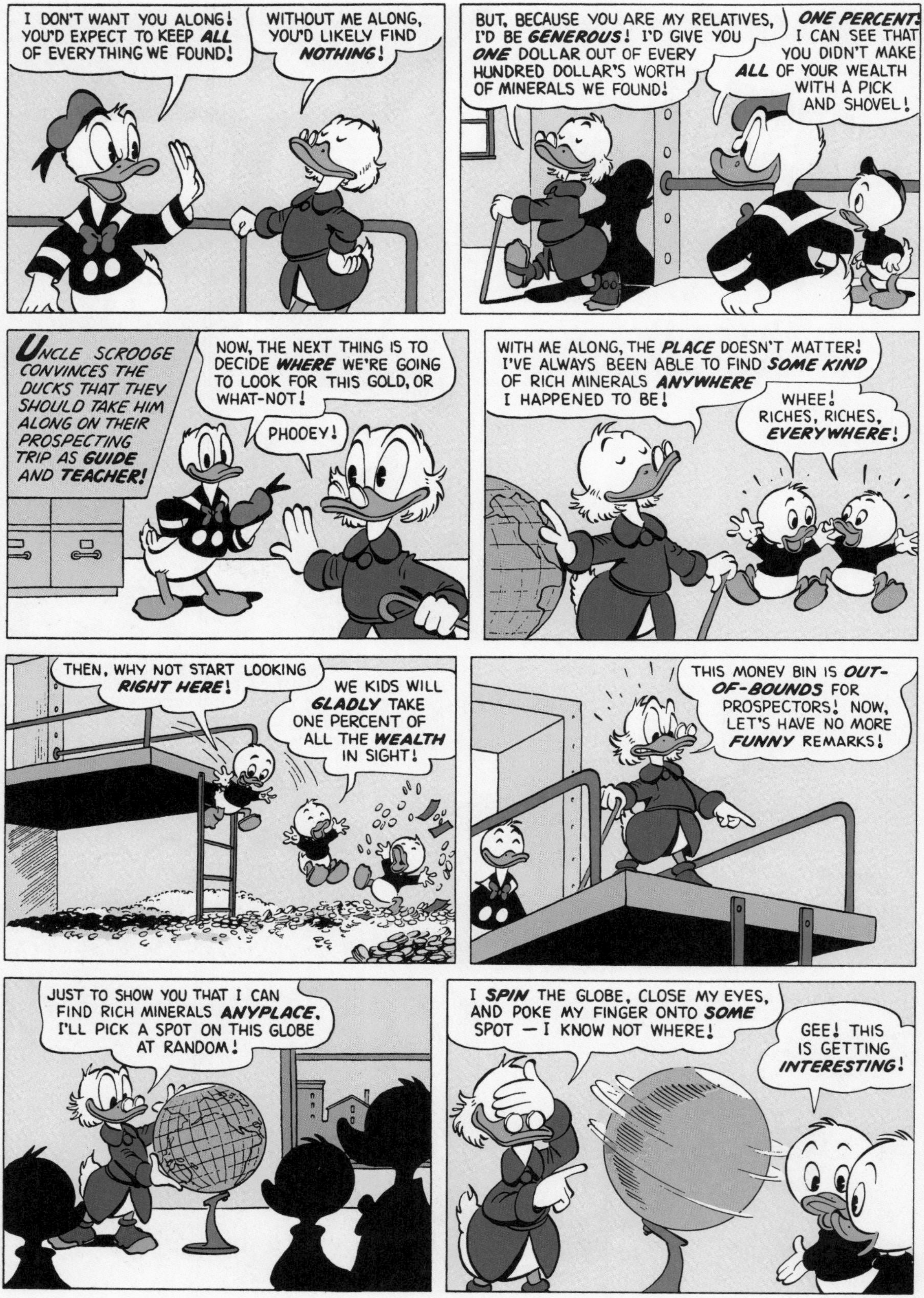
I DON'T WANT YOU ALONG! YOU'D EXPECT TO KEEP ALL OF EVERYTHING WE FOUND!
WITHOUT ME ALONG, YOU'D LIKELY FIND NOTHING!
BUT, BECAUSE YOU ARE MY RELATIVES, I'D BE GENEROUS! I'D GIVE YOU ONE DOLLAR OUT OF EVERY HUNDRED DOLLAR'S WORTH OF MINERALS WE FOUND!
ONE PERCENT! I CAN SEE THAT YOU DIDN'T MAKE ALL OF YOUR WEALTH WITH A PICK AND SHOVEL!
UNCLE SCROOGE CONVINCES THE DUCKS THAT THEY SHOULD TAKE HIM ALONG ON THEIR PROSPECTING TRIP AS GUIDE AND TEACHER!
NOW, THE NEXT THING IS TO DECIDE WHERE WE'RE GOING TO LOOK FOR THIS GOLD, OR WHAT-NOT!
PHOOEY!
WITH ME ALONG, THE PLACE DOESN'T MATTER! I'VE ALWAYS BEEN ABLE TO FIND SOME KIND OF RICH MINERALS ANYWHERE I HAPPENED TO BE!
WHEE! RICHES, RICHES, EVERYWHERE!
THEN, WHY NOT START LOOKING RIGHT HERE!
WE KIDS WILL GLADLY TAKE ONE PERCENT OF ALL THE WEALTH IN SIGHT!
THIS MONEY BIN IS OUT-OF-BOUNDS FOR PROSPECTORS! NOW, LET'S HAVE NO MORE FUNNY REMARKS!
JUST TO SHOW YOU THAT I CAN FIND RICH MINERALS ANYPLACE, I'LL PICK A SPOT ON THIS GLOBE AT RANDOM!
I SPIN THE GLOBE, CLOSE MY EYES, AND POKE MY FINGER ONTO SOME SPOT — I KNOW NOT WHERE!
GEE! THIS IS GETTING INTERESTING!

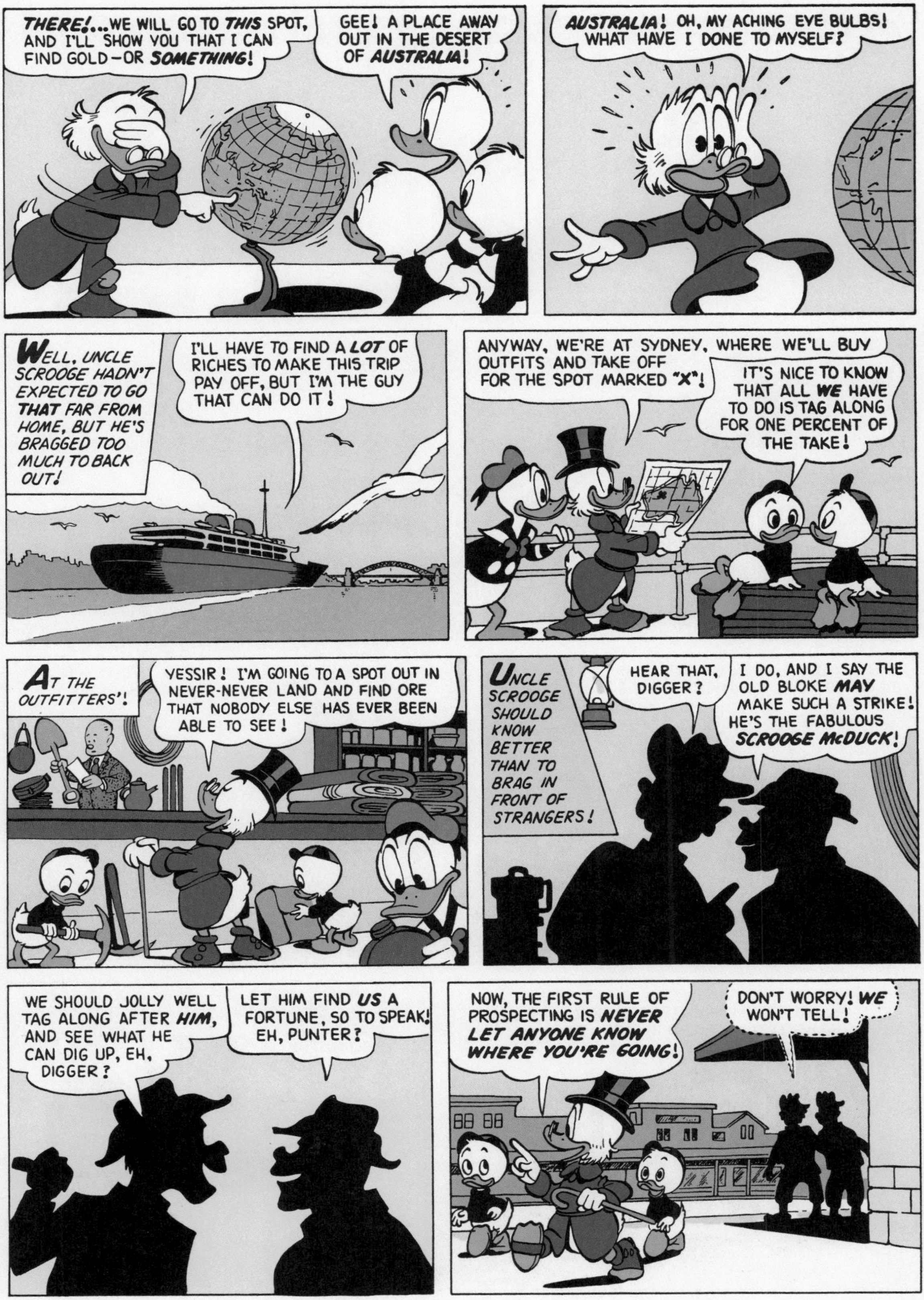
THERE!...WE WILL GO TO THIS SPOT, AND I'LL SHOW YOU THAT I CAN FIND GOLD—OR SOMETHING!
GEE! A PLACE AWAY OUT IN THE DESERT OF AUSTRALIA!
AUSTRALIA! OH, MY ACHING EYE BULBS! WHAT HAVE I DONE TO MYSELF?
WELL, UNCLE SCROOGE HADN'T EXPECTED TO GO THAT FAR FROM HOME, BUT HE'S BRAGGED TOO MUCH TO BACK OUT!
I'LL HAVE TO FIND A LOT OF RICHES TO MAKE THIS TRIP PAY OFF, BUT I'M THE GUY THAT CAN DO IT!
ANYWAY, WE'RE AT SYDNEY, WHERE WE'LL BUY OUTFITS AND TAKE OFF FOR THE SPOT MARKED "X"!
IT'S NICE TO KNOW THAT ALL WE HAVE TO DO IS TAG ALONG FOR ONE PERCENT OF THE TAKE!
AT THE OUTFITTERS'!
YESSIR! I'M GOING TO A SPOT OUT IN NEVER-NEVER LAND AND FIND ORE THAT NOBODY ELSE HAS EVER BEEN ABLE TO SEE!
UNCLE SCROOGE SHOULD KNOW BETTER THAN TO BRAG IN FRONT OF STRANGERS!
HEAR THAT, DIGGER?
I DO, AND I SAY THE OLD BLOKE MAY MAKE SUCH A STRIKE! HE'S THE FABULOUS SCROOGE McDUCK!
WE SHOULD JOLLY WELL TAG ALONG AFTER HIM, AND SEE WHAT HE CAN DIG UP, EH, DIGGER?
LET HIM FIND US A FORTUNE, SO TO SPEAK! EH, PUNTER?
NOW, THE FIRST RULE OF PROSPECTING IS NEVER LET ANYONE KNOW WHERE YOU'RE GOING!
DON'T WORRY! WE WON'T TELL!

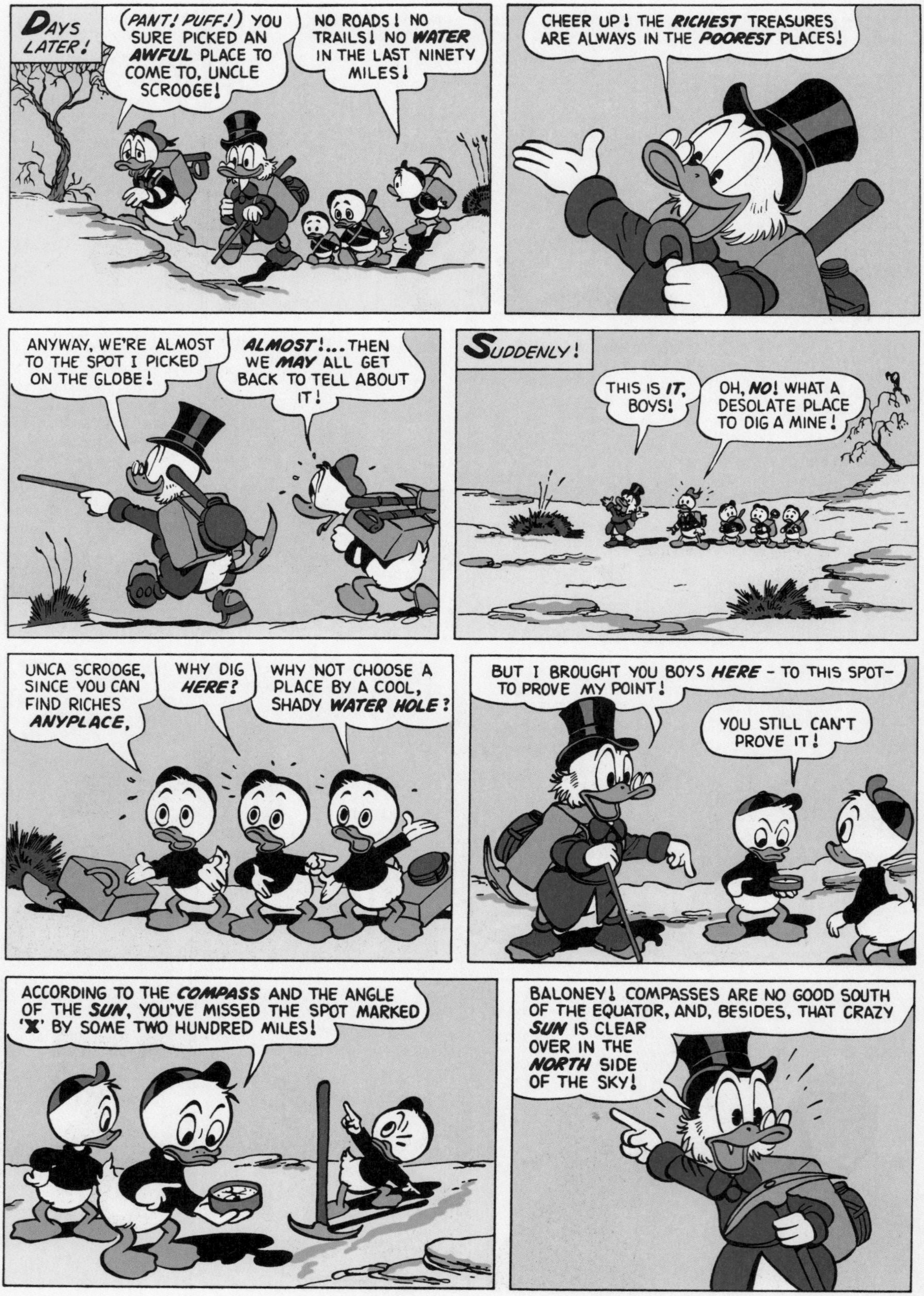
DAYS LATER!
(PANT! PUFF!) YOU SURE PICKED AN AWFUL PLACE TO COME TO, UNCLE SCROOGE!
NO ROADS! NO TRAILS! NO WATER IN THE LAST NINETY MILES!
CHEER UP! THE RICHEST TREASURES ARE ALWAYS IN THE POOREST PLACES!
ANYWAY, WE'RE ALMOST TO THE SPOT I PICKED ON THE GLOBE!
ALMOST!... THEN WE MAY ALL GET BACK TO TELL ABOUT IT!
SUDDENLY!
THIS IS IT, BOYS!
OH, NO! WHAT A DESOLATE PLACE TO DIG A MINE!
UNCA SCROOGE, SINCE YOU CAN FIND RICHES ANYPLACE,
WHY DIG HERE?
WHY NOT CHOOSE A PLACE BY A COOL, SHADY WATER HOLE?
BUT I BROUGHT YOU BOYS HERE - TO THIS SPOT - TO PROVE MY POINT!
YOU STILL CAN'T PROVE IT!
ACCORDING TO THE COMPASS AND THE ANGLE OF THE SUN, YOU'VE MISSED THE SPOT MARKED 'X' BY SOME TWO HUNDRED MILES!
BALONEY! COMPASSES ARE NO GOOD SOUTH OF THE EQUATOR, AND, BESIDES, THAT CRAZY SUN IS CLEAR OVER IN THE NORTH SIDE OF THE SKY!

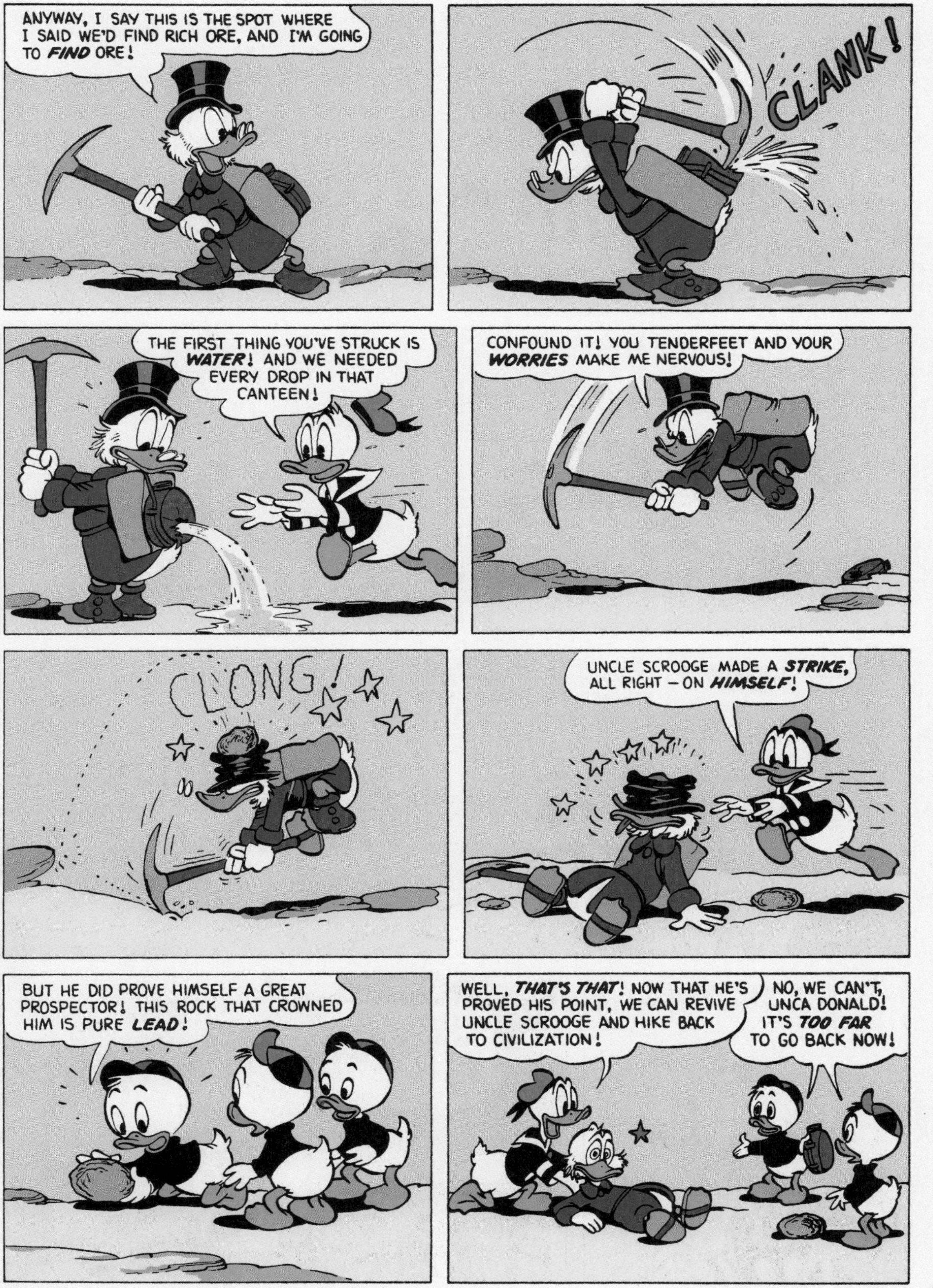
ANYWAY, I SAY THIS IS THE SPOT WHERE I SAID WE'D FIND RICH ORE, AND I'M GOING TO FIND ORE!
CLANK!
THE FIRST THING YOU'VE STRUCK IS WATER! AND WE NEEDED EVERY DROP IN THAT CANTEEN!
CONFOUND IT! YOU TENDERFEET AND YOUR WORRIES MAKE ME NERVOUS!
CLONG!
UNCLE SCROOGE MADE A STRIKE, ALL RIGHT — ON HIMSELF!
BUT HE DID PROVE HIMSELF A GREAT PROSPECTOR! THIS ROCK THAT CROWNED HIM IS PURE LEAD!
WELL, THAT'S THAT! NOW THAT HE'S PROVED HIS POINT, WE CAN REVIVE UNCLE SCROOGE AND HIKE BACK TO CIVILIZATION!
NO, WE CAN'T, UNCA DONALD! IT'S TOO FAR TO GO BACK NOW!

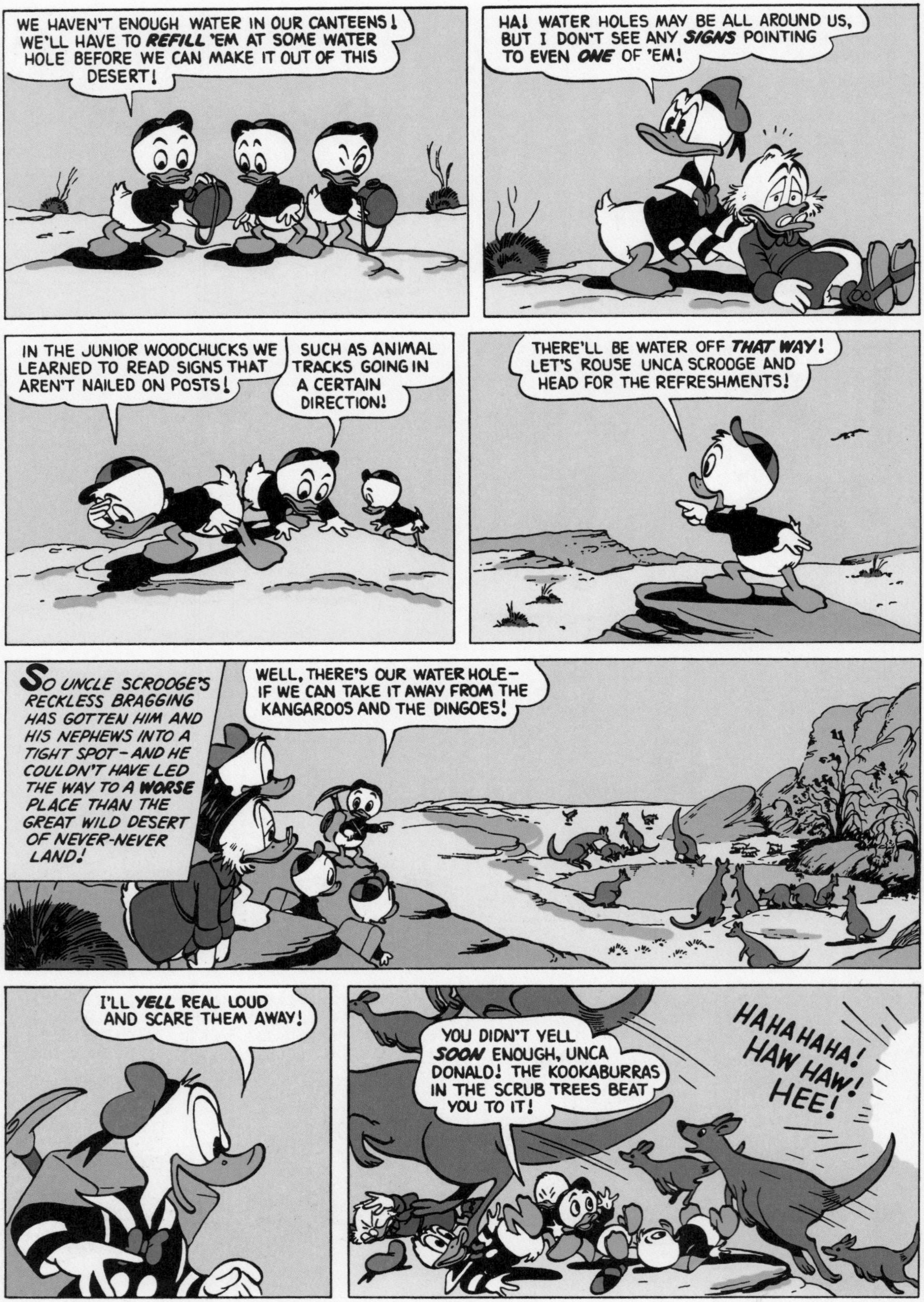
WE HAVEN'T ENOUGH WATER IN OUR CANTEENS! WE'LL HAVE TO REFILL 'EM AT SOME WATER HOLE BEFORE WE CAN MAKE IT OUT OF THIS DESERT!
HA! WATER HOLES MAY BE ALL AROUND US, BUT I DON'T SEE ANY SIGNS POINTING TO EVEN ONE OF 'EM!
IN THE JUNIOR WOODCHUCKS WE LEARNED TO READ SIGNS THAT AREN'T NAILED ON POSTS!
SUCH AS ANIMAL TRACKS GOING IN A CERTAIN DIRECTION!
THERE'LL BE WATER OFF THAT WAY! LET'S ROUSE UNCA SCROOGE AND HEAD FOR THE REFRESHMENTS!
SO UNCLE SCROOGE'S RECKLESS BRAGGING HAS GOTTEN HIM AND HIS NEPHEWS INTO A TIGHT SPOT - AND HE COULDN'T HAVE LED THE WAY TO A WORSE PLACE THAN THE GREAT WILD DESERT OF NEVER-NEVER LAND!
WELL, THERE'S OUR WATER HOLE- IF WE CAN TAKE IT AWAY FROM THE KANGAROOS AND THE DINGOES!
I'LL YELL REAL LOUD AND SCARE THEM AWAY!
YOU DIDN'T YELL SOON ENOUGH, UNCA DONALD! THE KOOKABURRAS IN THE SCRUB TREES BEAT YOU TO IT!
HAHAHAHA! HAW HAW! HEE!

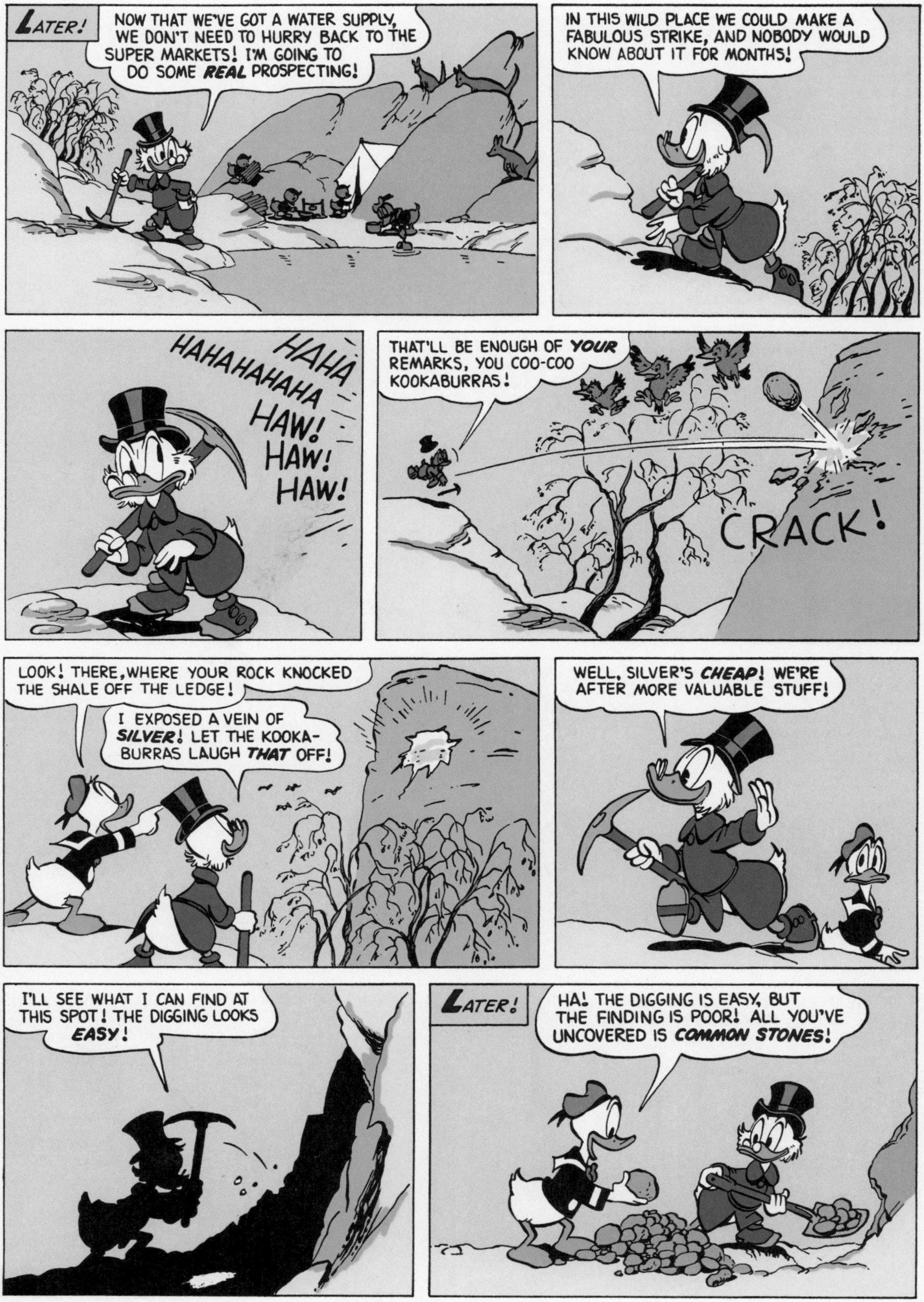
LATER!
NOW THAT WE'VE GOT A WATER SUPPLY, WE DON'T NEED TO HURRY BACK TO THE SUPER MARKETS! I'M GOING TO DO SOME REAL PROSPECTING!
IN THIS WILD PLACE WE COULD MAKE A FABULOUS STRIKE, AND NOBODY WOULD KNOW ABOUT IT FOR MONTHS!
HAHA HAHAHAHAHA HAW! HAW! HAW!
THAT'LL BE ENOUGH OF YOUR REMARKS, YOU COO-COO KOOKABURRAS!
CRACK!
LOOK! THERE, WHERE YOUR ROCK KNOCKED THE SHALE OFF THE LEDGE!
I EXPOSED A VEIN OF SILVER! LET THE KOOKA-BURRAS LAUGH THAT OFF!
WELL, SILVER'S CHEAP! WE'RE AFTER MORE VALUABLE STUFF!
I'LL SEE WHAT I CAN FIND AT THIS SPOT! THE DIGGING LOOKS EASY!
LATER!
HA! THE DIGGING IS EASY, BUT THE FINDING IS POOR! ALL YOU'VE UNCOVERED IS COMMON STONES!

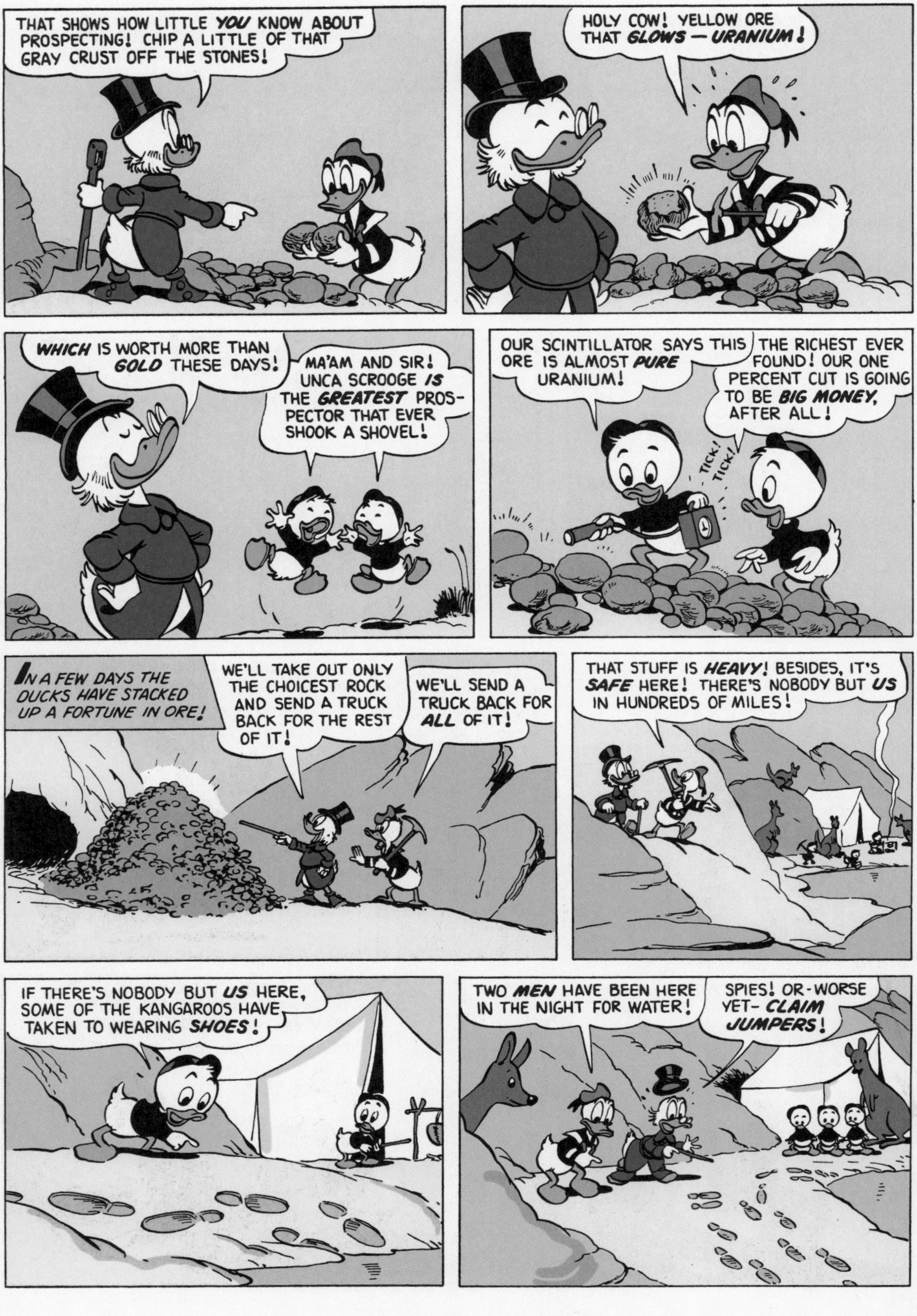
THAT SHOWS HOW LITTLE YOU KNOW ABOUT PROSPECTING! CHIP A LITTLE OF THAT GRAY CRUST OFF THE STONES!
HOLY COW! YELLOW ORE THAT GLOWS — URANIUM!
WHICH IS WORTH MORE THAN GOLD THESE DAYS!
MA'AM AND SIR! UNCA SCROOGE IS THE GREATEST PROSPECTOR THAT EVER SHOOK A SHOVEL!
OUR SCINTILLATOR SAYS THIS ORE IS ALMOST PURE URANIUM!
THE RICHEST EVER FOUND! OUR ONE PERCENT CUT IS GOING TO BE BIG MONEY, AFTER ALL!
TICK! TICK!
IN A FEW DAYS THE DUCKS HAVE STACKED UP A FORTUNE IN ORE!
WE'LL TAKE OUT ONLY THE CHOICEST ROCK AND SEND A TRUCK BACK FOR THE REST OF IT!
WE'LL SEND A TRUCK BACK FOR ALL OF IT!
THAT STUFF IS HEAVY! BESIDES, IT'S SAFE HERE! THERE'S NOBODY BUT US IN HUNDREDS OF MILES!
IF THERE'S NOBODY BUT US HERE, SOME OF THE KANGAROOS HAVE TAKEN TO WEARING SHOES!
TWO MEN HAVE BEEN HERE IN THE NIGHT FOR WATER!
SPIES! OR-WORSE YET- CLAIM JUMPERS!

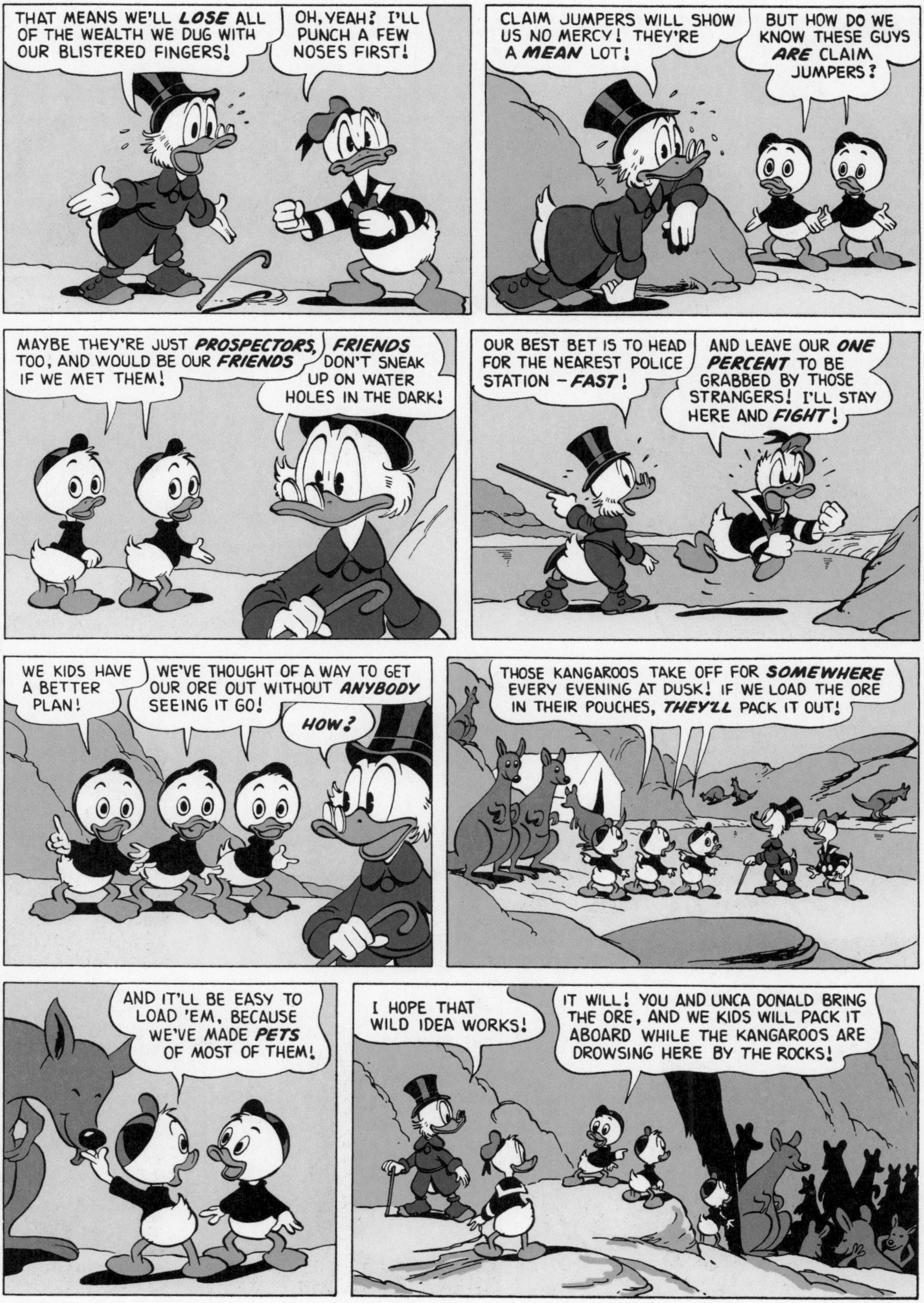
THAT MEANS WE'LL LOSE ALL OF THE WEALTH WE DUG WITH OUR BLISTERED FINGERS!
OH, YEAH? I'LL PUNCH A FEW NOSES FIRST!
CLAIM JUMPERS WILL SHOW US NO MERCY! THEY'RE A MEAN LOT!
BUT HOW DO WE KNOW THESE GUYS ARE CLAIM JUMPERS?
MAYBE THEY'RE JUST PROSPECTORS, TOO, AND WOULD BE OUR FRIENDS IF WE MET THEM!
FRIENDS DON'T SNEAK UP ON WATER HOLES IN THE DARK!
OUR BEST BET IS TO HEAD FOR THE NEAREST POLICE STATION – FAST!
AND LEAVE OUR ONE PERCENT TO BE GRABBED BY THOSE STRANGERS! I'LL STAY HERE AND FIGHT!
WE KIDS HAVE A BETTER PLAN!
WE'VE THOUGHT OF A WAY TO GET OUR ORE OUT WITHOUT ANYBODY SEEING IT GO!
HOW?
THOSE KANGAROOS TAKE OFF FOR SOMEWHERE EVERY EVENING AT DUSK! IF WE LOAD THE ORE IN THEIR POUCHES, THEY'LL PACK IT OUT!
AND IT'LL BE EASY TO LOAD 'EM, BECAUSE WE'VE MADE PETS OF MOST OF THEM!
I HOPE THAT WILD IDEA WORKS!
IT WILL! YOU AND UNCA DONALD BRING THE ORE, AND WE KIDS WILL PACK IT ABOARD WHILE THE KANGAROOS ARE DROWSING HERE BY THE ROCKS!

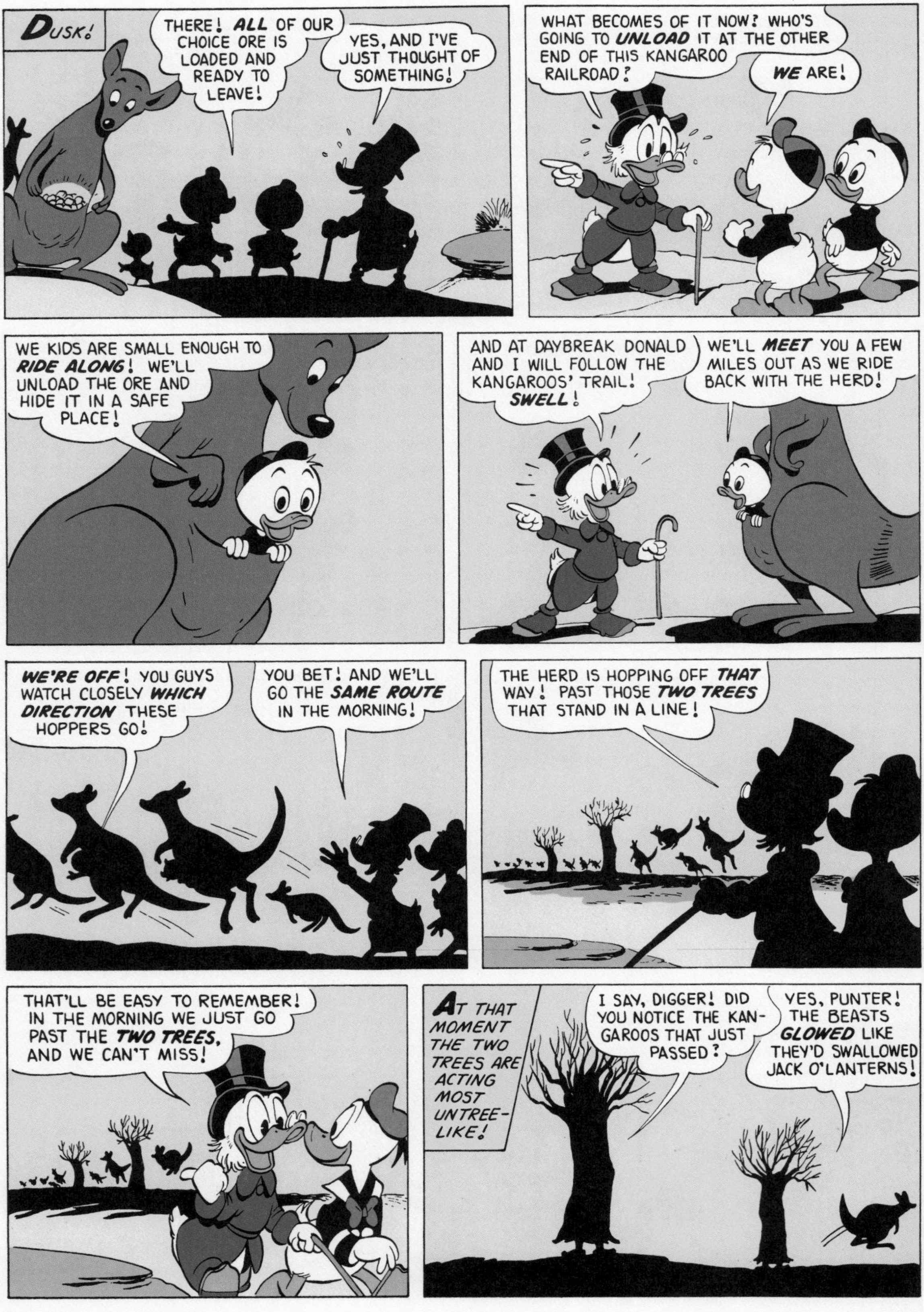
DUSK!
THERE! ALL OF OUR CHOICE ORE IS LOADED AND READY TO LEAVE!
YES, AND I'VE JUST THOUGHT OF SOMETHING!
WHAT BECOMES OF IT NOW? WHO'S GOING TO UNLOAD IT AT THE OTHER END OF THIS KANGAROO RAILROAD?
WE ARE!
WE KIDS ARE SMALL ENOUGH TO RIDE ALONG! WE'LL UNLOAD THE ORE AND HIDE IT IN A SAFE PLACE!
AND AT DAYBREAK DONALD AND I WILL FOLLOW THE KANGAROOS' TRAIL! SWELL!
WE'LL MEET YOU A FEW MILES OUT AS WE RIDE BACK WITH THE HERD!
WE'RE OFF! YOU GUYS WATCH CLOSELY WHICH DIRECTION THESE HOPPERS GO!
YOU BET! AND WE'LL GO THE SAME ROUTE IN THE MORNING!
THE HERD IS HOPPING OFF THAT WAY! PAST THOSE TWO TREES THAT STAND IN A LINE!
THAT'LL BE EASY TO REMEMBER! IN THE MORNING WE JUST GO PAST THE TWO TREES, AND WE CAN'T MISS!
AT THAT MOMENT THE TWO TREES ARE ACTING MOST UNTREE-LIKE!
I SAY, DIGGER! DID YOU NOTICE THE KAN-GAROOS THAT JUST PASSED?
YES, PUNTER! THE BEASTS GLOWED LIKE THEY'D SWALLOWED JACK O'LANTERNS!

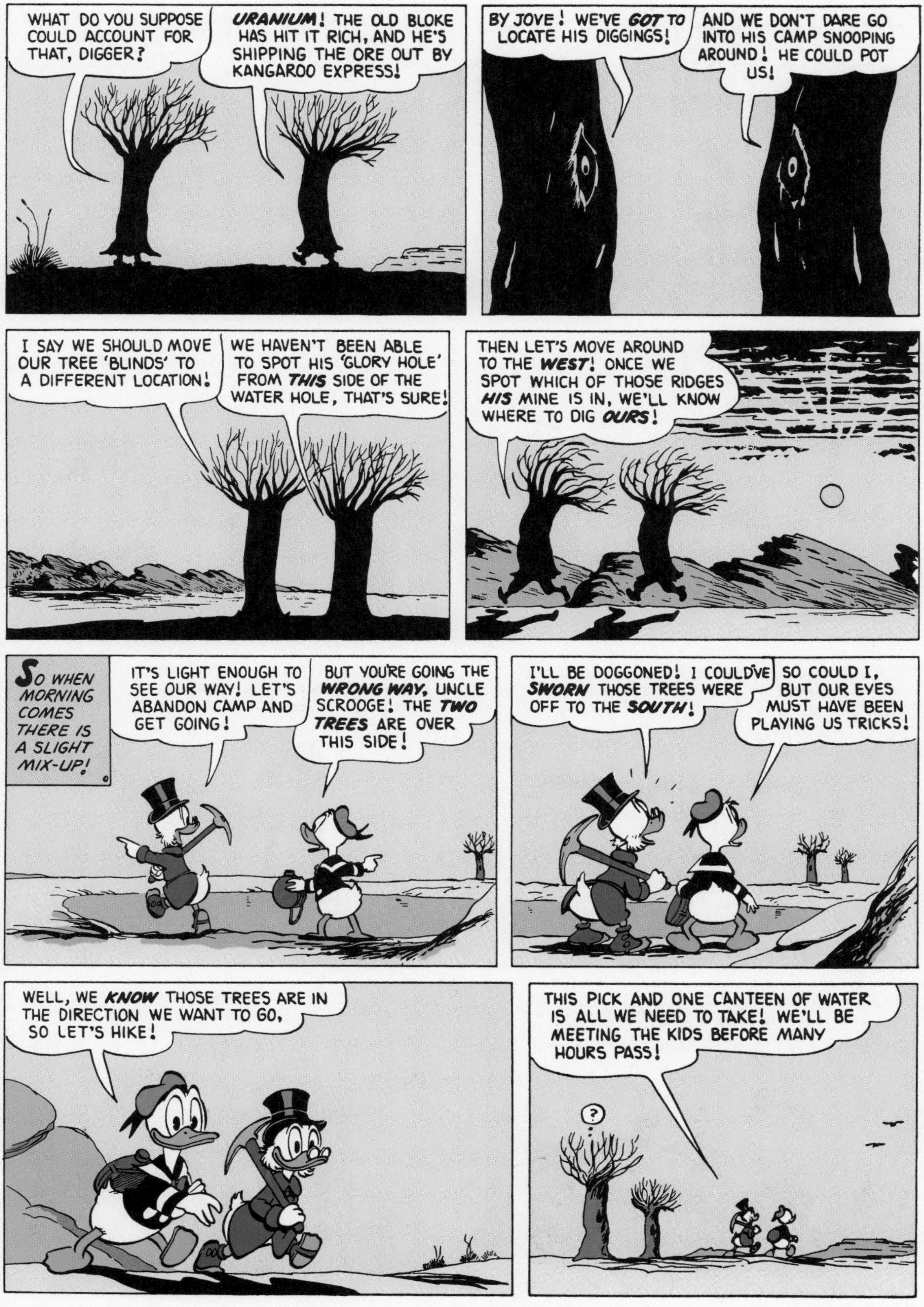
WHAT DO YOU SUPPOSE COULD ACCOUNT FOR THAT, DIGGER?
URANIUM! THE OLD BLOKE HAS HIT IT RICH, AND HE'S SHIPPING THE ORE OUT BY KANGAROO EXPRESS!
BY JOVE! WE'VE GOT TO LOCATE HIS DIGGINGS!
AND WE DON'T DARE GO INTO HIS CAMP SNOOPING AROUND! HE COULD POT US!
I SAY WE SHOULD MOVE OUR TREE 'BLINDS' TO A DIFFERENT LOCATION!
WE HAVEN'T BEEN ABLE TO SPOT HIS 'GLORY HOLE' FROM THIS SIDE OF THE WATER HOLE, THAT'S SURE!
THEN LET'S MOVE AROUND TO THE WEST! ONCE WE SPOT WHICH OF THOSE RIDGES HIS MINE IS IN, WE'LL KNOW WHERE TO DIG OURS!
SO WHEN MORNING COMES THERE IS A SLIGHT MIX-UP!
IT'S LIGHT ENOUGH TO SEE OUR WAY! LET'S ABANDON CAMP AND GET GOING!
BUT YOU'RE GOING THE WRONG WAY, UNCLE SCROOGE! THE TWO TREES ARE OVER THIS SIDE!
I'LL BE DOGGONED! I COULD'VE SWORN THOSE TREES WERE OFF TO THE SOUTH!
SO COULD I, BUT OUR EYES MUST HAVE BEEN PLAYING US TRICKS!
WELL, WE KNOW THOSE TREES ARE IN THE DIRECTION WE WANT TO GO, SO LET'S HIKE!
THIS PICK AND ONE CANTEEN OF WATER IS ALL WE NEED TO TAKE! WE'LL BE MEETING THE KIDS BEFORE MANY HOURS PASS!
?

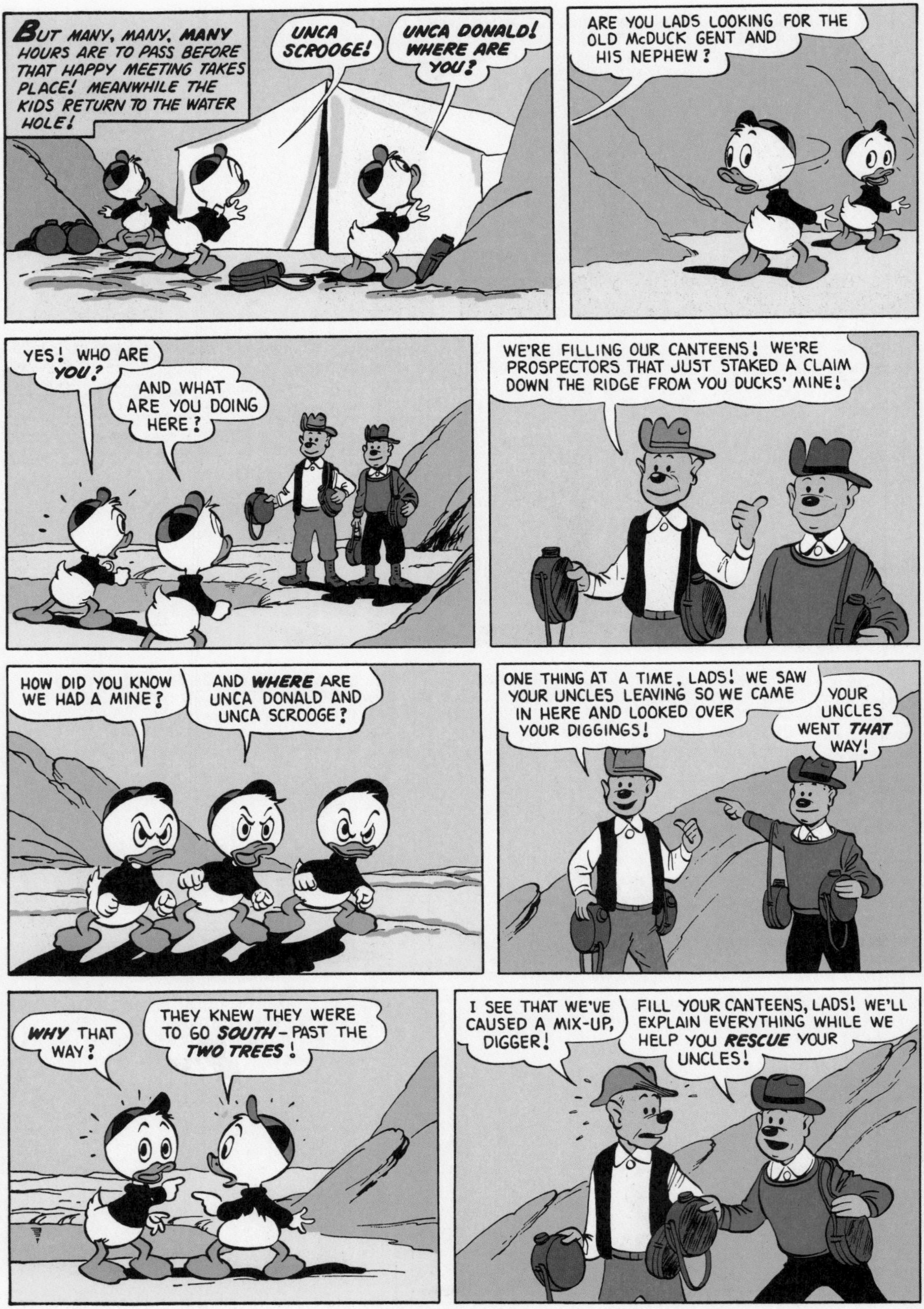
BUT MANY, MANY, MANY HOURS ARE TO PASS BEFORE THAT HAPPY MEETING TAKES PLACE! MEANWHILE THE KIDS RETURN TO THE WATER HOLE!
UNCA SCROOGE!
UNCA DONALD! WHERE ARE YOU?
ARE YOU LADS LOOKING FOR THE OLD McDUCK GENT AND HIS NEPHEW?
YES! WHO ARE YOU?
AND WHAT ARE YOU DOING HERE?
WE'RE FILLING OUR CANTEENS! WE'RE PROSPECTORS THAT JUST STAKED A CLAIM DOWN THE RIDGE FROM YOU DUCKS' MINE!
HOW DID YOU KNOW WE HAD A MINE?
AND WHERE ARE UNCA DONALD AND UNCA SCROOGE?
ONE THING AT A TIME, LADS! WE SAW YOUR UNCLES LEAVING SO WE CAME IN HERE AND LOOKED OVER YOUR DIGGINGS!
YOUR UNCLES WENT THAT WAY!
WHY THAT WAY?
THEY KNEW THEY WERE TO GO SOUTH — PAST THE TWO TREES!
I SEE THAT WE'VE CAUSED A MIX-UP, DIGGER!
FILL YOUR CANTEENS, LADS! WE'LL EXPLAIN EVERYTHING WHILE WE HELP YOU RESCUE YOUR UNCLES!

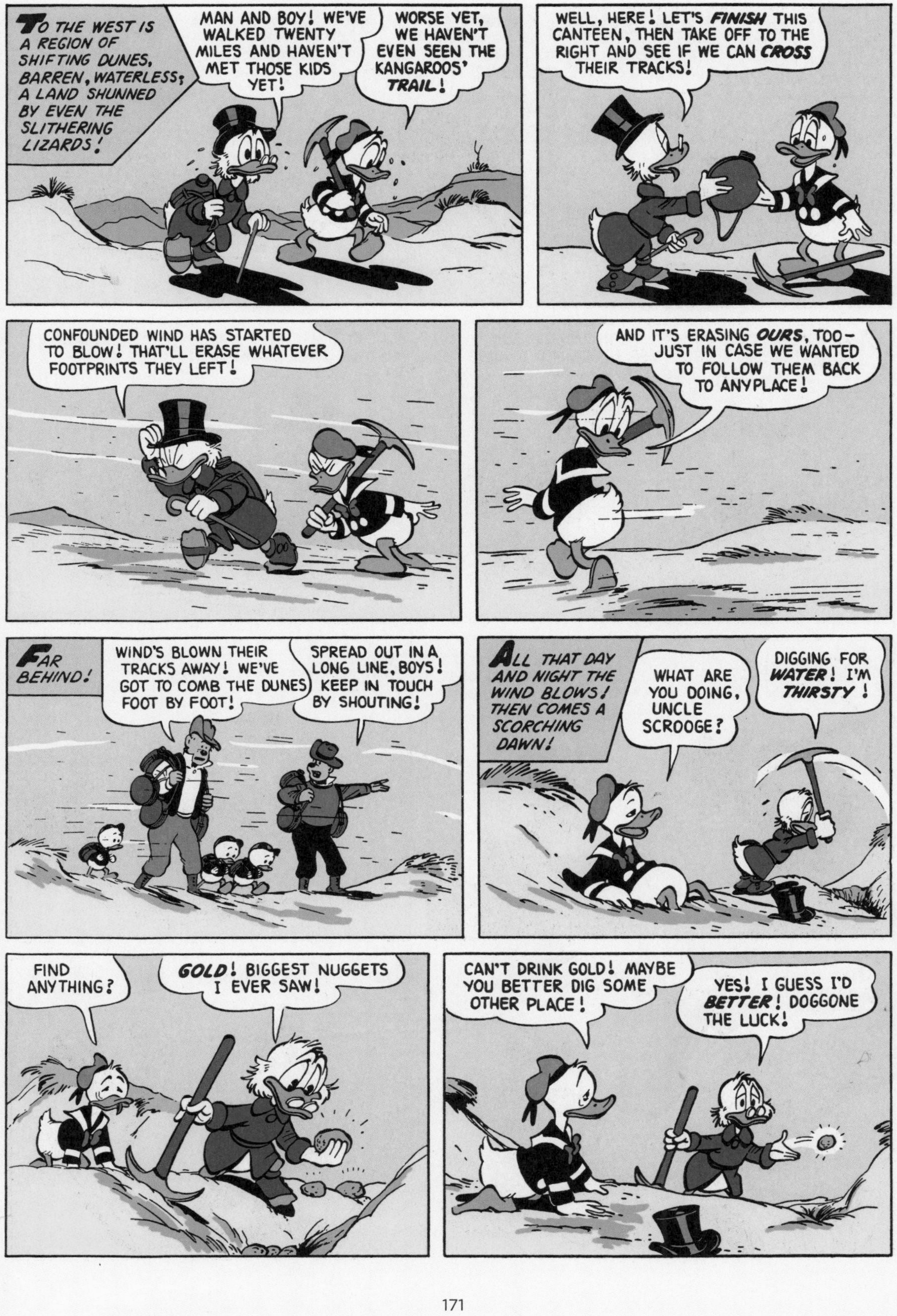
TO THE WEST IS A REGION OF SHIFTING DUNES, BARREN, WATERLESS; A LAND SHUNNED BY EVEN THE SLITHERING LIZARDS!
MAN AND BOY! WE'VE WALKED TWENTY MILES AND HAVEN'T MET THOSE KIDS YET!
WORSE YET, WE HAVEN'T EVEN SEEN THE KANGAROOS' TRAIL!
WELL, HERE! LET'S FINISH THIS CANTEEN, THEN TAKE OFF TO THE RIGHT AND SEE IF WE CAN CROSS THEIR TRACKS!
CONFOUNDED WIND HAS STARTED TO BLOW! THAT'LL ERASE WHATEVER FOOTPRINTS THEY LEFT!
AND IT'S ERASING OURS, TOO— JUST IN CASE WE WANTED TO FOLLOW THEM BACK TO ANYPLACE!
FAR BEHIND!
WIND'S BLOWN THEIR TRACKS AWAY! WE'VE GOT TO COMB THE DUNES FOOT BY FOOT!
SPREAD OUT IN A LONG LINE, BOYS! KEEP IN TOUCH BY SHOUTING!
ALL THAT DAY AND NIGHT THE WIND BLOWS! THEN COMES A SCORCHING DAWN!
WHAT ARE YOU DOING, UNCLE SCROOGE?
DIGGING FOR WATER! I'M THIRSTY!
FIND ANYTHING?
GOLD! BIGGEST NUGGETS I EVER SAW!
CAN'T DRINK GOLD! MAYBE YOU BETTER DIG SOME OTHER PLACE!
YES! I GUESS I'D BETTER! DOGGONE THE LUCK!

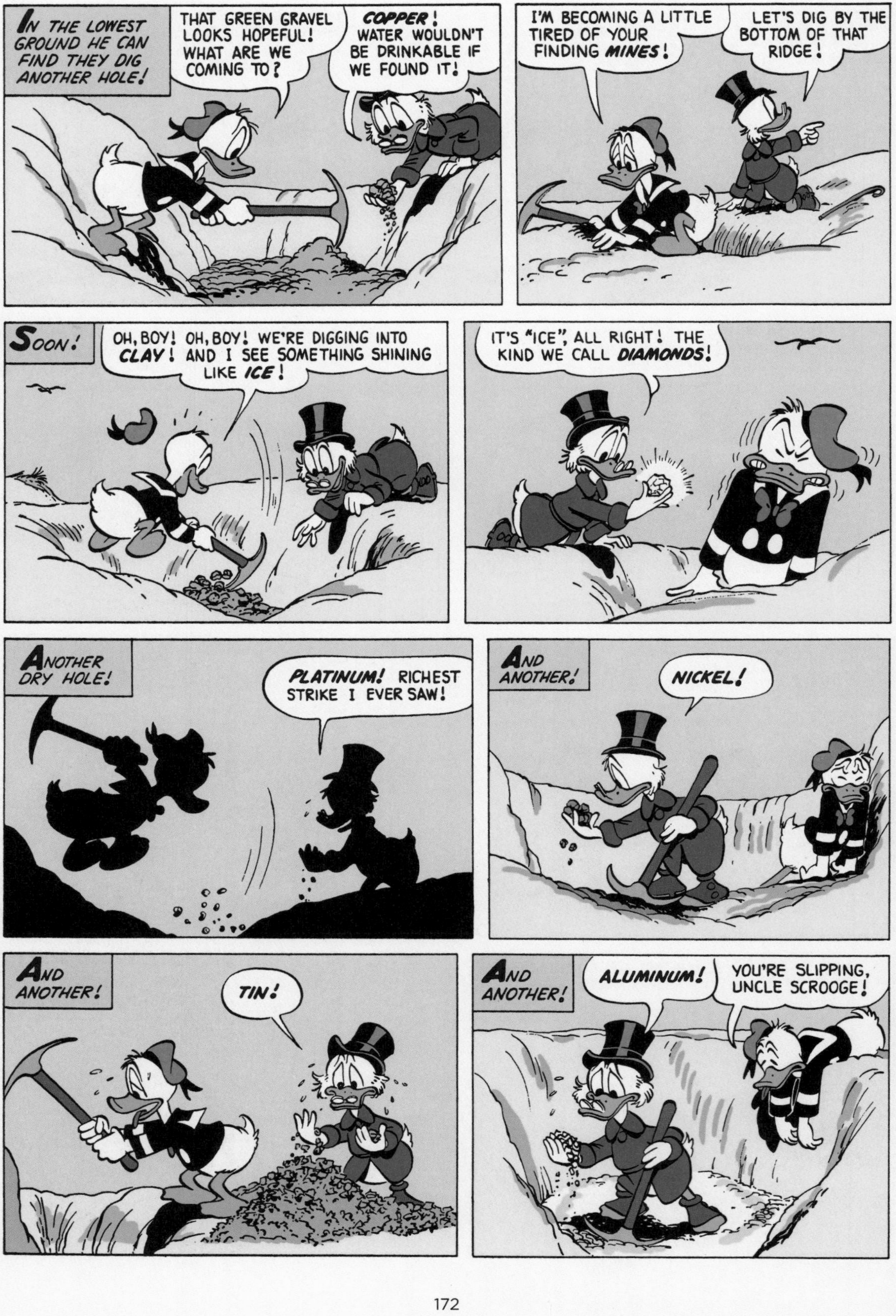
IN THE LOWEST GROUND HE CAN FIND THEY DIG ANOTHER HOLE!
THAT GREEN GRAVEL LOOKS HOPEFUL! WHAT ARE WE COMING TO?
COPPER! WATER WOULDN'T BE DRINKABLE IF WE FOUND IT!
I'M BECOMING A LITTLE TIRED OF YOUR FINDING MINES!
LET'S DIG BY THE BOTTOM OF THAT RIDGE!
SOON!
OH, BOY! OH, BOY! WE'RE DIGGING INTO CLAY! AND I SEE SOMETHING SHINING LIKE ICE!
IT'S "ICE", ALL RIGHT! THE KIND WE CALL DIAMONDS!
ANOTHER DRY HOLE!
PLATINUM! RICHEST STRIKE I EVER SAW!
AND ANOTHER!
NICKEL!
AND ANOTHER!
TIN!
AND ANOTHER!
ALUMINUM!
YOU'RE SLIPPING, UNCLE SCROOGE!

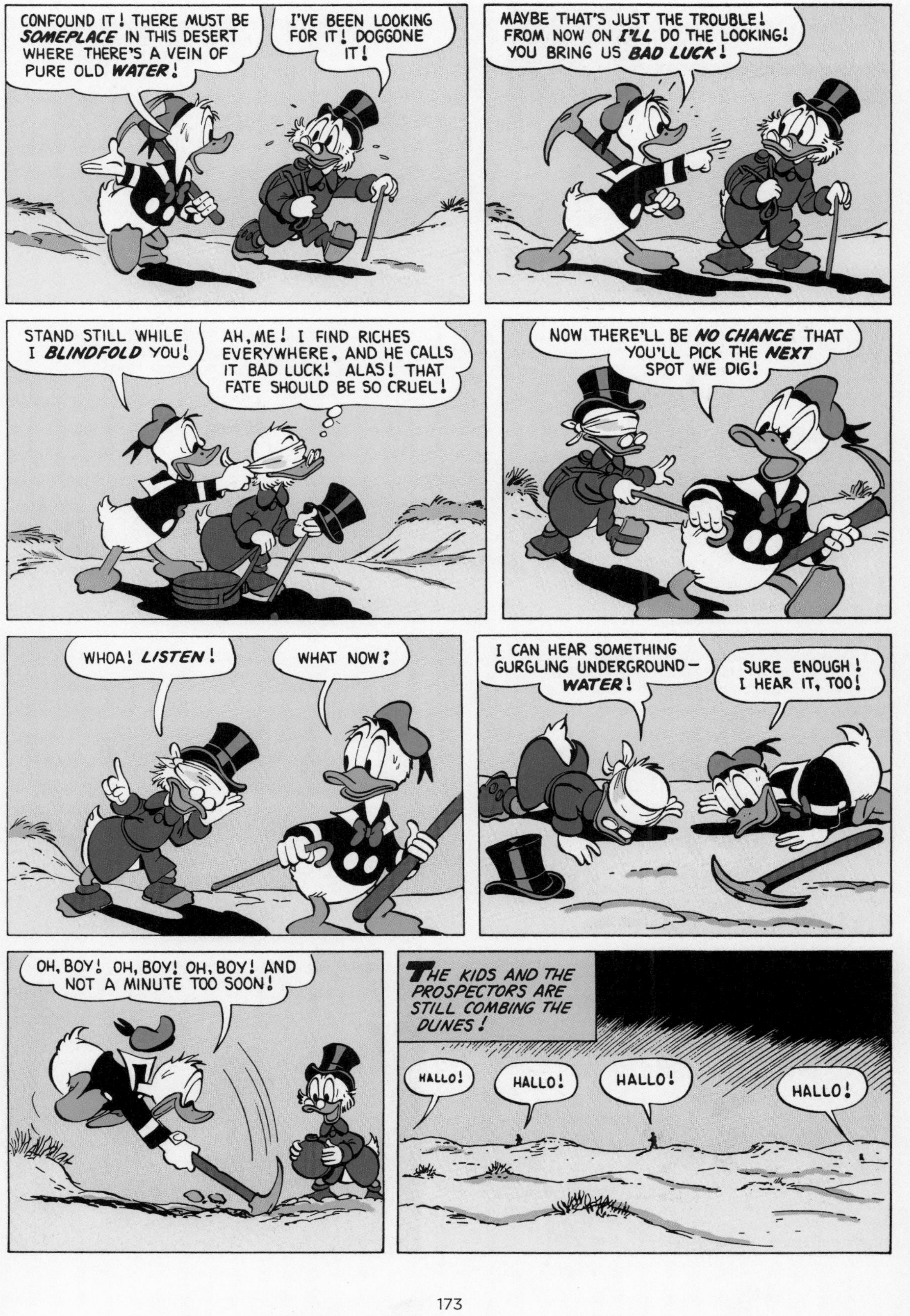
CONFOUND IT! THERE MUST BE SOMEPLACE IN THIS DESERT WHERE THERE'S A VEIN OF PURE OLD WATER!
I'VE BEEN LOOKING FOR IT! DOGGONE IT!
MAYBE THAT'S JUST THE TROUBLE! FROM NOW ON I'LL DO THE LOOKING! YOU BRING US BAD LUCK!
STAND STILL WHILE I BLINDFOLD YOU!
AH, ME! I FIND RICHES EVERYWHERE, AND HE CALLS IT BAD LUCK! ALAS! THAT FATE SHOULD BE SO CRUEL!
NOW THERE'LL BE NO CHANCE THAT YOU'LL PICK THE NEXT SPOT WE DIG!
WHOA! LISTEN!
WHAT NOW?
I CAN HEAR SOMETHING GURGLING UNDERGROUND— WATER!
SURE ENOUGH! I HEAR IT, TOO!
OH, BOY! OH, BOY! OH, BOY! AND NOT A MINUTE TOO SOON!
THE KIDS AND THE PROSPECTORS ARE STILL COMBING THE DUNES!
HALLO!
HALLO!
HALLO!
HALLO!

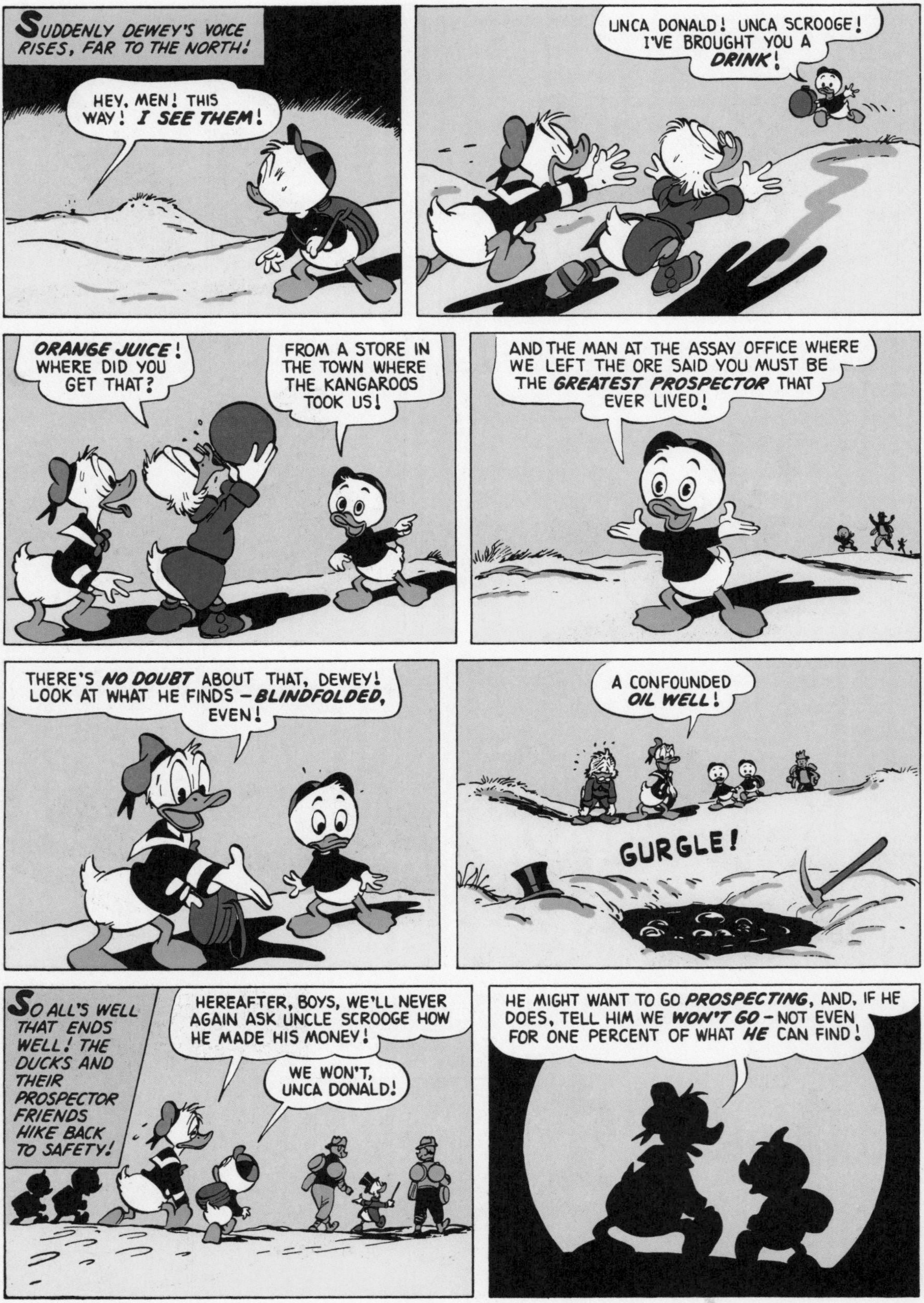
SUDDENLY DEWEY'S VOICE RISES, FAR TO THE NORTH!
HEY, MEN! THIS WAY! I SEE THEM!
UNCA DONALD! UNCA SCROOGE! I'VE BROUGHT YOU A DRINK!
ORANGE JUICE! WHERE DID YOU GET THAT?
FROM A STORE IN THE TOWN WHERE THE KANGAROOS TOOK US!
AND THE MAN AT THE ASSAY OFFICE WHERE WE LEFT THE ORE SAID YOU MUST BE THE GREATEST PROSPECTOR THAT EVER LIVED!
THERE'S NO DOUBT ABOUT THAT, DEWEY! LOOK AT WHAT HE FINDS—BLINDFOLDED, EVEN!
A CONFOUNDED OIL WELL!
GURGLE!
SO ALL'S WELL THAT ENDS WELL! THE DUCKS AND THEIR PROSPECTOR FRIENDS HIKE BACK TO SAFETY!
HEREAFTER, BOYS, WE'LL NEVER AGAIN ASK UNCLE SCROOGE HOW HE MADE HIS MONEY!
WE WON'T, UNCA DONALD!
HE MIGHT WANT TO GO PROSPECTING, AND, IF HE DOES, TELL HIM WE WON'T GO—NOT EVEN FOR ONE PERCENT OF WHAT HE CAN FIND!

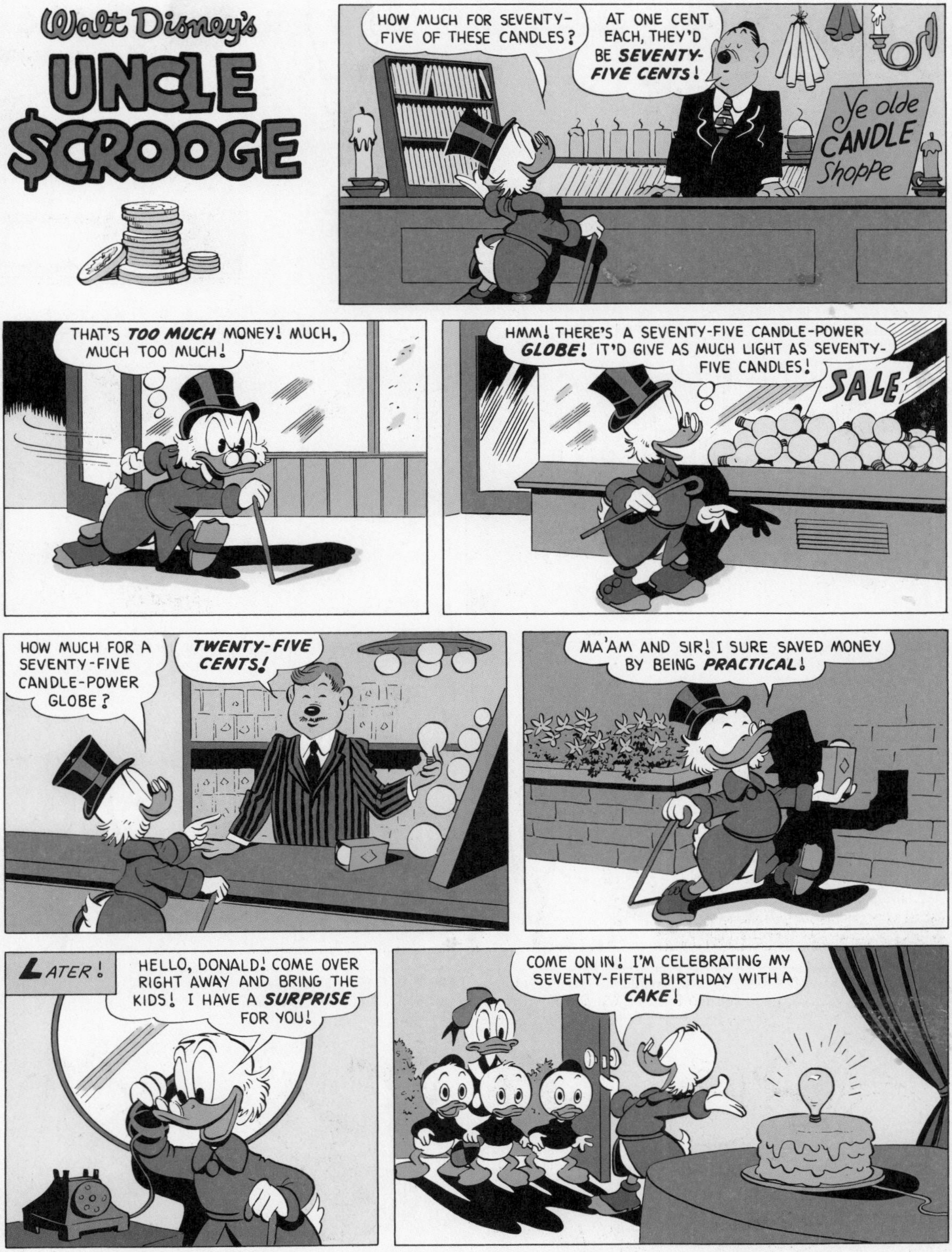
Walt Disney's
UNCLE $CROOGE
HOW MUCH FOR SEVENTY-FIVE OF THESE CANDLES?
AT ONE CENT EACH, THEY'D BE SEVENTY-FIVE CENTS!
Ye olde CANDLE Shoppe
THAT'S TOO MUCH MONEY! MUCH, MUCH TOO MUCH!
HMM! THERE'S A SEVENTY-FIVE CANDLE-POWER GLOBE! IT'D GIVE AS MUCH LIGHT AS SEVENTY-FIVE CANDLES!
SALE
HOW MUCH FOR A SEVENTY-FIVE CANDLE-POWER GLOBE?
TWENTY-FIVE CENTS!
MA'AM AND SIR! I SURE SAVED MONEY BY BEING PRACTICAL!
LATER!
HELLO, DONALD! COME OVER RIGHT AWAY AND BRING THE KIDS! I HAVE A SURPRISE FOR YOU!
COME ON IN! I'M CELEBRATING MY SEVENTY-FIFTH BIRTHDAY WITH A CAKE!

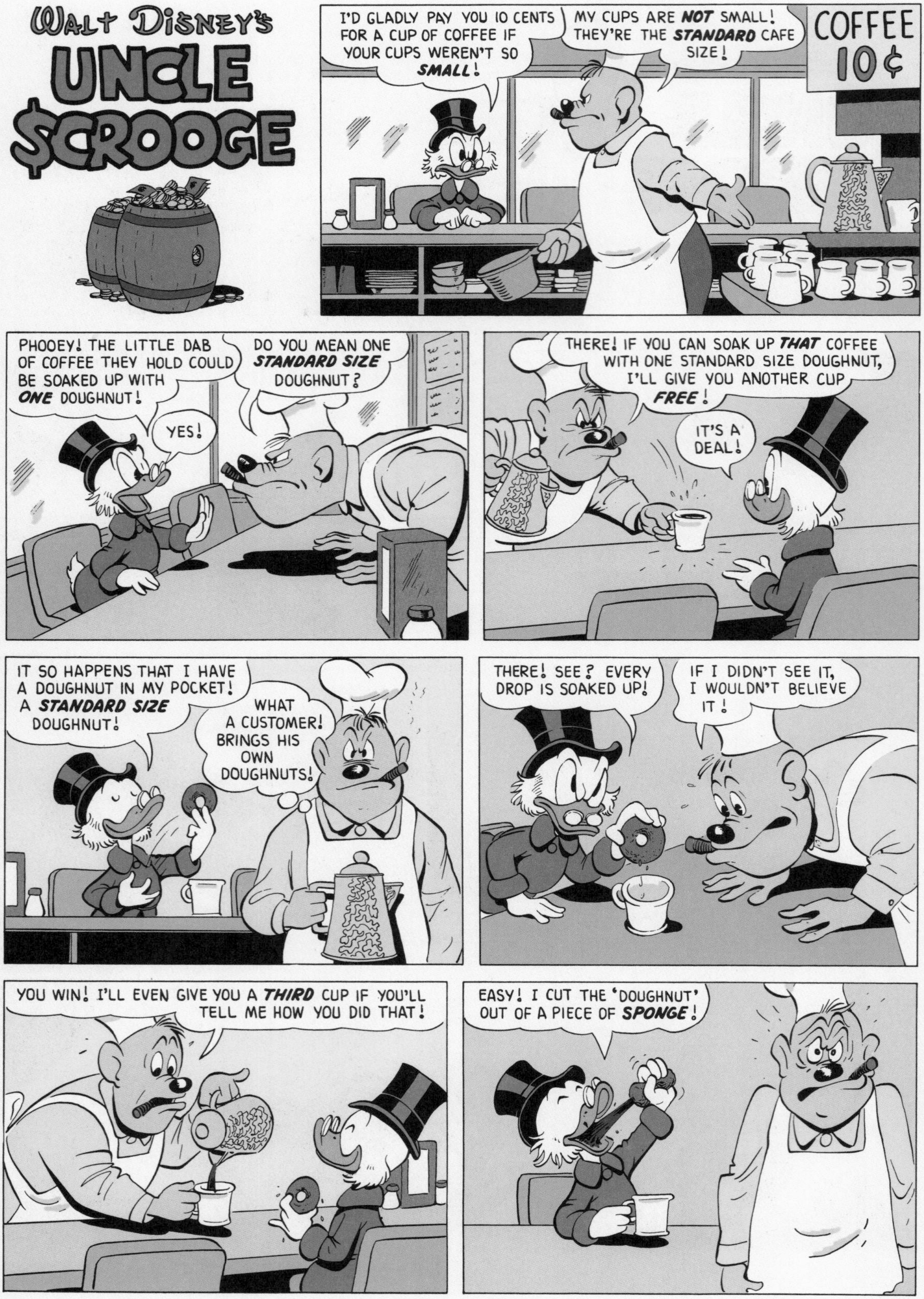
WALT DISNEY'S
UNCLE $CROOGE
I'D GLADLY PAY YOU 10 CENTS FOR A CUP OF COFFEE IF YOUR CUPS WEREN'T SO SMALL!
MY CUPS ARE NOT SMALL! THEY'RE THE STANDARD CAFE SIZE!
COFFEE 10¢
PHOOEY! THE LITTLE DAB OF COFFEE THEY HOLD COULD BE SOAKED UP WITH ONE DOUGHNUT!
DO YOU MEAN ONE STANDARD SIZE DOUGHNUT?
YES!
THERE! IF YOU CAN SOAK UP THAT COFFEE WITH ONE STANDARD SIZE DOUGHNUT, I'LL GIVE YOU ANOTHER CUP FREE!
IT'S A DEAL!
IT SO HAPPENS THAT I HAVE A DOUGHNUT IN MY POCKET! A STANDARD SIZE DOUGHNUT!
WHAT A CUSTOMER! BRINGS HIS OWN DOUGHNUTS!
THERE! SEE? EVERY DROP IS SOAKED UP!
IF I DIDN'T SEE IT, I WOULDN'T BELIEVE IT!
YOU WIN! I'LL EVEN GIVE YOU A THIRD CUP IF YOU'LL TELL ME HOW YOU DID THAT!
EASY! I CUT THE 'DOUGHNUT' OUT OF A PIECE OF SPONGE!

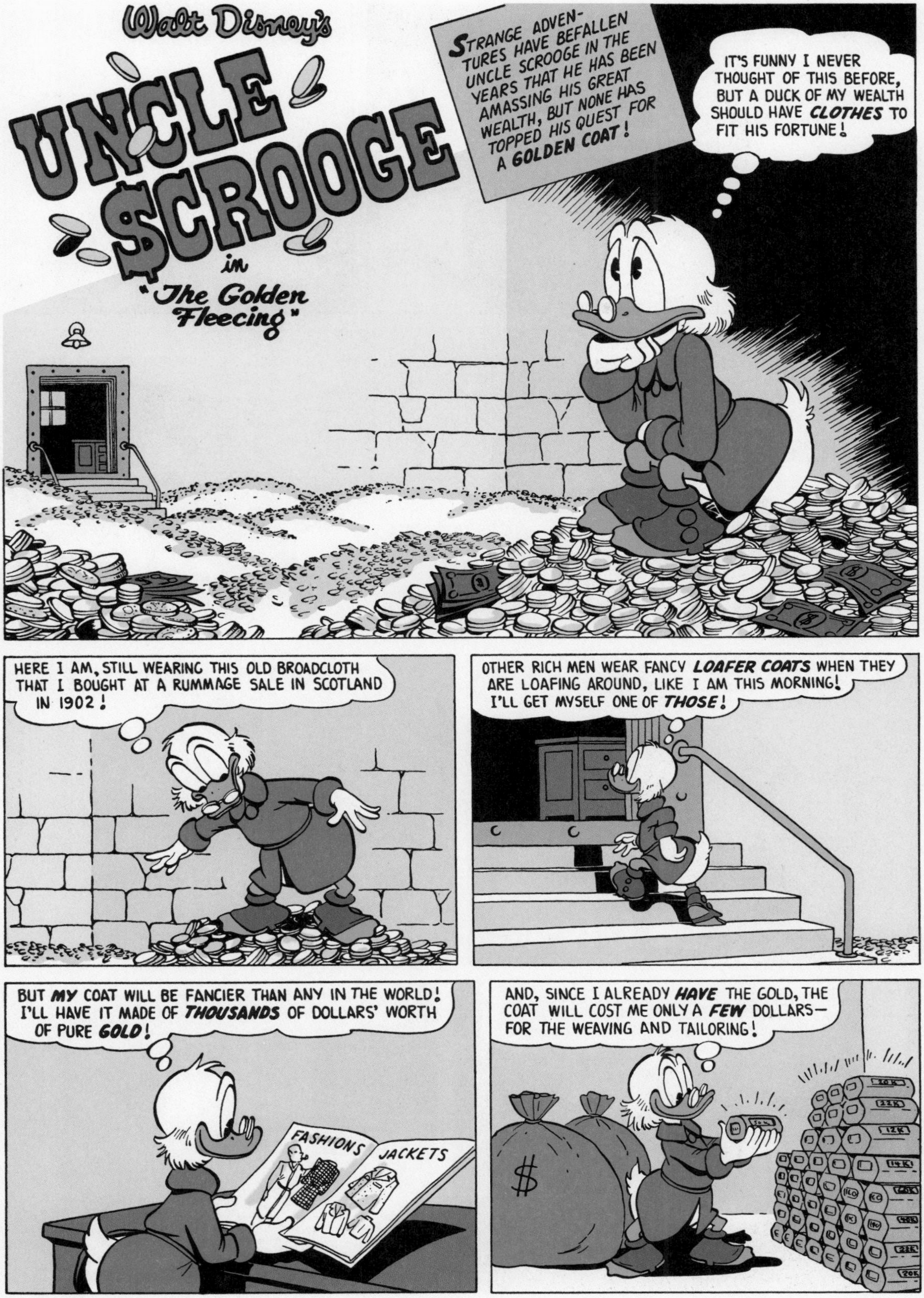
Walt Disney's
UNCLE $CROOGE
in
"The Golden Fleecing"
STRANGE ADVENTURES HAVE BEFALLEN UNCLE SCROOGE IN THE YEARS THAT HE HAS BEEN AMASSING HIS GREAT WEALTH, BUT NONE HAS TOPPED HIS QUEST FOR A GOLDEN COAT!
IT'S FUNNY I NEVER THOUGHT OF THIS BEFORE, BUT A DUCK OF MY WEALTH SHOULD HAVE CLOTHES TO FIT HIS FORTUNE!
HERE I AM, STILL WEARING THIS OLD BROADCLOTH THAT I BOUGHT AT A RUMMAGE SALE IN SCOTLAND IN 1902!
OTHER RICH MEN WEAR FANCY LOAFER COATS WHEN THEY ARE LOAFING AROUND, LIKE I AM THIS MORNING! I'LL GET MYSELF ONE OF THOSE!
BUT MY COAT WILL BE FANCIER THAN ANY IN THE WORLD! I'LL HAVE IT MADE OF THOUSANDS OF DOLLARS' WORTH OF PURE GOLD!
FASHIONS
JACKETS
AND, SINCE I ALREADY HAVE THE GOLD, THE COAT WILL COST ME ONLY A FEW DOLLARS— FOR THE WEAVING AND TAILORING!

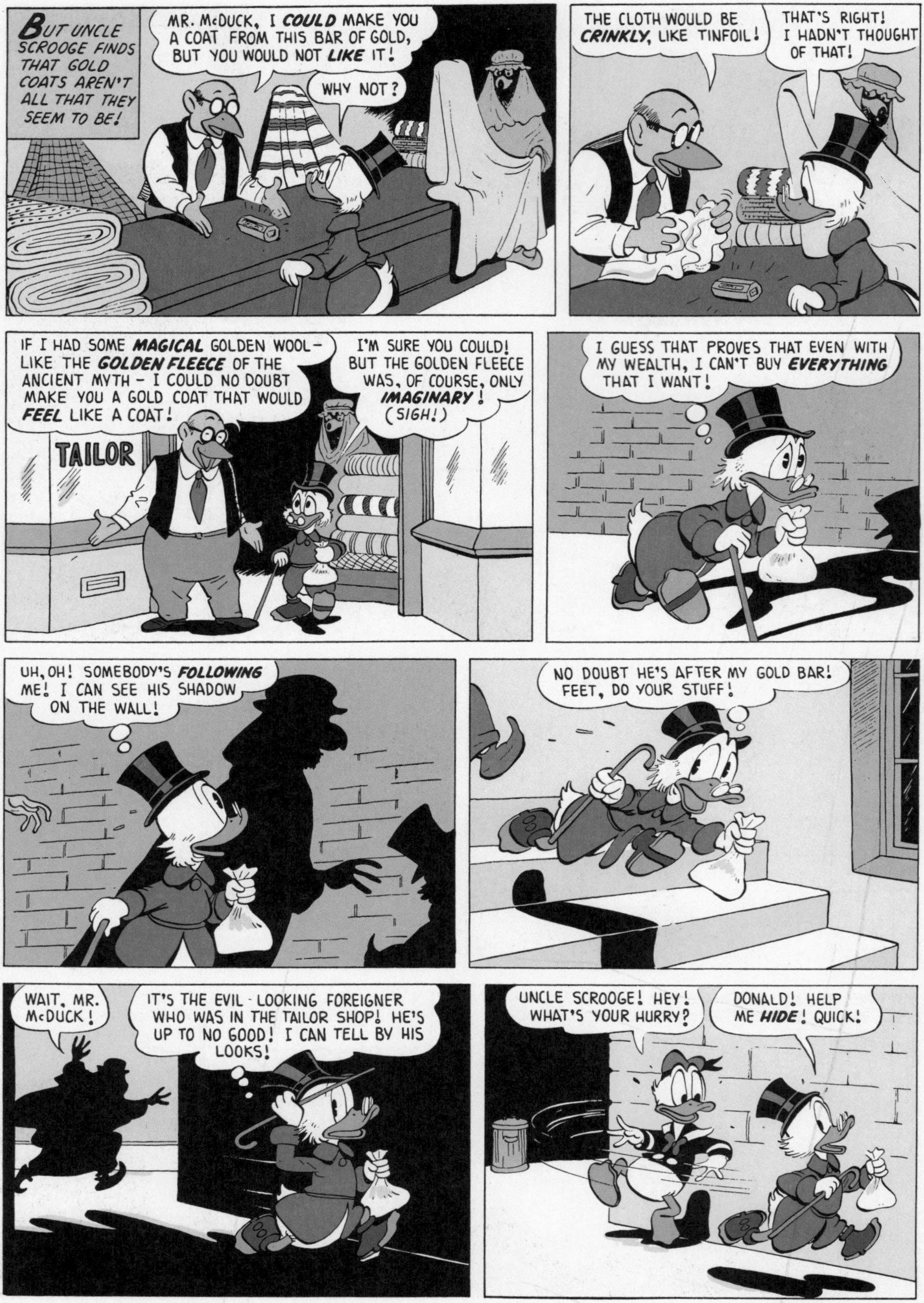
BUT UNCLE SCROOGE FINDS THAT GOLD COATS AREN'T ALL THAT THEY SEEM TO BE!
MR. McDUCK, I COULD MAKE YOU A COAT FROM THIS BAR OF GOLD, BUT YOU WOULD NOT LIKE IT!
WHY NOT?
THE CLOTH WOULD BE CRINKLY, LIKE TINFOIL!
THAT'S RIGHT! I HADN'T THOUGHT OF THAT!
IF I HAD SOME MAGICAL GOLDEN WOOL— LIKE THE GOLDEN FLEECE OF THE ANCIENT MYTH — I COULD NO DOUBT MAKE YOU A GOLD COAT THAT WOULD FEEL LIKE A COAT!
I'M SURE YOU COULD! BUT THE GOLDEN FLEECE WAS, OF COURSE, ONLY IMAGINARY! (SIGH!)
TAILOR
I GUESS THAT PROVES THAT EVEN WITH MY WEALTH, I CAN'T BUY EVERYTHING THAT I WANT!
UH, OH! SOMEBODY'S FOLLOWING ME! I CAN SEE HIS SHADOW ON THE WALL!
NO DOUBT HE'S AFTER MY GOLD BAR! FEET, DO YOUR STUFF!
WAIT, MR. McDUCK!
IT'S THE EVIL-LOOKING FOREIGNER WHO WAS IN THE TAILOR SHOP! HE'S UP TO NO GOOD! I CAN TELL BY HIS LOOKS!
UNCLE SCROOGE! HEY! WHAT'S YOUR HURRY?
DONALD! HELP ME HIDE! QUICK!

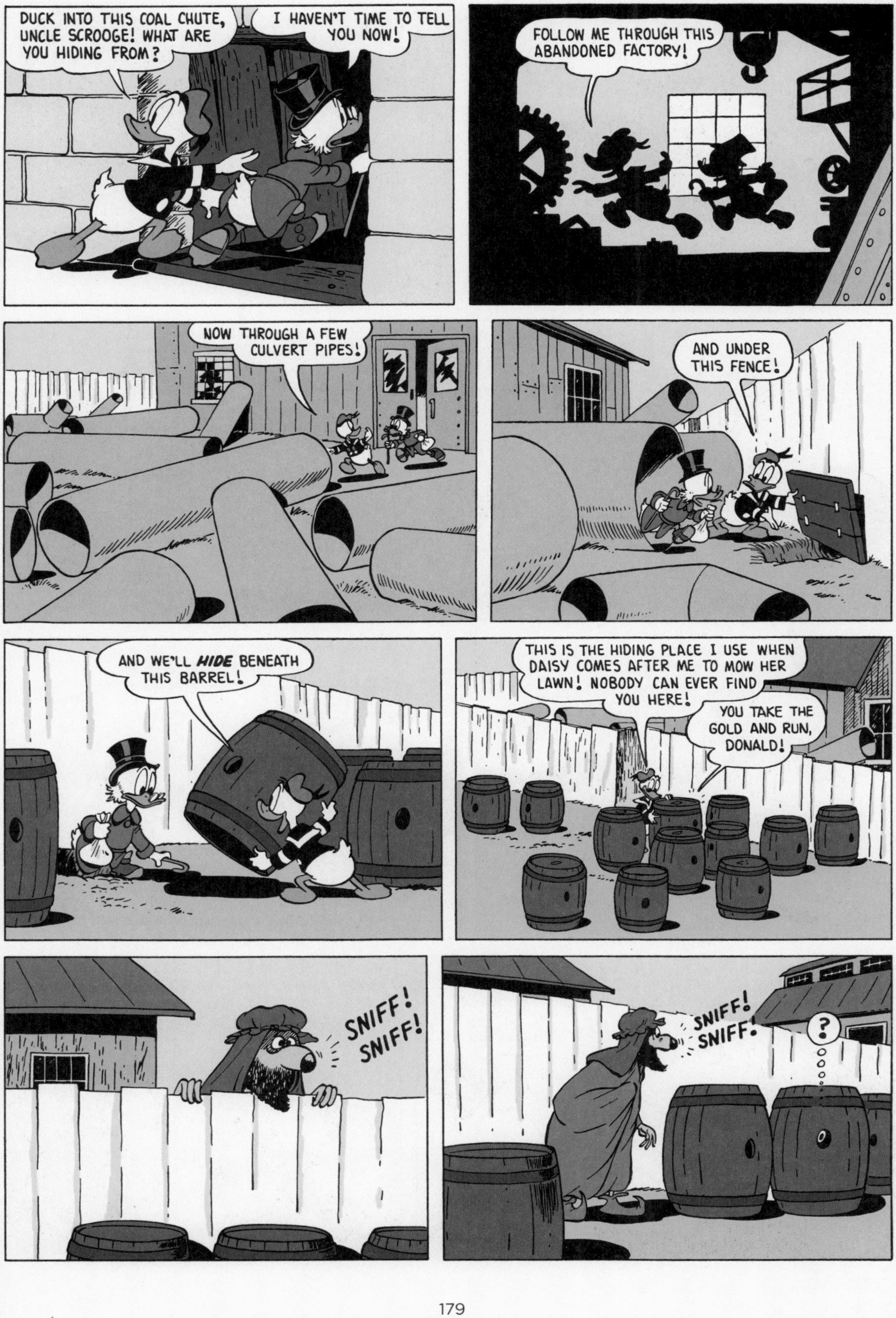
DUCK INTO THIS COAL CHUTE, UNCLE SCROOGE! WHAT ARE YOU HIDING FROM?
I HAVEN'T TIME TO TELL YOU NOW!
FOLLOW ME THROUGH THIS ABANDONED FACTORY!
NOW THROUGH A FEW CULVERT PIPES!
AND UNDER THIS FENCE!
AND WE'LL HIDE BENEATH THIS BARREL!
THIS IS THE HIDING PLACE I USE WHEN DAISY COMES AFTER ME TO MOW HER LAWN! NOBODY CAN EVER FIND YOU HERE!
YOU TAKE THE GOLD AND RUN, DONALD!
SNIFF! SNIFF!
SNIFF! SNIFF!
?

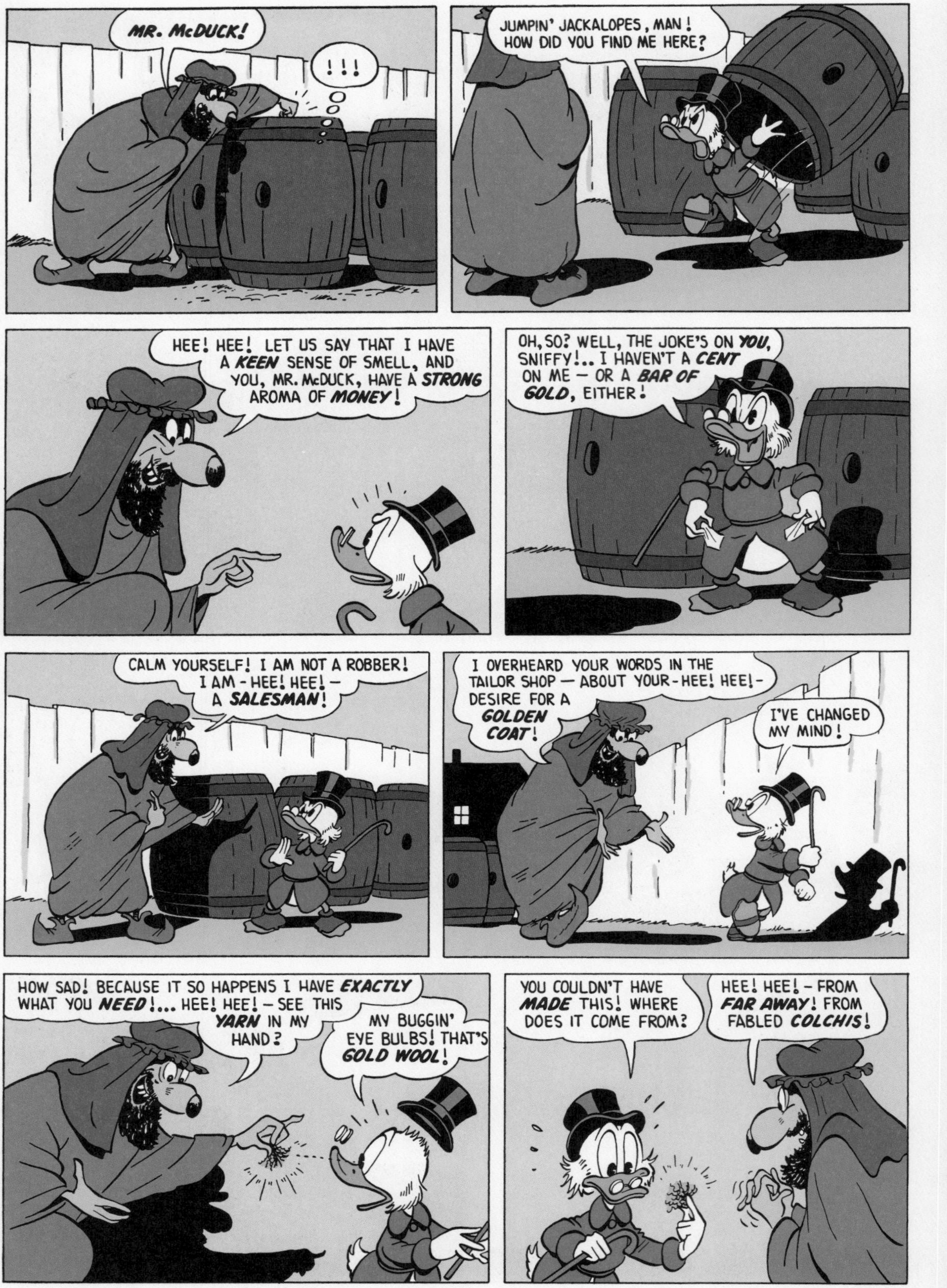
MR. McDUCK!
!!!
JUMPIN' JACKALOPES, MAN! HOW DID YOU FIND ME HERE?
HEE! HEE! LET US SAY THAT I HAVE A KEEN SENSE OF SMELL, AND YOU, MR. McDUCK, HAVE A STRONG AROMA OF MONEY!
OH, SO? WELL, THE JOKE'S ON YOU, SNIFFY!.. I HAVEN'T A CENT ON ME — OR A BAR OF GOLD, EITHER!
CALM YOURSELF! I AM NOT A ROBBER! I AM - HEE! HEE! - A SALESMAN!
I OVERHEARD YOUR WORDS IN THE TAILOR SHOP — ABOUT YOUR - HEE! HEE! - DESIRE FOR A GOLDEN COAT!
I'VE CHANGED MY MIND!
HOW SAD! BECAUSE IT SO HAPPENS I HAVE EXACTLY WHAT YOU NEED!... HEE! HEE! — SEE THIS YARN IN MY HAND?
MY BUGGIN' EYE BULBS! THAT'S GOLD WOOL!
YOU COULDN'T HAVE MADE THIS! WHERE DOES IT COME FROM?
HEE! HEE! - FROM FAR AWAY! FROM FABLED COLCHIS!

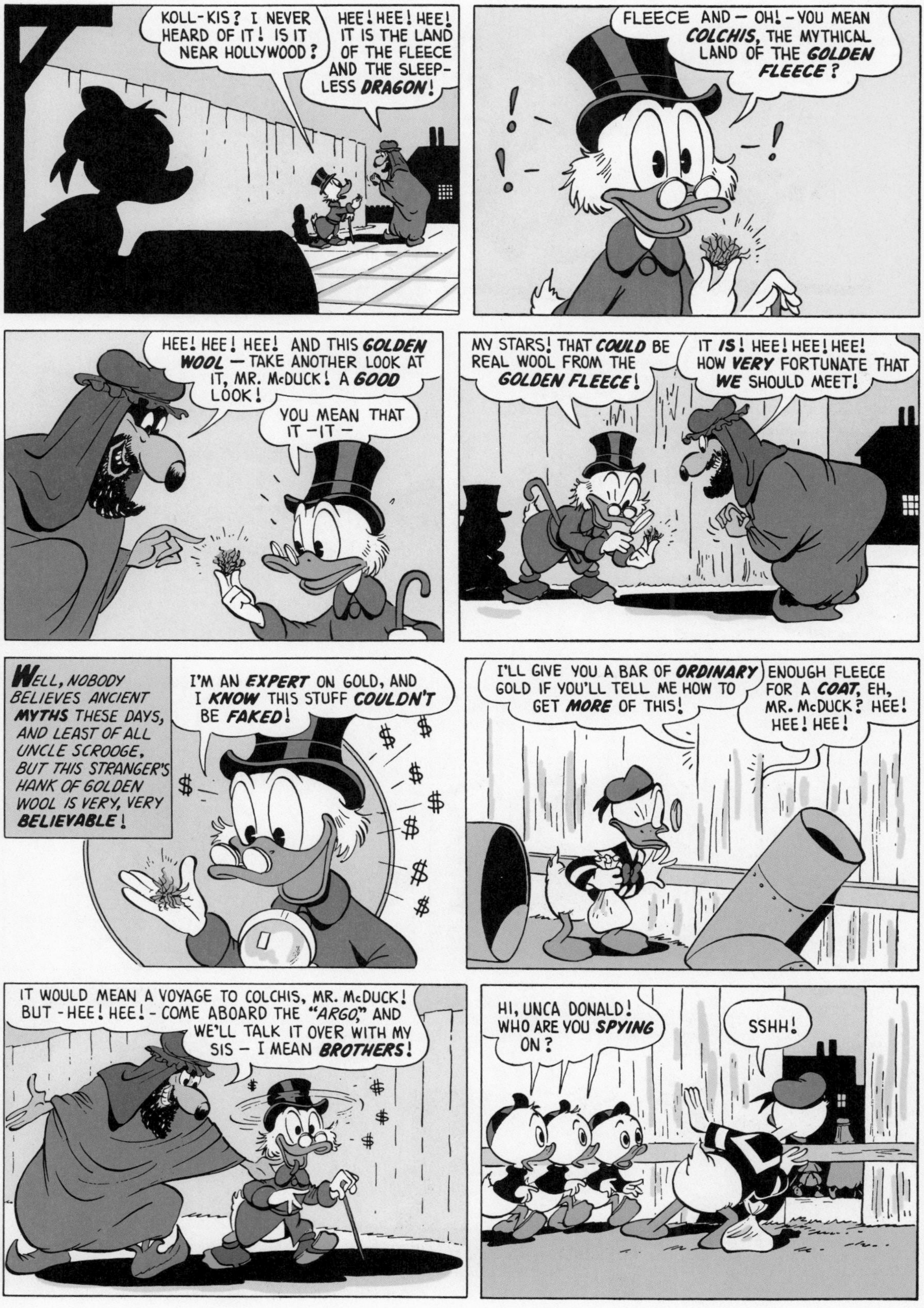
KOLL-KIS? I NEVER HEARD OF IT! IS IT NEAR HOLLYWOOD?
HEE! HEE! HEE! IT IS THE LAND OF THE FLEECE AND THE SLEEP-LESS DRAGON!
FLEECE AND — OH! — YOU MEAN COLCHIS, THE MYTHICAL LAND OF THE GOLDEN FLEECE?
HEE! HEE! HEE! AND THIS GOLDEN WOOL — TAKE ANOTHER LOOK AT IT, MR. McDUCK! A GOOD LOOK!
YOU MEAN THAT IT — IT —
MY STARS! THAT COULD BE REAL WOOL FROM THE GOLDEN FLEECE!
IT IS! HEE! HEE! HEE! HOW VERY FORTUNATE THAT WE SHOULD MEET!
WELL, NOBODY BELIEVES ANCIENT MYTHS THESE DAYS, AND LEAST OF ALL UNCLE SCROOGE, BUT THIS STRANGER'S HANK OF GOLDEN WOOL IS VERY, VERY BELIEVABLE!
I'M AN EXPERT ON GOLD, AND I KNOW THIS STUFF COULDN'T BE FAKED!
I'LL GIVE YOU A BAR OF ORDINARY GOLD IF YOU'LL TELL ME HOW TO GET MORE OF THIS!
ENOUGH FLEECE FOR A COAT, EH, MR. McDUCK? HEE! HEE! HEE!
IT WOULD MEAN A VOYAGE TO COLCHIS, MR. McDUCK! BUT - HEE! HEE! - COME ABOARD THE "ARGO," AND WE'LL TALK IT OVER WITH MY SIS — I MEAN BROTHERS!
HI, UNCA DONALD! WHO ARE YOU SPYING ON?
SSHH!

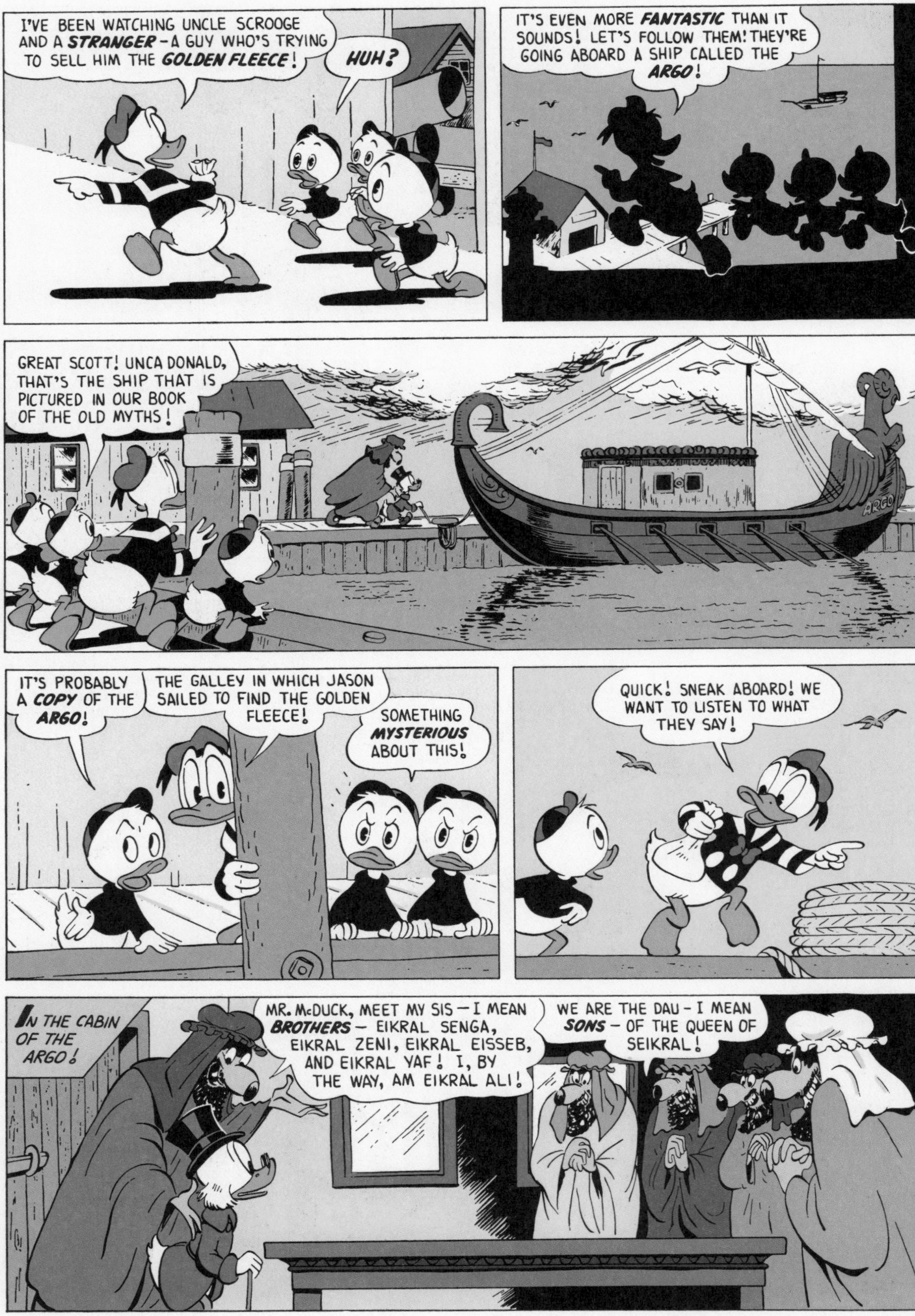
I'VE BEEN WATCHING UNCLE SCROOGE AND A STRANGER – A GUY WHO'S TRYING TO SELL HIM THE GOLDEN FLEECE!
HUH?
IT'S EVEN MORE FANTASTIC THAN IT SOUNDS! LET'S FOLLOW THEM! THEY'RE GOING ABOARD A SHIP CALLED THE ARGO!
GREAT SCOTT! UNCA DONALD, THAT'S THE SHIP THAT IS PICTURED IN OUR BOOK OF THE OLD MYTHS!
ARGO
IT'S PROBABLY A COPY OF THE ARGO!
THE GALLEY IN WHICH JASON SAILED TO FIND THE GOLDEN FLEECE!
SOMETHING MYSTERIOUS ABOUT THIS!
QUICK! SNEAK ABOARD! WE WANT TO LISTEN TO WHAT THEY SAY!
IN THE CABIN OF THE ARGO!
MR. McDUCK, MEET MY SIS — I MEAN BROTHERS — EIKRAL SENGA, EIKRAL ZENI, EIKRAL EISSEB, AND EIKRAL YAF! I, BY THE WAY, AM EIKRAL ALI!
WE ARE THE DAU – I MEAN SONS – OF THE QUEEN OF SEIKRAL!

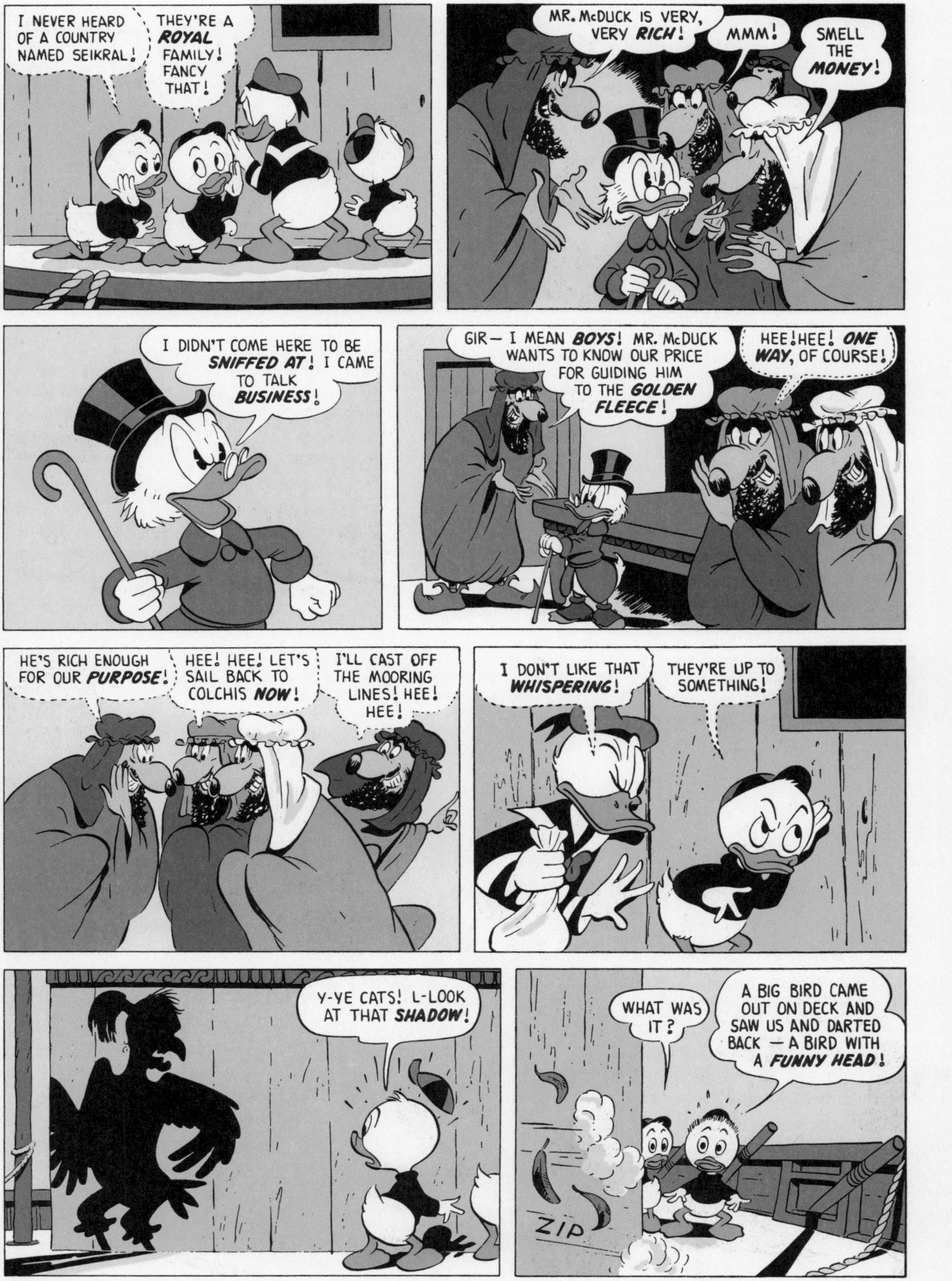
I NEVER HEARD OF A COUNTRY NAMED SEIKRAL!
THEY'RE A ROYAL FAMILY! FANCY THAT!
MR. McDUCK IS VERY, VERY RICH!
MMM!
SMELL THE MONEY!
I DIDN'T COME HERE TO BE SNIFFED AT! I CAME TO TALK BUSINESS!
GIR— I MEAN BOYS! MR. McDUCK WANTS TO KNOW OUR PRICE FOR GUIDING HIM TO THE GOLDEN FLEECE!
HEE! HEE! ONE WAY, OF COURSE!
HE'S RICH ENOUGH FOR OUR PURPOSE!
HEE! HEE! LET'S SAIL BACK TO COLCHIS NOW!
I'LL CAST OFF THE MOORING LINES! HEE! HEE!
I DON'T LIKE THAT WHISPERING!
THEY'RE UP TO SOMETHING!
Y-YE CATS! L-LOOK AT THAT SHADOW!
WHAT WAS IT?
A BIG BIRD CAME OUT ON DECK AND SAW US AND DARTED BACK — A BIRD WITH A FUNNY HEAD!
ZIP

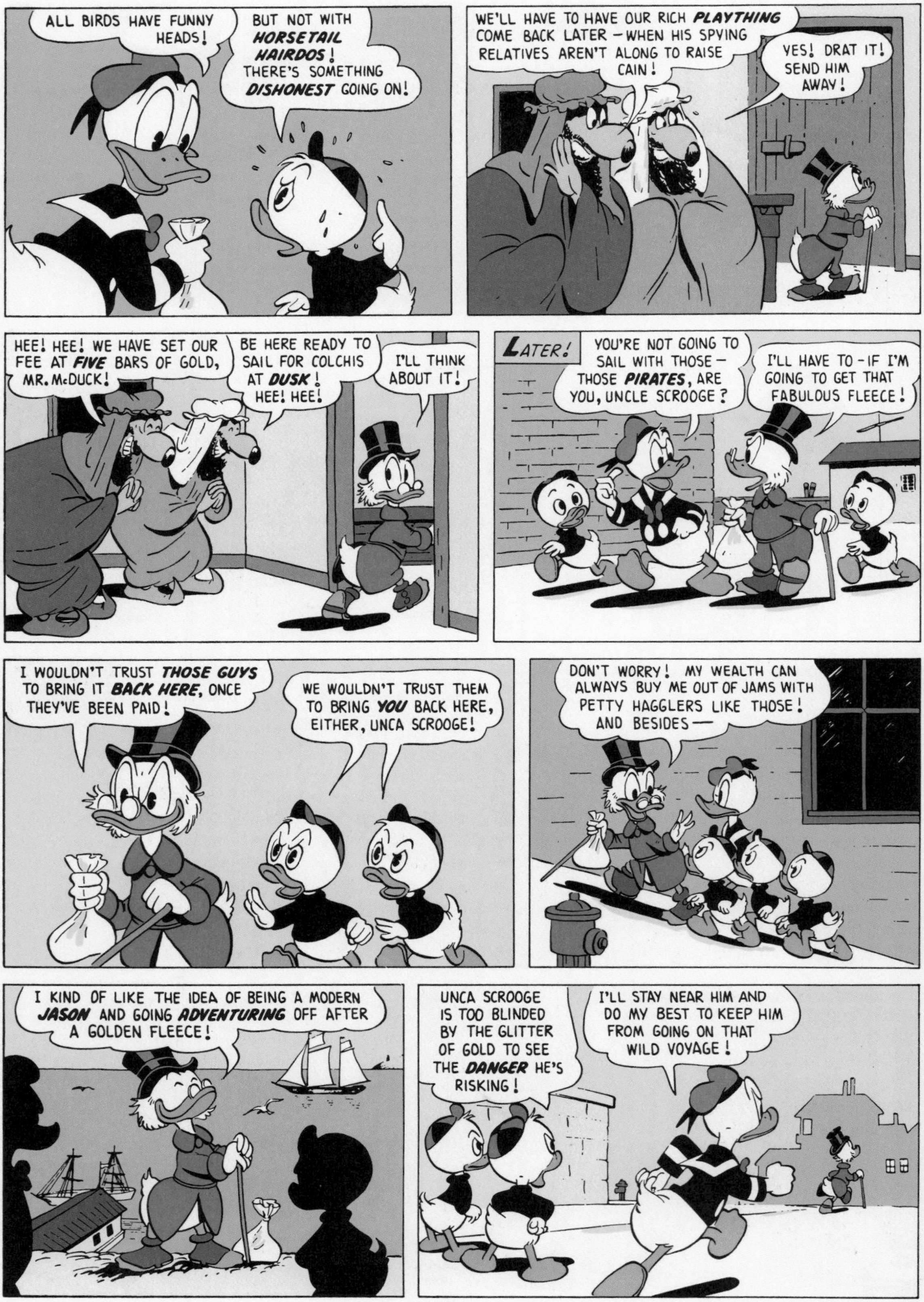
ALL BIRDS HAVE FUNNY HEADS!
BUT NOT WITH HORSETAIL HAIRDOS! THERE'S SOMETHING DISHONEST GOING ON!
WE'LL HAVE TO HAVE OUR RICH PLAYTHING COME BACK LATER — WHEN HIS SPYING RELATIVES AREN'T ALONG TO RAISE CAIN!
YES! DRAT IT! SEND HIM AWAY!
HEE! HEE! WE HAVE SET OUR FEE AT FIVE BARS OF GOLD, MR. McDUCK!
BE HERE READY TO SAIL FOR COLCHIS AT DUSK! HEE! HEE!
I'LL THINK ABOUT IT!
LATER!
YOU'RE NOT GOING TO SAIL WITH THOSE — THOSE PIRATES, ARE YOU, UNCLE SCROOGE?
I'LL HAVE TO — IF I'M GOING TO GET THAT FABULOUS FLEECE!
I WOULDN'T TRUST THOSE GUYS TO BRING IT BACK HERE, ONCE THEY'VE BEEN PAID!
WE WOULDN'T TRUST THEM TO BRING YOU BACK HERE, EITHER, UNCA SCROOGE!
DON'T WORRY! MY WEALTH CAN ALWAYS BUY ME OUT OF JAMS WITH PETTY HAGGLERS LIKE THOSE! AND BESIDES —
I KIND OF LIKE THE IDEA OF BEING A MODERN JASON AND GOING ADVENTURING OFF AFTER A GOLDEN FLEECE!
UNCA SCROOGE IS TOO BLINDED BY THE GLITTER OF GOLD TO SEE THE DANGER HE'S RISKING!
I'LL STAY NEAR HIM AND DO MY BEST TO KEEP HIM FROM GOING ON THAT WILD VOYAGE!

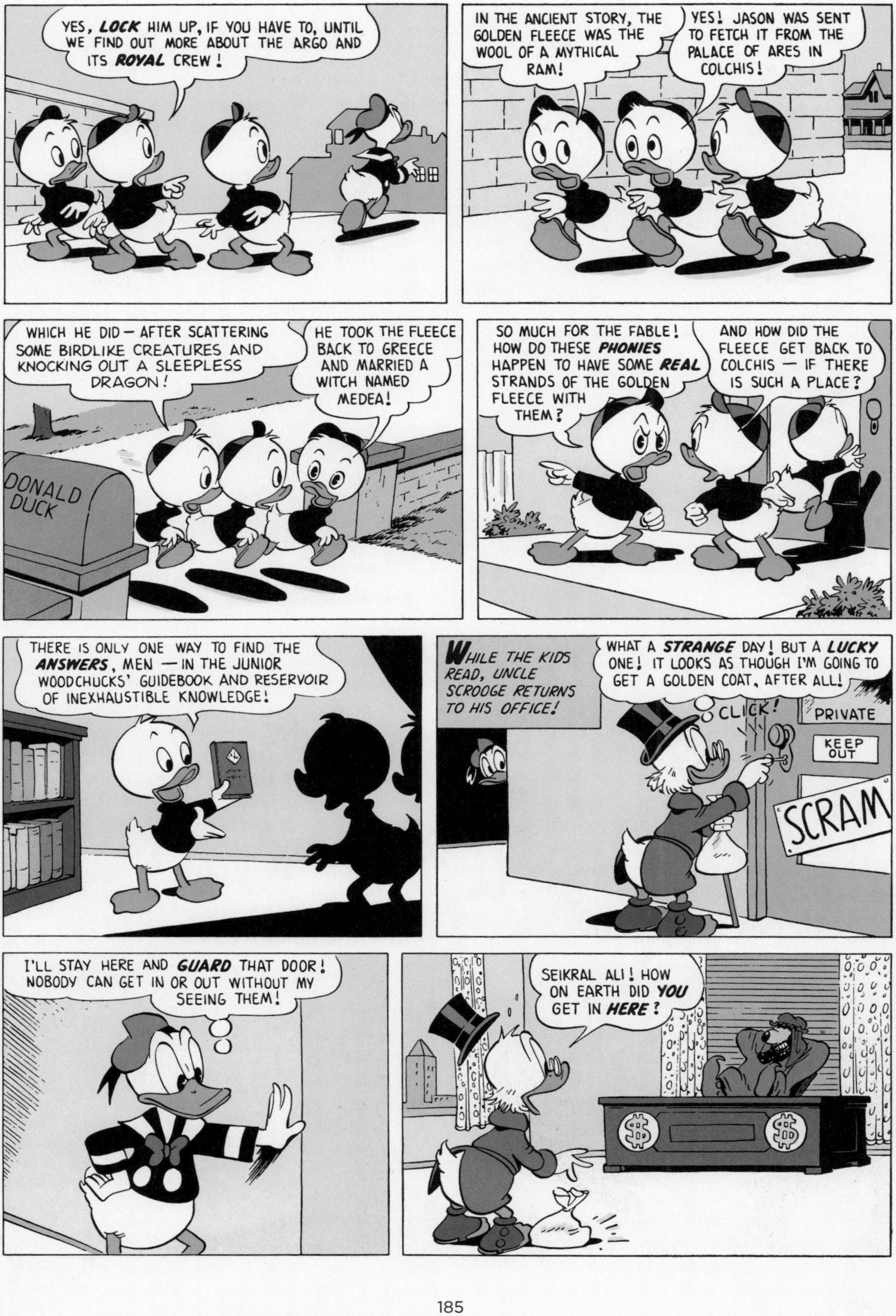
YES, LOCK HIM UP, IF YOU HAVE TO, UNTIL WE FIND OUT MORE ABOUT THE ARGO AND ITS ROYAL CREW!
IN THE ANCIENT STORY, THE GOLDEN FLEECE WAS THE WOOL OF A MYTHICAL RAM!
YES! JASON WAS SENT TO FETCH IT FROM THE PALACE OF ARES IN COLCHIS!
WHICH HE DID — AFTER SCATTERING SOME BIRDLIKE CREATURES AND KNOCKING OUT A SLEEPLESS DRAGON!
HE TOOK THE FLEECE BACK TO GREECE AND MARRIED A WITCH NAMED MEDEA!
DONALD DUCK
SO MUCH FOR THE FABLE! HOW DO THESE PHONIES HAPPEN TO HAVE SOME REAL STRANDS OF THE GOLDEN FLEECE WITH THEM?
AND HOW DID THE FLEECE GET BACK TO COLCHIS — IF THERE IS SUCH A PLACE?
THERE IS ONLY ONE WAY TO FIND THE ANSWERS, MEN — IN THE JUNIOR WOODCHUCKS' GUIDEBOOK AND RESERVOIR OF INEXHAUSTIBLE KNOWLEDGE!
WHILE THE KIDS READ, UNCLE SCROOGE RETURNS TO HIS OFFICE!
WHAT A STRANGE DAY! BUT A LUCKY ONE! IT LOOKS AS THOUGH I'M GOING TO GET A GOLDEN COAT, AFTER ALL!
CLICK!
PRIVATE
KEEP OUT
SCRAM
I'LL STAY HERE AND GUARD THAT DOOR! NOBODY CAN GET IN OR OUT WITHOUT MY SEEING THEM!
SEIKRAL ALI! HOW ON EARTH DID YOU GET IN HERE?

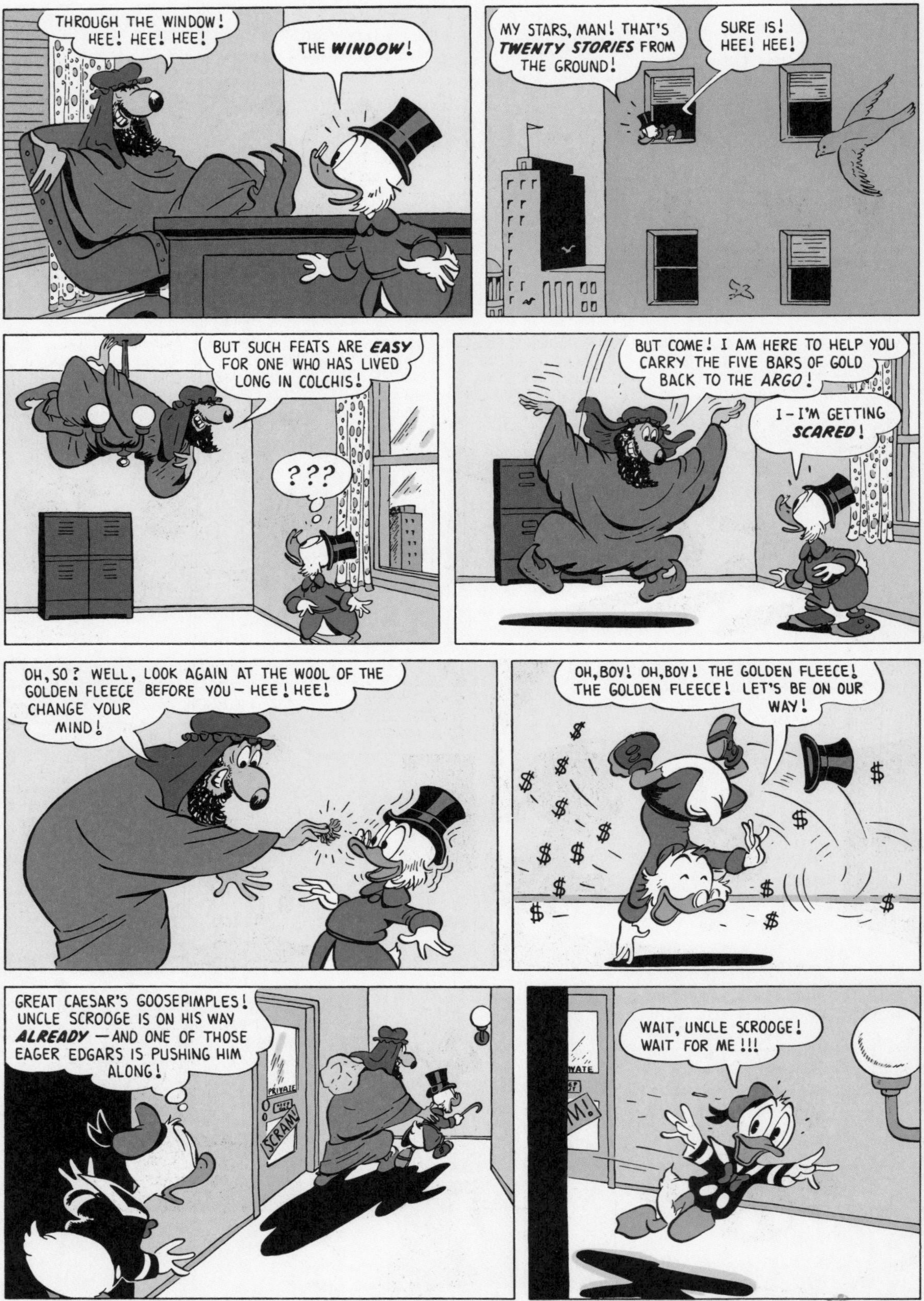
THROUGH THE WINDOW! HEE! HEE! HEE!
THE WINDOW!
MY STARS, MAN! THAT'S TWENTY STORIES FROM THE GROUND!
SURE IS! HEE! HEE!
BUT SUCH FEATS ARE EASY FOR ONE WHO HAS LIVED LONG IN COLCHIS!
???
BUT COME! I AM HERE TO HELP YOU CARRY THE FIVE BARS OF GOLD BACK TO THE ARGO!
I-I'M GETTING SCARED!
OH, SO? WELL, LOOK AGAIN AT THE WOOL OF THE GOLDEN FLEECE BEFORE YOU—HEE! HEE! CHANGE YOUR MIND!
OH, BOY! OH, BOY! THE GOLDEN FLEECE! THE GOLDEN FLEECE! LET'S BE ON OUR WAY!
GREAT CAESAR'S GOOSEPIMPLES! UNCLE SCROOGE IS ON HIS WAY ALREADY—AND ONE OF THOSE EAGER EDGARS IS PUSHING HIM ALONG!
PRIVATE
SCRAM!
WAIT, UNCLE SCROOGE! WAIT FOR ME!!!

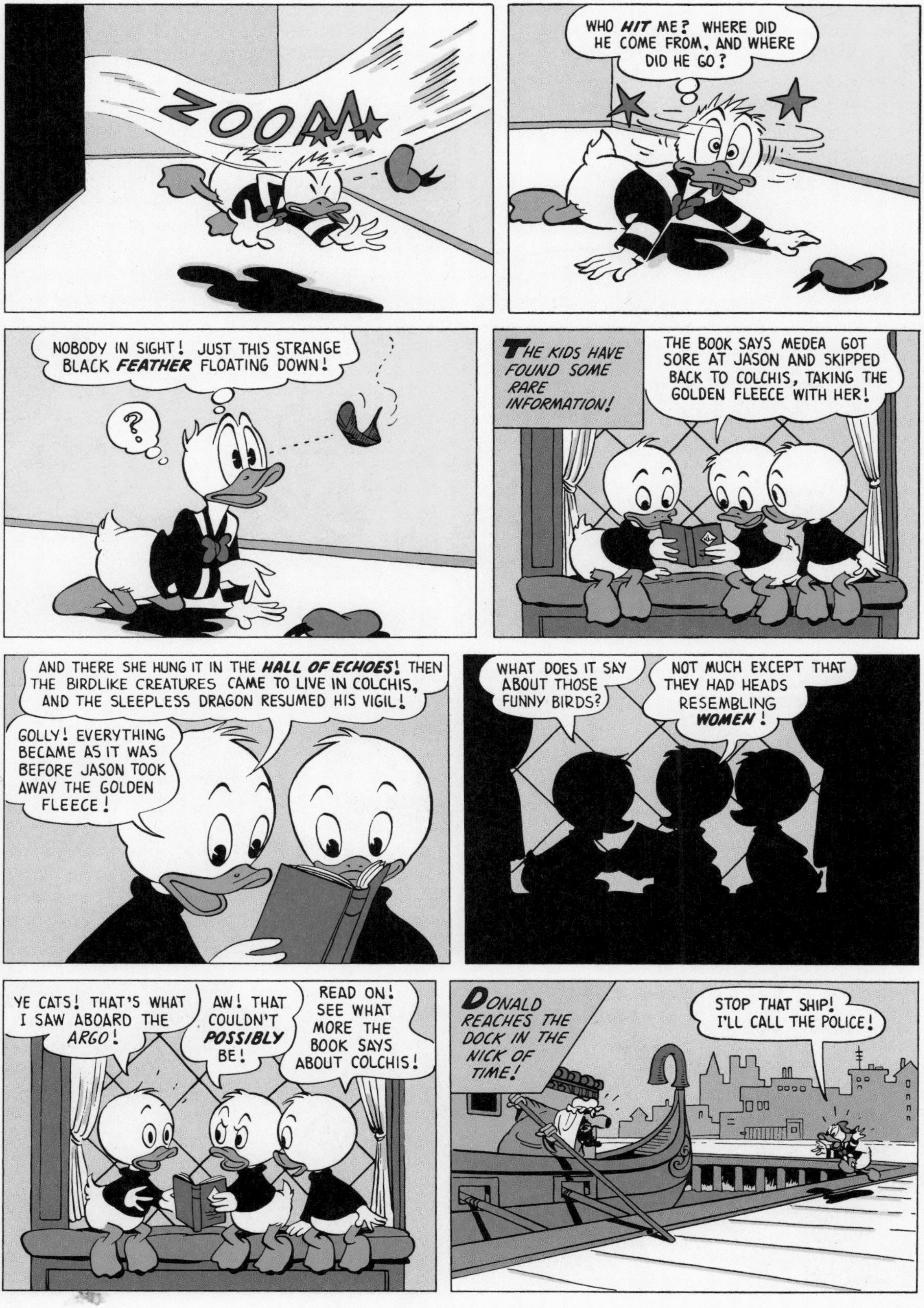
ZOOM
WHO HIT ME? WHERE DID HE COME FROM, AND WHERE DID HE GO?
NOBODY IN SIGHT! JUST THIS STRANGE BLACK FEATHER FLOATING DOWN!
?
THE KIDS HAVE FOUND SOME RARE INFORMATION!
THE BOOK SAYS MEDEA GOT SORE AT JASON AND SKIPPED BACK TO COLCHIS, TAKING THE GOLDEN FLEECE WITH HER!
AND THERE SHE HUNG IT IN THE HALL OF ECHOES! THEN THE BIRDLIKE CREATURES CAME TO LIVE IN COLCHIS, AND THE SLEEPLESS DRAGON RESUMED HIS VIGIL!
GOLLY! EVERYTHING BECAME AS IT WAS BEFORE JASON TOOK AWAY THE GOLDEN FLEECE!
WHAT DOES IT SAY ABOUT THOSE FUNNY BIRDS?
NOT MUCH EXCEPT THAT THEY HAD HEADS RESEMBLING WOMEN!
YE CATS! THAT'S WHAT I SAW ABOARD THE ARGO!
AW! THAT COULDN'T POSSIBLY BE!
READ ON! SEE WHAT MORE THE BOOK SAYS ABOUT COLCHIS!
DONALD REACHES THE DOCK IN THE NICK OF TIME!
STOP THAT SHIP! I'LL CALL THE POLICE!

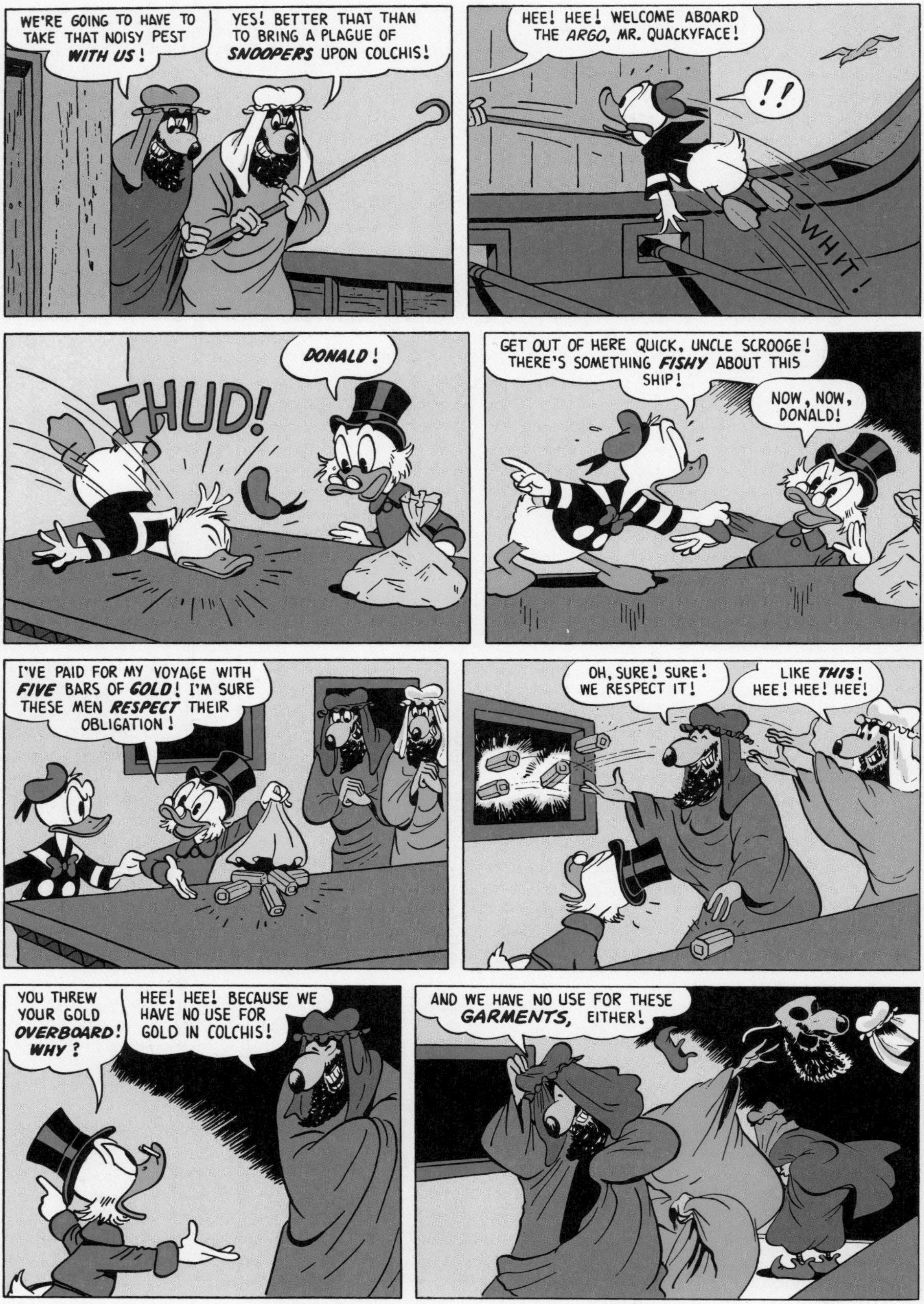
WE'RE GOING TO HAVE TO TAKE THAT NOISY PEST WITH US!
YES! BETTER THAT THAN TO BRING A PLAGUE OF SNOOPERS UPON COLCHIS!
HEE! HEE! WELCOME ABOARD THE ARGO, MR. QUACKYFACE!
!!
WHIT!
THUD!
DONALD!
GET OUT OF HERE QUICK, UNCLE SCROOGE! THERE'S SOMETHING FISHY ABOUT THIS SHIP!
NOW, NOW, DONALD!
I'VE PAID FOR MY VOYAGE WITH FIVE BARS OF GOLD! I'M SURE THESE MEN RESPECT THEIR OBLIGATION!
OH, SURE! SURE! WE RESPECT IT!
LIKE THIS! HEE! HEE! HEE!
YOU THREW YOUR GOLD OVERBOARD! WHY?
HEE! HEE! BECAUSE WE HAVE NO USE FOR GOLD IN COLCHIS!
AND WE HAVE NO USE FOR THESE GARMENTS, EITHER!

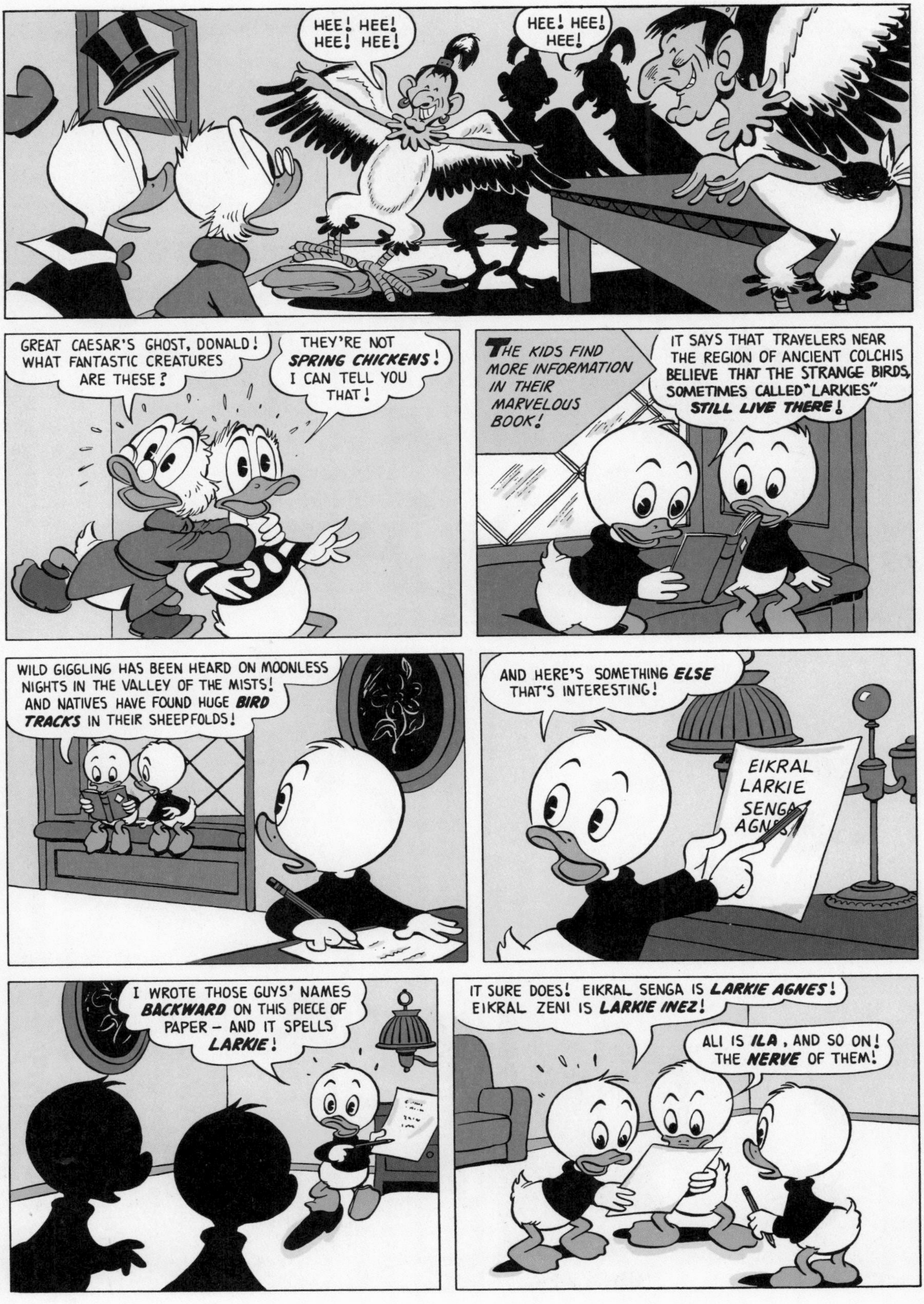

HEE! HEE! HEE! HEE!
HEE! HEE! HEE!
GREAT CAESAR'S GHOST, DONALD! WHAT FANTASTIC CREATURES ARE THESE?
THEY'RE NOT SPRING CHICKENS! I CAN TELL YOU THAT!
THE KIDS FIND MORE INFORMATION IN THEIR MARVELOUS BOOK!
IT SAYS THAT TRAVELERS NEAR THE REGION OF ANCIENT COLCHIS BELIEVE THAT THE STRANGE BIRDS, SOMETIMES CALLED "LARKIES" STILL LIVE THERE!
WILD GIGGLING HAS BEEN HEARD ON MOONLESS NIGHTS IN THE VALLEY OF THE MISTS! AND NATIVES HAVE FOUND HUGE BIRD TRACKS IN THEIR SHEEPFOLDS!
AND HERE'S SOMETHING ELSE THAT'S INTERESTING!
EIKRAL
LARKIE
I WROTE THOSE GUYS' NAMES BACKWARD ON THIS PIECE OF PAPER – AND IT SPELLS LARKIE!
IT SURE DOES! EIKRAL SENGA IS LARKIE AGNES! EIKRAL ZENI IS LARKIE INEZ!
ALI IS ILA, AND SO ON! THE NERVE OF THEM!

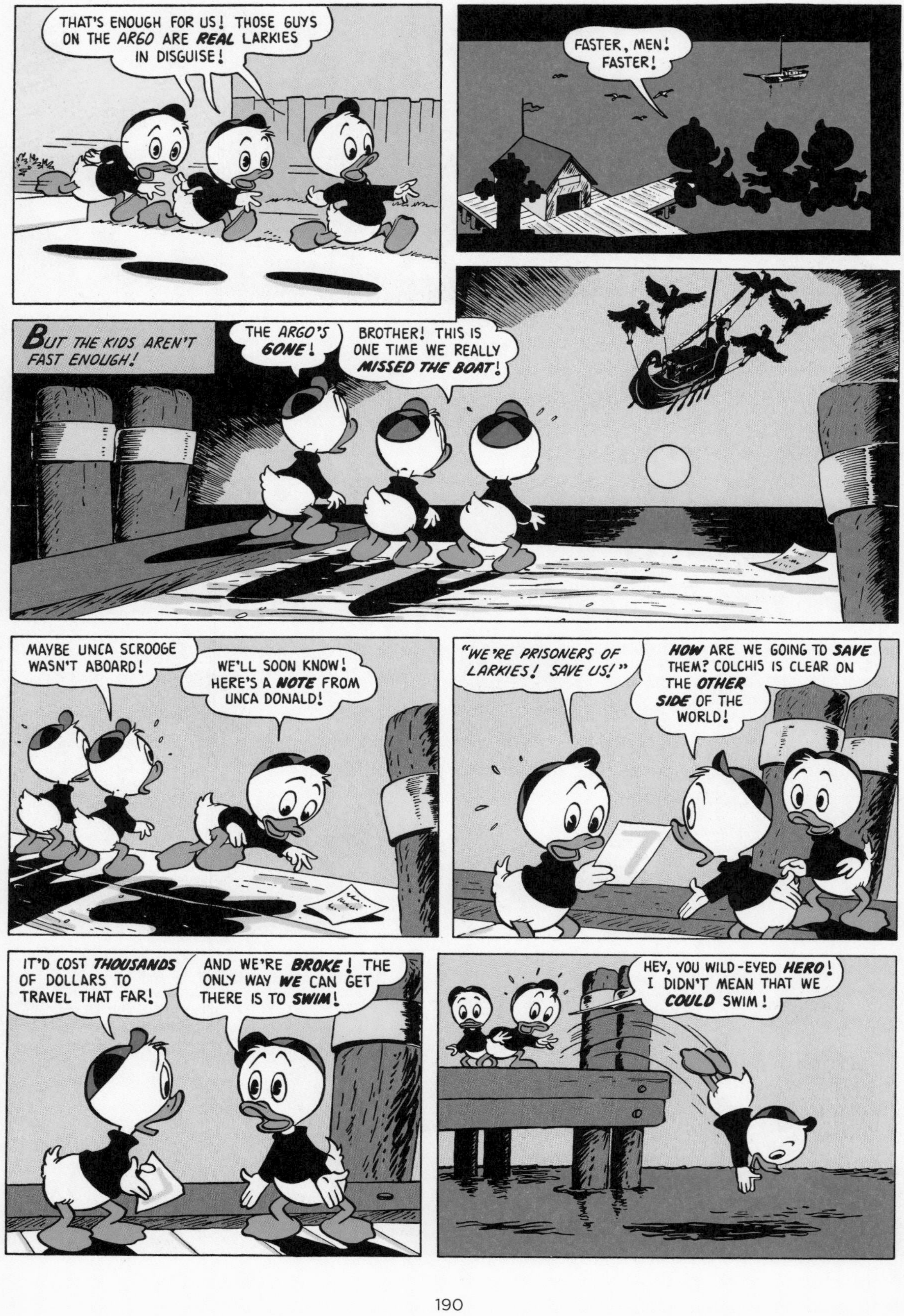
THAT'S ENOUGH FOR US! THOSE GUYS ON THE ARGO ARE REAL LARKIES IN DISGUISE!
FASTER, MEN! FASTER!
BUT THE KIDS AREN'T FAST ENOUGH!
THE ARGO'S GONE!
BROTHER! THIS IS ONE TIME WE REALLY MISSED THE BOAT!
MAYBE UNCA SCROOGE WASN'T ABOARD!
WE'LL SOON KNOW! HERE'S A NOTE FROM UNCA DONALD!
"WE'RE PRISONERS OF LARKIES! SAVE US!"
HOW ARE WE GOING TO SAVE THEM? COLCHIS IS CLEAR ON THE OTHER SIDE OF THE WORLD!
IT'D COST THOUSANDS OF DOLLARS TO TRAVEL THAT FAR!
AND WE'RE BROKE! THE ONLY WAY WE CAN GET THERE IS TO SWIM!
HEY, YOU WILD-EYED HERO! I DIDN'T MEAN THAT WE COULD SWIM!

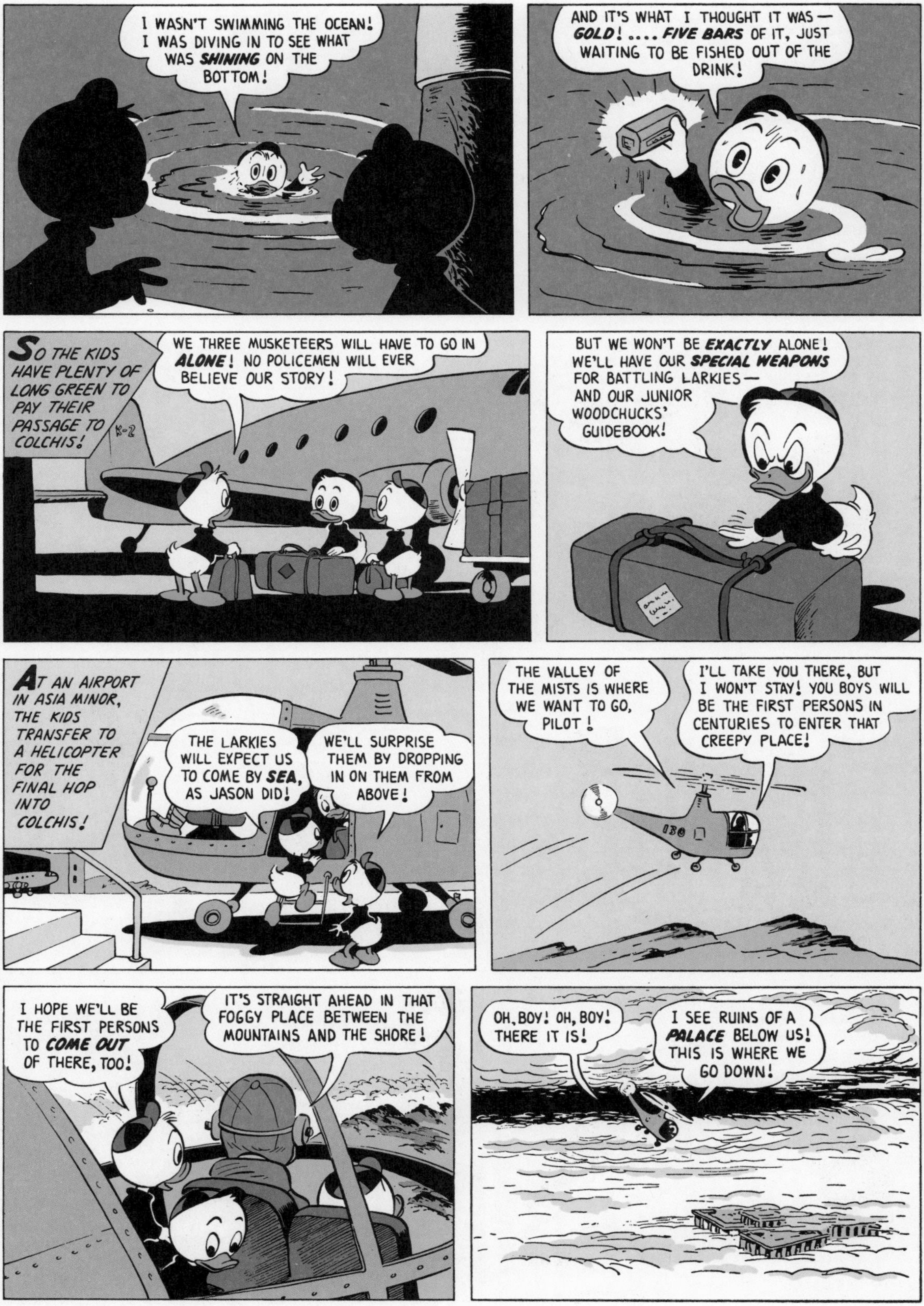
I WASN'T SWIMMING THE OCEAN! I WAS DIVING IN TO SEE WHAT WAS SHINING ON THE BOTTOM!
AND IT'S WHAT I THOUGHT IT WAS— GOLD! .... FIVE BARS OF IT, JUST WAITING TO BE FISHED OUT OF THE DRINK!
SO THE KIDS HAVE PLENTY OF LONG GREEN TO PAY THEIR PASSAGE TO COLCHIS!
WE THREE MUSKETEERS WILL HAVE TO GO IN ALONE! NO POLICEMEN WILL EVER BELIEVE OUR STORY!
BUT WE WON'T BE EXACTLY ALONE! WE'LL HAVE OUR SPECIAL WEAPONS FOR BATTLING LARKIES— AND OUR JUNIOR WOODCHUCKS' GUIDEBOOK!
AT AN AIRPORT IN ASIA MINOR, THE KIDS TRANSFER TO A HELICOPTER FOR THE FINAL HOP INTO COLCHIS!
THE LARKIES WILL EXPECT US TO COME BY SEA, AS JASON DID!
WE'LL SURPRISE THEM BY DROPPING IN ON THEM FROM ABOVE!
THE VALLEY OF THE MISTS IS WHERE WE WANT TO GO, PILOT!
I'LL TAKE YOU THERE, BUT I WON'T STAY! YOU BOYS WILL BE THE FIRST PERSONS IN CENTURIES TO ENTER THAT CREEPY PLACE!
I HOPE WE'LL BE THE FIRST PERSONS TO COME OUT OF THERE, TOO!
IT'S STRAIGHT AHEAD IN THAT FOGGY PLACE BETWEEN THE MOUNTAINS AND THE SHORE!
OH, BOY! OH, BOY! THERE IT IS!
I SEE RUINS OF A PALACE BELOW US! THIS IS WHERE WE GO DOWN!

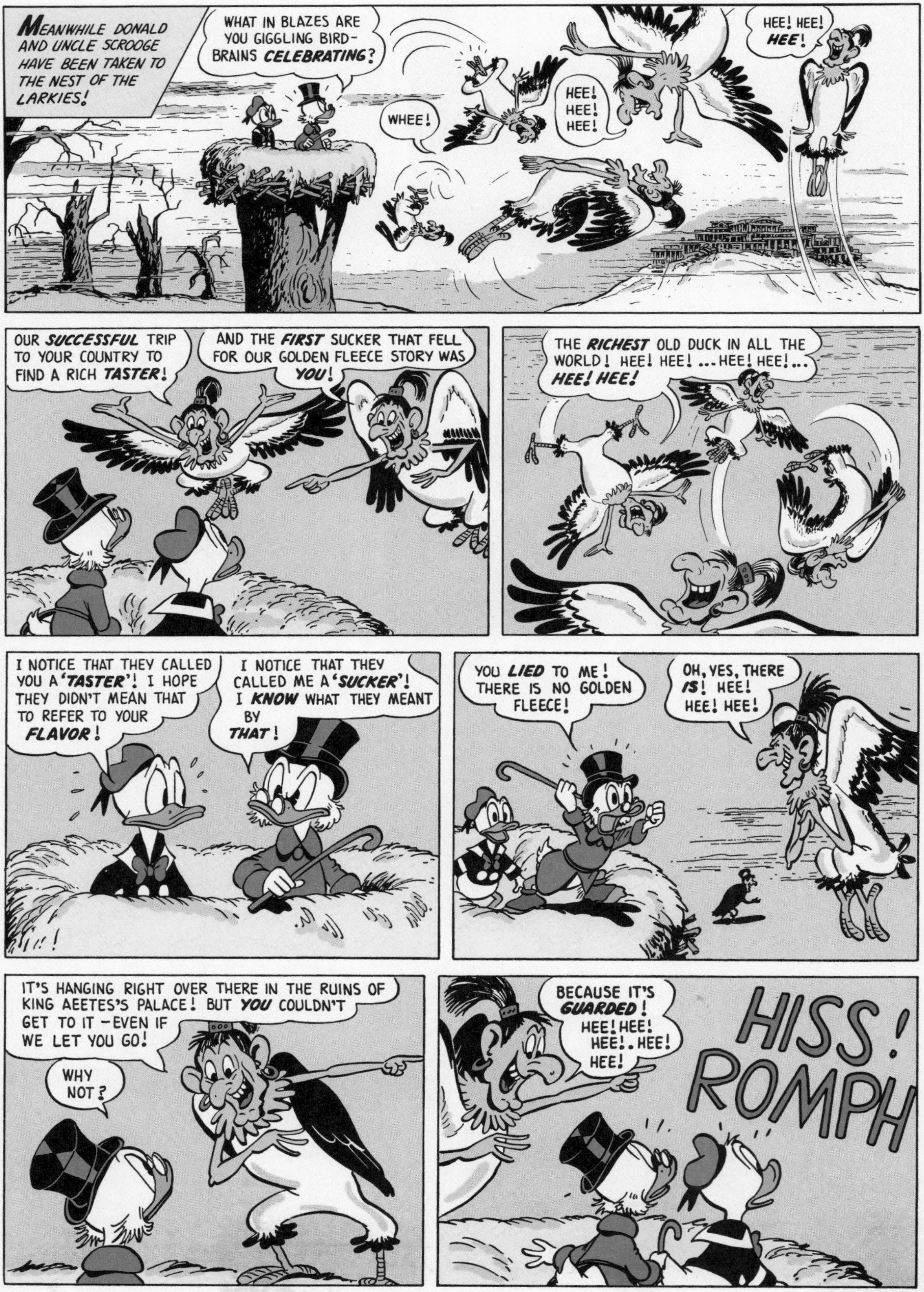
MEANWHILE DONALD AND UNCLE SCROOGE HAVE BEEN TAKEN TO THE NEST OF THE LARKIES!
WHAT IN BLAZES ARE YOU GIGGLING BIRD-BRAINS CELEBRATING?
WHEE!
HEE! HEE! HEE!
HEE! HEE! HEE!
OUR SUCCESSFUL TRIP TO YOUR COUNTRY TO FIND A RICH TASTER!
AND THE FIRST SUCKER THAT FELL FOR OUR GOLDEN FLEECE STORY WAS YOU!
THE RICHEST OLD DUCK IN ALL THE WORLD! HEE! HEE! ...HEE! HEE!... HEE! HEE!
I NOTICE THAT THEY CALLED YOU A 'TASTER'! I HOPE THEY DIDN'T MEAN THAT TO REFER TO YOUR FLAVOR!
I NOTICE THAT THEY CALLED ME A 'SUCKER'! I KNOW WHAT THEY MEANT BY THAT!
YOU LIED TO ME! THERE IS NO GOLDEN FLEECE!
OH, YES, THERE IS! HEE! HEE! HEE!
IT'S HANGING RIGHT OVER THERE IN THE RUINS OF KING AEETES'S PALACE! BUT YOU COULDN'T GET TO IT—EVEN IF WE LET YOU GO!
WHY NOT?
BECAUSE IT'S GUARDED! HEE! HEE! HEE!. HEE! HEE!
HISS! ROMPH

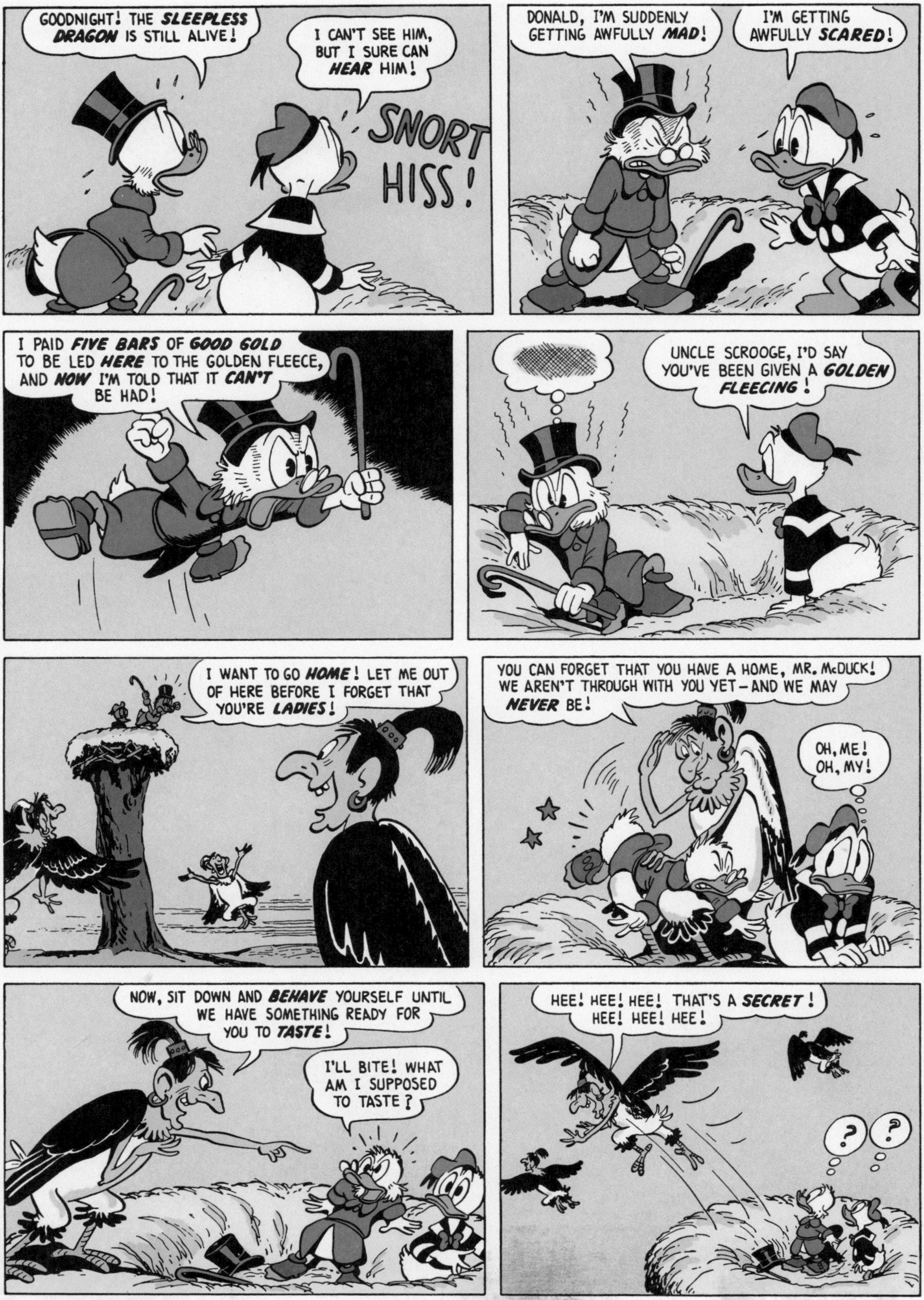
GOODNIGHT! THE SLEEPLESS DRAGON IS STILL ALIVE!
I CAN'T SEE HIM, BUT I SURE CAN HEAR HIM!
SNORT HISS!
DONALD, I'M SUDDENLY GETTING AWFULLY MAD!
I'M GETTING AWFULLY SCARED!
I PAID FIVE BARS OF GOOD GOLD TO BE LED HERE TO THE GOLDEN FLEECE, AND NOW I'M TOLD THAT IT CAN'T BE HAD!
UNCLE SCROOGE, I'D SAY YOU'VE BEEN GIVEN A GOLDEN FLEECING!
I WANT TO GO HOME! LET ME OUT OF HERE BEFORE I FORGET THAT YOU'RE LADIES!
YOU CAN FORGET THAT YOU HAVE A HOME, MR. McDUCK! WE AREN'T THROUGH WITH YOU YET—AND WE MAY NEVER BE!
OH, ME! OH, MY!
NOW, SIT DOWN AND BEHAVE YOURSELF UNTIL WE HAVE SOMETHING READY FOR YOU TO TASTE!
I'LL BITE! WHAT AM I SUPPOSED TO TASTE?
HEE! HEE! HEE! THAT'S A SECRET! HEE! HEE! HEE!
? ?

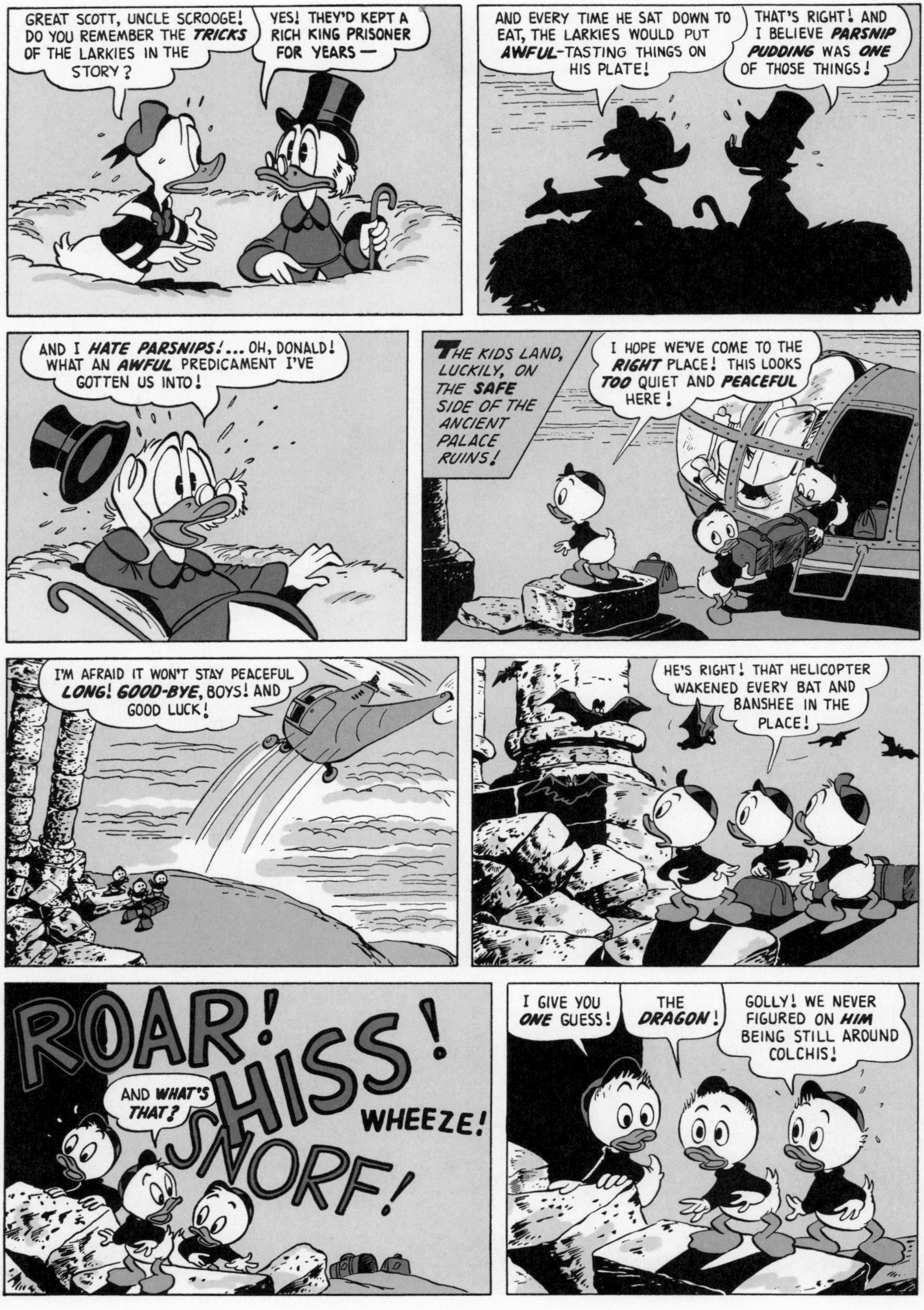
GREAT SCOTT, UNCLE SCROOGE! DO YOU REMEMBER THE TRICKS OF THE LARKIES IN THE STORY?
YES! THEY'D KEPT A RICH KING PRISONER FOR YEARS —
AND EVERY TIME HE SAT DOWN TO EAT, THE LARKIES WOULD PUT AWFUL-TASTING THINGS ON HIS PLATE!
THAT'S RIGHT! AND I BELIEVE PARSNIP PUDDING WAS ONE OF THOSE THINGS!
AND I HATE PARSNIPS!... OH, DONALD! WHAT AN AWFUL PREDICAMENT I'VE GOTTEN US INTO!
THE KIDS LAND, LUCKILY, ON THE SAFE SIDE OF THE ANCIENT PALACE RUINS!
I HOPE WE'VE COME TO THE RIGHT PLACE! THIS LOOKS TOO QUIET AND PEACEFUL HERE!
I'M AFRAID IT WON'T STAY PEACEFUL LONG! GOOD-BYE, BOYS! AND GOOD LUCK!
HE'S RIGHT! THAT HELICOPTER WAKENED EVERY BAT AND BANSHEE IN THE PLACE!
ROAR! SHISS!
AND WHAT'S THAT?
WHEEZE!
SNORF!
I GIVE YOU ONE GUESS!
THE DRAGON!
GOLLY! WE NEVER FIGURED ON HIM BEING STILL AROUND COLCHIS!

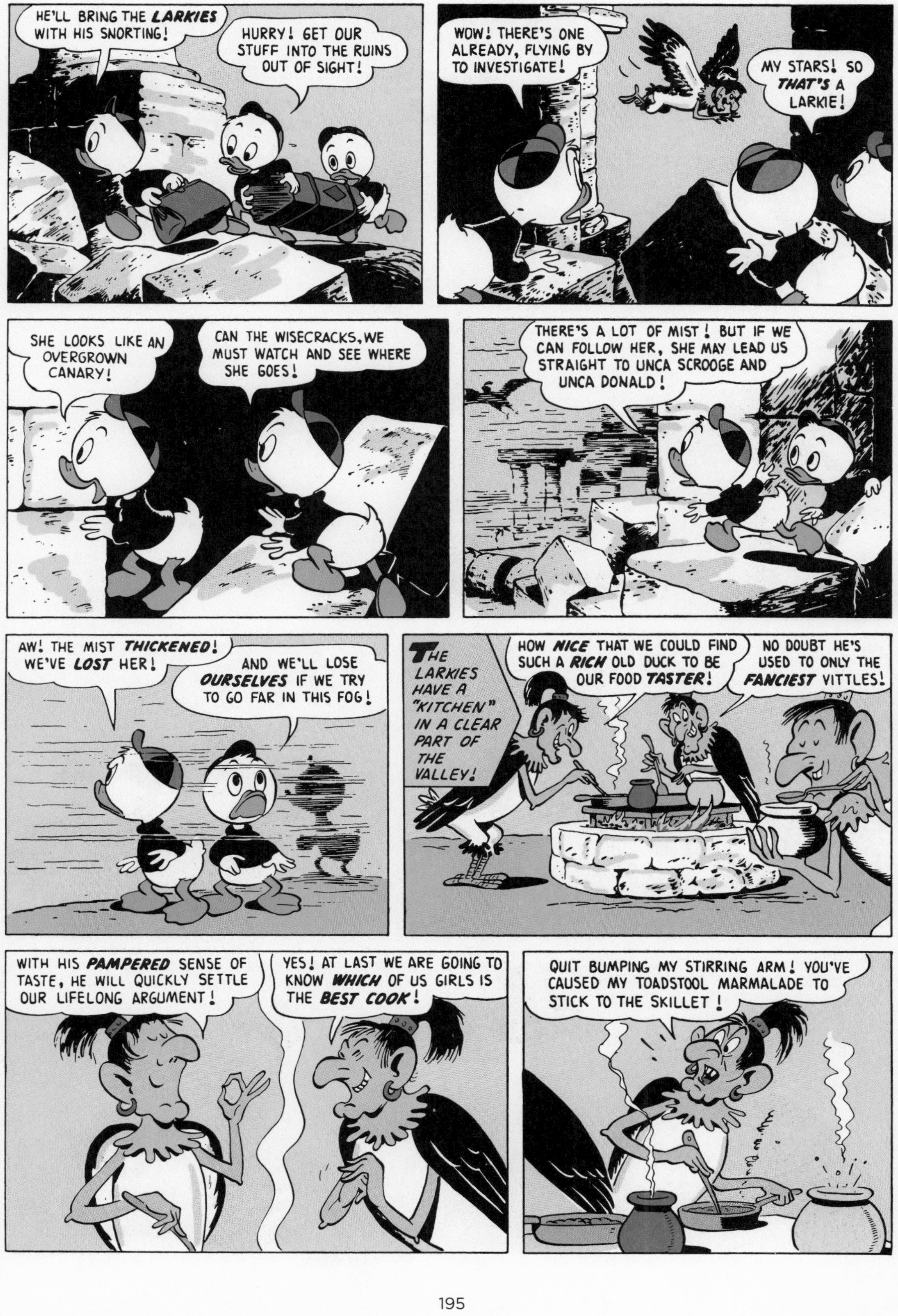
HE'LL BRING THE LARKIES WITH HIS SNORTING!
HURRY! GET OUR STUFF INTO THE RUINS OUT OF SIGHT!
WOW! THERE'S ONE ALREADY, FLYING BY TO INVESTIGATE!
MY STARS! SO THAT'S A LARKIE!
SHE LOOKS LIKE AN OVERGROWN CANARY!
CAN THE WISECRACKS, WE MUST WATCH AND SEE WHERE SHE GOES!
THERE'S A LOT OF MIST! BUT IF WE CAN FOLLOW HER, SHE MAY LEAD US STRAIGHT TO UNCA SCROOGE AND UNCA DONALD!
AW! THE MIST THICKENED! WE'VE LOST HER!
AND WE'LL LOSE OURSELVES IF WE TRY TO GO FAR IN THIS FOG!
THE LARKIES HAVE A "KITCHEN" IN A CLEAR PART OF THE VALLEY!
HOW NICE THAT WE COULD FIND SUCH A RICH OLD DUCK TO BE OUR FOOD TASTER!
NO DOUBT HE'S USED TO ONLY THE FANCIEST VITTLES!
WITH HIS PAMPERED SENSE OF TASTE, HE WILL QUICKLY SETTLE OUR LIFELONG ARGUMENT!
YES! AT LAST WE ARE GOING TO KNOW WHICH OF US GIRLS IS THE BEST COOK!
QUIT BUMPING MY STIRRING ARM! YOU'VE CAUSED MY TOADSTOOL MARMALADE TO STICK TO THE SKILLET!

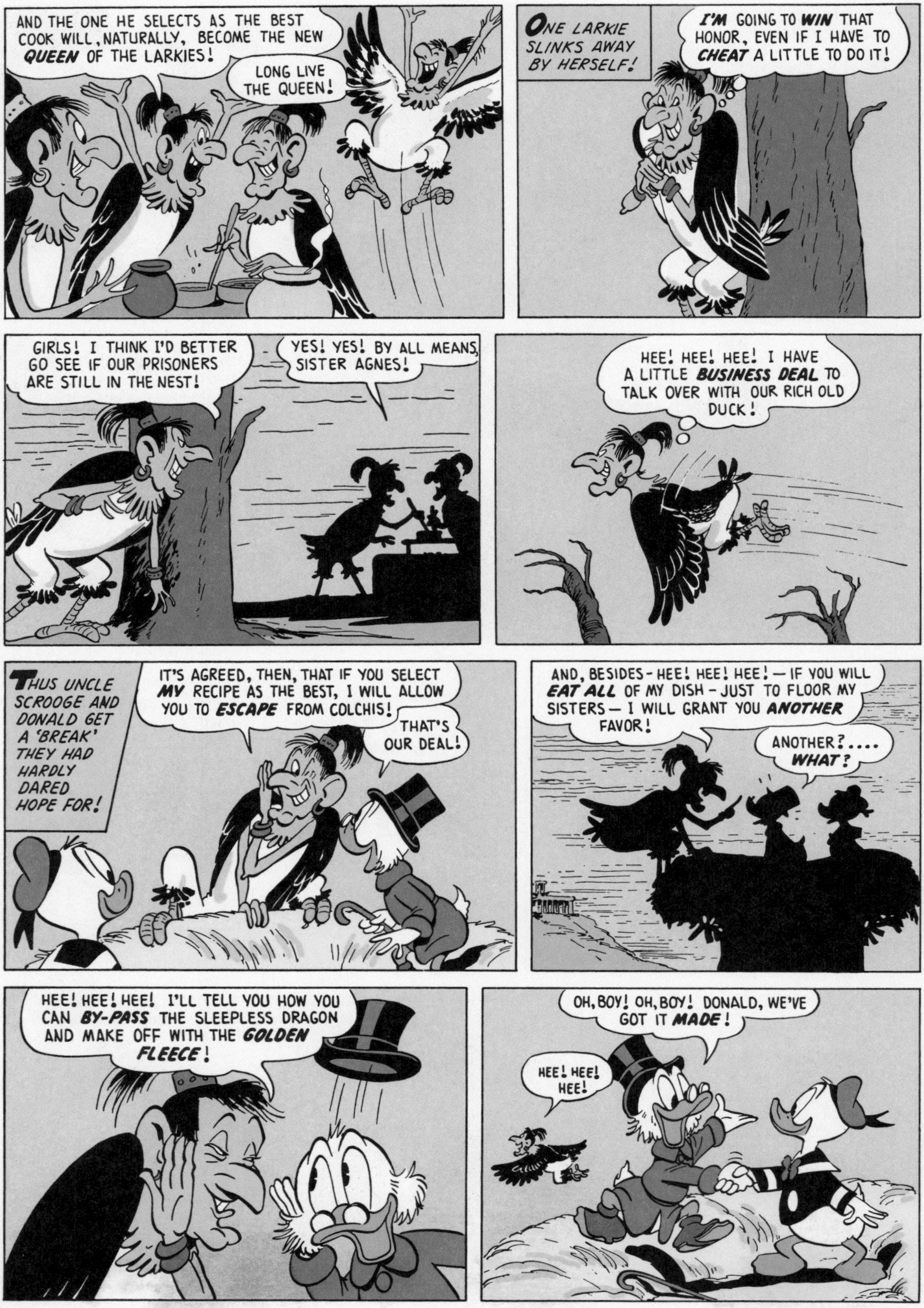
AND THE ONE HE SELECTS AS THE BEST COOK WILL, NATURALLY, BECOME THE NEW QUEEN OF THE LARKIES!
LONG LIVE THE QUEEN!
ONE LARKIE SLINKS AWAY BY HERSELF!
I'M GOING TO WIN THAT HONOR, EVEN IF I HAVE TO CHEAT A LITTLE TO DO IT!
GIRLS! I THINK I'D BETTER GO SEE IF OUR PRISONERS ARE STILL IN THE NEST!
YES! YES! BY ALL MEANS, SISTER AGNES!
HEE! HEE! HEE! I HAVE A LITTLE BUSINESS DEAL TO TALK OVER WITH OUR RICH OLD DUCK!
THUS UNCLE SCROOGE AND DONALD GET A 'BREAK' THEY HAD HARDLY DARED HOPE FOR!
IT'S AGREED, THEN, THAT IF YOU SELECT MY RECIPE AS THE BEST, I WILL ALLOW YOU TO ESCAPE FROM COLCHIS!
THAT'S OUR DEAL!
AND, BESIDES - HEE! HEE! HEE! — IF YOU WILL EAT ALL OF MY DISH - JUST TO FLOOR MY SISTERS — I WILL GRANT YOU ANOTHER FAVOR!
ANOTHER?.... WHAT?
HEE! HEE! HEE! I'LL TELL YOU HOW YOU CAN BY-PASS THE SLEEPLESS DRAGON AND MAKE OFF WITH THE GOLDEN FLEECE!
OH, BOY! OH, BOY! DONALD, WE'VE GOT IT MADE!
HEE! HEE! HEE!

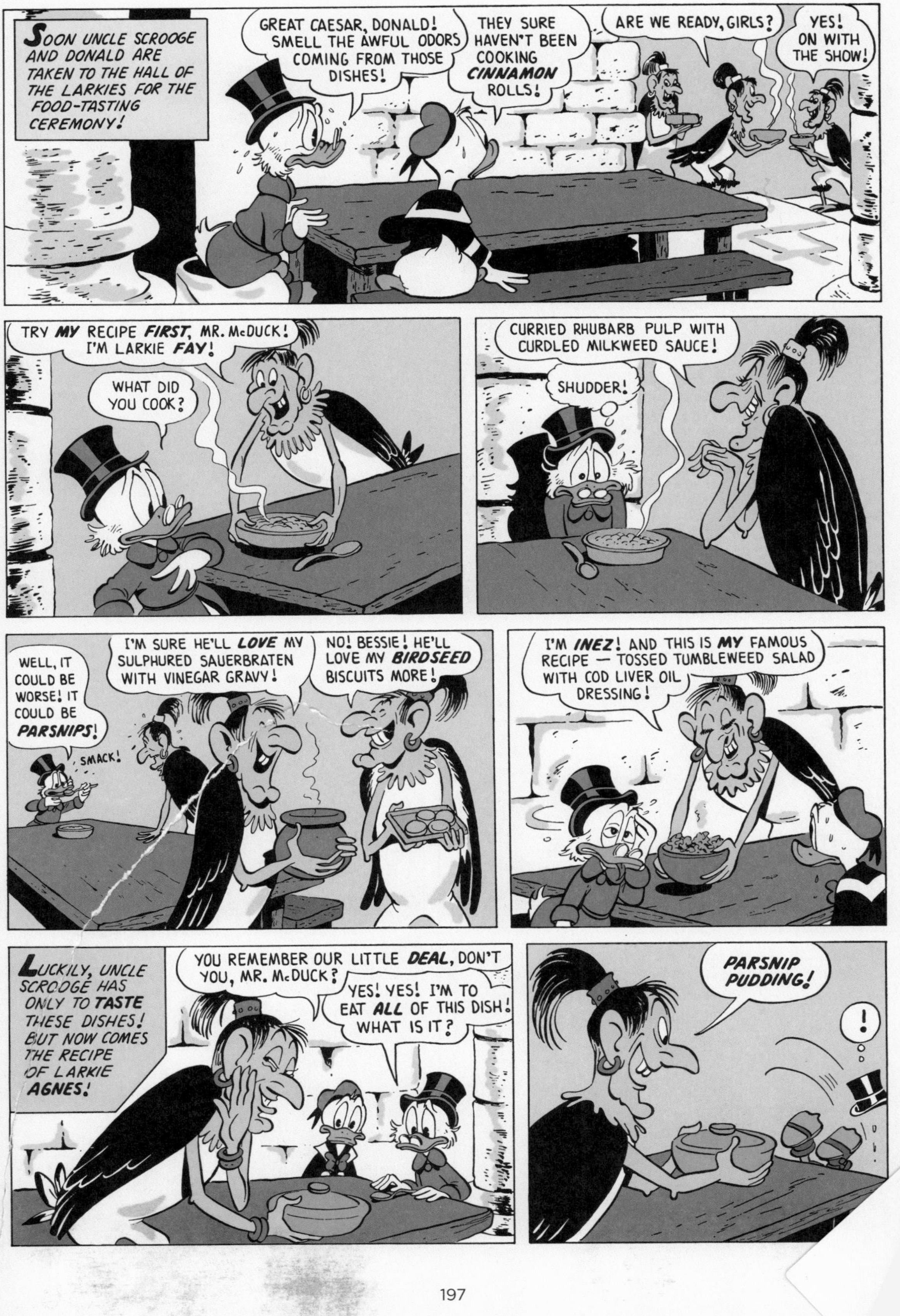
SOON UNCLE SCROOGE AND DONALD ARE TAKEN TO THE HALL OF THE LARKIES FOR THE FOOD-TASTING CEREMONY!
GREAT CAESAR, DONALD! SMELL THE AWFUL ODORS COMING FROM THOSE DISHES!
THEY SURE HAVEN'T BEEN COOKING CINNAMON ROLLS!
ARE WE READY, GIRLS?
YES! ON WITH THE SHOW!
TRY MY RECIPE FIRST, MR. McDUCK! I'M LARKIE FAY!
WHAT DID YOU COOK?
CURRIED RHUBARB PULP WITH CURDLED MILKWEED SAUCE!
SHUDDER!
WELL, IT COULD BE WORSE! IT COULD BE PARSNIPS!
SMACK!
I'M SURE HE'LL LOVE MY SULPHURED SAUERBRATEN WITH VINEGAR GRAVY!
NO! BESSIE! HE'LL LOVE MY BIRDSEED BISCUITS MORE!
I'M INEZ! AND THIS IS MY FAMOUS RECIPE — TOSSED TUMBLEWEED SALAD WITH COD LIVER OIL DRESSING!
LUCKILY, UNCLE SCROOGE HAS ONLY TO TASTE THESE DISHES! BUT NOW COMES THE RECIPE OF LARKIE AGNES!
YOU REMEMBER OUR LITTLE DEAL, DON'T YOU, MR. McDUCK?
YES! YES! I'M TO EAT ALL OF THIS DISH! WHAT IS IT?
PARSNIP PUDDING!
!

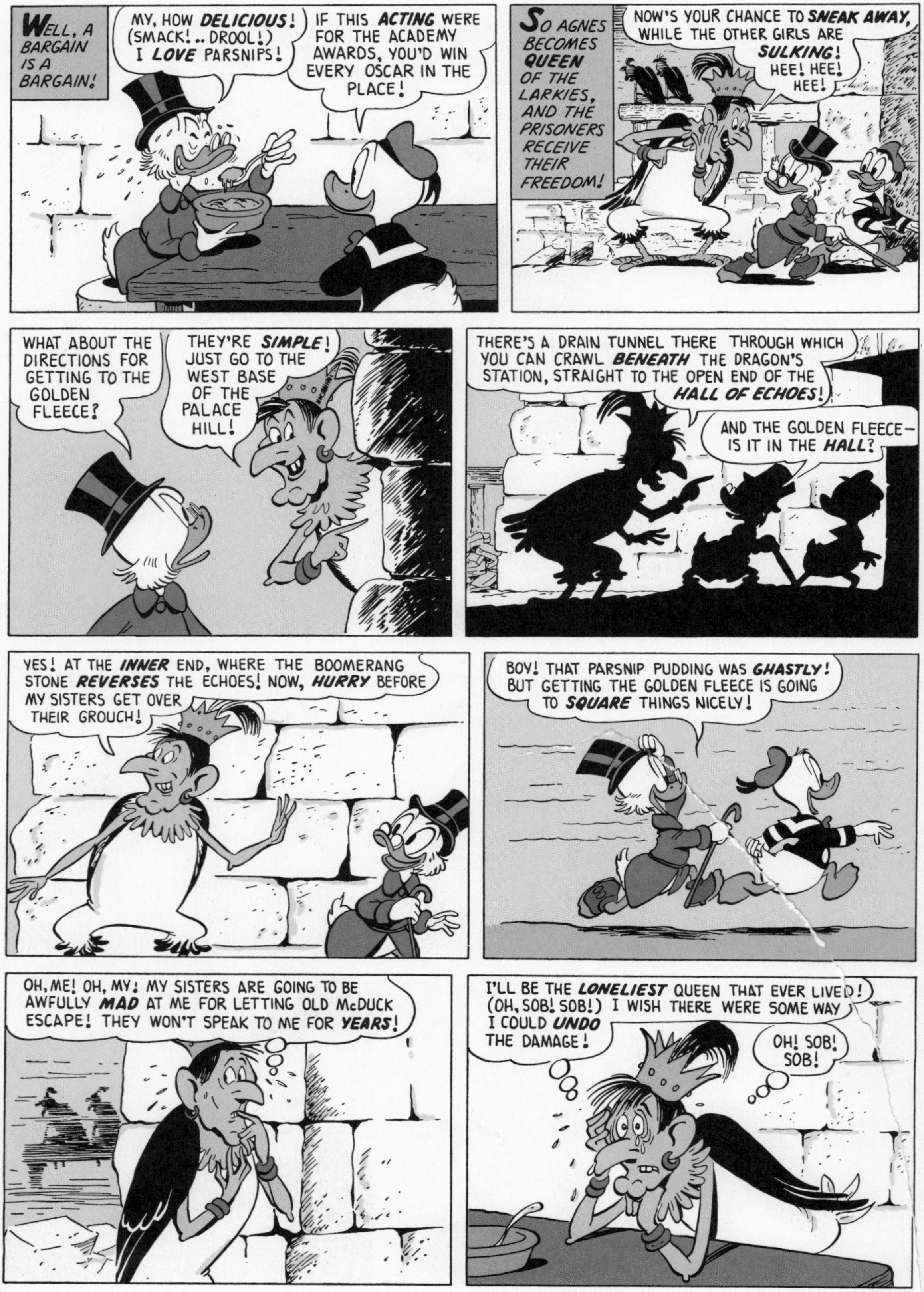
WELL, A BARGAIN IS A BARGAIN!
MY, HOW DELICIOUS! (SMACK!.. DROOL!) I LOVE PARSNIPS!
IF THIS ACTING WERE FOR THE ACADEMY AWARDS, YOU'D WIN EVERY OSCAR IN THE PLACE!
SO AGNES BECOMES QUEEN OF THE LARKIES, AND THE PRISONERS RECEIVE THEIR FREEDOM!
NOW'S YOUR CHANCE TO SNEAK AWAY, WHILE THE OTHER GIRLS ARE SULKING! HEE! HEE! HEE!
WHAT ABOUT THE DIRECTIONS FOR GETTING TO THE GOLDEN FLEECE?
THEY'RE SIMPLE! JUST GO TO THE WEST BASE OF THE PALACE HILL!
THERE'S A DRAIN TUNNEL THERE THROUGH WHICH YOU CAN CRAWL BENEATH THE DRAGON'S STATION, STRAIGHT TO THE OPEN END OF THE HALL OF ECHOES!
AND THE GOLDEN FLEECE— IS IT IN THE HALL?
YES! AT THE INNER END, WHERE THE BOOMERANG STONE REVERSES THE ECHOES! NOW, HURRY BEFORE MY SISTERS GET OVER THEIR GROUCH!
BOY! THAT PARSNIP PUDDING WAS GHASTLY! BUT GETTING THE GOLDEN FLEECE IS GOING TO SQUARE THINGS NICELY!
OH, ME! OH, MY! MY SISTERS ARE GOING TO BE AWFULLY MAD AT ME FOR LETTING OLD McDUCK ESCAPE! THEY WON'T SPEAK TO ME FOR YEARS!
I'LL BE THE LONELIEST QUEEN THAT EVER LIVED! (OH, SOB! SOB!) I WISH THERE WERE SOME WAY I COULD UNDO THE DAMAGE!
OH! SOB! SOB!

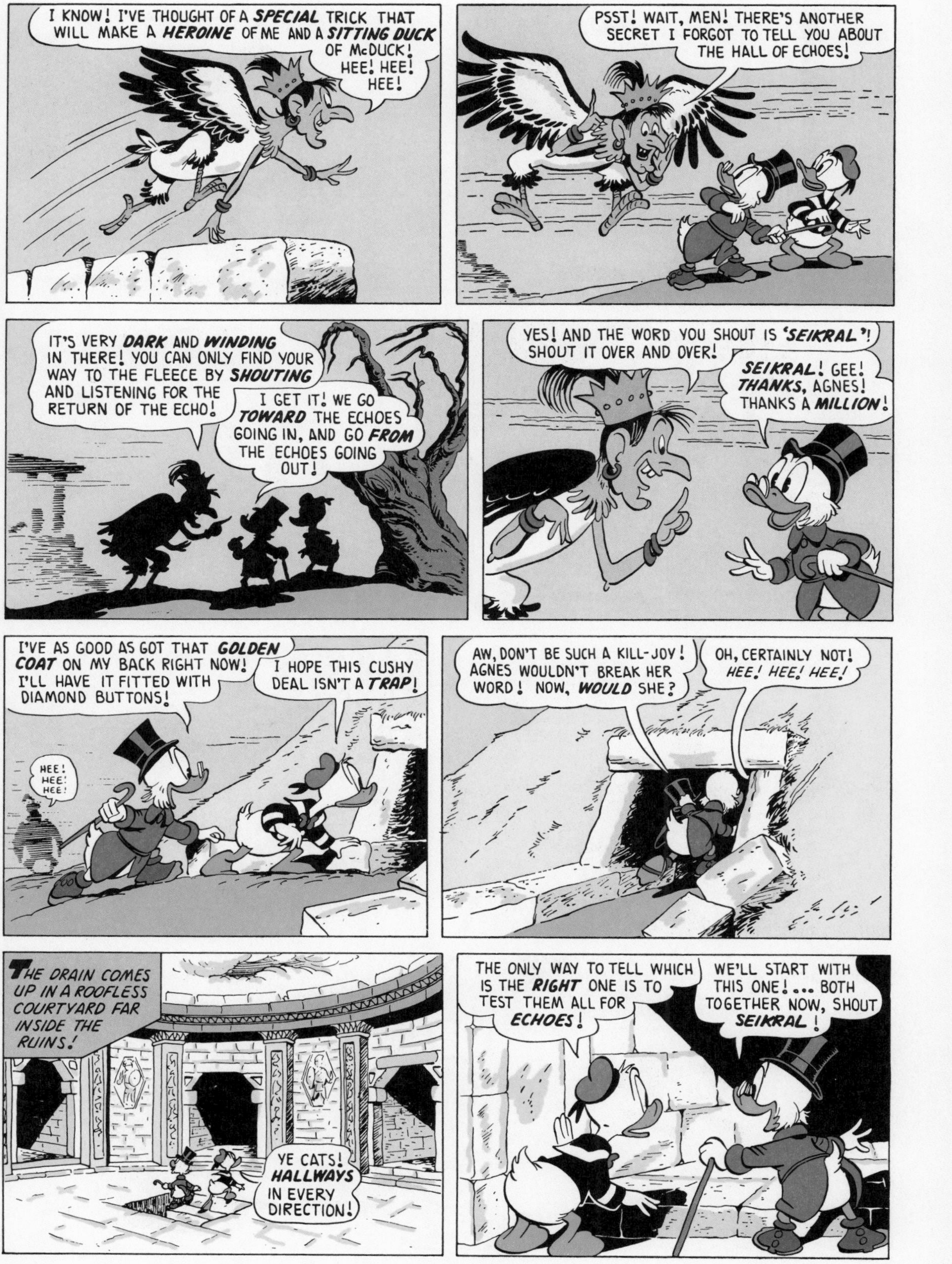

I KNOW! I'VE THOUGHT OF A SPECIAL TRICK THAT WILL MAKE A HEROINE OF ME AND A SITTING DUCK OF McDUCK! HEE! HEE! HEE!
PSST! WAIT, MEN! THERE'S ANOTHER SECRET I FORGOT TO TELL YOU ABOUT THE HALL OF ECHOES!
IT'S VERY DARK AND WINDING IN THERE! YOU CAN ONLY FIND YOUR WAY TO THE FLEECE BY SHOUTING AND LISTENING FOR THE RETURN OF THE ECHO!
I GET IT! WE GO TOWARD THE ECHOES GOING IN, AND GO FROM THE ECHOES GOING OUT!
YES! AND THE WORD YOU SHOUT IS 'SEIKRAL'! SHOUT IT OVER AND OVER!
SEIKRAL! GEE! THANKS, AGNES! THANKS A MILLION!
I'VE AS GOOD AS GOT THAT GOLDEN COAT ON MY BACK RIGHT NOW! I'LL HAVE IT FITTED WITH DIAMOND BUTTONS!
I HOPE THIS CUSHY DEAL ISN'T A TRAP!
HEE! HEE! HEE!
AW, DON'T BE SUCH A KILL-JOY! AGNES WOULDN'T BREAK HER WORD! NOW, WOULD SHE?
OH, CERTAINLY NOT! HEE! HEE! HEE!
THE DRAIN COMES UP IN A ROOFLESS COURTYARD FAR INSIDE THE RUINS!
YE CATS! HALLWAYS IN EVERY DIRECTION!
THE ONLY WAY TO TELL WHICH IS THE RIGHT ONE IS TO TEST THEM ALL FOR ECHOES!
WE'LL START WITH THIS ONE! ... BOTH TOGETHER NOW, SHOUT SEIKRAL!

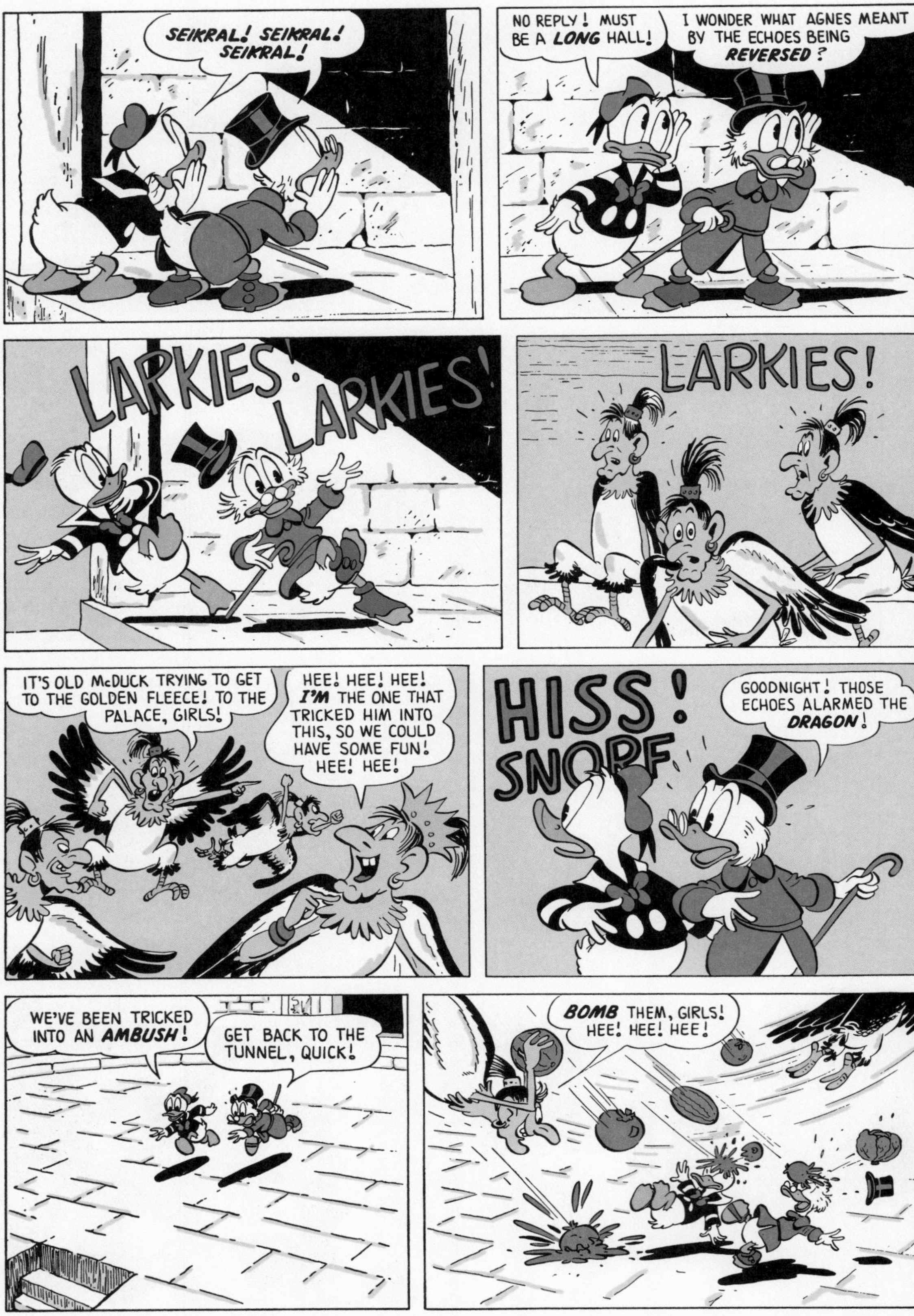
SEIKRAL! SEIKRAL! SEIKRAL!
NO REPLY! MUST BE A LONG HALL!
I WONDER WHAT AGNES MEANT BY THE ECHOES BEING REVERSED?
LARKIES! LARKIES!
LARKIES!
IT'S OLD McDUCK TRYING TO GET TO THE GOLDEN FLEECE! TO THE PALACE, GIRLS!
HEE! HEE! HEE! I'M THE ONE THAT TRICKED HIM INTO THIS, SO WE COULD HAVE SOME FUN! HEE! HEE!
HISS! SNORF
GOODNIGHT! THOSE ECHOES ALARMED THE DRAGON!
WE'VE BEEN TRICKED INTO AN AMBUSH!
GET BACK TO THE TUNNEL, QUICK!
BOMB THEM, GIRLS! HEE! HEE! HEE!

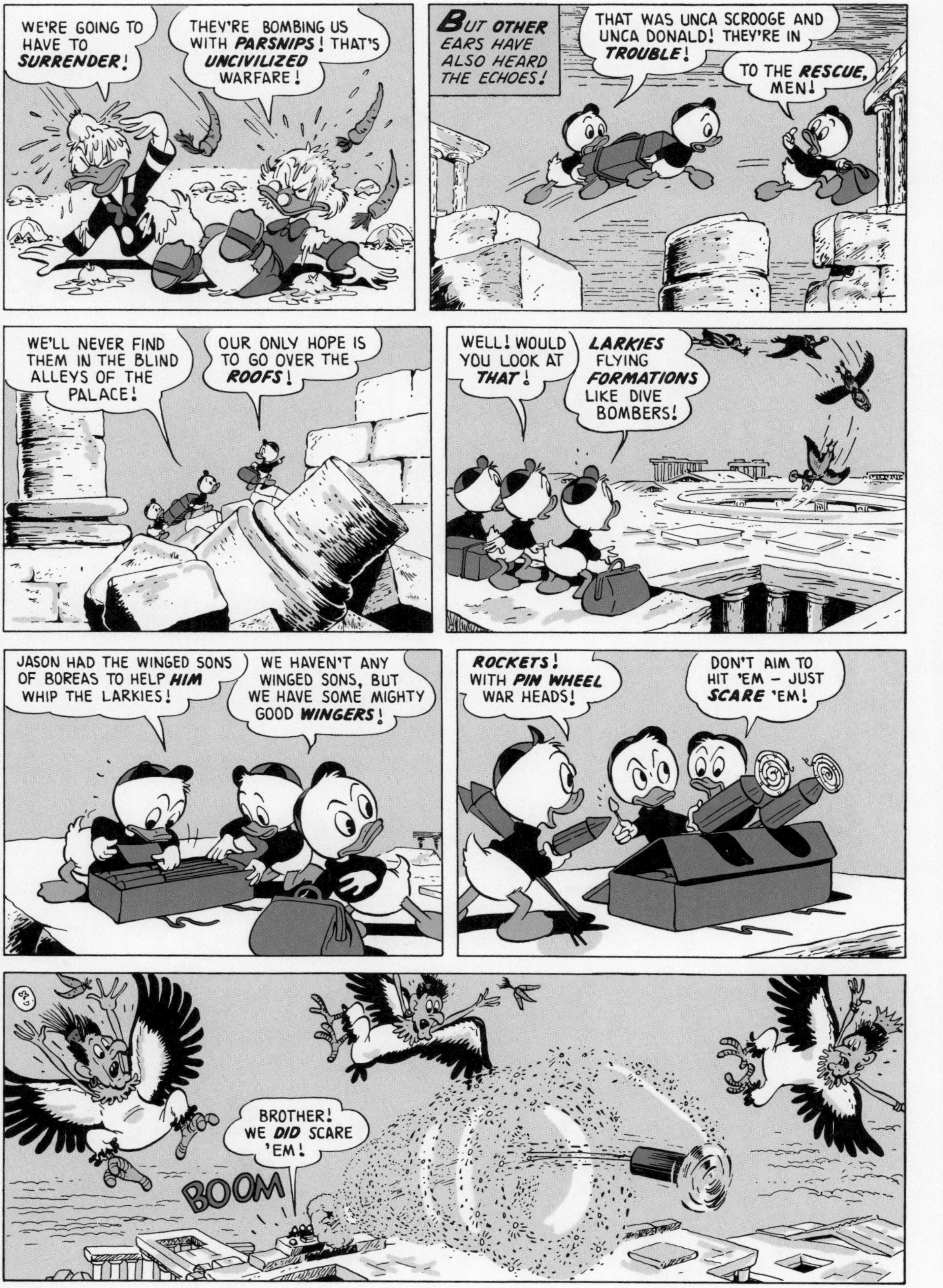

WE'RE GOING TO HAVE TO SURRENDER!
THEY'RE BOMBING US WITH PARSNIPS! THAT'S UNCIVILIZED WARFARE!
BUT OTHER EARS HAVE ALSO HEARD THE ECHOES!
THAT WAS UNCA SCROOGE AND UNCA DONALD! THEY'RE IN TROUBLE!
TO THE RESCUE, MEN!
WE'LL NEVER FIND THEM IN THE BLIND ALLEYS OF THE PALACE!
OUR ONLY HOPE IS TO GO OVER THE ROOFS!
WELL! WOULD YOU LOOK AT THAT!
LARKIES FLYING FORMATIONS LIKE DIVE BOMBERS!
JASON HAD THE WINGED SONS OF BOREAS TO HELP HIM WHIP THE LARKIES!
WE HAVEN'T ANY WINGED SONS, BUT WE HAVE SOME MIGHTY GOOD WINGERS!
ROCKETS! WITH PIN WHEEL WAR HEADS!
DON'T AIM TO HIT 'EM – JUST SCARE 'EM!
BROTHER! WE DID SCARE 'EM!
BOOM

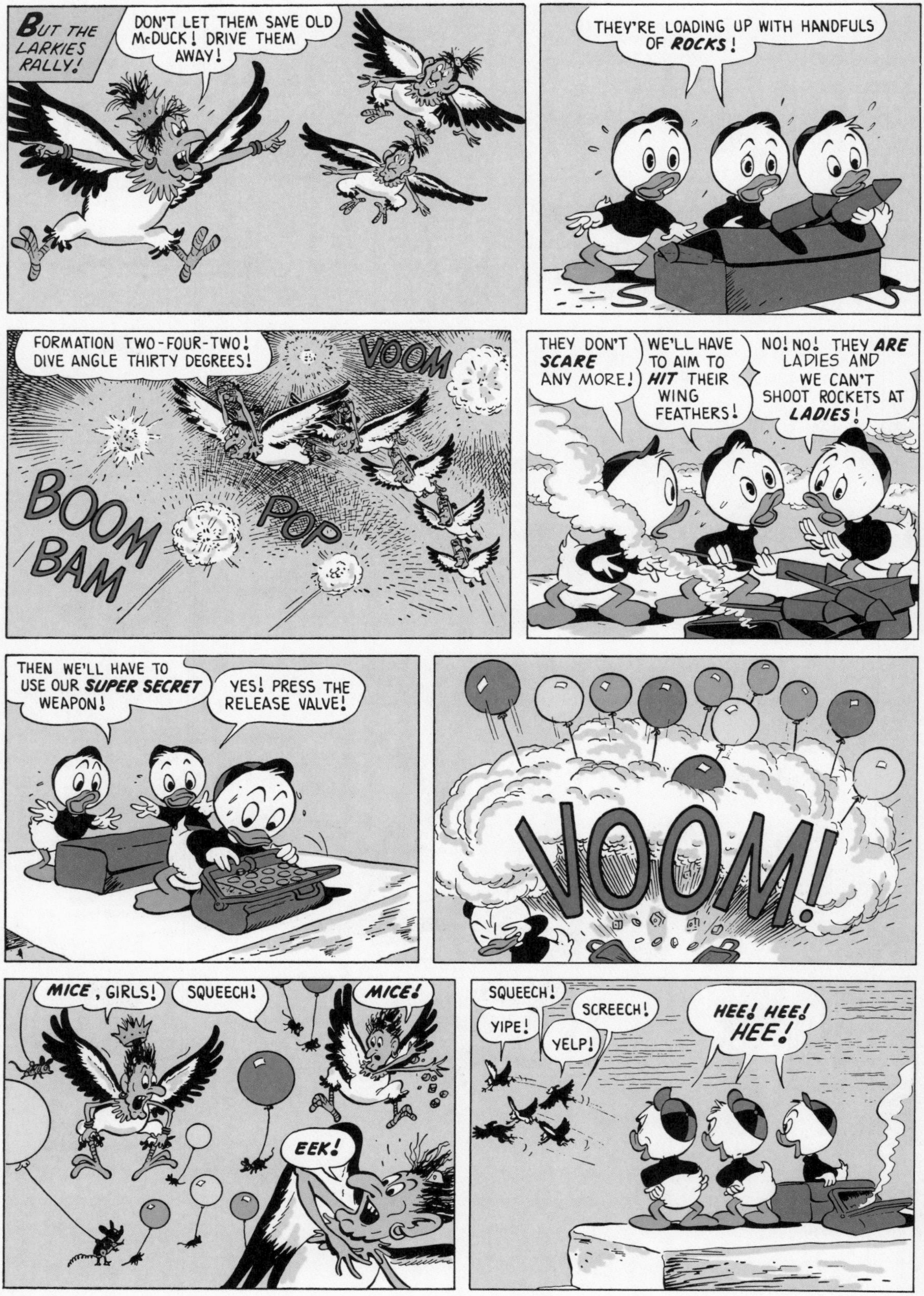
BUT THE LARKIES RALLY!
DON'T LET THEM SAVE OLD McDUCK! DRIVE THEM AWAY!
THEY'RE LOADING UP WITH HANDFULS OF ROCKS!
FORMATION TWO-FOUR-TWO! DIVE ANGLE THIRTY DEGREES!
VOOM
BOOM
BAM
POP
THEY DON'T SCARE ANY MORE!
WE'LL HAVE TO AIM TO HIT THEIR WING FEATHERS!
NO! NO! THEY ARE LADIES AND WE CAN'T SHOOT ROCKETS AT LADIES!
THEN WE'LL HAVE TO USE OUR SUPER SECRET WEAPON!
YES! PRESS THE RELEASE VALVE!
VOOM!
MICE, GIRLS!
SQUEECH!
MICE!
EEK!
SQUEECH!
YIPE!
SCREECH!
YELP!
HEE! HEE! HEE!

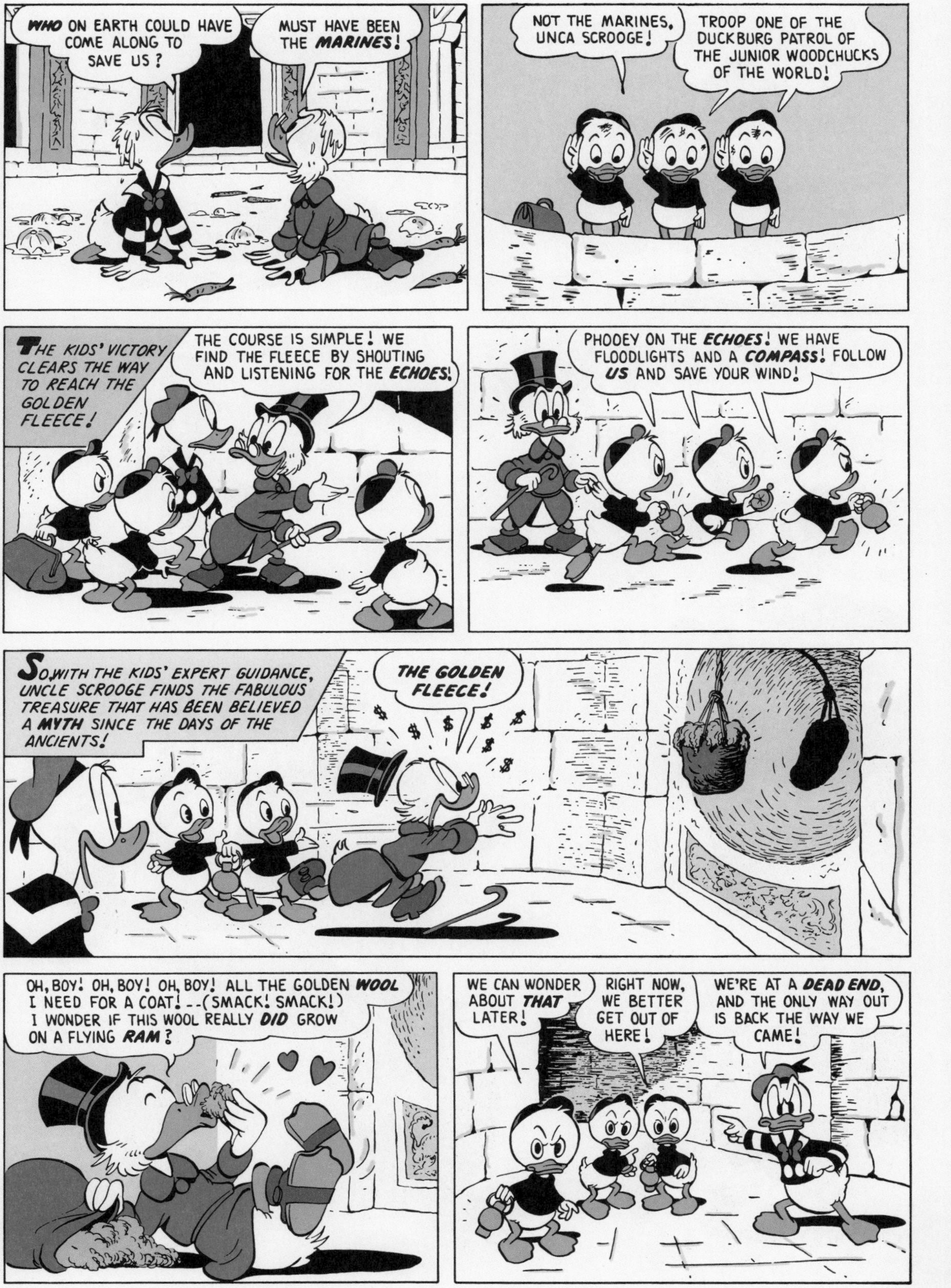
WHO ON EARTH COULD HAVE COME ALONG TO SAVE US?
MUST HAVE BEEN THE MARINES!
NOT THE MARINES, UNCA SCROOGE!
TROOP ONE OF THE DUCKBURG PATROL OF THE JUNIOR WOODCHUCKS OF THE WORLD!
THE KIDS' VICTORY CLEARS THE WAY TO REACH THE GOLDEN FLEECE!
THE COURSE IS SIMPLE! WE FIND THE FLEECE BY SHOUTING AND LISTENING FOR THE ECHOES!
PHOODEY ON THE ECHOES! WE HAVE FLOODLIGHTS AND A COMPASS! FOLLOW US AND SAVE YOUR WIND!
SO, WITH THE KIDS' EXPERT GUIDANCE, UNCLE SCROOGE FINDS THE FABULOUS TREASURE THAT HAS BEEN BELIEVED A MYTH SINCE THE DAYS OF THE ANCIENTS!
THE GOLDEN FLEECE!
OH, BOY! OH, BOY! OH, BOY! ALL THE GOLDEN WOOL I NEED FOR A COAT! --(SMACK! SMACK!) I WONDER IF THIS WOOL REALLY DID GROW ON A FLYING RAM?
WE CAN WONDER ABOUT THAT LATER!
RIGHT NOW, WE BETTER GET OUT OF HERE!
WE'RE AT A DEAD END, AND THE ONLY WAY OUT IS BACK THE WAY WE CAME!

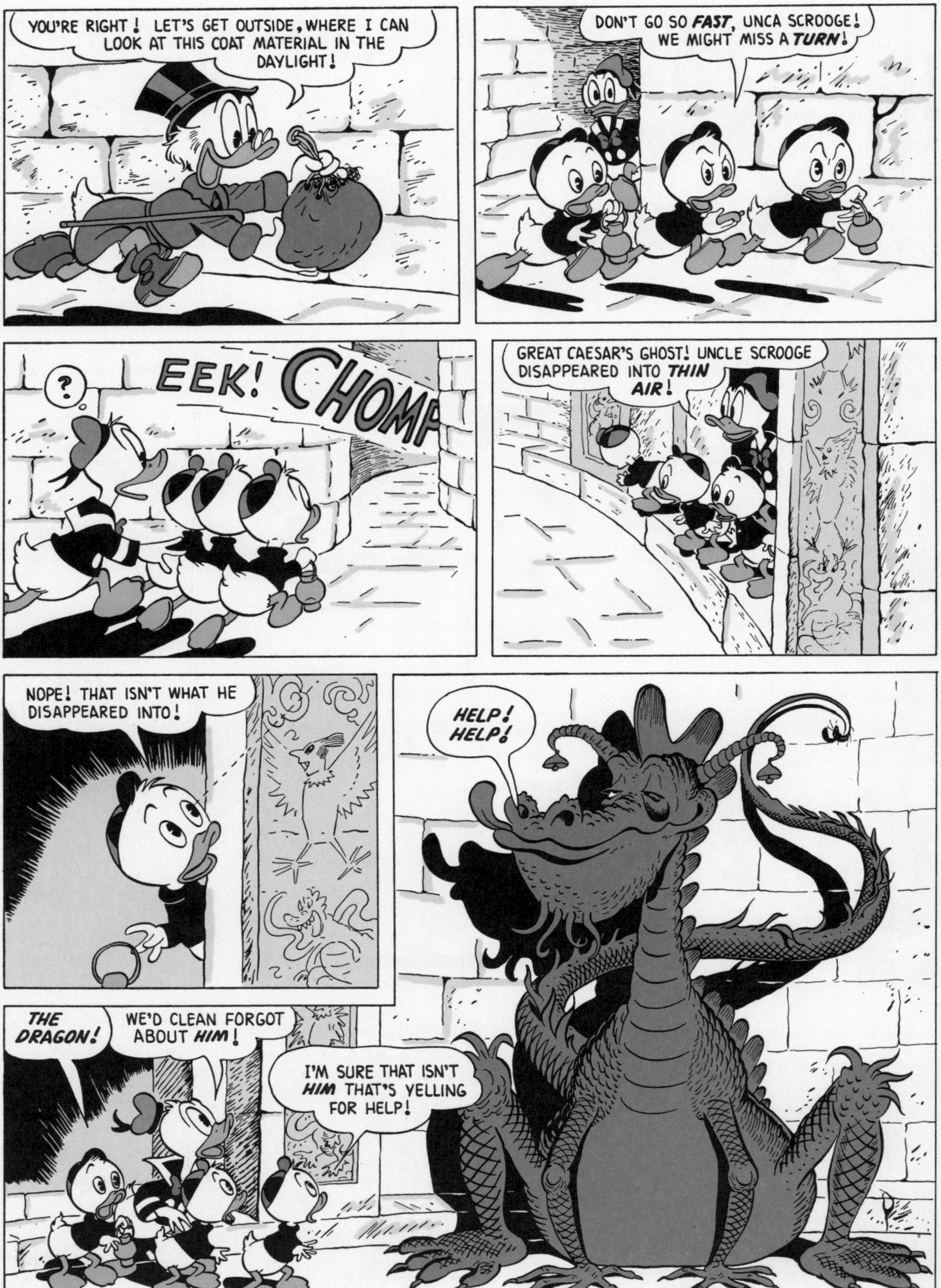
YOU'RE RIGHT! LET'S GET OUTSIDE, WHERE I CAN LOOK AT THIS COAT MATERIAL IN THE DAYLIGHT!
DON'T GO SO FAST, UNCA SCROOGE! WE MIGHT MISS A TURN!
?
EEK! CHOMP
GREAT CAESAR'S GHOST! UNCLE SCROOGE DISAPPEARED INTO THIN AIR!
NOPE! THAT ISN'T WHAT HE DISAPPEARED INTO!
HELP! HELP!
THE DRAGON!
WE'D CLEAN FORGOT ABOUT HIM!
I'M SURE THAT ISN'T HIM THAT'S YELLING FOR HELP!

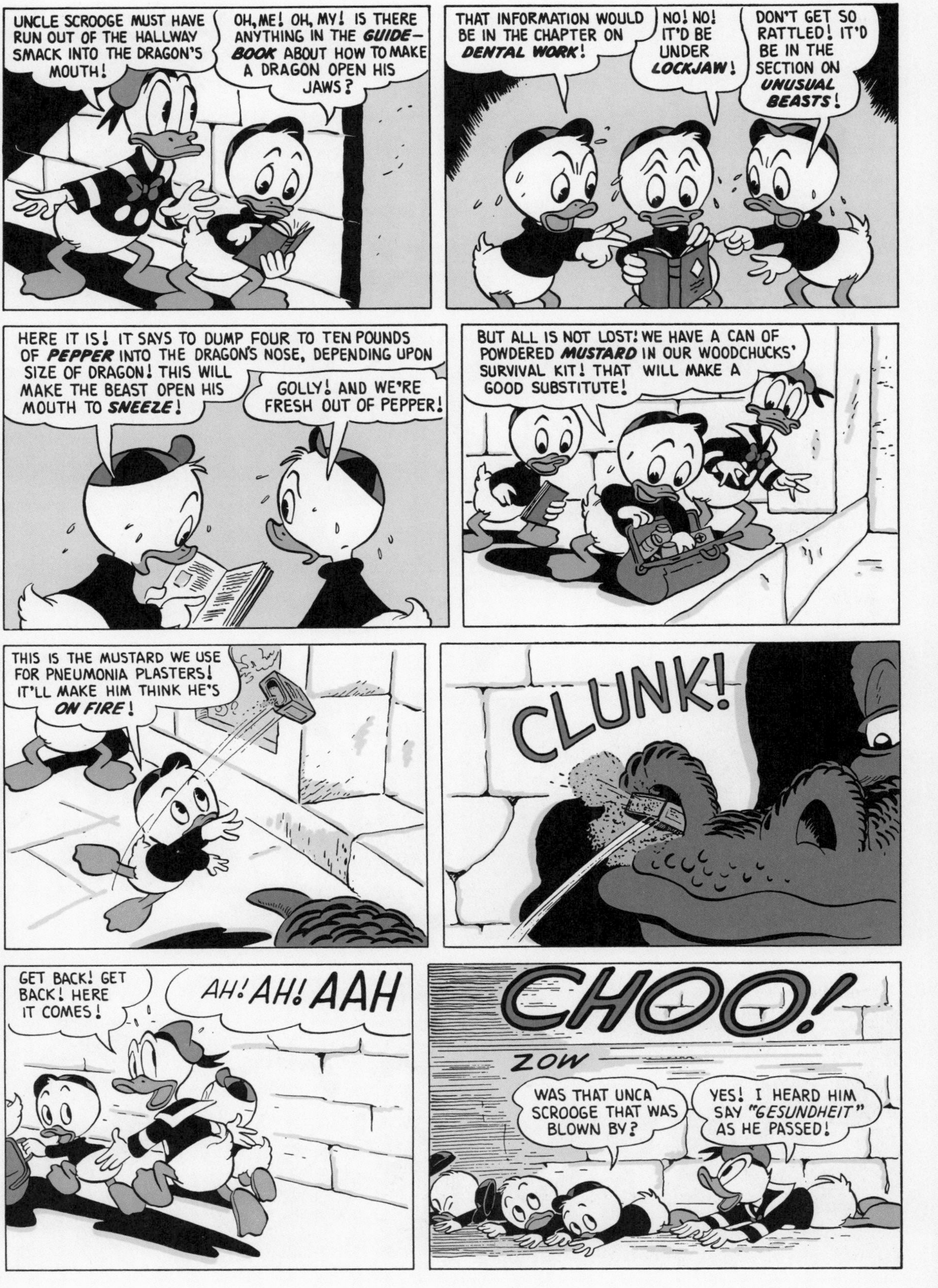
UNCLE SCROOGE MUST HAVE RUN OUT OF THE HALLWAY SMACK INTO THE DRAGON'S MOUTH!
OH, ME! OH, MY! IS THERE ANYTHING IN THE GUIDE-BOOK ABOUT HOW TO MAKE A DRAGON OPEN HIS JAWS?
THAT INFORMATION WOULD BE IN THE CHAPTER ON DENTAL WORK!
NO! NO! IT'D BE UNDER LOCKJAW!
DON'T GET SO RATTLED! IT'D BE IN THE SECTION ON UNUSUAL BEASTS!
HERE IT IS! IT SAYS TO DUMP FOUR TO TEN POUNDS OF PEPPER INTO THE DRAGON'S NOSE, DEPENDING UPON SIZE OF DRAGON! THIS WILL MAKE THE BEAST OPEN HIS MOUTH TO SNEEZE!
GOLLY! AND WE'RE FRESH OUT OF PEPPER!
BUT ALL IS NOT LOST! WE HAVE A CAN OF POWDERED MUSTARD IN OUR WOODCHUCKS' SURVIVAL KIT! THAT WILL MAKE A GOOD SUBSTITUTE!
THIS IS THE MUSTARD WE USE FOR PNEUMONIA PLASTERS! IT'LL MAKE HIM THINK HE'S ON FIRE!
CLUNK!
GET BACK! GET BACK! HERE IT COMES!
AH! AH! AAH
CHOO!
ZOW
WAS THAT UNCA SCROOGE THAT WAS BLOWN BY?
YES! I HEARD HIM SAY "GESUNDHEIT" AS HE PASSED!

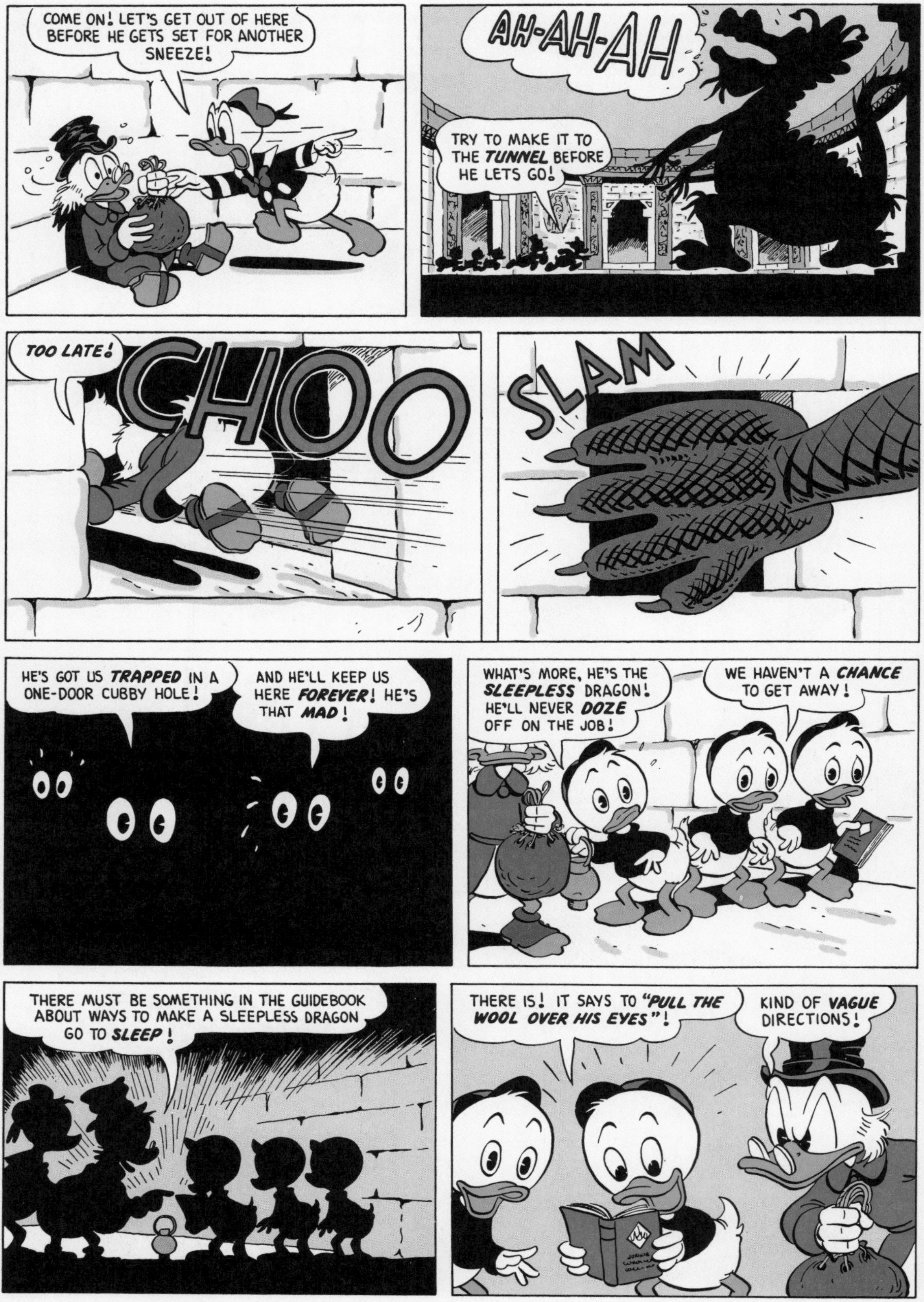
COME ON! LET'S GET OUT OF HERE BEFORE HE GETS SET FOR ANOTHER SNEEZE!
AH-AH-AH
TRY TO MAKE IT TO THE TUNNEL BEFORE HE LETS GO!
TOO LATE!
CHOO
SLAM
HE'S GOT US TRAPPED IN A ONE-DOOR CUBBY HOLE!
AND HE'LL KEEP US HERE FOREVER! HE'S THAT MAD!
WHAT'S MORE, HE'S THE SLEEPLESS DRAGON! HE'LL NEVER DOZE OFF ON THE JOB!
WE HAVEN'T A CHANCE TO GET AWAY!
THERE MUST BE SOMETHING IN THE GUIDEBOOK ABOUT WAYS TO MAKE A SLEEPLESS DRAGON GO TO SLEEP!
THERE IS! IT SAYS TO "PULL THE WOOL OVER HIS EYES"!
KIND OF VAGUE DIRECTIONS!

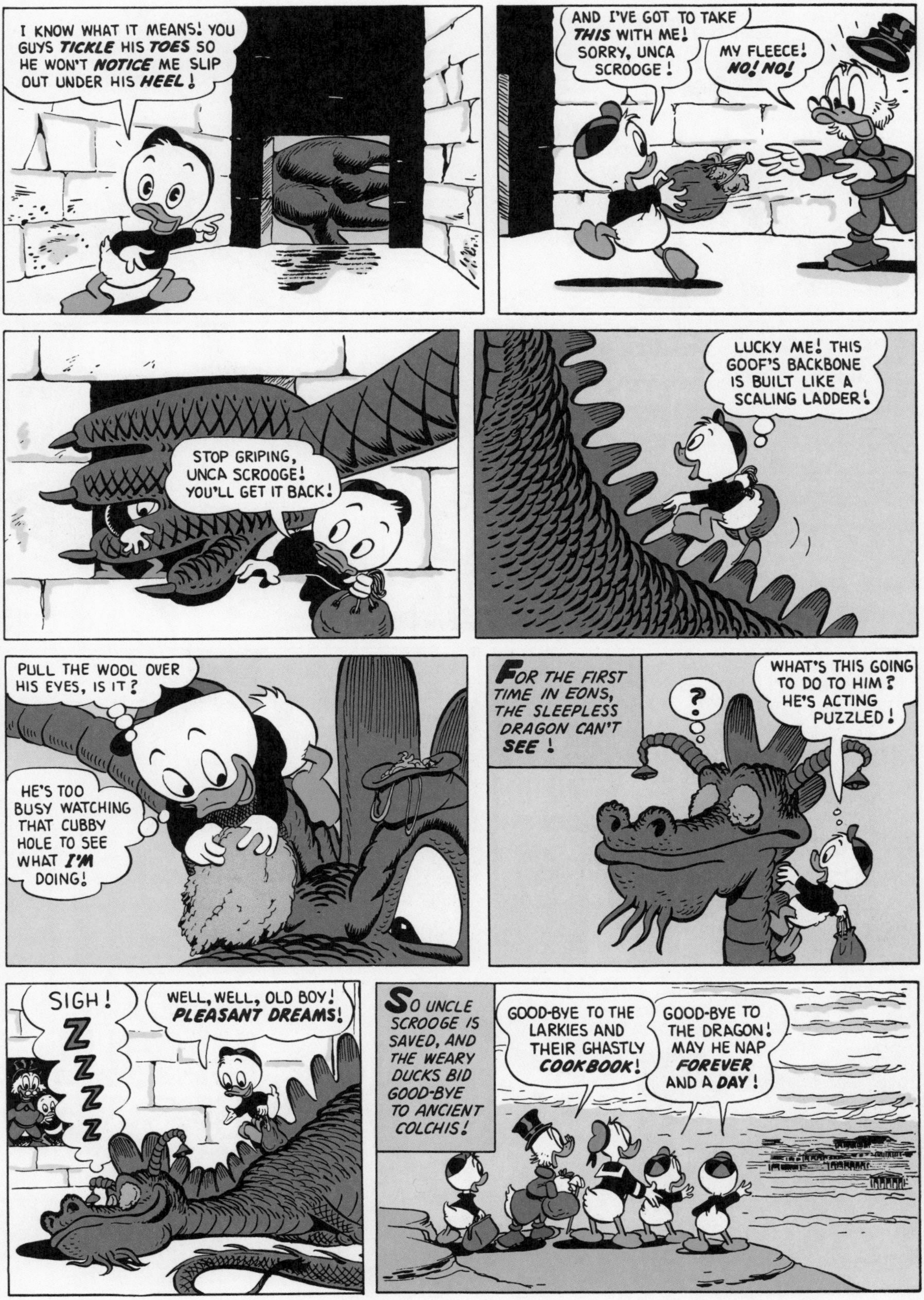
I KNOW WHAT IT MEANS! YOU GUYS TICKLE HIS TOES SO HE WON'T NOTICE ME SLIP OUT UNDER HIS HEEL!
AND I'VE GOT TO TAKE THIS WITH ME! SORRY, UNCA SCROOGE!
MY FLEECE! NO! NO!
STOP GRIPING, UNCA SCROOGE! YOU'LL GET IT BACK!
LUCKY ME! THIS GOOF'S BACKBONE IS BUILT LIKE A SCALING LADDER!
PULL THE WOOL OVER HIS EYES, IS IT?
HE'S TOO BUSY WATCHING THAT CUBBY HOLE TO SEE WHAT I'M DOING!
FOR THE FIRST TIME IN EONS, THE SLEEPLESS DRAGON CAN'T SEE!
?
WHAT'S THIS GOING TO DO TO HIM? HE'S ACTING PUZZLED!
SIGH! ZZZZZ
WELL, WELL, OLD BOY! PLEASANT DREAMS!
SO UNCLE SCROOGE IS SAVED, AND THE WEARY DUCKS BID GOOD-BYE TO ANCIENT COLCHIS!
GOOD-BYE TO THE LARKIES AND THEIR GHASTLY COOKBOOK!
GOOD-BYE TO THE DRAGON! MAY HE NAP FOREVER AND A DAY!

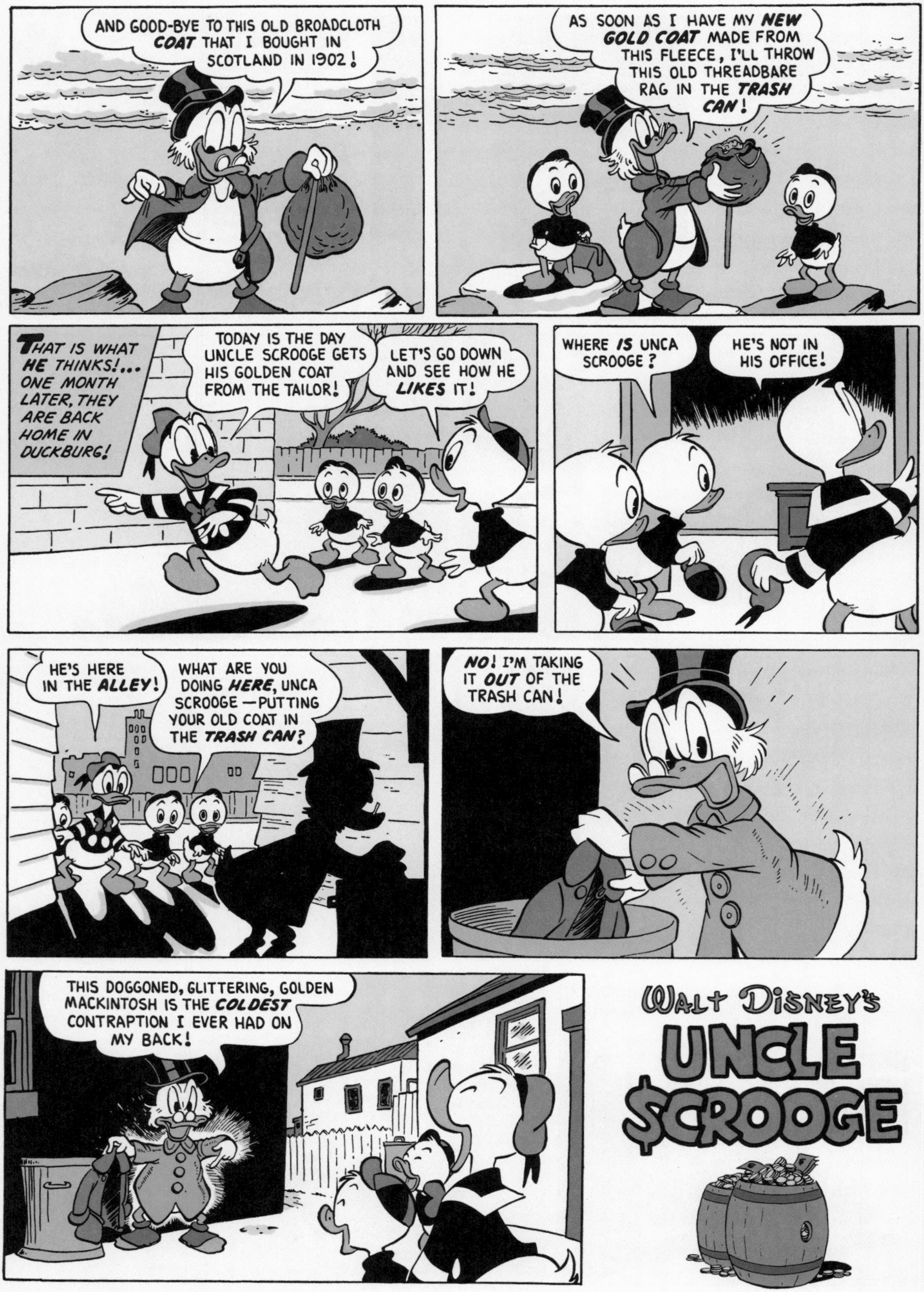
AND GOOD-BYE TO THIS OLD BROADCLOTH COAT THAT I BOUGHT IN SCOTLAND IN 1902!
AS SOON AS I HAVE MY NEW GOLD COAT MADE FROM THIS FLEECE, I'LL THROW THIS OLD THREADBARE RAG IN THE TRASH CAN!
THAT IS WHAT HE THINKS!... ONE MONTH LATER, THEY ARE BACK HOME IN DUCKBURG!
TODAY IS THE DAY UNCLE SCROOGE GETS HIS GOLDEN COAT FROM THE TAILOR!
LET'S GO DOWN AND SEE HOW HE LIKES IT!
WHERE IS UNCA SCROOGE?
HE'S NOT IN HIS OFFICE!
HE'S HERE IN THE ALLEY!
WHAT ARE YOU DOING HERE, UNCA SCROOGE—PUTTING YOUR OLD COAT IN THE TRASH CAN?
NO! I'M TAKING IT OUT OF THE TRASH CAN!
THIS DOGGONED, GLITTERING, GOLDEN MACKINTOSH IS THE COLDEST CONTRAPTION I EVER HAD ON MY BACK!
WALT DISNEY'S
UNCLE $CROOGE

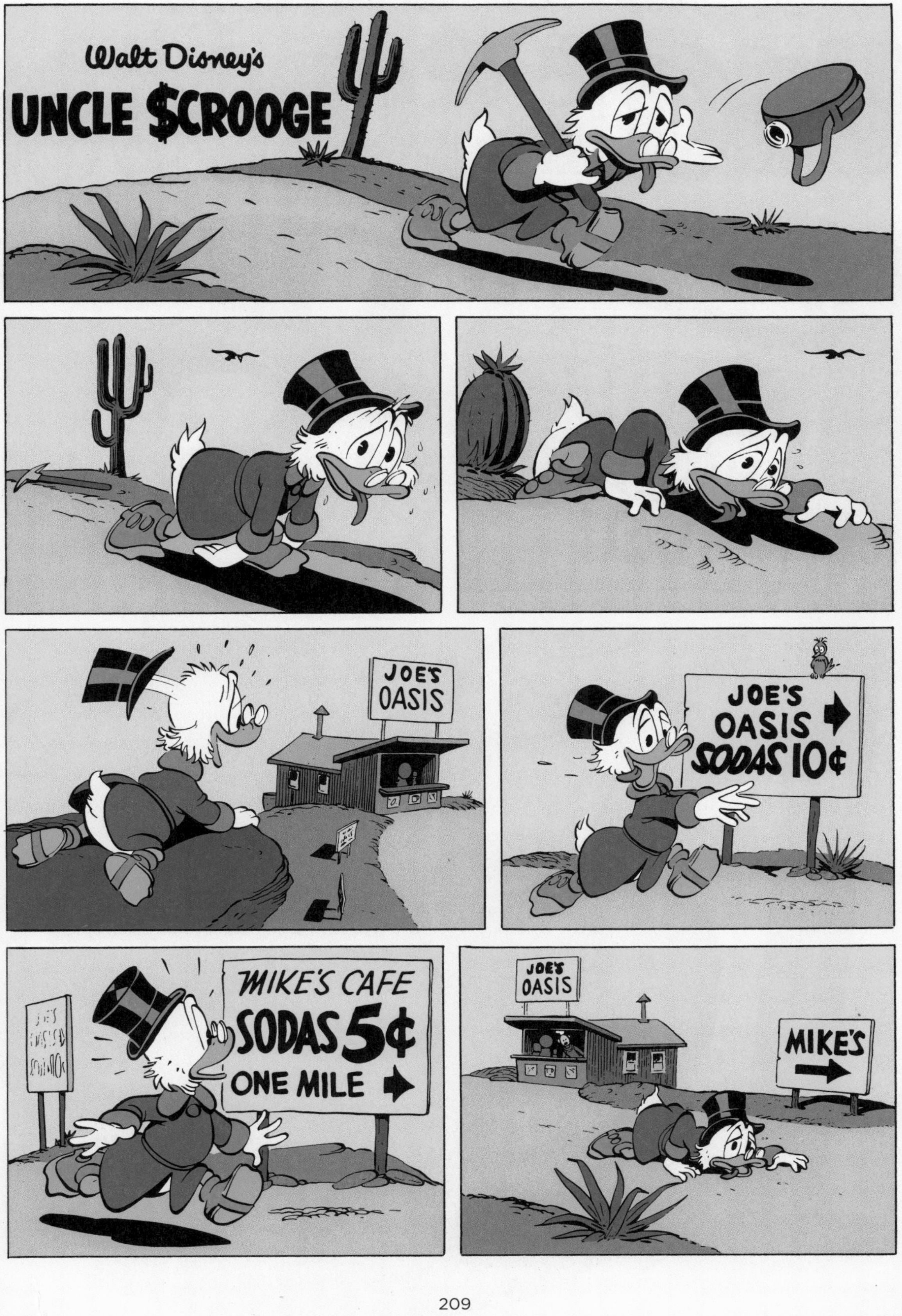
Walt Disney's
UNCLE $CROOGE
JOE'S OASIS
JOE'S OASIS SODAS 10¢
MIKE'S CAFE
SODAS 5¢
ONE MILE
JOE'S OASIS
MIKE'S

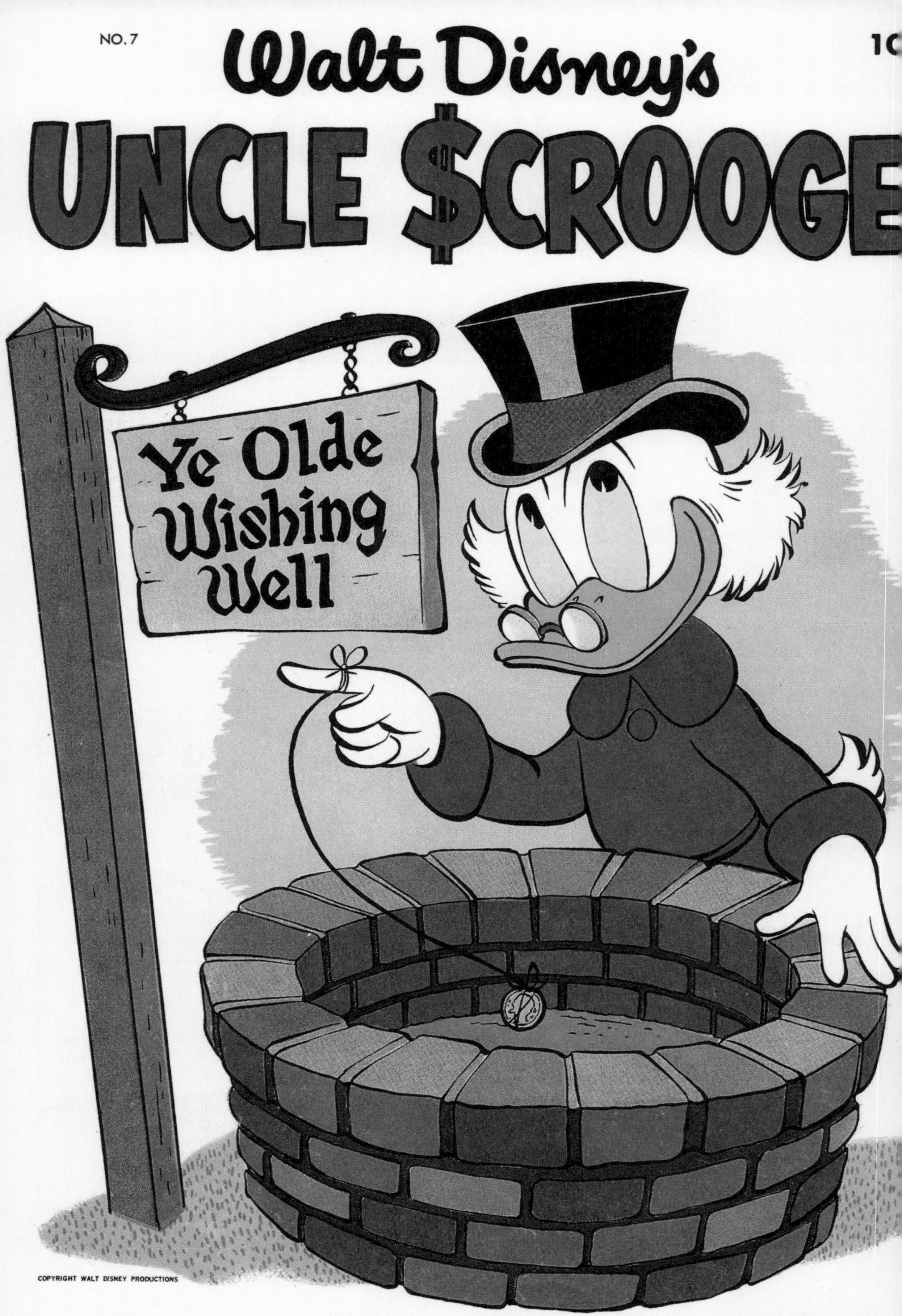
NO.7
Walt Disney's
UNCLE $CROOGE
Ye Olde Wishing Well

Story Notes

I BELIEVE IT IS A TRAIL!

WONDER WHERE IT'S TAKING US?

TO A SODA POP STAND, NO DOUBT!

WOULDN'T YOU BE SURPRISED IF IT DID?

THE SEVEN CITIES OF CIBOLA *p. 1*

Uncle Scrooge — the secret identity of Indiana Jones?

At the opening of *Raiders of the Lost Ark*, Indy is chased by a boulder after removing an idol from its altar.* That famous sequence is similar to the one on pages 23–26 of "The Seven Cities of Cibola." No big surprise when you understand that Indiana Jones creator George Lucas and his friend Steven Spielberg were both Carl Barks fans.

"My greatest source of enjoyment in Carl Barks's comics is in the imagination of his stories," wrote Lucas in his Barks appreciation (see *Walt Disney's Uncle Scrooge: "Only a Poor Old Man,"* volume 12 in this series).

In "The Seven Cities of Cibola" (originally untitled, it was given its name when reprinted in 1967), we see a fundamental evolution of Scrooge McDuck. He is no longer just a rich, miserly entrepreneur — now he becomes Uncle Scrooge the Adventurer, seeking treasure in exotic places. Barks wrote and drew many more such intrepid exploits in the following years, which inspired the TV series *DuckTales* (1987–1990) and the 1990 film *DuckTales the Movie: Treasure of the Lost Lamp.*

Barks cleverly mixes his storyline with legend. Two different legends, actually: one about

the Seven Cities of Cibola, all covered in gold (sought after in 1540 by Spanish conquistadores, led by Francisco Coronado), and one about a Spanish ship lost in the desert.

Barks plotted the story while drinking bourbon and beer with Al Koch, manager of the welfare offices in Indio, California. (Koch is shown on page 12, kicking the Beagle Boys out of his office.)

Scrooge, Donald, and the nephews, while looking for old Native American arrowheads, find an ancient amphora containing gold and jewels. A professor explains that they come from the legendary Seven Cities of Cibola, whose streets were covered with gold. Scrooge is, of course, very interested ...

Following an old Native American path through the desert and with the help of the know-it-all *Junior Woodchucks Guidebook,* the Ducks first discover an old ship in the desert, and Scrooge — reading the Captain's log (in Spanish, a language he knows) — discovers the way to the Seven Cities.

The Cities are wonderful, full of gold and jewels, but the Beagle Boys, who have secretly followed the Ducks, disturb an emerald idol (the sequence which inspired Spielberg and Lucas), and that triggers the Cities' destruction. The Ducks and the Beagle Boys escape to safety with bumps and bruises — but no memory of where they've been.

"The Seven Cities of Cibola" is not just an adventure story: the Cities are empty because the conquistadores from the lost ship brought a

Raiders of the Lost Ark, 1981. Starring Harrison Ford. Directed by Steven Spielberg. Screenplay by Lawrence Kasdan. Story by George Lucas and Philip Kaufman.

NO.8

Walt Disney's

UNCLE $CROOGE

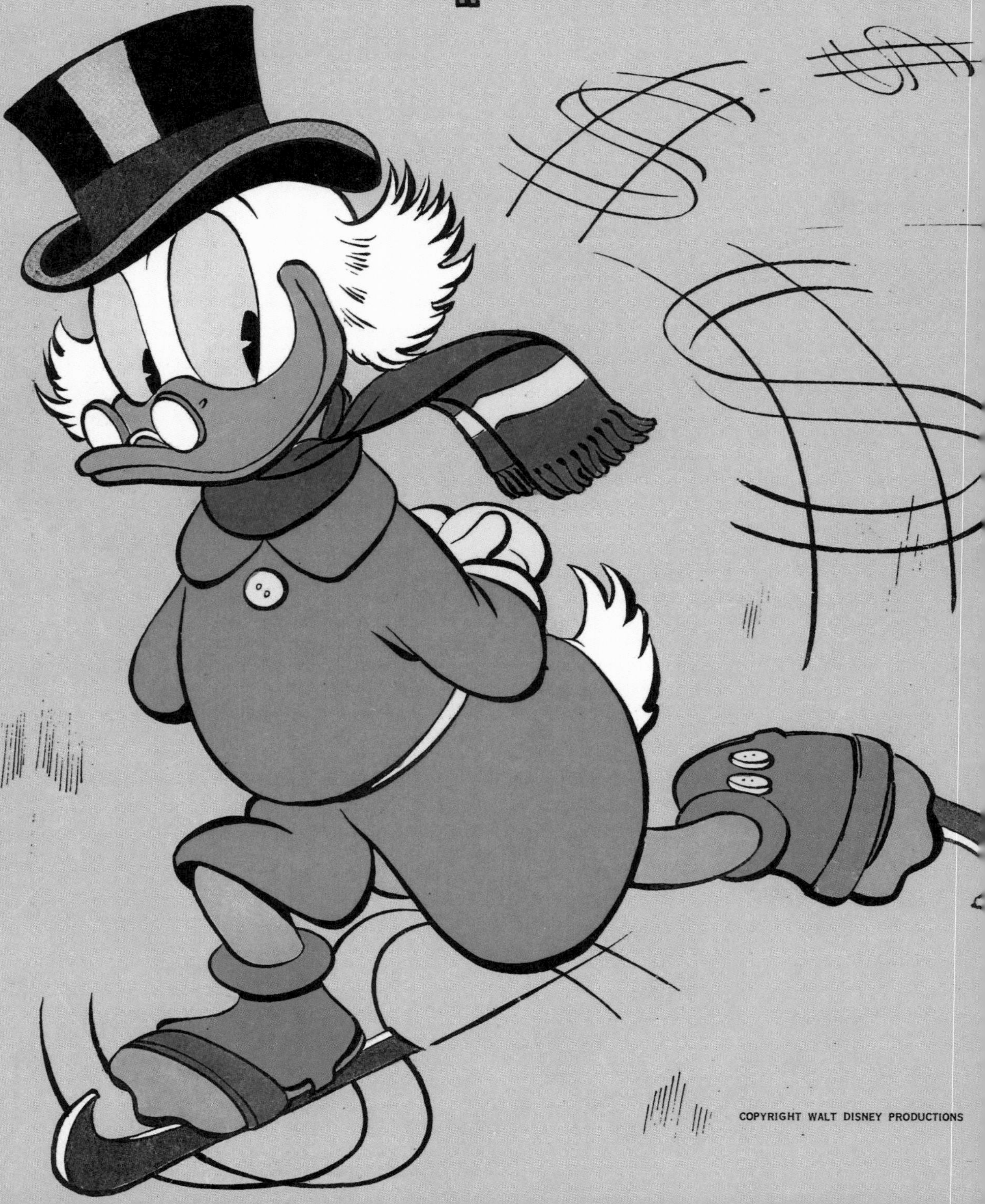

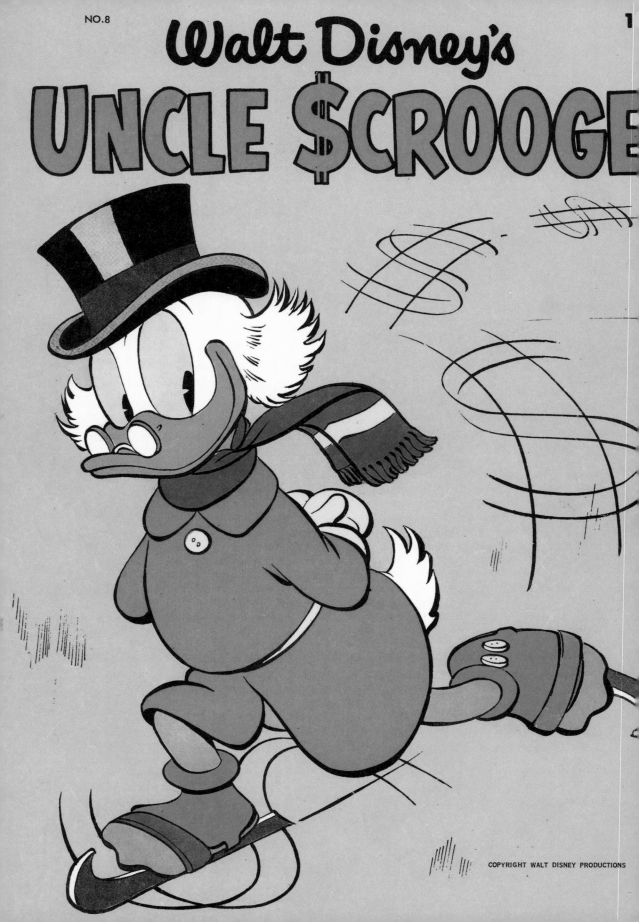

plague that exterminated the entire population — a bitter parable.

On a lighter note, there is a cameo by inventor Gyro Gearloose, the first time he and Scrooge actually meet in a story. Genial Gyro will come to be a close collaborator with Scrooge in the future.

— STEFANO PRIARONE

THE MILLION-DOLLAR PIGEON *p. 29*

With Carl Barks, four pages for a Duck story was an atypical length. Neither fish nor fowl, it's too long for a quick-hit gag and too short to develop a story. So instead, "The Million-Dollar Pigeon" might better be thought of as a character study.

Barks proceeds briskly. Scrooge's self-satisfaction over his thrift and his cleverness on the first page of the story ends with a blow to both. His confidence punctured, he imagines a host of unconsidered possibilities, even as he engages in a flurry of activities and strikes dynamically acrobatic poses. As a truer sense of his situation sets in, he moves from initial shock to angry resolve to resignation and, eventually, to a forced equanimity — almost.

Atypical, too, is the resolution. Scrooge, through no effort of his own, has seen his cash miraculously doubled, which he unaccountably accepts as an affirmation of his own original moneymaking "system." The intervening ordeal of dismay and powerlessness dismissed, his self-assurance re-emerges undiminished. He appears hardly the wiser, except perhaps for the generosity in tossing an extra grain of corn to his messenger.

— RICH KREINER

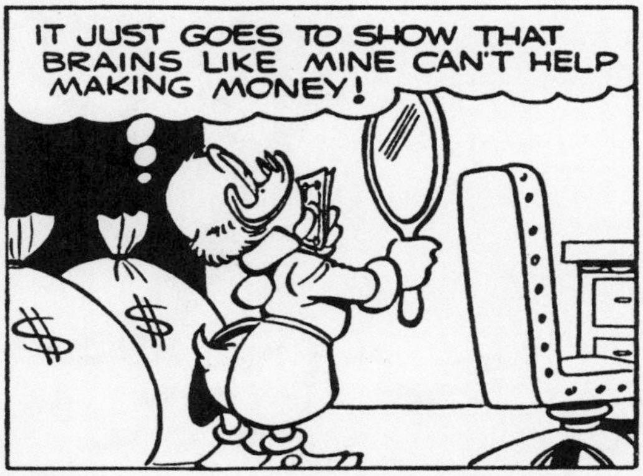
IT JUST GOES TO SHOW THAT BRAINS LIKE MINE CAN'T HELP MAKING MONEY!

THE MYSTERIOUS STONE RAY *p. 35*

This is perhaps Barks's most sophisticated foray into hard science fiction. Its poignancy is achieved through clever deployment of well-trodden genre devices: the mad scientist, the uncharted island, the death ray.

The story is shot through with an undertone of nausea. Most of the characters suffer at various points from food-related queasiness (cabbage, fish, prunes). Scrooge, however, is literally ailing from proximity to his money. This gives Barks the opportunity to craft not only a hilariously morose opening page, but also the priceless, twice-repeated gag wherein Scrooge is blushingly confronted by the fact that he lives out a common metaphor on a daily basis: "Do you roll in money?"

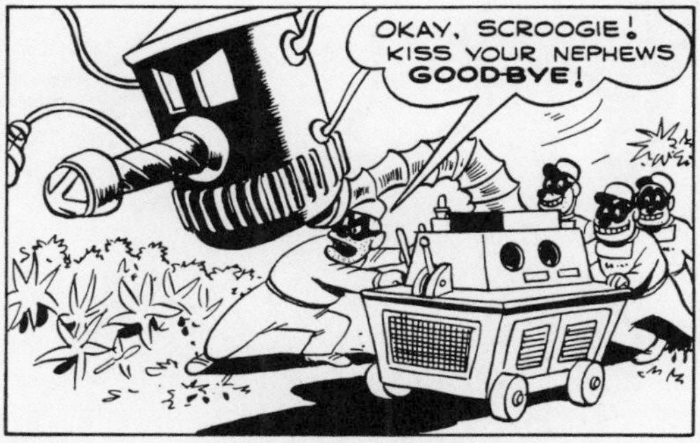
OKAY, SCROOGIE! KISS YOUR NEPHEWS GOOD-BYE!

It is a stroke of comic genius on Barks's part that Scrooge's gold-dust-clogged pores make him immune to the hellish invention at the story's center. Scrooge regards his money as an end in itself — not so much an accumulation of wealth but rather a beloved collection of coins and notes to be sorted and played with — and it is that very personal relationship with his physical money that saves him.

The menace of the stone ray is gradually seeded — first by the bottled message, then by the eerie, lifelike statues populating the island, and finally by its direct effect on our protagonists — culminating in the awesome half-page splash panel, where the metal basilisk rears its head at Scrooge (p. 53).

Ultimately, this delightful adventure story is a fable about the capriciousness and danger of science and human ambition. When the otherwise disturbingly aggressive scientist declares his pacifism — "there are too many masters in the

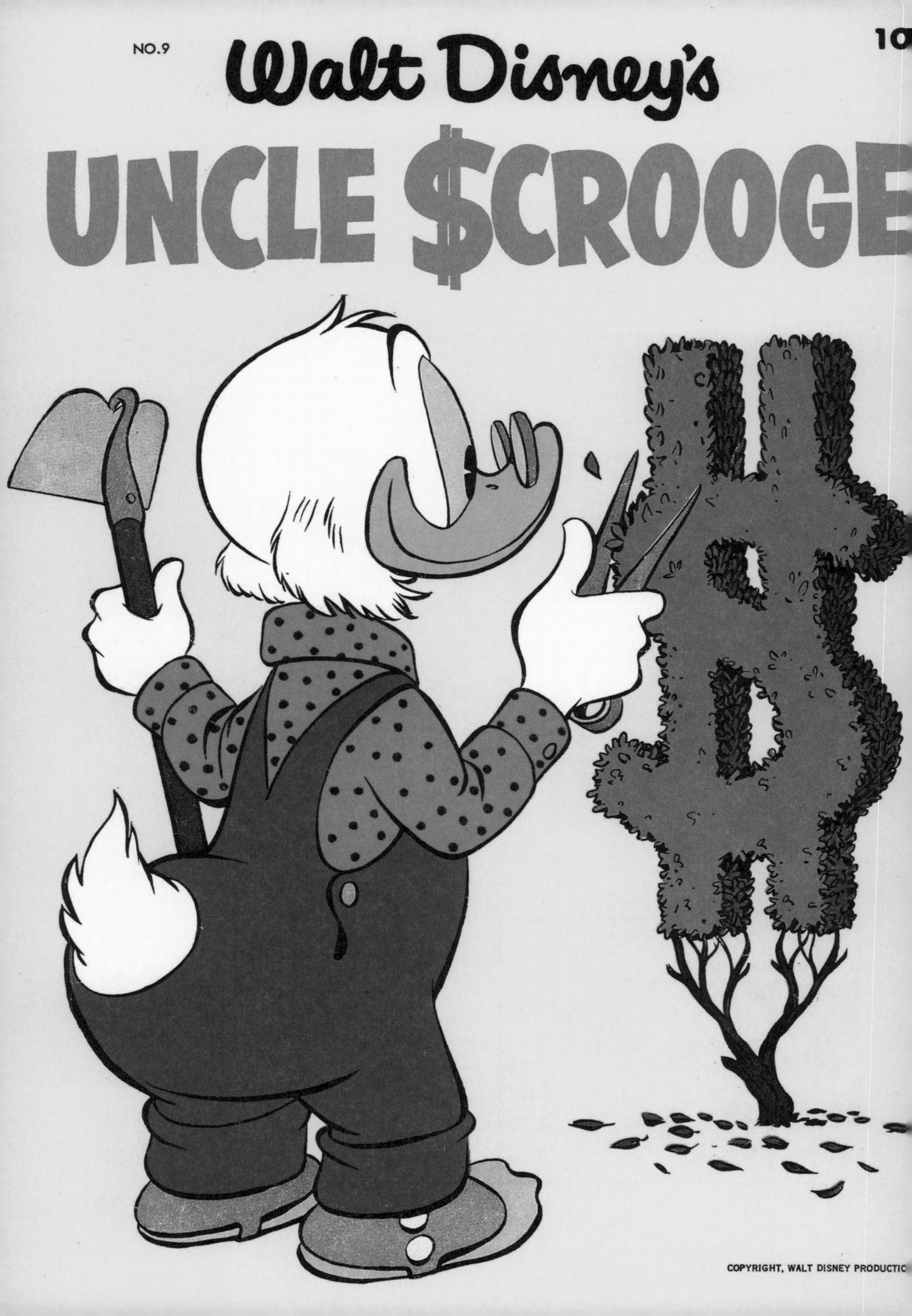
NO.9
Walt Disney's
UNCLE $CROOGE
10
COPYRIGHT, WALT DISNEY PRODUCTIC

world already, and not enough friends!" — he may be repeating a cliché, but it feels earned and even poetic in its wording.

Most powerful, though, is the image of Scrooge handing the petrified Dewey to his brother, terrified that he might break. This is as unsettling and beautiful a summary of human vulnerability and compassion as any in Barks's oeuvre.

— MATTHIAS WIVEL

A CAMPAIGN OF NOTE *p. 63*

It is often in the gag stories — the ones with seemingly the least room to give — that Barks expresses his cynicism. "A Campaign of Note" laments the shameful admixture of money and elections: a state of affairs almost as old as American democracy itself but newly visible in the 1950s.

While we tend to think of the outsized role of money in elections as a recent phenomenon, in fact it has been the norm since the postwar period, when candidate-focused fundraising began to displace the tradition of party-based fundraising, and when the new medium of television began to privilege the marketing of the candidate's personality over the selling of the party's platform.

"It's scandalous!" Scrooge bemoans the state of affairs. "All of that money being spent just to get one of them elected."

The role of money in elections was especially visible in the early 1950s, when Richard M. Nixon became embroiled in a scandal involving a fund that had been established to finance his future campaigns. Shortly after presidential candidate Dwight D. Eisenhower named Nixon as his running mate for the 1952 campaign, word of "the Fund" was leaked to the press. While the practice was not illegal, the media uproar brought the influence of money in American elections into stark relief — and Nixon's "Checkers speech," in which he defended himself against charges of impropriety in a nationally televised address, highlighted the new power of television to dramatically shape public opinion.

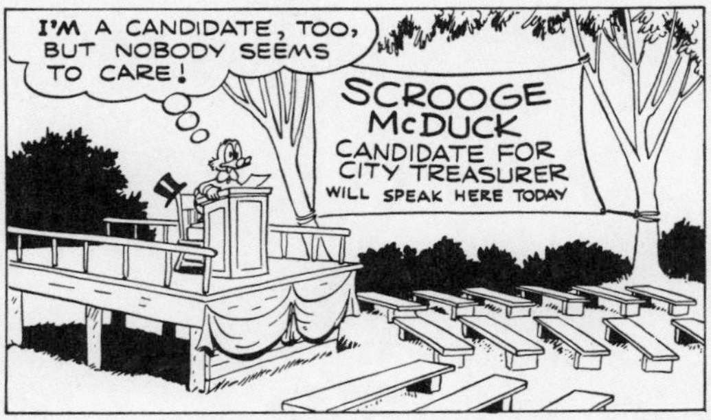
I'M A CANDIDATE, TOO, BUT NOBODY SEEMS TO CARE!
SCROOGE McDUCK
CANDIDATE FOR CITY TREASURER
WILL SPEAK HERE TODAY

In "A Campaign of Note," the trading of money for votes is represented as a series of back-alley exchanges and shadowy transactions, as cigars and candy are dispensed for the promise of favor in the voting booth. Predictably resistant to parting with his money, Scrooge's candidacy remains invisible to the electorate with the election only one day away.

With no money to contribute to the cause, Donald and the boys decide to contribute by rounding up the Junior Woodchucks and the "Firehouse Five" for a parade. (A reference to the Firehouse Five Plus Two, a Dixieland jazz band made up of Disney artists, led by Ward Kimball, which, by 1954, had released several popular albums.)

Marching alongside the Junior Woodchucks, art and civic pride seems at first to win the day over money. But of course, in the end, it is still just money — as Donald dispenses to the rapacious crowd the money Scrooge had squirrelled away in the tuba. At least Donald and the boys can retain their illusions that it was the music and the parade that won the day for Scrooge, and not the promise of free money.

— JARED GARDNER

THE LEMMING WITH THE LOCKET *p. 69*

As perhaps might be anticipated of someone who chronicled a character of incalculable wealth, Carl Barks was intrigued by huge numbers and enormous accumulations. This interest appears in meticulous renderings as routine as the coins and bills piled high in Scrooge's money bin and as unique as the rain of bottlecaps in Tralla La (*Walt Disney's Uncle Scrooge: "Only a Poor Old Man"*). And of course there are these lemmings ...

"The Lemming With the Locket" — inspired by a 1953 magazine article and *not* by a later controversial Disney documentary — divides neatly into three segments. The first is marked by intentions and tactics. Scrooge schemes to keep his fortune safe within an impenetrable vault, thereby initiating his predicament. In short order, he's bankrolling strategies to locate and rendezvous

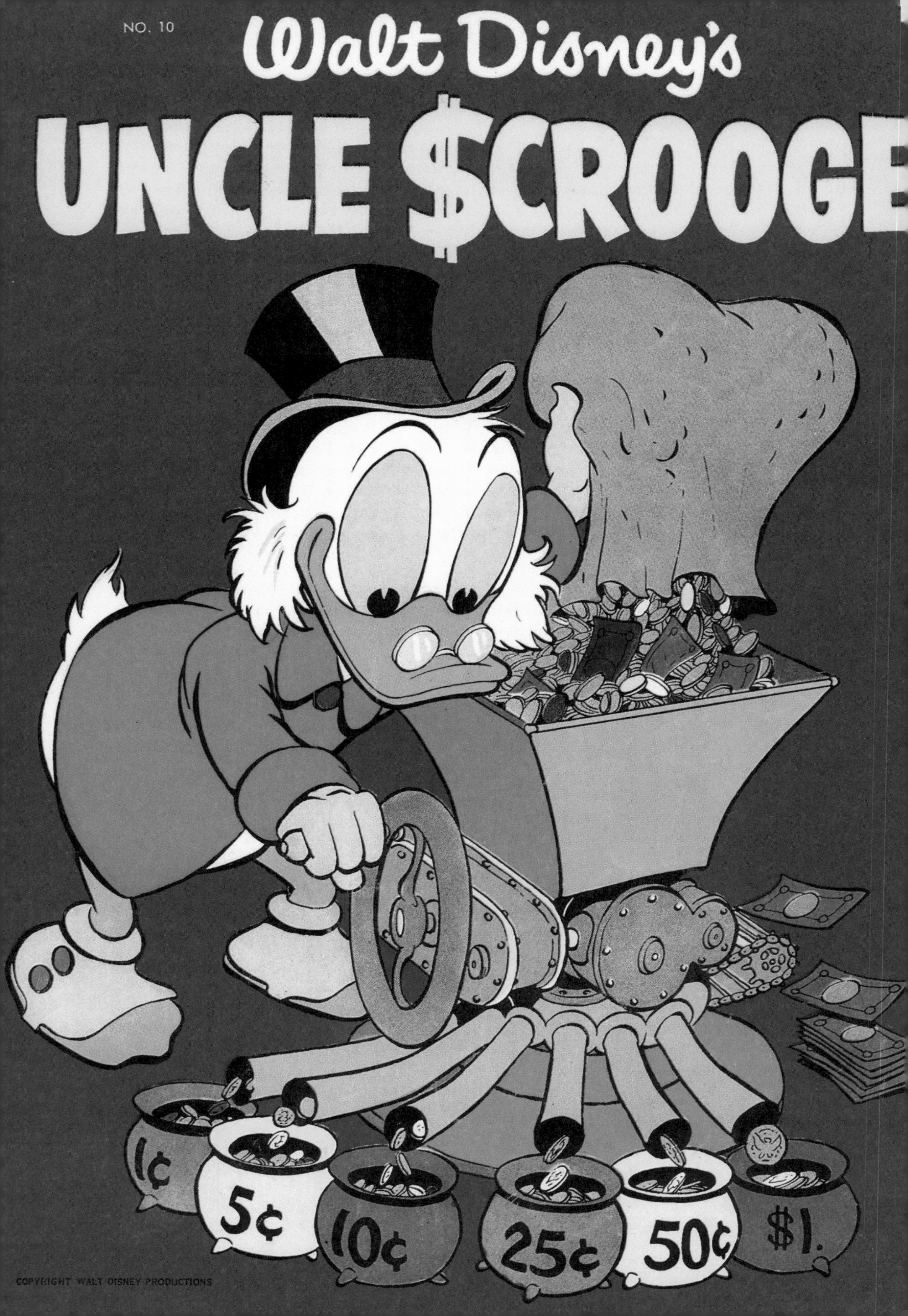

NO. 10
Walt Disney's
UNCLE $CROOGE
1¢
5¢
10¢
25¢
50¢
$1.
COPYRIGHT WALT DISNEY PRODUCTIONS

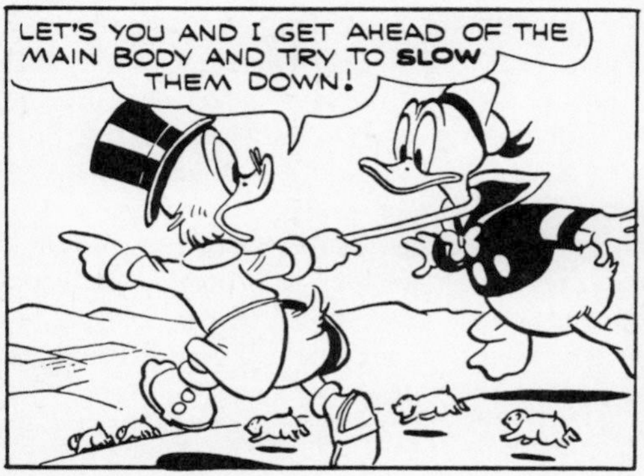
LET'S YOU AND I GET AHEAD OF THE MAIN BODY AND TRY TO **SLOW** THEM DOWN!

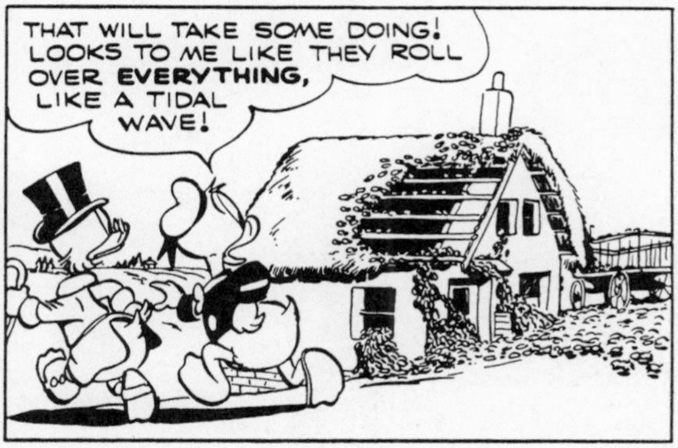
THAT WILL TAKE SOME DOING! LOOKS TO ME LIKE THEY ROLL OVER **EVERYTHING,** LIKE A TIDAL WAVE!

with the schooner *Moony Gull*. Shipboard, the stalked lemming evades his would-be captors with ploys and counter-measures reminiscent of the most innovative silent film comedians.

Once on Norway's shore, though, the story's tone changes, pronto, as nature demonstrates its disdain for niceties like enterprise. A lone lemming is replaced by several, then dozens, then

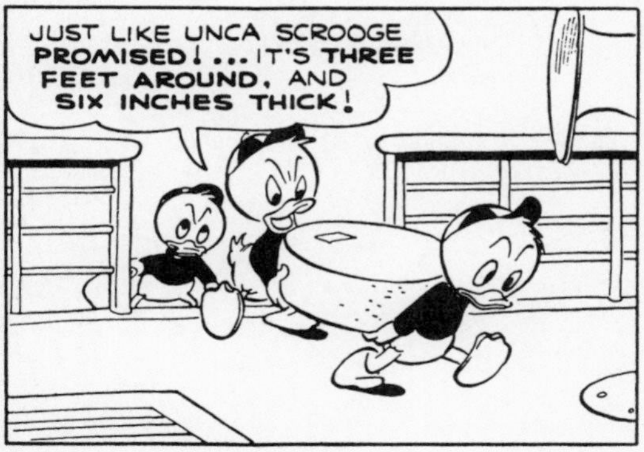
JUST LIKE UNCA SCROOGE **PROMISED! ...** IT'S **THREE FEET AROUND,** AND **SIX INCHES THICK!**

scores as Barks takes pains to turn a trickle into a tide. Residents retreat to the hills, possessions on their backs. Houses are destroyed!

Finally, the Ducks get a truer sense of the situation in that memorable half-page splash panel (p. 83) as they behold the sea of lemmings sweeping across the countryside, swarming toward their goal. Desperate improvisations involving barriers, switches, pine trees, and haystacks prove to be exercises in futility. Gone are any practical notions of planning. Nature has defeated design.

With this convincing show of supremacy, humor is tinged with poignancy. The page of the lemmings' final onslaught is fraught. Scrooge is frantic. While overwhelming everything and everyone, the lemmings have managed to become individuated and distinct, even en masse, their plunge into the sea affecting.

A spent and dejected Scrooges lies atop his makeshift wall, as inert as the stones he has just heaped up, reduced to posing what could be the rhetorical question of a child. The page ends with a somber panorama: of cliffs that had so recently boiled with life now barren and scrubbed clean, of a painfully wide expanse of empty ocean, of a broad sky's distant clouds along a devastatingly flat horizon. The Ducks are dwarfed, hunched.

After that sobering montage, it requires an extended denouement and narrative muscle to raise the mood. In the third and final segment, ingenuity resurfaces in the wake of nature's convulsion. The lone lemming's cleverness in constructing a scaffold provides him an immediate meal, even as it paves the way to a palatable finale.

Scrooge's last maneuver, his bait-and-switch of the nephews' reward, may be a shabby bit of chicanery but it remains consistent with an aspect of his character. And, after everything is said and done, the Ducklings do receive what is, by all accounts, a very fine cheese.

— RICH KREINER

THE TUCKERED TIGER *p. 93*

On the first page of "The Tuckered Tiger," something odd happens. The Ducks repeatedly refer to themselves and Duckburg's inhabitants as "people" and the creatures they race as "animals." When reading a *funny animal comics story*, we expect the main characters to exhibit human traits. Some, like the famous cat and

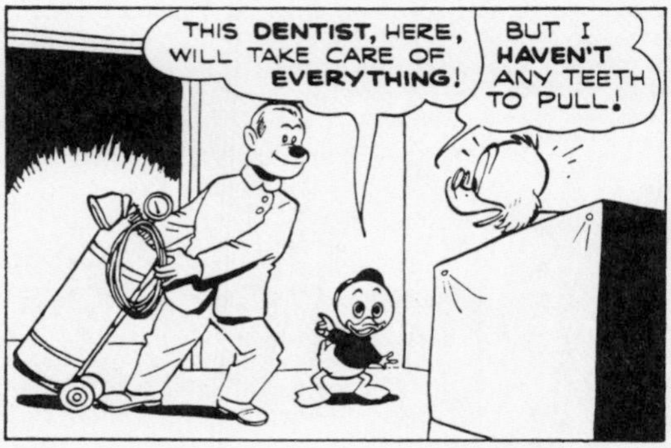
THIS DENTIST, HERE, WILL TAKE CARE OF EVERYTHING!
BUT I HAVEN'T ANY TEETH TO PULL!

mouse team Tom and Jerry, act like people *and* like animals.

But Barks's satire requires that we think of his characters not as animals acting instinctually, but as people acting deliberately. Barks is seeking more than laughs — he wants to expose the comically disturbing excesses of human nature.

Though Barks often lampoons greed and pride, "The Tuckered Tiger" highlights the foolishness of the story's antagonists by contrasting them with the docile creatures they control. Scrooge and the Maharajah each stand to lose a fortune if their respective animals lose, but something more important than money is at stake. Their competition gives each a chance to bolster his own ego: the winner is the better man. The need to prevail is so overpowering that Scrooge mistreats his prize horse — and himself. He and the Maharajah willingly abuse their own bodies, becoming freaks as they pursue victory.

In Duckburg, competition seems to infect everyone. Barks depicts the nephews racing frogs and provides a long list of townspeople who intend to race their animals. Perhaps this list hints

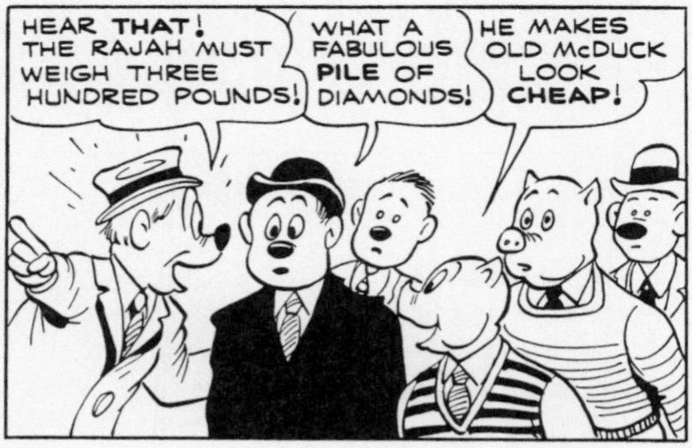
HEAR THAT! THE RAJAH MUST WEIGH THREE HUNDRED POUNDS!
WHAT A FABULOUS PILE OF DIAMONDS!
HE MAKES OLD McDUCK LOOK CHEAP!

at a truth about the relationship between competition and gender: all of the women withdraw from the race, leaving only males to battle it out.

While real-world animal antagonism generally stems from survival imperatives, the protagonists of "The Tuckered Tiger" fall victim to an all-too-human mix of vanity and insecurity. The Maharajah's tiger may be too tuckered to leave its cage, but Barks's males never weary of proving their manhood — or at least trying to. Maybe, for them, competition has become an instinct they can't — or won't — overcome.

— KEN PARILLE

THE FABULOUS PHILOSOPHER'S STONE

p. 105

The plot of a treasure hunt adventure may be relatively straightforward, but Carl Barks fortifies "The Fabulous Philosopher's Stone" with several enlivening wrinkles. The first is the addition of a dogged pursuer, here more odd than

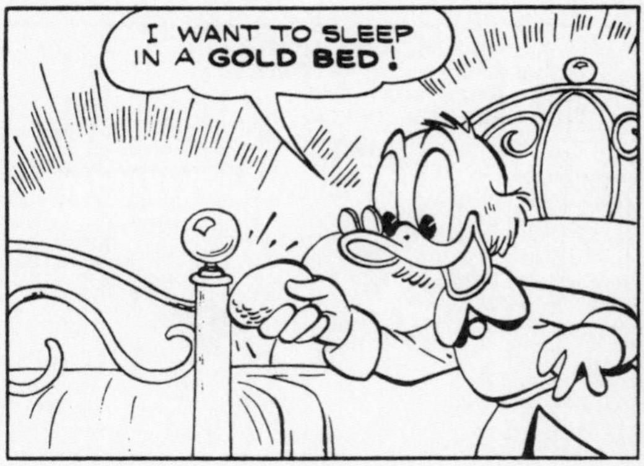
I WANT TO SLEEP IN A GOLD BED!

ominous. Eventually he stands revealed, not as a competitor or an antagonist, but as an authority figure on the side of the angels — evolving by story's end into a lifesaver. In a much wilder complication, Barks sends his cast ricocheting far and wide across Old World sites, as if the Ducks' quest was a pinball game.

With the enthusiasm of an autodidact, Barks spices his tale with an unusually large assortment of classical and academic references. Midas is invoked not only to communicate the fantasy of incomparable riches but also, in ominous foreshadowing, to remind of the curse accompanying his golden touch. The mythological and the historical versions of King Minos are effortlessly conflated, while Ostanes the Mede enjoys a rare modern salute. There's note made of fastidious Roman bookkeeping, ancient pirate routes and strongholds, legal niceties ("I know! I'll file a *claim* for it"), economic law of supply and demand ("destroy the value of all the world's gold coins!"), and some dubious causation attributed to miraculous atomic fission.

That's a lot of working parts to keep in motion, especially as it's critical to keep readers abreast and engaged. Barks holds everything together and keeps everyone in step using, among other techniques, one of a cartoonist's most multifaceted tools: pacing. The story gathers momentum through a steady quickening of action, beginning with a leisurely exposition (and they don't come much more leisurely than a trans-Atlantic passage) and accelerating straight through Scrooge's manic "gold fever" and the nephews' desperate race to intercede. In between, the cadence is ratcheted up incrementally: the segment in Germany takes almost three pages, that of the Italian coast little more than one page, and the stop in Sicily less than one. Damascus and Bagdad are each dispatched in a single panel before we land in Crete for the rest of the story.

Comics, of course, offer a handy formal means to instill a tale with rhythm. Throughout this volume, Barks frequently ends his pages on strong dramatic beats, and nowhere is that more consistently true than in "The Fabulous Philosopher's Stone." The most spectacular examples are the two consecutive pages that conclude at the mouth of the labyrinth and, following that, in front of the minotaur. In both cases, a final, irregularly shaped panel punctuates emphatically, widening from left to right, opening up the frame to dramatize the exotic, sensational mystery of the surroundings. That's the way to keep the pinballs careening.

— RICH KREINER

HEIRLOOM WATCH *p. 131*

This is one of those stories that McDuck genealogists cannot help but love. Scrooge receives word from Scotland that he has been named sole heir to his great-uncle Quagmire McDuck's estate, but only if he can produce the heirloom watch that has been in the McDuck family for 200 years — a watch that, of course, has just fallen into a hundred pieces as the story begins.

This story provides the first mention of Quagmire, Scrooge's great-uncle, and of the watch that will play a small role several decades later in weaving together the McDuck mythology. In the earlier "The Horse-Radish Treasure" (*Walt Disney's Uncle Scrooge: "Only a Poor Old Man"*), we had been introduced to Seafoam McDuck, who, in 1753, had been cheated out of his fortune by the devious Swindle McSue, escaping with only his gold teeth. In 1992, as part of his larger project of connecting the strands of the McDuck genealogy, Barks's most prominent successor, Don Rosa, added an additional item to Seafoam's meager salvage from his disastrous encounter with McSue: "the heirloom watch."

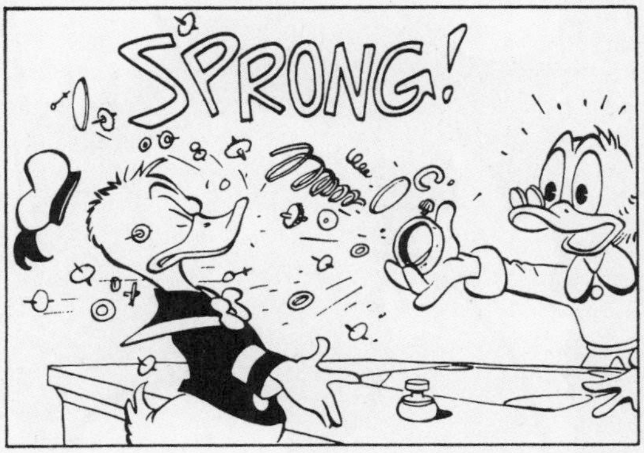
SPRONG!

In "The Horse-Radish Treasure," Scrooge had learned of an unwanted inheritance from Seafoam, the fine print of which provided the incentive for generations of McSues to pursue a breach of contract claim, now two centuries old, against the McDucks.

In "Heirloom Watch," Scrooge has reason to hope for a much happier inheritance, this time through Seafoam's descendent, Quagmire. But first the watch parts must be recovered and repaired, and it must prove it still retains the ability to predict a solar eclipse after 200 years of constant use.

As it happens, the longest total solar eclipse ever recorded occurred June 20, 1955, the same month that "Heirloom Watch" was published. The previous summer, shortly before Barks began working on the story, another total solar eclipse made headlines across the country due to its visibility in the continental United States.

Eclipses were therefore very much on people's minds. The 1955 event promised an unrivaled opportunity to prove one of the predictions

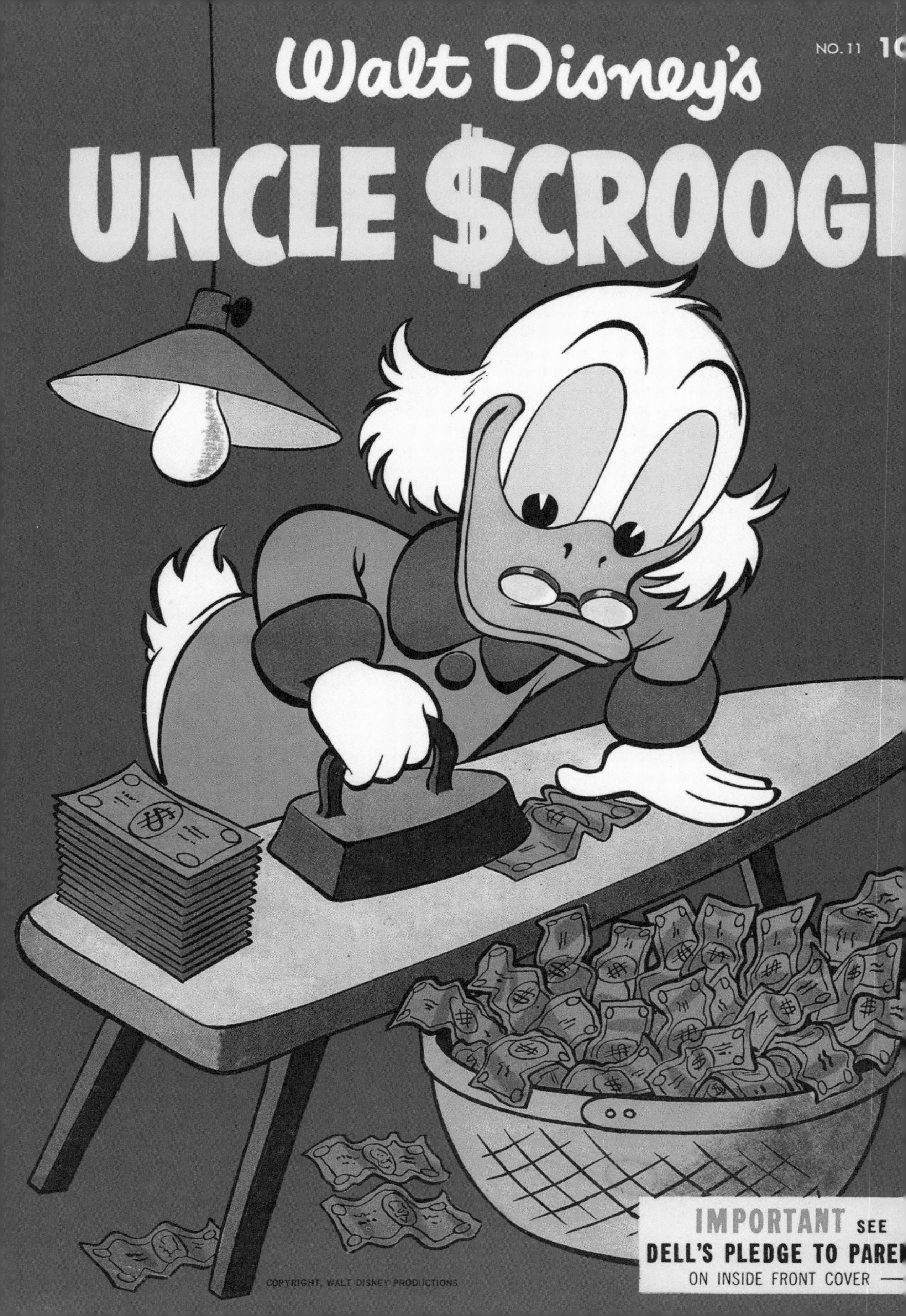
Walt Disney's
NO. 11
10
UNCLE $CROOGE
IMPORTANT SEE
DELL'S PLEDGE TO PARE
ON INSIDE FRONT COVER
COPYRIGHT, WALT DISNEY PRODUCTIONS

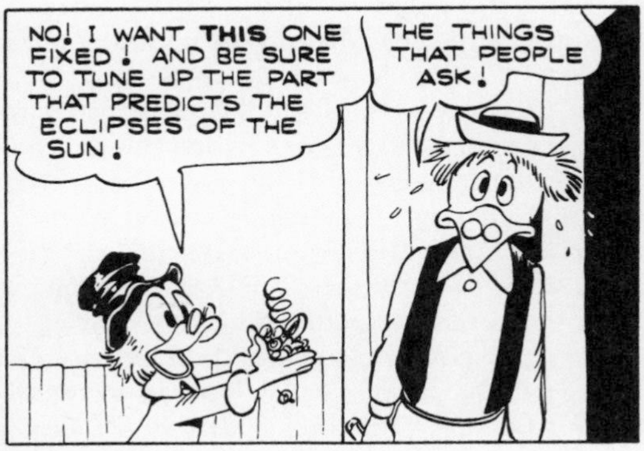
NO! I WANT THIS ONE FIXED! AND BE SURE TO TUNE UP THE PART THAT PREDICTS THE ECLIPSES OF THE SUN!
THE THINGS THAT PEOPLE ASK!

associated with Albert Einstein's theory of General Relativity — that time was relative to and inextricably bound up with space. As *The New York Times* put it, "The Einstein prediction that will be tested is that a ray of light, traveling close to a massive body, will be slightly deflected by the mass of the body."

Einstein had died in April of that year, and his legacy was very much in the news. Beginning with his theories of Special and General Relativity in 1905, Einstein had radically reoriented the foundations of physics, most especially with reference to time. Perhaps the most far-reaching consequence of Einstein's theories had been to disprove the idea that time was a clockwork-like universal constant.

It is somehow poetic that, on the eve of recorded history's longest eclipse and the opportunity to once again prove Einstein's predictions correct, that a watch serves at the center of Barks's tale. For a cartoonist working in a form in which space and time are always bound up with one another, "Heirloom Watch" is one way of acknowledging an inheritance far more valuable than the microscopic ruby Scrooge would gain for his troubles.

— JARED GARDNER

THE GREAT STEAMBOAT RACE *p.141*

The Great Steamboat Race features Uncle Scrooge, Donald, his three nephews, and one of Scrooge's porcine nemeses — the famous sportsman Horseshoe Hogg — in a race between two steamboats on the Mississippi River, from Natchez to Buzzards' Bend.

The purpose? To complete a contest begun in 1870 by their uncles: riverboat captains Porker Hogg in his side-wheeler steamboat, *River Belle*, and Pothole McDuck in his stern-wheeler, *Cotton Queen*. The reward? Ownership of Cornpone Gables, a beautiful old Southern mansion still standing by the Mississippi. Scrooge has no interest in racing, but his nephews talk him into it and agree to help him raise the sunken boat and win the race.

(Barks was a master of dialects as well as dialogues. To capture the cadence of the Southern gentleman's nuanced speech, read Hogg's sentences aloud and with a soft drawl.)

"The Great Steamboat Race" was written and drawn in early 1955, around the time Walt Disney and his crew of "Imagineers" were putting the finishing touches on Disneyland in Anaheim, California, in preparation for the park's grand opening on July 17.

One of the major features of Disneyland is the 105-foot long *Mark Twain* riverboat in Frontierland. Still in operation today, this was the first functional paddle-wheeler to be built in the United States after 1905, and saw its maiden voyage on July 13 (four days before the park officially opened) for a celebration of the 30th wedding anniversary of Walt Disney and his wife Lillian.

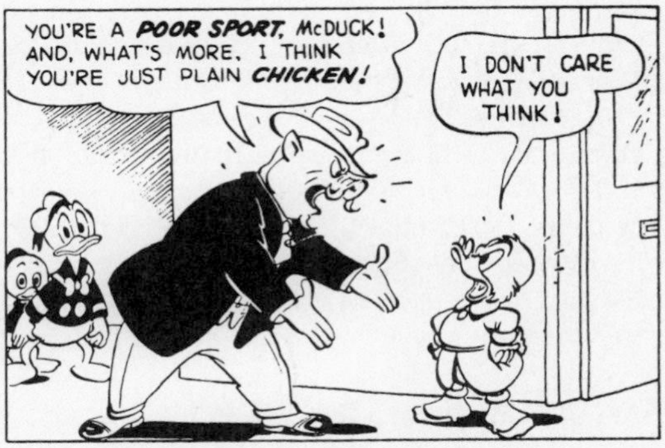
YOU'RE A POOR SPORT, McDUCK! AND, WHAT'S MORE, I THINK YOU'RE JUST PLAIN CHICKEN!
I DON'T CARE WHAT YOU THINK!

Riverboats have played an ongoing role in the history of The Walt Disney Company, beginning in 1928 with the first Mickey Mouse film (and first animated cartoon with synchronized sound), "Steamboat Willie." Barks's tale of riverboat racing carries on a grand Disney tradition.

Two further traditions show up in this 16-page tale of Mississippi River adventure. The first is Barks's use of inflation devices to raise sunken ships. In his earlier story, "The Sunken Yacht" (*Walt Disney's Donald Duck: "Lost in the Andes"*), Donald and nephews raise a sailboat by filling it with ping-pong balls. In "The Great Steamboat Race," they lash inner tubes to the vessel and pump air into them, resulting in one of the most impressive half-page splash panels in all of comics — where the emphasis is truly on "splash."

The other tradition is Barks's use of stupendous sneezes (something he was personally subject to) to bring about unexpected results throughout this story, where Scrooge wins the race by a nose — er, beak — but loses Cornpone Gables and his chance to become a goatee-sporting Southern Gentleman in a big hat, due to yet another Ah-ah-AH-AH-CHOO!

— JOSEPH ROBERT COWLES

RICHES, RICHES, EVERYWHERE! *p. 159*

Like an Old Master who takes years to complete his favorite painting, always coming back to it to add a further brushstroke, so did Carl Barks continually refine his masterpiece: adding another brushstroke to the personality of Uncle Scrooge with each new story.

Scrooge's passion for treasure hunting and his flair for prospecting are among his defining traits and constitute the foundation for this story. The twist that the additional brushstroke highlights is the subtle interplay between merit and fate, between self-determination and luck.

Scrooge famously made his fortune as a prospector by being "tougher than the toughest," and from the way he tells the tale to his nephews, he clearly holds strong, unshakable beliefs about his own abilities. Scrooge brags about his competence to the point of promising he'll find riches anywhere on a spinning globe, and to his credit, he doesn't back down when his finger lands on a desert at the antipodes. However, Barks tells us in this story, as much as Scrooge earns and deserves his luck, it ultimately remains just that: luck.

The two villains, shady figures whose facial features remain hidden for most of the story, add an unsettling sense of threat. We imagine them irredeemably evil, like Soapy Slick of "North of the Yukon" (1965) or Argus McFiendy of "Darkest Africa" (*Walt Disney's Donald Duck: "The Old Castle's Secret"*). They turn out to be merely two-bit crooks, but crooks with a conscience: after realizing that Scrooge and Donald are lost in the desert because of them, they help the nephews with the search and rescue expedition.

Ultimately, this tale echoes the better-known Barks classic of the "magic hourglass": there can be such a thing as too much good luck, and there are situations where gold and diamonds are worthless compared to what you really need (a sip of water). With "Riches, Riches Everywhere!" Barks adds ever more brushstrokes to his portrait of Scrooge, making him more poignant and three-dimensional.

— FRANCESCO STAJANO AND LEONARDO GORI

THE GOLDEN FLEECING *p. 177*

Like certain other Barks tales, "The Golden Fleecing" includes stereotypes that are somewhat disturbing for contemporary audiences. As the story opens, and "Eikral Ali" stalks Uncle Scrooge by smelling the Duck's "strong aroma of money," we're presented with a bizarre, contradictory mash-up of representational clichés:

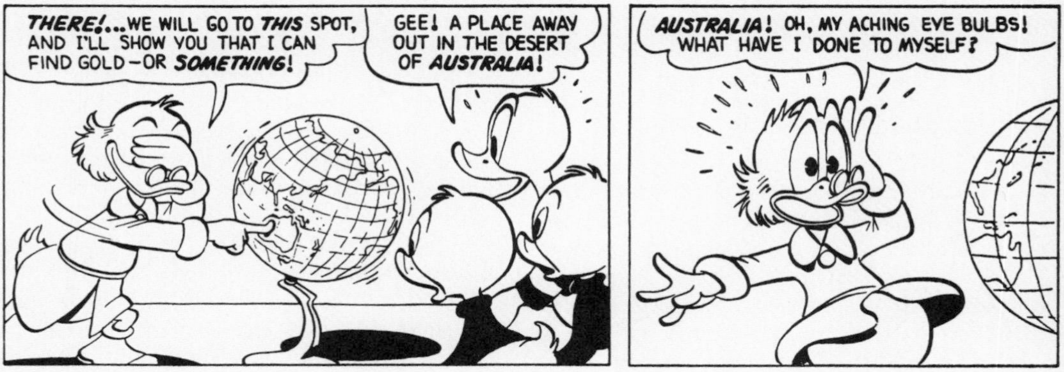
THERE!...WE WILL GO TO THIS SPOT, AND I'LL SHOW YOU THAT I CAN FIND GOLD—OR SOMETHING!
GEE! A PLACE AWAY OUT IN THE DESERT OF AUSTRALIA!
AUSTRALIA! OH, MY ACHING EYE BULBS! WHAT HAVE I DONE TO MYSELF?

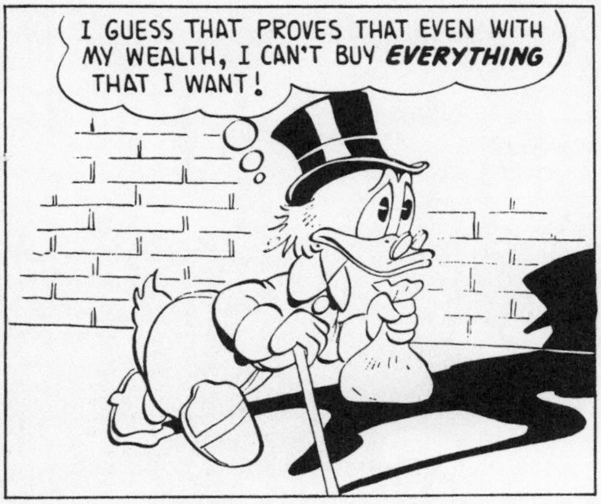
I GUESS THAT PROVES THAT EVEN WITH MY WEALTH, I CAN'T BUY *EVERYTHING* THAT I WANT!

Ali looks like a cartoon Arab with a big nose capable of sniffing money out of hidey-holes.

Ali, however, turns out not to be a "he" after all, but rather a monstrously feminine Larkie, who kidnaps Scrooge and Donald and forces them to judge a cooking contest. The only women in the story are the family of Larkies (Larkie Ila, Larkie Agnes, etc.), all of whom are defined by their interest in cooking and their desire to become queen. Like the nephews, the Larkies are visually interchangeable, and like Scrooge, the Larkies are driven by narrow, overwhelming passions. But the Larkies never transcend their limitations to become three-dimensional characters the way Scrooge, Donald, Huey, Dewey, and Louie do in Barks's best stories.

I find it hard to be too critical of "The Golden Fleecing," though, given Barks's troubled relationship with Western Publishing in 1955 (the year he wrote and drew "The Golden Fleecing"). In *Carl Barks and the Disney Comic Book: Unmasking the Myth of Modernity* (University Press of Mississippi, 2006), Thomas Andrae points out that Western's editors heavily altered and censored Barks's mid-to-late 1950s work (much more than they had his earlier stories), and that "The Golden Fleecing" was originally deemed wholly unfit for publication.

"I almost had to eat those 32 pages of drawings," Barks complained, according to Andrae. "It seems that Harpy or Harpie is an obscure name for a streetwalker. I managed to save the story by renaming the old girls LARKIES."

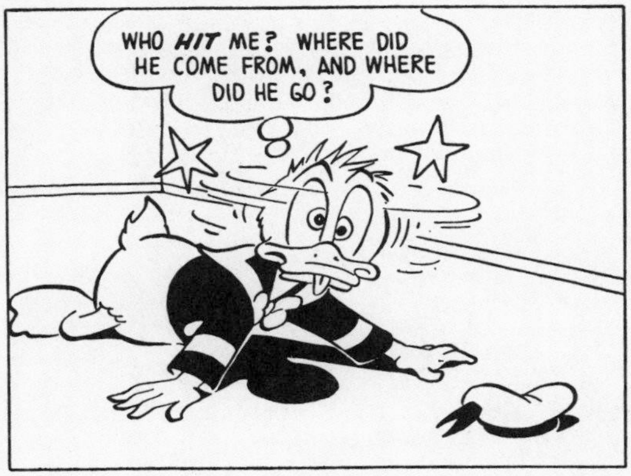
WHO *HIT* ME? WHERE DID HE COME FROM, AND WHERE DID HE GO?

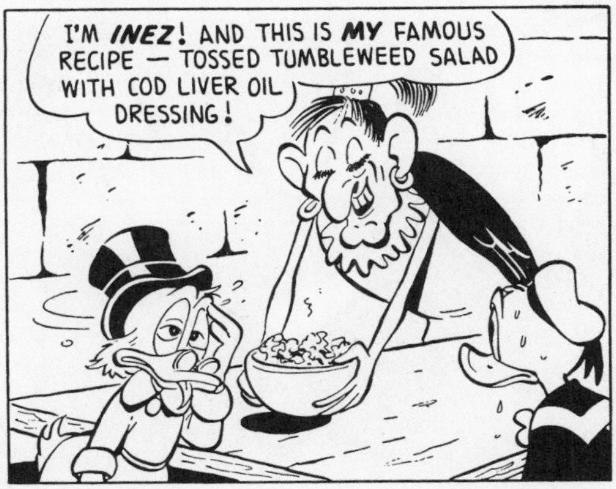
I'M *INEZ*! AND THIS IS *MY* FAMOUS RECIPE — TOSSED TUMBLEWEED SALAD WITH COD LIVER OIL DRESSING!

According to Andrae, a combination of factors — Western's interference, Barks's personal fatigue, his tendency during this period to recycle plot ideas from previous stories — define the mid-to-late 1950s as the weakest period in Barks's oeuvre, and "The Golden Fleecing" exemplifies that fallow time.

Barks diminished is still Barks, however, so much remains to recommend the story. My favorite part of the story is the climax, and Barks's cartoony design for the Sleepless Dragon. I love that one of the nephews hurls powered mustard to make the dragon feel "on fire" (aren't dragons supposed to breathe fire?) and that this dragon is too clueless to notice when the wool is literally being pulled over his eyes.

Barks also uses a neat formal device on pages 206 and 207, where his repetition of a close-up of the dragon's clawed foot allows us to read the second tier of panels as a continuous ribbon stretching across the spread of the

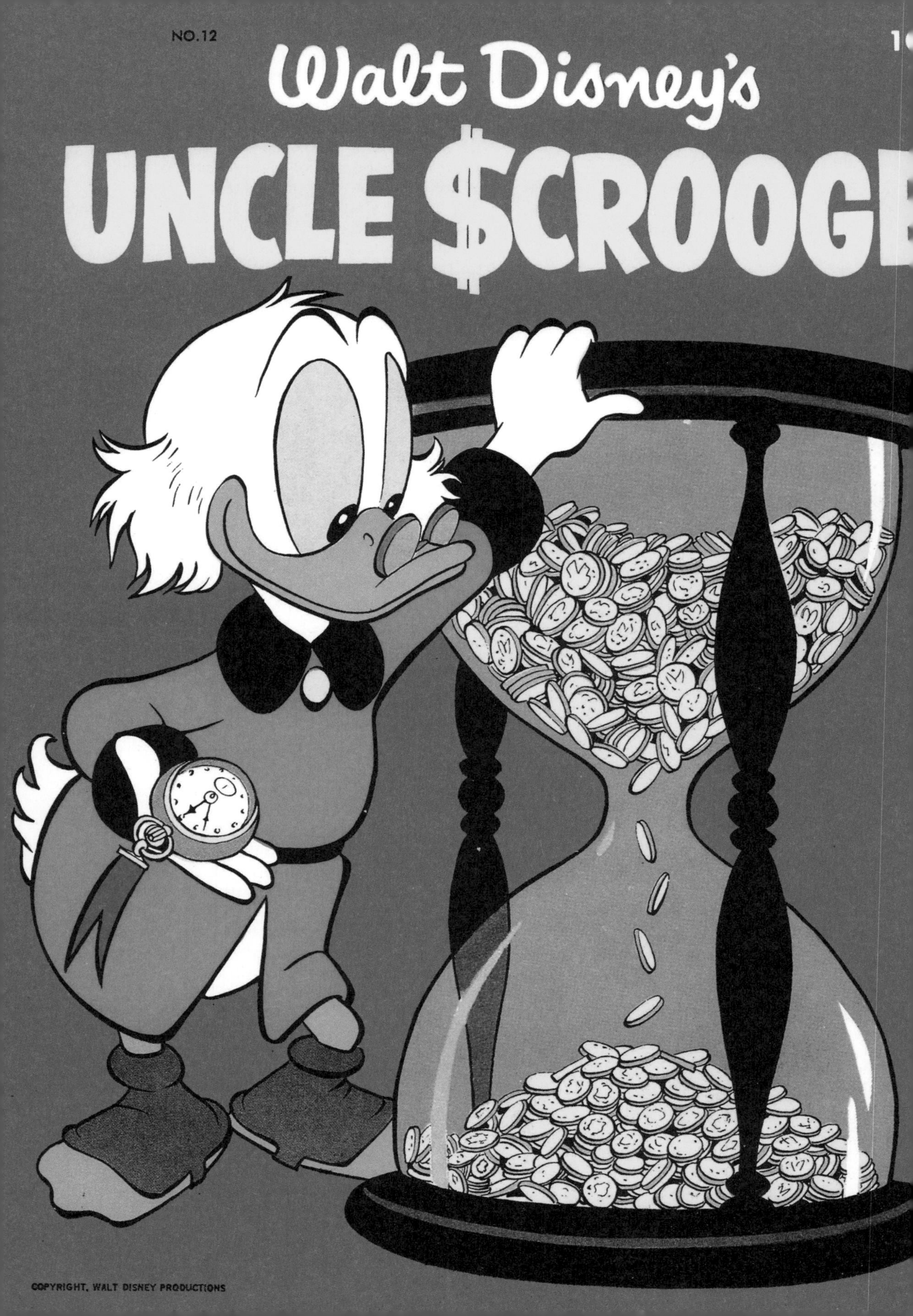
NO. 12
Walt Disney's
UNCLE $CROOGE
COPYRIGHT, WALT DISNEY PRODUCTIONS

two facing pages: on the second tier of panels on page 206, Scrooge dives into a hole in the stone wall ("Choo"), the Dragon's foot covers up the hole ("Slam"), and the action continues as we read downward to the third and fourth tiers on that page. But the layout also makes visual and narrative sense if we read rightward across the spread to the adjacent tier on page 207 where one of the nephews squeezes past the foot and crawls out of the wall.

This was a rough time for Barks as an artist, but he never stopped innovating, never stopped caring.

— CRAIG FISCHER

THE UNCLE SCROOGE ONE-PAGERS

Each of the 17 single-page vignettes of Barksian inspiration appearing in this anthology consists of six-to-eight panels in which Barks sets up a gag, plays it to completion, and grabs the reader with his punch line — or punch illustration. These brief tales of a miserly cartoon Duck whose wealth is measured in uncountable gazillions of dollars have plausible living-and-breathing reality for Carl Barks fans.

A disgruntled Scrooge isn't looking forward to first-of-the-month bill-paying in "Temper Tampering" (p. 33). He wants to tear into everything, and in the second panel he really gives that can a swift kick, doesn't he? Then he swipes at a leaf with his cane, further displaying his anger. But a

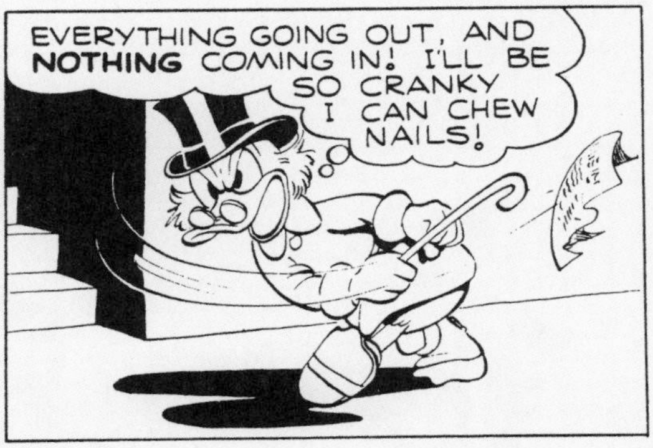
EVERYTHING GOING OUT, AND **NOTHING** COMING IN! I'LL BE SO CRANKY I CAN CHEW NAILS!

nickel on the sidewalk transforms Scrooge's day into pure delight ... thanks to two cagey McDuck employees who've planted the coin in his path. We all breathe a sigh of relief.

Ouch! It hurts to pay for a three-minute phone call and not reach who you're calling ("Wrong Number," p. 34). But why waste the dime? You may as well get your money's worth by chatting with whoever answered the phone. To put this gag into today's perspective, the U.S. minimum wage in 1954 was 75 cents an hour, and a single thin dime had big purchasing power: a soda pop, a candy bar, half a gallon of gas — even a Dell Disney comic book.

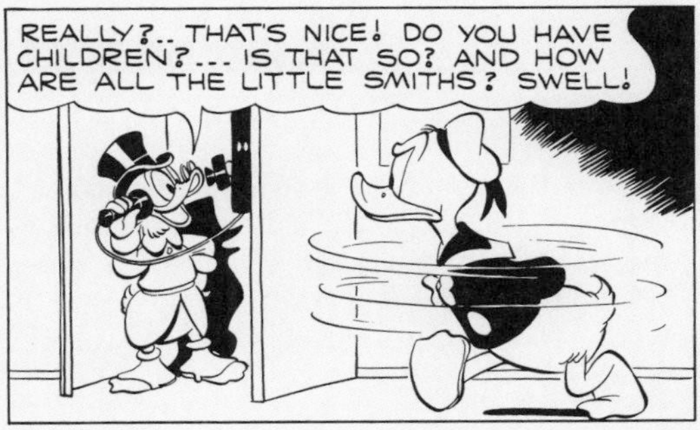
REALLY?.. THAT'S NICE! DO YOU HAVE CHILDREN?... IS THAT SO? AND HOW ARE ALL THE LITTLE SMITHS? SWELL!

"How much is a cup of coffee in this beanery?" is the opening line in "Diner Dilemma" (p. 67), which begins a sequence of coffee-in-a-café gags with our favorite miser devising numerous ways to mooch. These gags follow and elaborate on "Coffee For Two," the hobo-in-the-diner one-pager, in Fantagraphics's first Scrooge volume (*Walt Disney's Uncle Scrooge: "Only a Poor Old Man"*).

Inevitably, our hapless fry cook falls prey to Scrooge's short-con artistry, never quite catching on. In this episode, Cookie becomes willing to sell half a cup for three cents if it's the multiplujillionaire Duck's cup, and he doesn't have to wash it — but Cookie fails to specify how large Scrooge's cup can be.

Uh-oh. Mrs. McMooch always has both grasping hands out when she sees Mr. McDuck. In "Cash on the Brain" (p. 68), her social club is seeking donations. A check in any amount will do — perhaps a wheelbarrow of spare change. But when Scrooge turns his pockets inside out to convince her he's cash strapped, Mrs. McMooch puts her nose in the air and stomps off. The lady should have hung around to see the polite old gentleman doffing his hat to her in parting.

His money-lending business slacks off when it's raining so Scrooge heads home early — grumbling that he hasn't earned enough that day to

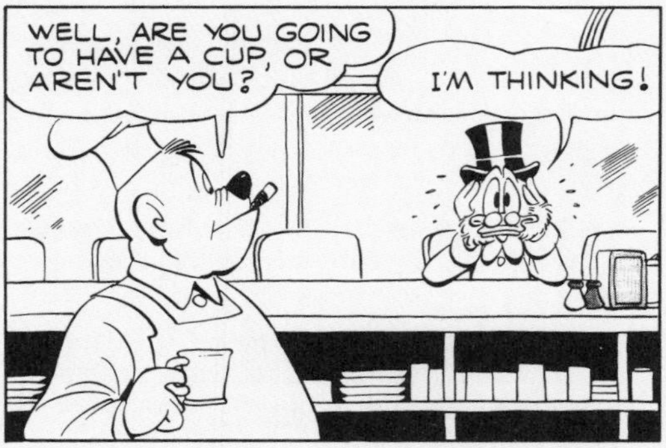
WELL, ARE YOU GOING TO HAVE A CUP, OR AREN'T YOU?
I'M THINKING!

pay for the gas in his huge limo, let alone the wages of his chauffeur. Then inspiration hits. Giving his driver the day off, Scrooge fills the limo with folding chairs and offers his services to folks who are caught in the rain and need a ride in "Classy Taxi!" (p. 91).

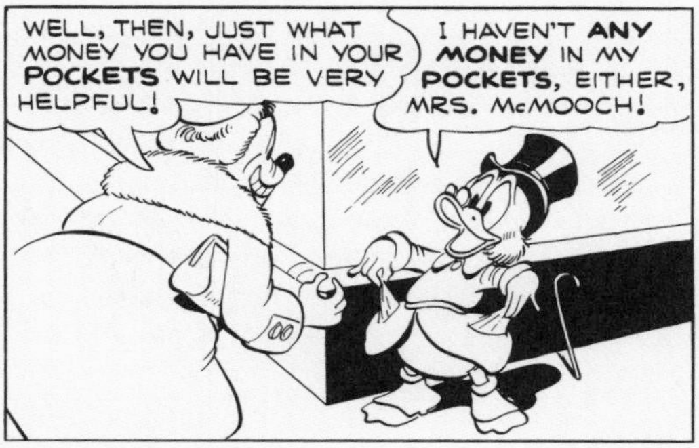
WELL, THEN, JUST WHAT MONEY YOU HAVE IN YOUR **POCKETS** WILL BE VERY HELPFUL!
I HAVEN'T **ANY MONEY** IN MY **POCKETS**, EITHER, MRS. McMOOCH!

Donald and the nephews are amazed to find their uncle snuggled under an electric blanket in "Blanket Investment" (p. 92). Such extravagance seems entirely out of character for the penny-pincher. The blanket wasn't cheap, it runs up the electric bill, and Scrooge only occupies a small part of it. So why'd he buy it? He uses the extra space to hatch chickens, making the blanket pay for itself. (It's a gag only a retired chicken rancher such as Barks could have dreamed up.)

When Donald brags to Uncle Scrooge about the new power mower he bought for a hundred dollars in "Easy Mowing" (p. 103), Scrooge replies that his mower cost only five dollars. For every power mower benefit Donald touts, his uncle brags that his mower is better and cheaper. Turns out it is, of course. *B-a-a-a-a!*

Uncle Scrooge has opened McDuck Mountain to skiers, and almost everything is free in "Ski Lift Letdown" (p. 104). The lift ride up the mountain is free, and Scrooge doesn't charge for the use of skis, yet the old fellow is raking in a nice profit. How so? It's that steep drop from the top of the mountain ... and the steep price Scrooge charges to ride the lift back down.

In "Cast of Thousands" (p. 129), a Doctor of Quackology advises Scrooge to take a break and go fishing. Scrooge can't take off because the government (someone in Congress, no doubt) is demanding a list of his paper money, which will require weeks to separate from the coins. But if he doesn't take the doc's advice, the old Duck may suffer a breakdown. Then comes inspiration! Scrooge discovers he can relax while practicing his casting and fishing for the big ones — in his money bin.

"Deep Decision" (p. 130) provides another example of Scrooge's ability to rook the cigar-smoking Cookie out of coffee. The old Duck only wants to spend a nickel for a small cup of java and brings his own cup for Cookie to fill: only half as high and not as wide as conventional cups — but oh so deep. (The next year, 1956, every sporting goods outlet in the country carried a line of collapsible cups for campers and travelers.)

In the 1950s, roadside stands featuring pottery items imported from Mexico were common along many sleepy country byways — especially in Southern California's beach towns and rural inland communities such as San Jacinto Valley, where Carl Barks made his home. Barks's inspiration for "Smash Success" (p. 139) is likely to have come from a local newspaper report of an out-of-control vehicle plowing through a pottery stand.

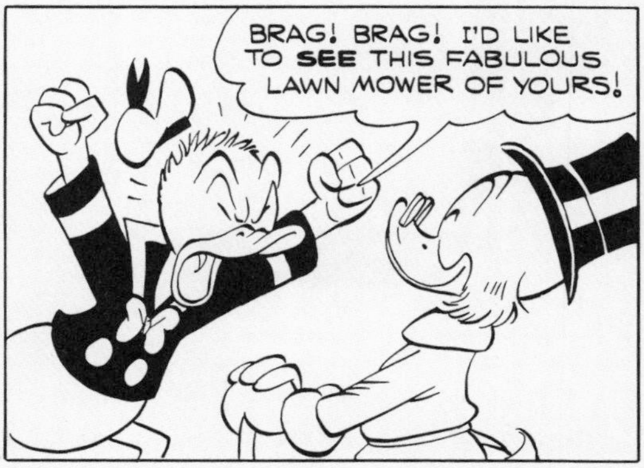
BRAG! BRAG! I'D LIKE TO **SEE** THIS FABULOUS LAWN MOWER OF YOURS!

"Luncheon Lament" (p. 140) was originally drawn for *Uncle Scrooge* #11, but was bumped from that issue and ran instead in #14. Fantagraphics has elected to publish it in this volume to keep it with the other work Barks created around the same time. Here, Grandma Duck is delighted with the meal to which Scrooge has treated her at the Ritzmore Café. Scrooge, however, develops gastric distress — not from what he's eaten, but from the price tag of Grandma's lobster dinner. And who can blame him? Prices were skyrocketing in the '50s; five or six years earlier, one could still enjoy a lobster luncheon in Southern California for only 75 cents.

For a while in the late '50s and early '60s, "Come-as-you-are" parties were popular events, staged just as Donald describes them to his uncle

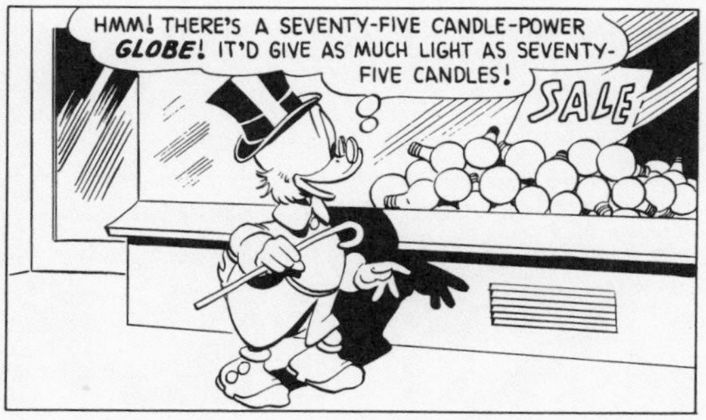
HMM! THERE'S A SEVENTY-FIVE CANDLE-POWER **GLOBE!** IT'D GIVE AS MUCH LIGHT AS SEVENTY-FIVE CANDLES!
SALE

in "Come As You Are" (p. 157). It's doubtful that many folks kept telephones next to their bathtubs (gotta love that old black dial phone), nor did they bathe in money, so Scrooge's invitation to a party while soaking in the tub *déshabillé* would have been unusual. But he can afford to go along with the gag.

Although Barks usually combined sight gags with dialogue, "Roundabout Handout" (p. 158) is a sight gag requiring no conversation or explanation. In this gentle pantomime, the happy squirrel gladly accepts a seemingly endless supply of nuts from Uncle Scrooge, who has the pleasure of endlessly replenishing the supply of nuts without having to pay for them.

Even when celebrating his own birthday, Scrooge remains the miser. His cake requires 75 candles, but at one cent each, that's too many pennies for the old Duck to spend. In "Watt an Occasion" (p. 175), he finds a 75-candlepower light bulb on sale for only two bits, and turns his birthday cake into a lamp. [This gag was published in 1955, indicating that Barks pegged Scrooge's birth year as 1880. So Scrooge will be celebrating his 135th birthday in 2015. Or do cartoon ducks remain the same age perennially?]

Cookie and his cigar are back in another coffee shop saga, "Doughnut Dare" (p. 176). This time the discussion is about how much coffee the beanery's cups hold, with Scrooge conning the fry cook to wager a second cup of coffee FREE if he can soak up the first cup with a single standard-size doughnut. Scrooge wins, of course, by producing a "doughnut" made from sponge.

We don't know the circumstances that brought this about (perhaps it's a dream), but in "A Sweat Deal" (p. 209), we find a thirsty Uncle Scrooge slowly making his way across the Arizona desert (note the saguaro and barrel cacti), having discarded his canteen and miner's pick. Scrooge looks down to see Joe's Oasis, a stand with 10-cent sodas, and races to it. But then he spots a second sign, for Mike's Cafe, one mile farther, where sodas are only 5 cents — and he elects to keep on crawling, just to save that nickel.

— JOSEPH ROBERT COWLES

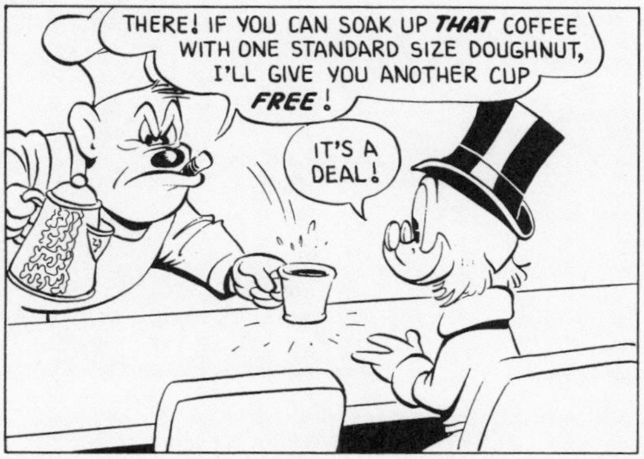
THERE! IF YOU CAN SOAK UP ***THAT*** COFFEE WITH ONE STANDARD SIZE DOUGHNUT, I'LL GIVE YOU ANOTHER CUP ***FREE***!
IT'S A DEAL!

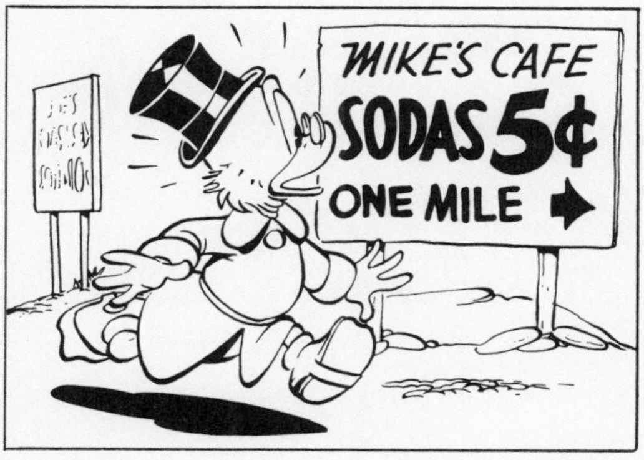
MIKE'S CAFE
SODAS 5¢
ONE MILE

The Panels That Never Were

If you compare the three-panel sequence below (A) to the panels on the top half of page 192, you will notice that panels 1 and 3 have been redrawn. (Panel 2 is unchanged.) Carl Barks's editor thought the behavior of the Larkies in those panels was too manic and asked Barks to tone things down. The story originally saw print with the panels below in place of those on page 192. For this edition, we have restored the story to what Barks originally intended. We offer Barks's tamer, redrawn panels here for your comparison.

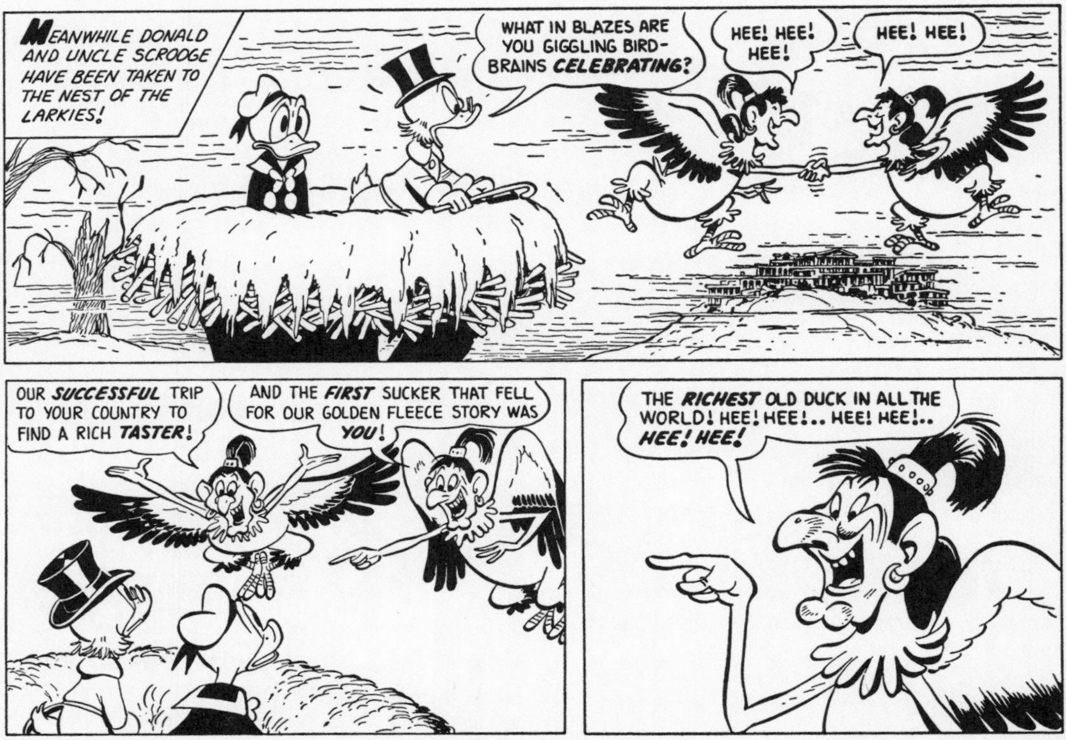
MEANWHILE DONALD AND UNCLE SCROOGE HAVE BEEN TAKEN TO THE NEST OF THE LARKIES!
WHAT IN BLAZES ARE YOU GIGGLING BIRD-BRAINS CELEBRATING?
HEE! HEE! HEE!
HEE! HEE!
OUR SUCCESSFUL TRIP TO YOUR COUNTRY TO FIND A RICH TASTER!
AND THE FIRST SUCKER THAT FELL FOR OUR GOLDEN FLEECE STORY WAS YOU!
THE RICHEST OLD DUCK IN ALL THE WORLD! HEE! HEE!.. HEE! HEE!.. HEE! HEE!

A

Here are three more instances of Barks changing a story, but this time they were changes he made on his own, while working out "The Mysterious Stone Ray" (p. 35). Compare the four panels below (B) with the corresponding panels on page 47. Barks discarded this sequence even before he finished inking it. Note the penciled "X" inside the Beagle Boy's mouth in panel 3, an indication to fill that area with black at the finishing stage. This sequence has never been shown in its semi-completed state before. Thanks to Kim Weston for providing it.

The four panels at the top of the next page (C) were originally intended to be the top half of page 50, with what is now the top half of that page as its bottom half.

The four panels at the bottom of the next page (D) originally made up the bottom half of page 51, but Barks eliminated the first row of two panels and redrew the second row with minor modifications to become what you see as the third row on page 51.

These sequences survive because Barks sold these clippings to fans and collectors. (Note his autograph on the artwork below.) In some cases, Barks completed the inking that he had earlier abandoned before handing over these "scraps."

Barks was always alert for ways to improve his stories. "I cut panels to shorten business which was getting tiresomely overstaged," Barks told Bruce Hamilton, Geoffrey Blum, and Thomas Andrae in a 1984 interview. It may also have been that Barks had originally planned this as a 32-page story and got word partway through that he had to cut it to 28 pages. It may have been a bit of both. But in each of these instances, you can see Barks's storytelling sense at work, as he refined and tightened the story.

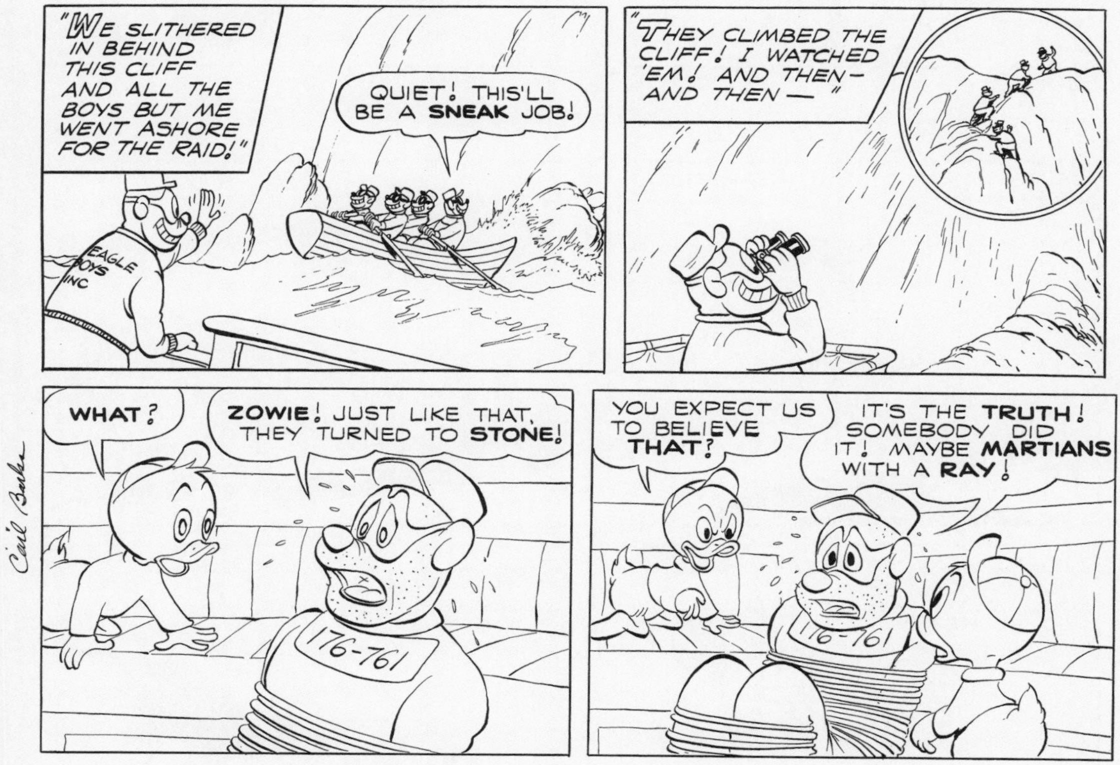
"WE SLITHERED IN BEHIND THIS CLIFF AND ALL THE BOYS BUT ME WENT ASHORE FOR THE RAID!"
QUIET! THIS'LL BE A SNEAK JOB!
BEAGLE BOYS INC
"THEY CLIMBED THE CLIFF! I WATCHED 'EM! AND THEN— AND THEN —"
WHAT?
ZOWIE! JUST LIKE THAT, THEY TURNED TO STONE!
176-761
YOU EXPECT US TO BELIEVE THAT?
IT'S THE TRUTH! SOMEBODY DID IT! MAYBE MARTIANS WITH A RAY!
176-761
Carl Barks

B

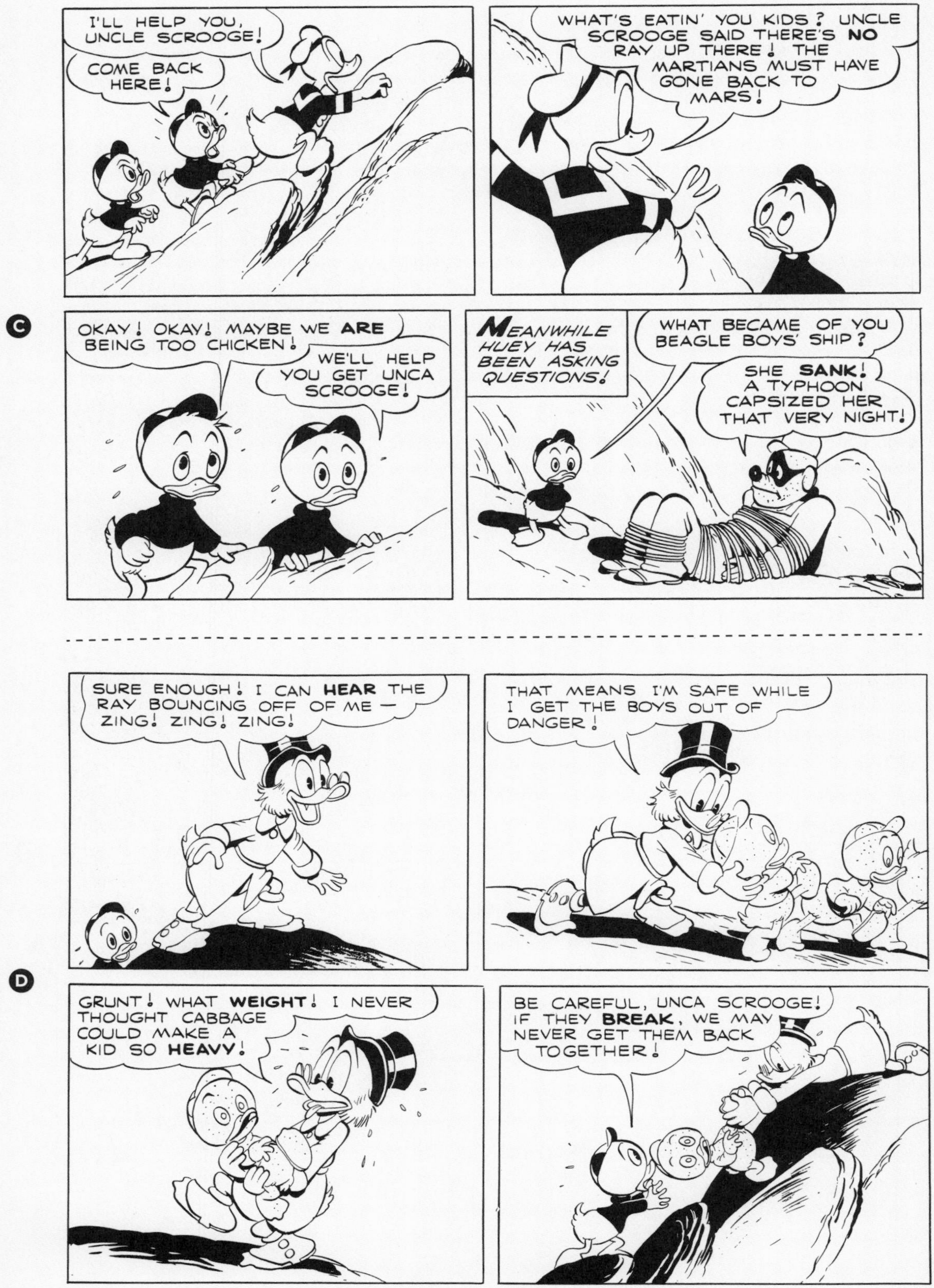
I'LL HELP YOU, UNCLE SCROOGE!
COME BACK HERE!
WHAT'S EATIN' YOU KIDS? UNCLE SCROOGE SAID THERE'S NO RAY UP THERE! THE MARTIANS MUST HAVE GONE BACK TO MARS!
OKAY! OKAY! MAYBE WE ARE BEING TOO CHICKEN!
WE'LL HELP YOU GET UNCA SCROOGE!
MEANWHILE HUEY HAS BEEN ASKING QUESTIONS!
WHAT BECAME OF YOU BEAGLE BOYS' SHIP?
SHE SANK! A TYPHOON CAPSIZED HER THAT VERY NIGHT!
SURE ENOUGH! I CAN HEAR THE RAY BOUNCING OFF OF ME — ZING! ZING! ZING!
THAT MEANS I'M SAFE WHILE I GET THE BOYS OUT OF DANGER!
GRUNT! WHAT WEIGHT! I NEVER THOUGHT CABBAGE COULD MAKE A KID SO HEAVY!
BE CAREFUL, UNCA SCROOGE! IF THEY BREAK, WE MAY NEVER GET THEM BACK TOGETHER!

Carl Barks

LIFE AMONG THE DUCKS

by DONALD AULT

ABOVE: *Carl Barks at the 1982 San Diego Comic-Con. Photo by Alan Light.*

"I was a real misfit," Carl Barks said, thinking back over an early life of hard labor — as a farmer, a logger, a mule-skinner, a rivet heater, and a printing press feeder — before he was hired as a full-time cartoonist for an obscure, risqué magazine in 1931.

Barks was born in 1901 and (mostly) raised in Merrill, Oregon. He had always wanted to be a cartoonist but everything that happened to him in his early years seemed to stand in his way. He suffered a significant hearing loss after a bout with the measles. His mother died. He had to leave school after the eighth grade. His father suffered a mental breakdown. His older brother was whisked off to World War I.

His first marriage, in 1921, was to a woman who was unsympathetic to his dreams and who ultimately bore two children "by accident," as Barks phrased it. The two divorced in 1930.

In 1931, he pulled up stakes from Merrill and headed to Minnesota, leaving his mother-in-law, whom he trusted more than his wife, in charge of his children.

Arriving in Minneapolis, he went to work for the *Calgary Eye-Opener*, that risqué magazine. He thought he would finally be drawing cartoons full time but the editor and most of the staff were alcoholics, so Barks ended up running the whole show.

In 1935 he took "a great gamble" and, on the strength of some cartoons he'd submitted in response to an advertisement from the Disney Studio, he moved to California and entered an animation trial period. He was soon promoted to "story man" in Disney's Donald Duck animation unit, where he made significant contributions to 36 Donald cartoon shorts between 1936 and 1942, including helping to create Huey, Dewey, and Louie for "Donald's Nephews" in 1938. Ultimately, though, he grew dissatisfied. The production of animated cartoons "by committee," as he described it, stifled his imagination.

For that and other reasons, in 1942 he left Disney to run a chicken farm. But when he was offered a chance by Western Publishing to write and illustrate a new series of Donald Duck comic book stories, he jumped at it. The comic book format suited him and the quality of his work persuaded the editors to grant him a freedom and autonomy he'd never known and that few others were ever granted. He would go on to write and draw more than 6,000 pages in over 500 stories and uncounted hundreds of covers between 1942 and 1966 for Western's Dell and Gold Key imprints.

Barks had almost no formal art training. He had taught himself how to draw by imitating his early favorite artists — Winsor McCay (*Little Nemo*), Frederick Opper (*Happy Hooligan*), Elzie Segar (*Popeye*), and Floyd Gottfredson, (*Mickey Mouse*).

He taught himself how to write well by going back to the grammar books he had shunned in school, making up jingles and rhymes, and inventing other linguistic exercises to get a natural feel for the rhythm and dialogue of sequential narrative.

Barks married again in 1938 but that union ended disastrously in divorce in 1951. In 1954, Barks married Margaret Wynnfred Williams, known as Garé, who soon began assisting him by lettering and inking backgrounds on his comic book work. They remained happily together until her death in 1993.

He did his work in the California desert and often mailed his stories into the office. He worked his stories over and over "backward and forward." Barks was not a vain man but he had confidence in his talent. He knew what

hard work was, and he knew that he'd put his best efforts into every story he produced.

On those occasions when he did go into Western's offices he would "just dare anybody to see if they could improve on it." His confidence was justified. His work was largely responsible for some of the best-selling comic books in the world — *Walt Disney's Comics & Stories* and *Uncle Scrooge*.

Because Western's policy was to keep their writers and artists anonymous, readers never knew the name of the "good duck artist" — but they could spot the superiority of his work. When fans determined to solve the mystery of his anonymity finally tracked him down (not unlike an adventure Huey, Dewey, and Louie might embark upon), Barks was quite happy to correspond and otherwise communicate with his legion of aficionados.

Given all the obstacles of his early years and the dark days that haunted him off and on for the rest of his life, it's remarkable that he laughed so easily and loved to make others laugh.

In the process of expanding Donald Duck's character far beyond the hot-tempered Donald of animation, Barks created a moveable locale (Duckburg) and a cast of dynamic characters: Scrooge McDuck, the Beagle Boys, Gladstone Gander, Gyro Gearloose, the Junior Woodchucks. And there were hundreds of others who made only one memorable appearance in the engaging, imaginative, and unpredictable comedy-adventures that he wrote and drew from scratch for nearly a quarter of a century.

Among many other honors, Carl Barks was one of the three initial inductees into the Will Eisner Comic Awards Hall of Fame for comic book creators in 1987. (The other two were Jack Kirby and Will Eisner.) In 1991, Barks became the only Disney comic book artist to be recognized as a "Disney Legend," a special award created by Disney "to acknowledge and honor the many individuals whose imagination, talents, and dreams have created the Disney magic."

As Roy Disney said on Barks's passing in 2000 at age 99, "He challenged our imaginations and took us on some of the greatest adventures we have ever known. His prolific comic book creations entertained many generations of devoted fans and influenced countless artists over the years.... His timeless tales will stand as a legacy to his originality and brilliant artistic vision."

Contributors

Donald Ault is Professor of English at the University of Florida, founder and editor of *ImageTexT: Interdisciplinary Comics Studies*, author of two books on William Blake (*Visionary Physics and Narrative Unbound*), editor of *Carl Barks: Conversations*, and executive producer of the video *The Duck Man: An Interview with Carl Barks.*

Joseph Robert Cowles is a lifelong Donald Duck fan who became friends with Carl and Garé Barks while a teenager working at Disneyland in the 1950s. He writes for the quarterly newsletter of the Carl Barks Fan Club, contributed materials and commentary to Egmont's Carl Barks collection, and is the author of *Recalling Carl*, a pictorial dissertation contending that Disney should be making feature films of Barks's stories. His Carl Barks website is TheGoodArtist.com.

Craig Fischer is Associate Professor of English at Appalachian State University. His *Monsters Eat Critics* column, about comics' multifarious genres, runs at *The Comics Journal* website (tcj.com).

Jared Gardner studies and teaches comics at the Ohio State University, home of the Billy Ireland Cartoon Library & Museum. He is the author of three books, including *Projections: Comics and the History of 21st-Century Storytelling* (Stanford University Press, 2011). He is a contributing writer to *The Comics Journal.*

Leonardo Gori is a comics scholar and collector, especially of syndicated newspaper strips of the '30s and Italian Disney authors. He wrote, with Frank Stajano and others, many books on Italian "fumetti" and American comics in Italy. He has also written thrillers, which have been translated into Spanish, Portuguese, and Korean.

Rich Kreiner is a longtime writer for *The Comics Journal* and a longertime reader of Carl Barks. He lives with wife and cat in Maine.

Ken Parille is the author of *The Daniel Clowes Reader* (Fantagraphics, 2012) and has published essays on Louisa May Alcott and boyhood, the mother-son relationship in antebellum America, TV bandleader Lawrence Welk, and, of course, comics. His writing has appeared in *The Nathaniel Hawthorne Review*, *The Journal of Popular Culture*, *The Boston Review*, *The Believer*, and *The Comics Journal.* He teaches literature at East Carolina University.

Stefano Priarone was born in Northwestern Italy about the time when a retired Carl Barks was storyboarding his last Junior Woodchucks stories. He writes about popular culture in many Italian newspapers and magazines, was a contributor to the Italian complete Carl Barks collection, and wrote his thesis in economics about Uncle Scrooge as an entrepreneur (for which he blames his aunt, who read him Barks Scrooge stories when he was 3 years old).

Francesco ("Frank") Stajano began reading Disney comics in preschool and never grew out of it — the walls of his house are covered in bookshelves and many of them hold comics. He has written on Disney comics, particularly with Leonardo Gori, and had the privilege of visiting Carl Barks at his home in Oregon in 1998. In real life he is an associate professor at the University of Cambridge in England.

Matthias Wivel is Curator of Sixteenth-Century Italian Painting at the National Gallery, London. He has written widely about comics for a decade and a half.

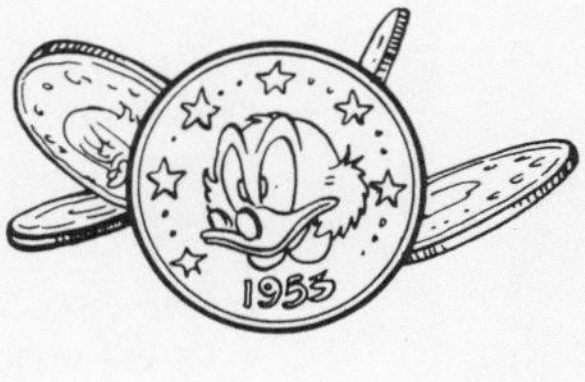
1953

Where did these duck stories first appear?

The Complete Carl Barks Disney Library collects Donald Duck and Uncle Scrooge stories by Carl Barks that were originally published in the traditional American four-color comic book format. Barks's first Duck story appeared in October 1942. The volumes in this project are numbered chronologically but are being released in a different order. This is volume 14.

Stories within a volume may or may not follow the publication sequence of the original comic books. We may take the liberty of rearranging the sequence of the stories within a volume for editorial or presentation purposes.

The original comic books were published under the Dell logo and some appeared in the so-called *Four Color* series — a name that appeared nowhere inside the comic book itself, but is generally agreed upon by historians to refer to the series of "one-shot" comic books published by Dell that have sequential numbering. The *Four Color* issues are also sometimes referred to as "One Shots."

Most of the stories in this volume were originally published without a title. Some stories were retroactively assigned a title when they were reprinted in later years. Some stories were given titles by Barks in correspondence or interviews. (Sometimes Barks referred to the same story with different titles.) Some stories were never given an official title but have been informally assigned one by fans and indexers. For the untitled stories in this volume, we have used the title that seems most appropriate. The unofficial titles appear below with an asterisk enclosed in parentheses (*).

The following is the order in which the stories in this volume were originally published.

Uncle Scrooge #7
(September-November 1954)
Cover
Temper Tampering (*)
The Seven Cities of Cibola (*)
[a.k.a. The Seven Cities of Gold]
The Million-Dollar Pigeon (*) [a.k.a. Billion-Dollar Pigeon, Pigeonholed Millions]
Wrong Number (*)
Diner Dilemma (*)

Uncle Scrooge #8
(December 1954-February 1955)
Cover
Cash on the Brain (*)
The Mysterious Stone Ray (*)
[a.k.a. Message from Mysterious Island]
A Campaign of Note (*)
Classy Taxi (*)
Blanket Investment (*)

Uncle Scrooge #9
(March-May 1955)
Cover
Easy Mowing (*)
The Lemming with the Locket
The Tuckered Tiger
Ski Lift Letdown (*)
Cast of Thousands (*)

Uncle Scrooge #10
(June-August 1955)
Cover
Deep Decision (*)
The Fabulous Philosopher's Stone
Heirloom Watch
Smash Success (*)

Uncle Scrooge #11
(September-November 1955)
Cover
The Great Steamboat Race
Riches, Riches, Everywhere!
Come as You Are (*)
Roundabout Handout (*)

Uncle Scrooge #12
(December 1955-February 1956)
Cover
Watt an Occasion (*)
The Golden Fleecing
Doughnut Dare (*)
A Sweat Deal (*)

Uncle Scrooge #14
(June-August 1956)
Luncheon Lament (*)